Reconstructing Indian History & Culture, no. 34

The Evolution of Historiographical Tradition in Ancient and Medieval India

G.P. Singh

D.K. Printworld (P) Ltd.
Publishers of Indian Traditions

Cataloging in Publication Data — DK
[Courtesy: D.K. Agencies (P) Ltd. <docinfo@dkagencies.com>]

Singh, G. P. (Girish Prasad), 1942-
The evolution of historiographical tradition in ancient and medieval India / G.P. Singh.
p. cm. — (Reconstructing Indian history & culture ; no. 34)
Includes bibliographical references (p.) and index.
ISBN 13: 9788124605561

1. India – History – To 324 BCE – Historiography.
2. India – History – 324 BCE - 1000 BCE – Historiography.
3. India – History – 1000-1765 – Historiography.
4. Literature and history – India. I. Title.
II. Title: Historiographical tradition. III. Series:
Reconstructing Indian history & culture ; no. 34.

DDC 954.0072 22

ISBN 13: 978-81-246-0556-1 ISBN 10: 81-246-0556-4
First published in India in 2011

Published and printed by:
D.K. Printworld (P) Ltd.
Regd. Office: '*Vedaśrī*', F-395, Sudarshan Park
Ramesh Nagar Metro Station
New Delhi-110 015-11
Phones: (011) 2545 3975; 2546 6019; *Fax*: (011) 2546 5926
E-mail: indology@dkprintworld.com
Website: www.dkprintworld.com

To

My dearly beloved wife

Kiran

whose constant help and co-operation
enabled me to complete
my all research works
past and present

By the Same Author

1. The Kirātas in Ancient India: A Historical Study of their Life, Culture and Civilization, Delhi, 1990.
2. Political Thought in Ancient India, Delhi, 1993.
3. Early Indian Historical Tradition and Archaeology, Delhi, 1994.
4. Facets of Ancient Indian History and Culture: New Perception, Delhi, 2003.
5. Ancient Indian Historiography: Sources and Interpretations, Delhi, 2003.
6. Republics, Kingdoms, Towns and Cities in Ancient India, Delhi, 2003.
7. Kingship in Ancient India: Genesis and Growth, Delhi, 2008.
8. Historicity of Rāma and Kṛṣṇa: Literary, Historical, Archaeological and Scientific Perspectives, Delhi, 2008.
9. Researches into the History and Civilization of the Kirātas, Delhi, 2008.
10. Perspectives on Indian History, Historiography, and Philosophy of History, Delhi, 2009.
11. Historical Researches into Some Aspects of the Culture and Civilization of North-East India, Delhi, 2009.
12. Indian Historians and Historiography in the Twentieth Century, Delhi, 2009.

Preface

THERE was, of course, continuity in the tradition of historical writing in India, but the trend of its evolution in ancient, medieval and modern periods was different from each other. Several traditions of historiography evolved in our country during the periods.

The object of this volume is to present a systematic and comprehensive history of historical writing in ancient and medieval India based on original sources and modern works. Some portions of my earlier work, *Ancient Indian Historiography: Sources and Interpretations*, have been reproduced in the volume with modifications and additions in the light of my further study and research in the subject and connected with further details of historiography in medieval India so as to provide a coherent/cohesive picture of the subject. An attempt has been made as far as possible to disentangle legends from authentic history.

The present work is an outcome of my research carried out over the past two decades in the subject. It is for the readers to judge as to how far I have succeeded in achieving my object.

I would like to express my indebtedness to all those scholars whose works I have utilised in this volume.

This work will, I believe, be of immense use to those interested in the study of the evolution of Indian historiography.

The subject dealt with here is vast and complicated. I am, however, conscious of the limitation of my knowledge of it.

The present author craves the readers' indulgence for any deficiencies or discrepancies that may be discernible to their eyes, although no pains have been spared to make the presentation of the subject accurate and perfect.

G.P. Singh

Abbreviations

AAR	*Annals and Antiquities of Rajasthan*
ABORI	*Annals of the Bhandarkar Oriental Research Institute.*
Agn.	*Agni Purāṇa.*
AICL	*Ancient India as Described in Classical Literature*
AIHA	*Aspects of Indian History and Archaeology*
AIHT	*Ancient Indian Historical Tradition*
AIIC	*Ancient India and Indian Civilisation*
AIMA	*Ancient India as Described by Megasthenes and Arrian*
AIOC	All India Oriental Conference
AISH	*Ancient Indian Social History*
Ait. Br.	*Aitareya Brāhmaṇa.*
AN	*Aṅguttara Nikāya*
Arth.	*Arthaśāstra* of Kauṭilya
ASB	Asiatic Society of Bengal, Calcutta
ASIR	*Archaeological Survey of India, Reports*
As. Res.	*Asiatic Researches (Comprising History and Antiquities, the Arts Sciences, Ethnology and Literature of Asia)*
ASS	Ānandāśrama Sanskrit Series
ASWI (or *Arch. SWI*)	*Archaeological Survey of Western India, Reports*
AV	*Atharvaveda*
BDCRS	*Bulletin of the Decan College Research Society*
BGP	Bhāratiya Jñānapīṭha, Kāśī.
Bhāg.	*Bhāgavata Purāṇa*

Bh. Sv. (or *Bh. Sāv*)	*Bhārata Sāvitrī* (an in-depth historical study of the *Mahābhārata*), by V.S. Agarwala.
Bhv.	*Bhaviṣya Purāṇa*
BIS	*Bibliotheca Indica Series* (a collection of Oriental Works), Asiatic Society, Calcutta.
Bmd.	*Brahmāṇḍa Purāṇa.*
Bmv.	*Brahmavaivartta Purāṇa.*
BORI	Bhandarkar Oriental Research Institute, Poona.
Br (or *Brh.*)	*Brahma Purāṇa.*
BRWW	*Buddhist Records of the Western Worlds.*
CAI	*Classical Accounts of India*, by R.G. Majumdar.
CCBM	*Catalogue of the Indian Coins in the British Museum, Ancient India.*
CCIM	*Catalogue of the Coins in the Indian Museum, Calcutta, Coins of Ancient India.*
CHI	*Cambridge History of India.*
Chro. Anct. Ind.	*Chronology of Ancient India.*
CII (or *Corp. Ins. Ind.*)	*Corpus Inscriptionum Indicarum.*
CMI	*Coins of Medieval India.*
Co. An. Ind.	*Coins of Ancient India from the Earliest Times down to the Seventh Century* AD.
Com Hist. Ind.	*Comprehensive History of India.*
CSARM	*Classical Studies in Ancient Races and Myths.*
Cul. Her. Ind.	*Cultural Heritage of India*, published by the Ramakrishna Mission Institute of Culture, Calcutta.
DDEI	*Dates and Dynasties in Earliest India.*
DHAS	Department of Historical and Antiquarian Studies, Gauhati.
DIP	*Dīpavaṁsa* (Ancient Buddhist Historical Record).
DN	*Dīgha Nikāya.*
EAB	*Ethnology of Ancient Bhārata.*

EB (or *En. Br.*)	*Encyclopaedia Britannica.*
EHI	*Early History of India from 600* BC *to the Muhammadan Conquest.*
EHIDS	*Early Hindu India: A Dynastic Study.*
EIHTA	*Early Indian Historical Tradition and Archaeology*, by G.P. Singh.
Ep. Car.	*Epigraphia Carnatica.*
Ep. Ind.	*Epigraphia Indica.*
ERE	*Encyclopaedia of Religion and Ethics.*
GDEP	*A Critical Study of the Geographical Data in the Early Purāṇas.*
Geographical Essays	*Geographical Essays Relating to Ancient Geography of India.*
Grd. (or *Gar.*)	*Garuḍa Purāṇa.*
HAI	*History of Ancient India.*
HASL	*History of Ancient Sanskrit Literature.*
HCSL	*History of Classical Sanskrit Literature.*
HHK	*Hindu History of Kashmir.*
HIL	*History of Indian Literature.*
HOS	Harvard Oriental Series.
HPL	*History of Pāli Literature.*
HSL	*History of Sanskrit Literature.*
Hv.	*Harivaṁśa Purāṇa.*
IETBJ	*India as Described in Early Texts of Buddhism and Jainism.*
IGI (or *Impl. Gaz. Ind.*)	*Imperial Gazetteer of India.*
IHC	Indian History Congress.
IHQ	*Indian Historical Quarterly.*
IHR	*Indian Historical Review.*
IIA	*Invasion of India by Alexander the Great.*
Ind. Ant.	*Indian Antiquary (Journal of Oriental Research in Archaeology, History, Literature, Language, Folklore, etc.).*

Ind. Co.	*Indian Coins.*
Ind. Stud.	*Indische Studien.*
JA	*Journal Asiatique.*
JAOS	*Journal of the American Oriental Society.*
JAS	*Journal of the Asiatic Society.*
JASB	*Journal of the Asiatic Society of Bengal.*
JAS(L)	*Journal of the Asiatic Society, Letters.*
JBBRAS	*Journal of the Bombay Branch of the Royal Asiatic Society.*
JBHU	*Journal of the Banaras Hindu University.*
JBIAS	*Journal of the Bharatiya Itihasa Adhyayan Samsthan.*
JBORS	*Journal of the Bihar and Orissa Research Society.*
JHR	*Journal of Historical Research.*
JIH	*Journal of the Indian History.*
JNSI	*Journal of the Numismatic Society of India.*
JRAS	*Journal of the Royal Asiatic Society of Great Britain and Ireland.*
JRASB	*Journal of the Royal Asiatic Society of Bengal.*
JRASB(L)	*Journal of the Royal Asiatic Society of Bengal, Letters.*
JSS	*Jaina Sahitya Samsodhaka*, Ahmedabad.
KAS	Kāmarūpa Anusandhan Samiti, Gauhati.
Km. (or *Krm.*)	*Kūrma Purāṇa.*
LAIJC	*Life in Ancient India as Depicted in the Jaina Canon and Commentaries.*
Lg. P.	*Liṅga Purāṇa.*
Mahā.	*Mahāpurāṇa.*
Manu.	*Manu-Smṛti.*
MAR	*Mysore Archaeological Reports.*
Mass.	Massachusetts, USA.
Mat. (or *Mts.*)	*Matsya Purāṇa.*
Mbh.	*Mahābhārata.*

Mbh. Ko.	*Mahābhārata Kośa (A Descriptive Index to the Names and Subjects in the Mahābhārata)*, by R.K. Rai.
MDJG	Manikchand Digambara Jaina Granthamala Series, Bombay.
ME	Mahāvīra Era.
Mhv.	*Mahāvaṁsa.*
Mhv. Comm.	*Mahāvaṁsa Commentary.*
Mkd.	*Mārkaṇḍeya Purāṇa.*
MN	*Majjhima Nikāya.*
MR	*Modern Review.*
Nat. Hist. (or *Hist. Nat.*)	*Naturalis Historia (Natural History)* or *Historia Naturalis (History Natural)*, by Pliny.
NEB	*New Encyclopaedia Britannica.*
NSP	Nirṇaya Sāgara Press.
OUP	Oxford University Press.
PDKA	*Purāṇa Text of the Dynasties of the Kali Age.*
Pdm.	*Padma Purāṇa.*
PHAI	*Political History of Ancient India.*
PIHC	*Proceedings of the Indian History Congress.*
PK	*Paurāṇic Kośa*, by R.P. Sharma.
PNEIHA	*Proceedings of North-East India History Association.*
POC	*Proceedings of the All India Oriental Conference.*
PTAIOC or *PTOC*	*Proceedings and Transactions of the All India Oriental Conference.*
PTS	Pāli Text Society, London.
Purāṇa	Half Yearly Bulletin of the Purana Department, All India Kasiraj Trust, Ramnagar, Varanasi.
QRHS	*Quarterly Review of Historical Studies.*
RPVU	*Religion and Philosophy of the Veda and Upanishads.*
R̥V	*R̥gveda.*
Śat. Br.	*Śatapatha Brāhmaṇa.*
SBA	*Sacred Books of the Aryan Series*, Delhi.

SBB	*Sacred Books of the Buddhists.*
SBE	*Sacred Books of the East*, Oxford.
SBLN	*Sanskrit Buddhist Literature of Nepal.*
SGAMI	*Studies in the Geography of Ancient and Medieval India.*
SHC	*Studies in History and Culture.*
SI	*Select Inscriptions Bearing on Indian History and Civilisation.*
SJG	Singhi Jaina Granthamala Series, Bombay.
SN	*Saṁyutta Nikāya.*
SOAS	School of Oriental and African Studies, London.
Tai. Aran.	*Taittirīya Āraṇyaka.*
TSS	Trivandrum Sanskrit Series.
v.	Verse.
Vāl. Rām.	*Vālmīki-Rāmāyaṇa.*
Vāl. Rām. Ko.	*Vālmīki-Rāmāyaṇa Kośa (Descriptive Index to the Names and Subjects of Rāmāyaṇa)*, by R.K. Rai.
VE	Vikrama Era.
VI	*Vedic Index of Names and Subjects.*
Vmn.	*Vāmana Purāṇa.*
VOJ	*Vienna Oriental Journal.*
Vrh.	*Varāha Purāṇa.*
VS	Vikrama Saṁvat.
Vṣṇ.	*Viṣṇu Purāṇa.*
Vṣṇ. Dh. (or *Vsh. Dh.*)	*Viṣṇudharmottara Mahāpurāṇa.*
vv.	verses.
Vy.	*Vāyu Purāṇa*
WZKM	*Wiener Zeitschrift für die Kunde des Morgenlandes.*
YCTI	*Yuan Chwang's Travels in India.*
ZDMG	*Zeitschrift der Deutschen Morgenländische Gesellschaft*, Leipzig.

Contents

Preface vii

Abbreviations ix

Book One
Introductory

1.1. Purpose, Scope, Method and Utility of the Work 3

1.2. Nature of Historiography, Schools of Historical Thought and Writing, and Forms and Kinds of History 28

1.3. Changing Approaches to Indian Historiography 41

Book Two
The Beginnings of Historical Tradition

Preliminary Remarks 47

2.1. The Itihāsa-Purāṇa Tradition and Its Impact on Historiography 51

2.2. The Vedic Tradition 66

- R̥gvedic History 66
- Historical Value of the R̥gveda: General Views 69

2.3. The Epic Tradition 74

- History in the Epics 74
- Historical Value of the Epics: A Critical Assessment 83

2.4. The Purāṇic Tradition 86

Antiquity and Historicity of the Purāṇas 86

Purāṇic History (Purāṇic Tradition of Historiography) 97

Book Three
Buddhist and Jaina Tradition of Historiography

General Remarks 127

3.1. Buddhist Historiography 131

3.2. Jaina Historiography 159

Book Four
The Tradition of Writing Historical Biography

Introductory Remarks 183

4.1. Historical Biographies 187

4.2. A Critical Evaluation of Biographical Writings 246

Book Five
The Tradition of Writing Chronicle, Vaṁśāvalī and Other Historical Works

General Remarks 253

5.1. Chronicles, Vaṁśāvalīs and other Historical Works of Northern India 255

Kashmir 255

Punjab 279

Sindh 281

Rajasthan 285

Nepal 286

5.2. Chronicles and Other Historical Works of Western India 290

Gurjaradeśa (Gujarat) 290

Maharashtra 324

5.3. Chronicles, Vaṁśāvalīs and Other Works of Eastern India 350
Orissa 350
Bengal 354
Assam 363
Manipur 377
Tripura 382

Book Six
The Tradition of Historical Writing in South India

Preliminary Remarks 389
6.1. Historical Writing in Tamiladeśa 394
6.2. The Tradition of Historiography in Karṇāṭadeśa 408
6.3. Historical Writing in Āndhradeśa 433
6.4. Historiography in Kerala 441

Book Seven
Chronological Tradition

Prefatory Remarks 451
7.1. The Purāṇic Tradition of Chronology 453
7.2. Chronological System in the time of Candragupta Maurya 459
7.3. The Buddhist Tradition of Chronology 462
7.4. The Jaina Tradition of Chronology 465
7.5. Eras and Their Historical and Chronological Significance 472

Conclusions and Observations 487
General Bibliography 497
Index 523

Book One
Introductory

1.1

Purpose, Scope, Method and Utility of the Work

> Historiography is a progressive science in the sense, that it seeks to provide constantly expanding and deepening insights into a course of events which is itself progressive.[1]

THE history of historical writing in ancient and medieval India has not been investigated to the extent it needs. We need "a constructive outlook over the past."[2]

India has had a rich tradition of historiography. There were various traditions of historical writing in ancient and medieval India. The historians are the guardians of those traditions.

The primary purpose of undertaking this research work is to trace the evolution of historiographical tradition in India from the time of Vedavyāsa to the end of the Medieval Age. One of our basic objectives is to estimate the contributions of the Hindus, Buddhists, Jainas, native Muslims and Sikhs to the evolution of this tradition. An attempt has been made as far as possible to bring to light the historical and semi-historical works of ancient and medieval historians of India and thereby to dispel the hitherto existing erroneous

---

1. E.H. Carr, *What is History?*, p. 124.
2. F. Powicke, *Modern Historians and the Study of History*, p. 174.

impression created by some Indian and foreign scholars that the ancient Indians (the Hindus, Buddhists and Jainas) had no sense of history and chronology and to disprove that there were neither historians nor historiography in India before the dawn of modern age. We have also examined the authenticity and relevance of the statements of some scholars that the ancient Indians were ignorant of the art of writing history; ancient India was barren of historical writings and it did not produce historians like Herodotus, Thucydides, Polybius and Xenophon of Greece and Livy and Tacitus of Rome, and that only few works bearing the historical character were produced in ancient India.

The ancient Indians, without entertaining the mythical concept of "*Clio* — the *Muse* of History" from whom the ancient Greeks are traditionally believed to have derived the inspiration to learn history, made a beginning in the field of historiography in the literary tradition. It will not be correct to say that the first lesson of history was taught in the school of Greece.

The ancient Indians had a clear conception and perception of history. They took history as the soul of the nation. They being conscious of the fact that the culture and civilisation of any country get reflected through its history took all possible pains to preserve the historical records of the past. They were not ignorant of an art which has been cultivated in other countries from almost the earliest ages. They, like the ancient Egyptians, Sumerians, Assyrians, Babylonians, Greeks, Romans, Chinese, Persians and Arabs, acquired the knowledge of the past and maintained the historical records. They were also aware of the fact that it is the past which determines the future of a country, and those who do not have knowledge of the past have neither present nor future. It has been rightly pointed out by E.H. Carr that "Past, present and future are linked together in the endless chain of history."[3]

It is an acknowledged fact that one of the chief functions of a historian is to discover the past and the documents it left behind or to study and record the facts relating to the society and culture of the past.[4] G. Barraclough correctly observed that there is nothing wrong in the realm of historiography to discover the past even on the basis of "imperfect and fragmentary evidence."[5] History in the words of J. Burckhardt is "the record of what one age finds worthy of note in another."[6]

The ancient Indians usually kept those records which they felt were significant and worth preserving.[7] "A sense of history can be defined as a consciousness of past events, which events are relevant to a particular society, seen in a chronological framework and expressed in a form which meets the needs of that society . . . the historical tradition can be culled from existing literature, whether specifically historical or not. Every society has a concept of its past and therefore no society can be called ahistorical. Furthermore, historical memory is frequently recorded in a chronological order."[8] It is also said that "Whether or not India had a sense

3. E.H. Carr, op. cit., p. 134.

4. See also Carr, op. cit., pp. 21-22, 26, 55; R.G. Collingwood, *The Idea of History*, p. 282.

5. *History in a Changing World*, pp. 29-30.

6. *Judgements on History and on Historians*, p. 158.

7. Romila Thapar, *The Past and Prejudice*, pp. 2-3.

8. Thapar, "The Tradition of Historical Writing in Early India", in her *AISH*, pp. 268-69.

of history, she had a lively sense of the past, though this past was generally visualised in legendary terms."[9]

It can scarcely be believed that the Indians, who applied their literary genius to almost all conceivable branches of study, failed to pay their attention to the chronicling of contemporary events and socio-economic, political, religious and cultural life of the people. In the words of James Tod:

> Is it to be imagined that a nation so highly civilised as the Hindus, amongst whom the exact sciences flourished in perfection, by whom the fine arts, architecture, sculpture, poetry and music were not only cultivated, but taught and defined by the nicest and most elaborate rules, were totally unacquainted with the simple art of recording the events of their history, the character of their princes, and the acts of their reigns? Where such traces of mind exist, we can hardly believe that there was a want of competent recorders of events, which synchronical authorities tell us, were worthy of commemoration.[10]

The above statements can fairly be attested to by M. Elphinstone's observation:

> As the rudest nations are seldom destitute of some account of the transactions of their ancestors it is a natural subject of surprise that the Hindus should have attained to a high pitch of civilisation without any work that at all approaches to the character of a history.[11]

However, it cannot be denied that only few of them attained perfection in the art of writing history or seriously took to it. One of the notable deficiencies in their writings is the

---

9. A.L. Basham cf. V.S. Pathak, *Ancient Historians of India*, Foreword.

10. *AAR*, I, Introduction, xiv.

11. Quoted in A.K. Majumdar, *EHIDS*, I, p. 41.

conspicuous absence of the details of political achievements of the kings and that of the rise and fall of kingdoms with few exceptions.

The correctness of the views expressed by the Indian and foreign scholars regarding the historical and chronological sense of the ancient Indians, particularly the Hindus, needs to be examined critically and objectively, and the progress achieved in the field of historiography during the medieval period needs to be ascertained so as to present a true history of historical writing in ancient and medieval India.

Alberuni was the first to remark that "The Hindus do not pay much attention to the historical order of things, they are very careless in relating the chronological succession of their kings. . . ."[12] This remark, which was made by him in CE 1030 in his Arabic work, *Tahqiq-i-Hind* (An Enquiry into India), has no relevance. The works of the Hindus especially the Purāṇa records were the principal sources of information for him for writing his book as admitted by himself. It is paradoxical that he calls his own work "a simple historic record of facts,"[13] but the sources on which it is based are spoken of as unhistorical.

In an attempt to justify Alberuni's statement, S.R. Sharma writes that his "version on the lack of historical sense of the Indians is largely justified by the paucity of historical works properly so called in our country coming down from ancient times. Material from which history can be constructed is undoubtedly available in abundance but very little of it shares the character of regular history."[14] But, on the other hand,

---

12. E.C. Sachau, *Alberuni's India*, II, pp. 10-11.

13. Ibid., Preface, p. 7.

14. *The Making of Modern India*, II, p. 308.

A.K. Majumdar asserts that ". . . we can't admit that the Hindus had incapacity for writing history and our ancestors have not bequeathed to us any reliable historical work for early period. They knew the simple art of writing history."[15]

L.J. Trotter and W.H. Hutton remarked that ". . . the old Hindus produced . . . not one historian of even the smallest mark."[16] Any sensible historian will never accept such kind of absurd remark. Some scholars have levelled the charge against the ancient Hindus that they "wrote no formal history at any period."[17] They did not have capacity to write history as stated by them. It has also been said that "Though genuine materials once abounded in India yet we find no national history of the Hindus."[18] H. Beveridge opines that "With the exception of a work on Kashmir, the literature of India has failed to furnish a single production to which the name of history can in any proper sense of the term be applied."[19] Such remarks can be dismissed as biased, prejudicial, misleading and fallacious.

A.A. Macdonell states that ancient India has bequeathed to us no historical works.

> History is the one weak spot in Indian literature. It is, in fact, non-existent. The total lack of historical sense is so characteristic that the whole course of Sanskrit literature is darkened by the shadow of this defect, suffering as it does from an entire absence of exact chronology. In the first place early India wrote no history because it never made any. . . . Secondly, the brāhmaṇas

---

15. *EHIDS*, I, p. 6.

16. *History of India from the Earliest Times to the Present Day*, p. 39.

17. J.N. Farquhar, *An Outline of the Religious Literature of India*, p. 3.

18. J.F. Fleet's paper on Epigraphy, *IGI*, II, p. 21.

19. *A Comprehensive History of India*, I, p. 18.

> whose task it would naturally have been to record the great deeds . . . have felt but little inclination to chronicle historical events.[20]

His statements amount to distortion of the history of historiography in ancient India.

Nothing can be farther from the truth than the statements that ancient India was without history and historians. The ancient Indians had "a distaste for history." The details of past events did not interest them and, therefore, they did not record them.[21]

It was Karl Marx who first stated in one of his articles published in the *New-York Daily Tribune*, 8 August 1853, that the Indians do not have their own history. His statement is not worthy of acceptance.

Parimal Kumar Das' statements, that there has been no tradition of historical writing in India and that there has been lack of historical consciousness on our part as a result of which very little history has been written in our country since ancient times,[22] are unworthy of credence.

It has been rightly said that "History, one of the oldest branches of human knowledge, has never been a neutral discipline standing outside of ideology and politics."[23]

R.G. Bhandarkar's observation, that "India has no real history. . . . The historical curiosity of the people was satisfied

20. *HSL*, pp. 10-11.

21. P. Masson-Oursel & c. AIIC, Foreword by Henri Berr, pp. xi-xii, xiv, and p. 22.

22. "Itihāsa Lekhan: Ek Dr̥ṣṭikoṇa" (History writing: A Perspective), in *Bias in Indian Historiography*, ed. D. Devahuti, p. 57.

23. B.I. Marushkin, *History and Politics*, Introduction, p. 7.

by legends what we find of a historical nature in the literature of the country before the arrival of the Muhammadans,"[24] can unhesitatingly be disposed of. He, like many other scholars, considers only Kalhaṇa's *Rājataraṅgiṇī* a historical work.

D.R. Bhandarkar (the worthy son of the worthy father), says that "historic sense had always been germane to the Indian mind, and if it did not manifest itself at any particular period by all sections of the people it was not on account of the extinctions of that faculty in them. It would be the height of absurdity to presume that prior to the medieval period the Indians never had any historic sense whatsoever."[25]

The view of S.R. Sharma is also worthy of notice. He holds that the *Rājataraṅgiṇī*, only historical work, is a poetic account of the rulers of Kashmir in which history is not a little vitiated by the art in which it is expressed. The bardic writers of Rajasthan also contributed to the historical writing in India. The "historical works and chronicles came into vogue in India more and more with the advent of the Muslims."[26]

Every scholar has his or her own view about Indian historiography.

J.W. McCrindle is of the view that:

> The Indians themselves did not write history. They produced, no doubt, a literature both voluminous and varied . . . but within its vast range history is conspicuous by its absence. Their learned men were brāhmaṇas whose modes and habits

---

24. *Early History of the Dekkan Down to the Mahomedan Conquest*, Introduction, pp. i-iv.
25. Cf. B.N. Puri, "D.R. Bhandarkar and Indian Historiography," PIHC (42nd session, Magadha University, Bodh Gaya, 1981), p. 37.
26. Op. cit.

> of thought almost necessarily incapacitated them for the task of historical composition . . . they allowed events, even those of the greatest public moment, to pass unrecorded, and so to perish from memory.[27]

The legitimacy of his view is questionable. His observation, that Sanskrit literature is deficient in history and chronology,[28] can also not be accepted as it runs contrary to the truth.

Some Indian and foreign scholars seem to have fallen into the grip of confusion about the historical value of ancient Sanskrit literature. The confusion has been made worse confounded by some recent writings on historiography in the context.

Some scholars are of the opinion that the Indians in the ancient past were not historians and did not have historical records like the Egyptians, Assyrians, Babylonians, Sumerians, Greeks, Romans, Chinese and Persians.[29] But the fact remains that each country has had its own tradition of historical writing and each tradition has its own value. The value of historiographical tradition in India should be judged independently and not by comparing with that in other countries. In every country, the art of history-writing developed gradually, and India is not an exception to this.

The statement, that "The Hindus have no history and no authentic chronology . . . and there is no certain date in

---

27. AICL, Introduction, p. xii.
28. IIA, Introduction, p. 6.
29. See Maurice Phillips, *The Teaching of the Vedas*, pp. 14-15; D.D. Kosambi, *The Culture and Civilisation of Ancient India in Historical Outline*, pp. 9-10.

the wide range of their literature except what is imported from Greek history,"[30] can outrightly be rejected. D.D. Kosambi's statements, that "India has virtually no historical records worth the name. . . . In India there is only vague popular tradition, with very little documentation above the level of myth and legend. We cannot reconstruct anything like a complete list of kings. Sometimes whole dynasties have been forgotten . . . no dates can be determined for any Indian personality till the Muslim period,"[31] can also be disputed.

Some of the historians of ancient India have opined that in all the large and varied literatures of the brāhmaṇas, Buddhists and Jainas there is not a single work which can be compared to the *Histories* of Herodotus, historical work of Thucydides or the *History* of Polybius of Greece or the *Annals* of Livy or Tacitus of Rome.[32] Any such comparison is unwarrantable. The historical works of the ancient Indians have their own merit and excellence.

E.J. Rapson has correctly stated that:

> . . . the ages were filled with stirring events; but these events found no systematic record. Of the great foreign invasions of Darius, Alexander the Great and Seleucus no mention is to be discovered in any Indian work. The struggles between native princes, the rise and fall of empires, have indeed not passed similarly into utter oblivion. The memory is to some extent preserved in epic poems, in stories of the sages and heroes of

30. Maurice Phillips, op. cit.
31. D.D. Kosambi, op. cit.
32. E.J. Rapson, "Sources of History", in *CHI*, I, *Ancient India*, ed. by himself, p. 51; E.J. Rapson, *Ancient India from the Earliest Times to the First Century AD*, p. 8; J. Allan, Wolseley Haig and H.H. Dodwell, *The Cambridge Shorter History of India*, p. 1; R.S. Tripathi, HAI, p. 1; Kosambi, *An Introduction to the Study of Indian History*, p. 1; H.C. Raychaudhuri, PHAI, p. 1.

> old, in genealogies and dynastic lists. Such in all countries are the beginnings of history; and in ancient India its development was not carried beyond this rudimentary stage.[33]

The literatures of brāhmaṇas, Buddhists and Jainas are deficient as records of political progress, and "By their aid alone it would be impossible to sketch the outline of the political history of any of the nations of India before the Muhammadan conquest."[34]

It will be a futile and unproductive exercise to draw a demarcation line between the historical writings in ancient India on the one hand and in ancient Greece and Rome on the other from the standpoint of degree of importance. In fact, all these three ancient countries were the repositories of historical wisdom. James Tod has rightly pointed out that:

> Those who expect from a people like the Hindus a species of composition of precisely the same character as the historical works of Greece and Rome commit the very egregious error of overlooking the peculiarities which distinguish the natives of India from all other races, and their intellectual productions of every kind. Their history like their philosophy, their poetry and their architecture are marked with traits of originality.[35]

He speaks very highly of historical sense, and historical works of all kinds, of the ancient Indians. He further adds that historical records, including the Purāṇas, and other works of a mixed historical character existed in ancient India.[36]

The ancient Greek and Roman historians produced only

33. "Sources of History," in *CHI*, I, p. 51.
34. Ibid., pp. 51-52.
35. *AAR*, I, Introduction, pp. xiv-xv.
36. Ibid., pp. xiii-xvii.

political histories[37] whereas the ancient historians of India touched upon all aspects of history — social, economic, political, religious and cultural. Both ancient Indian traditions and classical traditions of historiography have relative value. Max Müller is absolutely right in stating that history provides a comprehensive knowledge of all that happened in the past.[38] "There is history in the large and history in the small; each has its value, but their values are different."[39]

It is worthy of note that in every country and in every age the body of history has been shaped by the events of the contemporary age which were not identical at all. The events became the theme of historical writing or subject for historians to deal with. The historian makes history and the subject makes a historian. "Instead of the historian choosing the subject, the subject chooses the historian."[40] Sometimes history is produced by a historian and sometimes historian is produced by an event. "The historian, before he begins to write history, is the product of history."[41]

Greece was not the first country of historical composition as generally believed by the scholars. It is equally not correct to say that the Greeks first learnt the art of writing history. The history acquired its meaning and purpose and received the treatment in both ancient India and Greece concurrently. The contemporaneous growth of historical sense and development of historical writing in both the countries

37. See also B.B. Chakravorty, *Itihāsa of Bhāratavarṣa from the Bhāratīya Viewpoint (up to Gupta Period)*, pp. 25-26, 81-82.

38. *India: What can it Teach Us?* (London, 1883), pp. 25-27.

39. L. Gottschalk, *Understanding History: A Premier of Historical Method*, p. 10.

40. R.G. Collingwood, *The Idea of History*, p. 27.

41. Carr, op. cit., p. 40.

cannot be denied. And, thus, it will be unfair to highlight the importance of one and discard or depreciate the value of the other.

We do not find ourselves in agreement with E.J. Rapson that if "any ancient Indian literature, Brāhmaṇa, Jaina, or Buddhist", is compared with Greek and Latin classics, it will be found that "in none of them has the art of historical compostion been developed beyond its earliest stages."[42] He further observes that "Its sources — heroic poems, legendary chronicles, ancient genealogies — are indeed to be found in abundance. From the literatures and from the monuments we learn the names, and some of the achievements, of a great number of nations who rose to power, flourished, and declined in the continent of India during the twenty-two centuries before the Muhammadan conquest; but not one of these nations had found its historian." The literatures of ancient India "supply materials by means of which it is possible to trace the daily life of the people, their social systems, their religion, their progress in the arts and sciences, with a completeness which is unparalleled in antiquity; but events are rarely mentioned, and there is an almost total absence of chronology. Dynastic lists with, in some instances, the length of the different reigns are certainly to be found; but these in themselves supply no fixed point for the determination of Indian chronology."[43] In his observations, we find both acceptance and distortion of truth. All his statements are correct except that ancient India had no historian; and in ancient Indian literature historical events are not recorded and chronology is totally absent.

J. Allan, Wolseley Haig and H.H. Dodwell state that the

42. *Ancient India from the Earliest Times to the First Century AD*, p. 8.

43. Ibid., pp. 8-9.

only professedly historical work, the late twelfth-century chronicle of Kashmir, contains a certain amount of historical information. The epics, the Purāṇas, the biographical works, etc. are of little value from historical and chronological points of view.[44] As a matter of fact, all these works have considerable historical value. Some of the Purāṇas contain chronological data too. The chronicle of Kashmir in particular contains a bulk of valuable historical information.

Some balanced and rational judgements have been pronounced on the subject under discussion.

Affirming the historical sense of the ancient Indians and their historical writings, Maurice Winternitz (a German scholar) writes:

> . . . One must not believe as it has so often been asserted that the historical sense is entirely lacking in the Indians. In India too there has been historical writing and . . . we find in India numerous accurately dated inscriptions which could hardly be the case if the Indians have had no sense of history at all. It is only truth that the Indians in their writing of history never knew how to keep fact and fiction strictly apart, that to them the facts themselves were always more important than their chronological order and they attached no importance at all especially in literary matters to the question of what was earlier or later. Since the fifth century after Christ inscriptions too begin to give us information about the dates of many writers. . . .[45]

A.B. Keith is perfectly right in stating that "To the old complaint that India has no historians and no historical sense it has recently been objected, doubtless with a measure of truth, that there is certain amount of writing and a number

44. J. Allan, et al., op. cit.

45. *HIL*, I, pp. 29-30.

of facts attesting a degree of sense for history. In view of the antiquity and the developed character of Indian civilisation it would indeed be ridiculous to expect to find India destitute of historical sense. . . ."[46] But his statements that, "despite that abundance of its literature, history is so miserably represented, and that in the whole of the great period of Sanskrit literature there is not one writer who can be seriously regarded as a critical historian"[47] are not absolutely but partly correct. He, however, admits that some historical and semi-historical works were produced in ancient India. The Purāṇic genealogies, the *paṭṭāvalīs* of the Jainas and the works of the Buddhists, according to him, are of considerable historical value. The biographical works of Vākpatirāja Padmagupta, Bilhaṇa and others in his estimation are of greater historical value. The *Chronicle of Kings of Kashmir* in his opinion is the nearest approach to history. And its author Kalhaṇa is called by him "a true historian," who, according to him, is not a suitable match for Herodotus. We are in perfect agreement with him that the historians of Kashmir made substantial contributions to the evolution of Indian historiography. He points out that the national feeling, which is a powerful aid to the writing of history, was not evoked in ancient India. The political events that took place in India up to the twelfth century CE including the foreign invasions and the struggles and wars between rival dynasties and empires, were not recorded by the historians of ancient times because of absence of such feeling.[48] The struggles and wars between native rulers do find mention in some ancient Indian historical works; but the foreign invasions could not be recorded by ancient historians of India which may be attributed to non-availability of the sources

46. *HSL*, p. 144.

47. Ibid.

48. Ibid., pp. 144-48.

concerned in India during their times and not to the absence of national feeling among them.

A. Weber has categorically stated that the old Purāṇas and the works of Bāṇa, Bilhaṇa and Kalhaṇa are solid proofs of historical writings. Kalhaṇa's *Rājataraṅgiṇī* is a great work from both historical and chronological points of view. The family records preserved in ancient times are trustworthy. The ancient inscriptions, grants, etc. are also of considerable historical value.[49] M.A. Stein has also recorded his agreement with him on the points under discussion. He concurs with the scholars who are of the opinion that the ancient Indians possessed historical sense as well as historical works. He says:

> . . . advancing research has also proved that written records of events and traditions concerning them have by no means been wanting in ancient India.[50]

A.K. Warder, an acknowledged authority on Indian historiography, has strongly advocated the historical sense of the ancient Indians. In his work, he has presented abundant proofs of historical writing in ancient India. He says that it is a superficial misconception that ancient India produced little or no historical literature. He has firmly established that there was continuity in historiographical tradition in ancient India from Vedic antiquity to the twelfth century CE.[51] He has also conclusively proved that the tradition of historical writing further continued in medieval and modern India in an unbroken fashion.[52]

49. *HIL*, pp. 213-15.

50. *Rājataraṅgiṇī*, tr., I, p. 3.

51. *An Introduction to Indian Historiography*, Preface, p. vii, and pp. 15ff; see also C.H. Philips (ed.), *Historians of India, Pakistan and Ceylon* (vol. I of *Historical Writings on the Peoples of Asia*), pp. 44ff.

52. For details see his *An Introduction to Indian Historiography*.

U.N. Ghoshal,[53] A.D. Pusalker,[54] R.C. Majumdar,[55] R.C. Dutt,[56] Radha Kumud Mookerji[57] and Radhakamal Mukerjee,[58] the noted authorities on ancient Indian history, have proved beyond doubt that the ancient Indians had a true sense of history and produced historical and quasi-historical works of various kinds. They have acknowledged the facts that the tradition of historical writing was maintained in ancient India; the historical biographies, historical chronicles and other historical treatises were composed in different parts of India; the Hindus, Buddhists and Jainas made significant contributions to the evolution of historiography in ancient India.

Radha Kumud Mookerji has rightly pointed out that:

> History is not merely political and chronological and is not limited only to individual and datable facts and events. History is more important and interesting as a history of thought. It is social and cultural history.[59]

We are very much indebted to A.D. Pusalker for bringing to

53. *The Beginnings of Indian Historiography and Other Essays*, pp. 21-23, 50-52; *Studies in Indian History and Culture*, pp. 7-8, 15-18; "History and Historians of Ancient India in the Modern Age", *Indo-Asian Culture*, IX, 1961, pp. 353-84.
54. "Conception of History in Ancient Indian Literature", *Our Heritage*, XII, 2, 1964, pp. 35-52.
55. "Sources of Indian History," in *The Vedic Age*, ed. by himself, pp. 47-52; *Ancient India*, pp. 7-8; "Ideas of History in Sanskrit Literature", in *Historians of India, Pakistan and Ceylon (supra)*, 13-28.
56. *A History of Civilisation in Ancient India Based on Sanskrit Literature*, I (2000-320 BCE), pp. 2-4, 109-11; see also his *Ancient India (2000 BCE-CE 800)*, Delhi, 1980.
57. *Ancient India*, pp. 4ff.
58. *The Culture and Art of India*, pp. 33-34.
59. Op. cit., pp. 4-5.

light some of the Sanskrit histories and chronicles of the medieval period.[60]

It is not merely the genealogies, biographies and chronicles of kings but also other records that bear the evidence of historical writing.

Hiuen Tsang's testimony of the practice of preserving historical records in India[61] also deserves our notice. The practice of maintaining written records continued for centuries after Hiuen Tsang. At the courts of kings archives were maintained for preserving the records of important happenings. The archival records were used for composing or compiling mainly the chronicles and Vaṁśāvalīs.[62] There is enough evidence to show the historical consciousness on the part of the ancient Indians to preserve the records of the past events. A.L. Basham also observes that "At the courts of ancient Indian kings careful records were kept of the events of chief importance to the realm, but unfortunately these archives are completely lost to us."[63] He further adds that Kalhaṇa was the first to write the history of his native land, but his work although of great value for the study of the history of Kashmir has little to tell us about India as a whole. And no similar chronicles were composed elsewhere. It is unjust to maintain that the ancient Indians had no sense of history. The great empires which had risen and fallen in historical times did not receive their serious attention.[64]

60. See his "Sanskrit Histories and Chronicles", in *Cul.Her.Ind.*, V, ed. S.K. Chatterji (Calcutta, 1978), pp. 283-90.

61. See S. Beal (tr.), *BRWW* (London, 1906), I, p. 78; Thomas Watters, *YCTI* (London, 1904-05, Delhi, 1973), I, p. 154.

62. For details see G.P. Singh, *Ancient Indian Historiography*, p. 171.

63. *The Wonder That was India*, p. 45.

64. Ibid.

The evidence of historical writing in ancient India produced by C.V. Vaidya is very striking:

> The charge has often been brought against the Indians that they had no idea of history. . . . Work known as histories or *itihāsa*s were known even in Vedic times. The *Mahābhārata* itself was originally a history. Historical facts, especially genealogies, were most carefully recorded at all times in ancient India. The detailed figures given by Megasthenes himself clearly prove that this was done in his time. Hiuen Tsang has recorded it as a fact that annals were carefully recorded in each state. The *Rājataraṅgiṇī* speaks of ancient histories of Kashmir. In the presence of such evidence extending over such a long period, we cannot believe that history had no existence in India.[65]

The want of an authentic history of the ancient Hindus has been a matter of regret from the days of Sir William Jones. India was never without a history. A great nation never passes away without leaving records of its deeds and achievements. Ancient India was not bereft of such records. In ancient historical writings, there are some materials for our knowledge of the history and civilisation of ancient India. Each successive age has left in its literature a photograph of its thought and civilisation and when we bring all these photographs together we perceive at a glance the whole history of the "Hindu nation" and its civilisation, says R.C. Dutt.[66]

It is also believed that some of the ancient annals and other written records were destroyed or tampered with by the Muslims in the course of their invasions of India.

It is striking to note that the inscribed coins with dates

---

65. *The Mahābhārata: A Criticism*, pp. 58-59.

66. "An Introductory Essay on the History of Kashmira", in *Kings of Kashmira* (English tr. of Kalhaṇa's *Rājataraṅgiṇī*) by J.C. Dutt, II, pp. iii-v.

of rulers and events and dated inscriptions with historical information also bear testimony to the historical and chronological sense of the Indians.[67]

N.L. Dey observes:

> There is no systematic history of India before the Muhammadan conquest, the facts are meagre and scattered . . . the ancient Hindus did not possess any regular history, except the *Rājataraṅgiṇī*. Historiography was perhaps too secular to be worthy of the consideration of a people so much imbued with religious ideas. The *Rājataraṅgiṇī* . . . written by Kalhaṇa . . . is only the chronicle of the kings of Kashmir. But the ancient Hindus have left behind them innumerable works from which some idea of the civilisation . . . could be deduced. The several copper-plate inscriptions, inscriptions upon rocks and temples, and the various coins which are exhumed from time to time from the bowels of the earth, might also very well form a chapter of ancient Hindu history.[68]

Romila Thapar's conception of history, perception of the past and interpretations of the facts are really praiseworthy. The author of this work does not concur with her view that "The Indian tradition until the seventh century CE lacks any literature which can be specifically described as historical writings."[69] It is an acknowledged fact that the most important tradition of historical writing before the seventh century CE was Purāṇic one. A lot of valuable historical information is available in the Purāṇic literature of the pre-seventh century CE. Besides, some Buddhist and Jaina works composed before that century also contain historical writings. The author,

67. See also G.P. Singh, op. cit., pp. 172-73.

68. *Civilisation in Ancient India*, pp. 5, 175-76.

69. "The Tradition of Historical Writings in Early India", in her *AISH*, p. 268.

however, entirely agrees with her so far as the statements, that the historical biographies and histories of kingdoms produced between the seventh and the twelfth century CE form parts of historical literature[70] and that "the Indian historical tradition, particularly in the period prior to the seventh century CE, was not concerned primarily with keeping a record of essential political events . . . ,"[71] are concerned.

Expressing his views about Indian historiography, Jawaharlal Nehru wrote that the ancient Indians were not the historians like the Greeks, Chinese and the Arabs, and, therefore, we cannot safely depend on their works for determining the dates or putting the sequence of events in a proper chronological order. He also, like many other scholars, held that only Kalhaṇa's *Rājataraṅgiṇī* can be called a history. He, however, admitted that the Indian's knowledge of the past is also based on traditional accounts, Purāṇic stories and the *gāthā*s which have been handed down from generation to generation.[72]

Dismissing the false notion that the Indians, particularly the Hindus, did not produce any history, and upholding that there was tradition of historical writing in India, Dr Rajendra Prasad (the first President of Independent India), on the other hand, wrote that our ancestors have left behind them history of our past life describing all important events without specifying their dates. They also touched upon social and political life of the people. He further added that our Sanskrit literature is full of historical material. It contains

70. "The Tradition of Historical Writings in Early India", in her *AISH*, p. 268.

71. Ibid., p. 269.

72. *The Discovery of India*, p. 102; also its Hindi tr., *Hindustān kī Kahānī*, by Ramachandra Tandan, p. 114.

information about social formation, life and culture of the people, royal dynasties, mutual conflicts of the kings and their defeats and victories, etc.[73]

Ancient India was not devoid of either history or historians. The ancient Indian historians have bequeathed to us various types of historical work which include dynastic annals, genealogical records, historical biographies and local chronicles. The historical sense of ancient Indian writers is eloquently reflected in the works they have left behind. The richness of historical materials embodied in different kinds of literature also confirms their historical sense. Some of the Purāṇas, Pāli chronicles and commentaries, and the Jaina works, Kalhaṇa's work and the inscriptional records testify to their knowledge of chronology too. The tradition of historical writing further continued in medieval India. There was tremendous progress in the field of writing of historical biographies, chronicles and Vaṁśāvalīs. The regional histories and histories of kingdoms were also produced during the medieval period. The chronological tradition further developed. The chronological data furnished by the Hindu and Jaina writers of medieval period are very authentic. The medieval Indian historians made substantial contributions to the evolution of the tradition of historiography. We have enough evidence of historical writing in ancient and medieval India. In the light of the above facts, the hitherto existing belief that before the dawn of modern age historiography whatsoever was unknown in India can be dismissed without any hitch and hesitation.

There is ample scope for reconstructing the history of historical writing in ancient and medieval India.

---

73. *Sanskrit aur Saṁskṛti* pp. 9-13.

The Beginnings of Indian Historiography and Other Essays (1944), by U.N. Ghoshal, basically deals with Indian historical tradition. *Historians of India, Pakistan and Ceylon*, vol. I of *Historical Writing on the Peoples of Asia* (1961), edited by C.H. Philips, is not solely devoted to the study of Indian historiography. It contains only few articles by Indian and Foreign historians on the historical writings of the ancient Indians and other aspects of ancient Indian history. The remark of the editor of this volume (Introduction, p. 3), that "Historians of the peoples of the subcontinent have in the past operated rather like isolated guerrilla fighters in a jungle . . . ," can be dismissed as baseless and absurd. V.S. Pathak's *Ancient Historians of India* (1966) is a study in historical biography only. J.P. De Souza and C.M. Kulkarni (eds.), *Historiography in Indian Languages* (1972), contains 23 papers by different scholars on historical writings in eight Indian languages — Marathi, Bengali, Gujarati, Gurumukhi, Tamil, Telugu, Kannada and Malayalam. It is, no doubt, a collection of valuable papers from the point of view of Indian historiography. But it (as a whole) does not cover all relevant aspects of the subject under notice. A.K. Warder's *An Introduction to Indian Historiography* (1972) is, no doubt, the most excellent and the best of all the works on Indian historiography produced so far. It covers many important aspects of the subject, of course, but some of the traditions of historical writing have not received the full treatment at the hands of the author. We find some gaps in those portions of his work which deal with historiography in ancient and medieval India. Romila Thapar's paper "The Tradition of Historical Writing in Early India," in her *Ancient Indian Social History* (1978) deals with the main concepts of the historical tradition and some other pertinent aspects of the subject. The paper, however, does not cover all the traditions of historiography in ancient India.

B.N. Puri's *Ancient Indian Historiography* (1994) is, of course, a valuable work, but the information it contains about the subject is very scanty.

In view of the fact that enough works have already been done on the Muslim historians and their historical writings in Persian and Arabic by the historians of medieval india (like Jagadish Narayan Sarkar's work *History of History Writing in Mediaeval India*), only those Indian Muslim writers have been included in this work who wrote in regional languages in the Indian tradition of historiography. The inclusion of an Arabic work (later translated into Persian), that is the chronicle of Sindh, in this volume is an exception to this.

History in Modern Indian Literature (1975), edited by S.P. Sen, and *Historical Biography in Indian Literature* (1979), edited by S.P. Sen, are also worth mentioning here. Suffice it to say that their titles show what they deal with.

R.C. Majumdar's *Historiography in Modern India* (1970), S.P. Sen (ed.), *Historians and Historiography in Modern India* (1973) — an anthology of articles by forty eminent historians of modern India — and Subodh Kumar Mukhopadhyay's *Evolution of Historiography in Modern India* (1980) are useful only for the study of history of historical writing in modern India.

Ancient and medieval Indian traditions of historiography have not received as much serious attention as modern Indian historiography. Thus, there is a fair scope to highlight the different traditions of historiography in ancient and medieval India. Fresh light can be thrown on the antiquity of Indian historical tradition, nature of historiography, forms of history, ancient and medieval historians and their works, and evolution of historiographical and chronological traditions in India.

The work is broadly based on the original sources — texts and translations. The historical data contained in them have been critically analysed and scientifically interpreted. The information available in the modern works relating to the subject have also been incorporatd in this work as far as practicable. The work is divided into seven books further subdivided into chapters.

The present work will fill in the vacuums existing in our knowledge of the historians and historiography in ancient and medieval India.

1.2

Nature of Historiography, Schools of Historical Thought and Writing, and Forms and Kinds of History

INDIAN historiography began in literary tradition. The writing of history in this tradition began in the time of Vedavyāsa and continued until the beginning of the eighteenth century. History continued to flourish as a branch of literature in India and other countries of the world (where historical tradition was maintained) down to the close of the seventeenth century. It has been rightly pointed out by J.W. Thompson (a great authority on historiography) that the historical writing up to the seventeenth century was regarded predominantly as literature.[1]

The professional historians of today (with few exceptions) in their zeal for the truth, accuracy, objectivity and authentic chronology often deny the value of historical writings embodied in Indian literature. Highlighting the historical value of Indian literature, Tarasankar Banerjee writes:

> With few exceptions Indian historical writings have betrayed an aversion to the use of literature as source materials for reconstructing the contemporary history. The legacy we have

1. *A History of Historical Writing*, I, Preface, p. viii.

> inherited from the British historians of India is yet to be shaken off to give a new orientation to historical research which has hitherto been primarily document-based political history. Records-oriented research has its own merits. But it does not bring out the whole truth. Records speak other's language but literature has an inner language of its own. Hence, recently more attention is being given to literature for writing history.[2]

We have enough evidence of historical writing in ancient and medieval Indian literature. The history and civilisation of ancient and medieval India have been recorded in different classes of literary work. But only those works can be considered as historical which bear the character of a true history. The existence of historical literature in India is proved by the literary works of historical value, historical biographies, chronicles and other historical works which have come down to us. A. Weber has correctly stated that history was a part of literature. Indian literature has both history and chronology.[3]

Some scholars are of the view that ancient Indian literature in comparison to European literature is of little value from historical and chronological points of view. They hold that the biographical works of little historical value belong to literature rather than history.

> The historical data that can be gathered from Sanskrit and Pāli literature cannot be despised, but interpretation is often difficult and there is an entire lack of chronological data. It is with the help of synchronisms given by . . . mainly Greek and Chinese writers that the chronology of Indian history has been built up.[4]

---

2. "History in Bengali Literature", in *History in Modern Indian Literature*, ed. S.P. Sen, p. 22.
3. *HIL*, pp. 213f.
4. J. Allan, Wolseley Haig and H.H. Dodwell, *The Cambridge Shorter History of India*, p. 1.

History is not bunk in ancient Indian literature. It has only been coalesced with myths or legends. But one can be easily distinguished from the other. As already stated, historical biographies form parts of historical literature. Purāṇic and Pāli literatures are not deficient in chronological data and it is on the basis of this data that the chronology of ancient Indian history has been partly built up.

Maurice Winternitz asserts that there is an abundant wealth of historical information in ancient Indian literature which forms a necessary complement to the classical literature of ancient Greece and Rome.[5]

Writing to Noldke in 1877 about the contribution of the ancient Hindus in the field of producing historical literature, Prof Bühler remarked: "You are a little behind the age with your notion that Indians have no historical literature."[6] In his writing, he also referred to the works discovered by himself in which he found that the authors are contemporary with the events they describe. Max Müller has also attested to the historical value of ancient Sanskrit literature including the *Ṛgveda*. He has unequivocally stated that in order to understand the civilisation of ancient India one shall have to rely upon its historical literature. He does not give his assent to the views of some scholars that India had no historical work.[7]

J.T. Wheeler has rightly placed the *Ṛgveda*, the two epics and the Purāṇas under the category of semi-historical literature. He is, however, not wrong in stating that the "Sanskrit literature, whether Vedic or Brāhmanic, has no

5. *HIL*, I, pp. 30f.
6. Cf. *Modern Review*, January 1955, pp. 68-69.
7. *India: What can it Teach us?*, London, 1899, pp. 5-10, 90-96.

historical annals in the modern sense of the word, and that it is devoid of all real sequence or chronology."[8]

The Sanskrit, Buddhist and Jaina literatures are equally important from both historical and chronological points of view. Some of the works in Sanskrit and Prākṛt and the works in regional languages produced during the medieval period are also very useful for our historical purposes. The works of the Hindus and Jainas in particular composed during the period are important not only from the historical point of view but from the chronicle point of view as well. That there are histories in ancient and medieval Indian literatures cannot be questioned.

The Indian historiography before the dawn of modern age was by and large literary in character. The histories written in India in the literary tradition have been called by the Western scholars "literary history of the East." The evolution of historiography took place in both the East and the West in a literary tradition.

It may further be noted here that ancient India did not witness the compartmentalisation of knowledge. It was looked at in totality and presented in its entirety. History did not emerge as a separate discipline. It rather continued to flourish as a branch of literature till the end of the seventeenth century as noted before. It was unlike today not a subject of specialised knowledge. Nevertheless, its study and writing were never neglected. The writing of history was not a profession but a choice. There was no class of professional historians like today. There are some instances to show that the same writer combined in himself the

---

8. *India from the Earliest Ages (Hindu, Buddhist and Brahmanical Revival)*, vol. III of the *History of India*, Preface, p. viii, and pp. 5-6.

qualities of a poet, historian, geographer, grammarian and so on. The identity of history as an independent discipline was not established before the eighteenth century. Until then history and literature remained intertwined.

In all ancient countries, including India, Greece and Rome (three main centres of productions of historical works), history was treated more as an art than as a science.[9] The historiographers of ancient times usually adopted the artistic style of writing. They were least bothered about the creation of real, regular and scientific history. Almost all ancient historical works are more literary than scientific in nature. Their value is judged not only on the basis of the accuracy of facts but also by the style of expression. Some of the famous historians of the world have been called "literary artists." A.L. Rowse says: "Herodotus and Thucydides, Tacitus and Livy, Clarendon, Hume and Gibbon, Macaulay and Carlyle, were all great artists and among the greatest writers of their time . . . there will always remain history as an art."[10] This statement is obviously in defence of the artistic treatment of history.

As to the ancient Indians so also to the ancient Greeks and Romans history was an art and not "a critical science." Very few of them were critical historians. It is not the fact that the classical historians concerned produced purely scientific histories. In fact, they made both scientific and artistic approach to the study and writing of history. They too, like the ancient historians of India, adopted the literary style of writing. This is the reason why they have been called "literary artists" by the authorities on classical historiography.

9. For general idea about importance of history both as an art and as a science see A.L. Rowse, *The Use of History*, pp. 86-113.

10. A.L. Rowse, op. cit., pp. 112-13.

Even Herodotus, "the father of history" has been described by them as "a great artist" and "story-teller." It is a fact to reckon with that he has also mixed up history with myths and legends. All ancient historians, whether of India, Greece or Rome, were much more concerned with presentation of the truth than the presentation of a scientific history.[11]

It was from the late eighteenth or early nineteenth century onwards that the professional historians started attaching greater importance to scientific history than the literary one from the standpoints of truth, exactness and accuracy. It was J.B. Bury (1861-1927), a historian of Cambridge school, who for the first time in one of his lectures delivered at Cambridge University in 1903 emphatically asserted that "history is not a branch of literature" but "a science, no less and no more."[12] But G.M. Trevelyan (1876-1962), the British historian, on the other hand, stood for literary history which, according to him, is not unscientific as it also presents the accounts of the past events in the form of a narrative. According to him, the scientific and literary history is of equal importance.[13] G.J. Renier wrote: "History is a story, nothing more and nothing less, of the experience of men in civilised society."[14] He further

---

11. For details see Stephen Usher, *The Historians of Greece and Rome*, Introduction, pp. ix-xi and pp. 4-5, 7, 45-46; J.W. Thompson, op. cit., pp. 21-26, 76-77; Rowse, op. cit., pp. 112-13; H.E. Barnes, *A History of Historical Writing*, p. 29; J.T. Shotwell, *The History of History*, I, p. 185; NEB, VIII (15th edn., 1980), p. 946; G.P. Singh, "Was Herodotus of Greece the Father of History?", *Adhyayan*, JBIAS, III, 1 & 2, 1993, pp. 1-10.

12. *Selected Essays*, ed. H.W.V. Temperley, pp. 4, 6, 9, 19, 22.

13. *Clio: A Muse and Other Essays*, pp. 141ff. The views of both Bury and Trevelyan have been reproduced in F. Stem (ed.), *The Varieties of History: From Voltaire to the Present*, pp. 209-23 and 227-45.

14. *History: Its Purpose and Method*, ch. VI and p. 244.

adds that "history, though not a science, is a discipline which approaches its subject matter in the same spirit as science."[15] Lord Acton,[16] who belonged to Cambridge school of history, Renan, B. Croce (1866-1952),[17] a historian of Italy, and others stood for both literary and scientific history. The presentation of history both ways depending on the themes, context and time is justified. Rowse pleaded for an artistic history in the sense that a historian needs to be an artist to narrate the events. The famous British historian, A.J. Toynbee, aptly remarked: ". . . no historian can be great if he is not also a great artist."[18]

It was the German historian Ranke (1795-1886) who first laid stress on the critical approach to the writing of history.

It is an admitted fact that Indian historiography before the dawn of modern age was neither very scientific nor very critical.

With the foundation of modern historiography in the eighteenth century various schools of historical thought started emerging. Voltaire of France and Hume and Gibbon of England belonging to the school of Enlightenment historians, and also Macaulay and Carlyle of England took the past ages as unworthy of historical study, but we find in them the expression of genuine and valuable human achievements. But the historians of Romantic school, on the other hand, favoured the study of the past history. We have neither to love nor to discard the past. E.H. Carr has rightly pointed out that "The function of the historian is neither to

---

15. *History: Its Purpose and Method*, ch. VI and p. 245.

16. *Lectures on Modern History*, pp. 51f.

17. *The Theory and History of Historiography*, pp. 20-26; *History as the Story of Liberty*, pp. 19ff.

18. *A Study of History*, abridged edn. by D.C. Somervell, vol. I, p. 4.

love the past nor to emancipate himself from the past, but to master and understand it as the key to the understanding of the present."[19] The Indian historians never neglected the past. They rather contributed to the discovery of the past through their historical writings. They never distorted or glorified the past but rather reconstructed it.

The idealists and positivists represent two broad schools of historical thought. B. Croce, an idealist philosopher and a historian, in his *History as the Story of Liberty* pointed out that historian's task is not only to chronicle the past events but also to deal with socio-cultural and other problems, and as an artist he is to apply his imagination and freedom. The idealists stood for autonomy of history. The historians of the positivist school emphasised the importance of only political history ignoring the history of religion, culture and art. Karl Popper of that school propounded the theory that history is concerned with what people did and not what they failed to do. Karl Marx viewed history in the light of socio-economic transformation in the lives of men. The economic factors got prominence over other factors in the study and writing of history. But we should not lose sight of the fact that without social history economic history is barren and without them both the cultural history unintelligible.

It is pertinent to point out that no aspect of history, whether social, economic, political, religious or cultural, is missing in the writings of ancient and medieval historians of India.

The three prominent schools of historical writing were in Rajasthan, Gujarat and Kashmir. The historians of those three schools made substantial contributions to the evolution of historiography in India during the periods under our

19. *What is History?*, p. 26.

notice by giving fillip to the production of historical works which are relatively of greater importance.

History was written in India in different forms. The ancient Hindus wrote history in the form of *itihāsa* (record of the past events), Purāṇa (traditional dynastic history, genealogy and chronology), *ākhyāna* (narratives), *itivṛtta* (story of the past), *purāvṛtta* or *purākalpa* (accounts of persons and past events), *carita* or *ākhyāyikā* (biography of a king, ruler or any other historical personage), etc.

The Buddhist writers presented history mainly in the form of an *avadāna*. The other forms of their history are *vaṁsa* (dynastic account), *nikāya*, *carita* (biography) and chronicle.

The Jaina scholars presented history in various forms which include *paṭṭāvalī*s (political succession lists or dynastic lists), *guruvāvalī*s (pontifical succession lists or the lists of Jaina *guru*s and religious preachers and teachers), *rājāvalī*s (brief histories or chronicles of kings and rulers including those of Delhi), *prabandha*s (biographies and chronicles with historical narrative), *carita*s (biographies, semi-historical and historical or the life stories of kings, rulers and persons of note), *vākā*s (accounts of historical events), Purāṇas (traditional accounts of the life and culture of the people) and *praśasti*s (eulogistic records of the achievements of kings, inscriptional records, accounts of donors and of grants and charters, genealogical records, records of important events with their dates, etc.).

Historical biographies and chronicles were written in different parts of India in different forms in Sanskrit, Prākṛt and regional languages.

In Rajasthan, historical biographies were written in the form of *prabandha*, *rāso*, *caupāī*, *kathā*, *carita*, *vigat*, *vārttā*, *vācanika*, *haqīqat*, etc. The *khyāta* represents both historical biography and chronicle. As a history of dynasty it is a chronicle and as a history of king or ruler a biography. The *khyāta*s constitute the most important branch of historical literature of Rajasthan in prose. They were mostly written under the patronage of the rulers who were keen to perpetuate the memory of their exploits in various fields. There were two types of *khyāta* — the court *khyāta*s and the *khyāta*s which were known after the names of persons who wrote them. The court *khyāta*s were written under the supervision of the state. A number of *khyāta*s on individual rulers were composed. The biographies were written in both Sanskrit and Rajasthani but chronicles in only Rajasthani.

In Kashmir, chronicles of its kings were written in Sanskrit during ancient and medieval periods under various names/ titles the most prominent among which is *Rājataraṅgiṇī*. In the Punjab, the biography was written in the form of *janam-sākhī* (on the basis of traditions, both oral and written, and family records), *caritra*, etc. Besides, chronicles and Vaṁśāvalīs were also composed there. They all form parts of Punjabi historical literature. In Sindh, history was produced in the form of a chronicle (originally in Arabic, later translated into Persian, as noted before). It is also included in the list of the chronicles which were written in India. The tradition of composing or compiling chronicles and Vaṁśāvalīs in Nepal began in ancient times when it formed part of India. The tradition further continued. The chronicles or Vaṁśāvalīs were written there originally in *parbatiyā* with an admixture of Sanskrit and Newārī and then in Sanskrit and partly in old Newārī.

In Gujarat, the biographies were written in the form of *carita* and also *prabandha*. The chronicles were mostly written in the form of *prabandha*. Some chronicles were written in the form of *praśasti*. They were written in Sanskrit, Prākṛt and Gujarati.

In Maharashtra, the annals or histories were written in the form of *bakhar* (chronicle), *powaḍā* (historical ballad or bardic poem), *kaifiyat* (detailed narrative), and *śakāvalī* (noting the dates of events) in Marathi, and Vaṁśāvalī (genealogical record), *campū*, etc. in Sanskrit.

In Bengal, the historical works were produced in different forms. The biographical works written in the form of *carita* in Sanskrit and Prākṛt, and the works written in the form of *maṅgala kāvya* (dealing with contemporary social and cultural life), *aitihāsika gāthā* (historical ballad) and Purāṇa (dealing with contemporary political history) in Bengali form parts of historical literature. Some of the biographical works composed in Bihar in old Maithili mixed with Prākṛt and Apabhraṁśa are included in this work. In Orissa, histories were written in the form of chronicle and Vaṁśāvalī in Oriya.

In Assam, historical works were composed in the form of *burañjī* (chronicle) and Vaṁśāvalī (dynastic history) in Assamese. In Manipur and Tripura, histories were written in the form of chronicle in Manipuri and Sanskrit and Bengali respectively.

In Tamiladeśa, history was written in several forms — *paraṇī* (war poems dealing with wars and battles of Coḷa kings), *uḷā* (peace poems throwing light on the life and deeds of Coḷa kings), *pillaittamil* (a biographical work like *paraṇī* and *uḷā*), *vaṁśacarita* (history of a dynasty, e.g. *Coḷavaṁśacaritam* — history of Coḷa dynasty), *praśasti* (songs in praise of Coḷa king, genealogy of the king and achievements of his predecessors), *ammānai* (historical ballad), *kalambakam* (biographical works on the Pallava kings — who ruled the kingdom with its capital at Kāñcī) and *kovai* (a collection of poems dealing with political history of the Pāṇḍyas with details of the wars and battles fought during their rule). Besides, a Tamil chronicle dealing with the history of Koṅgudeśa was written in the seventeenth century.

In Karṇāṭadeśa, historical compositions were in the form of biography (in Sanskrit called *carita* and in Kannada *caritre* dealing with the life and achievements of king or ruler), Purāṇa (traditional story of Jaina *tīrthaṁkara*), epic poems (in Sanskrit dealing with the histories of Hoysaḷa kings, Vijayanagara rulers), *rāja*Vaṁśāvalī or *rājakulavaṁśa* (in Sanskrit and Kannada dealing with history of dynasty of kings), *rājavijaya* (history of kings, in Sanskrit), *kāvya* (political history, in Kannada), *kathā* (history of Bījāpur Sultān) chronicle (in Sanskrit and Kannada), Vaṁśāvalī (family history, in Kannada), etc.

Carita in Sanskrit or *caritra* in Telugu (biography), epic (political history, in Sanskrit), *prabandha* (political history, in Telugu), Vaṁśāvalī (family record, in Telugu), and *purāṇam* (history of the Reḍḍīs) were some of the important forms of history written in Āndhradeśa.

In Kerala, the history was first written in the form of *vaṁśa* in Sanskrit (e.g. *Muṣikavaṁśa* — dynastic history of the Muṣikas). Further, the writing of history continued in different forms — *maṇipravāla* (in Malayalam mixed with Sanskrit, throwing light on contemporary socio-cultural and political life of the people of Kerala), epic (in Sanskrit, describing socio-political history of Kerala), *sandeśakāvya* (in Sanskrit and Malayalam, dealing with history of Zamorins of Calicut), Ballad (in Malayalam, dealing with political history) and chronicle (in Malayalam, dwelling upon some aspects of the history of Kerala).

All kinds of history — social, economic, political, biographical, dynastic, genealogical, religious and cultural — received the attention of ancient and medieval historians of India. Histories were written both in regional and Indian contexts.

1.3

Changing Approaches to Indian Historiography

THE approach to the writing of history in India went on changing with the developing historical and chronological sense, growing historical consciousness, prevailing historical tradition in a contemporary age and events of the time.

Historical writing in ancient India was more or less based on the Itihāsa–Purāṇa tradition. The approach to the writing of history in pre-seventh century was purely traditional.

The approach to historiography started changing from the seventh century onwards. During the period from the seventh to the twelfth centuries, a number of important historical biographies, few chronicles and other historical and semi-historical works were written. A considerable progress was made in the field of historical writing. The political history also received the attention of ancient historians of India to a reasonable extent. Political events found the place in their biographical works and chronicles written during the period.

With the dawn of Medieval Age, history writing in India took a new turn. A new approach to the writing of history began. The historical outlook also changed. There was a fundamental departure from the earlier Itihāsa–Purāṇa tradition. The traditional concept of history underwent significant changes. The works produced during the medieval period were more historical than literary in nature. One of the noticeable changes in the literary style of presentation of history during the period was due to emphasis on truth and accuracy discarding myths and legends. Most of the literary works of medieval period bear historical accuracy. The medieval historians of India paid more serious attention than the ancient ones to the presentation of factual history. The history was generally written within a broader framework during the period. The historical data received rational interpretation at the hands of the Indian historians of the period.

Historical biographies, local chronicles, Vaṁśāvalīs (family histories, and dynastic histories) and other works bearing historical character were written in different parts of India. The art of writing a historical biography considerably changed during medieval period. The biographies written during the period highlighted not only the achievements or exploits of the kings or rulers, who were the patrons, but also the contemporary political and other historical events and episodes based on eyewitness accounts. Historical biographies were written not only in the courts under royal patronage but also independently, whereas during the ancient period they were usually written by the court-poets-cum-historians extolling the virtues and glorifying the achievements of their patrons. The biographies of medieval period are less eulogistic in nature and panegyric in tone than those of ancient period. The biographers of the medieval period wrote the biographies with greater emphasis on historical facts. Likewise, the chronicles were written during medieval period in greater details with wide coverage of historical subjects. They deal not only with political history but also socio-economic, religious and cultural life of the people. The medieval chroniclers did not give prominence to political history over other subjects of historical importance. As historical records the Vaṁśāvalīs of medieval period are more authentic than those written during the earlier period. As a result of growing historical consciousness on the part of Indian historians, the historical records were preserved for the posterity.

The tradition of historical writing in medieval India evolved at much faster speed than in ancient India.

Indian historiography became by and large regional in character in medieval period. The writing of regional history as a complement to Indian history gradually started assuming significance. The pattern of writing regional history was different from that of writing history in Indian context. Regional histories were written during the period encompassing the social, political, religious and cultural life of the people. The approach to the writing of history of a kingdom also changed.

South Indian historians of medieval times adopted a new approach to the writing of historical biography, chronicle, genealogical and dynastic history, and other historical works. In south India, histories were written from CE 1700 onwards with critical approach departing from traditional approach. Tremendous progress was witnessed in the field of historiography in south India during the medieval period.

The medieval period witnessed a significant change in the approach to the writing of history from the chronological point of view. The chronology given by the ancient Indians (the Hindus, Buddhists and Jainas) in their respective works is purely traditional and only partly and not fully reliable. Applying their developed chronological sense, the Hindu and Jaina writers of the medieval period gave the correct dates of the accession and the last year of the reigns of kings and of some important historical events in their biographical works, chronicles and other works of historical value. In some of the chronicles, the lengths of reigns of kings are also given which have been found absolutely correct. Some of the Jaina writers have given even the dates of Muslim invasions of some Indian kingdoms during the Sultanate period which are very authentic. Apart from the Hindus and Jainas, some of the Sikh historians of the Punjab of medieval period also supplied chronological data in their respective works.

The schools of history that existed in Rajasthan, Gujarat and Kashmir in ancient times further flourished. The historians of these three schools adopted constructive approach in the field of historiography. They wrote several biographies, chronicles and other historical works during the medieval period.

The Hindu, Jaina, Muslim and Sikh historians of India deserve our credit for all the progress achieved in the field of historiography during the medieval period.

History attained a new status and high dignity in medieval India.

Book Two
The Beginnings of Historical Tradition

Preliminary Remarks

INDIAN historical tradition virtually began with the Itihāsa–Purāṇa tradition.

The historical tradition is preserved in the *Ṛgveda*, the epics (*Rāmāyaṇa* and *Mahābhārata*) and the Purāṇas. The historical data regarding kings and rulers, kingdoms and dynasties and Aryan and non-Aryan peoples bearing some similarities are contained in them. Their details are available more in the Purāṇas than in the Vedas and epics. The Purāṇas present an elaborate account of particularly the kingdoms and royal dynasties. The collation of Vedic literature, epics and Purāṇa texts reveals the fact that the Purāṇic genealogies (royal lineages) in some cases refer to the same kings figuring in the *Ṛgveda* and the epics. The Purāṇic data about some of the kings find confirmation in the *Ṛgveda* and the *Mahābhārata*. Ancient Indian historical tradition is, no doubt, best represented by the Purāṇas. It is significant to note that the importance of dynastic history, genealogies and chronology was first realised by the ancient *purāṇakāra*s of India. But it will not be fair to glorify one tradition and deprecate the other. In fact, the Vedic, epic and Purāṇic traditions are complementary to each other. It is well-nigh impossible to write a traditional history of India without placing our reliance on the combined testimony of these three traditions.

J.T. Wheeler has rightly placed the *Ṛgveda*, the two epics and the Purāṇas under the category of semi-historical literature. He has admitted that the materials preserved in these sources are useful for writing the history of India prior to the advent of Buddhism. He has correctly stated that the "Sanskrit Literature, whether Vedic or Brāhmanic, has no historical annals in the modern sense of the word."[1]

Assessing the comparative value of the Vedas and the Purāṇas as sources of traditional history, A.D. Pusalker writes:

> Some of the kings mentioned in the *Ṛgveda* can be fitted in the gaps in the Purāṇic lists. The *Ṛgveda*, no doubt, offers the proper corrective to the Purāṇic lists, but, when we find Purāṇic accounts to be corroborated by the Vedic evidence, it is legitimate to take their testimony as valid even in matters on which the *Ṛgveda* is silent. The proper procedure for the writing of traditional history is to take into account the joint testimony of the Vedic and Puraṇic texts wherever available and to try to bring harmony into the apparently conflicting texts.[2]

Making a general survey of ancient Indian historical tradition, F.E. Pargiter observes:

> Our knowledge of the most ancient times in India rests mainly on tradition. . . . The Purāṇas, the *Mahābhārata* and in a minor degree the *Rāmāyaṇa*, profess to give accounts from tradition about the earliest occurrences. The Vedas, the Brāhmaṇas and other Brāhmanic literature supply information also. The oldest of these, the *Ṛgveda*, contains historical allusions, of which

1. *India from the Earliest Ages* (*Hindu, Buddhist and Brahmanical Revival*), vol. III of the *History of India*, Preface, p. viii, and pp. 5-6.

2. "Traditional History from the Earliest Time to the Accession of Parikshit," in *The Vedic Age*, ed. R.C. Majumdar, p. 310.

some record contemporary persons and events, but more refer to bygone times and persons and are obviously based on tradition.[3]

The evidence in the *Ṛgveda*, whether contemporary notices or matter concerning the past borrowed from tradition, consists of statements more or less isolated; they are merely allusions and make up no connected account. Even the contemporary notices, though having all the trustworthiness of first-hand evidence, yet fix little or nothing definitely of themselves, because they have no certain chronological setting with reference to other events.[4]

Even contemporary historical notices in the *Ṛgveda* therefore remain chronologically vague, and by themselves yield little information that can be co-ordinated for historical purposes. Statements of a historical kind in the Vedic literature become serviceable, if they can be linked up with other statements from elsewhere, and that can be only from tradition. It is tradition that gives many of them a chronological position. . . . Tradition therefore becomes all-important. It is the only resource, since historical works are wanting, and is not an untrustworthy guide. In ancient times, men knew perfectly well the difference between truth and falsehood. . . . It was natural therefore that they should discriminate what was true and preserve it; and historical tradition must be considered in this light."[5]

He further states that Vedic literature is authoritative in historical matters, where it notices contemporary matters, but conclusions drawn from it are not criteria for testing the results yielded by historical tradition in the epics and

3. *AIHT*, p. 1.

4. Ibid., p. 2.

5. Ibid., pp. 2-3.

Purāṇas. Those results should be judged independently on their own merits.[6]

The Purāṇas and the *Mahābhārata* can be taken as the chief and authoritative basis of historical reconstruction of ancient past without disregard for historical tradition in the *Ṛgveda* and the *Rāmāyaṇa*.

Ancient Indian historical tradition is not to be put aside as wholly unworthy of attention. It may be examined and weighed with the aid of all information available to us. Its general trustworthiness can be tested by the results of discoveries and excavations. The tradition is human testimony concerning the long past. It is not to be discarded simply because it contains discrepancies.

---

6. *AIHT*, p. 14.

2.1

The Itihāsa-Purāṇa Tradition and Its Impact on Historiography

It was the Itihāsa–Purāṇa tradition which marked the beginning of historical tradition in India. Itihāsa (past events), Purāṇa (any old tale or ancient lore) and *ākhyāna* (narratives) were the three main constituents of the historical tradition. These three constitute rudimentary specimens of history. In fact, they contained the seeds of history. The said three constituents need historical interpretations within a broader framework. Itihāsa in real sense of the term signifies history which appears in ancient Indian literature not only as a record of the past events but also as a trustworthy guide to contemporary cultures and civilisation. In its broader sense, it comprises ancient events arranged in the form of a story based on the historical truth. The writers of the Itihāsa tradition took history in a very comprehensive sense and attached more importance to the delineation of social, economic, political, religious and cultural life of the people than to a mere description of wars and battles and political achievements of kings and rulers. It is worthy of note that the traditional concept of Itihāsa was different from the modern concept of history. In ancient India, history was more or less a part of literature. This is the reason why it is generally called a literary history. Purāṇa as a term is generally applied to tales of primaeval antiquity or ancient stories whether quasi-historical or mythological. The Purāṇa as a body of literature is a record of the past. It is, therefore, linked to Itihāsa which is often referred to as Itihāsa–Purāṇa in ancient Indian literature. The general use of the compound word *itihāsa-purāṇa* in the Vedic, epic and Purāṇic literature indicates the close relation and affinity between the two. The writers of the Purāṇa tradition have presented histories coalescing them with myths and legends. Itihāsa or Purāṇa in the widest application of the term denotes actual traditional history. The traditional history of India, in fact, has been presented in the Itihāsa–Purāṇa tradition. Various legendary and historical accounts of the past events or primordial events have been incorporated in the *itihāsa*s and Purāṇas. *Ākhyāna* signifies a narrative of an event of the past. It has often been used as a narrative story. The literature of both Vedic and post-Vedic times contains the rudiments of history — Itihāsa, Purāṇa and *ākhyāna*.

The earliest form of Itihāsa based on oral tradition emerged in the early Vedic age. The written records of the tradition appeared much later. The written form of history began with the written tradition.

The antiquity of Itihāsa–Purāṇa tradition can be traced back to the Vedic Age. The allusion to Itihāsa, the nearest equivalent Sanskrit word for history, occurs in one of the later Vedic texts.[1] It is clearly stated in the text that Itihāsa, Purāṇa, *gāthā*s (hero-lauds) and *nārāśaṁsī*s (eulogies of the warriors and princes of the past) were known to the people.[2] They being repositories of age-old traditions attracted their attention, ". . . the Indian word for *history*, viz. Itihāsa is India's

1. *AV*, XV.6.11-12.
2. Ibid.

greatest contribution to the world of historiography."[3] There is no denying the fact that in the later Vedic Age Itihāsa assumed greater importance than the Purāṇa. But the fact remains that both continued to be equally popular and remained indistinguishable for a considerable period of time. In later times, of course, some distinction was made between the two.[4] The connotation of Itihāsa gradually changed. Itihāsa was often used as a general term as it embraced all the old, historical and related traditions and also the Purāṇas.

The earliest reference to the term *purāṇa* is found in the early Vedic text.[5] It has been used in the form of a tale of hoary antiquity. In the later Vedic text, it has been mentioned first singularly[6] and then conjointly with Itihāsa.[7] The Purāṇic *ākhyānas* in the Vedas were purely based on contemporary tradition.[8]

The earliest mention of *ākhyāna* (i.e. story) is in a Brāhmaṇa text of the *Ṛgveda*.[9] And the "knowers of stories" have been called therein *ākhyānavida*.[10] In ancient Indian Sanskrit, Buddhist and Jaina literature, history has been presented also in a narrative style. Some of the narrative stories therein do contain historical facts.

---

3. B.N. Mukherjee, "Reflections on Trends in Indian Historiography", Presidential Address, 61st session, IHC, Calcutta, 31 December 2000 - 3 January, 2001, PIHC (Calcutta, 2000-2001), 1, p. 21.

4. For details see A.D. Pusalker, *Studies in the Epics and Purāṇas*, pp. 44-45; Baldeva Upadhyaya *Purāṇa Vimarśa*, pp. 6, 11.

5. *ṚV*, III.54.9; III.58.6; IX.99.4; X.130.6.

6. *AV*, XI.7.24.

7. Ibid., XV.6.11-12.

8. See S.N. Ray, *Historical and Cultural Studies in the Purāṇas*, p. 5.

9. *Ait. Br.*, III.3.25; VII.3.13-18.

10. Ibid., III.3.25.

In the later Vedic Age, the three families of the Bhṛgus, the Aṅgirasas and the Atharvans (the families of priest-poets) merged and the resultant composite family of the Bhṛgvāṅgirasas successfully carried on the tradition of the Itihāsa, Purāṇa and *ākhyāna*. Mainly the two clans of priests, Bhṛgu (Bhārgava) and Aṅgiras (Bhāradvāja), were associated with the writing of Itihāsa, Purāṇa and some other literary texts.[11] There is an evidence to show that the Brāhmanical historical school especially the Bhṛgvāṅgiras school revived the Itihāsa–Purāṇa tradition.[12]

Yāska (800-700 BCE), who is known for his etymological interpretation of Vedic words, in his *Nirukta* refers to Itihāsa, and Purāṇa as records of past events. He cites the Kuru dynasty in particular as an example of Itihāsa, which according to him, may be distinguished from the *gāthā*s. From his work we learn that there was a Vedic school known as the *aitihāsika*s — so named because its members made use of the Itihāsa in expounding the *mantra*s.[13] According to Durgācārya (CE 1300-50), a commentator on his work, the *aitihāsika*s were those who interpreted the Veda with the help of Itihāsa.[14]

While examining the relationship between the Itihāsa and Purāṇa, Sāyaṇa (CE 1300-80), a commentator on the Vedas, tried to distinguish one from the other but he did not obtain any consistent result. We find that by the former

11. V.S. Pathak, *Ancient Historians of India*, pp. 21f; also A.K. Warder, *An Introduction to Indian Historiography*, pp. 18-25.

12. Warder, op. cit., pp. 18f.

13. *Nirukta* (ed. and tr. Uma Shankar Sharma), 2.10; 3.19; 3.27; 4.6.

14. *Nirukta* (ed. with Durgācārya's comm. by V.K. Rajavade), 2.10; 2.16; 12.1-2; 12.10.

he meant the *Mahābhārata* and by the latter the *brahmāṇḍa*. They, according to him, form parts of the sacred literature.[15]

In some of the Brāhmaṇas, Itihāsa and Purāṇa have been mentioned as the Itihāsa Veda and the Purāṇa Veda.[16] The stories narrated in the Brāhmanical literature are also based on the Itihāsa–Purāṇa tradition. In one of the *Āraṇyaka*s, Itihāsa and Purāṇa have been mentioned together with those *gāthā*s and *nārāśaṁsī*s which have historical significance.[17] In the Upaniṣads, Itihāsa finds mention invariably in conjunction or combination with Purāṇa.[18] The general use of the compound word *itihāsa-purāṇa* indicates the close relation and affinity between the two. One of the Upaniṣads specifically refers to Itihāsa–Purāṇa as the fifth Veda (*itihāsapurāṇaḥ pañcamo vedānāṁ vedaḥ*), the other four Vedas being the *Ṛg*, *Yajur*, *Sāma* and *Atharva*.[19] It distinctly appears from the Upaniṣads that Itihāsa–Purāṇa and the Vedas were important subjects of study. In one of the Śrauta-Sūtras, Itihāsa–Purāṇa *par excellence* is spoken of as a Veda.[20] One of the Gṛhya-Sūtras also speaks of exactly the same.[21] We also learn from a Gṛhya-Sūtra that *itihāsa*s, Purāṇas, the Vedas, the Brāhmaṇas, the *gāthā*s and *nārāśaṁsī*s were recited by the people on certain occasions specially in honour of kings and heroes. The histories of the great men

15. Sāyaṇa, *An Introduction to the Ṛgveda Saṁhitā*, pp. 12, 23, cf. F. Max Müller, *HASL*, p. 37, note 1 and p. 38; see also *Ṛgveda Saṁhitā*, ed. and tr. with Sāyaṇa's comm. by Max Müller, vol. I.

16. *Gopatha Brāhmaṇa*, I.1.10; I.2.10; *Śat. Br.*, XI.I.6.9; XI.5.6.7-8; XIII.4.3.12-13; XIV.5.4.10.

17. *Taittirīya Āraṇyaka*, 2.9.

18. *Bṛhadāraṇyaka Upaniṣad*, II.4.10; IV.I.2; *Chāndogya Upaniṣad*, III.4.1-2.

19. *Chāndogya Upaniṣad*, VII.I.2 and 4.

20. *Śāṅkhāyana Śrauta-Sūtra*, XVI.2.21.27.

21. *Śāṅkhāyana Gṛhya-Sūtra*, I.24.8.

were also recited on some occasions. Both Itihāsa and Purāṇā were subjects of learning.[22] In one of the Gṛhya-Sūtras, Purāṇa has been mentioned in the sense of tales.[23] Kauṭilya, who flourished in the latter half of the fourth century BCE, also calls the Itihāsa a Veda.[24] The said Itihāsaveda (Itihāsa-Purāṇa) must have existed in his time. In one of the early Pāli texts also, Itihāsa is called the fifth Veda.[25]

The question as to which Itihāsa-Purāṇa or Itihāsa has been called the fifth Veda in Sanskrit and Buddhist texts concerned still remains to be answered. K.F. Geldner on the basis of the evidences whatsoever available in ancient Indian literary texts has reasonably concluded that there existed a single work called Itihāsaveda or Itihāsa-Purāṇa.[26] But he has not spelt out either the name of its author or whether it may be called the fifth Veda. His view has been contradicted by Maurice Winternitz,[27] A.A. Macdonell and A.B. Keith.[28] According to them, the Itihāsaveda is not any particular book but that branch of learning which consists of stories, legends, etc. They are of the view that Itihāsa-Purāṇa representing the great body of mythology and legendary history may roughly be classed as fifth Veda. Emil Sieg, while dealing with ancient Indian Itihāsa tradition, pointed out that there existed a collection of Itihāsas, or Purāṇas under the title Itihāsa, Itihāsaveda, Purāṇa or Itihāsa-Purāṇa. He holds the

22. *Āśvalāyana Gṛhya-Sūtra*, III.3.1-3; IV.6.6.

23. *Gobhila Gṛhya-Sūtra*, I.6.6.

24. *Arth.*, I.3 (7, 9ff).

25. *Sutta Nipāta*, III.7 (Sela Sutta).

26. *Vedische Studien*, I, p. 290f cf. A.A. Macdonell and A.B. Keith, VI, vol. I, pp. 76-78.

27. *HIL*, I, pp. 312-14.

28. Op. cit.

view that the "ancient Itihāsapurāṇa was an independent collection of legends and stories not specially connected with any particular Veda." That "Itihāsaveda or Itihāsapurāṇaveda has left distinct traces of its existence in the great epic." On the basis of the evidence available in the *Mahābhārata*, he has called it the fifth Veda.[29] It is true that this epic contains all the characteristic features of *Itihāsa-Purāṇa* literature. But the fact remains that the ancient Purāṇa was the precursor of the later literary works bearing the same name (or called both Itihāsa and Purāṇa). And, hence, the original Purāṇa has a better claim than the *Mahābhārata* for being considered as the fifth Veda. The view expressed by J. Hertel[30] is also worthy of our attention. But it does not provide the correct answer to the question concerned. The evidence furnished by the scholars (with few exceptions) so far is all about the existence of a work, Itihāsa–Purāṇa, called the fifth Veda by some ancient Indian writers, and not about its antiquity, composition or authorship. The so-called fifth Veda is no other than the Itihāsa-Saṁhitā or Purāṇa-Saṁhitā of Vedavyāsa which has been interchangeably called the Itihāsa–Purāṇa and the Purāṇa–Itihāsa. This can irrefutably be proved on the combined testimony of the Purāṇa texts themselves.[31] The original Purāṇa appeared as writ-large (or in the enlarged form) of the Vedas. That is why the Itihāsa–Purāṇa has been mentioned in the Vedic and Purāṇic literature as the fifth

---

29. *Die Sagenstoffe Des Ṛgveda und die Indische Itihāsa Tradition*, I, pp. 22, 24 ff, cf. J. Hastings (ed.), *ERE*, vol. VII (1914), pp. 461-62.

30. *VOJ*, XVIII, p. 59; XXIII, p. 273.

31. *Bhāg. P.*, I.4.20; III.12.39; *Km. P.*, I.I.3 and 5; I.50.13-14; *Vy. P.*, 103.48.51, 55-58; *Bmd. P.*, I.I.173; IV.4.47.50, 54-58; *Vmn. P.*, 12.3; *Vṣṇ. Dh. P.*, III.15.1; *Pdm. P.*, V.2.53 (all for *Purāṇa-Saṁhitā, Itihāsa-Purāṇa* or *Purāṇa-Itihāsa); Bmv. P.*, I.33.5 (for *Itihāsa-Saṁhitā*); see also Radhakamal Mukherjee, *The Culture and Art of India*, pp. 24-25.

Veda along with other four Vedas. In fact, the Purāṇa contains details of Itihāsa given particularly in the *Ṛgveda* about Aryan peoples and kings. The Itihāsa–Purāṇa and the Vedas were closely related and equally important. The Purāṇas were considered relatively more important than the Vedas. For achieving proficiency in the correct interpretation, explanation and analysis of the data contained in the Vedas, the sound knowledge of the Itihāsa and Purāṇa was essential for the brāhmaṇas as evidenced by the *Mahābhārata*,[32] the Purāṇas[33] and one of the Smṛtis.[34] The Purāṇa (Itihāsa–Purāṇa) as a subject was one of the main fourteen branches of learning.[35] According to well-established tradition, Itihāsa and Purāṇa were regularly studied by the learned members of the society.[36]

The ancient traditions preserved in Purāṇas (also called Itihāsa–Purāṇa) about the kings of various dynasties and their genealogies, chronology and famous deeds are of great historical value. The Purāṇas deal with various aspects of ancient Indian history which are the glaring examples of *itihāsa*s.

---

32. Ādi Parva, I.204.

33. *Vy. P.*, I.200-03; *Pdm. P.*, V.2.50-52; *Nārada Purāṇa*, 2.24.17-18.

34. *Vāsiṣṭha-Smṛti*, I.362 (cf. *Twenty Smṛtis*, ed. with Hindi tr. Shri Rāma Sharma Ācārya).

35. For details see *Vṣṇ. P.*, III.6.28-29; *Yājñavalkya-Smṛti*, I.3 (cf. *Twenty Smṛtis*). The other thirteen branches of learning were the four Vedas; six Vedāṅgas — Śikṣā (phonology), Kalpa (ritual), Vyākaraṇa (rules of grammar), Nirukta (rules for etymological interpretation of Vedic words), Jyotiṣa (astronomy) and Chanda (metre useful for correct pronunciation of Vedic hymns) — and Nyāyaśāstra (jurisprudence), Mīmāṁsā (one of the six systems of Indian philosophy) and Dharmaśāstra (law).

36. *Yājñavalkya-Smṛti*, I.101.

The value of Itihāsa–Purāṇa tradition is fairly illustrated in the Purāṇa texts. In some of the Purāṇas, Itihāsa, Purāṇa and *ākhyāna* have been treated as almost identical. The texts call themselves by all these terms. No clear-cut distinction has been maintained between them. However, as collective terms Itihāsa and Purāṇa are often mentioned as distinct.[37] They actually became separate from each other much later. The Purāṇic evidence in this regard is more explicit than the Vedic and Brāhmanic ones.

The two epics — the *Rāmāyaṇa* and the *Mahābhārata* — include almost all the constituent elements of historical tradition. The texts themselves bespeak the truth concerned. Vālmīki himself calls his *Rāmāyaṇa* a *purātana* (ancient) *itihāsa*[38] whose justification lies in the historical data contained in the text. Histories of various dynasties recorded in it are the most notable examples of Itihāsa. The *Mahābhārata* is called *purātana-itihāsa* (ancient history), Purāṇa (a traditional history), *ākhyāna* (narrative), *purāvṛtta* (records of past events) and *purākalpa* (descriptive accounts of persons, events, etc.) which are different forms or manifestation of Itihāsa. The word *itihāsa* occurs several times in this epic along with *purāvṛtta, ākhyāna, purāṇa, kathā,* etc. which are all synonymous. It embodies several *ākhyāna*s (lengthy narratives), *upākhyāna*s (short narratives or episodes), etc.[39] In this epic, there are numerous references to Itihāsa and Purāṇa as ancient works

---

37. *Vy. P.*, 54.1-3.115; 103.48.51, 55-58; *Bmd. P.*, IV.4.47.50, 54-58; *Br. P.*, 131.2; 161.27; 234.4; 245.27.30; *Mat. P.*, 69.55; *Pdm. P.*, V.32.8-9; VI.29.1-3; 192.16; 193.90-01; *Lg. P.*, I.39.61.

38. *Vāl. Rām.*, Yuddha (Laṅkā) Kāṇḍa, 131, 116.

39. Ādi Parva, I.17-19, 24-25, 48-52, 61-63; 54.23; 56, 18f; see also Sabhā Parva, 14.4; 29.72; 61.58; Āraṇyaka Parva 29.1; 31.20; Śānti Parva, 50.34; Anuśāsana Parva, 3.207; 97.5; V.S. Agrawala, Bh. Sv., vol. III, p. 262.

that were studied together with the Vedas. This epic is also called *Arthaśāstra* and Dharmaśāstra.[40] It is further said in the text (original one) by its author that it is well supported by the Vedic and Purāṇic evidence.[41] The dynastic history and genealogies of the kings of Lunar family of both pre- and post-Bhārata war period contained in the *Mahābhārata* represent Itihāsa.

According to E.W. Hopking, the *Mahābhārata* (great epic of the Bharatas) indifferently called the Itihāsa and Purāṇa also claims the title of the fifth Veda. The epic accounts in the present form is based upon that of the Purāṇa.[42] He further states that the "historical tales embedded in this epic is not wholly without scholastic affinities."[43] The *Mahābhārata*, no doubt, contains evidence for being called the fifth Veda. However, the present writer is of the firm opinion that the work called the fifth Veda was originally the Purāṇa called Purāṇa-Saṁhitā and Itihāsa-Saṁhitā as noted before. And the *Mahābhārata* took the place of the fifth Veda later because of being both Itihāsa and Purāṇa. The *Mahābhārata* is relatively more important than the *Rāmāyaṇa* from a historical point of view. It is, no doubt, a semi-historical work. It is encyclopaedic in nature containing a plethora of materials relating to some conceivable aspects of ancient Indian history and culture. F.E. Pargiter has correctly observed that "The Purāṇas, the *Mahābhārata* and in a minor degree the *Rāmāyaṇa* profess to give accounts from tradition about the earliest occurrences."[44]

40. Ādi Parva, 56.21.

41. Ibid., 56.15.16.

42. *GEI*, pp. 47f, 50, 53, see also his "The Princes and Peoples of Epic Poems", in CHI, I (*Ancient India*), ed. E.J. Rapson, p. 224.

43. *CHI*, I, p. 225.

44. *AIHT*, p. 1.

The former two constitute main pillars of the edifice of early Indian historical tradition. In the literature of the later period, names like Itihāsa, *ākhyāna* and Purāṇa are by no means restricted to the *Mahābhārata*, the *Rāmāyaṇa* or the Purāṇas, some Buddhist and Jaina works are also based on Itihāsa–Purāṇa tradition to a considerable extent.

The historical data contained in the *Ṛgveda*, the epics, the Purāṇas and the Buddhist and Jaina works have been highlighted here separately along with other historical works.

Kauṭilya's comprehensive view of Itihāsa (history) is worthy of our notice. According to him, Itihāsa is not a single work but a class of literature consisting of Purāṇa (traditional account of past events), *itivṛtta* (an account of past events, a narrative or an ancient story), *ākhyāyikā* (biography of a historical personage), *udāharaṇa* (an illustrative story containing historical truth), Dharmaśāstra (the works dealing with Hindu laws, ancient society, economy, polity and religion, etc., e.g. the Smṛtis) and the *Arthaśāstra* (science of polity or state and government),[45] composed by himself in or about 300 BCE. These were the six constituents of traditional Itihāsa or history. Purāṇa here means Purāṇas which, according to him, were most important of all components of Itihāsa. His description of the Itihāsa goes well in accord with what we find in one of the Jaina Purāṇas of the ninth century CE.[46]

> In fact, in ancient times both Itihāsa and Purāṇa denoted history. The school of *aitihāsikas* or historians . . . delved in *purāvṛtta* or records of past events, and included the *vaṁśa* . . . (genealogy) . . . part of the Purāṇas. . . . The element of royal *vaṁśa* . . . was

45. *Arth.*, I.5.13-14.

46. *Ādi Purāṇa* of Jinasena, I.24-25.

> adopted from Itihāsa or the works of the *purāvid*s. The halcyon days for Itihāsa or history were there from the time of Yāska to Kauṭilya — making the domain of this discipline both extensive and compact.[47]

The Itihāsa, Purāṇa, *ākhyāna* and *ākhyāyikā* also received the notices of Kātyāyana (second half of the fourth century BCE)[48] and Patañjali (*c*. 184-148 BCE)[49] as different forms of literary history. Manu (*c*. 200-100 BCE) also refers to Itihāsa, Purāṇa and *ākhyāna* (*ākhyānānitihāsāṁśca purāṇāṇi*) which were learnt and taught.[50] It has been affirmed on the basis of his evidence that works on history embodying ancient traditions, stories, etc. did exist.[51] Amara Siṁha (fifth century CE) in his lexicon defines *itihāsa* as *purāvṛtta* (an account of past events). The commentator on his work includes also the *Mahābhārata* in it.[52] The author in his lexicon further says that the Purāṇa is based on traditions and *ākhyāyikā* has a historical basis.[53] In the time of Bāṇa popularly known as Bāṇabhaṭṭa (the first half of the seventh century CE), Itihāsa and Purāṇa were the two main subjects of study and teaching. He was familiar with the Itihāsa–Purāṇa tradition. He himself studied Itihāsa, Purāṇa, *ākhyāna* and *ākhyāyikā* and taught them to his pupils from royal families. He had his own conception of history.

---

47. B.N. Puri, "D.R. Bhandarkar and Indian Historiography", PIHC (42nd session, Magadha University, Bodh-Gaya, 1981), p. 37.
48. *Vārttika* (on Pāṇini's *Aṣṭādhyāyī*), IV.2.60; also Weber, *Indische Studien*, I, p. 147.
49. *Mahābhāṣya* (great commentary on Pāṇini's *Aṣṭādhyāyī*), ed. F. Kielhorn, vol. II, pp. 284, 8f.
50. *Manu.*, III.232.
51. V.S. Agrawala, *India as Described by Manu*, pp. 2 and 9.
52. *Amarakośa*, I.6.4.
53. Ibid., I.6.5.

According to him, history is that branch of knowledge which not only provides the details of past events in a chronological order but also deals with the causes, course and effects of the events.[54] He records that Harṣa encouraged the teaching of Itihāsa. In the *gurukula*, history was taught along with other subjects. Rājaśekhara, who belonged to the last quarter of the ninth and first quarter of the tenth centuries CE, identifies the Purāṇa (consisting of eighteen parts) with Itihāsa. According to him, there are two different kinds of Itihāsa, viz. *parakriyā* and *purākalpa*. The former focuses on one hero such as in the *Rāmāyaṇa* and the latter on several heroes such as in the *Mahābhārata*.[55]

The ancient Indian writers do not appear to be consistent in their use of the expression, Itihāsa, Purāṇa and *ākhyāna*. They sometimes use them as synonymous or identical and other times describe them as different forms of history. They have not drawn any hard and fast line of distinction between them. They have rather treated them as interrelated and complementary to each other. The statement of V.S. Agrawala, that in ancient India a clear-cut demarcation line between Itihāsa and Purāṇa was never drawn,[56] is absolutely justified.

The three legitimate constituents of the Itihāsa–Purāṇa tradition were myth, genealogy and historical narrative. "The remote past was described in the form of myths and probably

54. *Kādambarī* of Bāṇa, ed. K.P. Parab, 1, pp. 24, 398; II, pp. 293-94; tr. C.M. Ridding, 1, pp. 24, 39; M. Bharatiya, *Bāṇabhaṭṭa aur unakī Kādambarī*, II, p. 172.

55. *Kāvyamīmāṁsā*, pp. 5-8.

56. "Itihāsa-Darśana", in *Itihāsa-Darśana* (collection of his papers), ed. P.K. Agrawala, pp. 21-22; see also A.D. Pusalker, "Conception of History in Ancient Indian Literature", *Our Heritage*, XII.2, 1964, pp. 35ff.

fabricated genealogies. . . . The more immediate past was recorded almost entirely in the form of genealogies filled out with historical narrative."[57] Some events of the remote past despite having historical basis are often taken as myths. A.J. Toynbee, a well-known British historian, in his monumental work has pointed out that history grew out of myths, stories, legends and traditions.[58]

The Itihāsa–Purāṇa tradition finds reflection not only in the Vedas, the epics and Purāṇas but also in the Buddhist and Jaina works. The historical writings in ancient India at least to the end of the Gupta period were broadly based on this tradition. In the post-Gupta period, there was, no doubt, slight departure from the earlier tradition. However, the impact of Itihāsa–Purāṇa tradition is discernible even on the historical literature (biographies, chronicles and other literary works containing historical narratives) of that period. The traditional concept of history gradually started changing from the seventh century BCE onwards. And the Itihāsa and Purāṇa developed as two distinct subjects of study. But the older tradition had not completely died down even in the post-seventh century CE. Even the writings of Kalhaṇa, a distinguished Kaśmīrī historian of the twelfth century CE and the best of all ancient historians of India, bear the stamp of the Itihāsa–Purāṇa tradition as is evident from the earlier parts of his work, *Rājataraṅgiṇī* (a chronicle of kings of Kashmir).[59] Ancient Indian historiography from the age of Vedavyāsa down to the time

57. Romila Thapar, "The Tradition of Historical Writing in Early India", in her *AISH*, P. 291; see also her "Origin Myths and the Early Indian Historical Tradition", in *AISH*, pp. 294, 297.

58. *A Study of History*, an abridged edition by D.C. Somervell, I, pp. 4ff, 44-45.

59. Eng. tr. J.C. Dutt, 1, Books I-IV; also H.H. Wilson, *The Hindu History of Kashmir*, pp. 8-39, 122-50.

of Kalhaṇa was more or less based on the Itihāsa–Purāṇa tradition.

During ancient period, various traditions of historiography, including the Vedic, epic, Purāṇic, Buddhist and Jaina, flourished one after another. It has been rightly pointed out that "Traditions, whether epic or Purāṇic, Jaina or Buddhist or purely local, have an important role to play in helping unravel our past cultures and civilisation."[60]

The reasons why some historians are not inclined to accept the forms of ancient Indian Itihāsa as historical find reflection in the following statement of V.S. Pathak:

> . . . conditioned by the language and ideas of modern historiography, historians viewed them rather as the monsters of the fable, who callously tortured and disfigured the fairy princesses of history, and from whose clutches the historians as gallant kings were duty-bound to liberate them; at the best these texts were thought to be full of irrational accretions which should be removed before the pure gold of history could be seen.[61]

60. H.D. Sankalia, "Archaeology and Tradition", in S.P. Gupta and K.S. Ramachandran (ed.), *AIHA*, p. 281.

61. *Ancient Historians of India*, p. 138.

2.2

The Vedic Tradition

Ṛgvedic History

THE earliest literary work of some historical value which the Aryans have left to posterity is the *Ṛgveda*. It is a Saṁhitā or collection of total 1028 (1017 + 11) hymns composed by various priest-poets or sages of great antiquity and arranged into ten *Maṇḍala*s or books. The hymns containing historical information reflect the historical sense of those who composed them. They were carefully preserved by the brāhmaṇas and handed down from generation to generation. The knowledge of the past was originally transmitted from one to other through the oral tradition. After the introduction of writing, the tradition connected with men and events of bygone times, contemporary persons, the culture and civilisation of the Aryans and other subjects was recorded by the brāhmaṇas. They were actually the keepers or preservers of the records of the past. Here it is worthwhile to mention that the Vedic hymns on the whole composed by various authors were collected, compiled, properly arranged and divided or classified into four Saṁhitās by the great sage, Kṛṣṇa Dvaipāyana Vyāsa (the son of Parāśara), in the beginning of the Dvāpara Age. And thereafter he became popularly known as Vedavyāsa. It is believed that Vasukra, a famous Kaśmīrī brāhmaṇa, undertook the task of explaining the Veda and committing it to writing.

The *Ṛgveda* contains a lot of historical data about the life and culture of the Aryans. The data contained in the text about their original homeland within the geographical boundary of India and their settlement patterns are of exceptional value. It is this text from which we learn that the Aryans were originally settled in the territory lying along the rivers, Kubhā (Kabul), Suvāstu (Swāt), Krumu (Kurram), Gomatī (Gomal) and Hariyūpiā (Hariruda of Herat) in Afghanistan,[1] and the Sindhu (Indus) and its principal tributaries, Vitastā (Jhelum), Asiknī (Cenāb), Paruṣṇi (Rāvī), Vipāśā (Beās) and Śutudri (Sutlej) — the five rivers of the Punjab on the west — and the Sarasvatī on the east called the Sapta-Sindhu region (the land of seven rivers).[2] There are some indications in the text about their original settlements in Bālhika or Bāhlika region (the Vaṁkṣu Valley) also.[3] The allusions to the rivers — the Gaṅgā and the Yamunā — in the text[4] indicate that they were partly settled in the Gangetic doab. In early Vedic times, the Gaṅgā-Yamunā Doab and "the territory between the rivers, Sarasvatī and Dṛṣadvatī, were occupied by the Bhāratas" (3, 23, 4). The areas inhabited by the Aryans in the Ṛgvedic Age extended from Afghanistan to the Gangetic Valley. The information contained in the text about the social, economic, political, religious and cultural life of the Aryans and their internal

1. *ṚV*, V.53.9; V.61.19; VI.27.5; VIII.19.37; X.75.6; see also X.64.8-9.

2. *ṚV*, X.75.1-8; II.12.12; II.41.16-17; 3.33.1-3; IV.30.11; V.52.9; V.53.9; VI.61.1-14; VII.36.6; VII.95.1-6; VII.96.1-5; VII.185.89; VIII.24.27; VIII.28.25; X.43.3; X.49.9; see also A.C. Das, *Ṛgvedic India: Cultural History of India as Depicted in the Ṛgveda*, vol. I, pp. 8ff, 19-67, 122f; J. Muir, *Original Sanskrit Texts*, vol. II, p. 322; Z.A. Ragozin, *History of Vedic India*, pp. 63f.

3. Das, op. cit., vol. I, p. 72.

4. *ṚV*, X.75.5.

divisions and mutual hostility and conflicts with the non-Aryans, inter-tribal warfare, the Dāsas or Dasyus, the expansion of Aryan culture by the Paṇis (a trading class) outside India, etc. are of great historical value.

There are incidental allusions in the *Ṛgveda* to the five allied Aryan peoples, viz. Anus, Druhyus, Yadus, Turvasas and Purus[5] who were the dwellers of the Sārasvata region. Besides these, the Bhāratas (who later merged into the Kurus), Tritsus, Śṛñjayas, Kṛvis, and other minor groups are also mentioned in the text. One of the notable events of the Ṛgvedic Age known as the Battle of 10 kings also finds mention in the text (VII.18; VII.83.1-8). This great battle was fought on the river Paruṣṇi or Rāvī in which Sudāsa, king of the Bharatas, defeated, with the help of Indra, the confederate peoples led by 10 kings (five of whom were heads of the above-mentioned allied Aryan groups and remaining five were the chiefs of non-Aryan tribal groups, viz. Alinas, Pakthas, Śivas, Bhalānases and the Viṣāṇins of the north-west) and established the political supermacy of the former over the latter. This event constitutes one of the significant aspects of the Ṛgvedic history dealing with political life of the Aryans.

The *Ṛgveda* refers to some important kings like Manu, the son of Vivasvān (X.63.1), Ikṣvāku (X.60.4), the dynastic history of which is available in the *Rāmāyaṇa* and Purāṇas, Purūravā (X.95.11), Kuruśravaṇa (X.33.4), who is identical with Saṁvaraṇa's son Kuru mentioned in the *Mahābhārata* and Purāṇas, Nahuṣa (I.122.8; VII.95.2; IX.91.2) and his son

5. *ṚV*, I.108.8; VII.18.6, 12-14; X.62.10; see also A.A. Macdonell and A.B. Keith, VI, I, pp. 466-67; II, pp. 11-13; R.C. Jain, *EAB*, pp. 70-92; Hopkins, *JAOS*, XV, p. 260; D.D. Kosambi, "The Vedic Five Tribes," *JAOS*, 87, 1967, pp. 33-39.

and successor, Yayāti (X.63.1). Their dynasties and genealogies are not given in the text, but their historicity is beyond doubt. The text also mentions the names of Divodāsa, Mudgala, Śṛñjaya, Cyavana and his son Sudāsa and one of his descendants named Somaka,[6] who were the rulers of North Pañcāla dynasty. However, it cannot be denied that the contemporary historical notices in the *Ṛgveda*, in spite of having all the trustworthiness of first-hand evidence, have not chronological setting, and by themselves yield little information that can be co-ordinated for historical purposes.

Historical Value of the Ṛgveda: General Views

The *Ṛgveda* is admittedly the oldest record of the Aryans. It deals with their origin, culture and civilisation. It constitutes the safe basis of reconstruction of their early history. The materials furnished by it are of great value for presenting a real history of the Aryan people.[7]

"The dawn of history is heralded in India by the hymns sung by the ṛṣis and enshrined in the *Ṛgveda Saṁhitā*."[8]

Louis Renou has correctly stated that some of the Ṛgvedic hymns are "historical." They contain the "rudiments of history."[9] Adolf Kaegi also observes that these hymns were composed "with the intention of protecting the heritage of ancestral times from further corruption, and from destruction"; and the "*Ṛgveda* is therefore, to an extent, a

---

6. See also C. Chakraberti, *CSARM*, pp. 26-27 for the kings mentioned in the *Ṛgveda*.
7. See Das, op. cit., Preface, pp. v-x.
8. R.P. Chanda, *The Indo-Aryan Races: A Study of the Origin of Indo-Aryan People and Institutions*, p. 1.
9. *Vedic India* (tr. from the French by Philip Spratt), p. 6.

scientific, historical collection."[10] "We have in these hymns," writes L. Geiger, "the picture of an original, primitive life of mankind, free from foreign influences. . . ."[11] "They are not narration of events, but provide incidental evidence on the life of the Aryans. They can be treated as being historically fairly authentic, since their composition was contemporary with the period described."[12]

Muir calls the *Ṛgveda* a "historic Veda."[13] Its historical value as the most ancient record of the Aryans has been acknowledged by a number of scholars.[14] A.A. Macdonell describes it as a "unique monument of a long vanished age" and further adds that it contains some materials of historical interest.[15] "The Indian conception of history is skilfully embodied in one of the early extant Vedic Aryan culture."[16]

According to F. Max Müller, the Veda is the earliest history of the Aryan family. It is the safe basis of Indian history. It has

10. *Life in Ancient India* (Studies in Ṛgvedic India), tr. from the German by R. Arrowsmith, pp. 11-12.

11. Quoted in ibid., p. 37.

12. Romila Thapar, *A History of India*, vol. I, p. 30n.

13. J. Muir, op. cit., p. 201.

14. Ragozin, op. cit., pp. 274ff, 334; A. Weber, *HIL*, pp. 5-8; M. Winternitz, *HIL*, pp. 119f, 169, 290; A.B. Keith, *HSL*, pp. 3f; *RPVU*, HOS, vol. XXXI, pt. I, p. 15; R.T.H. Griffith, *The Hymns of the Atharvaveda*, vol. 1, Preface, pp. iv-v; W.D. Whitney, *On the Vedas* (tr. of the *Atharvaveda Saṁhitā*), vol. I, pp. 10 and 21; H. Beveridge, *A Comprehensive History of India*, vol. I, p. 19; R.C. Dutt, *A History of Civilization in Ancient India based on Sanskrit Literature*, vol. 1, *c. 2000-320* BCE, pp. 2, 4-5, 9-12, 30-32, 109-11; Radha Kumud Mookerji, *Ancient India*, p. 5; Viśveśvaranath Reu, *Ṛgveda par ek Aitihāsika Dṛṣṭi*, pp. 119ff.

15. *HSL*, pp. 140-41.

16. Radhakamal Mukerjee, *The Culture and Art of India*, p. 37.

importance not only in the history of India but also in the history of the world.[17] In one of his essays, he writes:

> . . . for a study of man, or . . . for a study of Aryan humanity, there is nothing in the world equal in importance to the Veda. I maintain that to everybody who cares for himself, for his ancestors, for his history or for his intellectual development, a study of the Vedic literature is indispensable . . . it is far more improving that the reigns of Babylonian and Persian kings, even than the dates and deeds of many of the kings of Judah and Israel.[18]

U.N. Ghoshal has clearly stated that the oldest Indian historical tradition is preserved in the Vedic literature. The historical sense, according to him, had dawned upon the Indians at the beginning of their history.[19] This can more or less be corroborated by the statements of A.K. Warder.[20]

F.E. Pargiter admits that the *R̥gveda*, which is the oldest and the greatest Brāhmanical book, "contains historical allusions, of which some record contemporary persons and events, but more refer to bygone times and persons and are obviously based on tradition."[21] He further observes that the "historical tradition preserved in the Vedic literature has one great merit over that in the epics and Purāṇas that the literature has been very carefully preserved and what it contains now is the statements of the contemporary age." Its statements "being ancient are nearer accuracy than

17. *HASL*, pp. 11, 57-59; see also M. Krishnamachariar, *HCSL*, Introduction, p. vii, Maurice Phillips, *The Teaching of the Vedas*, pp. 26-27.
18. *The Vedas*, Introduction, p. ix.
19. *The Beginning of Indian Historiography and Other Essays*, pp. 22-23.
20. *An Introduction to Indian Historiography*, pp. 15-16.
21. *AIHT*, p. 1.

statements in the epics and Purāṇas which were not so scrupulously preserved."[22] But, on the other hand, he contradicts his own statements by saying that "Vedic literature is not authoritative in historical matters ('except where it notices contemporary matters'), and conclusions drawn from it are not criteria for estimating the results yielded by historical tradition in the epics and Purāṇas."[23] He has repeatedly mentioned that the Vedic texts are not books of historical purpose nor do they deal with history.[24] But such view is no longer tenable. A.B. Keith while dealing with the nature of Vedic Itihāsa has attached considerable importance to the Ṛgvedic history.[25] He says: "That the Vedic texts, the Saṁhitās and the Brāhmaṇas, are not books of historical purpose is notorious."[26]

The Vedic historical tradition cannot be brushed aside as wholly unworthy of attention. It has been truly said that "The evidences derived from the Vedic literature are indeed very strong and generally carry more authority inasmuch as many of them are either directly contemporary records or are traditions derived from contemporary evidences."[27] In fact, it is only the *Ṛgveda* which deals with history and culture of the early Vedic period. L.J. Trotter observes:

> The history of that olden (Aryan) civilisation has been written for us, not in chronicles like those which form the boast of Muhammadan India, but in the sacred writings of Sanskrit-

22. *AIHT*, p. 10.
23. Ibid., p. 14.
24. Ibid., pp. 2, 9-12, 61.
25. *JRAS*, 1911, pp. 979-95; 1912, pp. 429-38.
26. Ibid., 1914, pp. 739, 1031n; 1915, p. 143n.
27. S.N. Pradhan, *Chro. Anct. Ind.*, Preface, p. xi.

speaking Hindus, and in poems which portray the social life of pre-historic India as vividly as Homer portrayed the social life of pre-historic Greece.[28]

---

28. *History of India from the Earliest Times to the Present Day*, pp. 2-3.

2.3

The Epic Tradition

History in the Epics

THE epic tradition of presenting the history was completely different from the Vedic one as appears from the *Rāmāyaṇa* and the *Mahābhārata*. Both the epics have considerable historical value.

The two great epics embody a lot of historical data about ancient kings, kingdoms, dynasties, society, religion, polity, administration, towns and cities, *janapadas*, Aryans, non-Aryans, etc. They furnish plenty of valuable information about social and cultural organisation and the political institutions of the epic age. The expansion of the Aryans and the spread of the Aryan culture and civilisation — one of the significant aspects of ancient Indian history — also find depiction in the epics. The tradition preserved in the epics in this regard is of historical importance.

The *Rāmāyaṇa* of Vālmīki has been rightly called a historical epic.[1] The author himself calls it a *purātana itihāsa* (ancient history)[2] which gets vindicated by his incorporation of dynastic history of the Solar and Lunar families and other historical details of various kingdoms and principalities,

1. *Vāl. Rām.*, Bāla-Kāṇḍa (ed. with Hindi tr. of Yudhiṣṭhira Mīmāṁsaka by Pt. Akhilānanda), p. 13, note 2.
2. *Vāl. Rām.*, Yuddha-Kāṇḍa, 131, 116.

towns and cities, polity and administration, the condition of the Aryan society in the time of the *Rāmāyaṇa,* life and culture of some tribal people, etc. in it. The historicity of *Rāmāyaṇa* can, no doubt, be proved to a certain extent.[3] But K.K. Dasgupta's view that it is "the first historical biography produced in India"[4] cannot be accepted.

The genealogy of the kings of Ayodhyā (the capital of Kosala kingdom) from Ikṣvāku down to Rāma of the Solar family is preserved in Vālmīki's *Rāmāyaṇa.* The genealogy is, no doubt, systematically arranged. But it is incomplete as it contains only some 35 kings.[5] As a matter of fact, there were 64 kings in pre-Rāma period as it appears from the Purāṇic records. A brief history of two other dynasties (the Videha dynasty and the Vaiśāla dynasty) of the same Solar family is also given in the text. The Videha dynasty sprang from Ikṣvāku's son Nimi who is also called Videha. He was the founder of the royal family of Mithilā. He was succeeded by his son Mithi whose son was Janaka I who was further succeeded by several kings down to the time of Śiraḍhvaja (identical with Janaka II). From the genealogical order of the kings of this dynasty it appears that in the line of Nimi there were 52 kings after him who ruled over the kingdom of Videha with its capital at Mithilā (Janakapur, which now lies just within the border of Nepal).[6] The text is replete with some valuable information about the history and antiquity

3. See S.C. De, *Historicity of Rāmāyaṇa and the Indo-Aryan Society in India and Ceylon,* pp. 37ff.

4. "Historical Biography in Sanskrit Literature", in *Historical Biography in Indian Literature,* ed. S.P. Sen, p. 6.

5. Bāla-Kāṇḍa, 70, 21-44; Ayodhyā-Kāṇḍa, 110, 6-35; see also *Vāl. Rām. Ko.,* p. 136 (for genealogical list).

6. Bāla-Kāṇḍa, 71, 3-20; see also *Vāl. Rām. Ko.,* pp. 114-16, 171.

of the Vaiśāla dynasty. The King Viśāla was the founder of this dynasty or kingdom with its capital at Vaiśālī also called Vaiśāla. From the genealogical list of the kings of this dynasty as given in the text it appears that he was succeeded by nine other kings down to Sumati.[7]

The *Rāmāyaṇa* furnishes us with the history of the Lunar family also. We are told that Purūravā ruled at Pratiṣṭhāna (modern Jhunsi opposite Allahabad) the capital city of Madhyadeśa.[8] Nahuṣa[9] was succeeded by his son, Yayāti, whose five sons, Yadu, Turvasa or Turvasu, Druhyu, Aṇu and Puru[10] ruled over different kingdoms. Brahmadatta, the king of Kāmpilipurī (Kāmpilya), the capital of South Pañcāla kingdom, also finds mention in the text.[11] The information supplied in it about the Haihaya dynasty is of paramount historical importance. The Haihayas constitute one of the branches of the Yādavas in Yadu's line. The King Haihaya and his successors are generally called the Haihayas. Their genealogy is also partly given in the text. The Haihayas extended their rule to the Narmadā Valley during the time of Kṛtavīrya's son Arjuna. The latter is said to have conquered Māhiṣmatī, situated on the banks of the Narmadā, by defeating Karkoṭaka, a Nāga chief who had settled over there and subsequently made it his fortress capital. The Haihayas established themselves in that part of India by overthrowing the Nāgas of the Narmadā region.[12] The hostile relations of

7. Bāla-Kāṇḍa, 47, 11-17; also 45, 8-12.
8. Uttara-Kāṇḍa, 56, 26; also 90, 92.
9. Ibid., 56, 27-28.
10. Ibid., 58, 8-13.
11. Bāla-Kāṇḍa, 33, 19; *Vāl. Rām. Ko.*, p. 57.
12. Uttara-Kāṇḍa, 31, 7-10; 32, 1-7.

the Haihayas and Tālajaṅghas with the Kosala kingdom during the time of one of its kings, Asita, also find reflection in the text.[13] Some fragments of information about the s are also found therein.[14]

Vasu (Uparicara Vasu, fourth in succession from Kuru's son, Sudhanvan) and his five sons, including Bṛhadratha, who was the founder of the kingdom of Magadha with its capital at Girivraja, and Kuśa or Kuśāmba, who founded Kauśāmbī (the capital of Vatsa kingdom), also find mention in the *Rāmāyaṇa*.[15]

A number of towns and cities like Pratiṣṭhāna, Prāgjyotiṣapura, Ayodhyā, Mithilā, Vaiśālī, Mathurā, Hastināpura, Girivraja (Rājagṛha) Māhiṣmatī, Kāmpilya and Kuśāvatī also figure in the *Rāmāyaṇa*. The text not only deals with the history of their foundations but also gives their vivid description and provides a glimpse into an urban life. It also abounds in information about the rights and duties of a king, nature and functioning of about the rights and duties of a king, nature and functioning of the state, administration of justice, war and politics, the social and religious life of the Aryans, etc.

The *Rāmāyaṇa* throws a good deal of light on the historical geography also with regard to various kingdoms, principalities, *janapada*s and urban centres, and various races and tribes existing in different parts of India in those days.[16]

The *Mahābhārata* was originally composed by Vyāsa exactly three years after the Great Bhārata battle came to an end as

13. Bāla-Kāṇḍa, 70, 28-29.
14. Uttara-Kāṇḍa, 38, 15-20.
15. Bāla-Kāṇḍa, 32, 1-9; also *Vāl. Rām. Ko.*, pp. 71, 73, 83, 103, 315.
16. See Kiṣkindhā-Kāṇḍa, chs. 37-50.

recorded in the text.[17] It was first named *Jaya Itihāsa*. In the text itself, it has been repeatedly called an *itihāsa* (history).[18] It is further said that this *Bhārata Itihāsa*, full of the details of valuable subjects, is the most excellent and the best of the *itihāsas*.[19] It was laso called *Bhārata Saṁhitā* because of being a history of Bharat dynasty. It consisted of 24,000 verses.[20] Further, many stories and contemporary events were incorporated and many additions were made in it which led to the increase in the number of its verses to 100,000. And thereafter it became popularly known as the *Mahābhārata*. The text in the present enlarged form (divided into eighteen *parvans* or books) consists of exactly the same number of verses. It is believed to have been redacted twice, once in the Śuṅga period and then in the Gupta period.

Some scholars are of the view that *Mahābhārata* is "a work of history,"[21] which is not unworthy of acceptance. C.V. Vaidya considers it both an epic and a history.[22] He further writes: ". . . Works known as Histories or *itihāsas* were known even in Vedic times. The *Mahābhārata* itself was originally a history. . . ."[23] V.S. Agrawala opines that it is not that type of history in which historical events are chronologically arranged. It has its own historical value.[24] It is, no doubt, an

17. Ādi Parva, 56, 32.
18. Ibid., I.24-25, 48, 52; 56, 16, 18-20, 25-27; Svargārohaṇa Parva, 5, 39 and 43; also *Bh. Sv.*, vol. 3, p. 230.
19. Ādi Parva, 2, 31-33; also 56, 15-16.
20. Ibid., I.61; I, 208-09.
21. K.K. Dasgupta, op. cit., p. 6; Umashankar Dikshit, *Maharṣi Vedavyāsa: A Historical and Cultural Biography*, p. 13.
22. *The Mahābhārata: A Criticism*, pp. 37ff, 50ff.
23. Ibid. p. 59.
24. *Bh. Sv.*, vol. I, pp. 27f.

encyclopaedia of historical knowledge. It sheds light on different aspects of ancient Indian history.

The *Mahābhārata* as a whole contains valuable historical information about the dynastic history and genealogies of the Lunar family of both pre- and post-Bhārata War period, towns and cities, kingdoms and republics, kingship and state, polity and administration, Aryans and non-Aryans, the contemporary social and religious conditions of the people, etc.

The genealogies of the kings of the Lunar dynasty of the pre-War period given in the *Mahābhārata* include that of Purūrava, of the five sons of Yayāti, Aṇu, Druhyu, Turvasu, Yadu and Puru, of the kings of Puru's descendants called Pauravas, the kings of Bharata and Kuru dynasties in the line of the Pauravas and the kings of Pañcāla dynasty.[25] The histories of the kingdoms and dynasties of the Āṇavas (descendants of Aṇu),[26] the Yādavas in general including the Andhaka-Vṛṣṇīs,[27] the Bhojas[28] and the Haihayas,[29] the Yādavas from Mathurā to Dvārakā (which include the details of the reasons of shifting the capital from the former place to the latter, their fratricidal war and destruction and sinking

25. Ādi Parva, I.44-45, 138; 69, 49; 70, II.45; ch. 71; 80, 26; 82, 5; 89, 5-55; 90, 7-96; also *Bh. Sv.*, vol. I, pp. 83-87, 150-72.

26. Ādi Parva, 88, 6, 17-19; also I.172-75; 207, 9-10; Sabhā Parva, 29, 5-6; Droṇa Parva, 6, 2-7; Bhīṣma Parva, 10, 7.

27. Ādi Parva, 210, 15-20; 213, 23-55; Sabhā Parva, 13, 3-55; Śānti Parva, 82, 8-29.

28. Sabhā Parva, 13, 4-7, 24-25; 28, 1-15, 37-43.

29. Ādi Parva, 31, 5-8; 98, 1; Anuśāsana Parva, 152, 3-4; Udyoga Parva, 19, 22-23; Sabhā Parva, 28, 17 and 24; see also Sorensen, *Index to the Names in the Mahābhārata*, I, p. 458; II, p. 457.

of Dvārakā city in the sea),[30] the Pauravas, Bhāratas, Kurus and Pañcālas,[31] etc. are also depicted therein. The dynastic history of the Kāśī[32] and Magadha kingdoms[33] described in the text is of equal historical value. The details provided therein about the Kuru kingdom of Hastināpura ruled by the successors of Parīkṣit II in the post-War period are also of considerable historical importance.[34] There are also some fragments of information about the Nāga dynasty.[35] However, the dynastic genealogies are not mutually consistent, and the chronological sequence of events is broken to a certain extent. These are the two deficiencies which are noticeable in the presentation of the historical accounts of the kingdoms and dynasties in this epic.

The *Mahābhārata* also throws light on early phase of urban settlements in the Gangetic Valley as well as in other parts of India. It contains information about the foundations and growth and some urban features of some towns and cities like Hastināpura, Indraprastha, Kauśāmbī, Ahicchatra,

30. Ādi Parva, 210, 15-20; 213, 23-55; Sabhā Parva, 13, 5-55; Āraṇyaka Parva, 16, 5-23; 17, 1-33; Mausala Parva, 2, 1-20; 3, 1-22; 4, 32-41; 6, 1-15; 7, 9-22; 8, 4-10, 32-74; Mahāprasthānika Parva, I.43 (for sunken Dvārakā city in the sea beheld by the Pāṇḍavas with their own eyes during the course of their wanderings); see also *Bh. Sv.* vol. 1, pp. 143-44; vol. 3. pp. 221-23; *Mbh. Ko.*, p. 100.

31. For all see Ādi Parva, 89-5-90; 90, 10-96; also I.44-45; 55, 22-25; 105, 17-22; 213, 13, 22-35; 3, 144-46; 37-9; Sabhā Parva, ch. 48; Virāṭa Parva, 1, 9-14; *Bh. Sv.*, vol. I, pp. 84-85, 99; *Mbh. Ko.*, pp. 199-200.

32. Anuśāsana Parva, 31, 10-26.

33. Ādi Parva, 57, 1-2, 7-12, 27-30; Sabhā Parva, 17, 4-9-21-23; 18, 21-30; 19, 1-18; 13, 29-32; *Bh. Sv.*, vol. I, pp. 143, 146-47.

34. Ādi Parva, 3, 10-18, 144-46, 179-80; 40, 6-8; ch. 94; *Bh. Sv.*, vol. I, p. 53; *Mbhn. Ko.*, p. 293.

35. Ādi Parva, 3, 119-22, 140, 144-46, 166-69; 31, 5-18; 52, 5-19; *Bh. Sv.*, vol. I, pp. 128-29.

Kāmpilya, Girivraja (Rājagṛha), Campā, Kāśī (Vārāṇasī) and Māhiṣmatīpur. Their existence has already been archaeologically proved. The history of Dvārakā city in Gujarat in particular from its foundation to its submerging into the sea exactly 36 years after the war or Great Bhārata battle is recorded in the epic. The information provided in it about the seals made out of shell bearing the engravings of *padma* (lotus) symbol (Āraṇyaka Parva, 80, 83) is quite consistent with the findings of distinguished marine acrhaeologist, S.R. Rao. He discovered exactly the same seals from Beṭ-Dvārakā some time between November 1987 and February 1988. It is striking to note that the political importance and economic value of the seals of Dvārakā in Kṛṣṇa's time have also been highlighted respectively in the above *parva* of the *Mahābhārata* (16, 19) and the *Harivaṁśa* (Viṣṇu Parva, 58, 57-66). The archaeological discovery of the remains of sunken Dvārakā city from the Arabian Sea and that of the said seals by Shri Rao proves not only the historicity of Kṛṣṇa but also the historical authenticity of the epic account of the city. Some other urban centres like Tāmralipti, Bharukaccha Śūrapāraka, Virāṭanagar, Madra's capital Śākala, Daśapura, Tripurī, Prāgjyotiṣapura, Bhojakaṭapura, Kuṇḍinapura, Sūktimatipura, Uragapura (one of the early capitals of Coḷa kingdom), Rājapura, the capital of Kamboja and Maśaka (Massaga in the Swāt Valley which was in a flourishing condition at the time of Alexander's invasion of north-west India) also find mention in the Great Epic.

A long list of kingdoms (states) and *janapada*s (territorial units and peoples) existing in different parts of India[36] and

36. Sabhā Parva, 23, 13-26; 24, 1-27; 25, 1-18; 26, 1-16; 27, 1-28; 28, 1-50; 29, 1-19; 31, 6-25; 47, 10-16; 48, 3-42; Bhīṣma Parva, 10, 37-68; 12, 33-35; Droṇa Parva, 4, 4-5; 6, 2-27; 10, 15-16; Chs. 17-19, 22-28, 31 and →

that of republican communities, notably the Andhaka-Vṛṣṇīs, the confederate Yādava tribes of Mathurā[37] and the Śivis, Kuṇindas, Trigarttas, Ambaṣṭhas, Oḍambaras, Yaudheyas and Kṣudraka-Mālavas of the Punjab[38] are furnished in the *Mahābhārata*. The details of evolution of the institution of kingship, the origin or formation of the state and its seven constituents (based on *saptāṅga* theory), nature and types, aims and functions and growth and decline, inter-state relations, etc. have also been provided in this work.[39] The monarchical and republican forms of government are said to have prevailed. The information contained in it about the administrative system followed in a monarchical state, the powers and functions of the king and his *mantrīpariṣad*, councillors, subordinate rulers and officers, military administration, judicial administration, village and city administration, *gaṇa* form of government, i.e. the rule of the many, etc. are of great value.

The original settlements of the Aryans in the region extending from the western coast of the Yamunā to

→ 114; Karṇa Parva, 27, 71-91; 30, 9-81; Udyoga Parva, 19, 7-32; Virāṭa Parva, I, 9-14; 5, 3-21; 29, 1-28; ch. 30; 31, 1-24; 32, 3-12; Āśvatthamedhika Parva, 84, 1-19; *Bh. Sv.*, vol. I, pp. 150-53; vol. 2, pp. 121-47, 159, 169-72, 247-76; *Mbh. Ko.*, pp. 14ff; see also S.N. Pande, *Geographical Horizon of the Mahābhārata*, pp. 119-43.

37. Śānti Parva, 82, 8-29; 108, 8-31; see also K.P. Jayaswal, *Hindu Polity*, App. A, pp. 355-60; G.P. Singh, *Republics, Kingdoms, Towns and Cities in Ancient India*, pp. 8ff.

38. Sabhā Parva, 23, 13-15; 29, 1-8; 48, 12-14; Droṇa Parva, 6, 2-7; 10, 16; *Bh. Sv.*, vol. 3, pp. 89-95, 259-60; see also B.P. Roy, *Political Ideas and Institutions in the Mahābhārata*, pp. 166-88; G.P. Singh, op. cit., pp. 32-33, 45f, 56-66, 77-80.

39. Śānti Parva, 56, 2-36; 57, 4-42; 58, 1-24; 59, 13-18; 67, 2-14; chs. 69, 81, 84, 87, 91-95, 162; 104, 11-30; 108, 8-31; ch. 308; *Bh. Sv.*, vol. 3, pp. 23, 41-58, 67-69; see also Roy, op. cit., pp. 88-165, 335-82; G.P. Singh, *Political Thought in Ancient India*, pp. 21-130.

Kurukṣetra on the bank of the Sarasvatī (which formed a part of the Sārasvata region) are also described in the Great Epic.[40] Kurukṣetra was situated to the south of the Sarasvatī and the north of the Dṛṣadvatī. Several non-Aryan races and tribes, and foreign invaders like Śakas, Pahalavas (Pārthians), Yavanas (Bactrian Greeks) and Hūṇas also find mention in it.

The picture of contemporary social life with details of caste system, the position of nobles, the brāhmaṇas, slaves and women, the custom of *satī*, the practice of polygamy, marriage system and the religious beliefs, etc. is vividly portrayed in the Great Epic.

Historical Value of the Epics: A Critical Assessment

Both the epics are regarded as the true history of India. They contain the kernel of historical truth about several aspects of ancient Indian history and culture.

The *Rāmāyaṇa* of Vālmīki, according to R.S. Tripathi (one of the authorities on history of ancient India), bears historical character to some extent. He observes: "The *Rāmāyaṇa* is superb indeed both as regards form and matter, and it portrays ideal characters in almost all aspects of human life."[41] R.C. Dutt has also acknowledged the historical value of this epic.[42] Monier Monier-Williams,[43] H. Jacobi,[44] and A.B. Keith[45] admit that it has a historical basis. Parimal Kumar Das

40. Āraṇyaka Parva, 81, 1-7; also *Bh. Sv.*, vol. I, pp. 255-56.
41. *HAI*, p. 63.
42. *A History of Civilisation in Ancient India*, I, p. 211.
43. *Indian Epic Poetry*, p. 8.
44. *Das Rāmāyaṇa* (Bonn, 1893).
45. *HSL*, p. 43.

categorically stated that the *Rāmāyaṇa* and the *Mahābhārata* are the two best specimens of contemporary social history.[46]

It may, however, be noted here that the genealogical lists of some dynasties contained in the *Rāmāyaṇa* are truncated. The achievements of the kings mentioned in the dynastic genealogies are not highlighted in detail except few.

Estimating critically the historical value of the *Mahābhārata*, R.S. Tripathi writes: "In the main the story of the *Mahābhārata* is based on historical truth."[47] ". . . there are undoubted deviations from historical accuracy in the *Mahābhārata*, but the central theme is authentic, and its characters, whose exploits were first popularised by story-tellers and minstrels, are by no means imaginary."[48]

Assessing the historical importance of the *Mahābhārata*, V.S. Agrawala says that it is an encyclopaedia of knowledge of history of ancient India. Originally, it was written by Vyāsa as a history of Bharata dynasty. Later, various other historical subjects were incorporated in it. It is a unique storehouse of information regarding polity, religion, Aryan culture, etc.[49] He unequivocally states that it is different from those historical works in which historical events are chronologically described. It is a historical work of its own kind.[50] He has thrown a good deal of light on its historical value.

"The struggles between native princes, the rise and fall of empires, have indeed not passed . . . into utter oblivion.

46. "Itihāsa Lekhana: Eka Dṛṣṭikoṇa", in *Bias in Indian Historiography*, ed. D. Devahuti, p. 57.

47. *HAI*, p. 67.

48. Ibid., pp. 68-69.

49. *Bh. Sv.*, vol. I, pp. 17f; vol. 3, pp. 235-37, 262ff.

50. Ibid., vol. I, pp. 27-28.

The memory is to some extent preserved in epic poems, in stories of the sages and heroes of old, in genealogies and dynastic lists. Such in all countries are the beginnings of history; and in ancient India its development was not carried beyond this rudimentary stage," says E.J. Rapson.[51]

The dynastic and genealogical histories recorded in the *Mahābhārata* are neither complete nor systematic.

It is said that the two great epics are of little importance for political history.[52] This statement contains some substratum of truth.

Both the epics are deficient in chronology.

51. *CHI*, I (Ancient India), p. 51.

52. J. Allan, Wolseley Haig and H.H. Dodwell, *The Cambridge Shorter History of India*, p. 1.

2.4

The Purāṇic Tradition

Antiquity and Historicity of the Purāṇas

THE Purāṇas have their own history. There was originally a single text called both *Purāṇa Saṁhitā* and *Itihāsa-Saṁhitā* whose authorship has been ascribed to the great sage, Vedavyāsa, twenty-eighth in the line of Vyāsas who were known by different names. He inherited the tradition of preserving and compiling the Purāṇic data from his predecessors. The Purāṇas themselves record that after having classified the single Veda into four Saṁhitās, he first composed the Purāṇa divided into eighteen parts consisting of *ākhyāna*s, *upākhyāna*s, *gāthā*s, etc. and then an Itihāsa (history) named the *Mahābhārata* (originally called both *Bhārata Itihāsa* and *Bhārata Saṁhitā*) incorporating in it some Purāṇic data in the *Dvāpara-yuga* itself.[1] The said 18 Purāṇas contain, among other things, historical tradition of the Aryans. A.K. Warder's view, that the original Purāṇa was composed in the eighth century BCE

1. *Mts.*, 52, 3-11, 68-69, also 3, 3-4; *Vṣṇ.*, III.3.2-21; III.4.1-10; III.6.15; *Km.*, I.I.3 and 5; I.50.10-14 and 20-21, also II.44.145; *Vy.*, 103, 48-51, 55-58; *Bmd.*, II.173; IV.4.47-50, 54-58; *Bhāg.*, I.4.20; III.12.39; *Bmv.*, 133, 5; *Vmn.*, 12, 3; *Pdm.*, V.2.53; *Vṣṇ. Dh.*, III.15.1; *Devī Bhāgavat*, I.3.17, 25-33. The eighteen Purāṇas consisting of four lakh verses are listed in order of their antiquity in some of the Purāṇas texts like *Mts.* (53, 12-66), *Vṣṇ* (III.6, 20-24) and *Bhāg.* (XII.7, 22-24; also XII.13, 3-9). For historical significance of the words like *ākhyāna*, *gāthā*, *nārāśaṁsī*, *vaṁśa*, etc. see V.S. Pathak, *Ancient Historians of India*, pp. 1-21.

during the reign of Adhisīmakṛṣṇa of the Kaliyuga (sixth in the succession from Abhimanyu) or may have existed in some form earlier,[2] appears to be confusing. In fact, the Purāṇa was narrated and not composed during the reign of the said king. In reality, it was the *Dvāpara-yuga* which marked the beginning of the tradition of historical writing in early India.

It is significant to note that Maharṣi Vedavyāsa in his Purāṇas and the *Mahābhārata* also included some important historical subjects like dynastic genealogies of pre-Bhārata war period, contemporary events, etc. And it is perhaps on this ground that Umashankara Dikshit has called him *itihāsakarttā* (composer of historical work) and "a great historian."[3] N.S. Rajaram also observes: "In ancient times Vedavyāsa was considered a great historian. Tradition credits him with the authorship of the historical epic *Mahābhārata* and also with the responsibility for preserving ancient records found in the Purāṇas."[4] Their views find support in A.K. Warder's statement that Vyāsa was "the original historian of the *Bhārata Ākhyāna* and Purāṇa."[5] It is practically not possible to chronologically arrange all his works. Nor can he be placed in a chronological framework. He was not a mythical figure but a historical personage. In fact, it were *ṛṣi*s and *maharṣi*s who built up the tradition of preserving the historical records of the past.

It was Vedavyāsa who taught the first lesson of history to his pupils. There are some concrete evidence in the Purāṇa

2. *An Introduction to Indian Historiography*, pp. 17-18.

3. *Maharṣi Vedavyāsa: A Historical and Cultural Biography*, p. 13.

4. "Distortions of Indian History from Harappa to Ayodhya", in B.V. Raman (ed.), *The Astrological Magazine*, vol. 87 no. 1 (Bangalore, January 1998), p. 75.

5. Op. cit., pp. 116-17.

records to show that he taught the Itihāsa-Purāṇa to his famous disciple, Romaharṣaṇa or Lomaharṣaṇa (called *sūta*) who further taught it to his son, Ugraśravā, and six disciples at least five of whom were brāhmaṇas.[6] The Purāṇic brāhmaṇas belonging to a class of *sūta* had developed historical sense. Their concept of history was fundamentally based on the precepts of the said Vyāsa. In all probability, the work begun by Vyāsa might have been completed by Romaharṣaṇa and his disciples. The tradition of studying, teaching and interpreting the Itihāsa and Purāṇa set by Vyāsa and followed by his disciples was handed down from generation to generation.

The original Purāṇa contained the details of the kingdoms and dynasties with genealogies of only the pre-Bhārata war period. It saw several recensions with additions between *c.* 500 BCE and CE 500. Only some Purāṇas contain the historical information covering the period from the seventh to the twelfth centuries CE. The *purāṇakāras* (composers of the Purāṇas) had clear conception of history. Applying their historical sense, they time to time incorporated in the Purāṇas the historical events of the past along with other subjects during the aforesaid period.

The Purāṇic *sūtas*, who belonged to both brāhmaṇa and kṣatriya class, played very important role in the preservation of ancient Indian historical tradition. According to some Purāṇas, it was their special duty to compose, arrange and preserve the genealogies (Vaṁśāvalīs) of the kings of various dynasties which constituted the source-material for the Itihāsas and Purāṇas.[7] They used to compile the royal genealogies

6. *Vṣṇ.*, III.4.8-10; III.6.16-19; *Bhāg.*, I.4.22; XII.7.5-7; *Vy.*, 61, 55-58; *Km.*, I.1.2-7; I.50.12-14; *Bmd.*, IV.4.67f; *Pdm.*, V.I.11-14.

7. *Vy.*, I.31-32; *Pdm.*, V.I.27-28; see also Pargiter, *AIHT*, p. 15.

on the basis of the information collected from the royal families and the families of the priests and others. The materials collected by them were incorporated in the Purāṇa texts. They were also employed by the kings in their courts to record the events of their reigns as well as that of the reigns of their ancestors. Thus, they were preservers of historical tradition (both Brāhmanical and kṣatriya), custodians of genealogical records and chroniclers of events of the past. We are also informed by Kauṭilya, who flourished in the latter half of the fourth century BCE that "the *paurāṇika*, the *sūta* and the *māgadha*" were three officials of salaried class retained by a king or prince for listening to the Itihāsa and Purāṇa. The former two are said to have been well conversant with their subjects. The *itihāsa*s and Purāṇas were explained by them to a king or prince to educate him or to make him perfect, wise and great.[8] Maurice Winternitz also admits that the *paurāṇika*s and *aitihāsika*s were professional story-tellers in very ancient times.[9] The *paurāṇika*s and *aitihāsika*s are applied respectively to those who knew or studied the Purāṇas (the works containing purely traditional accounts of past history) and the Itihāsas (the works containing historical accounts of the past events, stories based on historical truth, etc.).

According to V.S. Pathak, the *sūta*s belonged to brāhmaṇa class. He has connected them with Bhṛgu (Bhārgava), Aṅgiras (Bhāradvāja) and Kaśyapa clans of priests of whom the first two were associated with historiography or writing of history (Itihāsa, Purāṇa and later some other texts).[10] The *sūta*s were also of the warrior or kṣatriya class or of mixed parentage.

8. *Arth.*, I, 5 (line 15); V. 3; V, 6; XIII.1.

9. *HIL*, I, p. 313; see also B.P. Sinha, "Race, Religion, Region and Ideology", in *Bias in Indian Historiography*, ed. Devahuti, p. 37.

10. Op. cit., pp. 21f; see also Warder, op. cit., pp. 18-25.

The Bhṛgu partly merged with Aṅgiras to form a Bhṛgvāṅgiras. There is an evidence to show that from the end of Paurava period to the foundation of the Magadha empire a school of Bhṛgvāṅgiras historians revised the Itihāsa-Purāṇa tradition.[11]

The contributions made by the *sūtas* in the field of historiography was no less significant than that of any historiographer (or *itihāsakāra*) of the contemporary age.

The *sūtas* are often equated with bards[12] as they used to bestow extravagant praise on great kings and heroes of the past while writing or singing about their deeds. But the bards as such did not get official recognition in the royal courts before the dawn of the seventh century CE. Nor did their office become professional or hereditary before that period. The *sūtas* gradually lost their importance. "In the early Medieval Age when the heroic tradition of history changed into the courtly one, the wandering *sūtas* and the Bhṛgvāṅgirasas were replaced by salaried court-poets. . . ."[13]

Ancient Indian historical tradition has been classified by Pargiter broadly into two groups, the brāhmanic and the kṣatriya, for judging their comparative historical value. The events described in Brāhmanic tradition, according to him, do not bear historicity. Kṣatriya tradition, on the other hand, professes to deal with history. He further states that the Vedic and other Brāhmanic literature give us notices of ancient times from purely the Brāhmanical point of view and they do not deal with history, while kṣatriya tradition

11. Warder, op. cit.

12. Romila Thapar, *AISH*, pp. 270-72; see also her *From Lineage to State*, p. 130; Pargiter, *AIHT*, p. 13.

13. Pathak, op. cit., p. 21.

preserved in the Purāṇas enables us to have a picture of ancient India and its political conditions from the kṣatriya standpoint. He continues to maintain that before the introduction of writing the brāhmaṇas had to rely on tradition when referring to men and events of the bygone age as well as to contemporaneous occurrences, and even after writing was introduced they discountenanced it so far as their religious books were concerned. There was a total lack of the historical sense among the brāhmaṇas who composed the Brāhmanical literature. They failed to compose genuine history. They hardly maintained distinction between history and mythology. And there was a constant tendency on their part to confuse the two by mythologising history, on the one hand, and historifying the mythology, on the other. They have been also charged by him with fabricating incorrect stories and fables. They often neglected to revise or harmonise historical tradition. The Purāṇic brāhmaṇas are said to have preserved a large mass of kṣatriya and popular tradition which was inconsistent with Brāhmanic stories and tenets. He further adds that kṣatriya tradition preserved in the Purāṇas is not deficient in the historical sense. This tradition is concerned chiefly with kings and heroes and their great deeds, genealogies, etc. Kṣatriya tales and ballads have some historical consistency. Royal genealogies certainly do not betray the lack of historical sense.[14] The Purāṇic "genealogies are essentially chronological; and the old tales, especially those narrated in the course of the best versions of the genealogies, have also a historical character."[15] The above observations amount to exaltation of the kṣatriya tradition and depreciation of the Brāhmanic tradition. But

14. *AIHT*, pp. 58-63.

15. Ibid., pp. 60-61.

the fact remains that the Vedic texts and the Purāṇas constitute joint testimony for writing traditional history.[16] It is an erroneous opinion about the ancient Indians that they had neither history nor did possess any historical instinct. The historical treasures buried in the Purāṇas are of great value. "The literature of the brāhmaṇa was always supplemented from the earliest times by the literature of the kṣatriya kings."[17] As a matter of fact, the Vedic, epic and Purāṇic traditions are supplementary to each other, and no coherent picture of early India can be presented without placing our reliance on the combined testimony of the three. It is an altogether different thing that the Purāṇic account of the subject is more elaborate and amplified than the Vedic and epic ones.

The Purāṇas deal with five subjects or topics, viz. (a) *sarga* (original creation), (b) *pratisarga* (dissolution and recreation), (c) *vaṁśa* (genealogies), (d) *manvantara* (an epoch of each Manu or division of time), and (e) *vaṁśānucarita* (histories of dynasties of kings mentioned in the genealogies).[18] These are the five attributes (*pañca-lakṣaṇa*) of a Purāṇa. Of these five, the two — *vaṁsa* and *vaṁśānucarita* — are purely historical subjects. These two are extremely important for dynastic history of early India. The *purāṇakāras* had obviously very comprehensive view of history.[19] Some

---

16. See *Cul. Her. Ind.*, vol. V (1978), p. 284 (for A.D. Pusalker's view).

17. S.C. Vidyarnava, "Paurani Chronology", in *The Matsya Purāṇa*, SBA, vol. I (ed. with Eng. tr. of various oriental scholars and notes of B.C. Majumdar, S.C. Vasu, H.H. Wilson, Bentley, Wilford and others by J.D. Akhtar). App. VIII, LXX-XCIII.

18. *Mts.*, 53, 64; *Vṣṇ.*, III, 6-25 and 27; *Bmv.*, 133, 6; *Km.*, I, 1, 12; *Bhāg.*, XII, 7, 9-10.

19. See also Pusalker, "Conception of History in Ancient Indian Literature", *Our Heritage*, XII, 2, 1964, pp. 35-46.

of the Purāṇas are very authentic records of dynastic genealogies and chronology. The dynastic genealogies in particular constitute the nucleus of the political history whatsoever in the Purāṇas. V.A. Smith says:

> . . . the most systematic record of the Indian historical tradition is that preserved in the dynastic lists of the Purāṇas . . . modern European writers have been inclined to disparage unduly the authority of the Purāṇic lists, but closer study finds in them much genuine and valuable historical tradition.[20]

Acknowledging the historical value of Purāṇic genealogies of the royal families, F.E. Pargiter observes:

> Though historical works about ancient India are wanting, yet tradition has handed down fairly copious genealogies of the ancient dynasties. These state the succession of kings, and in that way are historical. They are almost the only historical data found in Sanskrit books as regards ancient political development; and the list of teachers in professed chronological order set out in some Brāhmanical books supplies evidence as regards Brāhmanical succession. The genealogies form the basis by which the investigation of tradition for historical ends may be tested. They supply the best chronological clue, for the Vedic literature . . . is not a sure guide in historical matters."[21]

". . . traditional genealogies are rarely faithful records of times past."[22] And the traditional chronology is partly reliable.

Some scholars are of the opinion that the Purāṇas, whose authors may be compared to "medieval chroniclers, are mainly legendary and mythological collections." But they

20. *EHI*, revd. 4th edn., p. 11.

21. *AIHT*, p. 11.

22. Thapar, "Genealogy as a Source of Social History", in her *AISH*, p. 326.

"contain certain amount of genealogical matters, the historical significance of which it is very difficult to estimate."[23]

James Tod includes Purāṇas in the historical works of the ancient Indians. He specifically refers to Purāṇas as "Historical records."[24] Little different from it, he writes:

> In the absence of regular and legitimate historical records, there are, however, other native works, which, in the hands of a skilful and patient investigator, would afford no despicable materials for the history of India. The first of these are the Purāṇas and genealogical legends of the princes, which, obscured as they are by mythological details, allegory; . . . contain many facts that serve as beacons to direct the research of the historian.[25]

The Purāṇas in general are partly legendary and partly historical. Of the 18 main Purāṇas, the six — *Matsya, Vāyu, Viṣṇu, Brahmāṇḍa, Bhāgavata* and *Bhaviṣya* — are very very important from a historical point of view. The first two have been called by their authors *purātana itihāsa* (ancient history)[26] in support of their historicity, as they (like other four Purāṇas) deal with historical events of the past. These six Purāṇas really constitute very faithful historical records. They have preserved highly valuable accounts of different dynasties of both pre- and post-Bhārata war period with the help of which we can throw some new light on the dark or obscure aspects of ancient Indian political history of those

23. J. Allan, Wolseley Haig and H.H. Dodwell, *The Cambridge Shorter History of India*, p. 1.
24. *AAR*, I, Introduction, xiii-xvii.
25. Ibid., xv.
26. *Mts.*, 72, 6; *Vy.*, 103, 48; see also *Pdm.*, VI, 77, 30; 243, 3.

periods. They have great historical value from dynastic, genealogical and chronological points of view. A. Weber has also admitted that some of the old Purāṇas contain historical portions with dynasties of kings, genealogies and chronology.[27]

The Purāṇas are not the productions of one age or of one brain. As stated earlier, the original Purāṇa was composed by Vyāsa some time before the Great Bhārata battle began. And then time to time several additions were made into it by the *purāṇakāras*. The process of incorporating the past events in some of the Purāṇas began as early as the sixth or fifth century BCE and generally continued till the fourth or fifth century CE but in some cases even beyond that period.

Since the *Vāyu* and *Viṣṇu* provide dynastic history up to the beginning of the Gupta rule, they in the present form must have existed about the middle of the fourth century CE. The *Matsya* (one of the early Purāṇas) was compiled with new additions towards the end of the reign of King Yajña Śrī Śātakarṇi (*c.* CE 165-95) of the Āndhra or Sātavāhana dynasty. Its compilation was further carried up to CE 236. It was finally completed before the end of the third century CE as it covers the dynastic accounts only up to the end of the rule of the Āndhras or Sātavāhanas. The *Brahmāṇḍa* in the present form existed in or about CE 400.

The *Bhaviṣya Purāṇa* existed before *c.* 500 BCE as appears from the *Āpastamba Dharmasūtra*. The *Kaliyugarājavṛttānta* (details of the dynasties of the Kaliyuga) given in this Purāṇa appears to be the oldest of all other Purāṇic details thereof. The dynastic accounts of the rulers of the Kaliyuga was first included in it towards the end of the second century CE. The text in the revised form very much existed in the middle of

27. *HIL*, pp. 213 f.

the third century CE which is supported by the fact that the *Matsya* borrowed its account of the dynasties of the Kaliyuga from it before the end of that century, and the *Vāyu* and *Brahmāṇḍa* borrowed their accounts of the same dynasties from it in the next century, as the internal evidence therein indicates. The *Bhaviṣya Purāṇa* contains the accounts up to the times of the famous Rājpūt ruler Pṛthvirāja Cauhāna (CE 1179-92) so far as the ancient period is concerned. The events of the subsequent periods also appear to have been recorded in it. Therefore, no definite date can be assigned to it in the present form.

The *Bhāgavata Purāṇa* existed in the middle of the third century CE. Some additions were, of course, made into it some time between CE 600 and 800 as appears from the text itself. Some other important Purāṇas like the *Brahma* (the oldest of all) and *Padma* (next to it in order of antiquity) must have existed at least as early as the beginning of the fifth century BCE.

"Verses praising gifts of land are quoted in various land-grants that are dated; and some of those are found only in the *Padma*, *Bhaviṣya* and *Brahma Purāṇa* and thus indicate that those Purāṇas were in existence before CE 500 and even long before that time. Some of those verses, which occur in grants of the years 475-76 and 482-83, are declared in some grants to have been enunciated by Vyāsa in the *Mahābhārata*."[28]

The *Agni Purāṇa* in its original form can be placed much earlier than the fourth century CE. However, some additions were made into it between *c.* CE 500 and 900. The *Kūrma*, *Mārkaṇḍeya*, *Brahmavaivartta*, *Liṅga*, *Vāmana* and other Purāṇas were also in existence before CE 500.

28. Pargiter, *AIHT*, p. 49.

Purāṇic History (Purāṇic Tradition of Historiography)

One of the most important traditions of historiography in ancient India was the Purāṇic one. And, hence, this tradition deserves our special attention.

The Purāṇic historiography is important especially from dynastic, genealogical and chronological points of view.

The Purāṇas contain a lot of valuable historical data regarding ancient Indian kings, kingdoms, dynasties, society, polity, religion, culture, *janapadas*, towns, cities, etc.

The historical reliability of the Purāṇic accounts of the kingdoms and dynasties with genealogies of the Ikṣvāku rulers of Kosala with its capital at Ayodhyā[29] and that of the rulers of Videha with its capital at Mithilā (Janakapur),[30] of Vaiśālī which was itself the capital (in north Bihar)[31] and of the Śaryātas in the line of Śaryāti (who reigned at Kuśasthalī, the ancient name of Dvārakā or Dvāravatī in Gujarat, which was named Ānarta after king Ānarta)[32] of the Solar family of the pre-Bhārata war period is beyond doubt. Likewise, the details provided in some of the Purāṇas of the kingdoms and dynasties with genealogies of the lineal descendants of Purūravā, the progenitor of the Lunar family and ruler of Pratiṣṭhānapura on the confluence of the Gaṅgā and the Yamunā in Prayāga, of the same period are of great historical

---

29. *Vy.*, 88, 3-212; *Vṣṇ.*, VI, 2, 34, 70; IV, 3, 1-28; IV, 4, 5-40, 75-112; *Mts.*, 12, 34-35, 42-57; *Bmd.*, III, 63, 115, 120-41, 186-91; *Bhāg.*, IX, 6, 20-39; IX, 8, 17-19; IX, 13, 1-16; Pargiter, AIHT, pp. 90-94.

30. *Vy.*, 89, 1-23; *Vṣṇ.*, IV, 5, 1-34; *Bmd.*, III 64, 1-19; *Bhāg.*, IX, 13, 1, 11-27; *AIHT*, pp. 95-96.

31. *Vy.*, 86, 14-22; *Vṣṇ.*, IV, 1, 43-61; *Bmd.*, III 61, 12-17; *Bhāg.*, IX, 2, 33-36; pk, 481; *AIHT*, pp. 96-97.

32. *Vy.*, 86, 22-28; *Mts.*, 12, 21-24; *Vṣṇ.*, IV, 1, 62-64; *Bmd.*, III 61, 18-24; *Bhāg.*, IX, 3, 1-2; *27-36; Br.*, 7, 27-29; *Agn.*, 273, 12-16; *AIHT*, pp. 97-98.

value. The Purāṇic description of Purus of Madhyadeśa or Gaṅgā-Yamunā doab, the Yādavas in Yadu's line including the Haihayas of northern, western, central and southern India, the Āṇavas of north, Druhyus of north-west and Turvasus of south-east — all five branches which sprang up from Yayāti — and that of Kāśī and Kānyakubja dynasties, of Kurus in the main Paurava line, of Pañcālas, and of five kingdoms, notably, Magadha founded by Bṛhadratha (who was succeeded by another nine rulers during the period concerned) and Kauśāmbī founded by Kośāmba — two of the five descendants of Vasu-uparicara of Cedideśa in Kuru's line[33] — are historically and archaeologically well tested.

It is significant to note that the first phase of Paurava's settlements in the Sārasvata region and upper doab and Yādavas' settlements in Narmadā, Mālwā, Gujarat and Gaṅgā-Yamunā doab are archaeologically associated with Ochre Coloured Pottery (OCP) of late Haṛappan period (*c.* 2200-1700 BCE) and Chalcolithic Black and Red Ware (BRW) ascribed to *c.* 2000 BCE respectively. The Kurus of upper Sarasvatī and upper doab and the Pañcālas of Gangetic doab

33. For details see *Vy.*, 91, 1-103; 92, 1-75; 93, 26-27, 87-92; 94, 1-54, 95, 14-47; 96, 1-160; 99, 6-12, 25-28, 167-70, 194-249; D.R. Patil, *Cultural History from the Vāyu Purāṇa*, pp. 8-13; *Vṣṇ.*, IV.8, 1-21; IV.10, 1-32; IV.11, 1-30; IV.12, 2-45; IV.13, 1-20, 35-70, 108-61; IV.14, 1-45; IV.17, 1-5; IV.18, 1-30; IV.19, 1-85; IV.20, 1-53; *Mts.*, 43, 7-52; 44, 14-36, 45-85; 45, 1-34; 46, 1-29; 48, 6-9, 22-29; 49, 1-59; 50, 26-33; *Bmd.*, III.65, 45-46; III.66, 1-75; III.67, 1-79; III.68, 27, 90-92; III.69, 3-55; III.70, 14-48; III.71, 1-144; III.74, 7-12; *Bhāg.*, IX.14, 1ff; IX.15, 1-36; IX.17, 2-10; IX.20, 1-39; IX.21, 1-35; IX.22, 1-18; IX.23, 1-39; IX.24, 6-45; *Br.*, 10.13-68; 12.18-19; 13.154-207; 14.14-25; 15.30-45; 16.9-49; *Agn.*, 274.1-23; 275.1-51; 277.4-4; 278.27-41; Pargiter, *AIHT*, pp. 99-119 and ch. XXIV ("Ancient History from Tradition"), pp. 258-84; A.D. Pusalker, "Traditional History from the Earliest Time to the Accession of Parikshit", in *The Vedic Age*, ed. R.C. Majumdar, pp. 277 ff; G.P. Singh, *EIHTA*, pp. 50-98.

belonged to Painted Grey Ware (PGW) period (the first half of the first millennium BCE).[34]

The Purāṇic history of the early Aryans has its own importance. The Purāṇic data about their origin and expansion is really valuable. According to some Purāṇas, their original homeland was Pratiṣṭhāna from where they expanded all over the Gangetic doab.[35] The Purāṇic evidence goes to prove their indigenous origin in contradistinction to their foreign origin.

> The Purāṇas profess to give us the ancient history of Aryan India. In doing so they begin from the earliest Ṛgvedic period describing genealogies of kings who established kingdoms and principalities and thus parcelled out and ruled ancient India. Occasionally the feats and achievements of kings . . . are related, battles mentioned and described, noticeable incidents and happenings recorded and very valuable synchronisms noted down.[36]

William Jones opines that the traditions of pre-Kaliyuga periods are purely mythological and that of the Kaliyuga historical.[37] But the fact remains that the traditions of both pre- and post-Kaliyuga are historical. It may, however, not be denied that the Purāṇic history of the Kaliyuga is relatively

---

34. See Thapar, "Purāṇic Lineages and Archaeological Culture", in her *AISH*, pp. 242 ff and Genealogical Table facing p. 262.

35. For details see *Vy.*, 91.5-8 and 51; 92.1-7; *Vṣṇ.*, IV.1, 16-17; *Br.*, *chs.* 10-12; *AIHT*, pp. 296-302; *EIHTA*, pp. 50ff; H.D. Sankalia,"Prehistoric Literary Colonization in India: Archaeological and Evidence", in *AIHA*, pp. 308-10; J. Kennedy, "The Purāṇic Histories of the Early Aryas", *JRAS*, 1915.

36. S.N. Pradhan, *Chro. Anct. Ind.*, Preface, xi.

37. "On the Chronology of the Hindus", *As. Res.*, vol. 2 (Delhi, 1979), p. 111.

more reliable. The best form of traditional history is recorded in the Purāṇas. The Purāṇic descriptions of the Solar and Lunar dynasties of pre-Bhārata war period are filled with myths and historical narratives but that of the dynasties of the post-Bhārata war period or Kaliyuga are historical in character.

A.S. Altekar has rightly pointed out that the pre-Bhārata war dynasties mentioned in the Purāṇas are as historical as the dynasties of Kaliyuga like Maurya, Sātavāhana, etc. He further adds that the history of India of pre-Bhārata war period can be reconstructed with the help of epic and Purāṇic evidence.[38]

The traditional history of India from the earliest times to the accession of Parīkṣit II (36 years after the war) is well recorded in the Purāṇas.

The kingdoms and dynasties of the post-Bhārata war period extending from the accession of Parīkṣit or the beginning of Kaliyuga down to the sixth or fifth century BCE have also been covered in the Purāṇa records. Twenty-nine kings of Puru dynasty called the Pauravas of the Lunar family who ruled over Hastināpura, Indraprastha and Vatsa (Kauśāmbī),[39] 30 kings of Ikṣvāku dynasty of Kosala of the Solar family including the predecessors and successors of Prasenajit[40] and 22 kings of the Bṛhadratha dynasty of

38. "Can we Reconstruct Pre-Bhārata War History?", *JBHU*, IV, pp. 183-223; also his presidential address, section I: "Archaic and Early cultural History", IHC, 3rd session, Calcutta, 15-17 December 1939.

39. *Vy.*, 99.249-79; *Vṣṇ.*, IV.21, 1-18; *Mts.*, 50.57-89; *Bhāg.*, IX.22, 33-44; Pargiter *PDKA*, pp. 4-5, 24, note 16.

40. *Vy.*, 99.280-93; *Vṣṇ.*, IV.23, 1-13; *Mts.*, 271.4-18; *Bmd.*, III.74, 104-7; *PDKA*, pp. 10-11, 66-67.

Magadha (with their regnal years)[41] have all been incorporated in the dynastic lists of kings. The genealogical lists containing the names of kings of the said dynasties have also been furnished. The information supplied by the Purāṇas about the shifting of capital from Hastināpura to Kauśāmbī during the reign of Nicakṣu (one of the successors of Parīkṣit), the rule of famous king Udayana over Kauśāmbī, the pedigree and progeny of the Buddha of the Śākya clan and the kingdoms of Pañcāla, Śūrasena, Videha, Aṅga and Kāśī have historical validity. That ten dynasties of the Kaliyuga ruled contemporaneously in northern, central and eastern India have also historical credibility.

The five kings of Pradyota dynasty who ruled the kingdom of Avantī are mentioned in the Purāṇas with their regnal years and total duration of their rule. They are said to have ruled for 138 years.[42] But, in fact, they ruled for 102 years (*c.* 513-411 BCE).

The Purāṇic accounts of the major dynasties of early historical period are of exceptional value. Ten kings of Bimbisārian and Śiśunāga dynasties including Bimbisāra (*c.* 558-491 BCE) and Ajātaśatru (*c.* 491-459 BCE), both contemporaries of the Buddha (*c.* 563-483 BCE), Udāyin, Śiśunāga and others are said to have ruled for 360 or 362

41. *Vy.*, 99.294-308; *Vṣṇ.*, IV.23, 1-13; *Mts.*, 271.18-30; *Bhāg.*, IX.22, 46-49; *Bmd*; III.74, 107-21; *Hv*; I.32, 63-78; *PDKA*, pp. 13-22; *PK*, p. 356; see also *AIHT*, pp. 285-87; *EIHTA*, pp. 141-54; Pusalker, "Traditional History from the Accession of Parikshit to the End of the Bārhadratha Dynasty", in *The Vedic Age*, pp. 323-33.

42. *Vy.*, 99.308-14 *Vṣṇ.*, IV.24, 1-8; *Mts.*, 272.1-5; *Bhāg.*, XII.I, 2-4; *Bmd.*, III.74, 121-25; *PDKA*, pp. 18-21, 68-69; H.H Wilson (tr.), *Viṣṇu Purāṇa*, p. 372; *PK*, p. 333.

years.[43] They actually ruled for 200 years (*c*. 543-343 BCE). The nine Nandas are said to have ruled for 28, 40 or 100 years.[44] In reality, only two of them, the first (Mahāpadmānanda, the founder of the dynasty) and the last (Dhanānanda, identical with Agrammes or Xandrammas of classical (Greek and Roman) writers, and contemporary of Alexander) were the reigning kings who altogether ruled for 22 years (*c*. 343-321 BCE). We are also informed that a period of 1050 years had elapsed between the birth of Parīkṣit and the coronation of Mahāpadmānanda.[45] It is also clearly stated in some of the Purāṇas that it was Cāṇakya (Kauṭilya) who uprooted the Nandas and installed Candragupta Maurya on the throne of Magadha (in 321 BCE)[46] which is a historical fact. Ten kings of the Maurya dynasty including Candragupta, Bindusāra, Aśoka and his seven successors are said to have ruled for 137 years (*c*. 321-184 BCE)[47] which is perfectly accurate. In one of the Purāṇas,* it is also mentioned that Candragupta Maurya was married to the daughter of Sulūva[48] (Seleucus, a general of Alexander called "Paurasādhipati," one who subdued king Poros) following the peace treaty concluded between the two in 303 or 302 BCE. It is also recorded in the Purāṇas that

43. *Vy*., 99.314-21; *Vṣṇ*., IV.24, 9-19; Wilson, op. cit., pp. 372-75; *Mts*., 272.5-13; *Bhāg*., XII.1, 5-7; *Bmd*., III.74, 127-33; *PDKA*, pp. 21-26, 67-69; see also Max Müller, *HASL*, pp. 265-66; *PK*, p. 496.

44. *Vy*., 99.321; *Vṣṇ*., IV.24, 20-24; Wilson, op. cit., p. 374; *Mts*., 272.14-21; *Bhāg*., XII.1, 8-11; *Bmd*., III.74, 139-44; *PDKA*, pp. 23-24, 69; *HASL*, p. 266; see also *PK*, pp. 257 and 407.

45. *Vy*., 99.415; *Vṣṇ*., IV.24, 104; Wilson, op. cit., p. 389; *Mts*., 273.36.

46. *Vy*., 99.329-31; *Vṣṇ*., IV.24, 25-28; *Mts*., 272.21-22.

47. *Vy*., 99.331-36; *Vṣṇ*., IV.24, 29-32; Wilson, op. cit., pp. 374-76; *Mts*., 272.22-26; *Bhāg*., XII.1, 12-15; *Bmd*., III.74, 145-49; *PDKA*, pp. 28-30; *EITHA*, pp. 177-80; *PK*, p. 434, *HASL*, p. 266.

48. *Bhv*. (ed. with Hindi tr. R. Sharma Ācārya), I, pp. 334-35, v. 43, also v. 44 (for Mauryan rulers from Candragupta to Aśoka).

Bṛhadratha, the last Maurya king, was treacherously murdered by his own commander-in-chief, Puṣyamitra Śuṅga, who established himself on the throne of his master and founded a new dynasty named after him, Śuṅga dynasty.[49] Ten rulers of this dynasty from Puṣyamitra to Devabhūti are said to have ruled for 112 years (*c.* 184-72 BCE)[50] which is absolutely correct. Four kings of the Kaṇva dynasty from Vasudeva to Suśarman ruled exactly for 45 years (*c.* 72-27 BCE).[51] These six dynasties ruled successively Magadha and other kingdoms on the whole from the sixth to the first century BCE. The Purāṇas also contain some information about the rise and fall of these dynasties. Thirty rulers of the Sātavāhana dynasty from its founder Śimuka to Pulumāvī IV are said to have ruled for 456 or 460 years.[52] The Purāṇas also supply the information that a period of 836 years intervened between Mahāpadmānanda and the last

---

49. *Vy.*, 99.336-37; *Mts.*, 272.26-27; *Vṣṇ.*, IV.24, 34.

50. *Vy.*, 99.336-42; *Vṣṇ.*, IV.24, 33-37; Wilson, op. cit., pp. 376-77; *Mts.*, 272.26-33; *Bhāg.*, XII.I, 16-18; *Bmd.*, III.74, 150-55; *PDKA*, pp. 30-32, 70.

51. *Vy.*, 99.343-47; *Vṣṇ.*, IV.24, 38-42; Wilson, op. cit., p. 377; *Mts.*, 272.32-37; *Bhāg.*, XII.1, 19-21; *Bmd.*, III.74, 155-60; *PDKA*, pp. 33-38, 71.

52. *Vy.*, 99.348-58; *Vṣṇ.*, IV.24, 43-50; Wilson, op. cit., pp. 378-80; *Mts.*, 273.1-17; *Bhāg.*, XII.1, 22-28; *Bmd.*, III.74, 160-70; *PDKA*, pp. 38-43, 71; see also V.A. Smith, *EHI*, pp. 216-17, 220; R.G. Bhandarkar, *Early History of the Dekkan down to the Mahomedan Conquest*, pp. 15-23; *A Peep into the Early History of India*, pp. 36-37; S.P. Sen (ed.), *Historians and Historiography in Modern India*, pp. 32-34; *AIHT*, pp. 286-87.

    For details of pre- and post-Maurya dynasties up to Sātavāhana, as recorded in the Purāṇas, see G.P. Singh, *EIHTA*, pp. 161-86; "A New Approach to the Study of Historical Data in the Epic and Purāṇic Literature Regarding Ancient India", *Proceedings of the UGC Sponsored National Seminar on History and Literature* (Sardar Patel University, Vallabh Vidyānagar, Gujarat, 9-11 February 1991), p. 4.

Sātavāhana king Pulumāvī.[53] According to this chronological data, the Sātavāhanas' rule began 376 years after the Nanda and lasted for 460 years. According to our chronological calculation and computation, they reigned (in Maharashtra and Andhra Pradesh) for not more than 252 years (*c.* 27 BCE – CE 225). There are some epigraphic and numismatic evidences[54] to partly confirm the historicity of Purāṇic genealogy of this dynasty. The genealogical list of the dynasty contains the names of many actual rulers like Śrī Śātakarṇi I, Śātakarṇi II, Gautamīputra Śātakarṇi, Pulumāvī and Yajña Śrī Śātakarṇi. The political achievements of some kings of some of the aforesaid dynasties have also been highlighted in the Purāṇas. Some information supplied in this regard are very useful for our historical purpose.

It is worthy of note that the above-mentioned seven dynasties that ruled over different kingdoms are historically authenticated. Their genealogies are chronologically arranged. Most of the kings mentioned in the genealogical lists are real. Only few of them are fictitious. The length of reign of each individual king as well as the total duration of the rule of each dynasty are given. Some figures are, of course, inflated and arbitrary, but some are accurate. There are some variations in the Purāṇas with regard to the number of kings and their names, order of succession, regnal years and total

53. *Vy.*, 99.416-17; *Mts.*, 273.37.

54. Bühler's Report, *Arch. Surv. of West India*, vol. IV, pp. 98, 110; vol. V, pp. 60-71; Lüders, "A List of Brahmi Inscriptions from the Earliest Times to About CE 400", pub. as an Appendix to *Ep. Ind.*, X, 1910, p. 160, nos. 1113, 1114, 1144; *JIH*, LVI, I, 1978, pp. 48-49, 52-53; D.C. Sircar (ed.), *SI*, vol. I, pp. 176-80, 197-201; *Ep. Ind.*, VIII, 5, pp. 36-49, 60-61 (1,5,7), 73-74; E.J. Rapson, *Catalogue of Coins in the British Museum, the Andhra Dynasty, etc.*, 1908, p. xxx; K.P. Jayaswal, *JBORS*, XVI, 3 & 4, pp. 265-66; also *JNSI*, III, I, June 1941, pp. 43-45.

duration of their rule. The chronological sequence of kings in case of some dynasties is also broken to some extent because of anachronism. However, the total duration of the rule of some dynasties given in some Purāṇas are absolutely correct which can be utilised for the purpose of chronological computation and interpretations to determine the period of the end of one dynasty and the beginning of the other. The total duration of reigns of the Mauryas, Śuṅgas and Kaṇvas given in the Purāṇas have been accepted by almost all the historians of ancient India. The Purāṇic data are no doubt extremely important for genealogical and chronological reconstruction of ancient Indian history of the periods concerned.

The historical value of the Purāṇic data from dynastic, genealogical and chronological points of view has been acknowledged by some noted authorities on the Purāṇa and some other scholars.[55]

55. D.R. Mankad, "Studies in Purāṇic History, Genealogies and Chronology in Modern Times", *Purāṇa*, IV, I, 1962, pp. 3-22; *Purāṇic Chronology* (Vallabh Vidyānagar, 1951); A. Banerji Shastri, "On Ancient Indian Historical Tradition", *JBORS*, XIII, pp. 62-79; V.R.R. Dikshitar, "The Purāṇa: A Study", *IHQ*, VIII, pp. 747-67; R. Morton Smith, *DDEI*, pp. 38 ff; "The Early Chronology of India", *JAOS*, vol. 77, no. 2, April-June 1957 and no. 4, December 1957; Pargiter, *PDKA*, pp. 4 ff; "Ancient Indian Genealogies and Chronology", *JRAS*, 1910, pp. 26-56; "Earliest Indian Traditional History", *JRAS*, 1914, pp. 267 f; Max Müller, *HASL*, pp. 265-68; K. Venkatachalam, *The Plot in Indian Chronology*, pp. 23 ff, 38 ff, 80-100; *Chronology of Ancient Hindu History*, I, pp. 34 ff; Thapar. "Origin Myths and the Early Indian Historical Tradition", in her *AISH*, pp. 294-325; "Genealogy as a Source of Social History", in *AISH*, pp. 326-60; see also William Jones, "On the Chronology of the Hindus", *As. Res.*, vol. II (I[st] pub. 1799, rept. Delhi, 1979), pp. 107-13 (all about Purāṇic dynasties); Lord Teignmouth (ed.), *The Works of Sir William Jones* (in 13 vols.), vol. IV (London, 1807), pp. 36-46; F. Wilford, "Chronology of the Hindus", *As. Res.*, vol. V (Delhi, 1979), pp. 241-92; "An Essay on the Sacred Isles in →

The later Sātavāhanas and some contemporary minor dynasties of the kings of both indigenous and foreign origins that ruled over different parts of India some time between the third century BCE and the sixth century CE which include the dynasties of the post-Sātavāhana period also are vividly portrayed in the Purāṇas. The genealogies and chronology of some dynasties are also given therein which are partly correct.

The later Sātavāhanas or the successors of the Sātavāhanas of the Deccan have been referred to in the Purāṇas as Āndhravr̥tyas. They belonged to the lineage of the servants or feudatories of the Āndhras. There were seven kings in this line. The Śrīparvatīya-Āndhras (of Telaṅgānā) have been assigned a reign-period of 52 years. One of the five minor dynasties that came into being after the dismemberment of the Sātavāhana empire was that of the Abhīras of western India (Maharashtra). The ten Abhīra kings are said to have ruled for 67 years. The kings of the Āndhra dynasty (who established themselves in the Deccan and western India some time after CE 236) are said to have ruled for over a period of 300 years. The eight Yavana kings (Greek princes of Bactria lying between the Hindukuśa and the Oxus who ruled from the third century BCE to the middle of the first century BCE) are said to have ruled for 80 to 87 years. The 10, 16 or 18 Śaka kings (Indo-Scythians, second century BCE – second century CE) are said to have ruled (over Afghanistan, northern, central

→ the West with other Essays . . ." Essay III, *As. Res.*, vol. IX (Delhi, 1979), pp. 116-210 (for kings and their chronology); J. Bentley, "On the Principal Eras and Dates of Ancient Hindus", *As. Res.*, vol. V, pp. 315-43 (about different dynasties of the post-war period as given in the Purāṇas); "On the Hindu System of Astronomy and their connection with History in Ancient and Modern Times," *As. Res.*, vol. VIII (1st pub. 1809, rept. Delhi, 1979), pp. 225 ff.

and western parts of India and in the upper Deccan) for 183 or 380 years. The 14 Tuṣāras (the tribes settled on the banks of the river Cakṣu or Oxus in the north-western region) are said to have ruled for 500 years. The seven Gardabhinas or Gardabhillas (who established themselves in Avantī region with their seat of power at Ujjayinī anterior to the Śakas) ruled for 72 years. The 13 Murūṇḍas (a branch or kinsmen of the Śakas) along with other kings of the śūdra class are said to have ruled for 200 to 450 years. The 18 or 19 Hūṇas (or Maunas) ruled for 300 years. The eleven kings of the contemporary *mleccha* dynasty are also said to have reigned for 300 years.[56] The kings of the said dynasties altogether are said to have ruled for 1090 to 1099 years.[57]

The historicity of the above-mentioned dynasties is well proven. Here it may further be added that the Murūṇḍas established their rule in some parts of central India some time after CE 230. They continued to rule till the time of Samudragupta (CE 335-75) which can be substantiated by the epigraphic evidence and other relevant sources. The Allahabad Pillar inscription confirms that the "Śaka-Murūṇḍas" were one of those foreign powers who acknowledged Samudragupta as their overlord.[58] They were probably ruling as the Śaka lords or chieftains in the regions of Surāṣṭra and Ujjain at his time. The Gardabhinas were actually Gardabha princes who once ruled over Mālwā region

56. *Vy.*, 99.359-64; *Vṣṇ.*, IV.24, 51-54 and 58; Wilson, op. cit., pp. 380-82; *Mts.*, 273.18-24; *Mts.*, *SBA*, I, pp. 339-41; *Bhāg.*, XII.I, 27-32; *Bmd.*, III.74, 170-77; *PDKA*, pp. 42-48, 540-51; also R.K. Arora, *Historical and Cultural Data from the Bhaviṣya Purāṇa*, pp. 37 f; Patil, op. cit., p. 262.

57. *Vṣṇ.*, IV.24, 53; *Bhāg.*, XII.I, 30-32.

58. Fleet, *CII*, vol. III, no. 1, pp. 1-17; J. Allan, *Catalogue of the Coins of the Gupta Dynasty*, Introduction, pp. xxix-xxx.

of central India and some parts of western India.[59] This dynasty ruled over western Mālwā with its capital at Ujjain before the Śaka kings established their supremacy there.

The details of Vikramāditya (son of Mahendrāditya) of Ujjain and his dynasty have been provided in the Pratisarga Parvan of the *Bhaviṣya Purāṇa*.[60]

Vikramāditya regained his ancestral kingdom of Ujjain by expelling the Śakas from there after nine years of their rule (which began in 66 BCE). In order to commemorate his victory over them, he introduced a new era called Vikrama Saṁvat (or Mālwā Saṁvat) in 57 BCE. He reigned for 60 years and his four successors, including Śālivāhana, altogether for 75 years[61] which comes to total 135 years.

According to the same Purāṇa (*Bhaviṣya*), Vikramāditya was succeeded by his son Devabhakta who ruled for 10 years only. He was either overthrown or killed by the Śakas.[62] His son, Śālivāhana, of the same dynasty conquered the Śakas and celebrated his victory by commencing a new era called Śālivāhana Śaka Era in CE 78.[63] He is believed to have established his rule over his kingdom with its capital at Ujjain in about CE 32. He was succeded by 10 rulers. The Śālivāhana dynasty and some other dynasties that ruled over Ujjain are briefly described in the same Purāṇa. The reign-period of individual rulers, the total duration of the rule of each

59. For details see *As. Res.*, VI, p. 35; IX, p. 147; *JASB*, December 1835, p. 688; *JRAS*, III, p. 385.

60. *Bhv.*, I, pp. 337-40, vv. 8-26; II, pp. 161-64, vv. 13-21.

61. Ibid., I, pp. 416-19, vv. 17-19, 33, 419-20, vv. 1-4, 425, vv.1-2; II, pp. 163-64, vv. 22-23, 164-67, vv. 24-42.

62. Ibid., II, pp. 163-64, v. 22.

63. Ibid., pp. 163-64, v. 23; I, pp. 416-19, vv. 17-19, 33.

dynasty and achievements of some of the rulers of some dynasties are also given therein.[64]

Some unanointed kings of Kilakila have also been depicted in the Purāṇas. They are stated to have belonged to either Yavana race or śūdra class.[65] They actually succeeded the Ābhīras of Maharashtra after overthrowing them. The Kilakila princes were succeeded by the rulers of the dynasty founded by Vindhyaśakti. After the extinction of this dynasty three Vāhlika kings ruled for 30 years.[66] Sakyma, the famous king of Māhiṣmatī, seven kings who ruled over Mekala (situated on the bank of the Narmadā River), nine kings who governed Kosala, etc. also find mention in the Purāṇas.[67] They were all contemporary provincial rulers.

The Purāṇas also provide description of the rulers (called Mitras) who governed Mekala and Māhiṣmatī regions for about 30 years. Puṣyamitra was one of the famous rulers. The "Puṣyamitras" are said to have ruled for 13 years.[68] The Bhītarī Pillar Inscription bears witness to the fact that towards the closing years of Kumāragupta's reign (CE 414-55) the Puṣyamitras' invasion led to the eclipse of the Gupta power. It was Skandagupta (CE 455-467) who crushed them and restored the fallen fortunes of his family.[69]

---

64. *Bhv.*, II, pp. 164-67, vv. 24-42; I, 2 pp. 419-20, vv. 1-4, 425, vv. 1-2.

65. *Vy.*, 99.363-64; *Vṣṇ.*, IV.24, 55; *Mts.*, 273.23-24; *Bhāg.*, XII.I, 32-33; also *PK*, p. 338.

66. *Vy.* 99.372-73; *Vṣṇ.*, IV.24, 57.

67. Ibid., 99, 374.

68. Ibid., *Vṣṇ.*, IV.24, 58; Wilson, op. cit., p. 384; *Bmd.*, III.74, 187-88; *Bhāg.*, XII.I, 34; *PDKA*, p. 51, note 14; see also K.P. Jayaswal, *Hindu Polity*, pp. 156-57.

69. Fleet, *CII*, vol. III, pp. 53-55; H.R. Divekar, "Puṣyamitras in the Gupta Period", *ABORI*, 1919-20, pp. 99-103.

We come across some inaccuracies and discrepancies in the Purāṇas with regard to the number of kings of the dynasties concerned and total duration of their rule. The trustworthiness of some reign periods is doubtful. Sometimes one dynasty is merged or interwoven into another; sometimes dynasties are lengthened owing to various corrupt readings, sometimes their accounts appear to be conflicting and confusing because of fabrications, interpolations and distortions. History and myths have been jumbled up to an extent that sometimes it becomes difficult to extricate one from the other. However, they cannot be put aside as wholly unworthy of credence.

The Purāṇas do contain some useful information about the rule of the Nāga dynasties at Vidiśā (the capital of eastern Mālwā), Y (modern Padam Pawaya near Narwar in the Gwalior State, Madhya Pradesh), Kāntipurī (modern Koṭwār, about 25 miles north of Gwalior) and Mathurā (Uttar Pradesh) between the second century BCE and the fourth century CE.

The Nāga dynasty of Vidiśā has been divided into two parts in the Purāṇas. To the first part belonged those kings who flourished before the end of the Śuṅgas and to the second belonged those who ruled in the post-Śuṅga period. The Purāṇas mention the names of Śeṣanāga, Bhogin, Rāmacandra, Sadācandra, Dharmavarman, Vaṅgara (who ruled during the Śuṅga and Kaṇva periods), Bhūtīnandī, Madhunandī, Śiśunandī, Yaśonandī and his descendants, Dauhitra, and Śiśuka, Śivanandī, etc. (who ruled in the post-Kāṇva period).[70] The historicity of most of the Nāga kings mentioned above has been proved, and they have been chronologically arranged by K.P. Jayaswal.[71]

70. *Vy.*, 99.366-70; *Vṣṇ.*, IV.24, 56; Wilson, op. cit., pp. 382-83.

71. *History of India* (CE *150-350*), pp. 3-15.

The Purāṇas refer to nine Nāga kings of Padmāvatī without mentioning their names. Kāntipurī is said to have been one of the chief seats of their power.[72] The said nine kings known from coins and inscriptions were Bhavanāga, Gaṇapatināga, Nāgasena, Bhīmanāga, Skandanāga, Bṛhaspatināga, Devanāga, Vibhanāga and Vyāghranāga.[73] The archaeological excavation at Koṭwār has proved that Kāntipurī mentioned in the Purāṇas was once the seat of power of the Nāga kings.

The Purāṇas also refer to the seven Nāga kings who ruled at Mathurā[74] after the fall of the Kuṣāṇas. These seven kings from Mathurā continued to rule over Doab for 383 years which can also be confirmed on the testimony of the Purāṇas.[75] The coins discovered from Mathurā bear the names of the said seven kings as Puruṣadatta, Uttamadatta, Rāmadatta, Kāmadatta, Śeṣadatta, Bhavadatta and Balabhūti.[76]

Pargiter on the authority of the Purāṇas has stated that the Nāga families ruled from more than one place, viz. Vidiśā, Padmāvatī and Mathurā.[77] K.P. Jayaswal while throwing light on the Hindu republics in the Nāga period (CE 150-284) has

---

72. *Vy.*, 99.382-83; *Vṣṇ.*, IV.24, 63; Wilson, op. cit., p. 385; *Bmd.*, III.74, 194, 197; *PK*, p. 267.

73. E.J. Rapson, *Ind. Co.*, p. 28 and plate V; V.A. Smith, *CCIM*, I, pp. 176-77 (Some Nāga coins of Padmāvatī belong to the second century CE); *JRAS*, 1897, p. 643 (coins of the fourth century CE); Cunningham, *CMI*, pp. 20-21; *JASB*, 1865, p. 115; Fleet, *CII*, vol. III, no. I, lines 20-21.

74. *Vy.*, 99.382-83; Wilson, op. cit., p. 385; *PK*, p. 393.

75. Ibid., 99, 453; *Bmd.*, III.74, 194-95, 267; *PK*, p. 267.

76. V.A. Smith, *CCIM*, I, pp. 176-77.

77. *PDKA*, p. 49.

opined that the Nāgas of Mālwā and Padmāvatī were by and large republican communities.[78]

The archaeological evidence, including coins and inscriptions, about the Nāga kings and seats of their rule mentioned in the Purāṇas proves the historicity of the Purāṇic accounts of the Nāga dynasties. The Purāṇic style of presentation of subject matter is completely different from what we find in other sources. There are, of course, some vacuums in the Purāṇic accounts of the subject. However, from the twilight of the Purāṇic history it appears that Nāgas (mostly serpent-worshippers) had spread far and wide in central and northern India. Some Nāga rulers became powerful during the times of the later Kuṣāṇas in the second century CE and some of them re-established themselves after the expulsion of the Kuṣāṇas from some parts of northern India in the early third century CE. Some Nāga chiefs ruling in the Yamunā Valley and central India were exterminated by the Gupta ruler (Samudragupta) about the middle of the fourth century CE.

The information contained in the Purāṇas about the Vākāṭakas is very meagre but authentic.

The founder of the Vākāṭaka dynasty, Vindhyaśakti (who flourished about the middle of the third century CE), figures in the Purāṇas. He is said to have ruled for 96 years. His son and successor, Pravīra, is said to have ruled for 60 years. Kāñcanapurī was the capital of his kingdom. Being an ambitious ruler he carried his arms to the Narmadā and succeeded in annexing the kingdom of Purika, which was being ruled by a king named Śiśuka. He is said to have performed *Vājapeya* sacrifices after assuming the title "Samrāṭ." He had sons but all of them did not become

78. *History of India (c. CE 150-350)*, pp. 53-54; *Hindu Polity*, pp. 154-55.

rulers.[79] Other details are conspicuous by their absence in the Purāṇas.

There are some inscriptional and other reliable evidences to partly prove the historical authenticity of the information supplied by the Purāṇas about the Vākāṭakas, particularly about their genealogy and chronology. Vindhyaśakti and Pravīra have been identified on the basis of inscriptions with Vindhyaśakti I and Pravarasena I respectively. The former is said to have ruled from CE 250 to 270. It is said that he had his base in central India from where he occupied parts of Vidarbha or Berār in western India and the Deccan (Andhra Pradesh). The latter is said to have ruled from CE 270 to 330 (which is in full accord with the Purāṇic length of his reign, i.e. 60 years). It has also been established that out of his four sons only the second one, Sarvasena, had set up a separate dynasty with his capital at Vatsagulma in the Akolā district of Vidarbha and ruled from CE 330 to 335. This also confirms the authenticity of the Purāṇic testimony that he had four sons and all of them did not rule. The other rulers of the dynasty further continued to rule till CE 500. After the defeat of the Vākāṭakas at the hands of the Kalacuris (descendants of Kārttavīrya Arjuna of the Haihaya race mentioned in the epics and Purāṇas) of Māhiṣmatī in the second quarter of the sixth century CE, the dynasty ultimately came to an end or ceased to exist.[80]

---

79. *Vy.*, 99.365, 370-72; *Vṣṇ.*, IV.24, 56; Wilson op. cit., pp. 382-83; *Bmd.*, III.74, 184-86; *PDKA*, p. 44; also *PK*, pp. 337-38.

80. For details see V.V. Mirashi, "Some Purāṇic Passages Corroborated by Inscriptional and Numismatic Evidence", *Purāṇa*, I, pp. 31-38; "The Vākāṭaka Chronology," *IHQ*, XXIV, pp. 148-55; Govinda Pai, "Genealogy and Chronology of the Vākāṭakas", *JIH*, XIV, 1935, pp. 1-26, also 165-204; R.C. Majumdar, "Note on the Genealogy and Chronology of the Vākāṭakas", *JRASB* (L), XII, p. 150; S.K. Aiyangar, "The Vākāṭakas →

The information available in some Purāṇas about the earliest phase of the Gupta rule (CE 275-300) is very valuable.

It is fairly stated in the Purāṇas that the "Guptas set up their rule over Anugaṅgā (the middle Gangetic basin), Prayāga (Allahabad), Sāketa (adjoining Ayodhyā) and Magadha (south Bihar).[81] It is a historically proven fact that the kingdom of the Guptas originally comprised only some parts of Uttar Pradesh and Bihar at the end of the third century CE. The earliest centre of their power was in Uttar Pradesh which can be confirmed by the discovery of early Gupta coins and inscriptions mainly from this part of India. They gradually expanded from Prayāga over the neighbouring regions and the whole of Magadha in south Bihar. The founder of the Gupta dynasty was Śrīgupta who ruled as a minor chief over a small territory in Magadha from CE 275 to 300. The Purāṇic passage shows the extent of the Gupta dominions of pre-Candragupta's period and not of Candragupta's time (CE 319-35) as held by Pargiter.[82] The *Bhaviṣya Purāṇa* informs us that the seven kings of the Gupta dynasty ruled for 245 years.[83] But we find that in the imperial Gupta line there were 12 or 13 kings (from Śrīgupta to Bhānugupta) who ruled for 235 years (CE 275-510).

A.K. Warder opines that Purāṇas provide a comprehensive view of ancient Indian history, a universal

→ and their place in the History of India", *ABORI*, V, pp. 31-54; V.A. Smith, "The Vākāṭaka Dynasty of Berar in the 4th and 5th Centuries," *JRAS*, 1914, pp. 317-18; K.P. Jayaswal's views cf. *JBORS*, March-June 1933, p. 67.

81. *Vy.*, 99.383; *Vṣṇ.*, IV.24, 63; Wilson, op. cit., p. 385; see also D.R. Patil, "Gupta Inscriptions and Purāṇic Tradition", *BDCRS*, II, pp. 2-58; V.A. Smith's views cf. *Ind. Ant.*, 1902, p. 258, note.

82. *PDKA*, Introduction, p. xii, and p. 20.

83. See also Krishnamachariar, *HCSL*, Introduction, pp. xlviii-xlix.

history from the origin of the state through the earliest recorded kings, and the ancient dynasties down to the early fourth century CE. They mention Guptas and the history of early Vākāṭakas.[84] H.H. Wilson has also stated that the dynastic lists of kings of the post-war period (Kaliyuga) have been preserved in the Purāṇic historical records with greater precision which offer political and chronological particulars. Their general accuracy has been incontrovertibly established. Some Āndhra and Gupta rulers mentioned in the Purāṇas find confirmation in the inscriptions on columns of stones or rocks and on coins deciphered by archaeologists and others.[85]

The Purāṇic history of the post-Harṣa period (CE 650-1200) is very reliable. It is only the *Bhaviṣya Purāṇa* (Pratisarga Parvan) which provides data about the Pratihāras (Parihāras), the Paramāras, the Cāhamānas (Cauhānas) and the Cāḷukyas or Solaṅkīs (Śuklas), the four Rājpūt families of the Agnivaṁśa or Agnikula, and the Rājpūt rulers of other dynasties. They (except Cāḷukyas) actually dominated the politics of northern India after the death of Harṣa in CE 647. They established their rule in this part of India and founded several petty independent kingdoms which lasted for nearly five centuries and then one by one succumbed to the Muslim invaders.

The Pratihāras have been described in the said Purāṇa as the Parihāras. It is a well-known fact that prior to the conquest of Kannauj (Kānyakubja), they established their rule in Avantī with its capital at Ujjain. A notable ruler of this dynasty named Vatsarāja (identified by all historians with the father of Nāgabhaṭa II, CE 805-33) figures in the

---

84. A.K. Warder, op. cit., p. 157.

85. Op. cit., preface, pp. lxviii-lxx.

Purāṇas as a king of Avantī.[86] He ascended the throne in about CE 778. His empire initially comprised Mālwā and eastern and central Rājpūtānā. Gradually he established his supremacy over a large part of northern India. Bhoja I (CE 836-85) and Bhoja II (CE 910-12) were also the Pratihāra rulers of Kannauj. We find the description of the Bhojas in the Purāṇa,[87] but neither their periods nor the details of their achievements are given therein. However, the Pratihāras continued to exercise their sway over Kannauj and Madhyadeśa. The last king of this dynasty, Rājyapāla (CE 991-1018), also figures in the Purāṇa.[88] His capital Kannauj was invaded by Mahmud of Ghazni in CE 1018, but he could not defend it and fled away out of fear.

The Candellas, who established their sway over the kingdom of Bundelkhand (situated between the Yamunā and Narmadā) in the tenth century CE, were the feudatories of the great Pratihāra emperors of Kannauj. The Purāṇic tradition confirms it that Kāliñjar (which was earlier one of the strongholds of the Pratihāras and later occupied by the Candellas) was founded by the king named Parihāra, who ruled for 10 years.[89] The names of all his successors who ruled over Kāliñjar are given in the Purāṇa.[90] One of them called Karvarman can be identified with Kīrttivarman who ruled some time between CE 1100 and 1129.

The Paramāras of Mālwā, according to the Purāṇa, were the descendants of King Parmāra of Avantī. He is said to

86. *Bhv.*, II, p. 165, v. 32.

87. Ibid., I, pp. 419-20, 425; II, p. 165.

88. Ibid., II, pp. 165-66, v. 35.

89. Ibid., I, p. 366, vv. 1-2; II, pp. 184-85, vv. 1-4.

90. Ibid., II, pp. 184-90, vv. 5-37.

have ruled over Avantīpura (Ujjain, which had an extent of 4 *yojana*) for six years.[91] Muñja or Muñjavarman (CE 974-98), who was the seventh king of this dynasty, also finds mention in the Purāṇa. He is said to have defeated the Śavaras and Bhillas. The details about Sindhurāja are also given therein.[92] The most famous king of this dynasty was Bhoja (son of Sindhurāja) who ruled over Mālwā with its capital at Dhāra (60 km from Indore). He was popularly known as Rājā Bhoja. He ruled for about 42 years from CE 1018 to 1060. The Purāṇa explicitly mentions his name as a king of this dynasty.[93] The later Paramāra kings of Mālwā are also mentioned in the Purāṇa.[94] But the historicity of only two of them, Naravarman and Udayāditya, has been established. The copper plate of the former (nephew of Bhojarāja) preserved in Archaeological Museum of Indore proves that the latter (CE 1059-94) was a brother of Bhoja. According to the Purāṇa, Udaya (Udayāditya) was the founder of Udayapur[95] which can be confirmed by "Udepur" inscription,[96] which describes him as the successor of Bhoja.

The Purāṇic accounts of the Tomaras of Delhi and Cauhānas of Ajmer and Delhi are of paramount historical importance.

It is clearly mentioned in the Purāṇa that the Tomara dynasty founded by Anaṅgapāla I ruled at Indraprastha

91. *Bhv.*, I, pp. 335, vv. 49, 337, v.8; II, pp. 161-62, vv. 13-15.

92. Ibid., II, pp. 175-77, vv. 25-30.

93. *PK*, p. 385; see also Wilford, *As. Res.*, IX, pp. 176-77.

94. *Bhv.*, II, pp. 176-77, vv. 31-35.

95. Ibid., p. 176, v. 34.

96. *Ep. Ind.*, I, pp. 232-38.

(Delhi).[97] It is further said that Tomara also ruled for seven years. One of his descendants was Ajaya (or Ajayapāla).[98]

Ajayapāla (Ajayarāja) was one of the Cauhāna rulers of Ajmer. He is credited with having founded that city. One of the famous rulers of this dynasty was Viśāladeva (or Vigraharарāja IV, CE 1152-64) who captured Delhi about CE 1158 from the Tomaras. In the Purāṇic genealogy of the Cauhāna rulers, his name figures as Viśāla. One of the Tomara kings was Jayasiṁha who is said to have ruled for about 50 years. The two other noted rulers, Ānandadeva and Someśvara have also been mentioned in the Purāṇa.[99] The most famous and illustrious king of the Cauhāna family, Pṛthvīrāja (CE 1179-92), inherited the kingdom of Delhi from his maternal grandfather Anaṅgapāla II, the last king of the Tomara dynasty. It is clearly stated in the Purāṇa that after the death of Anaṅgapāla he became the full-fledged ruler of Delhi. He made it a fortified city. It became an extensive and magnificent city during this time.[100]

The further historical narratives of the subject in the Purāṇa show that Pṛthvīrāja's overlordship of northern India was disputed by Jayacanda of Kannauj, the most famous king of Gāhaḍavāla dynasty or Rāṭhor family, who ruled from CE 1170 to 1194. It is said that the former turned the latter into an enemy by forcibly carrying off his beautiful daughter, Saṁyogitā, from her *svayaṁvara*. The rivalry between the two ultimately resulted in the battle which was fought at Sūkar.

97. *Bhv.*, I, pp. 424, v. 5, 429-32, vv. 1-14.

98. Ibid; II, pp. 168-69, vv. 1-6.

99. Ibid., pp. 170-71, vv. 15-22 (the pedigree and progeny of King Viśāladeva are given); also I, p. 430, v. 4.

100. *Bhv.*, II, p. 171, vv. 22-25; I, pp. 430-34, vv. 1-15, 22-28.

In this battle the soldiers of both sides were killed. The hostility between the two potentates proved to be disastrous for the Agnivaṁśa[101] and blessing for Muhammad Ghori. The Purāṇa even records the "death of Pṛthvīrāja at the hands of Sahoddin (Shihabuddin Muhammad Ghori)"[102] which is indicative of the fact that the latter after having defeated the former in the second battle of Tarāīn (about 14 miles from Thāneśvar) fought in CE 1192 put him to death. And thereafter he occupied Delhi and Ajmer. It is also narrated in the same Purāṇa that after his death a large number of women of the Cauhāna family fell into the hands of the Muslims and their descendants were neither pure Aryans nor *mleccha*s. They were rather of mixed parentage. And the kṣatriyas sprang from the Cauhānas.[103]

The Purāṇa slightly touches upon the Cāḷukya (called Śukla) dynasty of Ānartta (Gujarat) in western India. The founder of the dyansty, Śukla, is said to have set up his rule at Dvārakā and ruled for 10 years. He was succeeded by Viśvaksena who ruled for 20 years, Jayasena for 30 years and Visena for 50 years.[104] But it is very difficult to establish their identities and to confirm their reign periods.

The Purāṇa accounts of some of the dynasties of Rājpūt princes shown above are neither systematic nor complete. There are some gaps in the dynastic accounts as well as in the genealogies. The overlapping of dynasties is also apparent. However, the historical validity of the information contained in the Purāṇa cannot be doubted. Some of the details are in

101. *Bhv.*, I, pp. 432-35, vv. 17-21, 29-38, 435-45, vv. 1-63, also 424-25, v. 4.

102. Ibid., II, p. 171, v. 25.

103. Ibid., pp. 171-72, vv. 26-28.

104. Ibid., I, p. 336, v. 4; II, pp. 172-76, vv. 1-28.

full accord with the facts recorded in ancient and early medieval history of India.

While critically judging the value of the Purāṇas, E.J. Rapson observed:

> The descriptions of ancient monarchs and of their realms (therein) are essentially historical. They may be compared to the Sagas and the medieval chronicles of Europe. They are the products of an imaginative and uncritical age in which men were not careful to distinguish fact from legend. It is the task of modern criticism to disentangle the two elements. . . .[105]

The historical material available in the Purāṇas about kingdoms and dynasties covers the period from primaeval king Manu Vaivasvata down to the times of Pr̥thvīrāja Cauhāna and not only up to the early fourth century CE as held by some scholars. It will not be correct to say that the Purāṇas provide dynastic history only up to the beginning of the Gupta rule.

There are some other aspects of ancient Indian history like towns and cities, *janapadas* (territories and peoples), state and government, polity and administration, society, religion and culture which are also recorded in the Purāṇas.

The Purāṇic data about the foundations, planning, naming, antiquity, growth and decay of towns and cities are very important for the study of history of urbanisation in ancient India. This is one of the aspects of judging the historical value of the Purāṇas. The Purāṇic records also throw light on the nature of urban settlements by showing the growth of towns as political, administrative, commerical, religious or educational centres. The towns and cities

105. "The Purāṇas", in *CHI*, I, p. 267.

described in the Purāṇas include Hastināpura and Indraprastha (the two capitals of Kuru kingdom), Ahicchatra and Kāmpil or Kāmpilya (the northern and southern capitals of Pañcāla kingdom), Mathurā (the capital of Śūrasena kingdom), Ujjayinī or Ujjain (the capital of Avantī kingdom, western Mālwā), Virāṭa (the capital of Matsya kingdom), Ayodhyā (the earliest capital of Kosala kingdom), Vaiśālī (the capital of king Viśāla and later metropolis of eight confederate republican clans), Girivraja or Rājagṛha (the earliest capital of Magadha kingdom), Pāṭaliputra (the later capital of Magadha kingdom), Kauśāmbī (the capital of Vatsa kingdom), Vārāṇasī (the capital of Kāśī kingdom), Māhiṣmatī (the capital of southern part of Avantī), Tripurī (the early medieval capital of Cedi kingdom), Tāmralipti (modern Tāmluk), Takṣaśilā and Puṣkalāvatī (the eastern and western capitals of Gandhāra kingdom), Śrāvastī (the capital of northern Kosala), Kuśāvatī (the capital of southern Kosala), Pratiṣṭhānapura (the capital of Purūravā and his descendants), Campā (the capital of Aṅga kingdom), Mithilā (the capital of Videha kingdom), Dvārakā, Bharukaccha (modern Baroach), Vidiśā (the capital of Daśārṇa, eastern Mālwā), Sūktimatipura (the early capital of Cedi kingdom), Kuṇḍinapura and Bhojakaṭapura (the earlier and later capitals of Vidarbha kingdom), Śūrpārka (modern Sopārā), Śākalapura (the Madras' capital) and Kāñcī (modern Kanjeevaram, originally belonged to the Coḷas and later became the capital of the Pallavas). These towns or cities belong to different parts of India including those of the upper and middle Gaṅgā Valley. The archaeological discoveries of the remains of most of the towns mentioned above not only confirm their existence but also prove the historicity of Purāṇic accounts of the subject. The archaeological evidences also throw light on the antiquity of the towns and settlement-patterns there. Of the towns mentioned above the first seven are archaeologically associated with PGW (Painted Grey Ware) and NBPW (Northern Black Polished Ware) phases of culture. The archaeologists on the basis of Carbon-14 dating place them in the first millennium BCE. The urban growth of next 12 are ascribed to NBPW phase or second half of the first millennium BCE. H.D. Sankalia, while placing his reliance on both tradition and archaeology, has reasonably concluded that the antiquity of towns and cities as occurring in the *Mahābhārata* and Purāṇas can also be proved by archaeological evidence.[106] The Purāṇas contain genuine historical tradition which also finds corroboration in archaeology. R. Morton Smith is perfectly correct in stating that ". . . the Purāṇa makes a good historical sense consistent with the idea of archaeology."[107]

The *janapadas* mentioned in the Purāṇas include Kuru, Pañcāla, Kāśī, Kosala, Śūrasena and Matsya of Madhyadeśa, Bāhlika, Gandhāra, Kamboja, Sindh, Sauvīra (northern part of Sindh), Madraka (northern part of the Punjab), Kashmir, the Śakas, Tuṣāras, Cinas, Kirātas, Pahalavas (Persians) and Ambaṣṭhas of Uttarāpatha (north-western region), Aṅga, Baṅga, Prāgjyotiṣa or Kāmarūpa, Puṇḍra, Videha (Mithilā), Magadha and Tāmralipti of Prācyadeśa (eastern region), Sārasvata, Saurāṣṭra, Ānartta and Bharukaccha of Aparānta (western region), the Pāṇḍyas, Keralas, Coḷas, Muṣikas, Śabaras, Pulindas, Māhiṣaka (Mysore), Kaliṅga (southern part of Orissa) and Aśmaka (southern part of Maharashtra) of Dakṣiṇāpatha (southern region), Avantī, Vidiśā, Tripurī, Daśārṇa and Bhojas of Vindhyan region, and the Kirātas,

---

106. *AIHA*, pp. 277-78 and 280.

107. *DDEI*, Preface, see also pp. 1-3.

Khasas, Dārdas, Mālavas and Trigarttas of mountain region.[108]

The Purāṇas throw a good deal of light on the evolution of kingship, emergence of the state and its seven constituent elements (based on the *saptāṅga* theory), interstate relations, administrative organisation (local, judicial, civil and military administration), revenue system, etc.[109] The data concerned have their own value in the realm of study of ancient Indian polity and administration.

The Purāṇic descriptions of socio-religious life of the people with references to the *varṇāśrama dharma* (fourfold stages of life), caste system, Śaiva, Śakti and Vaiṣṇava cults of Hinduism, etc. have considerable historical value.

Several broken chains in the political and cultural history of ancient India can be restored with the help of the historical data contained in the Purāṇas.

The present author is not in perfect agreement with Romila Thapar so far as her statement, that "The Indian

---

108. *Vy.*, 45.108-37; 47, 42-62; Patil, op. cit., p. 270; *Vṣṇ.*, 2.3, 15-17; *Mts.*, 114.34-57; *Mkd.*, 54.32-57; 55.6-32; 48-52; *Br.*, 19.15-18; 27.41-64; *Vmn.*, 13.35-57; *Km.*, I.45, 39-42; *Padma Purāṇa* (Svargakhaṇḍa), ed. Ashoka Chatterjee Śāstri, 15, 41-59; *Garuḍa Purāṇa*, Eng. tr. M.N. Dutta, I, ch. LV, p. 146; see also S.M. Ali, *The Geography of the Purāṇas*, pp. 133-76; D.C. Sircar, *SGAMI*, pp. 26-74; B.C. Law, "Countries and Peoples of India" (Epic and Paurāṇic Sources), *ABORI*, vol. XVII, pt. III, 1936, pp. 225 ff; *Geographical Essays*, pp. 119-71; M.R. Singh, *A Critical Study of the Geographical Data in the Early Purāṇas*, pp. 59 ff.

109. For details of all see *Mts.*, chs. 215-20, 225-27; *Agn.*, chs. 218-27; 233, 11-23; 234, 1-25; chs. 235-36; 239, 1-45; 240, 1-32; chs. 242-43, 251-52; B.B. Mishra, *Polity in the Agni Purāṇa*, pp. 27 ff; *Padma Purāṇa*, Svargakhaṇḍa (*supra*), chs. 36-37; 38, 1-40, 59-65; *Vṣṇ Dh.*, II. 65, 2-70; II, chs. 6, 18, 68, 150, 177-181; Patil, op. cit., pp. 47-54; J.L. Shastri, *Political Thought in the Purāṇas;* Om Prakash, *Political Ideas in the Purāṇas.*

tradition until the seventh century CE lacks any literature which can be specifically described as historical writing,"[110] is concerned. We find that the Purāṇic literature of pre-seventh century CE contains a lot of historical writing. Even prior to the seventh century CE, the *purāṇakāras* maintaining historical tradition kept a record of all important historical events in the form of a Purāṇa. As already stated, they time to time used to add historical information to what was already recorded in the existing Purāṇa.

The *purāṇakāras*, no doubt, made significant and substantial contributions to the evolutions of historiographical tradition in ancient India.

The historical portions of the Purāṇas do testify to the contributions of the ancient Hindus to the evolution of the tradition of historical writing in ancient India. This can best be qualified in the words of J.F. Fleet: "the ancient Hindus could write short historical compositions concise and to the point but limited in extent. The historical chapters of the Purāṇas do certainly indicate a desire on the part of the ancient Hindus not to ignore general history altogether and are clearly based on ancient archives which had survived in a more or less complete shape and were somehow accessible to the composers of those works. . . ."[111]

The historical data contained in the Purāṇas constitute one of the evidences to disprove the statements of some Indian and foreign scholars that the ancient Indians (mainly the Hindus) had no sense of history and chronology.[112]

110. "The Tradition of Historical Writing in Early India" in Romila Thapar's *AISH*, p. 268.

111. *Imp. Gaz. Ind.* (new edn.), vol. II, p. 17.

112. See also G.P. Singh, "The Purāṇic Tradition of Historiography in India", *IHR*, XXXI, 1 & 2, 2004, pp. 1-17.

Book Three

Buddhist and Jaina Tradition of Historiography

General Remarks

THE Buddhist and Jaina traditions of historiography are also worthy of our notice. Both the Buddhist and Jaina scholars made substantial contributions to the evolution of historiographical tradition in India, the former during the ancient period and the latter during the ancient and medieval periods. The Jainas in particular maintained continuity in their historical writing during the period which constitutes the distinguishing hallmark of their historiography. The Buddhists and Jainas also, like the Hindus, felt the need to record the past as well as contemporary events of historical nature in their respective works. They did not ignore the incorporation of historical subjects in their writings and their preservation. They, like the scholars of the Brāhmanical historical schools, presented history in literary form. They have both historical and semi-historical works to their credit. The historical narratives, dynastic genealogies and chronology, biographies and chronicles form very important parts of their historical writings. There were different schools of historical writing in the Buddhist and Jaina communities. The historical records were compiled and preserved by the Jainas and Buddhists of various schools. Like the Sanskrit literature, the Buddhist and Jaina literature too contain a good number of works of historical value. The Jaina historical literature, which is marked by its variety, vastness and richness, is of special importance. The Buddhist and Jaina historical traditions are preserved in different classes of works of different periods. Both the traditions have their own authenticity and value. Placing our reliance on the combined testimony of the Buddhist and Jaina works, we can throw fresh light on the socio-economic, political and religious history of India during the period in general and the history of Buddhism and Jainism in particular.

In ancient times, the Buddhists had apparently maintained a rich tradition of historiography. Their historical writings are well reflected in some of the Pāli canons, chronicles and commentaries, biographies and Vaṁśāvalīs works. However, they cannot be regarded as historical works in true sense of the words. Some of the *avadāna*s (Sanskrit Buddhist texts) are the most important of all the Buddhist works of historical value. These works as a whole are important for the study of history of ancient India from the time of the Buddha down to the time of Aśoka.

The historical writings of the Jainas are found in different categories of their literature. Some of their canonical and non-canonical works also contain such writings. Their other works which form part of historical literature include (besides some of the non-canonical texts) the *paṭṭāvalī*s, the *guruvāvalī*s, the *rājāvalī*s, the *vākā*s, *carita*s or biographies, Purāṇas, *praśasti*s and the *prabandha*s. The *paṭṭāvalī*s and *rājāvalī*s, the two important historical records, were compiled and preserved by the Jaina authors with great care. All these works are important from the point of view of historiography as they throw light on different aspects of ancient and medieval Indian history and culture. Besides the above-mentioned works, there are some other semi-historical and historical works of the period preceding and succeeding CE 900. The bulk of Jaina historical literature was produced during the medieval period. The

Jaina ancient works are no less authentic than the contemporary and similar Buddhist or Brāhmanical ones. It is an established fact that Jaina literature is more extensive than Buddhist one from the standpoint of its historical contents. It has been rightly pointed out that "The historical information contained in it is supposed to be of a more reliable nature, and is expected to add vastly to our existing knowledge."[1] Bühler also speaks very highly of the authenticity and historical importance of Jaina traditions.[2]

The historical works of the later period have been preserved in a better way than those of the earlier period by the Jaina historians unlike their Buddhist counterparts. The period of rule of the Cāḷukyas of Gujarat and the Rāṣṭrakūṭas of Deccan was a blooming one in the history of historical writing of the Jainas. Some very very important historical works were composed under the patronage of some Cāḷukya and Rāṣṭrakūṭa kings. A number of historical biographies and chronicles were produced by the Jaina scholars including those of Rajasthan and Gujarat during the medieval period. The Jaina writers, who made contributions to Indian historiography, belonged to both Śvetāmbara and Digambara schools.

> The Jaina books form one of the primary sources of our knowledge of the internal history of India from the seventh century BCE to the rise of the Mauryan Empire.[3]
>
> From the times of the Mauryas onwards right up to the advent of the Muslims, and in some respects even up to the end of the

1. B. Ch. Chhabra's Presidential Address at the History Section of the AIOC, 16th Session, Lucknow, 1951.
2. Bühler, "On the Authenticity of Jaina Traditions", in *The Indian Sect of the Jains* (tr. Burgess, London, 1903), pp. 21-23.
3. K.A. Nilakantha Shastri, *History of India*, I, p. 39.

> Muslim period, the Jaina material constitutes a good secondary source. In some cases, as that of Gujarat and several of the principal states of the Deccan and the south, histories of these regions could be reconstructed chiefly with the help of their respective Jaina sources. And for the prehistoric times, prior to the age of Mahāvīra and the Buddha, the Jaina traditions should have the same value and importance as the corresponding Brāhmanical traditions. Their mutual agreements and differences, if comparatively studied and critically examined, may reveal many a hitherto unknown fact and may push back farther the limits of historical times.[4]

Some of the Jaina works begin their accounts with the early period and bring them up to the dates of their respective completion. The works present a curious jumble of facts and fictions. In spite of their shortcomings, which scientific or authentic histories are generally free from, a close and careful study thereof yields reliable facts, figures and dates which no other contemporaneous work does. In some of the Jaina works, historical facts and chronological data have been found mixed up with narrative stories. The Jaina works are important for socio-economic, political and religious history of ancient and medieval India in general and early Muslim invasions of India in particular.

The Buddhist and Jaina historians of India also gave impetus to the writing of biographies and preservation of dynastic genealogies and chronology.

---

4. J.P. Jain, *The Jaina Sources of the History of Ancient India* (100 BC – AD 900), p. 3.

3.1

Buddhist Historiography

OF all the Buddhist works of some historical importance, mention may first be made of the three Piṭakas, *Vinaya, Sutta* and *Abhidhamma* which form parts of canonical Pāli literature ascribed to the period extending from the fifth century BCE to the first century BCE. Their historicity can be proved by the historical facts they contain.

The *Vinaya Piṭaka* contains valuable historical information about two powerful Magadhan rulers, Bimbisāra and his son Ajātasattu (Ajātaśatru), the events that took place during their times, socio-economic and political life of the people, towns and cities and kingdoms and republics in the time of the Buddha, Buddhism, etc. Bimbisāra is said to have ruled over the kingdom of Magadha with its capital at Rājagaha (Rājagṛha). The economic prosperity of this capital city is also highlighted. We are further told that Ajātasattu employed his two ministers, Sunidha and Vassakāra, to build a fort at Pāṭaligāma (which later developed as a city of Pāṭaliputta or Pāṭaliputra) to repel the invasion of the Vajjians. Brahmadatta, king of Kāśī, entered into a war with the king of Kosala in which the latter suffered most, but friendship was soon restored. The republican states of Pāvā and Kuśinārā of the Mallas were in a flourishing condition at the time of the Buddha. The towns and cities of Majjhimadesa (Madhyadeśa) which were intimately associated with the Buddha and

Buddhism include Rājagaha, Vesāli (Vaiśālī), Sāketa, Sāvatthī (Śrāvastī), Campā, Kośāmbī, Pāṭaliputta, Kapilavatthu (Kapilavastu) and Vārāṇasī. A brief account of the first two Buddhist Councils held at Rājagaha in 483 BCE (three months after the death of the Buddha) under the patronage of Ajātasattu, and at Vesāli in about 383 BCE during the reign of Kālāśoka respectively has also been provided in this *piṭaka*. Interesting sidelights are also thrown on the political history, and social and economic conditions of the people of the Buddha's time.[1] The *Mahāvagga* provides us with information about Gautama's attainment of enlightenment and the first sermon he delivered at Sārnāth near Vārāṇasī. The entire history of the foundation of the Buddhist community (*saṁgha*) is recorded therein. It records in chronological order the subsequent events of a century in that community. It presents a systematic history of the development of the Buddhist order. It also records a few important episodes in the life of the Buddha. It deals with his life history. In fact, it starts history just from the Buddhahood of Gautama.[2] The *Cullavagga* provides historical anecdotes connected with the life of the Buddha and history of constitution of the Order.[3] These two important sections of the said Piṭaka constitute very important sources of the history of Buddhism.

We find a wealth of historical material in the *Sutta Piṭaka*. It consists of the five Nikāyas, *Dīgha*, *Majjhima*, *Saṁyutta*, *Aṅguttara* and *Khuddaka*.

The *Dīgha Nikāya* contains a number of historical Suttas. The *Sāmaññaphala Sutta* furnishes us with valuable information

---

1. B.C. Law, "Historical and Geographical References in the Pāli Piṭakas" in his *HPL*, II, Appendix A, pp. 648-51.

2. Law, *HPL*, I, pp. 61 ff., 65.

3. Ibid., pp. 65 f.

about the crafts and occupations of the time. The weavers, potters and basket-makers have been mentioned as important occupational groups. Another important historical allusion in this Sutta is to the murder of Bimbisāra at the hands of his son Ajātasattu. The *Ambaṭṭha Sutta* refers to King Pasenadi of Kosala who was the contemporary of the Buddha. This Sutta also throws light on the social position of the Vaṇṇa Khattiya, brāhmaṇa, vessā and suddā. The *Sonadaṇḍa Sutta* refers to Campā visited by the Buddha with 500 monks, to King Bimbisāra of Magadha and King Pasenadi of Kosala. This Sutta also tells us how the Aṅga kingdom with its capital Campā was absorbed in the Magadhan empire. The *Mahāli Sutta* makes an incidental reference to the Buddha's dwelling at Vaiśālī. The *Lohicca Sutta* states that King Pasenadi used to collect taxes from the inhabitants of Kāśī-Kosala. He enjoyed the income not alone but with his subordinates. The *Mahāparinibbāna Sutta* contains the details of how the Magadhan monarch, Ajātasattu, hatched a plot to annihilate his Vajjian rivals. It relates that when the Buddha heard of this plot, he remarked that so long as the Vajjians remain united and fulfil the seven conditions of their welfare, there would be no danger to them. But soon Ajātasattu succeeded in annihilating them with the help of his two ministers, Sunidha and Vassakāra. These ministers are stated to have created dissensions among them which resulted in their fall and annexation of their metropolis Vaiśālī to Magadha kingdom. This Sutta further relates that Buddha on his way to Vesāli visited Pāṭaligāma where the said two ministers built a fort to crush the Vajjians. The same Sutta speaks of the Mallas of Kuśinārā. It further mentions Sāvatthī, Campā, Rājagaha, Sāketa, Kośāmbī and Vārāṇasī as great cities. The *Janavasabha Sutta* refers to Bimbisāra of Magadha as a righteous king. This Sutta also refers to Kāśī, Kosala, Vajjī, Cedī, Vaṁsa

(Vatsa), Kuru, Pañcāla, Maccha (Matsya) and Śūrasena kingdoms. The *Saṅgīti Sutta* informs us that Mahāvīra, the founder of Jainism, died at Pāvā. It also mentions the Mallas of Pāvā who were republican communities. The *Mahānidāna Sutta* and the *Mahāsatipaṭṭhāna Sutta* refer to the land of the Kurus where the Buddha dwelt for some time. The *Mahāsudassana Sutta* mentions Campā, Rājagaha, Sāketa, Sāvatthī, Kośāmbī, Vārāṇasī and Kuśinārā (also named as Kuśāvatī) as rich and prosperous cities. The *Mahāgovinda Sutta* refers to a number of great cities built by Govinda. They are Dantapura of the Kaliṅgas, Potana of the Assakas, Māhissati of the Avantīs, Roruka of the Sauvīra, Mithilā of the Videhas, Campā of the Aṅgas and Vārāṇasī of the Kāśīs. The *Dīgha Nikāya* is also an important record of the dialogues and discourses in which the Buddha expounded his doctrine.[4]

The historical information contained in the *Majjhima Nikāya* is mainly concerned with the life and itinerary of the Buddha. In this respect the *Ariyapariyesana Sutta* is very important. It deals with different phases of his life and activities. We are told that he in the course of his wanderings stayed at Rājagaha, Campā, Nālanda, Mithilā, Kuśinārā, Kośāmbī, Vaiśālī, Sāvatthī and other places. There are historical references in this Nikāya to the Vajjīs and Mallas, the Śākyas of Kapilavatthu, the Kāśīs of Vārāṇasī, the Aṅgas and the Magadhas, etc. It tells us of the Vajjīs and the Mallas as forming *saṁghas* and *gaṇas*, that is, clans governed by organised corporations. We are also informed that the political relation between the Licchavīs of Vesāli and King Pasenadi of Kosala was friendly.[5]

4. *DN*, I, pp. 47-126, 150-58; II, pp. 72-168, 220-52, 290-358.

5. *MN*, I, pp. 160-75, 231; II, pp. 100-101.

The *Saṁyutta Nikāya* refers to King Pasenadi of Kosala the capital of which was Sāvatthī. The whole of the *Kosala-Saṁyutta* is devoted to him. It contains historical narratives of a war that broke out between Ajātasattu, king of Magadha, and Pasenadi. Each claimed the possession of the township of Kāśī. At first the former was victorious but later on he was defeated and taken prisoner by the latter. Pasenadi, however, married his daughter, Vajirā, to Ajātasattu and granted to him the township of Kāśī.[6]

The *Aṅguttara Nikāya* contains a list of sixteen *mahājanapadas* (large territorial states) that existed in the age of the Buddha. These were Aṅga, Magadha, Kāśī, Kosala, Vajjī, Malla, Cetī, Vaṁsa, Kuru, Pañcāla, Maccha, Śūrasena, Assaka, Avantī, Gandhāra, and Kamboja.[7] The list includes the names of the people as well as states.

The *Khuddaka Nikāya* is of inestimable value from the point of view of the study of history of Indian civilisation in the pre- and post-Buddha period. The Jātaka records (assigned to the second century BCE) contain a lot of valuable historical data about political and socio-economic history of ancient India. It is clearly stated therein that Aṅga was once a powerful kingdom. Magadha was once under the sway of Aṅgarājā (*Jāt.*, Fausboll, VI, p. 272). It is said that King Manoja of Brahmavardhana (another name of Vārāṇasī) conquered Aṅga and Magadha (*Jāt.*, V, pp. 312-16). It appears from the same records that before the Buddha's time Kāśī was the most powerful kingdom in the whole of northern India (*Jāt.*, III, pp. 115ff; I, pp. 262ff). Mahākosala, father of King Pasenadi of Kosala, is said to have given his daughter in marriage to King Bimbisāra of Magadha. The pin-money was the village

6. *SN*, I, pp. 68-102.

7. *AN*, I, p. 213; IV, pp. 252, 256, 260

of Kāśī yielding a revenue of a hundred thousand (in terms of coins) for bath and perfume. We are also told that there took place many a fierce fight between the sons of Mahākosala and Bimbisāra, Pasenadi, and Ajātasattu respectively (*Jāt.*, II, p. 237; IV, pp. 342ff). In one of the Jātakas (IV, pp. 144ff) it is narrated that Viḍūḍabha, in order to crush the Śākyas who deceived his father Pasenadi by giving him a daughter of a slave girl to marry, deposed his father and became king. He marched out with a large army and succeeded in annihilating the Śākyas, But he with his army met also with destruction. The river Rohiṇī was the boundary between the territories of the Śākyas and Koliyas, the two republican communities. A quarrel flared up between the two over the possession of the river. But the Buddha succeeded in restoring peace among his kinsfolk (*Jāt.*, I, pp. 327 ff; IV, pp. 207 ff). A king of Vārāṇasī attacked the kingdom of Kosala and took the king prisoner. The king of Kosala had a son named Chatta who fled while his father was taken prisoner. Afterwards Chatta recovered his kingdom (*Jāt.*, III, pp. 115ff). The kingdom of Kāśī was seized by a king of Sāvatthī named Vaṅka. But it was soon restored to the king of Kāśī (*Jat.*, III, pp. 168-9). It is said that Campā, the capital of the kingdom of Aṅga, was at a distance of 60 *yojanas* from Mithilā (*Jāt.*, VI, p. 32). In the *Assaka Jātaka* (II, p. 155) we are told of the Assaka territory, the capital city of which was Poṭali. In the *Bhīmasena Jātaka* (I, pp. 356 ff) Takkaśilā (Takṣaśilā) is mentioned as a great centre of learning. From the *Śivi Jātaka* (IV, p. 401) we know that Ariṭṭhapura was the capital of the Śivi kingdom. The kingdom of Bāveru is referred to in the *Bāveru Jātaka* (III, p. 126). Bharukaccha, a seaport town, is referred to in the *Sussondī Jātaka* (III, pp. 187 ff). In the *Cetiya Jātaka* (III, p. 454) it is said that Sotthivatinagara was the capital of the kingdom of Cetī. In the *Gandhāra Jātaka* (III, pp. 363-69) the Kāśmīr-Gandhāra kingdom and the Videha kingdom are also mentioned. The kingdom of Kāśī with its capital Vārāṇasī also finds mention in the Jātakas. The extent of the city is mentioned as 12 *yojanas* (IV, p. 160). There are also references to the Kosala kingdom (*Jāt.*, III, pp. 211-13, 237). The Kamboja kingdom is also referred to in the Jātakas (IV, p. 208). There are innumerable references to the Magadha kingdom (*Jāt.*, IV, pp. 454-5; V, p. 316; VI, p. 272). The city of Mithilā, the capital of the Videhas, was seven leagues and the kingdom of Videha 300 leagues in extent (Cowell's *Jāt.*, III, p. 222). In the *Kumbhakāra Jātaka* (Ibid., III, p. 230) Kampilla has been mentioned as the capital of Uttara-Pañcāla. The river Campā formed the boundary between Aṅga and Magadha (*Campeyya Jātaka* — *Jāt.*, IV, p. 454). There are some Jātakas which throw light on different categories of the brāhmaṇas, their position in the society and different professions and occupations they chose, the position of the *khattiyas* who were warriors *par excellence,* agriculture and industry and trade and commerce both internal and external.

Apart from the Jātakas, the *Khuddaka Nikāya* contains some other books which are historically very important. The *Udāna* (p. 11) makes mention of King Bimbisāra of Magadha and King Pasenadi of Kosala. The *Sutta Nipāta* deals with social and economic conditions of the people of the time. The social position of the brāhmaṇas and various pursuits they followed as means of their livelihood are sufficiently highlighted in it (p. 122). It also speaks of internal trade system (vv. 1012-13). It contains historical references to Rājagaha and Kapilavatthu visited by the Buddha (pp. 86, 192), Patiṭṭhāna, Māhissati, Ujjayinī, Vidiśā, Kośāmbī, Kuśinārā, Magadha, etc. (p. 194). The *Mahāniddesa* speaks of India's commerce by sea with Yona and Paramayona. Towards the east, it mentions Kālamukha, Suvaṇṇabhūmi, Vesuṅga, Verāpatha, Takkola, Tamali,

Tambapaṇṇi and Java as countries visited by the Indian sea-going merchants and speaks also of the manner in which they followed the difficult land-route after reaching the harbour (pp. 154-5, 415). The *Cullaniddesa* (pp. 4-5) makes mention of a trade route from Patiṭṭhāna to Magadha. There are references to Mulaka, Patiṭṭhāna, Māhissati, Ujjayinī, Vedisā, Kośāmbī, Sāketa, Sāvatthī, Kapilavatthu, Kuśinārā, Pāvā, Bhoganagara, Vesāli and Magadha. The *Buddhavaṁsa* contains in verse the life history of Gautama Buddha. It also refers to the cities of Amarāvatī, Kuśinārā, Vaiśālī, Kapilavatthu, Allakappa, Rāmagāma, Pāṭaliputta, Avantīpura and Mithilā.[8] The *Cariyāpiṭaka* (a post-Aśokan work) mentions the city of Indapatta ruled by Dhanañjaya who met some brāhmaṇas from Kaliṅga, Kuśāvatī, Pañcāla where there was a king named Jayadissa in the city of Kappila or Kampil, etc. (pp. 74-5, 90f). The *Apadāna* contains a list of occupational groups like basket-makers (*nalakāra*), weavers (*pesakāra*), leather-workers (*cammakāra*), carpenters (*tacchaka)*, metal-workers (*kammāra*), blacksmiths, goldsmiths, tinsmiths, jewellers (*maṇikāra*), potters (*kumbhakāra*), cloth merchants (*dussika*) and dyers (*rajakāra*) (II, pp. 357 f). The hereditary craftsmen of those who followed different occupations and professions organised themselves into various guilds (called *seṇis, pūgas*) agreeing to be governed by their own laws and customs. This work also speaks of India's external trade relations with outside world. It bears witness to the fact that traders and merchants from various countries including Malaya (Malay Peninsula), Soṇṇabhūmi (Suvaṇṇabhūmi) and Cina (China) visited India (I, p. 2 and II, p. 357).

The *Kathāvatthu*, the third book of the *Abhidhamma Piṭaka*, also deserves mention here. It is a work of the Aśokan age. It

8. *Buddhavaṁsa*, Eng. tr. B.C. Law, PTS, London, 1938.

was composed by Thera Moggaliputta Tissa, president of the Third Buddhist Council held at Pāṭaliputra under the patronage of King Aśoka. It is important from the point of view of history of Buddhism and development of Buddhist doctrine of the ages after Buddha. It is evident from it that at the time of Aśoka there existed different schools of Buddhism.

The Tripiṭakas throw a good deal of light on social, economic, political and religious history of ancient India from the time of the Buddha or rise of the Magadhan empire to the third or second century BCE. They also provide the narratives of historical events that took place during the lifetime of the Buddha (sixth and fifth centuries BCE). It cannot, however, be denied that in the canonical Pāli texts the history is mixed up with legends.

The post-canonical Pāli literature of the period extending from the beginning of the Christian Era to the end of the fifth century CE also contains some works including the commentaries and chronicles which are very important from historical purposes.

The *Milindapañho* (a non-canonical or an extra-canonical work) preserves the history of rule of the Bactrian Greek king, Menander (165-145 BCE), over the Punjab with its capital at Sāgala (Śākala = modern Sialkot). He became popularly known as Milinda after being converted to Buddhism by Nāgasena, the learned Buddhist monk. It appears from this work that the capital city was adorned with splendid and magnificent buildings, parks, gardens, tanks, well-laid out streets, strong defences and marketplaces. It was one of the important centres of trade and commerce. It had shops for the sale of Benares muslin, jewels, and other costly articles indicating the wealth and prosperity of the kingdom. It had also trade relations with Pāṭaliputra.[9] The full details of conversations between King Milinda and Nāgasena have been provided in all the seven books of this work. It contains valuable information about the Buddhist monks who were persecuted by the brāhmaṇa ruler, Puṣyamitra Śuṅga (*c.* 184-148 BCE), and protected by Menander, a zealous Buddhist. The Śuṅga king was no doubt a persecutor of Buddhism and zealous champion of Brāhmanism. He, after having usurped the throne of Magadha in 184 BCE, actually extended his sway over Śākala in the Punjab. In one of the Buddhist Sanskrit texts, *Divyāvadāna,* also it is recorded that Puṣyamitra made the notorious declaration at Śākala setting a price of 100 gold *dīnāra*s on the head of every Buddhist monk.[10] There is hardly any reason to doubt the historicity of such information.

One of the important historical facts recorded in the *Milindapañho* is about Dhanānanda, the last reigning Nanda king, who was uprooted by Cāṇakya in a war in which Bhadraśāla was the commander-in-chief of the Nanda army and the carnage was terrible.[11] There are some other facts and contents of historical interest in this work. It contains a list of kingdoms, towns and cities, etc. It refers to the province of Yavana (Bactria in north Afghanistan watered by the Oxus) where the Bactrian Greeks established their rule, Alsanda (the town of Alexandria on the Indus founded by Alexander which was famous for coral trade), Bharukaccha (a seaport town equivalent to modern Broach), country of Cina (China), the kingdoms of Gandhāra (that

---

9. Eng. tr. from Pāli by T.W. Rhys Davids, *The Questions of King Milinda* SBE, XXXV, I, pp. 1-27.

10. *Divyāvadāna*, ed. E.B. Cowell and R.R. Neil, pp. 433-4

11. SBE, XXXVI, II, pp. 147-8.

had its capital at Puruṣapura), Kaliṅga (that had its capital at Dantapura ages before Buddha's time), Kashmir, Kosala, and Magadha with its capital at Pāṭaliputra, the cities like Sāgala, Sāketa, Ujjayinī, Madhurā (Mathurā) and Vārāṇasī and places like Sovira (Sauvira adjacent to Sindh), Suvaṇṇabhūmi (identical probably with Lower Burma and Malay Peninsula) and Takkola which were visited by Indian merchants.[12] It also throws some light on the socio-economic life of the people. It is explicitly stated in it that in a well-laid city or town, rooms had to be made for the residence of the various classes of khattiyas, brāhmaṇas, vessas, suddas, goldsmiths, silversmiths, workers in lead, tin, iron and brass, blacksmiths, jewellers, weavers, potters, leather-workers, wagon-makers, ivory-workers, basket-makers, dyers, money-exchangers, cloth-merchants, traders and merchants from various countries and places and other professional groups.[13]

The authorship of *Milindapañho* and date of its composition are controversial aspects of the subject. According to Mrs. Rhys Davids, the recorded conversations of Milinda and Nāgasena were edited in the new book form after the former's death by special commission by a brāhmaṇa of Buddhist collegiate training named Mānava. But it is disputable. The generally accepted view is that it had originally been written in northern India at or little after the beginning of the Christian Era in Sanskrit or in some north Indian Prākṛt by an anonymous author. It appeared again in an enlarged and modified form in the second century CE. It saw its Pāli recension before the fifth century CE.

The Buddhist historical writing in the commentatorial tradition is also worthy of our notice. Buddhaghoṣa, a native

12. *Milindapañha*, ed. V. Trenckner, pp. 327, 331, 359.

13. Ibid., p. 331.

of Bodha-Gayā, flourished in the first half of the fifth century CE. He went to Ceylon and wrote fourteen commentaries on the Pāli texts there during that period or between CE 410 and 435. Of all the commentaries written by him, the *Sāmantapāsādikā* (on the *Vinaya Piṭaka*) is the most important from a historical point of view. It provides dynastic history of Magadha from the sixth century BCE to the time of Aśoka. It gives dynastic genealogies and chronology of the kings of Bimbisāra, Śiśunāga, Nanda and Maurya dynasties who ruled over Magadha with its capital at Pāṭaliputra. Bimbisāra is stated to have ruled over the kingdom of Magadha maintaining a powerful army. He had many sons. He was succeeded by his eldest son Ajātasattu, who is said to have ruled for 24 years. He bore the cost of repairing at Rājagaha 18 *mahāvihāras* which were deserted by the Buddhist monks after the *parinibbāna* of the Buddha. The Buddha passed away in the eighth year of Ajātasattu's reign. Udāyi Bhadda, the successor or Ajātasattu, reigned for 16 years. The other two kings of Magadha are mentioned as Anuruddha and Muṇḍa. They altogether ruled for 18 years. Then came Nāgadāsaka who reigned for 24 years. He was banished by the citizens who anointed the minister named Śiśunāga as king. He ruled for 18 years. Kālāśoka ruled for 28 years. He had ten sons (the most prominent among whom was Nandivardhana). They altogether ruled for 22 years. Then came the Nandas who also ruled over Magadha for the same period. The Nanda dynasty was overthrown by Candagutta (Candragupta) Maurya who ruled the kingdom for 24 years (321-297 BCE). He was succeeded by Bindusāra who ruled for 28 years (297-269 BCE).[14] He was succeeded by Aśoka (Dhammāsoka) who

14. *Samantapāsādikā,* ed. J. Takakusu and M. Nagai, I, pp. 72-3, also 8-9, 41; see also B.C. Law; *The Magadhas in Ancient India*, p. 3, note 3, and p. 4.

is said to have enjoyed undivided sovereignty over the kingdom after slaying all his brothers except Tissa. It is clearly stated in this work that he reigned without coronation for four years[15] which means that he ascended the throne four years before he was formally crowned as a king. While furnishing an account of Aśoka this work also records that he followed his father for some time in making donations to non-Buddhist ascetics and institutions, and gave charities to the Buddhist *bhikkhus*. His income from the four gates of the city of Pāṭaliputta was 400000 *kahāpaṇas* daily. He is said to have built 84000 *vihāras* all over India. The missionaries who were sent to various places to preach the *dhamma* of Aśoka were all natives of Magadha.[16] These are positive evidences of historical writing in the said tradition. The other historical contents in this work are about Kuśinārā, the town of the Mallas, where Buddha passed away, the cities of Vārāṇasī, Vaiśālī, Campā, Sāvatthī and Kapilavatthu, the sea-port of Bharukaccha, Suvaṇṇabhūmi, visited by Indian traders, the kings of the Licchavīgaṇa, the places visited by the Buddha in the course of his wanderings, etc.[17] The historicity of the work is established by the facts stated above.

There are some other historically important commentaries of Buddhaghoṣa. The *Sumaṅgalavilāsinī* (on the *Dīgha Nikāya*) describes Ajātasattu as a patricide monarch. It further relates that he had hostile relationship with his father, Bimbisāra, whom he imprisoned and kept confined in a room and starved to death.[18] Ajātasattu's two ministers, Sunidha and Vassakāra, built a fortress at Pāṭaligāma to repel the attacks

15. *Samantapāsādikā*, I, p. 41.

16. Ibid., pp. 44, 52, 63 f, 115.

17. Ibid., pp. 175, 201, 212, 241.

18. *Sumaṅgalavilāsinī*, ed. Rhys Davids and J.E. Carpenter, I, pp. 133-40.

of Licchavīs of Vaiśālī.[19] The Śākyas, Koliyas and other republican tribes, the Aṅga kingdom with its capital Campā, the other two kingdoms of Kosala and Gandhāra, the towns of Rājagaha and Kośāmbī of the Buddha's time, the economic importance of Vārāṇasī as a trading centre and the weavers who produced soft and beautiful garments there, etc. are also recorded in it.[20] It also contains information about which grew as a town and a Buddhist university in the fifth century CE.[21]

The *Dhammapada-aṭṭhakathā* abounds in references to some of the important kings like Bimbisāra and Ajātasattu of Magadha and Pasenadi of Kosala, some principal cities like Takkaśilā, Kapilavatthu, Kośāmbī, Vārāṇasī, Rājagaha, Sāvatthī and Vaiśālī and the republican tribes like Licchavīs, Mallas, etc.

The *Sutta Nipāta* commentary is a mine of various sorts of valuable historical information. It deals with two important kingdoms of Magadha and Kosala. It states that Bimbisāra was a lord of Magadha, and being possessor of a big army was called Seniya. Kosalarāja Pasenadi is also described as a powerful ruler. It mentions Vārāṇasī, Sāvatthī, Kapilavatthu, Rājagaha and other famous cities of the Buddha's time. It also throws light on the socio-economic life of the people and trade and commerce of the time.

The *Aṭṭhasālinī* (commentary on the *Abhidhamma Piṭaka*) contains references to some historical personages including Udāyi Bhadda of Magadha. It supplies us with information about the kingdom of Kosala, the urban life of the people,

19. *Sumaṅgalavilāsinī*, II, pp. 516-17.

20. Ibid., I, pp. 132, 239, 258 f, 279. 317-19, 389.

21. Ibid., I, p. 35; III, p. 873.

the cities, Kāśīpura, Pāṭaliputta, Bharukaccha, Rājagaha, Sāketa and Sāvatthī, etc.

The *Khuddakapāṭha* commentary furnishes us with many important historical materials concerning political and religious history of ancient India. The details of the Licchavīs of Vaiśālī, the kingdom of Magadha, King Bimbisāra, growth of Buddhism, eighteen great monasteries in Rājagaha, the importance of Kapilavatthu in the time of the Buddha, etc. have been provided in it.

The above commentaries afford an ample testimony of Buddhaghoṣa's knowledge of history.

The two Ceylonese chronicles, the *Dīpavaṁsa* and the *Mahāvaṁsa,* are important historical records. Their association with Indian Buddhist historical tradition justifies their inclusion here. Both the chronicles deal with some aspects of ancient Indian history.

The *Dīpavaṁsa* was written at the end of the fourth century CE or the beginning of the fifth century CE by an anonymous Buddhist writer. Some of the kings of Magadha with the lengths of their reigns and the events of their times are mentioned in it. Bimbisāra is said to have ruled for 52 years, Udāyi Bhadda for 16 years and the ten sons of Kālāśoka for 22 years. Candagutta Maurya ascended the throne 162 years after the death of Buddha (i.e. 483 – 162 = in 321 BCE) and ruled for 24 years (i.e. till 297 BCE).[22] It further deals with the reign of the great Maurya king Aśoka (the grandson of Candagutta and son of Bindusāra) and the notable events that took place in his time. It was during his reign or in 246 BCE that Mahinda (Mahendra, his son) went to Ceylon and spread Buddhism there.

22. *Dip.*, ed. and tr. H. Oldenberg, III, 50-60, V, 97.

The *Mahāvaṁsa* (Great History) compiled by Mahānāma in CE 431 is an authoritative work. A dynastic list of the kings of Magadha to Aśoka with regnal years of most of them is preserved in it. It is recorded therein that Bimbisāra was fifteen years old when he was anointed king by his own father and then reigned for full 52 years. (Thus he was born in 558 BCE ascended the throne in 543 BCE, and reigned till 491 BCE.) His son Ajātasattu reigned for 32 years (491-459 BCE). It was the eighth year of his reign when the great Gautama Buddha died (i.e. in 483 BCE). Ajātasattu's successor Udāyi Bhadda reigned for 16 years. His lineal descendants, Anuruddha and his son Muṇḍa, conjointly ruled for 8 years and Nāgadāsaka for 24 years. The throne of Magadha was then offered by the citizens, ministers and officials of Pāṭaliputta to Susunāga (Śiśunāga) who ruled for 18 years. His son Kālāśoka ruled for 28 years. At the end of the tenth year of his reign a century had passed after the *nirvāṇa* of the Buddha. Kālāsoka's ten sons (including Nandivardhana and Mahānandin) together ruled for 22 years. All the above-mentioned rulers altogether ruled for 200 years (543-343 BCE). It is further stated in this chronicle that during the reign of Kālāsoka's sons the Nanda dynasty became powerful and usurped the sovereignty of Magadha. The nine Nandas have been assigned 22 years as the length of their reigns (343-321 BCE). It was Cāṇakya who uprooted this dynasty by putting Dhanānanda, the last reigning Nanda king, to death.[23] All the three traditions, Purāṇic, Buddhist and Jaina, are unanimous about this historic event. The genealogies and chronology of the kings mentioned above are very reliable. The genealogical lists of kings of the dynasties of pre-Maurya period do not agree with those of the Purāṇas in respect of

23. For all *Mhv.*, ed. W. Geiger, II.28-32, IV.1-8, V.14-15; tr. W. Geiger and M.H. Bode, introd. and pp. XL-XLVI, 12, 15, 21, 162 f, 168 f.

their names, order and regnal years and total duration of their rule. However, the Purāṇic and Buddhist lists are supplementary to each other so far as their names are concerned and they have relative value, but about the rest the latter stands as corrective to the former.

The Nanda dynasty came to an end in 321 BCE. It was supplanted by the Maurya dynasty. The *Mahāvaṁsa* also supplies us with information about the origin or parentage of its founder, Candagutta. He was the son of the chief queen of the king of Kṣatriya or Moriya clan (a branch of the Śākyas then ruling over Pipphalivana).[24] He is said to have ruled for 24 years which exactly agrees with the Purāṇic chronology. (Thus he ruled from 321 to 297 BCE) And his son Bindusāra ruled for 28 years (297-269 BCE). But according to the Purāṇas, the length of his reign is 25 years (297-272 BCE) which appears to be more appropriate than the former.

The *Mahāvaṁsa* as well as the *Dīpavaṁsa* state that Aśoka was formally crowned as a king 218 year after the death of the Buddha.[25] Thus it was (483–218 =) 265 BCE. Since he was crowned four years after his accession, the actual beginning of his reign, according to the Buddhist historical tradition, will go back to 269 BCE. However, there is another evidence to show that his coronation did not take place until 269 BCE[26] which means that he ascended the throne in 273 BCE which is near approximation to the truth. According to Purāṇic historical tradition he ruled for total 40 years (4 years before + 36 years after his coronation), i.e. from 272 to 232 BCE. This is the generally accepted reign period of this Maurya king. Both

24. *Mhv.*, tr. Geiger, p. 27; Comm. ed. Turnour introd. and pp. xxxviii-xlii.

25. *Dip.*, VI.1; *Mhv.*, V.21.

26. *Mhv.*, tr. Geiger, p. 28.

the chronicles deal with the propagation of Buddhism in Ceylon by Aśoka's son "Mahinda" and Buddhist establishments there. The historical statements are, of course, not always infallible. They also provide trustworthy accounts of three Buddhist Councils (already mentioned), eighteen different sects in the Buddhist order with their respective schools and systems that arose after the Second Council, and the Buddhist missionaries sent to far-off lands for spreading Buddhism after the Third Council. They furnish a good deal of information regarding towns and cities of the Buddha's time. The chronicles refer in common to all those places in India and Ceylon which are especially important in the history of Buddhism. The *Mahāvaṁsa* in particular throws some light on the relations between Coḷa-rattha and Ceylon. We are told that about the middle of the second century CE a Coḷa prince named Elāra conquered the Island and ruled there for a fairly long period. These two chronicles have great value as sources of authentic historical tradition and information.

A.K. Warder, while dealing with historical writing in ancient India, has correctly stated that some of the Pāli canons and commentaries, and the two chronicles are historical records.[27]

The Buddhists presented history also in the form of an *avadāna*. We have, of course, some *avadāna*s in Sanskrit in which we find some evidence of historical writing.

The *Aśokāvadāna* was composed in the first century of the Christian Era by an anonymous Buddhist writer of the Sarvāstivāda School. Some scholars suggest a later date of its composition, i.e. second or early third century CE.[28] It is

27. Cf. C.H. Philips (ed.), *Historians of India, Pakistan and Ceylon*, vol. I of *Historical Writing on the Peoples of Asia*, pp. 46-56.

28. *Aśokāvadāna*, ed. S.K. Mukopadhyay, p. lx.

basically a biographical work. It speaks of Aśoka and his times. Besides, it contains some other historical information too. It is primarily based upon the *Aśokasūtra* composed in Mathurā some time after the middle of the second century BCE or between 150 and 50 BCE which is no longer extent in original. It contains some stories of historical character about the great king Aśoka himself. The *Aśokāvadāna* consists of four chapters or sections titled *Pamsupradanāvadāna, Vitāśokāvadāna, Kunālāvadāna* and *Aśokāvadāna.*

The text throws light on the Aṅga kingdom with its capital at Campāpurī of the time of Bindusāra of Magadha. It refers to the Magadhan capital Pāṭaliputra as having been attacked by his son Susima when his younger brother Aśoka was reigning there, but the former was overpowered by the latter. It mentions the *vihāras* built during the time of Aśoka. It is also stated therein that Upagupta, the teacher of Aśoka, was the son of Gupta, a rich merchant of Mathurā. The information supplied in it about Aśoka and his successors particularly Kuṇāla are of great value.[29] There are, of course, some discrepancies in the stories narrated in it about them. It also contains some information about Prasenajit, king of Kosala, and Buddha's visit to Vaiśālī and other areas in its vicinity.[30]

The *Divyāvadāna* in its present form is datable to the fourth century CE. It is one of the important historical compositions. It throws light on the prosperity of the Magadha kingdom.[31] Its capital Rājagṛha is described as a rich, prosperous and populous city at the time of Bimbisāra and Ajātaśatru.[32] It

29. SBLN, pp. 8-11.

30. Ibid., pp. 12-13

31. *Divyāvadāna* (supra), p. 425.

32. Ibid., p. 545.

was an important centre of inland trade where merchants flocked from different quarters to buy and sell their merchandise.[33] From Rājagṛha to Śrāvastī there was a trade route for the merchants.[34] In and around the city of Rājaṛha there were a number of important localities hallowed by the history of their associations with the Buddha and Buddhism.[35] The Magadhan capital Pāṭaliputra at the time of the Buddha was a great city.[36] The Gaṅgā formed the boundary between the kingdom of Magadha and the territory of the Licchavīs, who were followers of the republican system of government. The Licchavīs and the Vaiśālikas have been mentioned as two different confederate clans. Vaiśālī was the metropolis of the entire confederacy of eight confederate clans including the Vṛjikas and the Licchavīs.[37] The wonderful city of Vaiśālī was visited by the Buddha more than once.[38] The Videha kingdom with its capital Mithilā (which had originally monarchical constitution) also finds mention in it.[39] The Mallas, who were a republican community, had their headquarters at Kuśinārā which became famous because of the Buddha's *parinirvāṇa* there.[40] Vārāṇasī, the capital of Kāśī kingdom, is described as a prosperous, extensive and populous city. It was a famous trading centre in King Brahmadatta's time. The traders in

33. *Divyāvadāna* (supra), p. 397.
34. Ibid., pp. 94-95.
35. Ibid., pp. 143, 554.
36. Ibid., p. 544.
37. Ibid., pp. 55-56, 136.
38. Ibid., p. 208.
39. Ibid., p. 424.
40. Ibid., pp. 208-09.

his time used to come from Uttarāpatha.[41] Hastināpura, capital of the Kuru kingdom, is described as a rich, prosperous and populous city which was visited by the Buddha.[42] *The Mākandika-avadāna* has preserved the tradition about King Udayana of the Vatsa kingdom.[43]

The existence of King Muṇḍa, one of the descendants of Udāyi Bhadda, and King Kālāśoka called Kākavarnin, son of Śiśunāga, of Magadha is attested by the *Divyāvadāna*.[44] This work also contains a genealogy of the rulers of Maurya dynasty from Candragupta down to Puṣyadharman (Śatadhanvan) who preceded the last ruler, Bṛhadratha.[45] Chapters XXVI to XXIX contain many legends about some pre-Maurya and Maurya rulers with some kernel of historical truth. The *Aśokāvadāna*, which forms a very important part of this work, mainly deals with Aśoka and his successors. It is also recorded in this work that the citizens of Takṣaśilā revolted against the oppression of the Maurya officials during the reign of Bindusāra. Prince Susima, his eldest son and viceroy there, could not quell the disturbance. Then Aśoka was deputed by his father to put down the revolt. He succeeded in restoring order.[46] The *Aśokāvadāna* states that Aśoka was immediately succeeded by his grandson, Samprati, and not by his son, Kuṇāla.[47] The historical tradition recorded in the Purāṇas is also conflicting about the immediate successor of Aśoka. It contains some anecdotes

41. *Divyāvadāna* (supra), pp. 73 and 510 ff.
42. Ibid., p. 435.
43. Ibid., pp. 515-44.
44. Ibid., Ch. XXVI, p. 369.
45. Ibid., pp. 370-71, 409, 433-34.
46. Ibid., pp. 234, 262, 371, 407-08.
47. Ibid., ch. XXIX.

about his son and grandson. It further offers a glimpse into the conditions prevailing during the last phase of the reign of the great monarch Bṛhadratha which led to the disintegration of the Maurya empire. The last king of the Maurya dynasty was murdered by his own commander-in-chief, Puṣyamitra, whose name also figures in this work.

The *Mahāvastu-avadāna* is one of the earliest extant works in Sanskrit composed before the beginning of the Christian Era by an anonymous writer of the Lokottaravāda school. Its *Rājavaṁśa* section is of exceptional value from a historical point of view. It deals mostly with the history of the life of the Buddha. It appears that the Buddhist historians were not ignorant of the biographical tradition. It also contains a traditional record of the 16 *mahājanapadas* or big states of his time.[48] It describes in detail the Licchavīs of Vaiśālī and their close association with him. It also states that there were twice 84,000 Licchavī rājās residing within the city of Vaiśālī.[49] It speaks of all important kingdoms and towns and cities which flourished before and after the rise of Buddhism. It refers to the Kuru kingdom with its capital Hastināpura, the Pañcāla kingdom with its capital Kāmpilya, the Aśmaka kingdom with its capital Poṭana, the kingdom of Magadha with its capitals Rājagṛha of Bimbisāra's time and Puṣpāvatī (identical with Pāṭaliputra) of later time, the Vatsa kingdom with its capital Kauśāmbī ruled by King Udayana in the Buddha's time, the Kosala kingdom with its capital Sāketa, the Aṅga kingdom with its capital Campā, the kingdom of Kāśī with its capital Vārāṇasī, the Videha kingdom with its capital Mithilā, etc.[50] It also highlights the political relation between

48. *Mahāvastu*, ed. E. Senart, I, p. 34; II, p. 2, line 15.

49. Ibid., I, pp. 253 ff.

50. Ibid., I, pp. 34 f, 120, 283, 289, 348 ; II, pp. 2, 94-95, 419; III, pp. 47, 57, 90 f, 172, 208-09, 231, 361-63, 402.

the kings of Kāśī and Kosala kingdoms. We are informed that Kāśī came in conflict with Kosala several times and each time the king of Kāśī was defeated. At last when he was going to make a desperate final attack the king of Kosala refused to fight and abdicated his throne.[51] Vārāṇasī's commercial importance is also highlighted in this work. The place is described as a great trading centre of Buddhist India. Rich merchants of the city used to travel to far-off countries with ships laden with merchandise. It is also stated therein that wealthy merchants came to Vārāṇasī from Takṣaśilā with the object of carrying on trade.[52] The history of the foundation of Kapilavastu and the settlement of the Śākyas (republican clan) there is also related in this work.[53]

In the *Avadānaśataka*, it is fairly recorded that the ancient Kosala kingdom was divided into two great parts the river Sarayū serving as the wedge between the two, and that there was a war between the kings of North and South Kosala.[54] The kingdom of Magadha with its capital Rājagṛha, the localities in and around this city important in the history of Buddhism, the city of Vaiśālī and the adjoining area and the Buddha's travels to all these places, the importance of Śrāvastī, the famous capital of the Kosala kingdom in the time of the Buddha, as a trading centre, etc. also find mention in it.[55]

The *Bodhisattvāvadāna-Kalpalatā* of Kṣemendra (CE 1028-63 or 1028-89), a historian of Kashmir school, is an extremely

51. *Mahāvastu*, III, p. 349.

52. Ibid., II, pp. 166-67; III, p. 286.

53. Ibid., I, pp. 350 ff.

54. *SBLN*, p. 20.

55. Ibid., pp. 17-25; *Avadānaśataka*, ed. J.S. Speyer, 2 vols., St. Petersburg, 1906.

important work. It refers to Hastināpura, the capital of the Kuru kings (3rd *pallava*, p. 116; 64th, pp. 9, 62), the kingdom of Pañcāla with its capital Kāmpilya (66th, p. 4; 68th, p. 9), the kingdom of Videha with its capital Mithilā ruled by a king named Puṣpadeva (83rd, p. 9), the Kāśī kingdom with its capital Vārāṇasī (6th, pp. 31-32), Kosala which was an important kingdom during the days of early Buddhism and its king Prasenajit (100th, p. 2) and one of its capitals, Sāketa, which was adorned with domes (3rd, p. 2) and the visit of merchants of Śrāvastī to Ceylon (7th, p. 50). It is stated therein that Kauśāmbī, the capital of Vatsa kingdom, was ruled by the King Udayana, the contemporary of the Buddha (35th, p. 3). It throws some light on the Licchavī republic. The Vaiśālikas or the inhabitants of Vaiśālī called *gaṇa*s are said to have followed the republican constitution (20th, p. 38). It mentions Buddha's visit to Vaiśālī and neighbouring places (90th, p. 73). It furnishes us with fragments of historical information about the rule of King Aśoka over Magadha with its capital at Pāṭaliputra and his different activities and *stūpa*s and *caitya*s built by him (69th, pp. 6-7). This work also contains many stories about the Buddha of both legendary and historical character.

The *avadāna*s constitute an important part of Buddhist historiography.

The *Lalitavistara,* an important Sanskrit Buddhist text of the early first century CE, is a memoir of the early life of the Buddha. The stories narrated about him therein are partly mythical and partly historical. Besides, it contains some other valuable information about kingdoms and republics, towns and cities, etc. of his time. Kapilavastu, famous in the history of Buddhist India and the home of the republican kṣatriya tribe Śākyas, is described copiously therein as *mahānagara* or great city with four gates, tower, marketplaces, etc. It gives 500 as the number of members of the Śākya council.[56] It also refers to the 16 kingdoms of the Buddha's time including those of Magadha, Kosala, Vatsa, Cedī, Avantī, Kāśī, Matsya, Śūrasena with its capital Mathurā which was a rich, flourishing and populous city, and Kuru.[57] It further stated therein that Rājagṛha, the capital of Magadha kingdom, was a *mahānagara* or great city. It was much frequented by the Buddha.[58] It also provides a description of the people of Magadha. Vārāṇasī, the capital of Kāśī kingdom, was very famous for manufacturing cloth called *Kāśika-Vastra*.[59] This city was also visited by the Buddha. Śrāvastī, the most important capital city of Kosala kingdom in the Buddha's time, was full of kings, princes, ministers, councillors, brāhmaṇas, kṣatriyas, householders, etc.[60] The Videha dynasty is described as wealthy and prosperous. The Licchavīs of Vaiśālī and the system of the government they followed are also recorded in it.[61]

The Sanskrit Buddhist texts, unlike some of the Pāli texts, contain hardly any contemporary evidence of a historical character. They deal mostly with past events.

The *Buddhacarita* of Aśvaghoṣa, who flourished in the first century CE and adorned the court of Kaniṣka, is a biographical work (semi-historical) in Sanskrit. It deals with

---

56. *Lalitavistara*, ed. R.L. Mitra, pp. 28, 58, 77, 98, 101-02, 113, 123, 136-37, 243.

57. Ibid., pp. 20-22, 27, 109, 405-06, 412-13.

58. Ibid., pp. 239, 243, 246, 318, 398.

59. Ibid., 215.

60. *Lalitavistara*, ed. and tr. P.L. Vaidya, Ch. 1.

61. Ibid., Ch. III, p. 21.

the main events of the life of the Buddha from his birth to his death or *mahāparinirvāṇa*, but the extant portion of this work covers only up to his attainment of enlightenment. It in the original form throws some light also on his teachings and Buddhist doctrine. Since the celebrated author does not treat of the Buddha as a historical personality, this work cannot be considered a historical biography. It was originally composed in 28 cantos as is proved by its Chinese translation of the fifth century CE. But the Sanskrit text is available only in 17 cantos.[62] It is significant to note that despite the absence of an established tradition of biographical writing in those days the Buddhist scholars made some contributions in this field as appears from this work as well as the *Aśokāvadāna* which deals with the life history of Aśoka and some of the other Sanskrit texts which deal with the life of the Buddha, mentioned before.

The *Mahābodhivaṁsa* composed by a monk Upatissa in the eleventh century CE has also some considerable historical value. A credible list of the names of King Kālāśoka's ten sons including the most prominent Nandivardhana of pre-Nanda period and that of nine Nandas including the last king Dhanānanda who ruled over Magadha is provided therein (p. 98). It also provides us with an account of attainment of enlightenment of the Buddha. There is a general historical reminiscence underlying the stories of the three Buddhist Councils recorded in it. The different Buddhist schools that arose after the Second Council also find mention in it (pp. 96-7). It deals partly with the history of *bodhi*-tree in Ceylon which has its own importance in the realm of spread of Buddhism there.

62. *Buddhacarita* of Aśvaghoṣa, Eng. tr. (cantos I-XVII) E.B. Cowell, in SBE, XLIX, I, pp. 1-200.

Each *vaṁśa* work is a part of history. The tradition of composing and preserving such work was handed down from age to age. This tradition of the Buddhists continued till the nineteenth century. It may casually be mentioned here that the *Śāsanavaṁsa* of Paññāsāmi which belongs to that century (1861) deals with the history of the growth of Buddhism from the time of the *parinirvāṇa* of the Buddha to the time of the author of the said work.

The early Buddhist literature is important for the history of ancient India from the time of the Buddha down to Aśoka. While estimating the historical value of this literature, B.C. Law observes:

> From a time when Indian history emerges from confusion and uncertainties of semi-historical legends and traditions to a more definite historical plane, that is from about the time of the Buddha to about the time of Aśoka the Great, the literature of the early Buddhists is certainly the main, if not the only, source of the historical . . . information of ancient India, supplemented, however, by Jaina and Brāhmanical sources here and there.[63]

The *Mañjuśrīmūlakalpa*[64] composed in the ninth century CE in Sanskrit is one of the ancient historical records of the Indian Buddhists. It carries the political history of ancient India down to the eighth century CE dealing with the Nandas, Mauryas, Guptas, Maitrakas (of Valabhī), Maukharīs, Puṣyabhūtis and the Pāla ruler of Bengal, Gopāla, though in a sketchy manner. The author of the work states that Cāṇakya survived his master (Candragupta) and further served

---

63. *Geographical Essays*, p. 2.

64. Ed. T. Ganapati Shastri, 3 vols. (70, 76 and 84), Trivandram Sanskrit Series (Trivandrum, 1920-25).

Bindusāra as minister for a few years. The information contained in this work about the succession of the Gupta emperors is very important. This Tibetan Buddhist work also throws light on the early history of Nepal from the fifth to the eighth centuries.

3.2

Jaina Historiography

THE Jaina tradition of historical writing began in the fourth century BCE with the biographical one preserved in the canon. Bhadrabāhu I, who was a contemporary of the last Nanda King Dhanānanda of Magadha, and Candragupta Maurya, wrote the biography of Vardhamāna Mahāvīra about 300 BCE which is contained in his *Kalpa-sūtra*. The work consists of three different sections. The first section contains the biographies of the 23 Jaina *tīrthaṁkara*s (prophets of Jainism) who preceded Mahāvīra, the last and 24th *tīrthaṁkara* and a historical personality like Buddha. The main part of this section contains the detailed biography of Mahāvīra. The 23rd *tīrthaṁkara* named Pārśvanātha who lived 250 years before Mahāvīra was a real historical figure. He was the son of King Aśvasena of Vārāṇasī. He is said to have founded the Jaina doctrine which Mahāvīra later followed. In the said work we find the history of Jainism from its inception to the close of the fourth century BCE. A short biography of Mahāvīra has also been preserved in the first book of the *Ācārāṅga-Sūtra* and in the *Bhagavatī-Sūtra.* According to these three sources, Mahāvīra was born in Kundagrāma, a suburb of Vaiśālī (in north Bihar), in 599 BCE in a rich kṣatriya family. His father Siddhārtha was the head of a kṣatriya clan called the Jñātrikas, and his mother, Triśalā was the sister of Cetaka, the most famous among the Licchavī princes and rulers of Vaiśālī. As King Bimbisāra (called Śreṇika) of Magadha had married Cellana, the daughter of Cetaka, Mahāvīra was related to the ruling family of Magadha. Mahāvīra was married to Yaśodharā. In 570 BCE or in his thirteenth year, on the demise of his parents he renounced the world, left his home and became an ascetic in the quest of truth. He wandered for thirteen years. In 557 BCE, when he was 42 he attained spiritual knowledge or enlightenment near the Pārśvanātha hills and thereafter became popularly known as Mahāvīra. For the next 30 years he moved from place to place and preached his doctrine. He paid frequent visits to Magadha during the first 16 years of Bimbisāra's rule. He died at Pāvā near Rājagṛha at the age of 72 in 527 BCE.[1]

The biographical writings embodied in the above three works form part of the Jaina canonical literature which was redacted thrice between the fourth century BCE and the fifth century CE. The Jaina canon of the Śvetāmbara sect was finally compiled in the present form in the latter half of the fifth century CE at Vallabhi in Gujarat. The Digambara section of the Jainas redacted their traditional canon by the beginning of the Christian Era.

The anonymous *Kālakācārya-Kathānaka* related in the *Kalpa-Sūtra* (a recension of the fifth century CE) and further repeated in a number of later works throws light on the role the Jaina saint Kālaka played in the overthrow of King Gardabhilla (Gandharvasena Mahendrāditya, 74-61 BCE) of Ujjayinī (Ujjain capital of the kingdom of Avantī or western Mālwā) who

1. *Ācārāṅga Sūtra*, II.3, 399-402; *Kalpa-Sūtra*, 2.27; 4.90, 96; 5.113-147; The *Ācārāṅga Sūtra*, and the *Kalpa-Sūtra* of Bhadrabāhu tr. from Prākṛt by H. Jacobi, in SBE, XXII, I, *Kalpa-Sūtra*, pp. 217-70 (for life of Mahāvīra), pp. 271-75 (life of Pārśvanātha) and pp. 281-85 (life of Ṛṣabha) ; see also J.C. Jain. (*Life in Ancient India as depicted in the Jain Canons and Commentaries* (*6th Century BC to 17th Century AD*), pp. 6-14.

was none other than the father of famous king Vikramāditya. The story tells us that Kālaka in his bid to depose Gardabhilla because of his hostility with him and opposition of his unjust and tyrannical rule proceeded to "Sagakula" (the Prākṛt version of the Sanskrit Śakakula, i.e. Śakasthān or the lands of the Śakas or Scythians in Sindh which they had conquered after entering India) whose king was styled as "Sāhānusāhī" (Prākṛt version), i.e. "King of Kings," stayed there for some time and persuaded the Śaka chiefs or Sāhīs to accompany him to the kingdom of Mālwā and to invade it and overthrow the dynasty of the ruler of Ujjayinī and occupy the rich kingdom. The Śaka Satraps, 96 in number, marched with their forces towards Mālwā. They crossed the Indus and first came to Surāṣṭra and encamped near Dhakkagiri.[2] We are further told that they entered Lāṭadeśa (Gujarat) and therefrom reached Mālwā and invaded it. They first entered Ujjayinī (in 66 BCE) and besieged the city. After having finally defeated Gardabhilla and expelled him from his homeland (in 61 BCE) they occupied Ujjayinī and settled there and continued to rule till they themselves were expelled from there. It was only after four years of their rule that the Mālwā people led by their valiant leader Vikramāditya, the son of Gardabhilla, rose in open revolt and ousted the Śakas from Ujjayinī. Thereafter the glorious king Vikramāditya re-established himself on the throne of his ancestors (*Kālak. Kathā*, p. 43). This national victory was celebrated, and to commemorate this event a new Mālwā or Vikrama Era (or Saṁvat) was introduced in *c.* 57 BCE. The Śaka chief or Sāhī who occupied Ujjayinī at the instance of Kālaka was probably the first Kṣaharāta, a predecessor of Nahapāna, and the Śaka overlord Sāhānusāhī probably the predecessor of Maues. The

2. See *Ind. Ant.*, XLIII, 1914, p. 125.

work provides a glimpse of the Scythian rule in western India during the first century BCE. The *Prabhāvakacarita* of Prabhācandra Sūri (CE 1276) also contains the details of some important episodes in the life of Kālaka. The story narrated in the ancient work *Kālakācārya-Kathānaka* has, undeniably, some historical basis. K.P. Jayaswal has also admitted that it records a genuine historical tradition.[3]

Of all those Jaina non-canonical works which are of historical importance, mention may first be made of the *Tiloyapaṇṇatti* of Yativr̥ṣabha (CE 150-80)[4] of Digambara school. This Prākr̥t text was originally composed by him in CE 176. Its later recension may be ascribed to either CE 478[5] or 483.[6] The work in the present form in any case cannot be placed later than the sixth century CE. It is divided into nine major chapters and contains 8,000 verses. It is the most important of the early texts from a strictly historical point of view. It contains a biographical description of all 24 *tīrthaṁkara*s and records Purāṇic traditions about them. There are also some incidental references to Jaina doctrine in it. Besides, it supplies pontifical genealogy of Mahāvīra's successors or a list of succession of Jaina *guru*s after Mahāvīra up to ME 683, i.e. CE 156 (IV, 1474-95). It also throws some light on the dynastic history of ancient India from the first century BCE to the fifth century CE. It provides information about the Śakas occupation of Ujjayinī and the beginning and end of their rule (IV, 1496, 1501-03), some rulers of Pradyota and Śuṅga dynasties, minor dynasties of the post-Sātavāhana period like the Muruṇḍas and the Gaḍḍava, and the Guptas

3. *JBORS*, XVI, p. 233.

4. Ed. A.N. Upadhye and H.L. Jain (Sholapur, 1951).

5. N.R. Premi, *Jaina Sāhitya aur Itihāsa*, p. 64.

6. J.K. Mukhtar, *Varṇi Volume*, p. 331.

with period of their respective rules, etc. The full dynastic list with chronological details is contained in the text (IV, 86-99; also IV, 1501-14). On the whole, the work is important for the study of social, political and religious history of ancient India to a considerable extent.

The *Vasudevahiṇḍi*, a Prākr̥t work of the fifth century CE by Saṁghadāsagaṇi Vācaka (also called Dharmadāsa) and later completed by other writers probably in the latter half of the sixth century CE contains some historical information about the Yadu dynasty that ruled the kingdom of Śūrasena with its capital at Mathurā, the Magadhan kingdom of Bimbisāra's time, trade and commerce during the period from the first century BCE to the third century CE, etc. It is a work of quasi-historical nature having half legends and half history.[7]

The *Kuvalayamālā*, a Prākr̥t work composed by Udyotana Sūri[8] of Jābālipur (Jālor) in CE 778, is very valuable as it supplies in the long colophon (27 verses) at its end much useful historical information. The colophon has both historical and chronological importance. Vatsarāja of the colophon is none else but the Gurjara-Pratihāra king of Avantī. We are further informed that his great-grandfather Nāgabhaṭṭa I had founded the kingdom of Bhinnamāla and had extended it up to Broach. He was a great conqueror. The epigraphic records also speak of his glory.[9] The work provides good source material for the history of Gūrjaradeśa

7. *Vasudevahiṇḍi*, tr. B.L. Sandesaria, pp. 55 f, 100 f, 187-92; for trade and commerce see Motichandra, *Sārthavāha*, pp. 166-68; G.P. Singh, "Trade and Commerce in Ancient India in the Light of Jain and Buddhist Traditions Bearing on its Economic and Cultural Contacts with the Asian Countries", *SHC*, IV, 1, 1996, pp. 5-6.

8. Ed. A.N. Upadhye, pts. I & II, revd. edn. (Bombay, 1970).

9. *Ep. Ind.*, XII, pp. 202-03.

around Bhinnmāl where Jainism had a big following. It furnishes a very reliable account of internal and external trade and commerce of India.[10] It is also stated in the said Jaina work that the Hūṇa chief, Toramāṇa, who had established his sway over a large part of north-western India in the late fifth and early sixth centuries CE, was converted to the Jaina faith.

Somadeva Sūri of Digambara school flourished in the reign of Rāṣṭrakūṭa king Kṛṣṇa III (CE 940-68). His *Nītivākyāmṛta* (composed in CE 959)[11] is an excellent treatise on the science and art of politics covering the period from 100 BCE to CE 900. It deals with evolution of kingship, state, government, etc. His another work, *Yaśastilaka-Campū*,[12] was composed in the same year (CE 959) at the capital of Baddiga, the eldest son of Cāḷukya prince Arikesari. He was probably patronised by the later Cāḷukyas of Bādāmi. The author himself tells us that "he finished that work in Caitra Śaka year 881 (CE 959) during the rule of the Cāḷukya prince Kṛṣṇarāja Deva" which shows both his historical sense and chronological consciousness. The work portrays a vivid picture of contemporary life and society. It also throws light on the economic life of the people with special reference to trade and commerce.

Jaṭila or Jaṭāsiṁhanandī in his *Varāṅgacarita* (CE 700), Vīranandī (CE 978) in his *Candraprabhā-carita* (*sarga* 5) and

10. See also J.C. Jain, "Trade and Commerce in Ancient India (from Less known Jain Sources"), *QRHS*, XVII, 1, 1977-78, p. 49. The history of trade and commerce recorded in other non-canonical Jain texts also forms the part of the article.

11. *MDJG*, Bombay, 1887-88.

12. Ed. Sivadutt and K.P. Parab (Bombay, 1901-03); tr. G.C. Jain, *Yaśastilaka kā Sāṁskṛtika Adhyayan* (Amritsar, 1967); K.K. Handiqui, *Yaśastilaka Champu and Indian Culture* (Sholapur, 1949).

Hariścandra (CE 900) in his *Dharma-Śarmābhyudaya* (*sarga* 18) have provided though meagre but very important information about state and government, practical politics, etc. These are useful works on political theories and institutions in ancient India. They are to some extent useful for historical purposes.

The *Jambūdvīpaprajñapti-Saṁgraha*, a Prākr̥t text in 13 chapters by Padmanandī (CE 700),[13] is almost a semi-historical work. It contains useful information about historical geography of ancient India in Jaina tradition.[14] It is also important for religious history. It contains a record of pontifical succession for about seven centuries after Mahāvīra's *nirvāṇa*. It also speaks of 18 settlements of Bhojas of the Yādava group of pre-Bhārata war period (1.12).

Haribhadra Sūri, a Śvetāmbara scholar, who belonged to the latter half of the eighth century CE, in his *Āvaśyakavr̥tti* (CE 775) in Sanskrit provides reliable information about Mahāvīra's last phase of life.

Dhanapāla, a Śvetāmbara poet, wrote *Tilakamañjarī*,[15] in or about CE 970 during the reign of Siyaka-Harṣa (CE 949-72), the father of Vākpati *alias* Muñja (CE 974-94) the two early Paramāra rulers of Mālwā. The work provides a trustworthy account of the social, economic, cultural and artistic life of the people during the early medieval period. It is said that it "ranks among the few first-rate works written after Bāṇabhaṭṭa."[16]

13. *Jambūdvīpaprajñapti* with the commentary of Śānticandra (Bombay, 1920). It is of limited historical value.

14. *IHQ*, XIV, pp. 188 ff; XIV, 2, pp. 388-91.

15. Ed. Bhavadatta Shastri, 2nd edn. (Bombay, 1938); also Virendra Kumar, *Tilakamañjarī kā Ālocanātmaka Adhyayan* (Ujjain, 1978).

16. G.P. Yadava "Position of Women as depicted in Dhanapāla's Tilakamañjarī", *QRHS*, XXI, 1, 1981-82, p. 28.

The *Trilokasāra* (CE 973), a Digambara work by Nemicandra, preserves a dynastic list containing the names of Śaka kings, and rulers of the Pradyota and Śuṅga dynasties with their reign periods. It also contains the information about the period of the rule of the Guptas and that of the post-Sātavāhana dynasties, etc.

The *Titthogāli-Painna,* an old Prākṛt text by an anonymous Śvetāmbara scholar, and *Tīrthoddhāra-Prakaraṇa* contain lists of some important dynasties like Pradyota that ruled over Avantī in central India; Nanda, Maurya and Śuṅga that ruled over a big empire of Magadha in eastern India; the Śaka of western India and Gardabhilla of Ujjayinī. The important kings of some dynasties are also mentioned, and the total reign periods of the kings and the dynasties are also given. The dynastic lists are incomplete and the total reign periods as given by the Jaina scholars are not fully reliable.

Hemacandra (CE 1125-72), a celebrated poet, grammarian, and historian of Śvetāmbara school, made significant contribution to the evolution of historiography in ancient India. He adorned the court of Jayasiṁha Siddharāja (CE 1093 1143), and also enjoyed the patronage of his successor Kumārapāla (CE 1143-72), the Cāḷukya king of Gujarat. His *Pariśiṣṭaparvan* (in Sanskrit) is a work of immense historical value. It deals with the history of Magadha from Bimbisāra down to the time of Candragupta Maurya. It furnishes a dynastic list containing the names of some of the prominent kings of different dynasties that ruled over this kingdom with their genealogies, chronology and other relevant details. We are told that Bimbisāra (called Śreṇika) was the real founder of the Magadhan imperial power. He governed Aṅga as a separate province with Campā as its capital. During his lifetime his son Ajātaśatru (called Kūṇika) acted as a viceroy at Campā. His son and successor, Udāyin before ascending the throne of Magadha also acted as his father's Viceroy at Campā. But being overpowered with sorrow at the death of his father he transferred his capital from Campā to Pāṭaliputra (*Pariśiṣṭa,* VI, 22-188, pp. 42-43) which accords with the Buddhist tradition but is at variance with the Purāṇic tradition, according to which, he shifted his capital from Rājagṛha to Kuśumapura (Pāṭaliputra). We are further informed that Udāyin was a powerful king. He defeated and killed in a battle the king of a certain country whose son went to Ujjain (ibid., VI, 189-91). He had political relation with the king of Avantī (VI, 208). Nandivardhana (one of the sons of Kālāsoka, successor of Śiśunāga) was offered the throne of Magadha five years before 415 BCE (i.e. in 420 BCE). Nanda (Mahāpadma, the founder of Nanda dynasty), the son of a courtesan by a barber, became king of Magadha 60 years after the death of Mahāvīra (i.e. in 417 BCE). He and his descendants continued to rule Magadha for 95 years or till the last Nanda king was deposed by Viṣṇugupta (Cāṇakya) 155 years after the death of Mahāvīra (VI, 231-43). Thus, according to Jaina Śvetāmbara tradition recorded in the said work, the Nanda dynasty ruled from 417 to 322 BCE. This dynasty is said to have been supplanted by the Maurya dynasty. The work further throws some light on the origin of the Mauryas. According to the said tradition, Candragupta was the son of a daughter of the chief of a village of peacock-tamers (*mayūra-poṣaka*) which belonged to the Nandas (VIII, 229, pp. 56f) which does not agree with Purāṇic tradition, according to which, he was the son of the last Nanda monarch by his śūdra wife named Mura after whom Candragupta and his descendants were styled as Mauryas. The author of the work further tells us that Candragupta ascended the throne of Magadha 155 years after Mahāvīra's *nirvāṇa* (VIII, 339) which may be probably 322 BCE. His son Bindusāra (whose mother's name was "Durdharā") succeeded him on the throne (VIII, 439-43). In the absence of corroborative evidence it is difficult to prove the historicity of the said queen mother. However, the succession of the king is well proven. Apart from dynastic history, the work also deals with the history of Jainism of ancient period.[17]

The *Vividhatīrthakalpa* composed in CE 1332[18] by Jinaprabha Sūri of Śvetāmbara school is one of the important historical works of the Jainas. It is partly in Prākṛt and partly in Sanskrit. It describes old Jaina places of pilgrimage and traces the history of rise and growth of Jainism. It provides valuable information regarding the imperial Magadhan ruler Bimbisāra (called Śreṇika in Jaina tradition) and his sons and successors, including Ajātaśatru (called Kūṇika). It also highlights the political and commercial importance of Rājagṛha, the earliest capital of Magadha kingdom. The dynastic list contained in it includes the Pradyotas, Nandas, Mauryas and Śuṅgas. It throws light on early towns and cities.[19] It makes an incidental allusion to *śāsanapaṭṭikā* (the rules or laws of administration) of Vikramāditya.

In *Vividhatīrthakalpa,* we find an accurate description of the conquest of the Cāḷukya ruler of Gujarat Jayasiṁha Siddharāja (CE 1093-1143). In 1114, he defeated his feudatory the Ābhira ruler Rā Kheṅgāra and imprisoned him. In the same year, he conquered Saurāṣṭra and founded the Siṁha Era to commemorate the conquest of Saurāṣṭra. Sajjana, the Jaina

17. *Pariśiṣṭaparvan* (*Sthavirāvali-carita*), ed. H. Jacobi, pp. 41-43; see also A.K. Warder, *An Introduction to Indian Historiography,* pp. 59-61.

18. The text was not composed between CE 1303 and 1306 or in 1308 as held by some scholars.

19. *Vividhatīrthakalpa*, ed. Jinavijaya, p. 22.

minister, was appointed as *daṇḍanāyaka* (military governor) of Saurāṣṭra and continued to act till 1119.[20] This supplements the information recorded in ancient Indian history.

One of the distinctive features of *Vividhatīrthakalpa* is that its author gives the date of the sacking of Gurjaradeśa (Gujarat) by "Gajjanavi" as "Vikrama Saṁvat 1081" (CE 1025).[21] It is historically a proven fact that on his arrival at Anhilwāḍa (modern Pāṭan in Gujarat) in January 1025, Mahmud of Ghazni learnt that Bhīma Deo (a Cāḷukya king) with most of his followers had fled from the place. Those who had remained behind were defeated. The said Jaina text also refers to Alauddin Khilji's conquest of Gujarat in "Vikrama Saṁvat 1356" (CE 1299).

In his *Pāṭaliputrakalpa*, Jinaprabha gives a brief historical account of the Mauryas down to Samprati, one of the successors of Aśoka.

The Jaina *paṭṭāvalī*s, which are very important historical documents of both the Digambaras and the Śvetāmbaras, were maintained from the early times. The Prākṛt *Paṭṭāvalī* of the Nandī Saṁgha, which is one of the oldest Digambara *paṭṭāvalī*s, and the equally old Śvetāmbara *Tapāgaccha-Paṭṭāvalī* belong to CE 500-900 and are sufficiently reliable. Most of the *paṭṭāvalī*s in their present form belong to later medieval times (i.e. fifteenth-seventeenth centuries). They are full of discrepancies and are not very reliable about early times. Some of the old *paṭṭāvalī*s supply useful historical, cultural and geographical information. Some of the Śvetāmbara *paṭṭāvalī*s refer to Magadhan dynasties of the pre-Maurya period (from Bimbisāra to the end of the Nanda dynasty).

20. *Vividhatīrthakalpa*, ed. Jinavijaya, p. 9.

21. Ibid., 29.

Śreṇika (Bimbisāra), Kūṇika (Ajātaśatru) and Udayana have been mentioned as powerful kings of Magadha. Pālaka mentioned in the lists was the son of King Caṇḍa Pradyota of Ujjayinī and in the period of 60 years allotted to him Kuṇika and Udayana were ruling at Pāṭaliputra (cf. *Paṭṭāvalī-Samuccaya,* p. 17). The dynastic lists include Pālaka, the Nandas, the Mauryas, some of the Śuṅga rulers, the Śakas and the Gaddabhas or Gardabhilla, and the periods of their rule are also clearly stated (ibid., p. 197: *Tapāgaccha-Paṭṭāvalī,* vv. 1-3). Śvetāmbara *paṭṭāvalī*s are important from dynastic and chronological points of view. Apart from dynastic succession lists, pontifical genealogy of Mahāvīra's successors in both Digambara and Śvetāmbara tradition are contained in some of the *paṭṭāvalī*s. The Prākṛt *paṭṭāvalī* of the Nandī Saṁgha gives the years of individual *gurus* who succeeded Mahāvīra during that period of 683 years.[22] On the basis of a close and comparative examination of the *paṭṭāvalī*s the history with a detailed and exact chronology of the Jaina *saṁgha* through the ages may be reconstructed, and an interesting detail about the political history of the country during those centuries may be furnished. The *paṭṭāvalī*s and *guruvāvalī*s of the different Jaina *saṁgha*s, *gaṇa*s, etc. that developed in both the sects, besides the respective genealogies, contain the faithful accounts of the achievements of important *gurus,* often give the names of the royal patrons and devotees of such *guru*s and also shed some light on religio-cultural history of the period. Dr Walthur Schubring observes:

---

22. *Paṭṭāvalī*s, Eng tr. of the Digambara *Paṭṭāvalī*s by Hoernle, *Ind. Ant.*, XIX, pp. 233-42; XX, pp. 341-61; XXI, pp. 57-84; also in *Jaina Antiquary*, Arrah, XV, 2, pp. 1-7; *Jaina Siddhānta Bhāskara*, Arrah, I, 1, p. 37; I, 2-3, p. 32; I, 4, pp. 43, 51, 71, 78, 81, 103; *Paṭṭāvalī-Samuccaya* (A Collection of Śvetāmbara *Paṭṭāvalī*s), ed. Muni Darśanavijaya, I, pp. 17, 46, 150, 166, 197, 199, 200.

> It was based upon some misunderstandings which naturally arose when India was measured with the scale found in China, Babylonia and Egypt. Her sources of history often flow not so plainly by far as those of other empires of the past, but there are some where no historian would have the right to deny the existence of historical exactness. It is specially Jaina authors who develop this praiseworthy quality. History cannot be told more exactly than has been done, for instance, in the Jaina *guruvāvalī*s and *paṭṭāvalī*s. The care with which the history of the primitive Jaina community is written by Hemacandra and other later authors is highly meritorious. Of course, the *Pariśiṣṭaparvan* (and such other Jaina works) contains much legendary by-work, but is it not the same thing in the West where nobody would think of not taking notice of our own medieval chronicles where history and legend so often intermingle . . .[23]

Some of the Jaina *paṭṭāvalī*s of medieval period are very important from a historical point of view. They were written in Rajasthani on the same pattern as they were written in Prākṛt or Sanskrit in ancient times. *Kaduha Sect Paṭṭāvalī* was written in VS 1685 = CE 1628. The other *paṭṭāvalī*s include *Nagauri Luṅkagacchiya Paṭṭāvalī, Bāgaḍ-gaccha Paṭṭāvalī* and *Pipalak Śaka Paṭṭāvalī.* These *paṭṭāvalī*s provide information regarding the origin, the growth and division and subdivision of the Jain's respective *gaccha*s, the names of their *ācārya*s or *guru*s with their biographical sketches, their contributions in disseminating the *dharma*, the functions organised during their priesthood, etc.

Equally important like the *paṭṭāvalī*s are the *rājāvalī*s — brief chronicles of kings and some important events that took place in their times. The *Rājāvalī Kathā* (an anonymous

23. Quoted in J.P. Jain's *The Jaina Sources of the History of Ancient India (100 BCE – CE 900)*, pp. 216-17.

work of unknown period) about Candragupta Maurya deals with his life and achievements. Some important *rājāvalīs*, particularly about the rulers of Delhi, have come down to us. They generally begin in the seventh or eighth century CE and end at the time of their respective compositions. The *rājāvalī* of Delhi in Hindi verse composed by poet Kisanadāsa starts with Anaṅgapāla Tomara of Delhi in CE 852. The exact date of its composition is not known. A number of important *rājāvalīs* were produced by the Jaina scholars during the medieval period. *Dillī kī Rājāvalī* (anonymous, preserved in a *guṭakā* manuscript at Mainpuri) begins with the foundation of Delhi by Rāṇā Jāju in CE 772 (VS 829) and ends in CE 1489, which marks the beginning of the reign of Sikandar Lodi. *Dillī kī Rājāvalī* (anonymous, preserved in a *guṭakā* manuscript in the Jaina temple of Delhi) begins with the foundation of Tomara dynasty of Delhi with Rāṇā Jāju as its founder in CE 782 (VS 839) and ends in CE 1628 with the accession of Shahjahan who is said to have succeeded his father Shah Salema.

The tradition of writing *Rājāvalī* further continued in modern period. *Rājāvalī-kathe* of Devacandra written in 1834 does not fall within the scope of this work.

A *vākā* (or chronicle of events), by Ṛṣi Rūghā written in CE 1792, beginning with the foundation of Ujjayinī by Rājā Bhoja in CE 674 and ending in CE 1707 mentions the death of Aurangzeb and after him of Dīdārbaksha and the accession of Azamshah at Delhi.

There are a number of biographical works or the *carita-kāvyas* in both Prākṛt and Apabhraṁśa which deal with the life-stories of some historical Jaina heroes, religious leaders and great teachers of early time. The tradition of writing *caritras* in Purāṇic style dealing with the lives of individual heroes had already begun by the sixth century CE, but only few of them were written prior to CE 800. In fact, such works in historical style began to appear from the ninth century onwards. Some of the important works in Prākṛt are the *Mahāvīracarita* of Asaga (CE 853),[24] of Guṇacandra (CE 1082),[25] of Guṇabhadra Sūri (CE 1139) and of Nemicandra (CE 1170)[26] which relate the life and teachings of Mahāvīra, the *Pārśvanāthacarita*,[27] which deals with the life of Pārśvanātha, the real founder of Jainism, the *Ādināthacarita* of Vardhamāna (1103), etc. They supply us with such salient facts about the lives of these heroes as may be taken to be credible. The contemporary royal personalities also find incidental mention in some of these works. The facts and fictions have jumbled up in the stories narrated about them. However, the works to a certain extent bear the character of historical biographies. The other works include the *Mallināthacarita*, the *Neminaha-cariu* and the *Sanakunara-cariu* of Haribhadra (CE 750-75), the *Karakandu-cariu* (in Apabhraṁśa) of Kanakamāra (tenth century). The *Sudarśanacarita* of Nayanandī (CE 1042), the *Jambu-carita* (in Prākṛt) of Guṇapāla (the post-eighth century CE), of Vīra (CE 1019) and of Sāgaradatta (CE 1020) the *Śāntināthacarita* of Devacandra (CE 1108), the *Sumatināthacarita* of Somaprabha, the *Nemināthacarita* of Maladhari Hemacandra, the *Supasanahacarita* of Lakṣmanāgani (CE 1142) and the *Sanatkumāracarita* of Śrīcandra (CE 1157). They chiefly deal with the spiritual life and religious deeds of the Jaina saints concerned. These works are more of a legendary than

24. *Vardhamāna-carita of Asaga* (Sholapur, 1931).

25. *Mahāvīracarita of Guṇacandra* (Bombay, 1929).

26. Premi, op. cit., pp. 74-91, 111-14, 199 (for all important Jain biographical works).

27. See *Pārśvanāthacaritam (The Life and Stories of the Jain Saviour Pārśvanātha)*, tr. M. Bloomfield (Baltimore, 1919).

historical character. Their values lie only in those facts which are related to the Jaina doctrine. The most important among the Jaina biographical works in Apabhraṁśa is Puṣpadanta's *Mahāpurāṇa*[28] which was composed some time between CE 940 and 968 under the patronage of the Jaina ministers of the Rāṣṭrakūṭa king Kr̥ṣṇa III. This work consists of biographies of nearly 63 *śalākāpuruṣas* (persons of great note). The work besides containing biographical accounts deals with socio-economic life in the early period. The two other notable works by the same author are the *Jasahara-cariu*[29] and the *Nayakumāra-cariu.*[30] The *Triṣaṣṭiśalākapuruṣacarita* of Hemacandra[31] also contains biographies of some important historical personages including Kumārapāla, the Cāḷukya king of Gujarat who was one of his patrons. The tradition of biographical writing was further carried on by the Jaina scholars in the medieval period. The *Śreṇika-carita* of Jinadeva (CE 1444) deals with the life of Śreṇika (Bimbisāra). These are semi-historical biographies. The historical biographies written during the medieval period are included in the fourth book of this work.

The period falling in between the accession of Dantidurga in CE 733 and the end of the rule of Amoghavarṣa I in CE 877 or 878 (the two famous Rāṣṭrakūṭa kings) produced a marvellous gallaxy of Jaina authors who produced a large number of valuable works in different languages on different subjects many of which are important for the political and cultural history of early India. The authors were actually patronised by the Rāṣṭrakūṭas. One of the authors was Swāmī

28. D.K. Jain, ed., 4 vols., *MDJG* (Delhi, 1979-83); P.L. Vaidya, 3 vols. (Bombay, 1937-41).
29. Edited with notes by P.L. Vaidya (Karanja, 1931).
30. Edited with notes by H.L. Jain (Karanja, 1933).
31. Tr. H.M. Johnson, I-VI (Baroda, 1931-62).

Vīrasena (CE 710-90) of Digambara school who wrote the *Dhavalā*, the *Jayadhavalā* and *Mahādhavalā* in Prākṛt and Sanskrit (mixed). He completed his famous work, *Dhavalā*, in CE 780 but his other works remained incompleted. His *Jayadhavalā*[32] was completed by his disciple Jinasena III in CE 837. The *Dhavalā* transmits information about some contemporary kings with their dates. The *Dhavalā* of Vīrasena and the *Jayadhavalā* of Jinasena contain almost idential dynastic lists with the names of the rulers of Pradyota and Śuṅga dynasty. The Śaka king, the post-Sātavāhana kings and dynasties, the Guptas, etc. also figure in the lists. The reign-periods of all are also mentioned. The historical and chronological data contained in the works are of equal importance. The genealogy of the 28 immediate successors of Mahāvīra divided into five groups together with the periods taken by each group has been preserved in both these works. This historic record of pontifical succession for about seven centuries after Mahāvīra's *nirvāṇa* is of unique value.

Some of the Purāṇic records of the Jains are also rich in historical contents. The *Padma Purāṇa* (CE 676-77) in Sanskrit (with 18,000 verses divided into 123 Parvas) of Ravisena;[33] the *Harivaṁśa Purāṇa* (CE 783) in Sanskrit (with 10,000 verses divided into 66 *sargas*) of Jinasena II[34] (Jinasena I of the third century CE being the author of the *Vardhamāna Purāṇa* about Mahāvīra), who flourished in the Rāṣṭrakūṭa age; the *Ādi Purāṇa* with 47 *sargas* of Jinasena III[35] (the religious preceptor of the Rāṣṭrakūṭa emperor Amoghavarṣa I (CE 815-77); and the *Uttara*

32. *BGP*, Kasi, 1947.

33. Ed. Pannalal Jain, 3 vols., 1st edn., *BGP* (Kasi, 1958-59).

34. Ed. Pannalal Jain, *BGP* (Kasi, 1962).

35. Ed. Pannalal Jain, 1st edn., *BGP* (Kasi, 1951); see also Nemicandra Shastri, *Ādi Purāṇa meiṅ Pratipādita Bhārata* (Varanasi, 1968).

Purāṇa (CE 898) with *sargas* 48-73 of Guṇabhadra[36] (who was patronised by the Rāṣṭrakūṭa king Kṛṣṇa II, CE 877-914) forming two different parts of the *Mahāpurāṇa* are valuable from a historical point of view. These Purāṇas contain some historical portions. Abundant wealth of historical material are embodied in them. They in common throw a good deal of light on different aspects of history and culture of India of ancient and early medieval periods. They deal with society, economy, trade and commerce, polity and administration, state and government, kings and kingdoms, towns and cities, religion and culture, art and architecture, Aryan and non-Aryan peoples, etc. The authors of the works furnish useful information about the life and society of their respective contemporary age.

Jinasena III defines history "as an account of past happenings, which must be authoritative, truthful and righteous" (*Ādi Purāṇa*, I, 24-25). This Purāṇa deals with the history of 63 famous men including kings, emperors and the Jaina heroes. Jinasena II, the author of the *Harivaṁśa Purāṇa* in particular, was more or less an *itihāsakāra*. He gives the history of Jainism down to his own time. He mentions Indrāyudha (CE 783-84), the ruler of Kānyakubja (Kannauj) in the north, Vatsarāja, the Gurjara-Pratihāra king of Avantī in central India, whose identity as the father of Nāgabhaṭṭa II (CE 805-33) is well established, and Dhruva Nirupama also called Śrī-Vallabha (CE 779-94), the Rāṣṭrakūṭa king of Deccan, who were all his contemporaries. The dynastic list furnished by him contains the names of some rulers of the Pradyota

36. Ed. Pannalal Jain, revd. edn., *BGP* (Kasi, 1954); see also R.B. Singh, "Jaina Purāṇas as a Source of Social History", *PIHC*, 38th Session (Bhubaneswar, 1977), pp. 127-29 for historical material in the *Ādi Purāṇa* and *Uttara Purāṇa* relating to social life in ancient India.

and Śuṅga dynasties. The Gaddava kings of Ujjayinī, the Śakas, the Hūṇas, the Guptas, etc. also figure in the said list with lengths of their respective reigns. He also supplies the dynastic chronology for the first 1,000 years beginning with Mahāvīra's *nirvāṇa* and ending with the termination of the age of the Hūṇas (*Harivaṁśa, sarga* 60, vv. 487-92, 551-52). The dynastic list given in this Purāṇa is almost identical with the corresponding list of the *Uttara Purāṇa.*

The Jaina *purāṇakāra*s were endowed with a remarkable historical sense. They have, in fact, preserved ancient Indian history in their respective works. They have maintained to a great extent the objectivity in their presentation of the subject matter. They have debunked Brāhmanical history and myth in the sense of making the narratives or stories more rational.

The *praśasti*s of Jaina authors also constitute a valuable literary source of ancient Indian history. These *praśasti*s occur in the works which were produced after the seventh century CE. They are generally found at the beginning or end of the works, or at the end of some or all chapters of a work. They are of various types. The *praśasti* of the author gives details about himself, his religious genealogy, when and for whom he wrote the work, etc. It sometimes mentions the name of the place and that of the ruler of the territory as well. The *praśasti* of the donor provides facts about his family and about the *guru* to whom the manuscript was given as a gift. We come across such information more in manuscripts from Gujarat and Central India than in those from Karnataka and Tamiladeśa. The works produced prior to the tenth or eleventh century CE contain mostly the first type of *praśasti.* The *praśasti*s of a number of later works contain useful historical information pertaining to older times, the most notable example of which is *Vaḍnagar Praśasti*s of Kumārapāla

(CE 1143-73), the Cāḷukya ruler of Gujarat, found in CE 1152, according to which, Vanraj Chavda founded the capital of Pāṭan in CE 746 and his dynasty ruled in Gujarat for about two centuries. The *praśastis* (inscriptions) were composed by Jaina poets to record important historical events. The *praśastis* composed in Gujarat during medieval period contain valuable historical information about kings and rulers and the events of their times. The notable examples of such *praśastis* are Śrīdhara's *Veraval Praśasti* and *Dabhoi* (or *Davoi*) *Praśasti* of Viśāladeva the Vāghelā king of Gujarat (CE 1244-62). The Veraval inscription of Bhīma II, the Cāḷukya king of Gujarat (CE 1178-1241), was composed by Śrīdhara. The inscription on the wall of Śiva temple renovated by King Viśāladeva in VS 1311 = CE 1254 at Davoi was composed by Someśvara, the author of *Kīrtikaumudī* and *Surathotsava*.

The inscriptions in the Jaina temples built by Vastupāla (during the rule of Vāghelā kings of Gujarat) on Mount Ābu and Girnār were also composed by Someśvara.

The *praśastis* (chronicles-cum-biographies) by Jaina scholars of Gujarat are included in the fifth book of this work.

The Jaina works of the ancient period mentioned above as a whole deal with different aspects of history and culture of India. They provide a systematic history of India from the time of Mahāvīra to the rise of the Maurya empire. The history of Jainism recorded in them is of exceptional value. They provide only little information about the post-Maurya dynasties, Gurjara-Pratihāras, Cāḷukyas, Rāṣṭrakūṭas, etc. We do not find continuity in the presentation of Jaina authors about them. They are selective in picking out the regions and historical personalities and usually do not give continuous history. Some historical works deal in part with the events of the post-Mahāvīra period. However, the details of contemporary life and society, general economy, polity, religion, art and culture, etc. provided in some of the works are of great historical value. The works of the period under discussion, in fact, provide the general history of ancient India as they cover various regions and touch on various dynasties. The Jaina works of medieval period are important for the study of kingdoms and dynasties, kings and rulers, early Muslim invasions of India, etc.

The *prabandha*s were written by the Śvetāmbara scholars of Gujarat during the period from the thirteenth to the fifteenth centuries. These works are purely of historical character and very valuable for a reconstruction of the history of Gujarat. The *prabandha*s of Rajasthan also belong to the medieval period. The *prabandha*s — historical biographies and chronicles — have been put in Book Four and Five respectively of this work. The chronological data furnished by the Buddhist and Jaina historians also figure separately in detail in Book Seven.

Book Four
The Tradition of Writing Historical Biography

Introductory Remarks

A HISTORICAL biography in the true sense of the words deals with the life, achievements and deeds of a historical personality, royal personage, eminent king, famous queen, great ruler, emperor, prince, chief or the great religious leader and reformer who occupies an important place in the local, regional or national history. The work on a prominent figure who has a place in the social, economic, political, religious or cultural history of any country may also be considered as a historical biography. It is based more on facts than fictions. It can easily be distinguished from a biography of an ordinary peron, literary figure or spiritual leader and a biography of semi-historical nature.

> Historical biography, though revolving round a person or persons, transcends the narrow limits of mere biological evolution. In a sense it partakes of the character of true history and even of universal history, involving due research, interpretation and historical thought processes. It is not only a reflection of the forces of the age but also a product of the dynamic personality or personalities, constituting the theme of the historical biography.[1]

The history of historical biography in India is not as old as in China, Greece and Rome. Though the Chinese historian

---

1. J.N. Sarkar, "Historical Biography in Mediaeval Indian (Persian) Literature", in *Historical Biography in Indian Literature*, ed. S.P. Sen, p. 46.

Ssu-ma Chien (145-58 BCE) initiated the tradition of biographical writing by dealing with the lives of a number of eminent personalities, all his contemporaries, in his *magnum opus* the *Shih-chi* produced in 100 BCE, it was the Greek historian Plutarch (CE 50-125) who got universal recognition as a "father of biography" because of writing the biographies of 46 famous historical personages of Greece and Rome in his *Parallel Lives* (also called *Lives of the Noble Grecians and Romans*). The *Life of Alexander the Great* by him also forms the part of his work. His contemporary the Roman historian Tacitus (CE 55-120), also became famous for his biographical works, *Life of Julius Agricola,* the *Annals* that covered the period from the death of Augustus to CE 69, and the history that covered also the Flavian emperors. The works of Plutarch and Tacitus can be regarded as the best specimens of historical biography that the ancient world produced. The art of writing biography appears to have developed in Greece and Rome in the first and second centuries of the Christian Era. In India, it was the seventh century which marked the beginning of the tradition of writing historical biography. The ancient Indians had their own conception of a biographical history which needs no comparison with that of the ancient Greeks and Romans. Their historical tradition including the biographical one was different from each other. And so is the case with the themes and qualities of their biographical works. However, the different traditions of biographical writing that evolved in China, Greece, Rome and India in different ages went a long way in according the biographical history a place it deserved.

Historical biographies in ancient and medieval India were generally composed in royal courts under the patronage of kings or princes concerned. The court historiographers not only enjoyed the royal patronage but also received the encouragement to record the history of their respective times which gradually led to the development of historical writing in India in pre-modern age. The writing of historical biographies in ancient India marked the significant stage in the development of the Itihāsa tradition. In medieval India in particular, many biographical works were composed independently giving detailed accounts of the lives and achievements of the kings and rulers concerned which are more authentic than what we find in the works completed under the royal patronage. The authors of historical biographies while dealing with the lives and deeds of kings, rulers or their patrons also touched on side by side their pedigree or genealogies, political relations with other kings and the historical events that took place before and during their times. Some authors have also focused on history and culture of the contemporary age.

A historical biography bears to some extent the character of a chronicle and vice versa. N.R. Ray has correctly stated that:

> . . . there is always a larger place for chronicle in a biography. . . . A historical biography is not worth its name if it does not attempt first to reconstruct the life of an individual it chooses as its subjects on the basis of unimpeachable evidence, and second to interpret and assess the impact of the personality on the age to which it belongs, or for that matter, the influence of the age and environs on the making of the individual whose life-story it delineates.[2]

Pointing to the place of biography in history, Carlyle observed: ". . . history is the biography of great men." Again, "History is no more than the sum total of innumerable biographies."

2. J.N. Sarkar, *Historical Biography in Indian Literature*, Preface, vi.

Historical biographies of ancient period as a whole are in Sanskrit, Prākṛit and Apabhraṁśa and those of medieval period in Sanskrit, Hindi and regional languages. Their writers in ancient period were mainly the Hindus and the Jains and in medieval period the Hindus, Jainas, Muslims and Sikhs. Various types of historical biography were produced in India during the period. The biographical works are by and large faithful records of the lives of kings, queens, rulers, emperors, princes, religious reformers and others who left indelible imprints of their personalities on the history of their respective periods.

The statement of a great orientalist, Maurice Winternitz, that "History and biography have in India never been treated other than by the poets and as a branch of epic poetry"[3] is very misleading. In fact, historical works including biographical ones have in India been written also by other than the poets and most of them are in prose. It is an established truth that such works were written both in verse and prose and some of their authors were well equipped with the skill of a historian.

The biographical tradition of historiography was fairly maintained in ancient and medieval India.

3. *HIL*, I, Introduction, p. 3.

4.1

Historical Biographies

Of all the extant historical biographies of ancient times, mention may first be made of the *Harṣacarita* of Bāṇa (Bāṇabhaṭṭa),[1] the court-poet-cum-historian of Harṣa (CE 606-48) of Sthānavīśvara (modern Thāneśvar in Haryana) and Kānyakubja (Kannauj). Bāṇa himself calls his work an *ākhyāyikā* as it has a historical basis. It consists of eight *ucchavāsa*s (chapters). In the first chapter, the author speaks of his own ancestry and lineage. According to the information supplied by him, he was the son of Citrabhānu in the Vātsyāyana line of the Bhārgava brāhmaṇas. His ancestral home was at Prītikūṭa, a village situated on the western bank of the river Śona within the limits of the kingdom of Kānyakubja. The first three chapters are devoted, of course, partly to the life and family of the author himself. He belonged to the family which was famous for scholary tradition. His inclination towards or interest in history was quite consistent with his family tradition.

Harṣa's ancestors find mention in the third chapter of the *Harṣacarita*. The author of the work informs us that it was Puṣpabhūti who founded the kingdom of Śrīkaṇṭha with

1. Ed. P.V. Kane (Bombay, 1918, rept., Delhi, 1965); K.P. Parab, 3rd edn. (Bombay, 1912); Eng. tr. E.B. Cowell and F.W. Thomas (RAS, London, 1897, 2nd edn., 1929); Hindi tr. V.S. Agrawala, *Harṣacarita: Ek Sāṁskṛtika Adhyayana* (Patna, 1964).

its capital at Sthānavīśvara (in the late fifth or early sixth century CE). He has been described also as the founder of the royal Vardhana dynasty. His successors, Naravardhana, Rājyavardhana and Ādityavardhana (mentioned in Madhuvana Copperplate Inscription of Harṣa) do not find place in the genealogy preserved in the work. These kings who flourished probably between CE 500 and 580 were the feudatory chiefs. They might have acknowledged the supremacy of the Guptas and the Maukharīs. The next king in the line of Puṣpabhūti, as mentioned in the work was Prabhākaravardhana who was blessed with two sons Rājyavardhana and Harṣavardhana, and a daughter, Rajyaśrī.

Prabhākaravardhana (CE 580-605) was an eminent and powerful king. After having expanded the frontiers of his paternal kingdom by annexing to it the territories of the conquered kings he assumed the titles, *mahārājādhirāja* and *paramabhaṭṭāraka*. His wars and conquests have been described in the fourth and fifth chapters. The information Bāṇa provides about him in the former, of course, in the metaphorical style is useful to a historian. He says that "he was a lion to the Hūṇa deer, a burning fever to the king of Sindhudeśa, a troubler of the sleep of Gurjara king, a bilious plague to that scent-elephant, the lord of Gandhāra, a destroyer of the pride of the Lāṭas, and an axe to the goddess of fortune and glory of Mālwā." He appears to have extended his political sway to the Hūṇa territories in the Punjab which marked the limit of the north-western frontier of his kingdom. In the east it was conterminous with the Maukhari state of Kannauj and on the west and south it just covered portions of the Punjab and the Rājpūtānā desert. He achieved partial success in subduing the king of Sindhudeśa. However, the latter accepted the political hegemony of the former. Gandhāra, which was then under the rule of Kuṣāṇas (a branch of those who had established themselves in the Kabul Valley), could not be brought within the limits of the kingdom of Prabhākaravardhana. The Gurjaras of Bhinnamāla and the king of Lāṭadeśa simply tendered their submission. Mālwā was, of course, annexed to his kingdom which can be substantiated by the fact that the two sons of the defeated Mālwā king, Kumāragupta and Mādhavagupta, were sent to his court to confirm their acceptance of his overlordship, as stated in the text. In the fourth chapter itself it is stated that Rājyaśrī was married to Grahavarman, the son of the Maukhari Prince Avantivarman of Kannauj.

The fifth chapter is devoted to Prabhākaravardhana's and his eldest son Rājyavardhana's conflicts with the Hūṇas. The former has been called "Hūṇahariṇakesarī" because of his resounding victory over the Hūṇas. The Hūṇas, who were defeated by him with the help of his relative, Avantivarman of Kannauj (in CE 575 or 582) were none other than the petty Hūṇa chief of the northern Punjab with their metropolis at Śākala where they continued to rule after the dismemberment of the Hūṇa kingdom in about CE 563 or 567. In order to strike another blow to the Hūṇas, Prabhākaravardhana sent Rājyavardhana on a military expedition against them in the Uttarāpatha. But before they could be finally subdued Rājyavardhana returned back to the capital on account of the illness of his father. His father had already expired and his mother had burnt herself to death on the bank of the Sarasvatī River. We are further told in the sixth chapter that Rājyavardhana because of being shocked and terribly upset offered the throne to his younger brother, Harṣa. The latter too was not willing to accept the throne and ultimately the former had to ascend the throne of Thāneśvar (in CE 605). No sooner had Rājyavardhana ascended the throne he received the sad news that the king of Mālwā or Avantideśa (who is identical with Devagupta of the Madhuvana and Bāṅskheṛā charter) had attacked and killed Grahavarman and imprisoned his wife Rājyaśrī and put her into the dungeon cell in Kānyakubja. He chalked out a plan to attack also Thāneśvar. However, Rājyavardhana in order to avenge the death of his brother-in-law and the humiliation of his sister at once marched with his troops for Mālwā leaving his younger brother Harṣa in the capital. He had successfully routed the Mālwā army and defeated King Devagupta but he was himself treacherously assassinated by the king of Gauḍa called Śaśāṅka (contemporary of Harṣa) who had come all the way from his distant kingdom to assist his ally, King Devagupta of Mālwā. This is the coalition of common enemies of Rājyavardhana which has been perhaps called by Bāṇa "Śaśāṅkamaṇḍala." He says that "Śaśāṅka threw Rājyavardhana off his guard by offering to marry his daughter to him as a token of submission and friendship and when he was weaponless, confiding and alone, the Gauḍa king despatched him to his own quarters and killed there." Having thus avenged the defeat of Devagupta of Mālwā the Gauḍa monarch Śaśāṅka occupied Kannauj and released the widowed Maukhari queen, Rājyaśrī, from captivity in her own capital. Bāṇa has maintained sequence and coherence to a considerable extent in the narration of events.

Harṣa was only sixteen years of age at the time he heard the news of the tragic end of Rājyavardhana. He was a bit reluctant to occupy the throne. But after being persuaded by the councillors of the state he agreed to take the reign in his hand, and ultimately ascended the throne of Thāneśvar (in CE 606). The immediate task before him was to rescue his sister, who, after having escaped from the prison, had entered the Vindhya forest, and to relieve Kannauj from the control of Śaśāṅka. When he was about to set out on his *digvijaya* (conquest) with a strong force, Haṁsavega, a messenger of King Bhāskaravarman of Prāgjyotiṣa (Assam), entered his court with gifts and message of friendship. A perpetual treaty of friendship between these two contemporary kings was concluded as stated by Bāṇa in the seventh chapter of his work. The said messenger in the course of narrating the early history of Assam told Harṣa the names of some of the prominent rulers of different dynasties including those of the predecessors of Bhāskaravarman of Varman dynasty who ruled over the kingdom concerned, as we find in the same chapter.

After the departure of Haṁsavega from Thāneśvar, Harṣa entered the Vindhya forest and made a vigorous search for his sister, Rājyaśrī, and at last with the help of forest chiefs like Vyāghraketu, Bhūkampa and Nirghāta and a Buddhist monk, Divākaramitra, rescued her at the moment when she was about to immolate herself. He along with his sister returned to his camp on the bank of the Gaṅgā, as described in the seventh and eighth chapters of the work. In these two very chapters Bāṇa has described in detail the life and culture of the tribal people of the Vindhya region with special reference to the Śabaras.

We are informed by Bāṇa that Harṣa made an elaborate preparation to wage war against the Gauḍa king Śaśāṅka, who is described as "the vilest of Gauḍas" and the "vile Gauḍa serpent." But he does not provide us with any detail of the war between the two. It seems that the friendly alliance between Harṣa of Thāneśvar and Bhāskaravarman of Kāmarūpa (one of the ancient names of Assam) struck fear in the mind of Śaśāṅka, and instead of facing an impending danger he withdraw from Kannauj which paved the way for Harṣa to establish his rule there. He probably in the last phase of his life transferred his capital from Thāneśvar to Kannauj and made it the seat of his power. Thus, he not only inherited the paternal kingdom but also got the Maukhari throne of Kannauj. The amalgamation of these two kingdoms helped him in consolidating his position and extending his authority and influence in all directions.

Bāṇa, while describing Harṣa as a warrior and conqueror, informs us (in the third chapter) that he conquered Sindhudeśa and annexed it to his kingdom and thereby completed the unfinished task of his father. The river Indus formed the western boundary of his empire. In the same chapter we are further informed that kings of the states in the Himalayan region were also subjugated by him. They after acknowledging his political supremacy started paying taxes to him. His conquest of Mālwā and its annexation to his kingdom finds mention in the seventh chapter of the author's work. These initial successes he achieved as a king of Thāneśvar. We do not get a clear picture of the extent of Harṣa's empire. However, it is true that he earned name and fame as the last great Hindu emperor of north India.

The information furnished by Bāṇa in the second chapter of his work regarding the administrative system and military organisation of Harṣa is of considerable historical value. He has highlighted the feudal structure of his administration. It may be stated here that the increase in the number of *sāmanta*, *mahāsāmanta* and feudatory chiefs after the disintegration of the Gupta empire had great bearing on the administrative system of Harṣa. Bāṇa has presented an enlarged picture of the feudal system that had already existed in ancient India prior to Harṣa's time. The same system continued in the time of Harṣa. According to Bāṇa, there were different categories of *sāmanta*, viz. *sāmanta*, *mahāsāmanta*, *āptasāmanta*, *pradhānasāmanta*, *śatrumahāsāmanta* and *pratisāmanta* who offered their services to Harṣa and his predecessors. The *sāmanta*s ruling over the territories assigned to them used to pay taxes annually to the said kings. They used to render all kinds of services to the kings. Those who occupied high positions among the *sāmanta*s were designated *pradhānasāmanta*. *Śatrumahāsāmanta*s were conquered chiefs who had to obey the orders of the king. They were treated with some respect. All other *sāmanta*s had to offer their services in the kingly court and royal palace whenever needed. The loyal and faithful *mahāsāmanta*s used to accompany the kings while going on military expedition. Some of the feudatory kings in the time of Harṣa also find mention in the work. Bāṇa has also focused on the inter-state relations in the time of Harṣa. The policies he followed towards kings are in perfect harmony with what we find in the *Prayāga-Praśasti* of Samudragupta. In the same chapter Bāṇa has provided the details of military strength of Harṣa with special description of elephant force and cavalry.

With regard to religious beliefs and faiths of the people, Bāṇa informs us that altogether 21 religious sects existed in India. He has referred to three popular cults of Hinduism, the Śaiva, Śakti and Vaiṣṇava, the Lokāyatika sect, Buddhism, Jainism, etc. that had already flourished before the dawn of the seventh century CE. On the combined testimony of the data available in the third, fifth and eighth chapters of his work it can plausibly be concluded here that Hinduism, Buddhism and Jainism were three popular forms of religion. Their coexistence is a proven fact. In the times of Harṣa and his predecessors, Brāhmanism and Buddhism flourished side by side. After having reigned for about four decades Harṣa passed away in CE 647 or 648.

A long list of 27 kings of different dynasties that ruled over different kingdoms in ancient India furnished by Bāṇa in the sixth chapter of his work on the basis of his knowledge of the past history also deserves our notice. The list includes Somaka of Paurava dynasty, Nāgasena of Nāga dynasty of Padmāvatī (Pavāyā), Vatsarāja Udayana (of Kauśāmbī), rulers of Ayodhyā, Śrāvastī, Videha, Kāśī, Kaliṅga, Mathurā, Aśmaka, Sovira and of Pradyota dynasty, and Kākavarṇa of Śiśunāga dynasty, Bṛhadratha of Maurya dynasty, Agnimitra, Sumitra and Devabhūti of Śuṅga dynasty and rulers of Gupta dynasty that ruled over Magadha, and Kṣatravarman of Maukhari dynasty. Even the killing of a Śaka king at the hands of Candragupta II attracted the attention of Bāṇa. Actually, his elder brother, Rāmagupta, after being defeated by the Śaka king agreed to surrender even his wife, Dhruvadevī, to him in compliance with his desire, but Candragupta in the guise of a woman killed that Śaka king in his camp itself, which Viśākhadatta in his *Mudrārākṣasa* has highlighted, already mentioned before. These are some of the additional historical information which Bāṇa has supplied in his work.

Bāṇa has not provided the life-history of Harṣa but also a true picture of social, economic, political, religious and cultural life of the people of India in his time. Some other historical information of great value have also been incorporated in his work. His historical knowledge was superb. He has nowhere in his work lavished extravagant praise on his patron. Nor do we come across any exaggeration in his presentation of the subject matter. He has dealt with the main theme of the work without much bias and prejudice. He has plainly stated the truth. Most of the facts stated by him are historically authenticated. However, it is undeniable that his work suffers from rhetorical descriptions and literary embellishment. The work after all belongs to a branch of literature called *kāvya* (epic).

> Indeed, it is possible to prove by a diligent and critical examination of our sources that the Indians in the ancient and the early medieval periods possessed a sense of history, which at present appears to be imperfect and rudimentary, and that they developed a tradition of writing historical biography, though its concrete evidence comparable to the lives of Plutarch is not avaliable. Were the sense of history or the tradition of biography-writing completely absent in ancient India, the emergence of Bāṇabhaṭṭa and Kalhaṇa would not have been possible. The works of Bāṇa and Kalhaṇa among others, represent the mature expression of historiography and historical biography and thus presuppose the continuity of literary and historical efforts and experiences of several generations.[2]

Cowell and Thomas have spoken very highly of Bāṇa and his work. They have observed that he in his Sanskrit works "has woven the story out of actual events." His work, in fact, is "based on real events." It contains "a living and contemporary picture wherein we can see something of the India of Alexander's time." The work "has another interest from the vivid picture which it offers of the condition of Indian society and the manners and customs of the period." Bāṇa's "descriptions of the court and village life abound with masterly touches which hold up the mirror to the time. . . . The court, the camp, the quiet village and the still more quiet monasteries and retreats, whether of brāhmaṇas or Buddhists, are all painted with singular power and his narrative illustrates and supplements the Chinese traveller's travel at every turn." Devahūti has also admitted that despite some defects typical of the courtly literature of the time, one can find a realistic picture of contemporary life and many

---

2. K.K. Dasgutpa, "Historical Biography in Sanskrit Literature", in *Historical Biography in Indian Literature*, ed. S.P. Sen, p. 5.

valuable facts about Harṣa's character and achievements in Bāṇa's *Harṣacarita*.[3]

Vākpatirāja in his Prākṛt work, the *Gauḍavaho*,[4] which consists of 1209 *gāthās*, describes the exploits of his patron, Yaśovarman (CE 725-752) of Kannauj, whose court he adorned as a poet. In fact, this work was composed by the said poet in CE 736 to celebrate with sense of honour and praise the victory of his patron over the king of Gauḍa. We are told that "the king of Magadha fled when Yaśovarman advanced, afterwards some of his vassals stood and fought in a great battle but were annihilated after which Yaśovarman pursued, defeated and killed the king of Magadha" who was most probably identical with Jīvitagupta II. He further continued his victorious march and conquered the king of Vaṅga (Bengal). The inclusion of Magadha in his great empire in north India and the extension of his political sway to the eastern sea in Bengal may be confirmed by Nālandā stone inscription and other reliable sources. The poet credits his patron with extensive conquests as far as the south. He is said to have defeated the king of the Deccan, crossed the Malaya mountain and reached the southern sea. The poet, while extolling Yaśovarman's success as a conqueror, further informs us that he conquered the Arabs who had occupied Sindh and expelled them from there, and also vanquished the Pārasikas (Persians) in the west. He received tribute from the regions of Western Ghāṭs, came to the banks of the Narmadā, entered into Marudeśa or Rajasthan and therefrom advanced towards Śrīkaṇṭha or Thāneśvar, passed through Kurukṣetra, proceeded to Ayodhyā and finally conquered the northern Himalayan region. But afterwards, in about CE 740,

3. *Harsha: A Political Study*, pp. 9-12.

4. Ed. S.P. Pandit, Bombay Sanskrit & Prākṛt Series, no. 34 (Bombay, 1887).

he was himself vanquished by King Lalitāditya (CE 724-60) of Kashmir but was allowed to rule as a feudatory. The poem of Vākpati contains, no doubt, little history in *kāvya* manner. Another work of the eighth century CE, the *Yaśoharacarita* (*Yaśodharacarita*) of Kanakasena Vādirāja,[5] is also important from a historical point of view. It is supplementary to Vākpati's work.

The *Navasāhasāṅkacarita* (in Sanskrit) of Padmagupta (also called Parimalagupta)[6] written about CE 1005 in 18 cantos deals with the history of the Paramāra king Sindhurāja Navasāhasāṅka of Mālwā. He was the younger brother and immediate successor of Vākpati-Muñja (CE 979-94). The author of the work first graced the court of the latter as a poet and later enjoyed the patronage of his two successors. In the twelfth canto of his work he has provided the description of all the rulers of the Paramāra dynasty preceding Sindhurāja in a chronological order whose historical authenticity is proved by the contemporary stone inscriptions. He has immortalised the achievements of Sindhurāja testifying to the success of his arms against a Hūṇa prince, Dakṣiṇa-Kosala (i.e. the Kalacuris of Tummāna), the Cāḷukyas of Lāṭa (Gujarat) and other neighbouring powers. After a short reign (CE 995-1005) Sindhurāja was followed by his son, Bhoja, the most striking and versatile Paramāra ruler. He ruled over Mālwā from 1005 to 1054 with Dhāra as its capital.

The *Rāmacarita* (in Sanskrit consisting of four cantos) of Sandhyākara Nandī[7] may be regarded as one of the best

5. Ed. T.A. Gopinath Rao (Tanjore, 1912).

6. Ed. V. S. Islampurkar (Bombay, 1895).

7. Ed. by R.C. Majumdar, R.G. Basak and N.G. Banerjee (Rajashahi, 1939).

specimens of historical biography produced in ancient India. It provides in detail the history of the life and achievements of Rāmapāla, one of the greatest Pāla kings of Bengal. He was the patron of the author who graced his court as a poet. The events which took place during the times of his two predecessors and successors are also recorded in the said work. The author begins with the origins of the Pāla dynasty, and just touches on his patron's ancestry. He throws little light on the parentage of Gopāla's son and successor, Dharmapāla (CE 780-815). Thereafter he relates the history from the time of Vigrahapāla III (CE 1055-70) onwards. He mentions his wars with the Kalacuri king, Karṇa of Tripurī. His death was followed by troublous times owing to the rivalry of his three sons (Mahipāla II, Sūrapāla II, and Rāmapāla) over the succession issue. However, Mahipāla II, being the eldest son of his father, succeeded him in about CE 1070 and ruled till about 1075. We are told that he imprisoned his two brothers relying on the mischievous rumours that they were plotting against him. "While they were fighting among themselves, the Varmans rose to power in eastern Bengal and the Pāla territories, which were already reduced to portions of Bihar and northern Bengal diminished still further." In Vārendra, a chief of the aboriginal Kaivarta tribe named Divvoka took advantage of the internal dissension in the imperial family and raised the banner of revolt. Mahipāla attempted to put it down but failed. We are informed that against the advice of his minister he marched to fight the rebels but was defeated and killed. Despite his ill-judged actions, he has been referred to by the author in a poetic style and laudatory term as a good king. After his death the rebel leader successfully established an independent kingdom in northern Bengal. The rebels, in fact, ruled over part of the empire confining the Pālas to the part south of the Gaṅgā. Taking advantage of the prevailing situation and the misfortune that assailed the Pālas, some of the feudatories also started raising their heads. Mahipāla was succeeded by his younger brother, Sūrapāla II, who ruled only for about a couple of years (CE 1075-77). His reign was not eventful at all.

When Rāmapāla ascended the throne (CE 1077) after the brief reign of his elder brother, Sūrapāla II, he found himself confronted with several problems. He appeared on the scene at a very critical moment. It appears from the *Rāmacarita* that the period immediately preceding his ascendency was the most turbulent in the history of the Pāla rule in Bengal. The immediate task before him was to restore the fallen fortunes of his family by overcoming the political adversaries. In order to achieve his goal he adopted a skilful policy. The author of the said work tells us that by his judicious presents and grants of land to the feudatories who were militarily very powerful he won them over and with their help raised a strong army. He sent his most able and loyal general Śovarāja ahead across the Gaṅgā to carry out military operation against the Kaivartas, and after his inital success he himself led the main army and had a pitched battle with the Kaivarta chief, Bhīma (the successor of his father Divvoka), who was defeated and captured. Hari, Bhīma's nephew, continued the war for some time but was ultimately forced to capitulate. The captive (Bhīma) was eventually put to death, and Hari was given a high position as a feudatory in recognition of his honourable capitulation. Thus, after being crowned with glorious victory, Rāmapāla was able to recover his paternal dominions in northern Bengal. He also overran the neighbouring kingdoms (Kaliṅga and Kāmarūpa). "His protection was even sought by the Yādava Varman rulers of eastern Bengal. The revival of Pāla supremacy was, however, only temporary." Towards the end of his rule he devoted his attention to the reorganisation of administration of the empire and promotion of learning. He entrusted the government to one of his sons, Rājyapāla. Rāmapāla died after a reign of about 45 years. The author further informs us that in the time of Rāmapāla's son, Kumārapāla, a revolt broke out in Kāmarūpa, but it was quelled by the minister, Vaidyadeva, who virtually became independent there. Kumārapāla's successor, Gopāla III, was weak and died trying to destroy his enemies. The narrative ends with the reign of Madanapāla (CE 1140-58). The author completed his work with an autobiography at its end only in the reign of this Pāla king. He has been praised for his successful, victorious and generous rule. But the fact remains that the feudatories reasserted themselves, and the rise of Vijayasena even resulted in his expulsion from northern Bengal. The spell of disaster befell the weak successors of Rāmapāla one after another, and they could not arrest the decline of the family.

> Sandhyākaranandin's object in this work seems primarily to be to contrast kings of good and bad judgement as demonstrated in their policies, with strong hints that they should submit to the guidance of the ministers, civil servants and of course writers like himself, scholars and poets, who generally belonged to the same bureaucratic class from which the administration was recruited.[8]

Sandhyākara Nandī has unhesitatingly bestowed praise on the rebel Kaivarta chief, Bhīma, "who had shaken the fortunes of the family of his patron, Rāmapāla" which is a fairly good specimen of objective treatment of history. The corroboration of some of the facts highlighted by him by inscriptions enhances the value of his work. "For instance, the defeat of the ruler of Pithi in Magadha, Devarakṣita, by Mahān, the uncle of Rāmapāla mentioned in the *Rāmacarita*

---

8. A.K. Warder, *An Introduction to Indian Historiography*, p. 54.

(II.8) gets confirmed by verse 7 of the Sārnāth inscription of Kumāradevī, Rāmapāla's daughter's daughter."

Sandhyākara Nandī's *Rāmacarita* possesses great value as a contemporary historical record on the Pālas' rule in Bengal from CE 1070 to 1155, though it is a poetical composition.

The *Rāmacarita* composed in the eleventh century CE by Abhinanda (also called Gauḍābhinanda) contains short biographies of two Pāla monarchs of Bengal, Dharmapāla and his son Devapāla (CE 815-55).

The *Kumārapālacarita* of Hemacandra (the celebrated Jaina scholar and historian of the twelfth century CE)[9] is another important historical biography.

In CE 1160, Hemacandra composed a historical epic in two parts one in Sanskrit and the other in Prākṛt, called the *Dvyāśrayakāvya*. It being a contemporary work is of immense historical value. The first part of it consisting of 20 cantos in Sanskrit constitutes a history of the Cāḷukya dynasty of Anhilwāḍa (identified with modern Pāṭan in Gujarat) from its founder Mūlarāja (CE 1093-1143), who accorded a place of honour at his court to the author of the said work. The second part consisting of eight cantos in Prākṛt deals with the life and achievements of Kumārapāla (CE 1143-72), the succcessor of Jayasiṁha Siddharāja. Hemacandra, in fact, enjoyed the royal patronage of both. He tells us that Kumārapāla, after having come under his influence, embraced Jainism and proclaimed it as a state religion. The author provides an extensive description of his discourse with the said Cāḷukya prince on the doctrine of Jainism. He has presented an authentic history of the Cāḷukyas of Gujarat in his work.

9. Ed. S.P. Pandit (Bombay, 1900); P.L. Vaidya (Poona, 1936).

We further learn from the *Kumārapāla-pratibodha* (composed at Pāṭan in Prākṛt by Somaprabhācārya towards the end of twelfth century CE or in about CE 1195) that Kumārapāla was converted to the tenets of Jainism. And it was due to Jaina influences that he issued stringent orders prohibiting the slaughter of animals throughout his vast dominions.

Jayasiṁha Sūri II, who is believed to have flourished in the middle of the fourteenth century CE, also wrote a historical epic called the *Kumārapālacarita*[10] in which he has given an authentic account of the achievements of Kumārapāla as a conqueror. We are told that "after having overcome all opposition to his accession he pursued a policy of active militarism. He attacked Arṇorāja, the Cāhamāna ruler of Śākambharī, and completely overpowered his forces. He also quelled the revolt of the Paramāra prince of Ābu, and reasserted the Cāḷukya authority in Mālwā, which had raised his head during his inital difficulties. He next turned his arms successfully against a chieftain of Saurāṣṭra, but his most remarkable exploit was the defeat of Mallikārjuna of Koṅkaṇa." The work contains some of those incidents or episodes connected with the life of Kumārapāla which are not found in earlier works available to us, such as his murder by his nephew. As a biography this is far more useful than the two other works mentioned above. However, these biographical works as a whole enable us to trace the history of Gujarat under the Cāḷukyas.

The school of historical writing in Gujarat developed under the influence of the Jainas.

Bilhaṇa in his *Vikramāṅkadevacarita*[11] recounts the exploits

---

10. Ed. Kṣantivijaya Gani (Bombay, 1926).

11. Ed. G. Bühler, Bombay Sanskrit Series, No. 14 (Bombay, 1875); tr. S.C. Banerji and A.K. Gupta (Calcutta, 1965); see also G.P. →

of his patron Vikramāditya VI Tribhuvanamalla (CE 1076–1126), the famous Cāḷukya ruler of Kalyāṇī (in the Kanarese district of Karnataka). The said work in Sanskrit consists of 18 cantos. The author originally belonged to Kashmir as it distinctly appears from his biography in the last and 18th canto of the work. He belonged to a branch (Sāravasta) of the Bhārgava clan of brāhmaṇas. He travelled all the way from his native place to the court of Vikramāditya VI in search of a good patron which he fortunately found in him. He flourished at his court under his royal patronage. He was known for his historical scholarship and poetic talent. He composed his work in about CE 1088. He has related in detail the history of the Cāḷukyas of Kalyāṇī up to CE 1088 in 17 cantos of his work which covers their origin, wars and conquests of Vikramāditya and of his father, Someśvara I Ahavamalla (CE 1043-68), and other historical themes.

Bilhaṇa, while dealing with the exploits of Someśvara I, informs us that he first inflicted crushing defeats on Coḷa princes and occupied their capital, Kāñcī. In his wars he was assisted by his son, Vikramāditya (VI), then a valiant youth. Further, he invaded Mālwā, defeated its Paramāra king Bhoja, and expelled him from his capital Dhāra. He also defeated the Kalacuri ruler, Lakṣmīkarṇa. These glorious victories enabled him to consolidate his imperial position. He founded a new capital at Kalyāṇī probably in CE 1053. He was succeeded by his eldest son, Someśvara II Bhuvanaikamalla. He did not attain any noteworthy distinction during a rule of about eight years (CE 1068-76). Vikramāditya VI, the most striking personality among the Cāḷukyas of Kalyāṇī and a valiant warrior, emerged victorious

→ Singh, "Historicity of Bilhaṇa's Account of Vikramāditya's Invasion of Kāmarūpa in the Eleventh Century", *Shodhaka, JHR*, 26, A, 76, 1997, pp. 3-5.

in some of the wars which he fought during the reign of his father. After having overrun Mithilā, Magadha, Aṅga and Vaṅga meeting with little or no opposition he vanquished the kings of Gauḍa and Kāmarūpa in the course of his northern incursions (some time between CE 1050 and 1053). The king of Gauḍa may be identified with Nayapāla. Vikramāditya VI met with feeble opposition from the decadent Pāla monarchy. But he along with his army was pushed back by king of Kāmarūpa who may be identified with Ratnapāla (CE 1030-53). The invasion of Kāmarūpa eventually ended in fiasco. We are further told by Bilhaṇa that after having subdued the ruler of Koṅkaṇa, Jayakeśin by name, the Coḷa monarch, Vīra-Rājendra of Kāñcī, and Kulotuṅga I (Rājiga) of Veṅgī, and deposed his elder brother, Someśvara II, who was tyrannical and distrustful, Vikramāditya VI assumed the reigns of government at Kalyāṇī in CE 1076. After becoming king he directed his energies more towards peace than military adventures. After the cessation of hostility and restoration of friendly relations with the Paramāras of Mālwā he soon got entangled into hostilities with the Cāḷukyas of Anhilwāḍa. Another storm he had to face was the revolt of his younger brother Jayasiṁha, whom he had appointed Viceroy of the Banavāsī province (northern Kanārā). But this uprising was suppressed with a firm hand. Further, he curbed the inroads of the Coḷa king and of the Hoysaḷa Viṣṇuvardhana, who challenged the might of the Cāḷukya manarch towards the close of his career. The contemporary social life has also been depicted in Bilhaṇa's work.

G. Bühler's remarks on the themes of the *Vikramāṅkadevacarita* deserves to be placed here:

> The main theme of this laudatory poem is royal wars and royal marriages. The poet begins with a short account of the

> Cāḷukya race and the kings of the restored dynasty which begins with Tailapa (CE 973-97); he dwells at some length upon the exploits of Vikramāditya's father and describes with all customary amplifications the conquests of Vikramāditya before his accession to the throne, his dethronement of his elder brother, Someśwara II, his defeat and capture of his younger brother and his numerous wars with the faithless Coḷas.[12]

Most of the facts stated by Bilhaṇa in his work with regard to Vikramāditya's conquests have been corroborated by contemporary epigraphical records. However, he is not free from bias. M.A. Stein has also opined that "The narrative of Bāṇa and Bilhaṇa, too, treats of historical facts yet their heroes are painted all white and their enemies all black."[13]

The *Vikramāṅkābhyudaya* of Someśvara III Bhūlokamalla (CE 1126-38), one of the later Cāḷukya rulers of Kalyāṇī, is an incomplete biography of his father, Vikramāditya VI. The author is a solitary example of a historian of royal family in ancient India. His work consists of three chapters which are fragmentary in nature. It is the third chapter which traces the history of the Cāḷukyas of Kalyāṇī from the time of Tailapa down to Vikramāditya VI. This chapter throws some light on the lives and activities of Vikramāditya including his anointment as an heir apparent and his military campaigns, and of other kings who preceded him. The first chapter provides a graphic description of the people of Karnataka, and the second deals with the splendour of the Cāḷukya capital Kalyāṇī.

Estimating the historical value of the *Vikramāṅkābhyudaya*, V.S. Pathak writes:

---

12. Op. cit., Introduction.
13. *Rājataraṅgiṇī*, Eng. tr., I, Introduction, pp. 32-33.

> Save the *Harṣacarita* of Bāṇa, this *Vikramāṅkābhyudaya* is the only historical prose-narrative of ancient India available to us, and hence its discovery is of more than usual interest to the study of the historical literary writings inasmuch as by comparison with the earlier *ākhyāyikā*, it affords an opportunity of discovering patterns, motifs and devices — the way through which the objective facts of history are moulded into a literary story. In the case of *Vikramāṅkābhyudaya*, there is an additional advantage as the authentic information on the life of Vikramāditya VI, the hero of the prose-narrative, is available from inscriptions containing much historical detail, which in the case of few inscriptions which mention Harṣa, celebrated in the *Harṣacarita* is sadly lacking.[14].

The *Somapālavijaya* of Jalhaṇa, the celebrated Kāśmīrī brāhmaṇa scholar of the twelfth century CE, is a short biography of King Somapāla (the son of Saṅgrāmapāla), who was his patron. The author was a minister at the court of Rājapurī, the capital of his patron. His work deals with the life and achievements of his patron. His delineation of the conquests of King Somapāla bears the impact of the writings of historians of Kashmir school.

Jayānaka in his *Pr̥thvīrājavijaya* (in Sanskrit consisting of 12 cantos)[15] provides the life-history of his patron, Pr̥thvīrāja III (CE 1179-92), the illustrious Cāhamāna (Cauhāna) king of Ajmer. Jayānaka, a Kāśmīrī brāhmaṇa, came to Ajmer, graced the court of Pr̥thvīrāja and flourished under his royal patronage as it appears from the 12th canto of his work. The author begins with the origin of the Cāhamānas. He has

14. *Ancient Historians of India*, p. 88.

15. Edited with commentary of Jonarāja by G.H. Ojha and C.S. Guleri (Ajmer, 1941); Hindi tr. in *Nāgarī Pracāriṇī Patrikā*, Kāśī, 5, 1981, pp. 133-83; Eng. abstract in *JRAS*, 1913, pp. 259-81.

traced their connection with the Solar dynasty. They are said to have descended from an eponymous Cāhamāna, born of the sun. He has narrated their earlier history in several cantos of his work. Of the several branches of the clan, the most important was that of Śākambharī or Sāmbhar. He has traced their genealogy to Vasudeva, who established a branch of the family in the Sapādalakṣadeśa (northern Rajasthan). He may be ascribed to the seventh century CE, and the family then served for three centuries as vassals of the emperors of Kānyakubja. From this period the account becomes more historical. The author seems to have used the records preserved in the Cāhamāna archives. He tells us that Ajayarāja (in the early twelfth century CE) founded the city of Ajayameru (modern Ajmer) made it his capital and issued new coins to mark the occasion. A resounding victory of his successor Arṇorāja over the Turks in the desert is celebrated with more poetic effect than factual detail. There is also reference to his marriage with the daughter of Siddharāja, the Cāḷukya prince of Gujarat.

In conformity with the prevailing literary conventions Jayānaka relates that Pṛthvīrāja III had to get rid of the *mlecchas* (i.e. the Muslim Turks) who had attacked and desecrated the sacred places and destroyed temples. In the concluding part of his work (which seems to have been lost) the author gives a picturesque description of the glorious victory (*vijaya*) of his patron-king (Pṛthvīrāja Cauhāna, the lord of the territories of Ajmer and Delhi) over Sahāvadina (Shihabuddin Muhammad Ghori) in the first battle of Tarāīn or Taroai (situated near Thāneśvar or Bhatinda) in CE 1191. Pṛthvīrāja thus freed Rajasthan and the Punjab from the Muslim invaders. In order to celebrate the victory of his patron be composed his work in about CE 1192. It also appears from his work that Pṛthvīrāja married Tilottamā (Saṁyogitā of

Pṛthvīrāja Rāso), a princess of perfect beauty. It appears that after the defeat and death of Pṛthvīrāja at the hands of his enemy, Jayānaka returned to Kashmir leaving his work incomplete on which the Kāśmīrī historian Jonarāja (fifteenth century) wrote a commentary.

Jayānaka has presented an authentic biographical history of the Cāhamānas of Śākambharī in his *Pṛthvīrājavijaya*. It, being a contemporary work, is of inestimable historical value. It constitutes a valuable source of information about Pṛthvīrāja the last independent Hindu sovereign of northern India, and some other Cauhāna rulers who preceded him. Many incidents narrated in it have found corroboration from inscriptions and other records. It is a near approach to genuine historical biography in its modern sense.

Another important biography of Pṛthvīrāja III is the *Pṛthvīrāja Rāso*[16] by his court-poet Canda Bardāī, who belonged to a class of bard. The said work consists of 1400 verses, mostly in Apabhraṁśa, then the spoken language in the greater part of northern India. It forms part of bardic literature. It has not been preserved in its original form. It saw several recensions with additions. A vast amount of additional material seems to have been incorporated in it over the centuries. Its considerable parts are believed to be much later than the fourteenth century.

Canda, while dealing with the origin of the Cāhamāna family in his *Rāso*, explicity states that like the Pratihāras and the Cāḷukyas (Solaṅkīs) the Cāhamānas belonged to "Agnikula". It is also traditionally believed that the descendants of those four persons who took the vow before the fire-altar in the presence of brāhmaṇas to repel the foreign invaders to defend the country were believed to be

16. Ed. S.S. Das (Benares, 1904); Pandia and Das (Benares, 1913).

of the Agni dynasty. It has, of course, some historical significance. However, the bardic tradition regarding the origins of the four Rājpūt families is not much relied upon in view of the evidence recorded in the extant inscriptions and other contemporary records of the Cāhamānas, the Pratihāras and the Cāḷukyas that the former two belonged to the Solar dynasty and the latter to the Lunar dynasty. We are told by Canda that Paramāra was assigned the region from Arbuda to Avantī, Cāḷukya Anhilwāḍa (modern Pāṭan in Gujarat), Pratihāra Marusthalī (the mostly desert country to the west of which the old capital was Māṇḍavyapura) and Cāhamāna Mahiṣadeśa (the middle Narmadā Valley with Mahiṣmatī as capital) from where the Cāhamānas eventually came to Sapādalakṣadeśa (northern Rajasthan) and settled there. The historical authenticity of the information concerned may be proved by the available evidences. His *Rāso* contains the genealogy of the Cāhamānas, the detailed information about the family of Pṛthvīrāja, etc.

Canda, while highlighting the herioc deeds (*vīra-gāthās*) of Pṛthvīrāja Cauhāna in his poems, informs us that he attacked and defeated the Candella king, Paramardi, in CE 1182 and occupied Mahobā, Kālañjara and other fortresses in Jejākabhukti (Bundelkhand). We are further informed that Pṛthvīrāja was not on friendly terms with Jayacanda (CE 1170-94) of Kānyakubja (Kannauj). The latter's daughter, Saṁyogitā, had heard much of the former's valour and wished to marry him, but her father did not approve of it. She could not keep her cherished desire secret for a long time. She conveyed her desire to Pṛthvīrāja through correspondence and invited him to come to Kānyakubja and take her away. When Jayacanda held a *svayaṁvara* (selection of bridegroom) for her daughter, Pṛthvīrāja appeared just in the midst of the ceremonies and carried her away fighting off the pursuing or chasing army of the enemy. This resulted in the hostility between the two which ultimately proved to be fatal for both. The said incident is supposed to have taken place immediately after Pṛthvīrāja's victory over Muhammad Ghori in CE 1191. It has without any doubt historical basis.

The poet, Canda, has furnished an eyewitness account of the second battle of Tarāīn which was fought in CE 1192 between Pṛthvīrāja Cauhāna and Muhammad Ghori. According to him, the former fell wounded from his horse in the course of the battle but at this instance killed the latter by an arrow and himself died which is not taken as worthy of acceptance. The information supplied in some of the later recensions of his *Rāso* that Ghori after having defeated Pṛthvīrāja made him captive, took him along with Canda to Ghazni and tortured him to death is taken equally incredible. What generally historians accept is that Pṛthvīrāja fled from the battlefield to save his life, but was captured near Sarasūti and taken to Ajmer where he was later put to death. And then Muhammad Ghori occupied Ajmer and Delhi. However, it is still a riddle or mystery of history as to how and where Pṛthvīrāja met his tragic end.

Canda's *Rāso* also records that the Tomara king Anaṅgapāla I (a feudatory of the Pratihāra king of Kannauj) founded a new city (on the ruins of Indraprastha which was devastated by the Śakas and Hūṇas) in VS 848 = CE 791 and named it Lāl Koṭ (a Rājpūt citadel) which was one of the seven names of modern Delhi. There are many other information in the said work which have kernel of historical truth. The *Pṛthvīrāja Rāso* has, no doubt, some historical value. The tradition of composing *rāso*s in Rajasthan was further carried on in the medieval period.

The school of historical writing in Rajasthan flourished

under the patronage of the Cāhamānas. The historical tradition of Rajasthan is different from that of other parts of India in terms of dynastic records or family histories.

The writers of the bardic tradition made some contributions to the development of historical writing in India. Bards may be regarded as the "Primitive historians of mankind." They (*bhāṭa*s) got recognition in the royal courts as a class of poetic writer not before the seventh century CE. The professional bards were conspicuous by their absence in the time of Purāṇic *sūta*s. The bards of Rajasthan played an important part in preserving its local history in oral tradition. They preserved it also by recording real events and commemorating real personages. The records and oral tradition of such bards were repositories of many valuable data and facts, incidents, past and contemporary events and other historical material. It was their profession to memorise events and put them in writing. This tradition among them was handed down from generation to generation. Traditionally the bard followed his father's profession. He learnt from him his techniques of writing and reciting poetry to chronicle historical facts and to glorify his Rājpūt patrons. The bards very carefully compiled the genealogies of the Rājpūt families. They earned their livelihood by this profession. They used to preserve with all meticulous care the genealogical records and the family histories of their Rājpūt patrons. At the death of a bard the records in his possession were passed to his son. Thus the bards became the permanent custodians of the family histories and genealogists of most of the ruling clans of Rajasthan. Histories of some princes or royal personages of Rajasthan were recorded by their respective family bards both in ancient and medieval periods. The heroic poems of the bards including that of Canda Bardāī constitute a valuable source of history. The bardic poems (*rāsos*) are historical records of Rajasthan. It is significant to note that when written historical records were being destroyed by the Muslim invaders in the course of their invasions of India, the bards thought it proper to memorise the contemporary historical events and to preserve them in their memories instead of recording them. History of Rajasthan (*Annals and Antiquities of Rajasthan*) of Tod was written chronologically on the basis of oral tradition preserved by bards (*bhāṭa*s and *cāraṇa*s) of Rajasthan (first published in 1829) which has been corroborated by written records also. J. Kennedy has correctly stated that "The true history of India is hidden under a thick veil of Brāhmanical or bardic fiction."[17] The institution of bards, which was hereditary, existed not only in Rajasthan but also in Gujarat, Kānyakubja in Uttar Pradesh, Jejākabhukti or Bundelkhand and other parts of Madhya Pradesh, Kashmir, Mysore and the Deccan. The historical value of Indian bardic literature of both ancient and medieval periods has been acknowledged by a number of scholars.[18]

The *Paramardi Rāso* (a poem generally called *Mahotsavakhaṇḍa*), an anonymous, is a biography of Paramardi (CE 1165-1203), the last prominent Candella sovereign of Jejākabhukti (Bundelkhand), east of Rajasthan and south of the Yamunā. He belonged to Candrātreya dynasty. The said work was composed originally in Jejākabhukti some time after 1182 or 1192 but not later than 1203. It was later modified and incorporated in the gradually growing *Pṛthvīrāja Rāso* corpus. It exists in different recensions. We learn from this work

17. *Imp. Gaz. Ind.*, 2, p. 309.

18. For details see Haimendorf, "The Historical Value of Indian Bardic Literature", in *Historians of India, Pakistan and Ceylon* (vol. I of *Historical Writing on the Peoples of Asia*), ed. C.H. Philips, pp. 87-93.

that Candravarman, the first Candrātreya king, built 85 temples at Kharjūravāhaka (Khajurāho), one of the most important cities in the Candella kingdom. He built a capital for himself named Mahotsava (Mahobā). It appears that these events took place in the first half of the ninth century CE. He and his successors ruled over the kingdom with its capital at Mahotsava.

An accurate historical account of a reverse the King Paramardi sustained in the war of 1182 at the hands of Pṛthvīrāja Cauhān III is given in the *Paramardi Rāso* or *Mahotsavakhaṇḍa*. We are told that the war occurred as a result of one of Pṛthvīrāja's expeditions when some of his troops were crossing the territory of Candella kingdom on their way home and became involved in a squabble with Paramardi's men. Paramardi's resulting attack on the Cāhamāna force was an "unchivalrous" and "impolitic" act. His general, Udayasiṁha, "tried to restrain him but Paramardi persisted, instigated by the mischievous advice of his brother-in-law, a Pratihāra prince who was his vassal but secretly wished to ruin him by embroiling him in war with a stronger army." After this the continuing intrigue of the Pratihāra prince forced Ālhā and his brother Ūdala, the two best generals of Paramardi, into exile. Pṛthvīrāja, kept informed of the situation by the Pratihāra prince, launched his expedition in retaliation against Paramardi. The latter finding himself unable to check the former retreated, but managed to secure a temporary truce which afforded him a chance to implore his generals to return to his aid. The battle ensued between the forces of Pṛthvīrāja Cauhāna and Paramardi in 1182 with very heavy losses on both sides. Ūdala and other leaders of the latter and one of the sons of the former were killed, and Ālhā was wounded. Paramardi fled to the fortress of Kālañjara and the victorious Pṛthvīrāja marched into Mahotsava. Afterwards Pṛthvīrāja sent a general to capture Kālañjara, and Paramardi was taken prisoner, but Ālhā's son, Indala, suddenly attacked the Cāhamānas with forces and freed his king. The city of Mahotsava eventually fell under the occuption of Pṛthvīrāja. Paramardi died in shame soon afterwards, but inscriptions of the Candella kings do not bear testimony to this fact but rather show that Paramardi escaped complete annihilation, and afterwards recovered the lost ground. He was in possession of his capital Mahotsava again within two years at most and ruled another 20 years until he died. It was the heroism of Ālhā, Ūdala and Indala which saved their king and his kingdom.[19] The original poem was composed to celebrate their marvellous feats of action, to commemorate the courage and valour displayed by Paramardi against his political adversary or to preserve the memory of the event that took place in 1182. The said work supplements the information supplied by Canda in his *Pṛthvīrāja Rāso*. Jejākabhukti seems to have maintained its own tradition of historiography.

Oral tradition has preserved in the Buṅdelī dialect of Hindu style an epic known as the *Ālhā Rāso* which is supposed to have been composed by Jagvik or Jagnik Rao, Paramardi's messenger. It supplies more information than the *Paramardi Rāso* about Paramardi. He has been called a magnanimous hero. There is some historical basis for this assessment of his character. It gives more detail of the intrigue of the Pratihāra prince. It gives a vivid description of the first battle between the Cāhamāna king Pṛthvīrāja III and the Candella king Paramardi resulting in a victory for the latter, Ālhā and Ūdala inflicting heavy losses on the former. We are further told

19. Warder, op. cit., pp. 80-83.

that the war was resumed for a different cause, and Pṛthvīrāja's kingdom was invaded by the forces led by Paramardi's son, who was killed during the expedition. Several more battles followed and finally the Candella kings were defeated after Ūdala's death and the city of Mahotsava fell in the hands of victors. Paramardi could not bear the disgrace and went on fast which led to his death and Mahotsava ceased to be the capital of Jejākabhukti.[20] The indication given in the work about a great event towards the end of Paramardi's reign was the stubborn resistance he offered to Qutb-ud-din Aibak in 1203 during the siege of Kālañjara, his military capital. Finding it not possible to stand with the odds which were altogether against him, Paramardi capitulated, but he died before fulfilling any of the terms imposed on him, according to the evidence available in standard historical works.

In medieval Rajasthan, historical biographies were produced in the form of *Rāso, Prabandha, Caupāī,* etc. in verse and *Khyāta, Vārttā, Vigat, Vācanika,* etc. in prose. As a matter of fact, the heroic deeds and noble achievements of the Rājpūt rulers, chiefs and heroes, and the bravery they displayed and the sacrifices they made while fighting against the Sultāns of Delhi and the Mughals inspired the writers to write their biographies to perpetuate the memory of events. The glorious deeds and military exploits of the princes and the warriors of the various states in Rajasthan also attracted the attention of biographers. Their valour, courage and sacrifices have been highlighted in the biographical works without any exaggeration or glorification. Scholars were also prompted to write on the lives of those who had distinguished themselves as king, ruler, patriot, or patron of arts, letters, religion and

---

20. Warder, op. cit., pp. 80-83.

so on. A biography of the Rājpūt queen Padminī, who gave wholehearted support to her husband Rāṇā Ratan Singh in his fight against Alauddin and sacrificed her life just to save herself from falling into the hands of the Muslim invader, was written by several writers. Several other biographical works bearing historical character were produced in Rajasthan in early and late medieval periods.

The Sanskrit epic, *Hammīra Mahākāvya*, composed by a Jaina writer Nayacandra Sūri in VS 1542 (CE 1485) is one of the important biographies of the Rājpūt rulers of Rajasthan. It gives a detailed biographical account of Hammīra Deva, the last ruler of the Cāhamāna dynasty of Raṇastambhapura (Raṇathambhor). The work is no doubt of great historical importance. It basically deals with the heroic deeds of Hammīra and his tragic end in the battle of Raṇathambhor fought with Ala-ud-din Khilji. However, before narrating the historical events of Hammīra's time the author Nayacandra traces the early history of the Cāhamāna dynasty. He has presented his work in 14 cantos which altogether consists of 1572 verses. In the first four cantos, he has dealt with the lives and achievements of the ancestors of Hammīra. The third canto exclusively deals with the victory of Pṛthvīrāja III in the first battle of Tarāīn (1191) fought with "Śāhavadina" (Shihabuddin, generally called Muhammad Ghori) and his defeat and death at the hands of the latter in the second battle of Tarāīn (1192). Nayacandra tells us that Pṛthvīrāja's general Skanda, who had won the former battle, was engaged in another war, thus the king himself advanced to meet the Turks overconfident and complacent but was defeated, captured and killed, and that after his death the Turks occupied Ajayameru (Ajmer) and Dilli (Delhi). We are further informed by him in the fourth canto that Pṛthvīrāja's son Govindarāja took over the reign of Ajmer as a vassal of the Turks. But Harirāja (brother of Pṛthvīrāja) soon deposed him and declared the independence of the Cāhamānas. On hearing this news, Qutb-ud-din, the trusted general of Ghori, invaded Ajmer, defeated Harirāja and annexed the Cāhamāna's territories. Govindarāja refounded the kingdom with its capital at Raṇathambhor where he and his descendants ruled as Cāhamāna kings till its capture by "Allāvadina" (Alauddin). Nayacandra briefly narrates their history until he comes to the reign of the hero of his epic, Hammīra, which began in CE 1283. These Cāhamānas sometimes acknowledged the supremacy of the Turkish *sultāns* at Delhi and sometimes asserted their independence. In the ninth canto of his epic, Nayacandra describes Hammīra's campaigns of conquest in the four directions, including Mālwā, Gūrjaradeśa (Gujarat) and Rājpūtānā. After the conquest of Gujarat (in 1299), Alauddin turned his attention to the subjugation of Rājpūtānā. Raṇathambhor was an important state of Rājpūtānā, and it had become independent of the Muslim rule. Its ruler Hammīra Deva, a descendant of the famous Cāhamāna king Pṛthvīrāja, was a brave Rājpūt. In 1299 itself, Alauddin despatched a strong force under their able general "Nisurata Khan" (Nusrat Khan) to besiege and conquer Raṇathambhor. In the eleventh canto of his work, Nayacandra narrates how Nisurata Khan was repulsed, defeated and killed by the defenders. Further, in the thirteenth canto, he informs us that after the death of general Nisurata Khan the Sultān (Alauddin) himself attacked the fort of Raṇathambhor and renewed its siege which lasted for one full year. Hammīra refused to submit and decided to give a fight to the finish. A huge funeral pyre was lit on which the Rājpūt women immolated themselves in keeping with their old tradition of *jauhara*, whilst the men under Hammīra died fighting. Hammīra "ascended to heaven" as told by Nayacandra.[21] He and his family and the remnant of the garrison were actually put to the sword. The fort of Raṇathambhor was captured in July 1301. Alauddin returned victorious to Delhi. "From the accession of Pṛthvīrāja Cauhāna to the death of Hammīra Deva the narrative is fairly historic."[22] The writings of the contemporary Muslim chroniclers, Amir Khusrau and Ziauddin Barani, on the subject also go to prove the historical accuracy of the information recorded in the work of Nayacandra.

Apart from the *Hammīra Mahākāvya* of Nayacandra Sūri, there are other biographical works on Hammīra Deva Cauhāna which include *Hammīra Rāso* (CE 1300) by Śāraṅgdhar in Hindi, and *Hammīra Rāso* or *Hammīrayān* (VS 1785 = CE 1728) by Jodharāja, *Hammīrayān Caupāī* (VS 1538 = CE 1481) by Bhāndav Vyās, *Hammīra Haṭha* (CE 1745) by Candraśekhara, *Hammīra Haṭha* by Gwal, and *Hammīra-ra Chanda* (VS 1798 = CE 1741) by Rājarūpa in Rajasthani. The details provided in them regarding Hammīra do not differ much from what we find in the *Hammīra Mahākāvya*. It is only the *Hammīra Caupāī* which provides some additional information. It gives the name of Hammīra's queen as Hasilade and of his daughter as Devalādevī. Of the two traitors, Raṇamalla and Ratipāla, the latter is mentioned as Rāyapāla. These works have, however, limited historical value.

The *Surajanacarita* (in Hindi) composed by Candraśekhara in the sixteenth century is a history of brave Rājpūt warriors

21. *Hammīra Mahākāvya*, ed. N.J. Kirtane (Bombay, 1878); also Jaganlal Gupta, "Hammīra Mahākāvya", in *Nāgarī Pracāriṇī Patrikā*, Banaras, 12, VS 1988, pp. 259-309; Abstract in *Ind. Ant.*, VIII, pp. 55 and 234.

22. M.S. Ahluwalia, "Historical Biographies of Early Mediaeval Rajasthan: Khilji Period — A Case Study", in S.P. Sen (ed.), op. cit., p. 176.

of Cāhamāna dynasty. It is somewhat less reliable than Nayacandra's work. Another *Surajanacarita* in Hindi was written by Sūdan in CE 1753.

The *Padmāvat* of Malik Muhammad Jāyasī (VS 1597 = CE 1540) in Hindi[23] and *Padminī Caritra Caupāī* of Kavi Labhdodaya (VS 1705),[24] *Gorā Bādal Padminī Caupāī* of Hemratna (VS 1646), *Gorā Bādal Caupāī* of Jatmal Nāhar (VS 1680), *Chitai Carita* (VS 1583), *Gorā Bādal Caupāī* of Bhāṣya Vijaya (VS 1803) and *Gorā Bādal Kathā* (anonymous) in Rajasthani, combined together, may be taken as useful for the study of the life of Rāṇā Ratan Singh, the king of Mewāṛ, and his queen Padminī (Padmāvatī of Jāyasī) famous for her beauty, Allāvadina's attack on Mewāṛ's capital Chittor and his persistent attempts to conquer it and to secure Padminī, fight of the Rājpūts under their brave leaders Gorā and Bādal in defence of Chittor, Ratan Singh's treacherous captivity and release by Padminī with the help of Gorā and Bādal, submission of the king, sacrifice of the queen and the ultimate fall of Chittor. The characters and events are described with little variations or minor changes in the aforesaid sources. The historical basis of the story narrated in Jāyasī's work in particular is supported by Nainsi, the famous historian of Medapāṭa (Mewāṛ) of the seventeenth century. In the words of A.L. Srivastava, a noted authority on medieval Indian history, ". . . Jāyasī wrote out a romance, the plot of which he had derived from Amir Khusrau's *Khazain-ul-Futuh*. Most of the romantic details of Jāyasī's *Padmāvat* are imaginary; but the main plot of the story that Padminī was coveted by Ala-ud-din . . . is most probably

23. Ed. Rāmacandra Shukla, Nāgarī Pracāriṇī Sabhā (Banaras, 1924).

24. Ed. B.L. Nahata (Bikaner, VS 2018).

based on historical truth."[25] Thus Jāyasī's work partly bears the stamp of historicity.

This is a historically proven fact that encouraged by his success against Raṇathambhor, the Sultān Ala-ud-din Khilji thought of conquering Mewāṛ, the premier state in Rājpūtānā. It was then under the rule of Ratan Singh. Early in 1303, Alauddin besieged its capital Chittor. His desire of its conquest was as intense as that of obtaining possession of the fair Padminī. The former was his ambition and the latter his passion. After Ratan Singh's arrest, the Rājpūts fell on the invaders and rescued him. In fact, Padminī along with some Rājpūt soldiers attacked the camp of Alauddin very cleverly and courageously by a stratagem and rescued her husband from captivity. The Rājpūts under their two brave leaders Gorā and Bādal fought desperately but were defeated. Amir Khusrau, who was an eyewitness, says that 30,000 Rājpūts were killed in the battle of Chittor. The reigning king Ratan Singh had to submit on 26 August 1303; Rani Padminī burnt herself on the funeral pyre along with other Rājpūt women to save her honour and chastity, and Chittor was thus finally conquered. In fact, the Sultān wanted to conquer the heart of Padminī and the captial of Mewāṛ, Chittor. The second he did but the first he could not.

The *Kanhadade Prabandha* composed by Kavī Padmanābha in CE 1456 is a detailed biography of Kanhadade (Kanhar Deva), the Cauhāna chief of Jālor. It was written in the court of Akhairāja, a descendant of Kanhadade. The poet belonged to Jālor where the latter was born, ruled and died. The work appears to be a historical *kāvya*. It is the most valuable treasure in old Gujarati or old western Rajasthani. It has been claimed equally by Gujaratis and Rajasthanis. "It is the most important

25. The *Sultanate of Delhi*, p. 169.

in the entire range of Rajasthani biographical literature pertaining to the Khilji period . . . judging from the historical point of view also, it is without a parallel in Rajasthani historical literature."[26] "The events narrated therein are mostly historical."[27] It deals with the heroic achievements of Kanhadade. We are told by the author Padmanābha that Kanhadade flatly refused Ala-ud-din Khilji to permit his troops to pass through Mārwāṛ when the latter was to attack Gujarat. By doing so he incurred the displeasure of the Sultān. Late in CE 1298 or early in 1299, "the Sultān's army conquered Gujarat and destroyed the temple of Somanātha in spite of the efforts of some Rājpūt clans to save it."[28] We are further informed by the author that the troops of the Turkish Sultān while returning from Gujarat halted near Jālor with a view to punishing Kanhadade but the latter inflicted a crushing defeat on Muslims. Kanhadade got the Hindus liberated. He also secured the fragments of an idol of Somanātha which he got installed at Prabhāsa, Bāgaḍa, Ābu, Javalipura and his palace garden.[29] "The second round of the struggle between Kanhadade and Alauddin Khilji began when the latter first besieged Siwāna (in or about 1308) which was under Kanhadade's nephew Śītaldeva."[30] "The Muslim army after capturing Siwāna besieged Jālor, the capital seat of Kanhadade. On the fifth day of the fighting Kanhadade met a soldier's death along with his 50 chosen warriors and

---

26. Ahluwalia, op. cit., p. 174.

27. Ibid., p. 175.

28. *Kanhadade Prabandha* of Padmanābha, ed. K.B. Vyas, Khaṇḍa (Part) I.

29. Ibid., Khaṇḍa I, vv. 250-56.

30. Ibid., Khaṇḍa II.

the ladies performed the sacred rite of *jauhara*."[31] K.B. Vyas has pointed out that the *Kanhadade Prabandha* "is perhaps the only *prabandha* that gives an accurate account of historical events. It is an epic poem divided into four *khaṇḍas*, grand in its design, vigorous in the portrayal of its characters, and masterly in its treatment of the sentiments."[32]

The evidence available in A.L. Srivastava's work that Sultān Ala-ud-din sent an army against Rājā Kanhar Deva (Kanhadade) of Jālor (in 1308); the army besieged Jālor and defeated the *rājā* in the battle and put him and his relations to death and Jālor was annexed,[33] go to prove the historical authenticity of what Padmanābha has recorded in his work about Kanhadade.

The *Vīram De Sonigara ki Vāt* written by an anonymous writer in VS 1761 is a biography of prince Vīram De, the son of Jālor chief Kanhadade. It deals with the chivalrous and romantic deeds of the said prince. The events narrated therein are, of course, based on historical facts but mixed with fiction. However, this biography provides some new and interesting historical details[34] which are supplementary to what we find in the *Kanhadade Prabandha*.

The tradition of writing historical biography in the *rāso* style in Rajasthan developed gradually and became common in the medieval period. The *rāso*s, which mainly comprise poems, were composed in Rajasthani to celebrate the heroic deeds of the Rājpūt rulers. Of the *rāso*s written during the

31. *Kanhadade Prabandha* of Padmanābha, ed. K.B. Vyas, Khaṇḍa IV, vv. 228-249; see also R.P. Vyas, "Biographical Sketches in Rajasthani Literature", in S.P. Sen (ed.), op. cit., pp. 186-87.
32. Op. cit., Introduction, pp. 1-2.
33. Op. cit., p. 170, see also p. 169.
34. *Vīram De Sonigara kī Vāt*, ed. P.L. Menaria, pp. 68-69.

period, mention may first be made of *Khuman Rāso* by Dalpat. Further, the *Khuman Rāso* was written separately by Brahma Datta in Hindi in the thirteenth century, and by Daulat Vijaya in Rajasthani some time before 1733. The said work basically deals with the life and achievements of King Khuman. He is said to have restored the principality of the Guhilas (called Guhilaputras) at Medapāṭa after it had been temporarily overthrown by a revolt of the Abhiras.

The most important *rāso* of the period is *Viśāladeva Rāso* by a Gujarati poet Narapati which was written in Rajasthani in the early sixteenth century. It contains some reliable information about Vigraharāja IV Viśāladeva (CE 1153-64) of the Cāhamāna dynasty. Some of the events narrated in it appear to be fictitious.[35]

The *Satrusal Rāso* by Dungal Singh, the *Rāṇā Rāso* by Dayaldas and the *Sagat Rāso* by Girdhar in Rajasthani are more of literary than historical value.

The *khyāta*s constitute the most important part of Rajasthani historical literature. They give the biographical data of the princes. They were mostly written under the patronage of the rulers who were keen to perpetuate the memory of their exploits in various fields. A number of *khyāta*s on individual rulers are available, viz., *Mahārājā Ajīt Singh-ri-Khyāta, Mahārājā Abhaya Singhji-ri-Khyāta* and so forth. The *khyāta*s which are known after the name of their writers include *Mutha Nainsi-ri-Khyāta, Bāṅkīdās-ri-Khyāta* and *Dayāldās-ri-Khyāta*. These *khyāta*s contain biographical sketches of various rulers of the various dynasties. They are described collectively and individually.[36] *Vāt*s are the shorter forms of *khyāta*s. These *vāt*s

35. See *Nāgarī Pracāriṇī Patrikā*, Banaras, 45, 2, pp. 163-71; *Menariya Rājasthānī Bhāṣā aur Sāhitya* (2006), pp. 85-90.

36. In his work on Indian historiography, Warder (op. cit., pp. 65- →

deal with individuals. *Rāo Jodhā-ri-Vāt*, *Rāo Sūthal-ri Vāt* and *Rāojī Amar Singhji-ri-Vāt* are noted examples of such *vāts*. In *Rāojī Amar Singhji-ri-Vāt*, a biographical sketch of Amar Singh of Jodhpur, the eldest son of Mahārājā Gaja Singh is given. We are informed that he was "excluded from the succession and met a violent death at the imperial court at Agra." At the end of the *vāt* it was stated that the *vāt* was a true copy from the original which was written in the year VS 1703 (CE 1646).[37]

Veer Mayan written by Bahadur Dhadhi is also an important work in Rajasthani. It provides us with biographical sketches of Rāṭhor Bīram. Bahadur Dhadhi was a Muslim poet but he wrote in Hindu style. We are told by him that Bīram was one of the four sons of Rāo Salkha. He had cordial relations with the Johiyās in the beginning. Originally, the Johiyās were Rājpūts but later on they embraced Islam. Bahadur Dhadhi was also in the service of Johiyās. Rāṭhor Bīram extended full support to the Johiyās against the Sultān of Delhi. But after some time trouble arose between the Johiyās and Bīram with the result that a battle was fought in which the latter as well as Madhu, the head of the Johiyās, lost their lives. The poet further informs that Cuṇḍa, the son of Bīram, later occupied Mandor. Rāo Cuṇḍa's brother Gogadev attacked the Johiyās to avenge the death of his father.[38] Since *Veer Mayan* was composed immediately after the death of Bīram, the reliability of the account given by the poet in regard to the life and deeds of

→ 79) has attached great importance to the *Rāsos*, *Hammīra Mahākāvya*, *Padmāvat*, *Khyātas* and other biographical works composed in Rajasthan and highlighted their historical importance.

37. R.P. Vyas, op. cit., p. 182.

38. Ibid., p. 187.

Bīram cannot be doubted. The poet's account is corroborated by other sources also.

Rai-Jetsi-Rau Chand, a Ḍiṅgal poem, composed by Vethu Sujo, a poet in the service of Rāo Jetsi of Bikaner, is another biographical work. It was composed in or about CE 1535 to celebrate a victory obtained by Jetsi over Babur's son Kamran, who from the Punjab had invaded his territory. Like all bardic poems it contains an introduction giving an account of the military exploits of Rāo Jetsi's predecessors from Rāo Cuṇḍa, who occupied Mando, to Rāo Lūṇakaraṇa, the valiant father of Jetsi.[39] The poet gives a picturesque description of the accession of Rāo Jetsi, the grandeur and splendour of his capital (Bikaner) and the prosperity of his subjects.[40] After the death of Babur, his son Kamran assumed independence in Lahore and invaded Bikaner to bring Jetsi under his subjection and domination.[41] He succeeded in capturing the fort of Bikaner. The fort of Bikaner fell to the Mughals after a fierce fight and terrible bloodshed. Rāo Jetsi with all the forces at his command attacked the enemies.[42] The Mughals were completely routed and the camp was in a pool of blood following a carnage.[43] Jetsi liberated his capital Bikaner from the control of the Mughals and thus attained a glorious victory over his enemies.[44] The poem appears to have been written shortly after the battle with Kamran was fought or after Jetsi met a soldier's death while trying to

39. *Rāo Jetsi Rau Chanda*, ed. L.P. Tessitori, vv. 2-93.

40. Ibid., vv. 94-103.

41. Ibid., vv. 142-62.

42. Ibid., vv. 371; p. 116.

43. Ibid., vv. 393-95.

44. Ibid., v. 398. The Ref. nos. 39-44 are cf. R.P. Vyas, op. cit., pp. 187-88.

defend Bikaner from the rapacious aggression of Rāo Maldeo of Jodhpur. In all probability, it was composed before CE 1541. Being a contemporary work its account is reliable with a few exceptions. In spite of minor inaccuracies and exaggerations which we generally come across in a work of this kind, the historical value of the poem is indisputable. The absence of the details of Kamran's episode in the works of Muhammadan historians enhances the value of the poem. The facts recorded in it help us fill in a small gap in the history of India of post-Babur or Humayun period.

The *Guṇarūpaka* composed by Keshavadas in CE 1624 is another Ḍiṅgal poem containing about 1,000 verses. The writer has given a vivid and poetic description of the life and deeds of Mahārājā Gaja Singh with special focus on the grandeur of his court, his pilgrimage and his principal wars. The Mahārāja was much so pleased with the poet that he conferred upon him a *jāgīra* worth Rs. 1,500 a year.[45]

There are some biographical works on the Rājpūt rulers of Medapāṭa (Mewāṛ) of the seventeenth century. The *Rājaprakāśa* (a Ḍiṅgal *kāvya*) written by Kishordas in CE 1662 deals with the glory of Mahārāṇā Rāj Singh. The poet gives a detailed account of his *Rājyābhiṣeka*, etc.[46] The *Rājavilāsa* composed by Mān in eighteen cantos (*vilāsa*) is an important biographical work. The author commenced his work in VS 1734 (= CE 1677) and completed it in VS 1737 (= CE 1680). It is a biography of Mahārāṇā Rāj Singh of Mewāṛ. It gives a full account of his life beginning from his birth till the last days of his life when he came in clash with Aurangzeb in order to uphold the claim of Ajit Singh for the throne of Mārwāṛ. The first two *vilāsas* trace the history of Mewāṛ from Bāpā to

45. B.N. Reu, *Mārwāṛ-kā-Itihās*, pt. I, p. 20 cf. R.P. Vyas, op. cit., p. 188.

46. *Rājaprakāśa*, vv. 89-92 cf. R.P. Vyas, op. cit., p. 189.

Mahārāṇā Jagat Singh. In the third *vilāsa*, the poet describes the early childhood of Rāj Singh, his education and his marriage with Hāḍā princess (Būndī).[47] The fifth *vilāsa* deals with the accession of Rāj Singh. The poet's description of his *durbār* and the personal qualities is more literary than historical in nature.[48] In the last nine *vilāsa*s, the poet has given a detailed historical account of the war between the Mughals and the Rājpūts (Rāṭhor–Sisodiās). It is a contemporary work and hence the information it contains regarding the life and the reign of the Mahārāṇā is fully reliable. The *Jagatavilāsa* is a biography of Mahārāṇā Jagat Singh.

The *Sūrya Prakāśa* composed by Karnīdān, and *Rājarūpaka* by Ratanu Veer Bhāna are two very important Ḍiṅgal *kāvya*s dealing with the lives of Mahārājā Ajit Singh in detail and Mahārājā Abhaya Singh up to his battle with Sarbuland Khan at Ahmedabad in October 1730. Both the poets were present with Mahārāja Abhaya Singh of Mārwāṛ at Ahmedabad and they were the eyewitnesses to that battle. With a view to commemorating the victory of their patron in the battle of Ahmedabad, they composed their respective Kāvyas. "As usual the Kāvyas commenced with the origin of the Sūryavaṁśa Rāṭhors from their cradle at Ayodia to Shia's migration, and in the same strain rapidly passed over all events until the death of Rājā Jaswant Singh. These Kāvyas chronicled the events that took place during the minority of Ajit Singh, his eventful reign, and that of Abhaya Singh to the conclusion of war against Sarbuland Khan, the *sūbedār* of Gujarat (1730). Karnīdān has devoted one full chapter (sixth) of more than 100 pages to present a biographical

47. *Rājavilāsa* of Mān, ed. M. Menaria, vv. 92-107.

48. Ibid., Vilāsa 5, vv. 59-95 cf. R.P. Vyasa, op. cit., p. 189.

account of Mahārājā Ajit Singh which encompasses his birth, his war with the Mughals, his entry into the capital (Jodhpur) after the death of Aurangzeb, his hostile attitude towards the Mughal Emperor Bahadur Shah, his meeting with Mahārājā Amar Singh II and Sawāī Rājā Jai Singh at Udaipur, his reoccupation of Jodhpur, his support to Sawāī Rājā Jai Singh in gaining Ajmer for him, his war with the Mughals at Sambhar, his war with the Mughals during the time of Farrukhsiyar and Muhammad Shah, and his death. Similarly, the poet has thrown light on the day-to-day activities of his patron Abhaya Singh up to the battle of Ahmedabad which was the principal theme of the *kāvya*. Ratna Veer Bhāna divided his *kāvya* into 45 *prakāśa*s (chapters) of which the first 37 were devoted to the depiction of the life of Mahārājā Ajit Singh. It is a detailed and reliable biography of this prince. The poet has also given a biographical account of Mahārājā Abhaya Singh covering the events of the first six years of his reign. The work ends with the victory of Mahārājā Abhaya Singh over Sarbuland Khan."[49]

There is one more Ḍiṅgal *kāvya* on Ajit Singh known as *Ajit Vilāsa* which is his biography right from his birth to his death. The name of the author of the *kāvya* is not known, but on the basis of the study of its text it has been pointed out that the author must have belonged to the period of Ajit Singh or his son Abhaya Singh. The poet is said to have given an account of the events of the reign of Ajit Singh in a chronological way mentioning their dates.[50]

The work that deals with the life of Jaya Singh II (1699-1743), the founder of Jayapura, is known as *Jayavilāsa*. Jaya Singh was succeeded by his son Īśvara Singh and the

49. Cf. R.P. Vyasa, op. cit., pp. 189-90.

50. Ibid., pp. 190-91.

contemporary poet Kr̥ṣna Śarmā wrote a Sanskrit epic, *Īśvaravilāsa* which is of considerable historical value. The work consists of 14 cantos. The cantos II-X deal with the reign of Jaya Singh, and the rest of the cantos contain the biography of Īśvara Singh from his accession to his death.

The *Mānacarita* (anonymous) is a biography of Rājā Mān Singh, one of the military officers of Akbar.

The *vācanika*s constitute an important branch of Rajasthani historical literature in prose. They also deal with the lives of princes and warriors with special reference to the significant events of their times. Of all the *vācanika*s, *Ratan Singh Mahesadasota-ri-Vācanika* is the most important which was written by Khiriya Jagga to commemorate the battle of Ujjain fought between Mahārājā Jaswant Singh and the combined forces of Aurangzeb and Murad, the sons of Shahjahan. The author was an eyewitness to the event. The most distinguished amongst the Rājpūts who sacrificed their lives for their king on that unfortunate day was Ratan Singh, the *rājā* of Ratlam in Mālwā, a kindred of Mahārājā Jaswant Singh. This *vācanika* was composed immediately or very shortly after the battle of Ujjain on Friday, the 9th day of the dark fortnight of Vaiśākha, VS 1715, just to commemorate the glorious death of Ratan Singh. The title it bears is indicative of the fact.

The *haqiqat* and *yādāsta* also have their place in the Rajasthani biographical literature. They do provide some reliable data concerning biographical sketches of certain historical personages. *Bādshāh Aurangzeb ri Haqīqat, Delhi ri Pādshāh ri Yād,* and *Rāo Jodhā ri Vedha Kiān ri Yād*[51] are the three notable instances of such works.

51. L.P. Tessitori, *Bibliotheca Indica: Descriptive Catalogue of Bardic and Historical Manuscripts,* Section I, part II, Bikaner State, pp. 18-19, cf. R.P. Vyas, op. cit., p. 184.

Vigat is another significant branch of Rajasthani literature of historical importance. In *vigat* too, we notice a vivid description of some historical personages. The most important example of *vigat* is *Mārwāṛ ra Parganā ri Vigat* composed by the historian Nainsi, "the Abul Fazl of Rajasthan," in VS 1721 (= CE 1664). The biographical accounts of the rulers of "Mārwāṛ" contained in it are very authentic from a historical point of view. The author has dealt with the exploits of Rāo Cuṇḍa up to the time of his death, which he met with at Nāgaur while fighting against a Muslim governor of Multan who received considerable help from Rāo Kalhan of Pugal. The account of Jodhā's sons, Santal and Sujā is fairly reliable. The detailed and date-wise biographical account of Rāo Maldeo not only constitutes the distinguishing feature of the work but also shows its historical value. Rāo Maldeo's "conquests and losses, his love for constructing forts and other buildings, his acts of charity, his relations with Rāṇā Udai Singh of Mewāṛ and annexation of Godwad to his dominion, his friendship with Haji Khan, his fights with Bhati Jaisa of Pugal, Vīramdev and Jaimal of Merta, Shershah Suri and the Mughal emperor Akbar, etc. are depicted with much accuracy. One very interesting fact discovered from the *vigat* is that Rāo Maldeo had eight daughters. Two of them were married to Muslims — one (Kanakavatī) to Sultān Muhammed II or Mahmud III of Gujarat, both of whom are known to have been Maldeo's contemporaries, and the second (Ratnāvatī) to Haji Khan, a well-known general of Emperor Sher Shah."[52] "After the demise of their husbands both abandoned the Muslim harem, one went to Jaisalmer to live with her sister, Sajana, a

52. *Mārwāṛ ra Parganā ri Vigat* of Nainsi, part I, ed. Narain Singh Bhati, pp. 20-26, 42-67, cf. R.P. Vyas, op. cit., p. 184. This *vigat* also contains some non-biographical writings.

queen of Harirāj and another came back to Jodhpur to live with her brother Candrasen."[53] From this *vigat* it is proved that Akbar was not the first Muslim ruler who entered into such matrimonial alliances without using any force.

Of the historical biographies of the *prabandha* type composed in Gujarat in the medieval period, mention may first be made of *Kumārapāla Prabandha* of Jinamaṇḍana Gaṇi. This *prabandha* written in the fifteenth century is supplementary to *Kumārapālacarita* written in the twelfth century by Hemacandra and in the thirteenth century by Jayasiṁha Sūri II, the two famous Jaina historians of Gujarat. Jinamaṇḍana's description of the *digvijaya* (conquest) of the Cāḷukya king of Anhilwāḍa (modern Pāṭan in Gujarat), Kumārapāla (CE 1143-72), is not at much variance with what Hemacandra and Jayasiṁha have described. In the *Kumārapāla Prabandha* (pp. 23, 33-36), it is explicitly related that Kumārapāla attained victory over Arṇorāja, the Cāhamāna ruler of Śākambharī. He reasserted the Cāḷukya authority in Mālwā, which was under the rule of the Paramāras. He subdued a chieftain of Saurāṣṭra. His most remarkable exploit was the defeat of King Mallikārjuna of north Koṅkaṇa. The story relating to his death narrated in the said *prabandha* (pp. 114-15) is slightly different from what we find in the work of Jayasiṁha.

The *Bhoja Prabandha* of Ballāla is a biography of Bhoja, the most striking and versatile Paramāra ruler of Mālwā. He raised Dhāra, the capital, to a position of eminence. The author (poet) has given the life sketch of Rājā Bhoja from his accession (in CE 999 or 1018) to the end of his reign (in 1054 or 1063). He is said to have conquered extensive territories, including Lāṭa (southern Gujarat), and annexed to his dominion.

---

53. R.P. Vyas, op. cit., p. 184.

The *Vimala Prabandha* composed by Lāvaṇyasāmay, "minister of Bhīmadeva Solaṅkī I," in CE 1512 is one of the important biographies in Gujarati. It is a life story of Vimala, who belonged to a class of merchants and left a mark of his own on the economic history of Gujarat during his time.[54]

Among Jaina historical biographies of the medieval period the most noteworthy is the *Prabhāvakacarita* of Prabhācandra Sūri of Gujarat who belonged to Śvetāmbara school. The author himself says that his work (completed in CE 1276 or 1277) is based on ancient historical and biograhical literature, and popular traditions.[55] It contains biographies of many historical personalities, including the famous kings and rulers, and Jaina saints and scholars. It gives accounts of several kings prominent among whom are Vikramāditya of Ujjayinī (Ujjain), Harṣavardhana of Thāneśvar and Kannauj, Yaśovarman of Kannauj, Dharmapāla of Bengal, Pratihāra Nāgabhaṭṭa II and Mihirabhoja of Kannauj, Paramāra Bhojadeva (Bhoja) of Mālwā, and Cāḷukya Bhīmadeva (Bhīma I), Jayasiṁha Siddharāja and Kumārapāla, the last two receiving detailed treatment. The historical accuracy of events of their reign recorded in it is beyond doubt. A dynastic list inclusive of Pālaka (Caṇḍapradyota) of Avantī, Nandas and Mauryas of Magadha, Gardabhilla of Ujjayinī and the Śaka in Ujjayinī is also given in it with duration of their rule in ME (*c.* 527 BCE) which is of chronological importance. The work also deals with the lives and activities of as many as 22 Jaina *ācārya*s beginning from Vajrasvāmī and ending with Hemacandra (the celebrated historian and the author of *Kumārapālacarita*). The last phase of life of Mahāvīra also received the attention of the author of the work.

54. For details see V.K. Chavda, "Historical Biography in Gujarati Literature", in S.P. Sen (ed.), op. cit., p. 199.

55. *Prabhāvakacarita*, ed. Jinavijaya Muni, v. 15.

The role Jaina *ācārya* Kālaka (a traitor) played in inviting and instigating the Śakas for invading and occupying Ujjayinī has been highlighted in the *Kālakācārya Kathānaka* (anonymous) which forms a part of *Prabhāvakacarita*. The story relating to the Śakas' occupation of Ujjayinī and King Vikramāditya prolixly narrated in it is not devoid of historical interest. It also throws some light on the antecedents and ancestors of Vikramāditya. The historical fact has indeed coalesced with legend in the course of treatment of the subject.[56]

Sarvānanda Sūri's *Jagaḍucarita* composed in the fourteenth century is a biography of Jagaḍu Shāh, a wealthy merchant and philanthrophist of Cutch. He flourished during the Vāghelā period. He gave a boost to Gujarat's external trade and commerce with the outside world. We are told by the author of the work that he had a very big fleet of vessels of his own for trade. He had his Gujarati broker stationed at Ormuz in the Persian Gulf. He has, no doubt, a place in the economic history of Gujarat of early medieval period. This work specifically describes the large maritime or overseas trade carried through ports like Bhṛgukaccha (Broach) and Cambay during the prosperity of Cāḷukya period.

Samara Ras, a work of 1315, by Ambadev Sur is a story of Samara Siṁha of Pāṭan who organised a pilgrimage of holy Jaina shrines in Saurāṣṭra. It contains valuable information

---

56. The *Kālakācārya Kathā* in *Prabhāvakacarita* attracted the notice of very few scholars. J. Charpentier ("The History of the Jains", in *CHI*, I, Ancient India, ed. E.J. Rapson, pp. 149-50), Sten Konow, (*Corp. Ins. Ind.*, vol. II, pt. I, Historical Background), A.S. Altekar, (*Nāgarī Pracāriṇī Patrikā*, VS 2000, pp. 85-86) and K.P. Jayaswal (*JBORS*, XVI, p. 233) have critically examined its historicity. The analysis and interpretation of the data contained in the said work by Raj Bali Pandey in his work (*Vikramāditya: Saṁvat Pravarta*, Hindi tr. of his *Vikramāditya of Ujjayinī: Founder of the Vikram Era*, in English, pp. 27-32, 44-45, 80-81) is the best of all.

regarding devastation caused by Ala-ud-din Khilji's armies in the course of invasion of Gujarat in 1299. Śrīdhara Vyāsa's *Raṇamalla Chanda* (1398) and poet Śāmal's *Rustam no Śaloko* (1725) are the other two important biographies in Gujarati. The history of important political events of their respective times is preserved in the respective works.[57]

Pasmanābha's Sanskrit work *Vīrabhadra Campū* (mixed prose and verse) completed in 1578 celebrates the achievements of Vīrabhadra, one of the Vāghelā rulers of Gujarat.

The *Śālivāhanacarita* of Śivadāsa is a biography of Śālivāhana who was no other than the king of Ujjain. He was one of the successors of Vikramāditya. He ascended the throne 135 years after Vikramāditya. The author narrates the early life and wars and conquests of Śālivāhana. His comparison with any of the Sātavāhana kings of Paiṭhan (Pratiṣṭhānapura on the Godavari in Aurangabad district of Maharashtra) will be unwarranted.

We have a biography dealing with Bundela history. Lāl Kavi (1657-1707) wrote an epic in Braj (the main classical form of Hindi), the *Chatraprakāśa,* to celebrate the deeds of King Chatraśāla (1646-1731) of Pannā near Kharjūravāhaka (Khajurāho) who made himself independent of the Mughals and worked to further the Indian resurgence and bring about the end of the Mughals' rule. The epic reviews the earlier history of Bundelkhand and then deals in detail with the lives of Chatraśāla and his immediate predecessors. Being a contemporary work, it has great historical value.

Jagannātha, the son of Perubhaṭṭa Tailiṅga of the village in Godavari district, was at the court of Mughal Emperor Shahjahan from 1628 to 1638, and prince Dara was his patron.

57. See Chavda, op. cit., p. 200.

He wrote *Āsaphvilāsa* (in prose) in praise of Nawāb Asaf Khan (a counsellor of Shahjahan) who died in 1646. His *Jagadābharaṇa* is a poem describing the deeds of his patron Dara Shah.[58]

In his *Śiva Bhārata* (in Sanskrit consisting of 31 chapters), Paramānanda describes the life and exploits of Śivājī (1627-80), the great Marāṭhā leader and a military genius. He is described as the glory of the Marāṭhās and the terror of the Mughal empire. The life of Śivājī's second son Rājārāma is sketched in *Rājārāmacarita*, a poem by Keśavapaṇḍita. The author (poet) has focused on his fight against the Mughal forces (during the reign of Aurangzeb) from 1689 till he died in 1700. The struggle for Marāṭhā independence in the Carnatic is also depicted in it. Both are contemporary works.

The bardic tradition did not die out completely. It was revived at the time of Hindu resistance to Aurangzeb's policy in the seventeenth century. In the same tradition, Bhūṣaṇa composed his *Śiva Rāj Bhūṣaṇa* in 1673 throwing considerable light on the achievements of Śivājī in an eulogistic style.

On Śivājī, works are in the form of *bakhar*. The *bakhar*s are chronicles and not historical biographies as such and hence they have been included in the fifth book rather than the present one of this work. They were written in late medieval period in Maharashtra.

The *Alī Nāmā* — a long historical poem — by Nusrati is also worth noting. It describes in detail the wars of the Adil-Shahis with the Mughals and the Marāṭhās and also gives an account of the valiant deeds of his master. This is considered as the first historical biography in Urdu.

58. M. Krishnamachariar, *HCSL*, p. 354.

The biographical tradition in the Punjab commenced in the sixteenth century and continued down to the end of the eighteenth century and even further. The eighteenth century in particular was a blooming period in the history of writing historical biography. During that century, a number of biographies bearing historical character were produced. Of the 10 Sikh *gurus*, Guru Nanak (the first) and Guru Gobind Singh (the last) attracted the utmost attention of the biographers. The former has a place in the history of the *bhakti* movement in India as well as in the religious history of the Punjab and the latter in the history of India of the Mughal period. Some of the hagiographers were the descendants of the Sikh *gurus*. The works on Guru Gobind Singh are historical in nature whereas those on other *gurus* both hagiographical and historical. The works were composed and compiled in Punjabi.

The *Janamsākhī* originally ascribed to Bhāī Bālā is the earliest biography of Guru Nanak (1469-1538), the founder of Sikhism and the great religious leader and reformer. It was written on the initiative of his immediate successor Guru Angad (1539-52). It was he who asked Bhāī Bālā, a companion of the Guru (Nanak) during his early life at Talwaṇḍī Rāī Bhoi (now called Nankānā Sāhib) in West Pakistan and Sultanpur Lodhi to reduce his reminiscences of the *guru* to writing. His work gives an account of the life of Guru Nanak and his travelling in different parts of the country, teachings and preachings in the form of stories. The book known as *Bhāī Bālā-wālī Janamsākhī* was enlarged by later hagiographers on the pattern of some earlier biographies of Hindu and Muslim saints.[59]

Another biography of Guru Nanak was compiled by

59. Ganda Singh, "Biography in Panjabi Literature", in S.P. Sen (ed.), op. cit., p. 158.

Manohar Das Sodhi also known as Manohar Das Meharban (1581-1640), the son of fifth Guru Arjan's elder brother Prithi Chand and the grandson of the fourth Guru Ram Das, which is known as *Meharbānwālī Janamsākhī*.[60]

The *Vilāyat-wālī Janamsākhī* or the *Purātan Janamsākhī* (1690) and *Śambhū Nāth Wālī Janampatrī Bābe Nānakjī kī*, popularly known as the *Ādi Sākhiāṅ* (1701, 1734), with a large number of *sākhīs* (stories) common to them, are also worth noting. It is said that "The dates when these *Janamsākhīs* were originally written are not inscribed on any of the available copies." It can only be inferred "from the dates of some of their transcriptions that they were written during the sixteenth and seventeenth centuries."[61]

The lives and personalities of the Sikh *gurus*, especially the tenth and the last Guru Gobind Singh (1666-1708), became a favourite subject for mainly the Sikh writers of the eighteenth century. The tenth Guru organised the Sikhs into a military organisation and fought against the Mughals all through his life. His heroic deeds and martyrdom inspired the writers to write his biography. The biographical works on him served the purpose of historical records for the posterity.

The *Janganāmāh Bhangani* and *Bhera Śrī Guru Gobind Singh kā* by anonymous authors and the *Janganāmāh Śrī Guru Gobind Singh* by the Guru's court-poet Ani Rai describe the battles fought by the Guru against the Śivālik Hill chiefs and government detachments. Ani Rai was an eyewitness to the

60. Ganda Singh, "Biography in Panjabi Literature", in S.P. Sen (ed.), p. 159; also J.P. De Souza and C.M. Kulkarni (eds.), *Historiography in Indian Languages*, pp. 238 f. The historical significance of the work has been highlighted by Kirpal Singh in his article, "Historical Significance of the Janamsakhi of Guru Nank by Meharban", in the *Proceedings of the 5th Session of the Punjab History Conference*, 1970.

61. Ganda Singh, op. cit., pp. 158-59.

events described by him. The *parchīān* (prosework) of Bhaī Sewā Dās, compiled by him in 1708, and the *Panjāb Sākhīān* compiled by an anonymous Sikh at about the same time, contain 50 *sākhīs* or stories from the lives of the Sikh *gurus* ending with the death of Guru Gobind Singh in October 1708. Within three years of the Guru's death was written (in 1711) the *Śrī Gur Sobhā* by poet Chander Bhan populary known as Sainapaṭ. The poet not only describes the greatness of the Guru but also records the events of his life to which he was himself an eyewitness. Though a great admirer of the Guru, he has refrained himself from eulogical or hyperbolical expression. He has rather painted a true picture of the Guru's life. All these works are of great historical value. The other two important works of the eighteenth century that have survived and have come down to us are *Gyān-Ratnāvalī Janamsākhī Guru Nānak Jī dī* compiled under the guidance of a scholar-saint Bhāī Maṇī Singh (by an anonymous author) also known as *Maṇī Singh-wālī Janamsākhī*, and the *Bhagat Ratnāvalī* also known as *Sikhāṅ-dī-Bhagat-Mal*, written in the same manner. The former is a biography of Guru Nanak and the latter gives accounts of some of the prominent Sikhs of the days of the *gurus*. Both these works belong to the hagiographic class of prose literature written before 24 June 1734, when Bhāī Maṇī Singh was cut to pieces limb by limb under the order of Nawāb Ẓakariyā Khān, governor of Lahore. The first detailed account of the life of Guru Gobind Singh was written by Koer Singh in 1751 in his *Gurbilās Pātshāhī Dās*, a work of rare historical value. It was based mostly on the *Śrī Gur Sobhā* of poet Sainapaṭ of the discourses of Bhāī Maṇī Singh. The last quarter of the eighteenth century also saw some important biographical works in Punjabi. In 1775, poet Sohan completed the *Gurbilās Pātshāhī Chevīṅ* devoted to the life of the sixth Sikh *guru*, Har Gobind, who is commonly credited with having imparted a militant character to the peaceful Sikh movement. In 1776, Sarup Das Bhalla, a descendant of the third Guru Amar Das, compiled the *Mahimā Prakāśa*. Over one-third of the book (in poetry) is devoted to the life of Guru Nanak and the rest to those of the remaining nine *gurus*. A part of the book gives in prose a brief account of Guru Nanak by Kirpal Singh. The work, though hagiographical in nature, is nearer to history. The *Gurbilās Pātshāhī Daswīṅ ke Caritar* written by poet Bhāī Sukhā Singh in 1797 is an important biography of the tenth *guru*, Gobind Singh.[62]

The eastern Indian tradition of historiography in medieval period also deserves our notice.

The *bhakti* movement of the fifteenth and sixteenth centuries gave fillip to the writing of a biography of the greatest Vaiṣṇava saint and religious reformer Caitanyadeva, who was born in 1485 at Nadia (Bengal) in a brāhmaṇa family. He fought against orthodoxy and casteism, preached the simple truths of religion (*bhakti*), took a Muslim into his fold and brought a socio-religious revolution in Greater Bengal and Orissa. He died in 1533 at the age of 48. The *Caitanya Maṅgala* (written between 1548 and 1560), *Caitanya Caritāmṛta* (not written before 1557) and *Caitanya Bhāgavata* in Bengali by Jayānanda, Kṛṣnadāsa Kavirāja and Vṛndāvan Dās respectively may be accepted to some extent as historical biographies and not merely hagiographies. Caitanyadeva of Bengal like Guru Nanak of the Punjab was a religious leader and reformer. Both were historical personages. Both have place in the history of *bhakti* movement in India.

Mana-Siṁha-pala written in verse by a Bengali poet deals

62. Ganda Singh, op. cit., pp. 159-61; also his "History in Panjabi Literature", in *History in Modern Indian Literature*, ed. S.P. Sen, pp. 112-16; De Souza and Kulkarni, op. cit., pp. 43-47, 165-73, 238 f.

with the story of Pratāpāditya, a local king of lower-Bengal, who fought against the Mughals but was later captured. This work is considered to be the first contribution by a Bengali poet in the field of writing historical biography.[63] It appears to have been written some time before 1757.

The *Kīrtilatā* written by Vidyāpati Ṭhākura (1360-1448), a celebrated poet of Mithilā (Bihar), in old Maithilī (mixed with Prākr̥t and Apabhraṁśa) in four *pallava*s (chapters) is a historical biography of Mahārājā Kīrtisiṁha, one of the rulers of Mithilā and a contemporary of Ibrahim Shah, the Turkish Sultān of Jaunpur (1401-40).

In the first *pallava* of his work, Vidyāpati throws light on the antecedents and ancestors of King Kīrtisiṁha. We are told that he was born in the Oinwar dynasty which was famous for both valour and learning. The dynasty was founded by one Kāmeśvara whose son Bhogeśvara was acclaimed as a friend by Sultān Feroz Shah Tughlaq. Bhogeśvara's son Gaṇeśvara had two sons, Vīrasiṁha, the elder, and Kīrtisiṁha (the hero of the story), the younger. All except Vīrasiṁha ruled the kingdom of Tirabhukti (Tirhut) with its capital at Mithilā in succession. At the end of this *pallava* and in the second one, it is clearly stated that a Muhammadan named Aslan attempted to seize the throne of Tirabhukti but was defeated by Mahārājā Gaṇeśvara Siṁha. The former later on cultivated friendship with the latter and murdered him (in 1372) and became the ruler of Tirabhukti. Further, from the third and fourth *pallava*s we learn that Kīrtisiṁha and his brother Vīrasiṁha inflicted crushing defeat on Aslan in a battle at Mithilā with the help of the forces of Ibrahim Shah of Jaunpur (in or about 1404 or

63. D. Bhattacharya, "Historical Biography in Bengali Literature", in *Historical Biography in Indian Literature*, ed. S.P. Sen, p. 84.

1405) and thus took revenge upon their father's murderer. Aslan fled away. Kīrtisiṁha's triumph was acclaimed and he was declared king of Mithilā and Sultān Ibrahim Shah himself anointed him.[64] In order to commemorate that historic event, Vidyāpati composed his work when Kīrtisiṁha was ruling. The poet has praised the valour and courage of the ruling king. The work is, no doubt, an excellent piece of history. K.P. Jayaswal has rightly stated that "It is more a piece of history than a *kāvya*."[65]

An equally important work of Vidyāpati is the *Kīrtipatākā* (in Maithilī) which deals with the life and achievements of his patron, Mahārājā Śivasiṁha, a worthy descendant of Kīrtisiṁha and worthy king of Mithilā. The poet gives an account of the battles fought between Śivasiṁha and some Muslim rulers. The biographical work is also of great historical value.

Vidyāpati wrote his *Puruṣa Parīkṣā* in Sanskrit at the beginning of the fifteenth century during the reign of Śivasiṁha. This work contains the details of several historical personalities in the form of stories. The illustrative stories go back to the time of the last Nanda Emperor Dhanānanda (fourth century BCE) who lost his empire to Candragupta Maurya. The Paramāra king Bhoja of Mālwā, King Lakṣmaṇa Sen of Vaṅga (Bengal), Candradeva, founder of the Gāhaḍavāla dynasty at Kānyakubja, and Jayacanda of the same dynasty who was defeated and slain by Sahāvadina (Sahabuddin Ghori), King Nānyadeva, the founder of Karṇāṭa dynasty that ruled Tirabhukti, and Harasiṁha of the same dynasty who was locked in a long war with

64. *Kīrtilatā*, ed. with Eng. tr. by Umesha Mishra, pp. 1-69 (text), 9-17 (tr.).

65. *JBORS*, XIII, 3-4, p. 298.

Mahamada (Muhammad Tughlaq), the Karṇāṭa prince Narasiṁha and his wars with Turkish Sultān, Hammīra Deva, the Cāhamāna ruler of Raṇastambhapur (Raṇathambhor), who was defeated and put to death by Allāvadina (Alauddin Khilji), Kīrtisiṁha, the king of Mithilā, and other kings and rulers and the events of their times are described in the work.[66]

A.K. Warder, a noted authority on Indian historiography, has also brought to light the contents of *Kīrtilatā* and *Puruṣa Parīkṣā* of Vidyāpati in his work.[67] The description of historical subjects in a poetic style by Vidyāpati bears witness to the fact that he combined in himself the qualities of a poet and a historian. There were many such poets in ancient and medieval India who contributed to the development of tradition of historical writing.

Mahesh Ṭhākura translated the *Akbarnāmā* into Sanskrit and named it *Sarvadeśavṛttānta Saṁgraha* (in prose) and he was presented by emperor Akbar with the Darbhaṅgā Rāj. The *Kīrti-Samullāsa* and *Nabākhānacarita* by the same author celebrate Jehangir.

The historical biographies of the ruling kings of Orissa (in prose in the Oriya language) form part of the *Mādalā Pāñjī* (the palm-leaf manuscripts preserved in the famous Jagannāth temple at Purī) whose date and authorship is controversial. Its composition began probably in the eleventh century during the reign of Choḍagaṅgadeva (1078-1147), the founder king of the Gaṅga dynasty and further continued. The lives and exploits of various kings and rulers with details of their wars and conquests, administrative system, economic policies, success and failures, etc. have

66. *Puruṣa Parīkṣā*, ed. and tr. by Nerulkar (Bombay, 1914).

67. Op. cit., pp. 85-86.

been incorporated therein. Anaṅgabhīma Deva (1211-38), a benevolent ruler, Kapilendra Deva (1435-66), the founder of Solar dynasty and the most powerful king, his son Puruṣottam Deva (1466-97) and some of their successors, including Pratāprudradeva (1497-1533), find mention therein. Sarala Das, the celebrated Oriya poet of the fifteenth century, wrote the *Mahābhārata*, a literary work of historical value. In his work, the poet has provided a faithful account of the reign of the great King Kapilendra Deva touching upon his heroic deeds and stable government.[68]

The tradition of writing historical biography in Assam began in the early seventeenth century. That tradition, in fact, commenced with the writing of hagiographies dealing with the lives and religious activities of Vaiṣṇava saints. Śaṅkaradeva (1449-1568), Mādhavadeva (1490-1596), Dāmodaradeva (1510-16), Gopāladeva, Vaṁśīgopāladeva (seventeenth century), Vanamālideva (seventeenth century), Aniruddhadeva (seventeenth century), Jadumaṇideva, Keśavadeva and Śrīrāmadeva were famous Vaiṣṇava saints and religious reformers and preachers. The most prominent among them was Śaṅkaradeva who ushered in a cultural revolution in Assam. They all have place in the religious history of medieval Assam. Their biographies were written in Assamese (both in verse and prose) during the seventeenth and eighteenth centuries. The biographers recorded facts and events personally witnessed by them. They also utilised materials handed down through tradition. Besides biographies dealing with particular individuals, there are a set of works which deal with the lives and activities of several religious preachers in the chronological order contained in

68. G.C. Misra, "Historical Biography in Oriya Literature", in *Historical Biography in Indian Literature*, ed. S.P. Sen pp. 109, 111-12.

a single volume the most notable example of which is the *Kathāgurucarita*, a voluminous prose work of the eighteenth century dealing with the lives and activities of all the renowned religious preachers of the sixteenth and seventeenth centuries. The family history and the early life of the preachers, their daily life and detailed activities as preachers have been minutely described. The biographical works besides dealing with the lives of the great Vaiṣṇava saints throw light on the socio-economic, political, religious and cultural life of the people. The patronage extended by different kings to the proselytizers and occasional repressive and oppressive measures of the kings towards the religious preachers are vividly described in some works. For instance, the *Keśavadeva-carita* by Ambarish Dvija of the eighteenth century gives a graphic account of the oppression over the Vaiṣṇavite preachers by the Ahom king Gadādhar Siṁha (1681-96).[69]

The hagiographical works, no doubt, fall little short of historical biography, but since they deal with the lives of religious personalities who have place in the medieval history of Assam, they may be considered the biographical works of historical importance. This may best be qualified in the words of S.N. Sarma:

> The hagiographies . . . without strictly conforming to the standard of historical biography serve the purpose of that category of biography to a considerable extent inasmuch as they not only project the lives of the preachers, but also afford us ample glimpse of the social, economic and religious conditions of early Assam.[70]

---

69. S.N. Sarma, "Historical Biographies in Assamese Literature", in *Historical Biography in Indian Literature*, ed. S.P. Sen, pp. 94-95; also his "History in Assamese Literature" in *History in Modern Indian Literature*, ed. S.P. Sen, pp. 46-47.

70. S.N. Sarma, "Historical Biographies in Assamese Literature", op. cit., pp. 95-96.

To Edward Gait has also placed the hagiographies (*carit-puthīs*) mainly on the life of Vaiṣṇava saints of Assam under the class of works that contain "historical writings." He further observes that:

> A huge mass of *carit-puthīs* was compiled during the period of the Ahoms, particularly in the *satra*-institutions. In these writings for the first time one comes into more intimate relations with the great saints of the period and sees them in the social surroundings in which they lived, and contemporary men and women with whom they worked and conversed daily.[71]

The *Campakavijaya* and the *Kṛṣṇa-mālā* (in Bengali) composed in Tripura are also worth noting. The former describes the life of Ratna Māṇikya II (1684-1712), the *rājā* of Tripura, and the events that took place during his reign. The latter work deals with the life and achievements of Rājā Kṛṣṇa-Māṇikya (1760-83). The dates of their composition and their authorship are not known.[72]

The tradition of writing historical biography does not appear to have developed in Manipur during the period of our study. There is no such work to be noted here. In this part of India, the tradition of writing and preserving chronicles was, of course, very rich which has been dwelt upon at length in the following book of this work.

---

71. *A History of Assam*, pp. 283-84.

72. See De Souza and Kulkarni, op. cit., p. 35.

4.2

A Critical Evaluation of Biographical Writings

THE historical biographies produced in India during ancient and medieval period belong to different classes. As most of the works were written by the poets in the courts of their respective patrons, it was but natural for the former to bestow praise on the latter and to glorify their deeds, extol their virtues and exalt their glory to keep them gratified. However, the main object of the authors of the biographical works was not the glorification of kings but to portray a true picture of their lives and times by applying their literary skill and ingenuity. The biographical writings are by and large eulogistic in nature and panegyric in tone but not devoid of historical contents. There are, of course, some inaccuracies and exaggerations in the author's presentation of subject matter but not distortions of historical truth. They have preserved all important historical facts in their respective works. All contemporary significant historical events have been incorporated in them. The biographical works on the whole are full of valuable historical information. The court-poets of medieval period wrote the biographies of their patrons generally casting off their flunkeyism to them and avoiding the tendency to glorify them unlike ancient court-poets. A few works were written not in the courts of their patrons but in those of their descendants during the period. The biographies were composed under the patronage of the rulers who were keen to perpetuate the memory of their exploits in various fields. The works which were written independently without any royal patronage during the same period are free from laudatory expressions. In such works, the authors have presented detailed accounts of the lives and achievements of the historical personages and events of their times based on facts. The works in general contain apart from biographical details other historical information.

Many events and incidents narrated in some biographical works of ancient period have been corroborated by inscriptions and other faithful records. Most of the facts regarding *digvijaya* (conquests) of the kings recorded in works have found support from contemporary epigraphical records and other valuable sources. Genealogies of kings and patrons given in some works have also been found reliable. All these go to prove the historicity of the works concerned. The biographers of famous kings and other historical personages were definitely endowed with a historical sense. The biographical works of historical character also bear testimony to the gradual progress in historical conception. Among the biographical writers of ancient and early medieval India there were few who were critical of their own men and liberal to the enemies of their patrons which is a distinct proof of the objective treatment of the subject. Admitting all these facts we cannot deny that the tradition of writng genuine historical biography had not fully developed in ancient India. In medieval India, of course, a number of genuine historical biographies were composed. However, only a few works can stand the test of rigorous scrutiny. Several works of the periods under notice suffer from the deficiency of chronology.

The biographical works composed in verse belong to a

class of literature called *kāvya*. This explains the reason why their authors could not avoid the use of metaphor and imagery and coalescing of facts and fictions in their writings. They have presented biographical histories by adopting *kāvya* style of writing which is characterised by literary ornamentation, high-flown expression and poetic embellishments. They actually followed the literary tradition of writing historical biography. The works in verse were, of course, written in literary style but they do contain a lot of historical facts. That is why they are often described as "w." In prose works, the lives and achievements of kings, rulers and other historical figures are described at greater length and with more accuracy than what we find in verse works.

The biographical works of medieval period belonging to hagiographic class deal with the lives and activities of great saints, religious leaders and reformers. They do not throw much light on the contemporary political events of their times. The authors of the works of such class have refrained themselves from making hyperbolical remarks. They have successfully distinguished histories from fanciful stories. There are, however, some panegyrical references in hagiographical writings.

The biographical works of ancient and medieval periods despite their shortcomings have relative value.

> Ancient Indian biographies, like their counterparts in other countries, are by no means perfect. By modern standards they fall short of the desired ideal. By and large their authors appear to have been believers in the "Great Man Theory of History," being ardent admirers of their patrons. Rarely they have succeeded in unfolding the full courses of the lives of their patrons and have seldom explored the quirks and crannies of their personalities. Yet viewed as a whole, their works have

enabled us to know many things about the lives and careers of eminent personalities of ancient and early medieval India and occasionally to recapture in our imagination all that they had lived and died for.[1]

The ancient biographies are . . . of very great importance to the modern student, because history is present in them not as a chart of events but as a detailed map in which the events are located with reference to contemporary values. We do not simply get a narration of events but their interpretations according to the culture of the time as well. These interpretations may appear grotesque to the modern historian as history viewed from the modern angle would have been to the ancient thinkers. . . . These historical biographies can well be utilised for reconstructing the history of the past, provided we carefully study the nature of the idealising agents and the contemporary methods of historical organisations and inferences.[2]

---

1. K.K. Dasgupta, "Historical Biography in Sanskrit Literature", in *Historical Biography in Indian Literature*, ed. S.P. Sen, p. 24.
2. V.S. Pathak, "Ancient Historical Biographies and Reconstruction of History", in *Problems of Historical Writing in India* (Proceedings of the Seminar held at the India International Centre, New Delhi, 21-25 January, 1963), pp. 20-21.

Book Five
The Tradition of Writing Chronicle, Vaṁśāvalī and Other Historical Works

General Remarks

THE chronicles (native, local or royal) and Vaṁśāvalīs (genealogical records or family histories) have their own place in the history of historical writing in India. They are very faithful records for the study of dynastic histories of India. They were composed or compiled in different parts of northern, southern, eastern and western India during ancient and medieval period. The royal archives were also maintained in some of the Indian states where all relevant records were preserved and made available to the composers or compilers of chronicles and Vaṁśāvalīs. The existence of historical chronicles in the states under our notice here bears testimony to this fact. "We are also under deep obligation to a great band of Indian writers — most of whose names are unknown to us — who have rendered eminent service to the cause of history; chief among these are the compilers of the Vaṁśāvalīs or genealogical rolls of the ancient rulers. From remote times it has been the custom in the royal and noble families of India to keep a careful record of their pedigree in a document called Vaṁśāvalī which possesses an accuracy of historical record," says Hutchison and Vogel.[1]

The tradition of composing and preserving chronicles and Vaṁśāvalīs was maintained in different parts of the country.

---

1. *History of the Punjab Hill States*, vol. I, pp. 2-3.

In Kashmir, there was a rich tradition of writing chronicle of its kings in ancient and medieval period. The tradition of writing such chronicle under the title *Rājataraṅgiṇī* was initiated by its famous historian Kalhaṇa in the twelfth century. He wrote it after thorough and critical examination of all past records, including the works of eleven chroniclers of Kashmir who preceded him. The tradition of writing *Rājataraṅgiṇī* was further carried on by Kalhaṇa's four successors — Jonarāja, Śrīvara, Prājyabhaṭṭa and Śuka — who belonged to his school. They were all brāhmaṇa chroniclers or historians. This tradition continued down to the sixteenth century.

The chronicles of Rajasthan and Sindh, the Vaṁśāvalī record of Punjab, the chronicles or Vaṁśāvalīs of Nepal, the chronicles by the Jaina writers of Gujarat school, the chronicles (*bakhar*s) of Maharashtra, the chronicles and Vaṁśāvalīs of Orissa, the chronicles (*burañjī*s) and Vaṁśāvalīs written in Assam under the patronage of the Ahom and Koch rulers respectively and the royal chronicles of Manipur and Tripura, and other historical and semi-historical works, including those written in Bengal, also deserve our attention.

The writing of chronicle and Vaṁśāvalī (taken together) in different forms during the periods under our notice was one of the important stages in the evolution of Indian historiography.

The chronicles, Vaṁśāvalīs and other historical works written in northern, western and eastern India have been covered here. The chronicles and Vaṁśāvalīs composed in south India are included in the Sixth book of this work along with other historical and semi-historical works.

5.1

Chronicles, Vaṁśāvalīs and Other Historical Works of Northern India

Kashmir

HERE mention may first be made of the *Rājataraṅgiṇī* (a chronicle or history of kings of Kashmir) by Kalhaṇa, a distinguished Kāśmīrī historian of the twelfth century CE. He was the son of Campaka, a minister of King Harṣa (CE 1089-1101). He adorned the court of King Jayasiṁha (CE 1127-59), the son of Sussala II. It was during his reign that he composed his great work. According to all available evidences, he began his work in CE 1148 and completed it in 1150. His *Rājataraṇgiṇī* became the most famous of all the ancient royal chronicles of Kashmir.

Kalhaṇa was gifted with all qualities of a true historian. He occupies the highest place among the ancient historians of India. With his appearance on the scene ancient Indian historiography took a new turn.

Kalhaṇa utilised the works of eleven chroniclers of Kashmir who preceded him as sources of his information for composing his work. The eleven chronicles (*rājakathā*s) used by him include the oldest extensive original works containing the royal chronicles (of Kashmir) condensed or abridged by Suvrata in the form of a handbook of the history of Kashmir (I.11), the *Nṛpāvalī* or *Rājāvalī* (list of kings) of Kṣemendra (CE 1028-63), who graced the court of King Ananta Deva (I.13), the *Pārthivāvalī* (list of kings in 12,000 verses) of Helārāja (I.17), the work (name not known) of Padmamihira containing the list of eight kings who preceded Aśoka (I.18), and the work (name unknown) of Śrīchavillākara (also called Śrīcchavillaka) containing the list of five princes from Aśoka to Abhimanyu out of 52 (lost ones) (I.19 and 20). In addition to the chronicles, he consulted also a Purāṇic record which is the *Nīlapurāṇa* of Nīlamuni. From this source he obtained the list of four kings, viz. Gonanda and his three successors (I.16). While acknowledging the aforesaid works Kalhaṇa observes: "I have examined eleven works of former scholars which contain the chronicles of the kings, as well as the Purāṇa containing the views of the sage Nīla" (I.14). He critically examined the existing historical records on Kashmir before wielding his pen. In fact, he adopted a critical method of historical research. Of all the works utilised by him for his purpose, only the said Purāṇa is now available and the rest have passed into oblivion. We do not possess any information about the use of the earliest historical *kāvya*, the *Bhuvanābhyudaya* of Saṅkula of Kashmir (*c.* CE 850), which describes the local battles, by him.

Kalhaṇa made a thorough use of royal charters, edicts, records of land grants, the contemporary documents, coins, inscriptions and other archaeological evidence, and with the help of these he corrected errors occurring in the earlier works. He has himself stated that by looking at the ordinances (*śāsana*) of former kings, at the inscriptions recording the grants and erection and consecration of temples and other monuments, at the laudatory inscriptions (*praśasti-paṭṭa*), and at the written records (*śāstras*), all worries arising from errors have been overcome and doubts have been set at rest (I.15). Like a serious historian or researchers of today he used all the relevant sources available to him for composing a chronicle of Kashmir.

The principles Kalhaṇa followed for carrying out his historical investigation also merit our attention. His strict adherence to the exposition of facts can best be qualified in his own words: "That virtuous (writer) alone is worthy of praise who, free from love or hatred, restricts his language to the exposition of facts" (I.7). He tells us that the discovery of truth was his sole object. He discarded all bias and prejudice which is the duty of a true historian. He laid stress on the fact that while writing a history of the past one has to pronounce his judgements like a judge. The mission of a historian, he says, is to "make vivid before one's eyes pictures of a bygone age" (I.4). He further says about the methodological technique he adopted for writing the history of the past: "How great a cleverness is required in order that men of modern times may complete the account given in the books of those who died after composing each the history of those kings whose contemporary he was! Hence in this narrative of past events, which is difficult in many respects, my endeavour will be to connect" (I.8-10). He had, no doubt, clear understanding of fundamental principles of historiography. His impartiality, honesty and objectivity find reflection in the statement of facts recorded in his work.

The *Rājataraṅgiṇī* (in Sanskrit containing nearly 8000 verses) is divided into eight books called *taraṅga*s. It embraces the history of Kashmir from the time of the first Hindu king Gonanda to CE 1149, the 22nd year of the reign of the last illustrious king Jayasiṁha. It contains the genealogies and chronology of kings of various dynasties that ruled Kashmir during this period. The achievements of all important kings and the details of all important events which took place during their times have been highlighted by the author in his work.

Of 52 kings who are said to have ruled Kashmir in the early phase, the list of only 17 which includes Gonanda I and his successors and some other kings has been provided in Book I. Kalhaṇa could not find the names of 35 kings as their records are lost. The same book contains the list of 21 kings who succeeded Gonanda III. Book II contains the list of six princes from Pratāpāditya I to Aryyarāja who belonged to Āditya dynasty. From Book III it appears that there was restoration of Gonanda dynasty and 10 princes of this dynasty from Meghavāhana to Bālāditya reigned in Kashmir. These three books contain more or less a traditional history from the time of the Great Battle of Kurukṣetra or beginning of the Kaliyuga to the end of the sixth century CE which is based on Itihāsa–Purāṇa tradition. Some kings are, of course, mythical but there are some kings like Aśoka and his son Jālauka, Kaniṣka and others whose historicity is well established. Their activities are also well recorded in Kalhaṇa's work. However, there is anachronism in the genealogical list furnished in Book I. And the chronology of some of the kings mentioned in the said three books is not reliable.

Of all the early kings mentioned in the first three books Aśoka is the most important. We are told by Kalhaṇa that in his time Kashmir formed part of the Maurya empire. He built there many *stūpas* and monasteries, and founded the city of Śrīnagara and made it capital (the ruins of which have been found at a distance of about 10 miles from modern Sri Nagar). He also "pulled down the wall of an old Hindu temple and built a new wall to it." In his time Buddhism was the prevailing religion. After Aśoka's death, one of his sons, Jālauka, became king of Kashmir. He drove back the *mlecchas* (Scythians?) from there and further extended his conquests to the eastern side of Kannauj. He professed the Śaiva sect of Hinduism. During his time Śaivism found many supporters, and Brāhmanical supremacy was established. But during the reigns of Kaniṣka and one of his successors, Huviṣka, Buddhism became once more a popular religion. Kashmir was never under the political sway of the Guptas. The Hūṇa chief, Mihirakula, is said to have usurped the throne of a Kashmir ruler, who was his contemporary, some time in the early sixth century CE and exercised his authority over a limited territory in the valley.

The information provided by Kalhaṇa in Books IV-VIII covering the period from early seventh century CE to about the middle of the twelfth century are more trustworthy than what we find in the earlier three books from both historical and chronological points of view.

Book IV contains the history of 17 kings from Durlabhavardhana to Utpalapīḍa who belonged to the Karkoṭa (also called Karkoṭaka) dynasty. Durlabhavardhana, the descendant of Nāga Karkoṭa or Karkoṭaka, founded this dynasty. He appears to have ruled from *c.* CE 598 to 634. His reign was chiefly distinguished by his encouragement of religion, the temples he founded, the endowments he bestowed upon the brāhmaṇas, and some other benevolent works he undertook for the general welfare of the people. He won the friendship of Harṣavardhana by presenting him a prised tooth-relic of the Buddha for installation in a shrine at Kannauj. The most powerful ruler of the line was Lalitāditya (CE 724-60), the third son of Durlabhaka *alias* Pratāpāditya. Lalitāditya has been described as an efficient administrator or, valiant warrior, great conqueror and patron of arts and culture. The author of the said work has given a faithful account of his *digvijaya* (conquest). He subjugated Yaśovarman of Kannauj (in CE 733, or in about CE 740) and a king (unnamed) of Gauḍa. He proceeded southwards and invaded Karṇāṭa, then subject to a queen Ratta, who submitted to the invader but was later restored to her dominions. He also subdued the coast and the islands opposite the banks of the Kāverī, and reduced seven Koṅkaṇas. He occupied Avantī and Kamboja, conquered a portion of the Punjab, launched his campaigns in Tukhāristān (the upper Oxus Valley) and Daradadeśa (Dardistān, north-west of Kashmir), carried his arms to the land of the Bhauṭṭas (Tibetans) and advanced to the realms of Uttarakuru. After having accomplished his task he returned to his own dominion and proclaimed himself the sovereign ruler of Kashmir. Next he went for revamping of the whole administrative structure. He set up various new administrative departments and appointed officials of all ranks for the good governance of the kingdom. He founded a number of cities which include Lalitapura and Parihāsapura. In the city of Parihāsapura he built temples for Brāhmanical gods — Bhūteśa (Śiva) and Parihāsa Keśava (Viṣṇu). In this city, he erected stone-image of Garuḍa, and constructed a colossal figure of the Buddha and a figure of Hari. In Huṣkapura, he erected an image of Mukta Svāmin and temple of Jyeṣṭha Rudra. He built Buddhist *vihāras* at Huṣkapura and other places. His most famous construction was the Mārtaṇḍa temple of the Sun whose ruins still testify to its former magnificence and splendidness. Jayāpīḍa (CE 779-810), one of the successors of Lalitāditya, was another illustrious monarch of Kashmir. The author has given detailed description of his military enterprises and other activities. He is said to have defeated and dethroned a king of Kannauj who may be identified with Vajrāyudha or Indrāyudha. His expeditions against Pauṇḍravardhana (north Bengal), then the residence of Jayanta, king of Gauḍa, who submitted to the victor, who submitted to the victor, and his conflict with king of Nepal are prolixly narrated in the author's work. One of the principal works of his reign was the construction of the fort of Jayapura and its embellishment by a temple of Śiva and by a Brāhmanical college. He was a great patron of learning, and his court was adorned by many literary celebrities and geniuses like Udbhaṭa, Vāmana and Dāmodaragupta. In hot pursuit of his passion to amass the wealth Jayāpīḍa adopted such measures which became fatal to his subjects. He levied heavy exactions on all ranks of people, and particularly oppressed the brāhmaṇas by taking back the endowments which he and his predecessors had bestowed upon them. He was followed by a number of weak and incompetent rulers. Their mutual conflict over the issue of possessing real sovereignty of Kashmir coupled with political convulsions led to the gradual decline of the power of the Karkoṭakas. About the middle of the ninth century their glory had totally eclipsed and they were supplanted by the Utpalas. Utpalapīḍa, the last monarch of the Karkoṭa dynasty, was deposed; and Avantivarman, the son of Sucavarman and founder of the Utpala dynasty, succeeded.

The narrative of fifteen princes from Avantivarman to Śūravarman II belonging to the Utpala or Varman dynasty has been provided in Book V. The accession of Avantivarman did not take place without opposition and he had to undergo many conflicts with his own cousins and even with his brothers before his dominion was established. By his valour, prudence, sagacity and wisdom aided by the wise counsel of minister, Sura or Suyya, to whom he was indebted for his crown, he overcame all opposition, restored order and tranquillity, ascended the throne in CE 855 and remained the undisputed sovereign of Kashmir till the end of his reign. "He was not in a position to embark upon any schemes of conquest as the kingdom had suffered greatly from economic and political troubles during the reigns of the later Karkoṭakas." He, however, took some steps to tone up the administration, establish internal security, mobilise resources and restore the health of state economy. He took some bold steps to curb effectively the power and influence of the Ḍāmaras, "a turbulent class of rural aristocrats." The minister of the king undertook some works of public utility. He constructed channels for irrigation which increased the fertility of the land resulting in higher agricultural production. This led to the economic prosperity of the kingdom. During the reign of Avantivarman many towns and temples were constructed which increased the grandeur of the kingdom. The king himself built temples and bestowed upon them the endowments. He also gave liberal grants in charity to brāhmaṇas. It is said that they also received the Agrahāras, Khaduya and Hastikarṇa, from Sūravarman who was nominated by the King Yuvarāja. The city, Avantipura, was founded by the king at Viśvakeśvara Kṣetra in which he also erected a temple and dedicated it to Avantīśvara or Śiva whose worship he had adopted in place of the Vaiṣṇava tenets in which he had been initiated. He also erected here three statues of the same deity under the names of Tripureśvara, Bhūteśa and Vijayeśa. But in the last phase of his life he again became the votary of Viṣṇu and popularised the Vaiṣṇava faith. The adoration of deities of Hindu pantheon during his time was on the increase. The king's minister built a town, Surapura or Suyyapura on the banks of Vitastā (Jhelum). The modern town of Sopur still preserves the name of the minister. The king also extended his patronage to literary figures amongst whom the most prominent was Ānandavardhana. Avantivarman after having ruled for 28 years passed away in CE 883.

After the death of Avantivarman, the reign of Kashmir passed into the hands of his son, Śaṅkaravarman. The latter reversed the peaceful policy of his father and kept himself engaged in wars and conquests. He invaded Darvābhisāra (the region between the Vitastā or Jhelum and the Candrabhāgā or Cenāb), extended his sway to Trigartta region (Kāṅgṛā) after subduing its king, Pṛthvīcandra, and defeated the Gurjara (i.e. Gujarat of Pakistan) chief Alakhāna and his ally Lalliya Shahi seizing the treasures and kingdom of the former and leaving him only Taccadeśa. Śaṅkaravarman also seized certain territories, conquered earlier by Mihirabhoja, from Mahendrapāla I Pratihāra, and transferred them to the Thakkiya chief. In order to replenish the treasury which became depleted because of his military operations, and also to satiate his desire to accumulate wealth, Śaṅkaravarman subjected his people to every kind of extortion. He levied heavy tolls and taxes, exacted undue proportions of the produce of the land, and let out to farm those lands which were the property of temples. He levied fees even on religious festivities and ceremonies. This oppressive taxation resulted in the gradual impoverishment of the people. Learning also suffered under his rule for want of patronage. He diverted the attention of his subjects by engaging them in military expeditions. He is said to have led an army to the north where he subdued the people along the Indus. He entered the Uraśā (Haẓārā) region where he was shot in the neck with an arrow by a mountaineer which resulted in his death. Thus Śaṅkaravarman after having reigned for 18 years died in CE 902.

Śaṅkaravarman was succeeded by his son, Gopālavarman. The only notable event during the reign of the latter was the defeat his minister Prabhākaradeva inflicted on a rebellious Śāhī king of Udbhāṇḍapura (Ohind, a few miles north of Attock) who may be identified with Alberuni's Samand (Śāmantadeva). His coins have also been found in large numbers in Afghanistan and the Punjab which are of the bull and horseman type and bear the legend "Śrī-Śāmantadeva" on the obverse. We also learn that the victor (Prabhākaradeva) placed Kamaluka on the Śāhī throne but he was later deposed because of being disobedient and unfaithful to the royal authority in Kashmir. It is noteworthy that in those days the Punjab and the territory beyond the Indus as far as Kabul were ruled by the Hindu princes of the Śāhīya dynasty. Gopālavarman, after having ruled for two years, died in CE 904. The author has narrated all the events in detail which took place in the succeeding period. We further learn that the last king but one, Unmattāvanti (CE 937-39), was "worse than wicked." He slew his father and starved all his half-brothers to death. After his death, with the brief reign of Śūravarman II, the Utpala dynasty came to an end in CE 939.

In Book VI, the author has provided the history of 10 kings in the lines of Yaśaskara and Parvagupta. We are informed that after Śūravarman II, Yaśaskara (son of Gopālavarman's minister, Prabhākaradeva), was elected by the brāhmaṇas as king. During his benevolent reign of nine years (CE 939-48) a new era of peace, progress and prosperity commenced in Kashmir. His son and successor, Saṁgrāma, was killed in CE 949 by the minister Parvagupta who usurped the throne himself. The most prominent and powerful ruler in this line was Diddā, granddaughter of Bhīma Śāhī and daughter of Siṁharāja, a chief of the Lohara (in the Punch state). It is said that "She was an ambitious and energetic woman, and for nearly half a century — first as queen-consort of King Kṣemagupta (CE 950-58), then as regent, and lastly as ruler (CE 980-1003) — she was the dominant personality in the politics of Kashmir." During this period there were constant court-intrigues which were suppressed by her with an iron hand. And in spite of the opposition of the Ḍāmaras (land-owning nobles) and the brāhmaṇas she maintained her position and exercised authority with the assistance of Tuṅga, a Khasa of low origin, for whom she had immense affection.

The history of six princes from Saṁgrāmarāja to Harṣa belonging to the so-called Lohara dynasty is contained in Book VII. Saṁgrāmarāja *alias* Kṣamāpati, nephew of Diddā and brother of the Lohara prince, Vigraharāja, ascended the throne in CE 1003 and continued to rule till 1028. Saṁgrāmarāja proved to be a weak king, and during the earlier part of his reign Tuṅga was virtually the ruler in the state. Kalhaṇa tells us that the latter went along with an army to help the Hindu Śāhī king against the aggression of a Turuṣka (Turk) named Hammīra, who, however, utterly routed the combined Hindu army. Tuṅga was murdered and thereafter Kāśmīrī soldiers fled back before conquering the Turuṣkas. And "Śāhīrājya" was annexed to the realm of Turuṣkas. Here Kalhaṇa speaks of Trilocanapāla (the Hindu Śāhī king of Lahore), who was defeated by Sultān Mahmud of Ghazni in CE 1021 despite being helped by his ally from Kashmir, and of the Punjab which was annexed to the Ghazni empire. The historical accuracy of the author's statement pertaining to this episode is well tested. We are also told that during the reign of Anantadeva (CE 1028-63) seven *mleccha* kings had entered Kashmir but were beaten back by Rudrapāla, the powerful Kāśmīrī general. Barring brief intervals of good government, the subsequent history of Kashmir is mainly a long tale of tyranny, misrule and fiscal oppression. Harṣa (CE 1089-1101), who began his political career as an able administrator, military leader, great conqueror, and "liberal patron of the softer arts of music and poetry, later degenerated into a profligate, cruel-hearted, and irreligious man." He is said to have conquered Rājapura (Rājorī). He employed Turuṣka generals in the army, and went on plundering the temples and defiling the images. At last, the powerful Ḍāmaras with chiefs, Ucchala and Sussala I, raised the banner of revolt against his excessive taxation and oppression, and consequently chaos and anarchy prevailed in the kingdom. Ucchala defeated Harṣa and his son Bhoja in a single battle, burnt the capital and after having killed the former in CE 1101 seized the throne of Kashmir. The political spectacle, however, changed, but the people almost began to groan under the weight of civil wars, misgovernment, and machinations of the aristocracy.

Kalhaṇa seems to be balanced in his value-judgements. He describes the periods of glory and misery, and greatness and weakness of rulers. He has highlighted both the bright and dark sides of the character of some kings. For instance, he describes Harṣa (the patron of his father) as tyrannical, but, on the other hand, counts his bravery as one of his good qualities. He praised Lalitāditya for his valour, benevolence and many other qualities but did not hesitate to criticise him for his betrayal of the king of Gauṇa. These are some of the instances which constitute a testimony to his objective treatment of the subject.

The last and the eighth book contains the history of seven kings from Ucchala (CE 1101-11) to Jayasiṁha (CE 1127-59), the last illustrious sovereign. The author has provided an eye-witness account of the events which took place about the middle of the twelfth century CE.

Kalhaṇa has presented the narratives of the kings of Kashmir from the early seventh century CE to his own time maintaining his perfect historical sense. The history of this period is not only authentic but also in proper chronological order.

On the whole, the reigns of the kings whose history is known cover a period of 2,330 years up to the time of Kalhaṇa.

The *Rājataraṅgiṇī* is a native chronicle of Kashmir. One of the characteristic features of this chronicle is that it contains information not only about kings but also about contemporary society, economy, religion and culture. It contains valuable information about the religious toleration, the prevalence of three popular cults of Hinduism, Śaiva, Śakti and Vaiṣṇava, and coexistence of Brāhmanism and Buddhism, in Kashmir. Thus, it is important for the study of dynastic, political, socio-economic and cultural history of ancient Kashmir. R.C. Dutt has rightly pointed out that the historical value of this chronicle can best be judged by its contents.[1] J. Hutchison opines that "Kashmir is the only country (state) in India of which we possess a written and detailed history of the Hindu period due to literary labours of poet-historian Kalhaṇa."[2] A.L. Basham is also of the view that ". . . No similar chronicles were composed elsewhere. . . ."[3] He observes: "Though every important Hindu court maintained archives and preserved genealogies of its rulers, Kashmir is the only region in India in which a tradition of historical writing is known to have existed in pre-Muslim times."[4] As a matter of fact, the tradition of historical writing not only existed in Kashmir but also in other parts of India. Tod has correctly stated that "It is now generally regarded as an axiom that India possesses no national history. . . . But the *Rājataraṅgiṇī* clearly demonstrates that regular historical composition was an art not unknown in Hindustan."[5] V.A. Smith has also acknowledged that "this work is nearest to the European notion of a regular history." The historical value of the work has been estimated by different scholars in different ways. This chronicle can undoubtedly be considered a valuable historical record. The statement of some scholars that this is the only work which can be called a history is not worthy of acceptance. In fact, this is the best of all ancient Indian historical works.

Kalhaṇa's name stands the foremost in the galaxy of chroniclers or historians of Kashmir school. A true

1. "A Note on Kalhaṇa's *Rājataraṅgiṇī*", in H.H. Wilson, *HHK*, Appendix X, p. 159; "An Introductory Essay on the History of Kashmira", in *Kings of Kashmir*, Eng. tr. of *Rājataraṅgiṇī* of Kalhaṇa, by J.C. Dutt, II, xxviii-xxix.
2. J. Hutchison and J.Ph. Vogel, *History of the Panjab Hill States*, I, p. 1.
3. *The Wonder that was India*, p. 45.
4. Cf. C.H. Philips (ed.), *Historians of India, Pakistan and Ceylon*, vol. I of *Historical Writing on the Peoples of Asia*, p. 57.
5. *AAR*, I, Introduction, xiii.

conception of history and the correct method of writing were not altogether unknown in ancient India. However, it was he who set several new landmarks in the history of historical writing in ancient India. He was the first Indian to understand the basic principle of historiography in the real sense of the term. The principles he laid down for writing history were far in advance of his age. He made a critical and objective approach to the study of history. He was the first to emphasise the need of a thorough critical examination of all past records useful for the purpose of producing a genuine historical work. A new age of critical historiography began. The first serious attempt at scientific presentation of history was made by him. And in that sense he is often called the father of scientific historiography in ancient India, though we cannot deny the fact that to some extent he adopted the literary style of writing as is evident from the earlier part of his work. However, his comparison with Herodotus, Thucydides or any Greek historian is unwarranted. The history writing in ancient India passing through several stages reached the height of its progress in the time of Kalhaṇa. He no doubt, made significant contribution to the development of historical writing in ancient India. His work is marked by high standard of accuracy. Its value can be judged even by the modern standard of historiography. He was the forerunner of many Indian historians in the realm of debunking the truth from falsehood. M.A. Stein has also observed that "Honesty in a historian has not unjustly been called a forerunner of critical judgement in regard to contemporary history. Kalhaṇa has manifestly endeavoured to be fair and impartial. May we not assume that the same feeling has helped to guide him rightly also in the opinions he formed of the past?"[6] Kalhaṇa was the source of inspiration for future historians of India.

6. *Rājataraṅgiṇī*, I, Introduction, p. 32.

His historical principles and laws were first followed by the Kāśmīrī chroniclers of the Medieval Age. In spite of possessing all the qualities of a historian, Kalhaṇa regarded himself not as a historian but as a poet which is his greatness. H.H. Wilson says that the work of Kalhaṇa Paṇḍit ". . . as a historical composition is clear and consistent, and contains fewer extravagances than most of the works to which the name of history has been assigned. . . ."[7]

While forming an estimate of Kalhaṇa as a historian and critically assessing the historical value of his work, J.C. Dutt writes,

> He has . . . made every effort to justify the conduct of the princes of the usurping dynasty, and to censure, often unjustly, the conduct of the last king of the previous line. . . . In several places, persons and events have been referred to by him so incidentally as to make it extremely difficult for us to identify them, though the sense was no doubt clear to people of his generation. And, lastly, his narration too is not faultless. Not only does he often attach undue importance to insignificant incidents, but he also travels from subject to subject without having the patience to complete the account of any one of them. He might have left us much more of useful and valuable information of his own times than he has done. As regards the history of times anterior to his, all that can be said is, that, in the absence of any other historical records, his must be considered very valuable. Wherever light has been received from other sources, his account appears to be meagre and incomplete, though generally correct. But whatever his defects may be . . . he is perhaps the only author in Sanskrit . . . who attempted to write a sober history. . . . To him belongs the credit of discovering, as it were, a new department in literature which it was the duty of his successors to improve.[8]

7. H.H Wilson, op. cit., Introduction, p. 6.
8. J.C. Dutt, op. cit., II, Preface, i-ii.

In the estimation of J.C. Dutt, Kalhaṇa may be called "the father of Indian history."[9]

The noted authority on medieval Indian History, J.N. Sarkar, has also unequivocally called Kalhaṇa a "historian."[10] According to him, ". . . the standard set by Kalhaṇa was not reached by any other Hindu historian of the medieval period, just as the lines chalked out by Ibn Khaldun do not appear to have been worked out by any other Arabic writer."[11]

The tradition of writing chronicle of Kashmir under different titles was further continued in the Medieval Age by the future successors of Kalhaṇa.

Jonarāja, who flourished about the middle of the fifteenth century, was next to Kalhaṇa to write a chronicle of Kashmir called *Rājāvalī-Dvitīya* (second) *Rājataraṅgiṇī*. After Kalhaṇa it was he who became famous as a historian of Kashmir. He maintained a library which was well equipped with books on literature and history.

In his *Rājataraṅgiṇī,* Jonarāja has presented a comprehensive history of Kashmir covering the events of 310 years. He begins with CE 1149, where Kalhaṇa closes his account with details of the reign of the last illustrious sovereign Jayasiṁha in his *Rājataraṅgiṇī*, and continues up to 1459. The work of Jonarāja contains the description of 24 kings and some *sultāns* of Kashmir. The details provided by him of the period 1149-1389 are not eyewitness accounts. However, their trustworthiness cannot be doubted. The details of the events of 70 years covering the period 1389-1459 appear to be authentic. We are told that Shamsuddin I founded the Muslim rule in Kashmir in 1339 after bringing

9. J.C. Dutt, op. cit., III, Preface, i.

10. "Thoughts on the Study of Indian History" General President's Address, 37th Session, *IHC* (Calicut, 1976), p. 11; *PIHC* (1976), p. 9.

11. "Ideas of History in Mediaeval India", *QRHS*, IV, 1-2, pp. 1-21.

the rule of Saṁgrāma dynasty to an end. Jonarāja's accounts of the last ten years (CE 1149-59) of the reign of Jayasiṁha is very faithful. The history of the first 39 years (1420-59) of the reign of Sultān Zain-ul-Abadin (called Jainollābhadina) in Kashmir provided by him in 223 verses is also reliable. In fact, he wrote the history of Kashmir from the King Jayasiṁha to Sultān Zain-ul-Abadin. Imitating Kalhaṇa's style of writing and deriving inspiration from his work, he brought the historical narratives down to his time. He died in Laukika Saṁvat 4535 = CE 1459 before completing his *Rājataraṅgiṇī*.

The next important chronicle called *Jaina Rājataraṅgiṇī* is the work of Śrīvara Paṇḍit, the pupil of Jonarāja. The name which the author has chosen to give his work has its own history. In fact, the author was a court-poet. He enjoyed the patronage of Sultān Zain-ul-Abadin who was very liberal to his Hindu subjects. He was under the paternal care of the Sultān. He received fatherly treatment, love and affection from him. And, thus, as a mark of expression of his gratefulness to and to perpetuate the memory of his liberal patron, Zain-ul-Abadin, he prefixed his short name Zain (which stands for Jaina) to his *Rājataraṅgiṇī*. That is the reason why his work is popularly known as *Jaina Rājataraṅgiṇī*. That he himself selected the title of his work is proved by his own writing (I.1, 18).

Śrīvara went through the works of Kalhaṇa and Jonarāja and derived inspiration from them to continue the tradition of writing a chronicle of Kashmir. But he adopted the style of the former more than that of the latter in his writing. He was committed to completing Jonarāja's work *Rājāvalī* which was left incomplete as stated by himself (I.1, 6-7). He started his third *Rājataraṅgiṇī* from the period where Jonarāja left and ended with the details of Fatteh Shah's ascendency.

The work of Śrīvara deals with the history of Kashmir from CE 1459 to 1486, i.e. from Zain-ul-Abadin's time to the accession of Fatteh Shah. The author has provided eyewitness accounts of historical events that took place during 27 years of reigns of four *sultāns* of Kashmir — Zain-ul-Abadin, Haidar Shah, Hasan Shah and Muhammad Shah — which cover the period 1459-86.

Śrīvara's work (which is now available) is divided into four *taraṅgas* (chapters). The first *taraṅga* is sub-divided into seven cantos. The rest of the *taraṅgas* are without cantos. The first *taraṅga* (pp. 1-251) has been entirely devoted by the author to his patron, Sultān Zain-ul-Abadin, as a compliment to him. He himself writes that being impressed by the merits and virtues of his patron he devotes his special attention to him (I.1, 11-12). He has provided a detailed history of the last 11 years of the rule of Zain-ul-Abadin (1459-70) in 820 verses. We learn from the author's account of the subject that the said Sultān was a benevolent ruler. His name and fame spread far and wide. His reign witnessed a tremendous and spectacular progress in all spheres of life. This chapter was written after his death in Laukika Saṁvat 4546 = CE 1470. In the second *taraṅga* (pp. 252-311), the author has described the rule of Haidar Shah (1470-72), the son and successor of Zain-ul-Abadin, in 219 verses. This chapter was written after 1472. The events that took place during the twelve years of reign of Hasan Shah (1472-84), son of Haidar Shah, are narrated in third *taraṅga* in 564 verses. The details of two years of rule of Muhammad Shah (1484-86), son of Hasan Shah, are elucidated in fourth *taraṅga* in 656 verses. The author begins with his accession and ends with his deposition. After completing the second *taraṅga*, the author undertook the writing of the third one after the death of Hasan Shah in 1484 and completed it together with the fourth one in 1486. He has written about four *sultāns* in four different chapters.

Śrīvara has supplied some relevant information about kings Lalitāditya and Jayāpīḍa on the authority of Kalhaṇa. Besides the kings and *sultāns* of Kashmir, he has made incidental references to King Jayasiṁha of Rājapur, King Māṇikya Deva of Madra (in central Punjab), prince Kumbha of Mewāṛ, King Ajayadeva of Madramaṇḍala, rulers of Gauḍa (Bengal), Māṇḍavya (Mālwā) and Surāṣṭra (Saurāṣṭra), Sultān Qayamdin of Sindh, Sultān Muhammad of Gujarat, Delhi Sultān Bahlol Lodi (1451-89) of Lodhi dynasty, Sultān Ābu-Sayyad of Khorasan and *sultāns* (unnamed) of Egypt and Iraq. The historicity of some of them is well proven. We are also informed that a fierce battle took place between the king of Jammu and the Mughals in which Bahrām Khan, the son of Sultān Zain-ul-Abadin, died fighting on behalf of the king (2.10) which is a well-established historical fact.

Śrīvara has given a graphic description of the contemporary social, economic, political, religious and cultural life of the people of Kashmir. While describing social life, he informs us that the Hindus, including those who were converted to Islam, could not do away with their age-old caste system. The old class and caste distinction continued to exist. Throwing light on the position and status of women in the society, he tells us that the women had an honourable place in the time of Kalhaṇa, but after the death of Zain-ul-Abadin in 1470 their position started degrading following social changes. They were placed under several bindings and restrictions. In the later medieval period, they completely lost their freedom. The custom of *satī* was no longer in existence among the Hindus. The *purdah* system (putting the veil on the face) was in vogue among the Muslim women. The professional women singers and dancers were looked down upon. They were not accorded any place of honour in the contemporary society. The endogamous marriage system which was earlier prevalent ceased to exist.

And the rule of exogamy prevailed for a considerable period of time. Jonarāja refers to matrimonial relations between the Hindus and Muslims. We are told by Śrīvara that inter-caste marriage system was not followed posterior to 1470. The divorce system was conspicuous by its absence among the Hindus but it was very much in practice among the Muslims. The despised class included the *cāṇḍāla*s and corpse-thrower. They received disdainful treatment in the society. He also makes mention of some tribes like the Khasas, Ābhīras, Kirātas, Dārdas and Kinnaras, and others including the Turuṣkas (Turks) who constituted the social segments and had their settlements in Kashmir in his time. It seems that the contemporary society was more or less heterogeneous in nature. We also learn from him that in the time of his patron, the economic condition of the people was very sound. Zain-ul-Abadin did everything possible to promote the economic prosperity of Kashmir. He also touches upon the system of governance during the reigns of the said four *sultān*s.

While dealing with religious history of Kashmir, Śrīvara informs us that the Hindus, including the neo-converts, continued to follow their traditional religious system, practices, rites and rituals. They had firm faith in their so-called Sanātana Dharma. The Śaiva, Tāntric and Vaiṣṇava cults of Hinduism were popular. But the major section of the Hindus had faith in the Śaiva sect. The idol-worship was prevalent among the Hindus. Zain-ul-Abadin's father Sikandar, who, because of being an iconoclast, got the name But-Shikan, was the sixth *sultān* of Kashmir. He ruled from 1394 to 1416. He was intolerant of other religions. He was out and out anti-Hindu. He destroyed icons of Hindu gods and goddesses. He forcibly converted a large number of Hindus to Islam. And several Hindu temples were razed to the ground by him. He was bent upon destroying all the vestiges of Hinduism. The Hindus suffered a lot due to his religious bigotry, dogmatism and fanaticism. The author has given a picturesque description of the sufferings of the Hindus at the hands of the said *sultān*. We are further informed by the author that Zain-ul-Abadin (the eighth *sultān* of Kashmir), who unlike his father Sikandar But-Shikan had extended very liberal and generous treatment to the Hindus and adopted the policy of religious toleration, got all those temples re-built which were demolished by his father and re-installed the idols therein for their worship and other images of Hindu gods and goddesses for their propitiation, and also returned to his Hindu subjects their wealth plundered by his father. He had great regard for the Hindus and great faith in Hinduism. He had knowledge of Sanskrit. He continued to study the Hindu religion and philosophy till he breathed his last. Even his minister Śrī Bhaṭṭa was from a Hindu family. His catholicity and magnanimity were greatly admired by his Hindu subjects. He is often called "the Akbar of Kashmir." The author has critically examined the religious policy of Muslim *sultān*s. He has dealt with different aspects of Islamic religion. In his time, Kashmir was a Muslim dominated province. Among the Muslims there were Sunnis, Shias and Sūfīs. Besides the Hindus and Muslims, there were also some Buddhists in Kashmir. He has also focused to a considerable extent on the Buddhist religious doctrine. It is quite apparent from his account of the subject that in his time Hinduism and Buddhism coexisted side by side with Islam.

In the fourth and last chapter of his work, Śrīvara closes his account with the details of dethronement of Muhammad Shah and enthronement of Fatteh Shah (the twelfth *sultān* of Kashmir) in Laukika Saṁvat 4562 = CE 1486. It appears that he died in the same year leaving his work incomplete. We are given to understand that he wanted to continue his work further but he could not do so owing to his sudden demise. Like Kalhaṇa and Jonarāja he also brought the history of Kashmir down to his time.

Śrīvara's work bieng a contemporary one is of inestimable value. His work is one of the priceless treasures of the historical world. It is both a history and a memoir. It focuses on several obscure aspects of medieval history of Kashmir as well as of India.

We are informed by Śrīvara that in his time there was another *Rājataraṅgiṇī* (anonymous) in Sanskrit containing the description of 10 *sultān*s which was translated into Persian by Shahmir by the orders of Zain-ul-Abadin and was made available to the public for its perusal. Neither the original text nor its Persian translation has come into light as yet.

The chronicle called *Rājāvalīpatākā* (fourth in the series of *Rājataraṅgiṇī*) is the production of Prājyabhaṭṭa and his pupil Śuka. It was begun by the former and completed by the latter.

Prājyabhaṭṭa began with 1486, where Śrīvara had left, and ended with description of the events of 1513 covering the history of 27 years from the time of Fatteh Shah to Nāzok Shah. His narratives of the events that took place during the reigns of Fatteh Shah (1486-93), Muhammad Shah II (1493-1505, Ibrāhim Shah and Nāzok Shah (1505-13) are valuable from a historical point of view. After he left his manuscript incomplete it was taken up by Śuka who brought the historical account of Kashmir down to 1586 — the year in which it was conquered by Akbar (after the capitulation of the then Sultān Yusuf Khan) and annexed to his empire and then ceased to be an independent kingdom. His eye-witness account of the events of 25 years covering the period 1513-38 constitutes an important part of his work. His account also covers the downfall of Shahmir dynasty. Some of the facts are narrated by him in a literary style but they do have historical accuracy. He has judiciously and meticulously disentangled the husk of legend from the kernel of historical truth.

Kalhaṇa and his four successors, Jonarāja, Śrīvara, Prājyabhaṭṭa and Śuka — all brāhmaṇa chroniclers or historians of Kashmir school — made significant contributions to the evolution of the tradition of historical writing in India in early and late medieval period by producing altogether four *Rājataraṅgiṇīs* — chronicles or histories of kings and rulers of Kashmir. Their works (in Sanskrit) are of immense historical value. They contain a wealth of historical material. Kalhaṇa has presented the history of Kashmir of 3597 years (traditionally) covering the period from the Laukika Era 628 = 653rd year of Kaliyuga to the Laukika Era 4225 = CE 1148-49 in exactly 7830 verses. In fact, the reigns of the kings whose history is known covered a period of 2,330 years up to the time of Kalhaṇa Paṇḍit; and those of the 52 kings of whom the history of only a few is known traditionally covered a period of 1,266 years, making a total of 3,596 years. Of the said 52 kings, the records or accounts of 35 were lost and that is why their history is blank. Kalhaṇa somehow could find the names of only 17 kings who are from Gonanda I to Abhimanyu mentioned in Book One of his work of whom some like Aśoka, Jālauka and Kaniṣka, though not placed in a proper chronological order because of an anachronistic list, all historical figures. Jonarāja wrote the history of 310 years (1149-1459) in 976 verses, Śrīvara history of 27 years (1459-86) in 2241 verses, Prājyabhaṭṭa history of 27 years (1486-1513) in 398 verses and Śuka history of 73 years (1513-86).

The history of Kashmir from CE 1098 to 1149 (51 years) presented by Kalhaṇa, from CE 1389 to 1459 (70 years) by Jonarāja, from CE 1459 to 1486 (27 years) by Śrīvara, from CE

1486 to 1513 (27 years) by Prājyabhaṭṭa and from CE 1513 to 1538 (25 years) by Śuka which cover the details of historical events of total 200 years are purely based on their eyewitness accounts whose historical authenticity can hardly be doubted.

Kalhaṇa and Jonarāja have presented both past and contemporary history, whereas, on the other hand, Śrīvara, Prājyabhaṭṭa and Śuka have dealt with only contemporary history. Events are narrated consecutively which show that the whole narration runs in one continuous flow. These writers were poets as well as historians. Kalhaṇa was a poet-historian of Hindu period — the period during which Kashmir was independent. He did enjoy the royal patronage but never adopted a panegyric style of writing. He wrote everything independently. His writings do not bear the stamp of his flunkeyism. The glory of Kashmir finds reflection in his writings. The other four were the historians of Muslim period. Being court-poets they were dependent on the *sultāns*. They have, no doubt, presented a realistic picture of the subject to a great extent. But at the same time we cannot deny that they extolled the virtues of their patrons. The conversion, oppressions and persecution of the Hindus, the demolition of temples and destruction of idols find reflection in the accounts of both Jonarāja and Śrīvara. During the inglorious reign of Sikandar But-Shikan, Kashmir had lost its ancient glory which was, however, restored by Zain-ul-Abadin. From the account of Śrīvara it appears that during the reign of the latter, peace, progress, and prosperity were witnessed in Kashmir. His reign proved to be a blessing for the Hindus. They regained everything which they had lost earlier. His reign marked a golden age in the history of Kashmir particularly from the point of view of religious freedom of the Hindus. Śuka's description of acquisition of Kashmir by Akbar and its annexation to Mughal empire is of unique value. Judging critically the authors and their accounts, J.C. Dutt writes:

> . . . valuable as the writings of these authors are from a historical point of view, in the absence of any other history of the country they relate to, we cannot unhesitatingly accept their estimation of persons and events when we remember that they were . . . court *paṇḍits*, and depended on the smiles of kings, whose accounts they wrote. . . . It is not unlikely that they often had to read out their writings in court . . . they begin the account of a king by extolling his virtues to the skies, and . . . they never wrote their censures on any king till he was dead or deposed. As court *paṇḍits* they had in full measure the vice of such people — fulsome adulation of their patrons. They did not hesitate to raise Muhammadan princes not only above the ancient heroes of their country, whom as Hindus they must have revered, but even above the gods of the Hindus. A strict impartiality of opinion cannot be expected from such writers. A true history cannot be written when the writer has a purpose to serve other than writing a true history. There is, however, no reason to disbelieve the correctness of their accounts, irrespective of the writers' views regarding the events narrated.[12]

One of the ancient chronicles of Kashmir had the impact even on the historical writing of the late eighteenth century. We find that the *Rājāvalī* (*A History of Kings of Hindustan from the pre-Kaliyuga Period Down to the Time of Warren Hastings*) was written by Vijaya Govinda some time after 1784 on the model of the *Rājāvalī* of Kṣemendra.

Punjab

The *Vaṁsāvalī Nāmā Dasan Pātshāhianka* by Kesar Singh Chibbar is a genealogical account of the 10 Sikh *gurus* (Nanak, Angad, Amar Das, Ram Das, Arjan Dev, Har Gobind, Har Rai, Har

12. J.C. Dutt, op. cit., III, Preface, ii-iii.

Kishan, Tegh Bahadur and Gobind Singh). It was completed in 1769-70 or 1779-80. The author claims to have based his account of the *gurus*, particularly of the tenth and the last *guru*, Gobind Singh (1666-1708), on some records of the time of the tenth *guru* preserved at Ānandapur. The work is full of useful information about the events up to about 1756 as he has recorded on his personal observation or first-hand knowledge.[13] It is said that "a number of chronological and other errors have crept into it in addition to his pro-Brāhmanical prejudices and Purāṇic influence."[14]

The two worth-noting historical works composed in the Punjab during medieval period include *Vār Amritsar Kī* by poet Darshan and *Ṅādir Shāh dī Vār* by Najabat.

Being inspired by the ideals of Guru Gobind Singh to resist tyranny — social, religious and political — his followers defeated in the summer of 1709 (within eight months of his death in October 1708) not only the local levies of the *amīna* of Paṭṭī Haibatpur and *caudhari* of Naushera Pannuan but also the detachments of the provincial army sent to help the latter by Nawāb Aslam Khan, the Governor of Lahore. This victory was indeed very significant for the Sikh people of the Punjab. Poet Darshan has presented an account of this victory lucidly in his *Vār Amritsar Kī*, written soon after the event.

Najabat's *Nādir Shāh dī Vār* contains an account of invasion of India by Nadir Shah of Persia (Iran) in 1739. The author has made a particular reference to the events in the Punjab and closes his account with the details of the battle of Karnal in which the army of the Mughal emperor Muhammad Shah

13. Ganda Singh, "Biography in Panjabi Literature", in *Historical Biography in Indian Literature*, ed. S.P. Sen, p. 161; "History in Panjabi Literature", in *History in Modern Indian Literature*, ed. S.P. Sen, p. 115.

14. Ganda Singh, "Biography in Panjabi Literature", op. cit., p. 161.

was defeated. Animated by the patriotic sentiment, the author goes to condemn the cowardly behaviour of the governor of Lahore, Zakariya Khan, who had submitted to the foreign invader without any resistance. Still stronger condemnation of the Mughal rulers of India, their Turānī officers, gunners and archers, and of the Indian *rājā*s, etc. is found in the second twelve-line stanza of the miscellaneous verses in the work which is in the form of a historical ballad. Therein they have been referred to as shameless cowards for their failure to defend the country against the Persian invader. The work seems to have been composed not long after the said invasion.

Sindh

The native chronicle of Sindh, which is popularly known as *Cācanāmā* (or *Chāchnāmā*), deserves mention here. It is an ancient history of Sindh from the Hindu period down to the Arab conquest. It was originally written in Arabic by an anonymous Muslim historian of Sindh incorporating some older sources for the Buddhist and brāhmaṇa rulers of the sixth and seventh centuries CE and adding an account of the Arab invasion early in the following century. It is difficult to fix the exact year of the composition of the original Arabic work. However, we have every reason to believe that the work was written not very long after CE 712, the year which marks the Arab conquest of Sindh. From the internal evidence of the narrative it appears that the work must have been written before CE 753. Later, in CE 1216, it was translated into Persian by Muhammad Ali bin Ābu Bakr Kufi. The work gives a brief account of Sindh and its inhabitants. It contains the details of all important incidents which took place in the course of Arab invasion of Sindh in the early eighth century CE. It throws light on the political condition of Sindh at the time of its conquest by the Arabs. It gives a fairly accurate picture of the circumstances that led to Muhammad bin Qasim's invasion of Sindh and the causes of his success and defeat of the Hindus.

In the sixth and early seventh centuries CE, the kingdom of Sindh with its metropolis at Alor (near modern Rohri), a large and well-fortified town adorned with magnificent palaces, was under the rule of kings of the Rāī family of śūdra origin. The five kings of this family ruled the kingdom altogether for 137 years during the period. At the beginning of the seventh century CE the reigning sovereign was Rāī Siharas, a believer in Buddhism. He was deposed by his brāhmaṇa minister Cāca (generally spelled as Chach), who put his royal master to death, unsurped the throne and founded the brāhmaṇa dynasty in CE 641. He was a great king. During his long reign of 40 years he extended the frontiers of the kingdom and held sway over them. After the death of Cāca his brother Candar succeeded him. He patronised the Buddhist monks and promulgated their doctrines. But he died soon after and a dispute arose for the throne between his son Duraj and the eldest son of Cāca named Dāhir. Eventually, Duraj was defeated and ousted, and Cāca's two sons, Dāhir and Daharsiah, divided the kingdom. On Daharsiah's death Dāhir became the sole ruler of Sindh. On the eve of the Arab conquest, Sindh was very much weakened owing to political instability and internal strife.[15]

It is further related in the *Cācanāmā* that Muhammad bin Qasim, an able general, marched with a strong army to invade Sindh in CE 712. At the time of this invasion the famous Hindu king, Dāhir, was ruling Sindh with its capital at Alor. Debal (modern Karachi), a port town of Sindh, was the first to bear the brunt of attack. It was colossal blunder on the part

15. *Cācanāmā*, Eng. tr. in H.M. Elliot and J. Dowson, *The History of India as told by Its Own Historians*, vol. I, pp. 138-55.

of Dāhir to remain inactive at his capital. He could not foresee the disastrous consequences of this invasion for himself as well as for his kingdom. He did not make any serious attempt to stem the tide of the progress of the invading army nor did he send any reinforcement to Debal which had a slender garrison of 4,000 troops as against the mighty invading army numbering over 25,000. The troops of Qasim besieged the town of Debal which was well protected by a strong stone wall. The troops stationed at Debal for its protection fought bravely but they were hopelessly outnumbered. "During the course of the siege a brāhmaṇa from the chief temple deserted to the Arabs and informed Muhammad that as long as the red flag, to the base of which a *talisma* (a charm consisting of a magical figure cut, and supposed to preserve the bearer from injury or sudden death) was tied, remained flying at the top of the temple, the town could never be taken." The people of the town were asked to choose between Islam and death. They preferred the latter to the former. The carnage, destructions and depredations that followed continued for three days. All the males of 17 years and above were put to death and their women and children were made slaves. Temples were desecrated and demolished and mosques built in their places. And finally Debal was conquered. From the chronicler's account of the subject it appears that a huge booty fell into the hands of the victor.[16]

Further, Muhammad bin Qasim and his troops crossed the Indus by a bridge of boats and attacked Rawar. Several pitched battles were fought between the troops of both the sides. A fierce battle which took place on 20 June 712, resulted in the defeat and death of Dāhir. Thereafter the women of Sindh led by Dāhir's widow, Rānī Bāī, made an attempt to expiate for the sins of their menfolk. The Rānī put up a heroic

16. *Cācanāmā*, op. cit., pp. 155-69.

defence within the fort of Rawar and her garrison numbering about 15,000 rained stones and missiles on the invading army causing them great damage. She left no stone unturned to push back the invader. But when she lost all hope of success she burned herself on the funeral pyre along with her women followers to save her honour and chastity. She became precursor of women of Rājpūtānā so far as this practice (*jauhara*) is concerned. The fort of Rawar was ultimately captured. Another round of battle was fought at Brāhmaṇābād (a city of brāhmaṇas at a distance of about 47 miles to the north-east of Hyderabad) between the remnants of Dāhir's troops numbering more than 8,000 and the troops of the enemy with casualties on both sides. Jai Singh, Dāhir's son, finding resistance useless retired to Chitrur. And thereafter Qasim with the help of his troops occupied Brāhmaṇābād with its treasures and Rānī Lāḍī, another widow of Dāhir, and the two maiden daughters of the latter, Sūryā Devī and Parmal Devī. The graphic description of the whole occurrences has been provided in the said local chronicle of Sindh. Alor (also called Aror), the then capital of Sindh, was the next target of invader's attack. This capital town was then held by another son of Dāhir. He along with the residents of the capital fought bravely against the invader and stoutly defended the town and abandoned it only when further resistance proved to be of no avail. With the capitulation of the fort of Alor the subjugation of Sindh became complete. The conqueror took in his possession Dāhir's territory with all its dependencies. And thus the Hindu kingdom of Sindh fell into the hands of the Arabs.[17] After the death of Muhammad bin Qasim his successors made continuous efforts to expand their territory but they failed to achieve their objective.

---

17. *Cācanāmā*, op. cit., pp. 170-211; see also A.L. Srivastava, *The Sultanate of Delhi*, pp. 17-19.

The *Cācanāmā* is a principal source of our information for the study of eary medieval history of Sindh.

Rajasthan

In Rajasthan, some of the *khyāta*s are known after the name of their writers. In this category, the most important is *Mutha* (or *Mūtā*) *Nainsi-ri-Khyāta* by Nainsi (1659-65), the famous historian of Medapāṭa (Mewāṛ). This work is in the form of more or less a chronicle. It is one of the best medieval histories by native scholars. In this work, the author has dealt with the history of several of the principal states of Rajasthan in a very scientific and secular way. He has also provided a very authentic history of a number of Rājpūt rulers and peoples. In such type of *khyāta,* we also find the biographical details of various rulers of the dynasties collectively and individually. The descriptions of the dynasties are historically very accurate. The *khyāta* of Nainsi provides the detailed account of the battle of Singoli which resulted in the defeat and captivity of Sultān of Delhi called Muhammad Shah Tughlaq. It is recorded in this *khyāta* that the Sultān was attacked and defeated near Singoli and made prisoner by Rāṇā Hammīra of Mewāṛ in Rajasthan. This event occurred some time after October 1335. The historicity of the details of event is, however, of doubtful nature.

Another important historical work by Nainsi is *Mārwāṛ ra Parganā ri Vigat,* composed in 1664. The *parganā*s dealt with in his *vigat* are seven, viz. Jodhpur, Sojat, Jaitaran, Phalodi, Merta, Siwana and Pokaran. The early history of these *parganā*s as given by Nainsi may not be authentic, but reliability of his account increases as we approach his own times. The *vigat* contains a lot of information regarding the life and culture of the people of that age. It also gives biographical accounts of the rulers of Mārwāṛ, notably, Rāo Maldeo. Its biographical contents appear in book four of this work.

The *Deśāvalīvivṛtti*, written by Jaganmohana at the request of King Baijala of Cauhāna family who died in Śaka 1570 = CE 1648, describes 56 kingdoms of India, including Rajasthan, with the names of the rulers of ancient and medieval times. It gives historical accounts of manners, customs, laws, religious institutions and the social life of the people of different parts of India before and after the Muhammadan conquest.

Nepal

The tradition of compiling and preserving the Vaṁśāvalīs in Nepal (i.e. "Jambūdvīpe Bhāratakhaṇḍe Nepālarājye") was handed down from generation to generation or age to age. It is difficult to determine the antiquity of this tradition with precision and accuracy. Some Vaṁśāvalīs in full still exist but parts of some old ones seem to have been lost. These records contain genealogies and chronology of kings of various dynasties with a few details, both mythical and historical. The lists of kings and the dates of their succession and duration of their reigns given therein are of exceptional value. The Vaṁśāvalīs which have survived till date are all based on ancient collections with new versions. These include a Vaṁśāvalī in Sanskrit (anonymous) probably written in CE 1350, the *Gopālarājā* Vaṁśāvalī, a composite work in three parts (VI, VII, and VIII) partly in Sanskrit and partly in old Newārī, apparently put together and supplemented in CE 1390 (preserved in the Darbar Library Kathmandu, discovered by C. Bendall in the course of his journey in Nepal in 1884-85) and the *Parbatīya* Vaṁśāvalī which was originally written in Parbatīya with an admixture of Sanskrit and Newārī and later compiled in the fourteenth century. The *Parbatīya* Vaṁśāvalī in particular saw its different recensions. According to its Buddhist recension, it was translated in 1867 by Munśī Śiva Śaṅkara Singh (attached to British Residency who lived in Nepal for almost 30 years) and Paṇḍit Śrī Guṇānanda (a native of Nepal residing at Pāṭan whose ancestors have been the compilers of Vaṁśāvalī history for many generations).[18]

Of all the Vaṁśāvalīs of Nepal, *Parbatīya* Vaṁśāvalī is the oldest and the most valuable. Daniel Wright calls it a genealogical history of Nepal.[19] It is, in fact, a replica of Purāṇic genealogical lists. Pandit Baladeva Prasad Mishra states that this Vaṁśāvalī with its Buddhist recension is the most important historical document. It gives a reliable account of Nepal. He further maintains that in spite of some of its discrepancies, it contains a lot of historical facts.[20] It gives in its own way a genealogy of kings with names and duration of their reigns, supplemented with a brief noting of the principal events. This Vaṁśāvalī in particular contains valuable information regarding the dynastic rule of the Kirātas in Nepal Valley from the epic age down to the seventh century CE. It also throws light on the rule of the Abhīras, later Licchavis called Sūryavaṁśī, Somavaṁśīs and others in the valley of Nepal but their chronology is not fully reliable.

It is worthwhile to note here that the said Vaṁśāvalīs (also called local chronicles) are based on the genealogical records of the Kirātas and the Licchavīs in Hindu and Buddhist traditions preserved by them during their rule in the valley of Nepal when it was an integral part of India. It has been established by Bhagawanlal Indraji, one of the noted

---

18. *Parbatīya* Vaṁśāvalī, Eng. tr. Daniel Wright, *History of Nepal*, pp. 109 ff; Baladeva Prasad Mishra, *Nepal kā Itihāsa*, p. 45; Bhagawanlal Indraji, *Some Considerations on the History of Nepal*; for his writings on the Vaṁśāvalī of Nepal see *Ind. Ant.*, XIII, 1884, pp. 411-12; A.K. Warder, *An Introduction to Indian Historiography*, pp. 88 ff; D.R. Regmi, *Ancient Nepal*, p. 41; *Gopālarājā* Vaṁśāvalī, ed. Regmi in his *Nepal: Mediaeval Period*, vol. III, pp. 112 ff, 158 ff; G.P. Singh, *The Kirātas in Ancient India*, pp. 47-48, 57-58 and 476.
19. Daniel Wright, op. cit., Preface, v.
20. Pandit Baladeva Prasad Mishra, op. cit., pp. 45, 55.

authorities on ancient Nepal and its Vaṁśāvalīs, that the tradition of writing genealogical or Vaṁśāvalī history or chronicles was maintained in Nepal from early times. The Vaṁśāvalīs were finally compiled in the fourteenth century with new additions and versions. After the break-up of the Gupta empire about the middle of the sixth century CE Nepal seems to have become independent. The events of the period preceding that century recorded in the Vaṁśāvalīs of Nepal form the part of ancient Indian historiographical tradition. The events of seventh to twelfth centuries were further incorporated in later compilation of the Vaṁśāvalīs.

The Vaṁśāvalī texts — *Parbatīya* Vaṁśāvalī, and *Gopālarājā* Vaṁśāvalī (first and second parts, VI and VII) — are authentic records on the ancient history of Nepal to the twelfth century CE. Their earlier portion, no doubt, represents the coalescence of both myth and history but the dynastic accounts and other details which follow from the sixth century BCE onwards are purely historical. The Gopāla dynasty founded by Nemuni first ruled over Nepal for about 521 years. This dynasty was supplanted by the Kirāta dynasty. According to the Vaṁśāvalī tradition, 29 Kirāta kings ruled in the valley of Nepal. Their rule virtually commenced towards the beginning of the Kaliyuga and continued uninterruptedly until the beginning of the first century CE. It was during their rule that the Buddha and Aśoka made historic visits to Nepal. The latter is said to have founded the town of Lalitapāṭan and built four Buddhist shrines there. After the appearance of the later Licchavīs on the political stage of Nepal in the first century CE their struggle with the Kirātas ensued for power and political supremacy which continued till the end of the third century CE. This period marked the beginning of the decline of the Kirātas' rule but not the disappearance or downfall of the Kirātas. According to the most reliable versions of the Vaṁśāvalīs, in the early centuries of the Christian Era Nepal was virtually ruled by the Licchavi dynasty. Jayadeva I is generally regarded as the real founder of this dynasty. The Licchavis ruled over Nepal from the first century CE down to the end of the eighth century. Candragupta II married the Licchavi princess, Kumāradevī, and brought under his sway all the frontier rulers of Nepal. During the period from the fifth century CE to the seventh century Nepal witnessed the vicissitude of its political fortunes. According to the Vaṁśāvalī tradition, a new Gupta dynasty was founded by Jayagupta. This dynasty ruled in Terai area up to Janakapura, the earlier capital of the Videha Kingdom, from CE 500 to 625. The Licchavi and Gupta dynasties ruled over Nepal simultaneously. But their relationship was very hostile of which the Kirātas took advantage and attempted to revive their position. Towards the close of the sixth century CE Aṁśuvarman, the minister of the Licchavi king, Śivadeva, founded the Ṭhākurī dynasty and ruled in the valley of Nepal for at least 45 years. It was during his time that Nepal came under the suzerainty of Tibet. There was restoration of the Licchavi rule. After Mānadeva I, one of the most prominent Licchavi rulers, the Kirātas again tried to restore the fallen fortunes of their dynasty. But they were defeated by the Guptas. The Ābhīras, who were the feudal chiefs during the Licchavis' rule, also ruled for sometimes between the fifth and eighth century CE. But they were defeated by Aṁśuvarman. The Kirātas were finally overthrown by the Ābhīra Guptas in the seventh century CE — the period which marked the end of the dynastic rule of the Kirātas in Nepal.[21]

---

21. See Daniel Wright, op. cit., pp. 109-12; Warder, op. cit., pp. 88-94; Regmi, *Ancient Nepal*, pp. 56-59; *Mediaeval Nepal*, I, pp. 21-22; G.P. Singh, op. cit., pp. 47-48, 395-411; K.P. Jayaswal, "Chronology and History of Nepal, 600 BCE to 800 AD", *JBORS*, XXII, III, 1936, pp. 157-264; R.S. Tripathi, *History of Ancient India*, p. 332; Sylvain Levi, *Le Nepal*, II, pp. 78-79.

5.2

Chronicles and Other Historical Works of Western India

Gurjaradeśa (Gujarat)

THE tradition of writing chronicles and other historical works was fairly maintained in Gūrjaradeśa in medieval period. The period from the thirteenth to the fourteenth centuries marks a significant phase in the history of historical writing in Gūrjaradeśa. A number of chronicles and some other historical works were produced during the period by the Jaina and non-Jaina scholars. The Jaina scholars in particular wrote several types of chronicle among which the *prabandha*s are the most important. They are of great historical value. The Jaina historians of Gujarat school admittedly made significant contributions to the development of historical writing in medieval India. The works bearing the character of a chronicle written in Gujarat in late medieval period also deserve our notice.

Among the works in the form of a chronicle composed in the thirteenth century in Sanskrit in Gurjaradeśa, mention may first be made of the *Kīrtikaumudī* of Someśvara (CE 1179-1262), a brāhmaṇa scholar, poet and historian. In his work, the author, Someśvara, has presented a dynastic history of the Cāḷukyas and Vāghelās of Gūrjaradeśa. The presentation of a historical account of a dynasty or dynasties in the order of time or in a chronological order constitutes the distinguishing feature of a chronicle. His work contains valuable information regarding different members of the Cāḷukya house of Gujarat and different historical personalities, and also other interesting details.

In the introductory portion of his work, Someśvara has given a brief account of the Cāḷukya dynasty of Anhilawāḍa (identified with modern Pāṭan in Gujarat) from its founder Mūlarāja I to the time of Karṇa which covers the period from about CE 940 to 1093.

Dealing further with the history of the Cāḷukyas, Someśvara states that Karṇa's successor Jayasiṁha Siddharāja (CE 1093-1143), one of the greatest kings of the dynasty, embarked upon the policy of conquering the neighbouring territories. He is said to have defeated the Paramāra potentates (Naravarman and Yaśovarman) and annexed Mālwā to his kingdom. He also annexed Bhinnmāl by defeating its Paramāra rulers. He further tells us that in CE 1139, Arṇorāja (CE 1139-53), the Cāhamāna ruler of Śākambharī submitted to Jayasiṁha who gave his daughter Kāñcanadevī to the former. Jayasiṁha also invaded the Candella kingdom and proceeded as far as Kālañjara and Mahobā (called Mahobaka). He invaded Bundelkhand and entered upon a war against Madanavarman of Mahobaka (CE 1129-63) but met with little success.[1] Madanavarman is recorded elsewhere as having defeated the king of Gūrjaradeśa.[2] Jayasiṁha is also believed to have gained victory over the Kalacuris of Cedi. He was, no doubt, one of the powerful monarchs, ruled over an extensive kingdom and raised the power and prestige of the Cāḷukyas to a great height.

Kumārapāla (CE 1143-72), successor of Jayasiṁha Siddharāja, came within the fold of Jainism after coming

1. *Kīrtikaumudī*, II, vv. 28 f, 37 f.

2. *JASB*, XVII, I, 1848, p. 318; *Ind. Ant.*, XXXVII, p. 144.

under the influence of his religious preceptor Hemacandra, as stated by Someśvara in the second canto of his work. He was succeeded by Ajayapāla who reigned for three years (CE 1173-75). He was further succeeded by his minor son Mūlarāja II who ruled from CE 1176 to 1178.

We are informed by Someśvara that in CE 1178 Shihabuddin (Muhammad of Ghur, also known as Muhammad Ghori) who was then the governor of Ghazni, invaded Gujarat. Young Mūlarāja II then in his teens opposed him at the head of the army of Gujarat. The two armies met near Ābu and a fierce battle followed. The army of Gujarat was led by loyal and seasoned warriors such as the brave Kalhaṇa of Mārwāṛ. In this battle, the forces of Ghori were defeated with great slaughter and the Turks escaped to Ghazni. Mūlarāja was crowned with victory. He obtained such a victory that Muhammad of Ghur did not venture to invade Gujarat again for another 20 years. According to *prabandhas*, Ajayapāla's queen, Naikādevī (also called Naiki), the daughter of the King Paramardin, was very brave. She with her son Mūlarāja II (the boy king) in her arms herself marched at the head of the army and inflicted a crushing defeat upon the Muslim forces near Mt. Ābu, securing for her son the title of the "Vanquisher of the king of Ghazni."[3]

Mūlarāja's victory over the Muslims called Hammīra is referred to in all the chronicles, including the Jaina *prabandhas* and some epigraphic records of the Cāḷukya rulers of Gujarat. The Veraval inscription of Bhīma II (successor of Mūlarāja II) tells us that Mūlarāja conquered Hammīra in the battle.[4] Four Kadi plates and two other Kadi grants of Bhīma II call Mūlarāja destroyer of *mleccha* (Muhammad of Ghur).[5] Another

3. *Kīrtikaumudī*, II, vv. 56-57.

4. Cf. *Bhāvanagar Prākṛt and Sanskrit Inscriptions*, 210, I, 20.

5. *Ind. Ant.*, VI, pp. 194 ff, 199; see K.M. Munshi, *Glory That Was Gurjaradeśa* (CE *550-1300*), pt. II, pp. 359-60 and 483.

epigraphic evidence also corroborates the attack of Turks on Gujarat in VS 1235 = CE 1178.[6] The defeat of Muhammad of Ghur at the hands of Mūlarāja can also be attested by the statement of a Muslim chronicler, Ferishta (1552–1623).[7] A.L. Srivastava, one of the noted authorities on Medieval Indian History, has also asserted that "Moola Raj" II was the Cāḷukya ruler of Anhilawāḍa (Pāṭan, the capital of the kingdom of Gujarat) at the time of Muhammad of Ghur's invasion.[8] But he has contradicted his own statement by saying that in CE 1178 Bhīma II inflicted a terrible defeat upon Muhammad of Ghur and drove him away from Gujarat.[9] All internal and external evidence go in favour of Muhammad of Ghur's invasion of Gurjaradeśa in CE 1178 in the time of Mūlarāja II and not Bhīma II as held by some historians.

Someśvara provides possibly the best history of the Cāḷukyas of Gujarat up to the time of Mūlarāja II. The later history of Gujarat provided by him is also valuable.

After the death of Mūlarāja in CE 1178, his younger brother Bhīma II, one of the later Cāḷukya monarchs of Gujarat, succeeded to the throne of Anhilawāḍa and ruled for 63 years (1178-1241). Many events one after another took place during his reign period. One of the events was Turkish invasion of Anhilawāḍa as referred to in Someśvara's work and other local chronicles of Gujarat. On the 3 or 4 February 1197, Qutb-ud-din Aibak plundered the capital city of Anhilawāḍa, occupied it and appointed a Turkish officer as its governor who was within a few months repulsed by the forces of Bhīmadeva, and the invader Aibak was driven out

6. *Ep. Ind.*, XI, p. 72.

7. *Tārīkh-i-Ferishta*, Eng. tr. in Briggs' *History of the Rise of the Mahomedan Power in India till the year 1612* CE, vol. I, p. 170.

8. *The Sultanate of Delhi*, p. 71.

9. Ibid., p. 76.

from Anhilawāḍa to Ajmer. Aibak did not venture to reinvade Gujarat. Neither he nor his master (Muhammad of Ghur) could conquer Gujarat. Bhīmadeva maintained its independence and in CE 1199 assumed the title of Abhinava Siddharāja. As a matter of fact, the entire Cāḷukya kingdom, including Ābu, remained in the hands of its legitimate ruler till as late as the year 1240.[10]

After 1199 the power of the Cāḷukyas was on the decline. The Vāghelā family tracing its descent from a sister of Kumārapāla took advantage of the situation and shot into prominence. For it appears that Lavaṇaprasāda (son of Arṇorāja[11] of Vāghelā branch of Cāḷukya family), who was the minister and feudatory of Bhīma II, established himself in an almost independent position in southern Gujarat, thereby reducing the latter's jurisdiction to its northern part. Gradually the Vāghelās took Anhilawāḍa and extended their sway over the whole of Gujarat.

The Vāghelā chief Arṇorāja loyally stood by the young king Bhīma II and subdued the rebellious elements. He lost his life in course of this struggle but his son Lavaṇaprasāda continued the task left unfinished by his father. He virtually carried on the administration of the state in the name of the king from his headquarters at Dhavalakapuri (modern Dholka). He had acquired the principality of that place between CE 1209 and 1220 as one of the feudatories called *mahāmaṇḍaleśvara rāṇaka*. He saved the state from internal dissensions and heroically struggled against external invasions.

10. See also Ibid., p. 83; Elliot and Dowson, *History of India as Told by Its Own Historians*, II, p. 226.

11. Arṇorāja belonged to the Cāḷukya clan and was related to Kumārapāla who granted him in recognition of his loyal and faithful service the village of Vyāghrapalli, 10 miles southwest of the Cāḷukya capital Anhilawāḍa. From the name of this village the family which settled there came to be known as the Vāghelās.

The author Someśvara (the family priest of the Cāḷukyas) advised Lavaṇaprasāda to save Gujarat from internal and external troubles. The latter on the advice of the former took the lead in saving Gujarat from its plight. This fact has been recorded by Someśvara himself in his work. He also speaks of the heroic deeds of Lavaṇaprasāda and his son Vīradhavala and his minister Vastupāla. They fought against several hostile forces between 1223 and 1226. By CE 1226, they brought the northern feudatories to order.[12]

Someśvara has given a contemporary account of an invasion of Gujarat by a Yādava ruler of Devagiri (modern Daulatābād), Siṅghana (CE 1210-47 or 1209-41), in the time of Lavaṇaprasāda and his son Vīradhavala. The Yādava prince was hostile to the Cāḷukyas of Gujarat. He continued the aggressive policy against them and formed an alliance with the Paramāra king of Mālwā and chief of Lāṭa for the purpose. In or about CE 1232, he attacked southern part of Gujarat (Lāṭa). He came with a large army and overran the country round Broach. Lavaṇaprasāda along with his son Vīradhavala and forces advanced to the banks of the Mahi to meet the enemy but suddenly stopped his march and turned back. Taking the Yādava forces invincible he submitted and concluded a treaty of alliance with the Yādava king Siṅghana in 1232 and retired from his service to the state as a chieftaiṇ of Bhīma II.[13]

Someśvara also narrates the history of the Vāghelā dynasty. He has chronicled all the important events that took

---

12. *Kīrtikaumudī*, II, vv. 86-107.

13. For details, see ibid., IV, vv. 43-63. From the Dabhoi and Devapāṭana *praśastis* it appears that detachment of the army of the Turks proceeded towards Cambay and Prabhāsa, but were driven back by Śrīdhara and Lavaṇaprasāda (cf. Śrīdhara's *Veraval-Praśasti*, *Ep. Ind.*, II, p. 437; *Dabhoi-Praśasti* of Viśāladeva, *Ep. Ind.*, I, p. 20). The *Dabhoi-Praśasti* was composed by Someśvara, the author of *Kīrtikaumudī* and *Surathotsava*.

place during the times of the later Vāghelā chiefs (of Rājpūt family) of Gujarat. He has highlighted the achievements of Lavaṇaprasāda's son Vīradhavala (CE 1180-1238). In CE 1220, he appointed Vastupāla and his brother Tejaḥpāla his principal ministers. He was a vigorous military leader. In 1220 itself, he led an expedition against Saurāṣṭra. He captured Cambay (called Stambhatīrtha) in the name of Bhīmadeva and appointed Vastupāla to govern the new territory.[14] From 1232 till his death in 1238 he ruled at Dhavalakapuri (Dholka) as a loyal chieftain of Gujarat during the reign of Bhīmadeva II. He acknowledged Bhīmadeva as the nominal ruler. In CE 1236, he conquered Lāṭa. After his death Bhīmadeva still continued to rule on in Anhilawāḍa.

Someśvara has described in detail the life and deeds of his patron Vastupāla. We are told by him that he was a valiant warrior. He defended with his army the kingdom against the attacks of the hostile forces.[15] He continued to work as a minister from CE 1220 till his death in 1240. After his death he was succeeded by his younger brother Tejaḥpāla who continued to function as the principal minister (*mahāmātya*) till his death in 1248.

In 1241, Bhīmadeva died and Tribhuvanapāla (1242-44) succeeded to the nominal kingship of Gujarat. The Vāghelā chief Viśāladeva (son of Vīradhavala) took charge of the affairs of the state under the title of *mahāmaṇḍaleśvara rāṇaka* in 1244 and continued to rule till 1262. The authors of the *Kīrtikaumudī* and the *prabandhas* have not taken notice of his reign.

Someśvara has also thrown some light on the

---

14. *Kīrtikaumudī*, IV, vv. 1-3.

15. The inscriptions on the stone-walls of the Jain temples of Mounts Ābu and Girnār were composed by Someśvara in praise of Vastupāla. These temples (constructed by Vastupāla himself) with inscriptions stand as monuments of his glory.

contemporary religion and culture. From his work[16] as well as the Jaina *prabandhas* it appears that Brāhmanism and Jainism coexisted in Gujarat during his time.

The whole narrative in the *Kīrtikaumudī*, one of the local chronicles (also called a "historical epic") of Gujarat, appears factual except for some exaggerated statements in traditional fashion about the earlier Cāḷukya kings. In his work, Someśvara has provided the history of Gurjaradeśa up to the death of Bhīma II in 1241. And hence his work must have been composed after 1241.

Someśvara's another work, *Surathotsava*, throws light only on some aspects of the history of the Cāḷukyas of Gujarat. Its first few cantos briefly deal with their early history which is, of course, mixed with legends. It is clearly stated therein that Ajayapāla, a brāhmaṇa, was the successor of Kumārapāla. His succession to the throne (in CE 1172) was opposed by one of the groups of disciples of Hemacandra (one of the exponents of the doctrine of Jainism). And this is the reason why he is described as an antagonist of Jains. He is represented by the Jaina chroniclers also as a persecutor of their religion. He continued to rule till CE 1175. He was succeeded by Mūlarāja II in CE 1176 who ruled up to 1178.

We are further told by Someśvara that in CE 1178, the very first year of the reign of Bhīma II, the successor of Mūlarāja, the Paramāra king of Mālwā, Vindhyavarman, the son of Jayavarman, raised a banner of revolt in Mālwā, but Kumāra, the father of Someśvara and also a General, was sent to Mālwā with the army of Gujarat to suppress the revolt. The rebel was defeated and Mālwā was brought under control.[17]

Someśvara describes allegorically the vicissitudes of

16. *Kīrtikaumudī*, IV, v. 17; IX, vv. 70-71.

17. *Surathotsava*, XV, vv. 36-37.

fortune of Bhīma II called Suratha. His reign period (CE 1178-1241) was eventful. He faced Muslim invasion of his capital Anhilawāḍa (in CE 1197) led by Qutb-ud-din. The capital city was captured and remained under occupation for some time causing political instability. Gujarat suffered from the inroads of the Paramāra king of Mālwā and the Yādava ruler of Devagiri. Taking advantage of the prevailing situation, Bhīma II's feudatory, Lavaṇaprasāda of Vāghelā family, established himself in an almost independent position in southern Gujarat, thereby reducing the formers's jurisdiction to its northern part.

The work concludes with the history of Someśvara's own family and eulogy of Vastupāla, the minister of Vīradhavala, son of Lavaṇaprasāda. The work seems to have been composed by Someśvara betweem 1250 and 1260.

It may be noted here that a revolutionary change in the writing of history of Gurjaradeśa had taken place between Someśvara (CE 1230) and Merutuṅga (CE 1300). Within a period of 70 years the technique of the Muslim chroniclers of providing dates, events and incidents and adjusting them to suit the continuity of the historical narrative had come into vogue. In the latter half of the thirteenth century, Someśvara, Merutuṅga and others were influenced by a new school of history which presumably drew its inspiration from the Muslim chroniclers. Historical legends of the Muslim chroniclers relating to Gujarat circulated in the camps of the Turks came to be accepted by the writers of the *prabandha*s and other works.

The chronicles and other historical works written in Sanskrit in the thirteenth century by the Jaina scholars of Gurjaradeśa also deserve our notice.

The *Sukṛtasaṁkīrtana* of Arisiṁha, a historian, and court-poet of the Vāghelā ruler of Gujarat, Viśāladeva (CE 1244-62), a patron of art and learning, is a historical epic or poem almost in the form of a chronicle. It consists of two cantos. In the first canto, the author deals with the history of Cāpotkaṭa or Cāvaḍa dynasty that ruled Gujarat from about the middle of the eighth century CE until the rise of the Cāḷukyas in or about CE 940. He has also provided the genealogy of the kings of former dynasty right from Vanarāja, the founder of "Anhilapāṭan," the capital city of the kingdom. In the second canto, he has given an account of the reign of the Cāḷukya kings from Mūlarāja I (CE 936 or 940-96), the founder of the dynasty, to Bhīma II (CE 1178-1241) and of the activities of Vastupāla and Tejaḥpāla, the two famous ministers of Gujarat appointed by Vāghelā chief Vīradhavala in 1220 during the reign of the latter Cāḷukya king. He has devoted more pages of his work to the delineation of the life and character of Vastupāla than to that of Tejaḥpāla. He concentrates on the religious aspects of Vastupāla's life rather than the political one. He speaks of his pilgrimages and religious and charitable activities, and also of the buildings and temples built by him for the welfare of the people.

In his work, Arisiṁha has given valuable information regarding life and culture under the Cāḷukyas of Gujarat. He tells us that there was growth of Jainism during their time, but Brāhmanism also flourished side by side with it. He further informs us that not only the Cāḷukya rulers (including the Hindus and Jains) but also Vastupāla (a devout Jaina) also offered prayers at the temple of Somanātha.

Arisiṁha appears to be much more rhetorical and less factual than Someśvara in the presentation of his account of the subject.

The *Hammīra-madamardana* of Jayasiṁha Sūri I, a Śvetāmbara Jaina scholar at Broach, is a historical drama in five acts. Like the chronicles of Gujarat it traces its history especially under the Cāḷukyas with fullness of details. The details of the events that took place during the reign of Bhīma II (CE 1178-1241) are especially worthy of our notice. We learn from it that Bhīma II ascended the throne of Anhilawāḍa in VS 1235 = CE 1178.[18] In CE 1199, he assumed the title of Abhinava Siddharāja. He ruled north Gujarat from his capital Anhilawāḍa. In 1209, Saurāṣṭra acknowledged his suzerainty. He has been referred to as Sīmāntamaṇi of Saurāṣṭra. Siṅghana, the Yādava king of Devagiri, invaded Lāṭa (southern Gujarat and reached the northern banks of the Narmadā, but with the timely assistance of Devapāla, the king of Mālwā, Saṁgrāmasiṁha (also called Śaṅkha), the son of Sindhurāja of Lāṭa who was a feudatory of Arjunavarman of Mālwā, drove him back. In CE 1219, the Yādava again invaded Lāṭa, the brave Śaṅkha was taken prisoner and sent to Devagiri. Subhaṭavarman, a Paramāra king of Mālwā, succeeded to the throne of Dhāra and later sacked Anhilawāḍa.[19] When the Yādavas of Devagiri, Paramāras of Mālwā and Śaṅkha were about to invade Lāṭa in concert, no Cāḷukya feudatory came forward to offer assistance.[20]

The information supplied by the author, Jayasiṁha Sūri, about the invasion of Gujarat by the Muslims (called Hammīras) and their failure to conquer it constitutes the nucleus of his work. The defeat of Muhammad of Ghur at the hands of the Cāḷukya ruler Mūlarāja II in CE 1178 and that of Qutb-ud-din Aibak at the hands of his successor Bhīmadeva II in CE 1197 are recorded not only in his work but also in some of the chronicles of Gujarat.

---

18. *Hammīra-madamardana*, p. 11.
19. Ibid., p. 17.
20. Ibid., p. 6.

The role Vīradhavala (a loyal Vāghelā chieftain of Gujarat during the kinship of Bhīma II) played in foiling the attempt of the Turkish Sultān of Delhi, Iltutmish, in conquering Mārwāṛ and northern Gujarat has been highlighted exclusively in the work of Jayasiṁha Sūri. We are informed by him that in 1226 Iltutmish invaded Mārwāṛ with the sole intention of pushing forward to Gujarat. Vīradhavala and his forces of Gujarat together with Udayasiṁha (1206-49), the Cāhamāna ruler of Jalore, and the old Dhārāvarṣa of Ābu and his son Somasiṁha (all loyal to their contemporary Cāḷukya ruler of Anhilawāḍa) offered stubborn resistance to the invader forcing him to beat a hasty retreat. Vīradhavala along with his forces returned triumphantly to his headquarters at Dholka.[21] In the battle of Mārwāṛ, Jaitrasiṁha, the king of Medapāṭa, stood aloof but paid heavy penalty of his betrayal the description of which given by Jayasiṁha is based on the statement of an eyewitness of the Muslim invasion of the capital city of the said king.[22]

Iltutmish invaded Gujarat between 1226 and 1234 (during the reign of Bhīma II) but his forces (called Turuṣkas and *mlecchas*) were repulsed by the armed forces of Gujarat led by Vīradhavala and Vastupāla and suffered a reverse.

M. Krishnamachariar opines that the author (Jayasiṁha) describes the repulsion of Muhammadan invasions of Gujarat before CE 1230.[23]

The Hammīras could not establish their sway over Gujarat. The flourishing kingdom of Gujarat with its capital Anhilawāḍa (Pāṭan) though raided by Turkish force more than once had never been subdued by any Turkish invader.

---

21. *Hammīra-madamardana*, 5-6, 16.
22. Ibid., 30.
23. *HCSL*, pp. 202-3.

The Hammīras — Ghori, Aibak and Iltutmish — failed to conquer Gujarat.

Jayasiṁha describes Vīradhavala as a valiant warrior, a great conqueror and an able administrator. The latter conquered Cambay in 1220 and Lāṭa in 1236. He formed alliances with those rulers and chieftains who were loyal to the Cāḷukya king Bhīma II to save Gujarat from external invasion. He is said to have left no stone unturned to thwart the attempt of hostile forces, including the Muslim invaders, to establish hegemony over Gujarat. He left this world in 1238.

In his *Vastupāla-Tejaḥpāla-Praśasti*, Jayasiṁha Sūri I throws light not only on the life and deeds of Vastupāla and Tejaḥpāla, the two famous personalities in the thirteenth-century history of Gūrjaradeśa (main theme of the work), but also on its two famous families, the Cāḷukyas and Vāghelās. This work is more a chronicle than a historical biography.

Jayasiṁha gives genealogy of Cāḷukya kings from Mūlarāja I (CE 936 or 940-96), the founder of the dynasty of Anhilawāḍa, to Kumārapāla (CE 1143-72).

The author further gives an account of Kumārapāla's battle with Arṇorāja, the Cāhamāna ruler of Śākambharī. The former assisted by his minister Sajjana fought against the latter. The forces of the enemy were routed. Arṇorāja was defeated and wounded in the battle and taken prisoner. As a result, he surrendered and gave his daughter in marriage to Kumārapāla. Kumārapāla also quelled the revolt of the Paramāra prince of Ābu, and reasserted the Cāḷukya authority in Mālwā, which had raised its head during his initial difficulties. He next turned his arms successfully against a chieftain of Saurāṣṭra.[24]

24. *Vastupāla-Tejaḥpāla-Praśasti*, 58, vv. 25-35.

We are also informed by the author Jayasiṁha Sūri that since the death of Kumārapāla, the Jaina community had faded into political obscurity, but it was powerful and wealthy. Vastupāla and Tejaḥpāla of that community were the two sons of Aśvarāja, whose father Caṇḍaprasāda was one of the ministers of the Cāḷukya king Jayasiṁha Siddharāja (CE 1093-1143). Both Vāstupāla and Tejaḥpāla had by their position, wealth, learning and statesmanship acquired a dominant position in their community. Both had done their best to consolidate Gujarat but as they were devout Jainas their power and influence were envied by others. However, they rose to prominence by virtue of their good deeds. The author has dwelt at length on the glorious deeds of both the brothers. He has highlighted the greatness of Vastupāla in particular as a warrior, a politician, an administrator and a scholar.

Vastupāla was, no doubt, a valiant warrior. As already stated, he defended with his army the kingdom of Gujarat by repulsing the hostile forces. He fought shoulder to shoulder with the Vāghelā chief of Dholka, Vīradhavala, against all the external enemies and invaders for maintaining the independence of Gujarat.

In 1220, Vīradhavala appointed Vastupāla and his brother Tejaḥpāla his principal ministers. In 1220 itself, Vīradhavala conquered Cambay and appointed Vastupāla as its governor. In 1239, Tejaḥpāla was functioning as the governor of Broach. Vastupāla died in 1240 or 1242. He was succeeded by his younger brother Tejaḥpāla who continued to function as the principal minister (*mahāmātya*) of Viśāladeva, the son of Vīradhavala, till his death in 1248.

Touching on religious activities of Vastupāla and Tejaḥpāla, Jayasiṁha Sūri informs us that they built many temples, including those of Dilwāṛā near Mt. Ābu and Śatruñjaya at Girnār. The former with the inscriptions in praise of Vastupāla stands as a monument of his glory. He made his memorable pilgrimage to Śatruñjaya in 1221. They built not only Jaina temples but Brāhmanical temples as well. Vastupāla upheld the tenets of Sanātana Dharma. He also offered prayers at Somanātha temple (as noted before). This testifies to the fact that Jainism and Brāhmanism flourished side by side in Gūrjaradeśa during the times of these two brothers.

Another work, *Vastupāla-carita*, of Jinaharṣa also eulogises Vastupāla as a warrior, statesman, philanthropist, constructor of temples, poet, patron of learning and founder of big manuscript libraries.

The *Sukṛtakīrti-Kallolinī* of Udayaprabha Sūri is a historical work. It was composed on the occasion of the pilgrimage of Vastupāla and Tejaḥpāla to Śatruñjaya (i.e. in 1221). It is partly a *praśasti* (eulogy) of the *sukṛtas* (pious or good deeds) and *kīrti* (glory) of these heroes. It contains, besides the genealogy of Vastupāla, the genealogy and an eulogy of the Cāpotkaṭa family and the Cāḷukyas of Gujarat.

The work of Udayaprabha Sūri deals with exploits of the Cāḷukya ruler Kumārapāla. He is said to have defeated the Cāhamāna ruler Arṇorāja of Śākambharī and the Paramāras of Mālwā and Ābu and thereby consolidated his position. He also established his sway over the Cāhamānas of Naḍḍula and Paramāras of Bhinnmāl. His most remarkable exploit was the defeat of Mallikārjuna of Koṅkaṇa.[25]

As in the *Hammīra-madamardana* so also in this work, we find that a confederate force consisting of the Yādava Siṅghana of Devagiri, Devapāla of Mālwā and Śaṅkha of Lāṭa himself advanced towards Cambay. Vastupāla and Tejaḥpāla's son Lāvaṇyasiṁha stood the ground. In the

25. *Sukṛtakīrti-Kallolinī,* GOS, X, Appendix II, p. 76.

meantime, Siṅghana and Devapāla fell out with each other and withdrew their forces. And Śaṅkha entered into a tready of friendship with Vastupāla. Vīradhavala, while on the battlefield of Mārwāṛ in 1226 fighting against the forces of Iltutmish, gave expression to his joy upon hearing that the son of Sindhurāja had become his friend.[26]

The *Vasantavilāsa* (a historical epic) of Bālacandra Sūri was written soon after Vastupāla's death in 1240 or 1242. The author of the work has given a historical account of the invasion of Gujarat by the Yādava kings of Devagiri during the time of the Cāḷukya ruler Bhīma II and of the reverses they suffered in the war with forces of Gujarat. He has also narrated the events that took place during the times of Vastupāla and his predecessors.

In Gūrjaradeśa, the *prabandha*s were written by the Jaina scholars of Śvetāmbara school in the thirteenth and fourteenth centuries. One of the characteristic features of the *prabandha* type of chronicle is the treatment of general history of India down to the ninth century CE covering various regions and various dynasties picking out only certain historical figures and certain events without maintaining continuity and coherence in its earlier parts and concentration on the history of Gūrjaradeśa in its later.

The earliest known *prabandha* is *Prabandhāvalī* of Jinabhadra (CE 1220). It contains priceless material of historical value. It includes stories relating to the Sātavāhanas of the Deccan, Cāhamānas of Śākambharī, Paramāras of Mālwā and the Cāḷukyas of Gujarat. It abounds in historical narratives of

26. *Sukṛtakīrti-Kallolinī*, vv. 138-40; see also *Hammīra-madamardana*, 5-6, 16.

For contents of the chronicles and other historical works composed in Sanskrit in the thirteenth century by the Jain scholar of Gujarat see also A.D. Pusalker, "Sanskrit Histories and Chronicles," in *Cul. Her. Ind.*, vol. V, ed. S.K. Chatterji, pp. 283-90.

the deeds of eminent kings of the concerned dynasties.[27]

The *Prabandhacintāmaṇi* (in Prākṛt mixed with Sanskrit) may be regarded as the best specimen of the Jaina chronicles of *prabandha* type. Its historical importance has been acknowledged by some of the noted scholars.[28] It was, according to the colophon of the work itself, completed at Vardhamānapura (modern Vadhvān) in Gūrjaradeśa in CE 1304 by a Jaina scholar Merutuṅga. This disproves the contention of some scholars that it was completed in CE 1306.

The author, Merutuṅga, occupies the most prominent place among the Jaina chroniclers of Gujarat school. He flourished in the later half of the thirteenth century.

Explaining his object of writing this work in its introductory part, Merutuṅga says: "Ancient stories because they have been so often heard do not delight so much the minds of the wise, therefore, I compose this work out of the life-histories of men not far removed from my own time." Equally interesting is his statement that he and his colleagues went through a number of manuscripts full of historical narratives exceeding hundred and collected materials from them. He was assisted in this work particularly by Dharmadeva. He also listened to oral traditions many times. And then he compiled his work.[29] More significant is the concluding verse in the introductory portion:

> Though somewhat obscure it seems to imply that since many different persons wrote on the same topics, there are bound to be differences among them, but the author has tried to select

27. *Prabandhāvalī* published with some shorter works of this class in *Purātanaprabandha Saṁgraha*, ed. Jinavijaya Muni, *SJG*, n.2 (Calcutta, 1936); see also A.K. Warder, *An Introduction to Indian Historiography*, p. 62.
28. C.H. Tawney (tr.) *Prabandhacintāmaṇi*, pp. 155 ff; M. Krishnamachariar, *HCSL*, p. 207.
29. *Prabandhacintāmaṇi*, ed. Jinavijaya Muni, pp. 1, 3-7; tr. Tawney, p. 2.

> the best views and hence does not deserve condemnation from those who happened to take a different view.[30]

The author's statements are truly reflective of his historical mind.

The work is divided into five *prakāśa*s (chapters) and each *prakāśa* into *prabandha*s. Each consists of narratives concerning kings of different dynasties and various other historical subjects.

In the *Vikramāṅka-Prabandha* section in the first *prakāśa* of his work, Merutuṅga describes Vikramāditya in the Jaina tradition as a king of Avantideśa (western Mālwā) with its capital at Ujjayinī (Ujjain). He has vividly portrayed his courage, wisdom and encounters with his adversaries. He is said to have introduced the Vikrama Era in 57 BCE in commemoration of his victory over the Śakas. He achieved that victory with the help of the Mālwās who fought under his banner against the Śakas.[31] Further, the author speaks of the Sātavāhanas of the Deccan.[32] The stories related by him about them represent a fusion of history and legend.

Furthermore, Merutuṅga provides histories of the Cāpotkaṭa dynasty and the Cāḷukya dynasty of Gurjaradeśa. The Cāpotkaṭa dynasty also known as Cāvaḍā dynasty after its founder, Vanarāja Cāvaḍā[33] ruled a part or the whole of Gujarat with its capital at Anhilawāḍa called Anhilapura (Pāṭan) from CE 746 until the rise of the Cāḷukyas. The genealogy of the kings of this dynasty is also given in Merutuṅga's work.

30. *Prabandhacintāmaṇi*, ed. Durgā Śankar Śāstrī, p. 1.

31. Ibid., ed. Jinavijaya, pp. 1-3; tr. Tawney, p. 4.

32. Ibid., p. 10.

33. Ibid., pp. 13, 21. The historical references to the Cāvaḍā dynasty are also found in the *Vaḍnagar Praśasti* (CE 1152) of Kumārapāla.

In the second, third and fourth *prakāśa*s of his work, Merutuṅga gives the complete history of the Cāḷukya of Gurjaradeśa systematically in a chronological order with their genealogy and chronology with special focus on the hostile relations of the Cāḷukya kings with their contemporary Cāhamānas of Śākambharī, and the Paramāras of Mālwā, especially the King Bhoja. He also provides dates of accession and death and also the regnal years of some of the Cāḷukya kings of Gujarat and the Paramāra kings of Mālwā which constitute one of the praiseworthy features of his work.

Mūlarāja, the founder of the Cāḷukya dynasty of Anhilawāḍa, was the son of Rāji, who from his mother's side belonged to the Cāvaḍā or Cāpotkaṭa line. Mūlarāja is said to have slain his maternal uncle and then seized the Cāpotkaṭa throne for himself. Merutuṅga distinctly refers to the origin of the Cāḷukya dynasty of Gujarat from the last Cāpotkaṭa king. According to him, Mūlarāja's accession to the throne of Anhilawāḍa took place in VS 993 = CE 936.[34] After having acquired the Sārasvat-maṇḍala by prowess of his arms he waged war against Bārappa, the ruler of Lāṭa (southern Gujarat), Vigraharāja, Cāhamāna of Śākambharī and other rivals of lesser importance. He ruled up to CE 996. According to Merutuṅga, his contemporary Vākpati-Muñja, the Paramāra king of Mālwā, who ascended the throne in CE 974, was a great warrior. He humbled Lāṭas. He entered the dominions of the western Cāḷukyas of Kalyāṇī (in Karṇāṭadeśa), but he was taken prisoner and put to death by Tailapa II in CE 994.[35]

Cāmuṇḍarāja succeeded his father Mūlarāja after his death in CE 996. The former while passing through Mālwā was deprived by its Paramāra king Sindhurāja of the insignia

34. *Prabandhacintāmaṇi*, ed. Jinavijaya, p. 16.

35. Ibid., pp. 17-21.

of state, the royal umbrella, and other valuables. He appears to have suffered a defeat at the hands of the king of Mālwā. Merutuṅga says that it was one of the reasons why the Cāḷukya king of Gujarat, Bhīma I, became hostile to the Paramāra king Bhoja. Cāmuṇḍarāja was succeeded by his brother Vallabharāja in CE 1009, but he soon died while besieging Dhāra which later rose to an eminence of a capital of Paramāra kings. His son Durlabharāja ruled at Anhilawāḍa from CE 1009 to 1021. But he did not succeed in extending his dominion beyond the territory which his father had inherited from Mūlarāja.[36]

Bhīma I, one of the famous Cāḷukya rulers of Anhilawāḍa, is said to have ruled for about 42 years (CE 1021-63). Soon after his accession, he had to face the storm of Sultān Mahmud (Mahmud of Ghazni) in 1025. As soon as Mahmud appeared before the gates of Anhilawāḍa, Bhīma fled to Cutch for his safety. After having sacked, desecrated and plundered the temple of Somanātha the former returned to Ghazni. After his departure the latter returned to his capital and revived the Cāḷukya power. He vanquished the Paramāra chief of Ābu and other rival forces.

In *Bhīma-Bhoja-Prabandha* of Merutuṅga's work, King Bhoja of the Paramāra dynasty of Mālwā has been depicted as an arch-enemy of the Cāḷukya king Bhīma. Merutuṅga states that the latter always apprehended the former's invasion of his kingdom. When Bhoja was about to launch an invasion against Bhīma, the latter sent his ambassador Ḍāmara to the court of the former with the message that he was also ready to invade Mālwā. Then Bhoja begged for peace to Bhīma. We are further told by the author that during Bhīma's compaign against the king of upper Sindh his capital Anhilawāḍa was stormed by Kulacandra, the general of Bhoja

36. *Prabandhacintāmaṇi*, ed. Jinavijaya, pp. 20-21.

Paramāra. This compelled Bhīma to enter into a coalition with the great Kalacuri king of Tripurī, Lakṣmī-Karṇa. The allied forces completely ravaged Mālwā and occupied the capital city of Dhāra. King Bhoja died in his capital in the course of the struggle, and the coalition was also dissolved subsequently. Hostilities broke out between the allies with the result that Lakṣmī-Karṇa suffered a reverse at the hands of Bhīma. The Paramāras took advantage of this conflict and Mālwā was free of foreign control.[37] The stories related by Merutuṅga about the events concerned are worthy of credence.

The information supplied by Merutuṅga about Bhoja, the most striking and versatile Paramāra ruler with capital at Dhāra, is also worthy of our attention. According to him, he ruled for fifty-five years, seven months and three days (CE 999-1054).[38] We find sufficient proofs in his work of his knowledge of history and chronology. He asserts that Bhoja conquered extensive territories. He first directed his energies towards the Cāḷukyas of Kalyāṇī (in Karṇāṭadeśa) with a view to avenging the execution of Muñja. He easily defeated his southern antagonist identified with Vikramāditya V. After having invaded Karṇāṭadeśa he annexed Lāṭa (southern Gujarat) to his dominion. He was the undisputed master of

---

37. *Prabandhacintāmaṇi*, ed. Jinavijaya, pp. 22, 25, 28, 30-32, 36. Merutuṅga's account of hostile relations between the Cāḷukya king Bhīma and the Paramāra king Bhoja is exactly similar to what we find in the *Bhojaprabandha* of Ballāladeva (pp. 80 ff).

    The historical authenticity of Merutuṅga's statement regarding Bhīma's invasion of Sindh can fairly be attested to by an epigraphic evidence ("Six Saindhava Inscriptions", *Ep. Ind.*, XXVI, p. 185). We learn from this epigraphic record that he had encroached upon the territory of the Saindhavas who ruled over west Saurāṣṭra with their capital at Ghumli, 25 miles north-east of Porbander.

38. *Prabandhacintāmaṇi*, ed. Jinavijaya, p. 22.

an empire which included the whole of peninsular Gujarat excepting the valley of Sārasvata which was in the hands of the Cāḷukyas. His general Kulacandra is stated to have sacked Anhilawāḍa. When the war with the combined forces of Bhīma and Lakṣmī-Karṇa was in progress, he passed away.[39]

According to Merutuṅga, the Cāḷukya king Bhīma I was succeeded by his younger son Karṇa, who ruled for about 30 years (CE 1063-93). He became the king of Sārasvat-maṇḍala. He conquered Mālwā. He invaded southern Mārwāṛ but was defeated by the Cāhamānas of Naḍḍula. He also subdued the Bhīla king of Āśāpallī (near modern Ahmedabad) and founded Karṇāvatī. In or about CE 1091, he assumed the title of Trailokyamalla on account of having conquered Lāṭa.[40]

Karṇa's successor, Jayasiṁha Siddharāja, was one of the greatest kings of the Cāḷukya dynasty of Anhilawāḍa. Merutuṅga says that he ascended the throne on Pauṣa vada 3 of VS 1150 (CE 1093).[41] He became popularly known as Mahārājādhirāja Parameśvara in CE 1108. He carried his victorious arms on all sides and defeated almost all his neighbours. Speaking of his conquest of Saurāṣṭra, Merutuṅga relates that the removal of the Cāḷukyan feudatory of Saurāṣṭra after CE 940 had strengthened the local Ābhīra ruler. During early years of Jayasiṁha's reign, Rā Navaghana, the Ābhīra chief, raised the banner of revolt. In the meantime, he died and was succeeded by his grandson Rā Kheṅgāra. Jayasiṁha now marched against his feudatory, defeated him in a battle and imprisoned him, and finally

39. *Prabandhacintāmaṇi*, ed. Jinavijaya, pp. 22 ff, 36 f, 45-48; see also PTOC, 1st session, Poona (1919), p. 327 for Bhoja's conquest of Karnataka, Lāṭa, and Gujarat during the reign of the Cāḷukya king Bhīma I.

40. *Prabandhacintāmaṇi*, pp. 53-58.

41. Ibid., p. 55.

annexed Saurāṣṭra to his kingdom. This event is said to have happened in CE 1114, the year in which Jayasiṁha founded the Siṁha Era to commemorate the conquest of Saurāṣṭra. Sajjana, the Jaina minister, was appointed as *daṇḍanāyaka* or military governor of Saurāṣṭra and continued to act as such at least till CE 1119. Jayasiṁha also conquered south Gujarat. He is said to have extended his sway up to Cambay. He annexed Bhinnmāl by defeating its Paramāra rulers. His brilliant campaigns against Paramāra potentates Naravarman and Yaśovarman ending in their defeats, capture of Dhāra and annexation of Mālwā have also been related. Jayasiṁha returned to his capital Anhilawāḍa with his triumphant army with the capture of Yaśovarman. He achieved this crowning glory of his life in CE 1135. The victor assumed the title "Avantinātha" in commemoration of the subjugation of Mālwā. Arṇorāja, the Cauhāna ruler, was amongst those who aided the Cāḷukya emperor to subdue Mālwā. The Cāhamāna rulers of both Naḍḍula and Śākambharī submitted to Jayasiṁha and ruled their states as his vassals. In CE 1139, Arṇorāja submitted to Jayasiṁha who gave his daughter Kāñcanadevī to the Cāhamāna. Merutuṅga further states that Jayasiṁha also invaded the Candella kingdom and proceeded as far as Kālañjara and Mahobā. The Candella monarch Madanavarman (of Bundelkhand) was forced to buy peace by returning Bhilsā which he had conquered from the Paramāras. Jayasiṁha was on terms of friendship with Kalacuri sovereign of Tripurī, Yaśaḥkarṇa (CE 1073-1120), and Govindacandra (CE 1114-54), of the Gāhaḍavāla dynasty of Kānyakubja (Kannauj). He also established diplomatic relations with them. Although the Paramāras of Mālwā and Cāhamānas of Naḍḍula recovered their dominions before the close of the reign of Jayasiṁha Siddharāja the Great, he ruled over an extensive kingdom and raised the power and prestige of the Cāḷukya to a height not reached before. We are also told by Merutuṅga that Siddharāja was a great patron of learning. He was also a great devotee of Śiva. He constructed a new temple of Rudramahālaya at Siddhapura. According to Merutuṅga himself, he died on Kārttika sudī 3 of VS 1119 (CE 1142).[42]

Jayasiṁha Siddharāja was succeeded by Kumārapāla. He ascended the throne of Anhilawāḍa, according to Merutuṅga, on Kārttika vadī 3, of VS 1199 (CE 1142).[43] He was the most striking personality among its rulers. He defeated all his political adversaries. Merutuṅga recounts the stories of his wars and conquests. He attacked Arṇorāja (CE 1139-53), the Cāhamāna ruler of Śākambharī, defeated him in a battle, made him wounded and completely routed his forces. He quelled the revolt of the Paramāra prince of Ābu who was dethroned and his nephew (loyal to him) was made the king. The Paramāra ruler of Mālwā was also attacked, and defeated and killed in the battle. His whole dominion up to Bhilsā was again annexed to the Cāḷukya kingdom. And thus Kumārapāla reasserted the Cāḷukya authority in Mālwā. He also put down the revolt of a chieftain of Saurāṣṭra. In or about 1150, he launched his campaign in Mārwāṛ and Sapādalakṣa. He also defeated and killed Mallikārjuna of Koṅkaṇa of the Śilāhāra dynasty in a battle with the help of his army led by Someśvara and his minister Āmrabhaṭa and conquered Koṅkaṇa (between 1160 and 1162). The conquest of Koṅkaṇa was the last exploit of the reign of Kumārapāla. The *prabandhas* look upon his reign as the golden age. We are also informed by Merutuṅga that on the advice of Hemacandra Kumārapāla abjured Śaivism and embraced Jainism. He

42. *Prabandhacintāmaṇi*, pp. 55-64, 74-76; tr. Tawney, p. 115; see also *Jaina-pustaka-praśasti-saṁgraha* (Singhi Jain Granthamālā), 100, no. 14, 103, nos. 36, 38.

43. *Prabandhacintāmaṇi*, p. 78.

constructed many Jaina temples and accepted the 12 vows of Jainism.[44] He died shortly before VS 1229 = CE 1172.

The earliest known date of Kumārapāla's successor, Ajayapāla is CE 1172. He succeeded to the throne after facing a lot of opposition from various quarters. He is said to have come to the throne by a *coup d'etat*. He got rid of the ministers and military leaders who were fighting for power. The streets of Anhilawāḍa witnessed a civil strife. The stories preserved in the works of Merutuṅga speak of him as a "low villain." He succeeded in putting down the revolt of his rival forces with the help of his feudatory Prahlādana, the brother of the Paramāra chief of Ābu. He is represented in the Jaina chronicles as a persecutor of their religion because of opposition of a section of Jainas to his accession. He appointed Someśvara his prime minister. He has been described by Merutuṅga as a powerful ruler. He crushed all his opponents. He defeated the Guhila chief Sāmantasiṁha who had invaded his dominions, and fought successfully against the Cāhamānas of Śākambharī. But he was stabbed to death by a Pratihāra named Vayajaladeva (in CE 1175).[45]

Mūlarāja II, the son of Ajayapāla, ruled for only three years (CE 1176-78). Taking advantage of the crisis faced by him owing to Muslim invasion of Gujarat in 1178, Mālwā successfully asserted her independence.

Mūlarāja II was succeeded by his younger brother Bhīma II in CE 1178. He was one of the powerful Cāḷukya monarchs of Gujarat. He ruled for long 63 years, i.e. up to 1241. Of all the events that took place during his reign (noted before) Merutuṅga records only Subhaṭavarman's (of Mālwā with

44. *Prabandhacintāmaṇi*, pp. 79-80, 86, 95; see also *Ep. Ind.*, IX, p. 72 for his campaign in Sapādalakṣa, and *JRAS*, 1913, p. 274 about role of Someśvara in his conquest of Koṅkaṇa.

45. *Prabandhacintāmaṇi*, pp. 96-97; see also *Ind. Ant.*, XI, p. 11.

throne at Dhāra) invasion of Saurāṣṭra and repulsion of his forces at Prabhāsapāṭan[46] in or about 1199.

After the death of Bhīma II in 1241, the crown of Anhilawāḍa passed to Tribhuvanapāla. He ruled from 1242 to 1244. But his reign and achievements have been passed over in silence by Merutuṅga.

Merutuṅga throws some light on the religious beliefs and practices of the brāhmaṇas during the rule of the Cāḷukyas of Gujarat. He refers to the offering of prayers at the temple of Somanātha by the Cāḷukyas. He says that Siddharāja abolished the tax on the pilgrimage to Somanātha. According to him, the Jainas also prayed at Brāhmanical shrines.[47] The evidence adduced by him testifies to the prevalence of Brāhmanical faith in Gujarat during Cāḷukya's times.

In the fifth and last *prakāśa* of his work Merutuṅga gives an account of the Vāghelās of Gujarat. He has highlighted the role Vīradhavala, the Vāghelā chief of Dholka, played in providing political stability to Gujarat between 1220 and 1238 during the reign of Bhīma II. Vīradhavala's eldest son Virama seized the throne of Anhilawāḍa in 1244 by driving away Tribhuvanapāla, but he was deposed by his younger brother Viśāla also called Viśāladeva who ruled from 1244 to 1262. From his time onwards the Vāghelās became full-fledged rulers of Anhilawāḍa, and gradually established their sway over the whole of Gujarat. Viśāladeva was succeeded by his nephew Arjunadeva who ruled from 1264 to 1274. Merutuṅga has correctly given the last year of his reign as VS 1331 = CE 1274. Merutuṅga's information about the contemporary Vāghelās of whom he had personal knowledge is absolutely worthy of our credence. In one of the wars with the Yādava

46. *Prabandhacintāmaṇi*, p. 97.

47. Ibid., pp. 73, 85; tr. Tawney, p. 84.

king of Devagiri, Rāmacandra (1271-1309), the forces of Arjunadeva was completely overwhelmed. Arjunadeva's Veraval grant of 1264 states that he was reigning victoriously at Anhilawāḍa. His successor Sāraṅgadeva ruled from 1274 to 1296. He defeated Arjunavarman II, the Paramāra king of Mālwā, and successfully defended his kingdom against the Yādava king Rāmacandra. After his death in 1296, his nephew Karṇadeva succeeded to the throne of Anhilawāḍa and ruled up to 1304 — the date which marked the end of the Vāghelā dynasty. Merutuṅga narrates the history up to last Vāghelā ruler Karṇa with some gaps in between. One of the very very important events of Karṇa's reign which Merutuṅga refers to in his work is Ala-ud-din Khilji's invasion of Gujarat. The former was contemporary of the latter (1296-1316). In his *Vicāraśreṇī*, Merutuṅga unequivocally states that the Muslim army (of Ala-ud-din) appeared before Anhilawāḍa during Karṇa's rule.

The concluding *prakāśa* of the *Prabandha-Cintāmaṇi* contains miscellaneous stories including those of Śilāditya of Valabhī (in Gujarat of the Maitraka dynasty that preceded the Cāpotkaṭas), Lakṣmaṇasena of Bengal, Pramardi (Candrātreya) of the Candella dynasty of Jejākabhukti (Bundelkhand), Pṛthvīrāja of the Cāhamāna dynasty of Śākambharī and Jayacandra of the Gāhaḍavāla dynasty of Kānyakubja (Kannauj). Merutuṅga narrates the death of the last two rulers in the wars with the Turks (Shihabuddin or Muhammad Ghori) in 1192 and 1194 respectively.

In his *Vicāraśreṇī*, Merutuṅga has given a dynastic list including Pālaka (of Pradyota dynasty of Avantī), the Nandas, the Mauryas, Puṣyamitra and Balamitra (of Śuṅga dynasty), Nahavahana Gaddabhilla and Śakas with length of reign of individual ruler and of the whole dynasty. He further adds that Vikramāditya (of Ujjayinī) and his dynasty ruled for 135 years. Merutuṅga himself points out that in

Jaina tradition a complete dynastic list in each case is not given and sometimes only a certain important king is mentioned under his name with his reign period. The total duration of the rule of the dynasty is also given. Total reign periods in all cases may not prove to be the exact ones. There may be some discrepancies. But in some cases we find them absolutely correct. For instance, the Śakas (of Ujjayinī) are said to have ruled for 4 years (61-58 BCE). In 57 BCE, they were defeated and expelled from there by the Mālwās under the banner of their leader Vikramāditya.

Critically estimating the historical value of the *Prabandha-Cintāmaṇi*, it may be observed that it contains some anecdotes about Vikramāditya and Sātavāhanas, but they do provide historical information about them in a scrappy manner. Merutuṅga, the author of the work, himself confesses that there were several contradictory accounts in existence as to the persons and events described by him. He is quite conscious of the uncertainty of the foundations on which his building rests. A large number of anachronism, omissions and other errors occur in all the parts of the *prabandhas*. However, the stories narrated therein regarding the kings of Cāḷukya, Vāghelā, Paramāra, Cāhamāna and other dynasties are not at all fanciful. They are rather truthful and historically authenticated. The dates of accession and death and the regnal years of some Cāḷukya, Paramāra and Vāghelā kings are accurate. Merutuṅga's knowledge of history and chronology is commendable. He was, no doubt, endowed with some of the qualities of a history writer. He usually gives a continuous account, particularly of the Cāḷukya dynasty of Anhilawāḍa, in chronological order. The portion dealing with time nearer to him is more authentic than other portions of the work. The information supplied by Merutuṅga is by and large trustworthy.

The *Prabandhakośa* written by Rājaśekhara Sūri II (of Gujarat) in VS 1405 = CE 1348 at Delhi under the patronage of Mahānasiṁha is a collection of 24 stories. This is the reason why it is also called *Caturviṁśati-Prabandha*. Of the 24 *prabandhas* or stories, seven deal with kings of different dynasties. While dealing with some of the Cāḷukya kings of Anhilawāḍa, the author informs us that Mīnaladevī, the queen mother, played an important part in shaping and moulding the character of her son, Jayasiṁha Siddharāja, in the early years of his life. She died a little before her son's conquest of Mālwā in CE 1135.[48] We are further informed by him that his successor Kumārapāla was poisoned by a person loyal to Ajayapāla which led to his death.[49] He died shortly before 1172, the earliest known date of his successor Ajayapāla. We are also told by the author that Lavaṇaprasāda (Vāghelā feudatory ruling at Dhavalakapuri or Dholka during the reign of the Cāḷukya king Bhīma II) also regained mastery over Saurāṣṭra by destroying some powerful enemy on the battlefield of Wadhwan.[50] This event happened shortly after 1221. An account of Someśvara's sojourn in the courts of the Vāghelā chief of Dholka Vīradhavala (1219-38), the son of Lavaṇaprasāda, and the Vāghelā king of Gujarat, Viśāladeva (1244-62), the son of Vīradhavala, is also given.

Rājaśekhara Sūri also described king Lakṣmaṇasena of Bengal and Madanavarman, the Candella king of Jejākabhukti (Bundelkhand). He has narrated the history of 37 Cāhamāna kings down to Hammīradeva who is said to have ruled from Saṁvat 1342 to 1358 and his ancestor Pṛthvīrāja III from Saṁvat 1236 to 1248. The list also mentions names of *sultāns* with whom some of the Cāhamāna kings were at war. The

48. *Prabandhakośa*, 115.
49. Ibid., 199-200.
50. Ibid., 104 ff, 210.

17 other stories narrated by Rājaśekhara are not for any historical purpose.

The *Purātana-Prabandha-Saṁgraha* is a collection of some shorter *prabandha* works. In the *Vikramāṅka-Sattva-Prabandha*, which constitutes a part of it, a good deal of light has been thrown on the life and achievements of King Vikramāditya of Ujjaiyinī in a metaphorical style.[51] Some of the *prabandhas* contain valuable historical information about some of the Cāḷukya kings of Anhilawāḍa. The early life of Jayasiṁha Siddharāja and his invasion of Mālwā, conquest of Dhāra and annexation of Mālwā to his kingdom are described in detail.[52] The achievements of other Cāḷukya kings of Gujarat (already noted before) have also been highlighted.[53]

The preceding chronicles and other historical works as a whole are very useful for reconstruction of the history of the Cāḷukyas and Vāghelās of Gurjaradeśa in early medieval period. There are many missing links in the recorded history of India of their times which can be restored with their help. The fullness of details we have therein about Gujarat is not found in case of any other kingdom except Kashmir.

Some other works bearing the character of a chronicle composed in early eighteenth century in Gujarat are also worthy of our notice. They throw some light on the political history of Gujarat of the period.

The *Rustamno Shaloko* or *Abrāhamkulikhanno Shaloko* written by Shamal Bhaṭ in 1725 gives a contemporary account of battles that were fought in 1723-24 at Ahmedabad, Kapadvanj and finally Adas near the Mahi River between the Mughal *sūbedār* Hamid Khan and the Nawāb of Surat Rustamkuli

51. *Purātanaprabandha-Saṁgraha*, ed. Jinavijaya Muni, pp. 1 ff.
52. Ibid., pp. 31-32, 35.
53. Ibid., pp. 36 ff.

Khan and his brothers Sujal Khan and Abrahamkuli Khan. At the end of his work, the author (poet) gives some more historical information about the political condition of Gujarat during the period.

There is another work, *Bhanno Shaloko*, composed in 1707 by Gaṅgādās Bhavānī of Khakarasar near Cambay which recounts the battle between Nawāb Alikhan of Cambay and the people of Padra village on the refusal to pay taxes and the defeat of the Nawāb.

The unpublished work *Gunbiradsingar Prabandha* by Karnidanji Gadhavi gives the history of Gujarat after the death of Aurangzeb in 1707. It is believed that the author was inspired by Abhaya Siṁha, who was the Mughal *sūbedār* of Gujarat from 1731 to 1733, to compose his work. The author opines that Abhaya Siṁha defeated Sarbuland Khan thrice.

Appendix

Ala-ud-din Khilji's Conquest of Gujarat as described in its Historical Literature

On the combined testimony of the *Vicāraśreṇī* (1304) of Merutuṅga,[1] the *Kanhadade-Prabandha* (1456) of Padmanābha[2] and the *Dharmāraṇya* (composed between 1300 and 1450),[3] it can irrefutably be proved that a Nāgara brāhmaṇa, Mādhava, who was a *mahāmātya* (minister) of the ruling Vāghelā king of Gujarat, Karṇa or Karṇadeva (1296-1304) invited Ala-ud-din (the Sultān of Delhi) to Gujarat for its conquest. As recorded in the *Dharmāraṇya*, Mādhava, wicked, traitor and hostile to King Karṇa, destroyed the rule of the kṣatriyas and established the rule of the *mlecchas* (Muslims) in Gujarat.[4]

We are told by Padmanābha that Kanhadade (Kanera Deva), a Cāhamāna chief of Jālor, refused Ala-ud-din Khilji to permit his troops to pass through Mārwāṛ when the latter was to attack Gujarat. Then Samarasiṁha of Chittor let the

---

1. *Vicāraśreṇī*, cf. *JBBRAS*, IX.
2. *Kanhadāde-Prabandha*, ed. K.B. Vyas, I, 13-15. This work was written by Padmanābha — a Nāgara brāhmaṇa from Visnagara — in 1456 at the court of his patron Akherāja (a descendant of Kanhadāde) of Jālore near Mārwāṛ. It is in old Gujarati or old western Rajasthani. Due to their close affinity, it has been claimed equally by Gujaratis and Rajasthanis.
3. *Dharmāraṇya*, LXVII, 68-69.
4. Ibid.; see also K.M. Munshi, *Gujarat and Its Literature*, p. 103.

army pass through his territory. He could not stop their march towards Gujarat. Pillaging, burning, and devastating, the Muslim army marched towards Anhilawāḍa.[5] The Musalmans, with Mādhava at their head, invaded the capital city. Mādhava advised King Karṇa to escape for his safety. Karṇa, having left Anhilawāḍa, evidently, gathered some of his forces at Āśāpallī (near modern Ahmedabad) but suffered defeat at the hands of Ulugh Khan. Gujarat passed immediately afterwards into the hands of Ulugh Khan.

That, in Vikrama Saṁvat 1356 = CE 1299 Sultān Ala-ud-din sent an army under Ulugh Khan from Delhi to conquer Gujarat (in the reign of Karṇa), can conclusively be proved by Jinaprabha Sūri's evidence funished in his *Vividhatīrthakalpa* (composed in 1332), which is as follows:

"अह तेरहस्य छप्पणविक्कमवरिसे अल्लावदीणसुरताण्णस, कणिट्ठो भाया उलुखानामाधिज्जो दिल्लीपुराओ गुज्जरधरं पट्ठिओ" ।[6] This can be corroborated by the statements of Muslim chroniclers of Sultanate period, Amir Khusrau (1253-1325)[7] and Barani (1286-1359),[8] both contemporaries of Ala-ud-din, Isami (1311-50),[9] and one of the noted modern historians of Medieval India, A.L. Srivastava.[10]

It is an established fact that in 1299 Ala-ud-din despatched an army under two generals, Ulugh Khan and Nasrat Khan, from Delhi for the conquest of Gujarat. The army besieged, sacked and plundered the capital city Anhilawāḍa and

5. *Kanhadāde-prabandha*, Khaṇḍa I.
6. *Vividhatīrthakalpa*, ed. Jinavijaya, 30.
7. *Khazain-ul-Futuh* (*The Treasure of Victories*), tr. M. Habib, p. 38.
8. *Tārīkh-i-Firozshāhī*, p. 251; tr. in Elliot and Dowson, op. cit., III, p. 164.
9. *Futuh-us-Salatin* (*Shahnama-i-Hind*), ed. Mahdi Hussain, pp. 242-44, 277.
10. *The Sultanate of Delhi*, p. 166.

captured it. Kamalā Devī, the wife of the Vāghelā ruler Karṇa, fell into the hands of the invaders. She was taken away to Delhi and married to Ala-ud-din. But Rājā Karṇa fled from his capital with his daughter, Devala Devī, to Devagiri and found an asylum in the court of its Yādava king Rāmacandra.

We learn from the literature of Gujarat that after having occupied Anhilawāḍa Ala-ud-din's army carried its carnage right up to Surat, Rander, Cambay and other places. Next, the army turned towards Saurāṣṭra, destroyed many of its towns and further proceeded to Prabhāsa. The Rājpūts mobilised their strength to protect the shrine of Somanātha, and fought the enemy valiantly. But the fortress fell and in front of the temple which they had vainly tried to protect, the heroic warriors fell fighting. The temple of Somanātha, which had already been previously destroyed by Mahmud, fell into the hands of the Turuṣkas (on 6 June 1299). Mādhava, instrumental in the invasion of Gujarat by Ala-ud-din, was also killed.[11] It is recorded in Indian history that every betrayer met the same fate. In his *Khazain-ul-Futuh*, Amir Khusrau has also stated that in 1299 Ulugh Khan was sent to destroy Somanātha and conquer Gujarat.

The whole of Gujarat was occupied in 1299 itself. Merutuṅga, who was a contemporary of Ala-ud-din, asserts in his *Vicāraśreṇī* that Karṇa's reign came to an end in 1304, after which the Muslims occupied Gurjaradeśa. But we do not find any evidence to support it.

The flourishing Gujarat kingdom with its capital at Anhilawāḍa, though invaded more than once, had never been subdued earlier by any Turkish invader. Ultimately, Ala-

11. *Kanhadāde-prabandha*, Khaṇḍa I; K.M. Munshi, *Gujarat and Its Literature*, pp. 103-04; For further details see his *Glory that was Gurjaradeśa* (CE *550-1300*), II, pp. 401-09.

ud-din Khilji conquered it. And thus the curtain fell on Hindu rule in Gujarat.

Maharashtra

The tradition of historical writing in Maharashtra began as early as the thirteenth century and further continued. The period extending from the thirteenth to the eighteenth centuries saw the composition of several historical and semi-historical works in Sanskrit and Marathi.

Of the Sanskrit historical works, mention may first be made of those which were composed and preserved during the rule of the Yādavas of Devagiri or Deogiri (modern Daulatābād). During the reign of Kṛṣṇa or Kanhara (1247-60), the *Sūktimuktāvalī* (a chronicle of Deccan) was composed in 1257 by Jalhana. It gives an account of the Yādava kings of Devagiri. The Yādavas were a feudatory family when the Rāṣṭrakūṭas of Mānyakheta and the western Cāḷukyas of Kalyāṇī held sway in the Deccan. After the decline of the latter, the Yādavas rose into prominence and in course of time established an extensive empire. The Yādava dynasty, in fact, supplanted the Cāḷukyas in Maharashtra towards the end of the twelfth century. The author of the said work refers to Bhillama V (1185-93) who was the first noteworthy figure in the dynasty. He took advantage of the moribund condition of the western Cāḷukya monarchy as a result of the Kalacuri usurpation and the aggressions of the Hoysaḷas, wrested in 1187 the territories to the north of the Kṛṣṇā from the feeble hands of Someśvara IV, acquired paramount sovereignty in the Deccan, fixed his capital at Devagiri and also assumed the imperial titles. The author informs us that Siṅghana was the most energetic personality, and during his long rule (1210-47) he conquered many lands. He is said to have routed Vīrabhoja (about 1215) and annexed the Śilāhāra realm of Kolhāpur after the fall of the fortress of

Parnāla or Panhola. He attacked Gujarat at least twice in the time of the Vāghelā princes. As a result of the military achievements of Siṅghana, the Yādava kingdom reached the height almost equal to that of the western Cāḷukyas. Kṛṣṇa, one of the later Yādava kings, is stated to have come into conflict with the rulers of Mālwā, Gujarat and Koṅkaṇa. He has been described as a devout follower of the brāhmanical religion.[12]

Hemādri or Hemādpant, who served under Mahādeva, one of the Yādava kings of Devagiri (1260-71), as a minister and an archivist and further flourished in the time of his successor Rāmacandra (1271-1309), wrote his *Caturavarga-cintāmaṇi*, divided into four parts and an appendix. The historical information contained in the work is, of course, meagre but valuable. The author gives the genealogy of the Yādava dynasty tracing it from Yadu with some sources on the later Gaṅgas of Kaliṅga. He gives a list of Yādava rulers who were evidently vassals of the Rāṣṭrakūṭas and Cāḷukyas, and then mentions the names of independent Yādava kings beginning from Bhillama V, the builder of Devagiri. He records Mahādeva's wars with Mālwā and the Kākatīyas of Warangal in his own time. After the Yādavas submitted to the Turks in the early fourteenth century (1307), the various local rulers in Maharashtra for the most part likewise became vassals of the Turkish rulers, but some of them tried to assert their independence.[13]

In the north-west of Maharashtra, a line of Rājpūts claiming their descent from the Rāṣṭrakūtas of Kānyakubja (of the eleventh century) maintained their autonomy in the state of Mayūragiri. The *Rāṣṭraudhavaṁśa* (an epic poem of 20

12. *Sūktimuktāvalī*, vv. 5-9, 11-13; see also R.G. Bhandarkar, *Early History of the Dekkan Down to the Mahomedan Conquest*, pp. 105-07; M. Krishnamachariar, *HCSL*, pp. 385-86.

13. A.K. Warder, *An Introduction to Indian Historiography*, p. 139.

cantos in Sanskrit) composed by the poet Rudra in 1596 deals with the history of these Rājpūts. The poet traces their origin to the King Rāṣṭraudha of Kānyakubja of a Solar dynasty. He describes the history of the Bagulas of Mayūragiri from Rāṣṭraudha, the founder of the dynasty, to Nārāyaṇa Śāha, his patron. In fact, he was patronised by King Nārāyaṇa Śāha and his son Pratāp Śāha of Mayūragiri. From what the poet relates it emerges that a younger brother of a king of Kānyakubja, contemporaneous with Jayasiṁha Siddharāja, the Cāḷukya monarch of Gujarat (1093-1143), sought his fortune in the Yādava Kingdom and married the daughter of King Rāmacandra. The great grandson of this adventurer, Nānadeva, conquered Mayūragiri from a local ruler and established himself there in the fourteenth century. He fought the Turks (called Turuṣkas and *mlecchas*) whose vast armies from Delhi overran many kingdoms and conquered and killed the Yādava king Rāmacandra. After a year's fighting Nānadeva was killed, but his son Ekadeva continued the war and defeated the Turks. Their successors carried out somewhat-like guerilla operations against the Turks, according to the poet. In Rudra's time, King Nārāyaṇa was defending his fortress against all enemies and taking part in successful wars of conquest. In the last 20th canto of the epic, the poet Rudra describes how Nārāyaṇa's son Pratāp distinguished himself alongside the son of the Mughal emperor Akbar in a war launched by the latter to extend his sway over Maharashtra putting down the local Turkish rulers who had been independent of Delhi since the fourteenth century. This gives us a glimpse of Akbar's policy of consolidating and extending his empire by conciliating the Indian princes respecting their religion and gaining their support. Rudra, however, eulogistically refers to his patron Nārāyaṇa as an emperor and to Akbar simply as "Lord of

Delhi." He concludes with the description of how Pratāp acquired his fortune.[14]

Historiography took a significant turn under the Marāṭhā Bhoṅsalā family. The Sanskrit historical works produced by the Marāṭhā writers in the seventeenth century and later here deserve our notice. The works deal mainly with the history of the Bhoṅsalā family. The principal Marāṭhā general who fought under the Turkish *sultāns* in the south and gradually strengthened his position was Śāhajī Bhoṅsalā (1594-1664), according to Jayarāma, who visited him when he had established himself in Karnataka as an independent, and wrote a Sanskrit *campū*, *Rādhāmādhavavilāsa*, which contains some references to contemporary history. Śāhajī (founder of the Bhoṅsalā dynasty) is said to have descended from the Sisodiyā branch of the Guhilaputra Rājpūts of Medapāṭa. This makes the Bhoṅsalā family a branch of the ancient Solar dynasty and asserts their claim to be legitimate rulers of India. The same *campū* mentions Śāhajī's victory over the army of the Sultān of Golacoṇḍā (on the outskirts of the city of Hyderabad) in 1651-52. Further account of Śāhajī's operations which appears to be fairly authentic (though contested) is included in an unfinished epic, *Sūryavaṁśa*, by Paramānanda, a poet and historian. It is indeed a unique work. It is also called *Śiva Bhārata* as it deals with the contemporary political life of Śivājī. It may undoubtedly be considered a faithful historical record. The *Sūryavaṁśa* describes itself as a work in 100 cantos but as far as it is now known not more than 60. Paramānanda describes Śāhajī's early victorious battles supporting one *sultān* against another such as one against the combined forces of the Sultān of Bījāpur and the Mughal emperor in 1624. Then he describes how Śāhajī fought for the Sultān of Bījāpur against a local

14. A.K. Warder, *An Introduction to Indian Historiography*, pp. 139-40.

Vijayanagara Nāyaka (in 1640). It is said with some exaggeration that Śāhajī conquered the whole of Karnataka and Tamiladeśa. In 1648, at the siege of Jinji the Sultān of Bījāpur suspecting that he (Śāhajī) was becoming leader of Indian opposition to the Turks got him arrested by another Marāṭhā general, as Paramānanda faithfully records, but afterwards released him in exchange for some territories. The Bhoṅsalās were recognised as ruling various territories in the south as well as ancestral lands in Maharashtra and seem to have become subordinate allies rather than mere vassals of the Sultān of Bījāpur. The Sultān did not expect them to maintain their loyalty to him and thus tried to keep them in check but could not suppress them because they were too strong. According to Paramānanda, Śivājī was the son of Śāhajī Bhoṅsalā by his first wife Jījāmbā (Jījābāī). Śāhajī's second wife Tukāmbā (Tukābāī) bore a son named Eka. Paramānanda has high praise for Śivājī's military skill during his father's time building up the strength of Maharashtra. Śivājī's activities in the beginning were mostly confined to Maharashtra itself, whilst Śāhajī continued his operation in the south. The narrative here (the first part of the epic) goes as far as 1661 when Śivājī repelled a Mughal attack on Kalyāṇa trapping the invaders in the Sāhyā mountains. Śivājī succeded his father Śāhajī as king in 1664, but Eka at the same time became effectively independent in the south. Paramānanda has devoted altogether thirty-one cantos of his work (*Śiva Bhārata*) to the description of Śivājī as a great Marāṭhā leader, great military genius, and founder of the Marāṭhā empire which dominated India for a century and a half. He describes his exploits in detail. After achieving great success against his enemies and strengthening his position as the Marāṭhā leader and great warrior he got himself consecrated as a king in 1674 at Rāyagiri (Rāigaṛh), celebrated his coronation with great pomp and rejoicing and assumed the imperial title of Chatrapati. It was on that occasion that he asked Paramānanda to compose the epic on his family. The first part as we now have it appears to be what he had completed before Śivājī's death in 1680. After that he had cause to continue it, but could not complete it due to his own death about 1687. In the cantos written after King Śivājī's death, Paramānanda dwells upon the events connected with the succession. He takes up the story from the year 1676 with important events between 1661 and 1676. He tells us that on Śivājī's death his second son Rājārāma, then 10 years old, was crowned at Rāigaṛh by his mother Soyarāmbā (Soyrā Bāī) in April 1680. She had persuaded Śivājī to make her son his successor and send Śambhājī away. But Śambhājī (Śivājī's eldest son by his first wife), who was arrested at the behest of his father in 1676 (being addicted to sensual pleasure) and kept under surveillance at Śṛṅgārapura, and later (in 1678) confined in the fort of Panhala put its commandant to death, obtained possession of the fort, won over the commander-in-chief, and proceeded to Rāigaṛh, captured it and threw Rājārāma and Soyrā Bāī (his stepmother) into prison. He ascended the throne on 30 July 1680 and appointed Nilo Pant (son of Moro Pant Piṅgle) as Peśawā (the prime minister). But his formal ceremony of coronation took place on 20 January 1681. He was consecrated by his ministers. He became the new patron of our historian Paramānanda. The whole work has been presented in the ancient Purāṇic tradition. In his narrative of events, Paramānanda (the author of the work) justifies the actions of his patron in disobeying his command of his father after he was sent to Śṛṅgārapura (southern Maharashtra). He further informs us that King Śivā (Śivājī) made a great expedition into Karnataka (in 1677-78) to extend his domain there. He describes how in due course Śambhājī became emperor after his father. We are further told by him that the Lord of Delhi, Aurangzeb, knowing that Śivājī was separated from his son and seeing in this a weakness which he might exploit to overthrow his enemies, ordered his general (or a military officer) Dalela (Diler Khan) to enter into a correspondence with Śambhā in order to win him over. Śambhā first waits for his father to return from the south, since he was entrusted with the government at Śṛṅgārapura. The author always insists on Śambhā's scrupulous sense of duty. King Śivājī was willing to divide his realms between his sons, but the minister warned him against Śambhā's relations with the Mughals. Consequently, he sent Śambhā away again to Sajjanagiri. Dalella did his best to win Śambhā over completely assisting him to collect troops ready to take part in campaign with him. Śambhā, however, refused to become the enemy of his deluded father. At the same time, he joined Aurangzeb's general and both of them jointly attacked and captured Bhūpāldurga (or Bhūpālgaṛh), an outlying Marāṭhā stronghold (in 1679), as told by the author. Before Paramānanda completes his description of the capture of Bhūpāladurga, his continuous narrative comes to an end. It is noteworthy that some of the events described by him are contemporaneous with those described in the Marathi *bakhar*s. The impression we get from Paramānanda's historical work is that it is generally faithful as to the events described but not credible as to the interpretations favourable to his patron Śambhā. Twelve more cantos so far recovered from the *Sūryavaṁśa* appear to be later part of the work following Śambhā's consecration. The extant fragments also refer briefly to the unsuccessful rebellion of Aurangzeb's son, prince Muhammad Akbar, against the fanatical policies of his father and his dealings with King Śambhā as an ally in the struggle (1682-87). Aurangzeb gradually strengthened his position by conquering Bījāpur (1686) and Golcoṇḍā (1687). He was then ready to attempt the conquest of Maharashtra, says the author.[15]

15. A.K. Warder, op.cit., pp. 140-44; Krishnamachariar, op. cit., pp. 240-41.

S.R. Sharma has aptly remarked that Paramānanda's *Śiva Bhārata* is of "great historical use in spite of its form."[16]

The historical authenticity of Paramānanda's statement regarding Śivājī's parentage, coronation and invasion of Karnataka, Śambhājī's desertion and joining Mughal camp at the persuasion of Aurangzeb's general, and events connected with succession after Śivājī's death can be proved by what A.L. Srivastava, one of the noted historians of medieval India, has recorded in his work.[17]

Another work composed in Sanskrit and bearing on an important theme in Marāṭhā history is Jayarāma's *Parnālaparvatagrahanākhyāna*. This epic's narrative celebrates the capture of the fortness of Parnāla (Panhāla, near Kolhapur) by Śivājī in 1660 after defeating Bījāpurī army. This major event seems to have escaped the attention of Paramānanda as we do not find it recorded in his work. However, the veracity of Jayarāma's statement cannot be questioned. The event he describes was a real one.[18]

Aniruddha composed a *Śivarājarājyābhiṣeka Kalpataru* on Śivājī's consecration or coronation (1674).

In order to form an alliance with the Marāṭhā king Śambhājī (also called Śambhūjī) to seek his co-operation for deposing his father Aurangzeb, prince Akbar undertook a journey to Maharashtra in 1681 and reached Pālī near Negothna, 25 miles north of Rāigaṛh. But no alliance was entered into between the two. In hot pursuit of his son, Aurangzeb arrived at Aurangabad in 1682. He sowed dissensions among the followers of Śambhājī and Akbar and won many of them over to his side. Akbar could not execute his design. In the massive invasion of Maharashtra which

16. *The Making of Modern India*, p. 308.
17. *The Mughal Empire* (*1526-1803*), pp. 390, 410, 414, 418 and 430.
18. See ibid., p. 396.

Aurangzeb launched in 1687, the Marāṭhās were forced to resort to guerilla warfare in the hope of exhausting the enemy. In 1689, Śambhājī was captured and taken prisoner to Aurangzeb's camp at Bahadurgarh. The former was asked by the latter to surrender all his forts and disclose the names of the Mughal officers who were in league with him but he refused to do so. Consequently, he was tortured to death. This tragedy occurred at Koregaon, 12 miles north-east of Poona, on 21 March 1689.[19] After the death of Śambhājī, Rājārāma, the younger son of Śivājī, was proclaimed king on 19 February 1689, and continued the war against the Mughals. Evading the Mughals he set out for the south in order to carry on the fight from Jinji. His expedition to Jinji and his struggle for Marāṭhā independence in Karnataka is well depicted in Keśava's *Rājārāmacarita*. The rulers of Karnataka rallied to support Rājārāma and crush the Mughals. Rājārāma died on 12 March 1700.

In continuation of the historiographical tradition in Maharashtra, early in the eighteenth century some more Sanskrit historical works were produced. The tradition further continued later in the same century.

In the far south, an independent Marāṭhā Kingdom flourished under Eka and his successors. In 1675, Eka captured Tañjanagara (Tanjore) from the Nāyakas (local rulers serving under the rule of Vijayanagara emperors) and declared himself king. After consolidating his new realm he abdicated in favour of his son Śāha. Early in the eighteenth century, Veṅkaṭeśvara wrote a *Bhoṅsalā*Vaṁśāvalī on these Marāṭhā kings of Tanjanagara. Ayyāvāḷ's epic *Śāhendravilāsa* likewise deals with these kings as a continuation of the Solar

19. For details see ibid., pp. 430-33; S.R. Sharma, *Mughal Empire in India*, pp. 312-14; *The Crescent in India: A Study in Mediaeval History*, pp. 496-97; Khafi Khan, cf. Elliot and Dowson, *History of India as Told by Its Own Historians*, VII, pp. 309 ff.

dynasty history with high praise of King Śivā for defeating the Mughals and describes how Eka returned after consecrating Śāha in 1684. He also focuses on how Śāha supported Rājārāma when the latter came to Jinji. The *campū Dharmavijaya*, by Nala (Bhuminātha), is also on the list of Śāha. Śāha had an official historiographer (*paurāṇika*) named Dhundhirāja who wrote a commentary on the *Rāmāyaṇa* with a long historical introduction regarding the life of the king. In both history and literature, Śāha appears to have been an enlightened and popular monarch. He was succeeded in 1712 by his brother Sarabha (Sarabhojī), the hero of Jagannātha's *Sarabharājavilāsa* and of Ananta Nārāyaṇa's *Sarabhojīcarita*. Sarabhojī occupies an important place among the Marāṭhā rulers of Tanjavur (Tanjore). Another *Bhoṅsalāvaṁśāvalī* by Gaṅgādhara is also important from a historical point of view. It gives a dynastic account of the Bhoṅsalā family.[20]

The tradition of composing chronicle called *bakhar* commenced in the thirteenth century, developed in the late seventeenth (sixteen years after the death of Śivājī) and further flourished during the succeeding two centuries.

The chronicles or *bakhar*s form part of Marathi historical literature. Some of them give historical accounts of important personalities in the annals of Maharashtra, especially the makers of Marāṭhā history, important places and the chief events. The word *bakhar* is believed to be a derivative from the Arabic *khabar*. The Muslim *durbar*s used to have writers to keep a record of daily events of the court. Getting inspired from this practice, the Marāṭhās coined the word *bakhar* which is a chronicle of events. However, in Maharashtra the *bakhar*s or chronicles were composed not merely to record the events but also to describe the lives and deeds of historical

20. Warder, op. cit., pp. 144-46.

personages. Usually written at the command of a king, Peśawā or Sardar they began with a salutation to the one who had ordered the *bakhar* to be written. Some of the *bakhar*s of persons, places and events were written without any command in pre- and post-Śivājī times.

We are here concerned with only those *bakhar*s which are chronicles in nature, fall within the purview of this work and possess historical value.

One of the oldest *bakhar*s is the *Śālivāhana Bakhar* narrating the history of Sātavāhanas (called Śālivāhanas) who ruled at Paiṭhan (modern Pratiṣṭhāna on the Godāvarī in Aurangabad district) in the first three centuries of the Christian Era. We do not know either the author or the date of composition of this *bakhar*. All we know is that it went through several hands and was revised. It is still available in manuscript copies. It was printed by Raghunath Shastri Datye at his own expense in 1840. It comprises 25 printed pages and is of little use to the historians of ancient India.

The *bakhar* of Siṅghana, the Yādava ruler of Devagiri (1210-47), has passed into oblivion.

The *Mahim Bakhar* covering a long period of the history of Mahim from 1138 to 1500 was written by the beginning of the seventeenth century. The importance of the *bakhar* lies in the fact that it records the history of "Maharashtra Dharma" which became a catchword of the Marāṭhās in the subsequent centuries. It is of limited value from the historical point of view.

It is significant to note that the chroniclers have immortalised certain historical events by producing their works soon after or not long after the event when the memory thereof was quite fresh. The *Rakṣastangadi Bakhar,* for instance, narrating the story of the battle of Talikoṭa (1565), which sealed the fate of the Vijayanagara empire for ever, was written in 1614. It is an established fact that the combined armies of Bījāpur, Ahmadnagar, Golcoṇḍā and Bīdar invaded Vijayanagara and inflicted upon her a defeat on the field of Talikota on 23 January 1565. Rāmarāya, the prime minister of Sadāśiva (Vijayanagara ruler), fought well but he was captured and put to death. The *Saśtici Bakhar* originally written in 1742 to which additions were made in 1782 mainly deals with the Vasai Campaign in which the Marāṭhās had registered a remarkable victory in 1739 against the Portuguese by capturing the fort of Vasai.[21]

Of the nine important *bakhar*s or chronicles on Śivājī, the earliest and the most authentic one is *Śivā Chatrapaticen Carita*, by Kṛṣṇājī Anant Sabhāsad,[22] a near contemporary of Śivājī. This work was written at the instance of Rājārāma (the younger son of Śivājī) during his stay at Jinji. Sabhāsad started his work in 1696 (sixteen years after Śivājī's death) and completed it in 1697 at Jinji itself. He was an important member of Rājārāma's court at Jinji. He must have personally witnessed the events of Śivājī's later life. Moreover, his chronicle has come to us practically intact. It has been rightly said that Sabhāsad's *bakhar* is the only one which can claim to be contemporary.[23] Sabhāsad composed his work in the form of a chronicle to satisfy the curiosity of his master Rājārāma. The latter commanded the former to write about his father Śivājī saying:

> Our father, the Great King, performed so many feats of bravery and subdued four different "Pādaśāhīs." In spite of his performing such prodigies of valour, Aurangzeb came and

21. See J.P. De Souza and C.M. Kulkarni (ed.), *Historiography in Indian Languages*, p. 9.
22. Ed. by V.S. Vakaskar, 4th edn. (Pune, 1973); Eng. tr. S.N. Sen, *Śiva Chatrapati* (Calcutta, 1920).
23. S.N. Sen, *Extracts and Documents relating to Marāṭhā History*, I, pp. 251, 272.

> captured many of the forts. What was the cause of this? You are a man well-informed of the affairs of the old kingdom. Write, therefore, a biography from the beginning.[24]

Sabhāsad's *bakhar* is, no doubt, a contemporary work.

> This is a piece of primary historiography by an eyewitness though the writer was handicapped by the conditions of the siege of Jinji during which he wrote having no access to archives.

The work is mainly based on personal knowledge and hearsay evidence. Sir Jadunath Sarkar says, even Sabhāsad's contemporary account is not based on state papers and written notes. According to him, Sabhāsad's work is "entirely derived from his memory."[25]

Sabhāsad gives pedigree of Śivājī starting with his great-grandfather. He describes Śivājī's deeds, exploits and some of the important events that took place during his lifetime. He describes how did Śivājī conquer Javli (at extreme north-western corner of the Satara district) which was in the possession of Chandra Rao More, a Marāṭhā nobleman. We are told by him that Chandra Rao had formed an anti-Śivājī coalition with the Bījāpurī governor of that region and blocked the expansion of Śivājī's domain in the south and south-west. So Śivājī formed a plot to get rid of him and capture Javli. He secured the murder of Chandra Rao by a hired assassin, attacked Javli immediately after the murder (25 January 1656) and captured the fort. The whole of Javli thus passed into Śivājī's possession. No adverse comment is made by the author on the murder of Chandra Rao and conquest of Javli. We are also informed by the author that in 1659 the Sultān of Bījāpur sent his general, Afzal Khan, to capture Śivājī dead or alive. In an encounter near the fort of

24. Sabhāsad's *Bakhar*, ed. K.N. Sane, 3rd edn. (Kalyan, 1912).

25. *Shivaji and His Times*, pp. 408, 431.

Pratāpgaṛh, Śivājī slew Afzal Khan with his steel claws and his army was attacked and routed. This, according to the author, was the most significant event in the early career of this hero. Giving a brief account of Śivājī's war with the Mughals, he tells us that in 1665 Aurangzeb sent Rājā Jayasiṁha of Ambāvatī (Amber), the most capable general in his service, against Śivājī. Jayasiṁha won a few victories, besieged Śivājī in Purandhur and persuaded him to make his submission to Aurangzeb and present himself at the imperial court at Agra. Śivājī also ceded some of his forts to the Mughals. It is a well-known fact that after reaching Agra in 1666 Śivājī found himself a prisoner. But he somehow managed to escape from there. He succeeded in reaching Rāigaṛh. The author gives a list of persons who accompanied Śivājī when he went to meet Aurangzeb. The information provided by the author that Jayasiṁha came out to great Śivājī is not authentic. Actually, he did not come out to receive Śivājī, but sent his secretaries, Udaisiṁha and Ugrasen Kachwa, to meet him. The author's statement, that the relationship between Jayasiṁha and the Mughal general Dilel (Diler) Khan was not harmonious, is also not true. In fact, they supported each other and moved hand in hand. One of the important achievements of Śivājī, as told by the author, was his victory over the Mughals in the battle of Sāleri (Salher) in 1672. Salher was reoccupied by the Marāṭhās. This was probably decisive in paving the way for Śivā's consecration two years later. This was also the culminating point of Śivā's war of independence which virtually began in 1670 after he rapidly recaptured a series of fortresses which he had previously surrendered to the Mughals. Sabhāsad also describes Śivā's expedition into southern India (in 1677). He is said to have conquered Jinji, Vellore and many other towns in Karnataka (1677-78). Sabhāsad has described the events without maintaining their chronological sequence.

He regards Śambhājī (the eldest son of Śivājī) as a renegade on account of his dealings with the Mughals which, no doubt, was Rājārāma's view. This view was upheld by almost all later Marāṭhā historians. Sabhāsad records the speech made by Śivājī to kindle the spark of patriotism in the hearts of his countrymen and to arouse them to fight the Mughals:

> Why should we be contented with presents from barbarian rulers and with our father's legacies? We are Indians. This country belongs to us, yet the barbarians hold it, desecrate our temples, plunder us, convert us by force, etc. We will suffer this no longer, but rely on our arms to defend our religion and our country. If we make an effort God will help us to win our freedom.

Sabhāsad describes the religious ceremonies of the times. His description of Śivājī's administration in general and his military organisation, including a fleet of warships, constitutes the quintessence of his work. He informs us that on Śambhājī's return from the Mughal camp (in 1679) Śivājī with his son surveyed the resources of his kingdom. Then he gives us the precise number of gold coins of every variety in the royal treasury. Towards the end of his *bakhar*, he relates that Śivājī and Śambhājī made a reckoning of the extent of their territory. An inventory is given of the 18 departments of government, the 12 *mahals*, the treasury, list of military and provincial officers, the names of 60 cavalry and 30 infantry officers, the names of 49 existing and 108 new forts constructed by Śivājī and of 70 forts in the south.[26] Victories and defeats of Śivājī are plainly and briefly told. The author is free from bias and prejudice in his presentation of the account of the subject. Sabhāsad's *bakhar*, in spite of its defects, is useful to the historians. R.V. Hervadkar is of the opinion

26. Sabhāsad's *Bakhar*; S.N. Sen, op. cit., pp. 6 ff, 29-33, 49-58, 89-95, 113-18, 132-48; Warder, op. cit., pp. 147 ff.

that it cannot be wholly relied on as history.[27] But Jadunath Sarkar after a thorough scrutiny regarded this *bakhar* as the most valuable Marathi account of Śivājī.[28] Later *bakharkāras* (*bakhar* writers) have largely used this *bakhar* as a source.

The next important *bakhar* or chronicle of Śivājī known as *Ninety-one Qalmi Bakhar* was originally composed by his *mantrī* or counsellor Dattājī Trimal Waqnavis (or Waqianavis) not long after 1680. This composite work in 91 sections (*qalms*) is believed to have been compiled between 1685 and 1760. It has survived only in few fragments. However, it contains authentic information regarding Śivājī's life and his administrative system, military operations and building of fortresses.

Dattājī merely jotted down certain notes clause-wise for a later compilation. These notes were copied by Anaji Ranganath Malekar, another civilian officer who served under Śivājī. The number of *qalm*s available in six different versions vary from 73 to 96. Dattājī was a member of the Council of Eight Ministers entrusted with the duty of compiling a daily record of the king's deeds, court incidents, etc.

In his chronicle, Dattājī records that Śivājī met Aurangzeb at Delhi and not Agra. Śivājī's coronation, the most important event in his life, is described just in three lines in clause 87. The chronicler (Waqianavis) has not provided the details of Śivājī's exploits after his coronation in 1674. However, his southern compaign has been covered in 10 clauses. And clause 89 records Śivājī's death.[29]

The chronicler had the best opportunity to use state

27. *Marathi Bakharas*, p. 50.

28. Jadunath Sarkar, op. cit., p. 392.

29. *Ninety-one Qalmi Bakhar*, ed. by V.S. Vakaskar (Pune, 1962); see also N.H. Kulkarnee, "Historical Biography in Marathi Literature (From Earliest Times to the Nineteenth Century)", in *Historical Biography in Indian Literature*, ed. S.P. Sen, pp. 232-33.

papers of Śivājī. In his famous work, *Shivaji and His Times*, Jadunath Sarkar describes *91-Qalmi Bakhar* as one of the most valuable *bakhar*s because its original author was Śivājī's own recorder of daily events, etc. According to him, this *bakhar* is "an authority of the highest value on Śivājī's history." *Tārīkh-i-Śivājī* is considered by him to be a Persian version of this *bakhar*.

The other important *bakhar* on Śivājī is the *Śiva Caritra* composed by Raghunath Yadav Citre *alias* Citragupta between 1760 and 1770. This *bakhar* is entirely based on that of Sabhāsad with some additions and elaboration. It is believed to have been written at the behest of "Śambhājī of Kolhapur." The author adopted a new style of chronicling the event to impress his patron Yashwantrao Shinde. Śivājī is a divinity to the author. He depicts Śivājī as a family man unlike any other *bakharkāra*.

Śivadigvijaya is one of the most valuable *bakhar*s on Śivājī. It has been ascribed to Khando Ballal, the son of Śivājī's secretary Ballaji Avaji. And it is said to have been written in 1712. But the author and date are disputed. In fact, it is based on old *bakhar*s and was finally compiled in 1818.

The author of *Śivadigvijaya* writes about Śivājī's conquest and his coronation. But the chronology is badly mixed up. Unlike Sabhāsad, he gives no details of the administration or military organisation of Śivājī.[30]

In his introduction to his fourth volume of *Sources of Marāṭhā History* (*Marathy anchya Itihasachi Sadhane*), V.K. Rajwade, the noted Marāṭhā historian, has rightly pointed out that by no stretch of imagination the *bakhar*s on Śivājī can be regarded as his historical biographies. They are chronicles. They fall short of the norms of historical biography.

30. For details see *Śivdigvijaya*, ed. P.R. Nandurbarkar and L.K. Dandekar (Baroda, 1895).

The *bakhar*s or chronicles relating to Śivājī are, no doubt, of great historical value. They are not untrustworthy. They are rather authentic sources of history of the Marāṭhās. They embody the features of both literature and history. Since they do not possess the elements of true historical writing, they cannot be called pure histories. However, it cannot be denied that "they are nearer to history. And they could be called perfect historical works."[31] Some of them give dynastic account of the Bhoṅsalā family to which Śivājī belonged. The recording of events are found in most of them, as stated by R.V. Hervadkar.[32] Some contain the description of the deeds and exploits of Śivājī.

Some state papers of Śivājī's period were available to all the *bakharkāra*s. Even then they relied more on hearsay evidence, traditional stories, myths, legends and their memory of events witnessed in the past than on documentary materials resulting in factual errors of omission and commission on their part, some inaccuracies and inconsistencies, contradictory dates and facts, anachronisms, etc. They did not properly test the historical credibility of the evidence and the reliability of their witnesses. There is a clear-cut reflection of credulity in the writings of the Marathi chroniclers of Śivājī. However, some of their statements can be corroborated and authenticated by what is recorded in some standard works on the history of Mughal India. It is true that some traditional beliefs were not tested by them on the touchstone of history. They presented some of the historical facts within the framework of ancient Indian traditions of historiography. It is altogether a different thing that in some *bakhar*s the events are not arranged chronologically. No dates are given except those of Śivājī's

31. See S.P. Sen (ed.), *Historians and Historiography in Modern India*, p. 218.

32. R.V. Hervadkar, op. cit., pp. 1-30, 256.

birth, coronation and death and some events. All are not absolutely correct. The full details of events are also conspicuous by their absence in them. Since the *bakhar*s were written at the express orders of the masters or patrons to whom their writers were loyal, they have been glorified and eulogised to some extent. The writers could not maintain freely the objectivity which is one of the primary requirements of history writing. During the days of Śivājī and the Peśawās, the *bakharkāra*s were also imbued with patriotic fervour. They were sometimes emotional and irrational in their assessment of personalities and recording of events.

Despite all defects of the *bakhar*s on Śivājī, some Indian and foreign historians of the Marāṭhās copiously used them in their historical writings. Edward Scott Waring, the earliest historian of the Marāṭhās (1810), though fully aware of the limitations of the *bakhar*s or chronicles concerned, considered them more valuable than the Persian chronicles in many ways. He writes:

> The Marāṭhā historians write in plain, simple and unaffected style, content to relate passing events using inflated phraseology. Victory and defeat are briefly related. They do not endeavour to bias or do not mislead the judgement, but are certainly deficient in chronology and in historical reflections.[33]

Grant Duff also preferred the Marathi *bakhar*s to the Persian *Tawārīkhs*, which were according to him, "laudatory accounts of the Muslims and are false in many respects whereas the accounts written by the Hindus were only half truth." He spared no pains in collecting, copying and translating the *bakhars* (while he was Political Agent of Satara 1818-22) for writing his *History of the Marāṭhās* which appeared in 1826 in

33. Cf. S.R. Sharma, *The Making of Modern India*, p. 309.

three volumes. He got a copy of Śivājī's life (probably the Sabhāsad's *bakhar*) from the Rājā of Kolhapur. He considered some of the *bakhars* as "mass of nonsense." Nevertheless, he used them extensively particularly that of Citnis which appeared to him on the whole most valuable as it gives a good account of Śivājī's expedition into Karnataka. It has been categorically stated that he "drew chief material from *bakhars*."[34] James Cunningham too made full use of the *bakhars*. Jadunath Sarkar, despite being highly critical of the Marathi chronicles, utilised Sabhāsad's *bakhar* and *91-Qalmi Bakhar* as sources for his *Shivaji and His Times* (1919) which is one of his monumental works. Surendranath Sen found Sabhāsad's *bakhar* very useful for Śivājī's administration. The two eminent Marāṭhā historians, V.K. Rajwade and N.J. Kirtane, have also underlined the importance of *bakhars* (also called chronicles) as sources in their respective works, *Marathyanchya Itihasachi Sadhane*, and *Marathyanche Bakharivar Tika*.

The *bakhars* or chronicles of the Peśawā period written in Marathi in the eighteenth century are worthy of our notice. They are to a great extent based on official records of the Peśawās or state papers of the period. However, some accounts are apparently based on memory, hearsay evidence and traditional beliefs. Like the earlier *bakhars*, they were written at the behest of some patron. And hence eulogy of the family of the patron and bias in favour of the persons written about are refelected therein. As in the earlier *bakhars* so also in the *bakhars* of the period, the writers could not overcome their patriotic fervour and emotional feeling.

Some of the *bakhars* of the period are faithful historical records. One of such *bakhars* is known as *Shri Shahu Maharajanchi Bakhar*. It was commanded by Govindrao Khanderao Citnis, an important *sardār*. It was composed sometime after 1749.

34. See S.P. Sen, op. cit., p. 403.

The author was in the personal service of Śāhu, the son of Śambhā (or the grandson of Śivājī). The author throws some light on Śāhu's early life in Mughal captivity. In his chronicle, he has depicted the deeds of the Peśawās (from the time of Balaji Vishwanath, the founder of the Peśawā dynasty, to Balaji Baji Rao) in greater detail than what we find in that of Malhar Ram Rao Citnis. The author had the knowledge about Śāhu's personality but could not comprehend how it influenced the politics of the period.

The most striking event in the eighteenth century was the third battle of Panipat fought in 1761 between Ahmad Shah Abdali and the Marāṭhās during the reign of the third Peśawā Bālājī Bājī Rāo (1740-61). The commander of the Marāṭhā forces was Sadāśiva Rāo (the Bhāo Sāheb), a cousin of the Peśawā. The Marāṭhās suffered a defeat at the hands of their enemy. This struck a severe blow to the prestige and power of the Marāṭhās. A number of chronicles narrating the tragic debacle of the Marāṭhās were written in the eighteenth century. Some of them contain eye-witness accounts of the battle.

The chronicles on the battle of Panipat 1761 include *Holkaranchi Thaili* (1761), *Shrimant Bhau Shahebanchi Kaifiyat* (1762), *Bhau Shahebanchi Bakhar* (1763), and *Panipatchi* (or *Panipatanchi*) *Bakhar* (1763), by Raghunath Yadav.[35]

The *Holkaranchi Thaili* was written to explain Holkar's conduct at Panipat. The writer is said to have "fabricated the story that Holkar ran away from the battlefield at the request of Bhāu in order to escort his wife Pārvatībāī."[36] Of all the chronicles on the said battle of Panipat, the most prominent one is *Shrimant Bhau Sahebanchi Kaifiyat*. It describes

35. De Souza and Kulkarni, op. cit., p. 9; Mani P. Kamerkar, "History in Marathi Literature (18th Century)", in *History in Modern Indian Literature*, ed. S.P. Sen, p. 149.

36. Kamerkar, op. cit., p. 150.

the life of Bhāo Sāheb, the commander of the Marāṭhā forces at Panipat. It describes the activities of the Marāṭhās in the north from 1753 onwards. The refusal on the part of Bhāo Sāheb to pay heed to the advice of several exprienced soldiers not to fight a pitched battle but to adopt guerrilla warfare not only triggered internal bickerings but also led to the defeat of the Marāṭhās. The said *Kaifiyat* throws a good deal of light on the weakness of the Marāṭhā camp. T.S. Shejwalkar points out that the reports about the events were collected from the people who had fled the battlefield.[37] In the *Kaifiyat* the failure of the Marāṭhās to win the battle of Panipat has been precisely attributed to the new tactics of the trained infantry. The fact that Govindpant Bundale did not attack Abdali from the rear and the broken and faint-hearted army was "burdened with a host of campfollowers" has not been highlighted by the writer which may be because of his prejudice. However, he has given a correct description of Bhāo's plan of the battle. According to Shejwalkar, the author was "well acquainted with the topography of the battlefield and its surroundings."[38] In all probability, the writer was personally present in the Marāṭhā camp. The narrative of the battle in *Bhau Sahebanchi Bakhar* is based on the *Bhau Sahebanchi Kaifiyat*. Their authors are unknown. These two seem to be the most reliable. They provide authentic information for the historians. With the help of these two works the history of the battle of Panipat 1761 can be reconstructed. Raghunath Yadav's *Panipat Bakhar* was written on the order of a member of the Peśawā's family.

Another noteworthy chronicle of the Peśawā period is the *Peswanchi Bakhar* by K.P. Sohoni.[39] This was written on the

---

37. *Panipat, 1761*, pp. 131, 141, cf. Kamerkar, op. cit., p. 150.
38. Op. cit., p. 132.
39. Ed. V.N. Kulkarni and others (Bombay, 1963).

order of Pant Daji by Sohoni who was a *sūbedār* in the service of Bājī Rāo II (1795-1818). It was written with the intention of glorifying the Peśawās. It covers the history from 1713 to 1818. It provides a glimpse into the Marāṭhā history from Śāhu and Balaji Vishwanath to Bājī Rāo II. It also gives information regarding the main events of the period.

> With the advent of the British, this form of writing naturally disappeared. The great Marāṭhā chieftains and *sardār*s were drowned in defeat and disgrace. The patriotism of Maharashtra was dealt a powerful blow and the spirit and urge for *Bakhar* writing gradually disappeared.[40]

The *bakhars*, including those on Śivājī, composed in the nineteenth century do not fall within the scope of this work.

The *Jedha Śakāvalī* or chronology of the Jedha family is another type of record which is of considerable historical importance.

The historical ballads of the Marāṭhās also merit our attention. The ballad or *powaḍā* was sung by the wandering minstrel called Gondhali and handed down from father to son. The *powaḍā*s were collected and put to writing. The name of the original author is generally given at the end of each ballad, but he cannot be easily identified. The traditional bardic style was used in the poetry by a band of poets in the seventeenth and eighteenth centuries such as Ram Joshi, Anant Phandi, Honaji Bala, Paraśurāma, Prabhākar, Tulsīdās and Agnidās. Of all the available *powaḍā*s, sixteen are of the Śivājī Era, and 42 of the Peśawā period, especially on Sawāī Mādhavrāo and Bājī Rāo II — the period of glory and the period of decline respectively. In the late nineteenth century, some 60 bardic poems were collected by H.A. Acworth,[41]

40. Kamerkar, op. cit., p. 151.
41. *Ballads of the Marāṭhās*, p. 129.

and published by him and S.T. Saligram.[42]

Some of the *powaḍās* are contemporary works. They record the warfare and valour of the Marāṭhās, the heroic deeds of brave men, bravery and defeat, battles and conquests, etc. "Their primary purpose was to unify the people of Maharashtra, to keep alight the torch of Marathi freedom by reminding them of their fight against oppressors."[43] History has been coalesced with folklore and traditional beliefs. Nevertheless, they are useful to the historians as source material.

There are some *powaḍās* which possess historical value. One of the most popular among them is of the days of Śivājī. It was sung by Tulsīdās, the famous Shahir ("as *powaḍā* composers and singers were called") on Tānājī's capture of Sinhgad.

> It describes in glowing terms Tānājī's scaling of the fort on a Ghorpad and the fight of the Marāṭhās against great odds with Udayban. The description of the strength of Udayban, the valour of Tānājī, the defeat of Udayban after the death of Tānājī are all very vividly recalled. The ballad is replete with exaggeration and imagination. It throbs with patriotic fervour.[44]

Agnidās' *powaḍā* on the death of Afzal Khan describes the meeting of Śivājī and Afzal Khan. "It gives the Marāṭhā version of the story that Afzal Khan first leapt upon Śivājī, who then struck him down. This is taken as a matter of fact."[45] This ballad also gives a brief account of Śivājī's conquests and rise to power.

The rise of the Peśawās marked an efflorescence of *powaḍās*. Ram Joshi, Honaji Bala, Sagan Bhau, Anant Phandi

42. *Powaḍās: As Historical Ballads of the Marāṭhās* (Poona, 1911).
43. Kamerkar, op. cit., p. 152.
44. Ibid., p. 153.
45. Ibid.

and Prabhakar — all Shahirs — wrote about the story of war, the bravery of the *sardārs*, social customs, religious practices, etc. They were hailed as poets of the people.

Bājī Rāo II, who patronised most of the Shahirs, bestowed the title of *kavirāja* on Ram Joshi who was the best loved of all the poets. He wrote many *powaḍās* on contemporary political and historical themes. In *Brahmani Rajya Jordar*, he describes the social reforms of Sawāī Mādhavrāo and prosperity of Maharashtra during his time. The bravery of the chieftains and *sardārs*, such as Bapu, Gokhale, Holkar, Ghorpade, Shinde and others is extolled. The religious practices of the people are also delineated. The contemporary social and cultural history can be gleaned from the *powaḍās*. In another *powaḍā*, *Peshwyancha Sukrawarvada*, a detailed description of the palace of the Peśawās is given. It gives very important information about the decorations, ornamentations and architectural styles of those days. In *Dushkal*, he traces the decline of Maharashtra, the moral and political degeneration caused by internecine war, the depredations of Holkar and the Piṇḍārīs, and the consequent sufferings of the common man.[46]

The history of the eighteenth-century Deccan was essentially a struggle for supremacy between Nizam and the Marāṭhās. The Marāṭhās inflicted crushing defeat on the Nizam in 1795 on the battlefield of Kharda. The *Khardyachiladhaichi Bakhar* composed a year later (i.e. in 1796) praises the achievements of the Marāṭhās.

There are about 10 *powaḍās* on the battle of Kharda in which the Marāṭhās defeated the Nizam. Anant Phandi and Honaji Bala both have considered this to be the most important and resounding victory of the Peśawās. Whilst the former has given details of the battlefield, arrangements,

46. Kamerkar, op. cit., pp. 153-54.

names and ranks of the *sardārs*, weapons and armaments, the latter has given a very short description of the war. A considerable part of the poem is an eulogy on Sawāī Mādhavrāo.[47]

The Shahir Paraśurāma's *Deshasthicha Powaḍā* describes the last days of Peśawā Bājī Rāo and the political and moral degeneration which was overtaking Maharashtra. The *powaḍā*s of Shahir Sagan Bhāu (a Maharashtra Muslim) reflect as much the patriotic fervour and praise of Marāṭhā heroes as those of other Shahirs. In his *powaḍā*s on Kharda and Panipat, he sings of Marāṭhā heroism.[48]

It is worthy of note that the *bakhar*s and *powaḍā*s were written for the purpose of arousing the national consciousness and patriotism of the Marāṭhās. Historically, they serve the purpose of making the historian understand the spirit of the age and the people and add to his knowledge of the social, cultural and religious practices of the period.

The existence of Sanskrit historical works including the Vaṁśāvalīs, chronicles, mainly the *bakhar*s on Śivājī and of the Peśawā period, *śakāvalī*s (annals), historical ballads (*powaḍā*s) and other historical and semi-historical works in Marathi (noted before) testifies to the rich tradition of historical writing in Maharashtra. The Maharashtrians (mainly the Marāṭhā historians and chroniclers) also made contributions in the field of historiography in medieval India. This can best be qualified in S.R. Sharma's words: "Among the natives of the soil, the Marāṭhās made the largest contributions in the field of historiography."[49]

The historiographical tradition in Maharashtra has continued with hardly a breakdown to the present day.

---

47. Kamerkar, op. cit., p. 154.
48. Ibid.
49. S.R. Sharma, op. cit., p. 308.

5.3

Chronicles, Vaṁśāvalīs and Other Works of Eastern India

THE tradition of preserving historical literature in the forms of chronicles, Vaṁśāvalīs and other works was maintained in different parts of eastern India.

Orissa

In Oḍradeśa or Oḍiśā (Orissa), archives were kept in the temples and some have survived such as those of the famous Jagannātha temple at Purī. These were primary sources for the compilers of chronicles, Vaṁśāvalīs and other historical works. The famous chronicle, *Mādalā Pāñjī*, in prose style in Oriya language was compiled from the Purī archives. This chronicle is believed to have been begun on the order of the king of Gaṅga dynasty, Anantavarman V Coḍagaṅga, at the beginning of the twelfth century CE and kept up to date since then. Manuscript copies of it are kept by various priests attached to the temple and they sometimes vary in detail. Anantavarman was called Coḍagaṅga because he was the son of Rājarāja Gaṅga by his Coḷa wife, Rājasundarī, daughter of Rājendra Coḷa. Coḍagaṅga ruled over Kaliṅga from CE 1077 to 1147. The Gaṅga family rose to the zenith of its power and height of its glory under him. Tradition ascribes to him the building of the famous temple of Purī. He is said to have extended the bounds of his realm. The said chronicle contains valuable information about the rule of Gaṅga dynasty over Kaliṅga. It records at some length the significant events which took place during the rule of the Gaṅga kings. Its Rājacarita section deals with the life and achievements of kings of Gaṅga dynasty. From the account furnished in the chronicle it appears that Anantavarman V was invited from the south by a certain brāhmaṇa official and then ruled over the whole kingdom. The building activities of some Gaṅga kings and also their organisation of the revenues of Kaliṅga are recorded in the chronicle. Anaṅgabhīma II at the end of the twelfth century was one of the greatest builders of temples and magnificent palaces. He conducted a new survey of the whole kingdom and reorganised the revenue administration. His speech on this subject addressed to the nobility is preserved in the chronicle. He proposed to build a new temple at Purī and their agreement is recorded.

The palm-leaf manuscripts or chronicles preserved in the archives of the temple of Jagannātha at Purī contain historical narratives about the lives of the rulers of Orissa right from the establishment of the Gaṅga dynasty and their military expeditions, battles, conquests, achievements, etc. The date and authorship of the chronicles are controversial. However, the materials and themes incorporated therein are important for the study of individual rulers of different dynasties and their mode of administration, economic policies, benevolent activities and success and failures. The chronicles are valuable documents regarding the royal dynasties of Orissa.[1]

The Vaṁśāvalīs (historical records of dynastic genealogies or genealogical histories) were compiled and maintained with great care.

---

1. See also G.C. Misra, "Historical Biography in Oriya Literature", in *Historical Biography in Indian Literature*, ed. S.P. Sen, p. 109.

In Orissa, the tradition of compiling the Vaṁśāvalīs began in the ancient period and continued till the fifteenth or sixteenth century. A number of Vaṁśāvalīs were written and revised with some additions during the period. These records contain lists of the kings and the length of their reigns and the dates of important events. The Eastern Gaṅgas of Kaliṅga maintained the Vaṁśāvalī records which are full of details of their kings. The *Gaṅgavaṁśānucarita* in Sanskrit (preserved at Purī) is based largely on the *Mādalā Pāñjī* and partly on the earlier writings. It was, in fact, revised by Vasudevaratha in the later half of the fifteenth century after the Gaṅga dynasty was supplanted by the Gajapati dynasty but under the patronage of a local ruler belonging to a branch of the Gaṅga family. This Sanskrit composition works up the matter of a chronicle in artistic form. But, actually it is a Vaṁśāvalī. This *Rājavaṁśāvalī* is a history of the Gaṅga dynasty. According to the testimony of this record, the Eastern Gaṅgas ruled Kaliṅga for nearly 1,000 years (CE 496-1435). The names of the kings of the Gaṅga dynasty who preceded and succeeded Anantavarman V are given therein with details of achievements of some of them. The details available in the chronicle, *Mādalā Pāñjī*, and the Vaṁśāvalī about the Gaṅga kings up to about the middle of the twelfth century are almost similar. Some later additions are there in the latter. We are informed that about the middle of the thirteenth century Narasiṁha I had emerged as a popular legendary figure in Kaliṅga. "He was a great general and builder of the splendid temple of the Sun at Koṇārka." Anaṅgabhīma (CE 1211-38), a benevolent ruler, Bhānu, Kapilendra (CE 1435-66), a nobleman of Solar ancestry, and other rulers find mention in the said Vaṁśāvalī. The names of rulers of the Gajapati dynasty and their deeds were further added to earlier genealogical details therein. Kapilendra's son and successor, Puruṣottama (CE 1466-97), is noted chiefly for his military exploits in the south as far as Tamiladeśa. His son and successor, Pratāparudra (CE 1497-1533), was a staunch follower of Caitanya cult of Vaiṣṇavism. He was the patron of Caitanya who arrived at Purī in 1510 and stayed there for eighteen years or so. A fanciful story is narrated about the decision King Pratāparudra took to suppress Buddhism in Kaliṅga. After his death his sons were murdered by the minister Govinda Vidyādhara who proclaimed himself king.[2]

A literary work, *Samar Taraṅga* (Wave of War), of Brajanath Bada Jena (1730-98) also deserves our notice as it is of great historical value. This work has been called a "historical document." It primarily deals with the war between the Marāṭhā *sūbedār* Rājārāma then stationed at Cuttack and the ruling chief of Dhenkanal:

> . . . the chief of Dhenkanal refused to owe allegiance to the Marāṭhā ruler and to pay the fixed tribute which infuriated Rājārāma, and the latter requested the Marāṭhā ruler at Nagpur to take suitable action against the defaulting Oriyā chief. All negotiations have failed, a fierce war ensued, and Rājārāma and his troops were miserably beaten by the brave soldiers of Dhenkanal under the command of Trilochan Mahendra Bahādur, the celebrated chief of Dhenkanal. This battle was fought about 1781 CE and the contemporary renowned poet Brajanath Bada Jena adopted it with subtlety as the subject matter of his long narrative poem *Samar Taraṅga* which, when recited in the Dhenkanal *durbār*, received much appreciation and roused feelings of patriotism. This poetic work breathes an air of contemporaneity and possesses a genuine historical character.[3]

---

2. A.K. Warder, *An Introduction to Indian Historiography*, pp. 133-38; for *vaṁśāvalīs* of Orissa see also *JASB*, VI, II, 1837, pp. 756 ff; for Chronology and History of Orissa see *As. Res*, XV, 1822.
3. G.C. Mishra, "History in Oriya Literature", in *History in Modern Indian Literature*, ed. S.P. Sen, pp. 62-63.

Bengal

The development of historical consciousness among the Beṅgālī writers of medieval period resulted in the presentation of more and more history through literature. The works produced during the period throw a good deal of light on the history of contemporary Bengal. Medieval Bengal saw the production of a number of literary works of historical value and a few important historical works.

The *Rājyacampati* of the poet Govind Das (1536-1620) deals with the history of eastern Bengal under Hussain Shah (1493-1519).[4]

The *Ratnasenakulapraśasti* of Bhavadatta contains a genealogical account of the Sena dynasty of Bengal.

The eighteenth century Bengal witnessed an evolutionary trend in the interaction pattern of history and literature. There was, of course, some influence of literature on contemporary society and politics in Bengal. But Bengali literature of the time was not divorced from its historical moorings either. The eighteenth century is the "seed time" for the study of history in literature in Bengal.

Among the eighteenth-century Bengali literary works of historical importance, mention may first be made of *Annadamaṅgala* composed by Bharatcandra Ray in 1752. He was a court-poet of Mahārāja Kr̥ṣṇa Candra of Kr̥ṣṇanagar, and died in 1760. It is interesting to note that the poet Bharatcandra had a history-awareness which was something new at that time. His work is full of valuable information regarding the socio-economic life and the political condition of Bengal. For the first time in the eighteenth century we find a projection of historical events on literature. The preface of the *Annadamaṅgala* is valuable for gaining the knowledge

4. De Souza and Kulkarni (ed.), *Historiography in Indian Languages*, p. 36.

of the genesis of the Marāṭhā invasion of Bengal. In author's opinion, Alivardi's attack on Bhubaneswar in Orissa created a sort of reaction as a result of which the Marāṭhās of Satārā were invited to rescue Bengal by subduing the Yavanas (Muhammadans). Raghurajah sent Bhāskar Paṇḍit to Bengal. The poet has depicted the historical events in a mythological fashion. If we are to accept his statement, then the Marāṭhā invasion of Bengal was the outcome of a Hindu reaction against the oppressive Muslim Nawāb Alivardi. We do not get any reference to this alleged Hindu reaction either from the Persian or the Marāṭhā sources. Professor K.K. Dutta has, however, remarked:

> ". . . it was also natural that the Muslim writers of Bengal should be largely out of touch with the undercurrents of discontent amongst Hindu subjects."[5] "In fact, Bharatcandra's account cannot be accepted without a grain of salt as he was himself biased against Alivardi for his oppressive treatment towards his patron Kṛṣṇa Candra. Being a court-poet of the Mahārāja, Bharatcandra very naturally could not maintain an impartial attitude so far as Alivardi was concerned. Notwithstanding this limitation, we must admit that Bharatcandra made an assertion in the historical perspective."[6]

The third part (*Mānsiṁha-pala*) of Bharatcandra's work is full of details regarding the engagements of Man Singh with Pratāpāditya (a local king of lower Bengal), the difficulties confronting the Mughal army, and its ultimate victory over Pratāpāditya. Critically speaking, Bharatcandra invented new events which actually did not take place. It is well known that Pratāpāditya was never imprisoned by Man Singh. In fact, it was 12 years after the departure of Man Singh that

5. *Alivardi and His Times*, p. 47 cf. Tarasankar Banerjee, "History in Beṅgālī Literature (Eighteenth century)", in *History in Modern Indian Literature*, ed. S.P. Sen, p. 5.

6. Tarasankar Banerjee, op. cit., p. 5.

Pratāp was held captive by Islam Khan, *sūbedār* of Bengal. There was, however, a popular saying that Pratāp was being sent to Delhi in a cage and on the way he died at Benares. Though we find departures here and there from actual facts, it is not fair to say that Bharatcandra distorted history deliberately to suit his literary style of writing. Though he blended history with fiction, truth with imagination and objectivity with personal interest, there is no denying the fact that he was conscious of the historical perspective. His writings do betray his sense of history. And his *Annadamaṅgala* is partially historical in nature.

In the eighteenth-century Bengal, several historical ballads or *Aitihāsika Gāthā* were composed by unknown village *kavial*s. They reflect upon the battle of Giria between Alivardi and Sarfaraz, Siraj-ud-Daula's downfall at Plassey, tension and war between the English and Mir Kasim, etc. A principal difficulty with these ballads is that they cannot be dated with accuracy. Secondly, their composers often blended history with popular stories and hearsay. None the less, they have some historical value and can be useful as corroborative evidence in reconstructing the local history of the period.

Gaṅgārām's *Mahārāṣṭra Purāṇa*, which forms an important part of the eighteenth-century Bengali historical literature, deserves our special attention. Though written in a Purāṇic style, it is in the nature of a chronicle or history of the Marāṭhā invasions of Bengal. This manuscript was discovered in 1904 by Sri Kedar Nath Mazumdar of Mymensingh. The available manuscript consists of only the first canto and deals with only the early part of the Marāṭhā invasions of Bengal. We do not know whether there were other cantos of the work. Dimmock and Gupta rightly observed: "whether or not the poet ever finished his narrative, of which only this part survives, or whether this was all he ever wrote, is still unknown."[7] Even then the portion of the manuscript handed down to us is rich in details about the occasional Marāṭhā raids in Bengal. There is no denying the fact that the geographical and political knowledge of Gaṅgārām about places outside Bengal was somewhat imperfect. Notwithstanding this imperfection, the historical correctness of what he had narrated in his work is beyond doubt. With regard to the socio-economic impact of the Marāṭhā invasions, his work is almost an eyewitness account. The minute observations of Gaṅgārām have lent the manuscript a great significance from the historical point of view.

Gaṅgārām's idea of the genesis of the Marāṭhā invasions was somewhat different from that found in other accounts, Persian, Marathi and English, and in the *Annadamaṅgala*, a contemporary literary work by Bharatcandra, noted before. Gaṅgārām's is a non-communal approach to the treatment of the subject. His *Mahārāṣṭra Purāṇa* is "basically a text of pure secular history." Gaṅgārām does not mention either any plot or an instigation by the Muslim partisans of Sarfaraz, as stated by contemporary Muslim chroniclers. About the origin of the invasion, Ghulam Hussain Khan writes:

> The Marāṭhā prince (Raghuji Bhonsle) either instigated by Nizam-ul-Mulk, or prompted by what he knew of the weakness of the Empire, undertook to make an irruption into the Kingdom of Bengal. His views were either to make a conquest of it, or at least to establish in it contributions to the full amount of the Chout (*cauth*), i.e. one quarter of the revenues, an odious yoke that had become established in many countries of Hindoostan and Deccan, but from which Bengal had yet remained entirely free. For this purpose he made choice of his

7. E.C. Dimmock and P.C. Gupta (ed. and tr.), *The Maharashtra Purana*, p. xi.

> own prime minister, Bhāskar Paṇḍit, and gave him the command of an army of 25,000 horses. . . .[8]

The element of instigation in the Marāṭhā invasion is also reflected in other Muslim chronicles as well as in the writings of contemporary Europeans.[9] If we are to accept G.S. Sardesai, the Marāṭhā invasion was mainly the result of the rivalry between Raghuji Bhonsle and the Peśawā Bājī Rāo for hegemony in Maharashtra. Sardesai writes:

> Raghuji Bhonsle of Nagpur looked on this eastern province of Bengal as his special sphere and had shown deep resentment when Peśawā Bāji Rāo made demands on the revenues of Bengal in his negotiations with Nizam-ul-Mulk at Bhopal in 1738. Raghuji's Karnataka expedition had added to his reputation and on his return to Nagpur in 1741, he was informed of the political changes in Bengal and of the offers received from Mir Habib and the disgruntled section of the new Nawāb's officers. Raghuji dreaded the new Peśawā's ambitious views towards the province and decided to forestall him by at once sending his army eastward. He was naturally anxious to have an independent field for his activities and readily grasped the offer made to him by Mir Habib.[10]

There is thus a general agreement on two points, instigation either by the Nizam-ul-Mulk or by a section of officers who did not like Alivardi, the usurper, and the lure of the *cauth* of Bengal. It is possible that the penetration of the Marāṭhās was easier because of the degraded socio-political condition of Bengal during the early years of Alivardi's regime. Gaṅgārām is silent on the question of instigation. But that the desire to exact *cauth* from Bengal was one of the factors responsible for the Marāṭhā invasion was reflected in his

8. *Siyar-ul-Mutakherin*, pp. 376-77.
9. See Tarasankar Banerjee, op. cit., p. 12; Jadunath Sarkar, *The Bengal Nawābs*, pp. 28, 96.
10. *New History of the Marathas*, vol. II, p. 222.

Mahārāṣṭra Purāṇa. He writes: "Sāhu Rājā told Raghuji Bhonsle that Bengal had not paid *cauth* for long."

It is also a historical fact that the Emperor of Delhi had promised that the Marāṭhās would have the *cauth* of Bengal. Thus the Emperor's indirect action precipitated the crisis and when Raghuji sent Bhāskar Paṇḍit to Bengal, the great Mughal became a helpless spectator. It is also known that to counteract Raghuji's invasion the Emperor had to take the help of the Peśawā. "After some initial confrontation between the two Marāṭhā leaders some patching up was effected and the Marāṭhās closed their ranks, much to the disadvantage of Bengal." Gaṅgārām was aware of the problem of *cauth*. He writes, "the Badshah ordered the *wazīr* to write to Sāhu about Bengal. Being a servant of the state, Alivardi killed the *sūbedār* (Sarfaraz); and after establishing himself did not pay the tributes for two years. As there were not enough troops with the emperor he could not take early steps. As a result, Alivardi was enjoying the spoils of Bengal and was strongly established. Therefore, Sāhu should send some people to exact the *cauth* of Bengal." Thus the historicity of Gaṅgārām's observations is proved by other evidences.

Marathi records do not throw much light on the initial attack by Bhāskar Paṇḍit and the consequent difficulties of the Nawāb. But Gaṅgārām gives us a vivid detailed account of what happened since the entry of the Marāṭhās through Pachet (60 miles east of Ranchi). He describes the march of the Marāṭhā army. He says that the Marāṭhā army was accompanied by a large number of retainers.

The Marāṭhā army entered Bengal through Midnapur and attacked Burdwan through Pachet. The Nawāb (Alivardi) at once left for Burdwan, and ultimately encamped on the embankment of Rānīdīghī near the town. At first he despatched his men to ascertain the reasons why the Marāṭhās had come.

The Marāṭhā army under the command of Bhāskar suddenly attacked the Bengal army, looted their baggage and completely surrounded them. The condition of the Nawāb became more critical because all the Afghans in his army were inclined to defection at that time. The Nawāb ultimately sent an officer to the Marāṭhā camp to negotiate with Bhāskar. Gaṅgārām did not fail to record this. According to him, the officer went to the Marāṭhā camp and proposed —

> "Take your army and go back. Tell the Emperor that tributes will be paid only on the receipt of a *sanad*; and you will get your *cauth* from there." But Bhāskar did not accept the proposal as he suspected the trick in it. The Marāṭhās attacked with full fury, carried on widespread devastation, encircled the toops of the Nawāb, and cut off all avenues of supply. The pitiable condition of the Bengal troops and the prevailing economic condition of the people find a clear expression in the *Mahārāṣṭra Purāṇa*.

After having won over the Afghans, Alivardi, the then Nawāb of Bengal, managed to break the cordon of the Marāṭhās and proceeded from Burdwan to Katwa. The reliability of Gaṅgārām's account of the condition of the Nawāb before his arrival at Katwa could be proved by what Ghulam Hussain has recorded in his *Siyar-ul-Mutakherin* and Yusuf Ali in his *Ahwal-i-Mahbatjangi*. Unable to cause any harm to Nawāb at Katwa, the Marāṭhās then wreaked their vengeance upon the innocent people of Bengal and unleashed a systematic devastation of the villages on their way. Bhāskar Rām started systematic ravages inflicting utmost cruelties and oppression upon innocent people. It is striking to observe that the Marathi sources are silent about the inhuman torture, loot and plunder committed by the toops of Bhāskar Rām who cursed himself for the escape of Alivardi. But Gaṅgārām has left a graphic description of this in his *Mahārāṣṭra Purāṇa*. His account of the events is well corroborated by the contemporary writings. Vaneswar Vidyalankar, the court-poet of the Mahārājā of Burdwan and an eyewitness of the events observed in his *Citra Campu*:

> Shahu Rajah's troops are niggard of pity, slayers of pregnant women and infants, of brāhmaṇas and the poor, fierce of spirit, expert in robbing the property of everyone and committing every kind of sinful acts. . . .[11]

Gaṅgārām gives a long list of villages plundered and burnt by the Marāṭhās. Practically speaking, the authority of the Nawāb was non-existent in Bengal. Even Murshidabad was not spared. The Marāṭhās under Mir Habib launched an attack on the capital before Alivardi could reach there.

During the rainy season of 1742, the activities of the Marāṭhās slowed down. Their spirit of attack was, however, not dampened. Pursuing their ambition they started their preparation for next course of action of which Gaṅgārām has given description in his work. Meanwhile Hooghly was captured and Sis Rao was appointed Governor of that important political and commercial centre. Gaṅgārām further informs us about the activities of the Marāṭhās and the events that took place. We are told by him that while the Marāṭhā general Bhāskar was busy in holding a grand celebration of his victory somewhere near Katwa during the Durgā Pūjā festivities, Alivardi suddenly attacked the Marāṭhās who fled away helter-skelter, leaving a large portion of their baggage behind. The Bengal army chased them up to the banks of the Ajoy and the Marāṭhās retreated to Orissa in a huff. The success of the Nawāb was temporary as the Marāṭhās regrouped themselves and launched another invasion in 1743 with renewed vigour. The same old method

11. Quoted in J.N. Sarkar (ed.), *History of Bengal*, vol. II, p. 458.

of loot and plunder was repeated. Gaṅgārām has provided the details thereof in a Purāṇic style.

Unable to contain the Marāṭhās by his power of arms, Alivardi hatched up a plot to assassinate Bhāskar Paṇḍit. The Nawāb employed Jānakīrām and Mustafa Khan to lure the Marāṭhā leaders to come for negotiation with him. Bhāskar Paṇḍit was hoodwinked by the false promises of those two persons and agreed to meet the Nawāb along with his prominent generals. If Gaṅgārām's account is to be relied upon, the Nawāb Alivardi took leave of Bhāskar and his associates after some initial discussion on the plea of attending the nature's call. As soon as Bhāskar along with other generals came out of the tent and mounted, the Nawāb's officers attacked them suddenly and killed them. Gaṅgārām's *Mahārāṣṭra Purāṇa* ends dealing with the defeat and murder of Bhāskar. But we know that the Marāṭhā invasions of Bengal did not come to an end with his murder.

> Fighting continued for several years more till the treaty of 1751 restored peace and normalcy in the province. Taken as a whole, Gaṅgārām's *Mahārāṣṭra Purāṇa* may be profitably utilised in reconstructing the contemporary history of Bengal. If we neglect the manuscript as a mere literary writing, we shall overlook authentic evidences particularly relating to the socio-economic conditions of the time. In spite of many shortcomings the manuscript presents a vivid account of what had taken place in the districts west of the Ganges. It would not be preposterous to describe the work as an eye-witness account.[12]

Gaṅgārām's *Mahārāṣṭra Purāṇa* can undoubtedly be considered as an important historical work. Its use by the famous historian K.K. Dutta in his *Alivardi and His Times* and the celebrated Marāṭhā historian G.S. Sardesai in his *New History of the Marāṭhās* (vol. II) testifies to its historical value.

12. Tarasankar Banerjee, op. cit., p. 20.

In north-east India, Assam, Manipur and Tripura have had the distinction of producing and preserving the chronicles and other historical works.

Assam

In Assam, the tradition of composing chronicle popularly known as *burañjī* virtually commenced after the advent of the Ahoms in CE 1228. Actually, the credit of initiating this tradition in Assam goes to them. They took keen interest in getting the contemporary historical events chronicled as well as in preserving the concerned records. The *burañjī*s are apparently historical records of the events that took place during the Ahom rule. It were the Ahoms who first introduced the art of writing chronicle or history which further developed in Assam during the medieval period. In fact, it was the early thirteenth century which marked the beginning of a new era in the history of historical writing in Assam.

> "The Ahoms were a tribe of Shans who migrated to Assam early in the thirteenth century. They were endowed with the historical faculty in a very high degree; and their priests and leading families possessed *burañjī*s, or histories, which were periodically bought up to date. These were written on oblong strips of bark (of the *sāci* tree), and were very carefully preserved and handed down from father to son."[13]

> "The science of history was unknown to the early inhabitants of Assam, and it is not till the Ahom invasion in CE 1228 that we obtain anything at all approaching a connected account of the people and their rulers."[14]

> The "Ahoms had the historic sense very fully developed, and many of the priests and nobles maintained *burañjī*s, or

13. E. Gait, *A History of Assam* (1st edn., 1905), Introduction, v.

14. Gait, op. cit. (rept. 2003), p. 1.

> chronicles, which were written up from time to time, and which contain a careful, reliable and continuous narrative of their rule."[15]

The *buraññjīs* dealing with the history of Assam from CE 1228 onwards may be regarded as trustworthy historical records.

The Ahom or Tai word *burañjī* literally means "a storehouse of knowledge." The *burañjīs* are really repositories of our historical knowledge of the events that took place during the Ahom rule of nearly six centuries (1228-1824). The term *burañjī* is generally applied to all those records and documents of the Ahom period which are historical in nature. The *burañjīs* as a whole deal with the history of Assam from the beginning to the end of Ahom rule, Ahom-tribal relations, political, cultural and diplomatic realtions with the neighbouring kingdoms, Ahom-Mughal conflicts, role of the people in the repulsion of Muslim invasions of Assam, Burmese invasion and British occupation of Assam, etc.

From the thirteenth century to the end of the sixteenth (the so-called early medieval period) the chronicles (*burañjīs*) were written in Ahom or Tai language[16] by Ahom scholar-scribes. With the gradual assimilation of the Ahoms with the indigenous people of Assam and with the absorption of the Hindu ideals and customs and adoption of the Assamese as an additional court language by them after their conversion to Hinduism, the recording of contemporary political events began in Assamese. The compilation of *burañjīs* in Assamese began in early seventeenth century and continued unabated till the end of the Ahom rule or till the occupation of Assam

---

15. Gait, op. cit. (rept. 2003), p. 71.

16. Gait (op. cit., 1905, Introduction, v) is of the opinion Ahom language is "similar to that of other Shan tribes, and is written in a character derived from the Pāli. The knowledge of it is now confined to a few old men of the *Deodhai* or priestly caste."

by the British in 1826. The period from the beginning of the seventeenth century to 1826, which in the context of Assam is called the late medieval period or pre-British period witnessed a spectacular progress in the field of historiography. A large number of chronicles were compiled in Assamese language during the period. It is important to note that the chronicles in Assamese containing accounts of the pre-seventeenth-century period of the Ahom rule are but translations of contemporary Ahom records and not original compilations. The chronicles in Ahom language relating to the early period of Ahom rule are more authentic than those in Assamese. They are very important for the reconstruction of the history of Assam of the early medieval period.

Dealing with historiographical tradition in Assam in medieval period, A.K. Warder, a noted authority on Indian historiography, says that a series of prose chronicles were written largely in the seventeenth century and later. He categorically states that "they belong to the Indian tradition."[17] Giving details of contents of the *burañjī*s, he opines that the *burañjī*s are numerous, very extensive and authentic, and collectively they supply an elaborate history of Assam down to the beginning of the nineteenth century.[18]

> The art of writing chronicles was not confined to the Ahom gentry alone, it gradually percolated to the non-Ahom officers and nobles also. Some of the notable chroniclers, like Ratna Kandali, Kashinath Tamuly Phookan, Maniram Barbhander Barua, Haliram Dhekiyal Phookan, and a few others, belonged to non-Ahom communities.[19]

Several *burañjī*s bearing the title *Assam Burañjī* were written.

17. *An Introduction of Indian Historiography*, p. 95.
18. Ibid., p. 96.
19. S.N. Sarma, "History in Assamese Literature", in *History in Modern Indian Literature*, ed. S.P. Sen, p. 42.

More than 100 are extant. Most of them are based on old ones, and are unpublished and preserved in the Department of Historical and Antiquarian Studies, Gauhati University.[20] They form part of Assamese historical literature. It has been rightly pointed out that:

> "The *burañjīs* constitute an unprecedented golden chapter in Assamese literature."[21]

> "The Assamese are justly proud of their national literature. In no department have they been more successful than in a branch of study in which India is, as a rule, curiously deficient. Remnants of historical works . . . are still in existence. The chain of historical authenticity can be relied upon. These historical works or *burañjīs*, as they are styled in Assam, are numerous and voluminous."[22]

The contributions of indigenous Assamese scholars in the field of compilation of the chronicles or *burañjīs* during the period from the seventeenth century to 1826 cannot be underestimated.

"One of the milestones of the development in Assamese literature under the Ahoms was reached in the *burañjīs*, the chronicles of the Ahom court. These *burañjīs* contain a careful, reliable and continuous narrative of the Ahom rule . . . these documents were the digests of periodic reports transmitted to the court by military commanders and frontier governors, diplomatic epistles sent and received from foreign rulers and allies, judicial and revenue papers

20. S.K. Bhuyan collected and edited a large number of chronicles (*burañjīs*). They were mostly published from DHAS, Gauhati. He has surveyed the *burañjīs* in his *Studies in the Literatures of Assam* (Gauhati, 1962).

21. Gait, op. cit. (2003), p. 283.

22. G.A. Grierson, *Linguistic Survey of India*, vol. I, pt. I, p. 156; also quoted in Gait, op. cit.; J.P. Wade, *An Account of Assam*, ed. Benudhar Sharma, Introduction to the first impression (1927) by Benudhar Sharma.

submitted to the kings and ministers for their final orders and the day-to-day annals of the court which incorporated all the transactions done, important utterances made, and significant occurrences reported by eye-witnesses."[23]

> "The chronicles were prepared generally by men who cammanded a comprehensive knowledge about state affairs, and we have several *burañjī*s whose authors held high government office. Records as they are of concrete facts, they have been put in a language which is ordinarily free from sentimental rhetoric. Couched in easy, straightforward and unambiguous language, they are charming and admirable writings. Scattered throughout the entire *burañjī* literature are patches of political wisdom and original thought."[24]

The chronicles or *burañjī*s were written under the patronage of the Ahom kings and nobles. They were "compiled under the supervision of the government officials, and the chroniclers were given free access to the state papers and documents, diplomatic correspondence and court proceedings. Most of the chroniclers were high-ranking state officials and a few of them were connected with diplomatic missions. The accounts of the chroniclers are, therefore, authentic, mutually corroborative and supplementary."[25] The Assamese *burañjī*s have been categorised under four heads:

> (i) desultory chronicles of the early Hindu kings of Kāmarūpa prior to the advent of the Ahoms, the accounts being mostly scrappy, mixing myths and legends with historical traditions; (ii) chronicles of the Ahom kings from CE 1228 to the terminations of their rule in CE 1826, this class of chronicle being more numerous than others; (iii) chronicles dealing with the accounts of neighbouring states like Jayantia, Kachari,

23. Gait, op. cit., pp. 282-83.
24. Ibid., p. 283.
25. S.N. Sarma, op. cit., p. 43.

Chūṭiyā and Koch with whom the Ahoms had frequent diplomatic relations and conflicts also; and (iv) chronicles of countries or states other than Assam, the *Tripurā Burañjī* and the *Pādshāh Burañjī* being two notable examples.[26]

There are also four types of chronicles in Ahom language. Some chronicles contain historical accounts of all important events that took place during the reign of each successive Ahom monarch. The events are recorded therein in chronological order which is one of the chief characteristic features of a chronicle. The concised chronicles contain only the name, the dates of accession and death, and the total reign period of each king. They are important from chronological point of view. Few chronicles contain, besides the names and the dates of accession and death of each king, the names of ministers and chief officials with their family origins. There are some shorter chronicles containing the names of the kings and their sons.

In his introduction to the first edition of his *A History of Assam* (1905), Edward Gait, one of the pioneers in the field of historical research in Assam, gives two different lists of the *burañjīs*, one Ahom and the other Assamese:

The following is a list of the Ahom *burañjīs*:

1. From the earliest times to the end of Ahom rule. This is a very complete and valuable record.
2. From the earliest times to Mir Jumla's invasion of Assam, 1662-63.
3. From the earliest times to CE 1681.
4. From the earliest times to CE 1695.
5. From the earliest times to CE 1764.
6. From the earliest times to CE 1810.

---

26. S.N. Sarma, op. cit., p. 43.

Assamese *burañjīs* are the following:

1. From the earliest times to the end of Ahom rule.
2. From CE 1228 to 1660.
3. From CE 1228 to 1714.
4. From CE 1497 to 1714.
5. From CE 1598 to 1766. It deals very fully with the events of Rudra Siṁha's reign.
6. From CE 1681 to 1790.
7. From CE 1790 to 1806.
8. An account of the tribute paid to Mir Jumla.
9. An account of the relations with the Muhammadans in the years immediately following Mir Jumla's invasion.
10. An account of the Moamarias.
11. An account of the political geography of Assam in the seventeenth century.

The *burañjīs* which deserve our notice here are given below with full details thereof:

Ahom Burañjī (ed. and tr. G.C. Barua, Calcutta, 1930, rept. Gauhati, 1985) deals with events concerning the Ahoms only from the earliest times to the end of their rule in Assam. It was written by many hands to record or chronicle the contemporary events. In its original form, it was divided by the writer (anonymous) into six chapters only dealing with the rule of Ahom kings. In its modern translated form, it gives the history of Assam from Sukāphā (the founder of the Ahom dynasty in Assam) to the time of Purandar Siṁha. It gives accounts of the events that took place during the reigns of Ahom kings. It also provides dates of accession and death of some kings. This chronicle is a treasure-house of information regarding the relations of the Ahom kings with the Nāgā, Chūtiyā, Kachārī, Jayantiā and Mikir tribes and some North-Eastern Frontier tribes like the Mīrīs and Adis; political, cultural and commercial relations of the Ahom kings with the Nāgās and clashes and conflicts between the two in the sixteenth and seventeenth centuries; the Ahom wars with the Chūtiyās, the Kachārīs and other tribes of Assam; politico-cultural relations between Assam and Manipur — the two neighbouring kingdoms — in the sixteenth and seventeenth centuries; relations of the Ahoms with the Koch kings; Muhammadan invasions of Assam including those by Mir Jumla (Aurangzeb's General), Rām Siṁha and Mansur Khan (1662-1682); role of the people of Assam in the repulsion of these invasions; the rise and fall of Ahom rule; the advent of British in Assam, etc. The accounts of events given in this *burañjī* go in harmony with those given in other *Ahom Burañjī*s as well as with those given by Muhammadan writers. Edward Gait got sufficient materials from this *burañjī* for his *History of Assam*.

Deodhai Assam Burañjī (with several shorter chronicles of Assam compiled from old Assamese *burañjī*s, ed. S.K. Bhuyan, DHAS, Gauhati, 1932) covers the period from origin of the Ahom royal family to the accession of Jayadhvaja Siṁha (1648). It provides copious information about the origins of the Jayantiās, the Chūtiyās and the Mikirs, their early kings and kingdoms, religious customs and their political relations with contemporary Ahom monarchs, Ahom-Koch relations, the contemporary political, religious and administrative conditions of Assam, etc.

Jayantiā Burañjī (ed. S.K. Bhuyan, DHAS, Gauhati, 1937) is a chronicle or history of Jayantiā from the earliest times to the reign of the Jayantiā Rājā Lakṣmī Siṁha (1669-97) and the Ahom king Śiva Siṁha (1714-44). We learn from this *burañjī* that the Jayantiā rulers maintained their political, diplomatic and matrimonial relations with Ahoms from the sixteenth century onwards to 1729.[27]

Kachārī Burañjī (ed. S.K. Bhuyan, DHHS, Gauhati, 1936) is a history of the Kachārīs of north Cachar from the earliest times to the reign of Kachārī Rājā Tāmradhvaja Nārāyaṇa (1706-08) and the Ahom king Rudra Siṁha (1696-1714). The information contained in it regarding the early history of the Kachārīs and their kings and kingdoms are very trustworthy. It deals with the Ahom-Kachārī relations up to 1714. The diplomatic relations of the Kachārī kings with the Ahom monarchs with special reference to the epistles exchanged betwen the two (like Ahom-Jayantiā diplomatic relations) also find description in it. It also provides the narrative of the wars between the Kachārī and Ahoms in the sixteenth century and that of the conflicts of Kachārī kings with Koch rulers, Jayantiā rulers and Maṇipurī kings during the period from the sixteenth to the eighteenth centuries.

Tripura Burañjī (ed. S.K. Bhuyan, DHAS, Gauhati, 1938), a chronicle of Tripura, originally called *Tripura Deshar Kathar Lekha*, was written in 1724 by Ratna Kandali Sarma Kataki and Arjun Das Bairagi Kataki — the two Assamese envoys — who had visited the royal court of Tripura as agents of the Ahom king Rudra Siṁha on three different occasions between 1710 and 1715 during the reigns of Ratna Māṇikya II (1684-1712) and Mahendra Māṇikya (1712-14). They give a historical and descriptive account of Tripura up to 1714 (pp. 32-34). This *burañjī* has been collated from the original manuscript in the British Museum, London.

Kāmrūpar Burañjī (ed. S.K. Bhuyan, DHAS, Gauhati, 1930) is a history of Assam from ancient times up to the reign of Gadādhar Siṁha (1681-96), compiled from a number of old

27. See also Lakshmi Devi, *Ahom-Tribal Relations* (*A Political Study*), pp. 106 ff.

chronicles. It contains valuable information about ancient Kāmarūpa. It also deals with the history of the Koches. It gives a detailed account of Ahom-Mughal conflicts in the seventeenth century covering the invasions of Allahyar Khan, Mirja Nathan, Mir Jumla, Rām Siṁha and Mansur Khan and the ultimate victory of the Ahoms in 1682. Eighteen diplomatic epistles are also incorporated in it.

Purāṇī Assam Burañjī (ed. H.C. Goswami, KAS, Gauhati, 1922) is a history of Assam from the beginning of the Ahom rule to the time of Gadādhar Siṁha. It deals with the diplomatic relations of the Koches with the Mughals, the Afghans and the Ahoms.

Satsari Assam Burañjī (ed. S.K. Bhuyan, Gauhati University, 1960) is a collection of seven old Assamese chronicles, four of which contain references to the Koches and their political relations with the Ahom.

Assam Burañjī (a history of Assam from the beginning to the end of Ahom rule in Assam, an enlarged version of Kasinath Tamuli Phukan's chronicle, by H.K. Barua, ed. S.K. Bhuyan, DHAS, Gauhati, 1930); *Assam Burañjī* (a history of Assam from 1648 to 1681 based on old Assamese Manuscript chronicles, ed. S.K. Dutta, DHAS, Gauhati, 1938); and *Assam Burañjī* (a chronicle of Assam from Sukāphā to Gadādhar Siṁha obtained from the family of Sukumar Mahanta, ed. S.K. Bhyan, DHAS, Gauhati, 1945) are equally important. They throw a good deal of light on Ahom-tribal relations and Ahom-Koch relations.

Tungkhungia Burañjī (a history of Assam 1681-1826, Eng. tr. Srinath Barbarua's Assamese chronicle 1671-1806, by S.K. Bhuyan, Oxford University Press, London, 1933, DHAS, Gauhati, 1968) contains a lot of valuable information regarding the relations of the Ahom kings with the hill tribes of Assam and Maṇipurī kings; the Burmese invasion and the British occupation of Assam; rise and fall of the Ahom power, etc.

Pādshāh Burañjī (an old Assamese chronicle, originally pub. by KAS, Gauhati, 1935, tr. into English by S.K. Bhuyan under the title *Annals of the Delhi Badshahate*, DHAS, Gauhati, 1947) is of extraordinary importance. It basically deals with the history of the *sultāns* and emperors of Delhi. It embodies numerous details closely connected with the Assam-Mughal conflicts comprising Jai Siṁha's subjugation of eastern India; Mir Jumla's and Rām Siṁha's invasions of Assam in the seventeenth century; the visits of the Assamese ambassadors to the imperial courts at Delhi and Agra, etc. Other interesting details are also recorded in this chronicle.[28] The contemporary events are prolixly narrated in it. This *burañjī* was written probably in the later half of the seventeenth century when the Assam-Mughal relation was strained.

> The historicity of *burañjī*s is proved not only by the way in which they support each other, but also by the confirmation which is afforded by the narratives of Muhammadan writers, wherever these are available for comparison. Their chronology is further supported by the dates on various records which have been collected and collated for the purpose of checking it, including those on about 70 Ahom coins, 48 copperplates, nine rock, and 28 temple inscriptions and six inscriptions on cannon.[29]

It is significant to note that J.P. Wade's *An Account of Assam*, compiled during 1794-1800, is basically a translation of three historical documents, or *burañjī*s: (1) History of the Ahom kings from the earliest times to the reign of Lakṣmī Siṁha;

28. See also G.P. Singh, "Sources of the History of Medieval Assam", in *Sources of the History of India*, vol. III, ed. by N.R. Ray, p. 125.
29. Gait, op. cit. (1905), Introduction, vii.

(2) History of the Koch kings; and (3) Account of the wars with the Muhammadans.

As historical records, the *burañjī*s are as valuable as other similar works. In this very regard, it has been observed by S.K. Bhuyan:

> The *burañjī*s were to the Assamese what the *bakhar*s were to the Mahrattas (Marāṭhās), the *Tawārīkhī*s to the Mughals and the Persians, the *Yazawins* or *Rajawins* to the Burmese and the *P'ongsawadans* to the Siamese.[30]

In Assam, the historical record or chronicle was also compiled in the *satra* — a religious institution of the Vaiṣṇavites. The *satra* chronicles are found both in verse and in prose forms. They throw a considerable light on the socio-religious and political conditions of Assam during the seventeenth and eighteenth centuries. Not only do they contain the day-to-day activities of the religious preachers and *satra* heads of the medieval period, but they also throw some light on the religious practices of the people, the manner of propagation of the faith by different religious leaders, the expansion of their religious activities in different parts of the country, the difficulties and impediments faced by the preachers in their proselytising activities, the religious policies of different rulers, etc. The chronicle of Mayamara *satra* by Cidānandadeva contains accounts of the conflict of the Moamariyas (followers of Mayamara *satra*) with the royal forces towards the last quarter of the eighteenth century. The Moamariyas temporarily occupied the capital and ruled over eastern Assam for a year or so after defeating the royalists. The oppression of King Gadādhar Siṁha (1618-96) on Vaiṣṇavite preachers and monks is described in a biographical work — the *Keśavadeva-Carita* of Ambarish Dvija of the eighteenth century. Similarly, the *Thakur-Atacarit* — a *satra* chronicle by

30. *Tungkhungia Burañjī*, Introduction, xv.

Vidyānanda Ojhā — gives a graphic description of the demolition of the Vishnupur *satra* by the Muslim invaders under the leadership of Abdus Salam in the middle of the seventeenth century. The biographies and the *satra* chronicles are equally important and reliable records for dealing with socio-religious history of Assam during the seventeenth and eighteenth centuries. The biographers and *satra* chroniclers recorded facts and events personally witnessed by them. Sometimes the facts ascertained from contemporary eye-witnesses were also recorded by them. They also utilised materials handed down through tradition.[31]

The Ahom chronicles focus more on the political history than on the socio-religious aspects of the contemporary society, whereas the *satra* chronicles provide us with all relevant information about the socio-religious history of Assam during the period. The latter are also important to some extent for reconstructing the religious history of Assam during the period of the Vaiṣṇava revivalism (fifteenth-seventeenth centuries).

The *Gopicandrer Pañcālī*, a local chronicle of Cachar, composed by Kavi Kr̥ṣṇamohan in 1670 Śaka = CE 1748, deals with the growth of Śaivism in the hill areas of Cachar. The chronicle refers to the worship of Bhuvaneśvara (Śiva) in the cave temples of Bhuvan Hill in Cachar. The presiding deity of Bhuvan Parbat has been called Kirāteśvara Śiva, being worshipped by the local Kachārī tribe popularly known as Kirāta.

The other classes of historical writings prominently include Vaṁśāvalīs, which "sketch the lives and careers of the important nobles. It seemed important for various reasons to preserve an authentic record of the noble families for receiving royal grant and office. These Vaṁśāvalīs thus

31. For details see S.N. Sarma, op. cit., pp. 46-48.

supplement and corroborate information in the *burañjīs*," says E. Gait.[32]

The chronicles composed in verse in metrical Assamese under the patronage of Koch kings are titled as Vaṁśāvalīs. The two notable works of this category are *Darrāṅg Rājavaṁśāvalī* written by a well-known Assamese writer, Sūryakhari Daivajña, in 1798 at the instance of Samudra Nārāyaṇa, the Koch king of Darraṅg (1791-1806), and *Koch Rājavaṁśāvalī* compiled in 1802 by Ratikānta Dvija. These two are famous Vaṁśāvalī records of Assam. They deal with dynastic histories of the Koch kings ruling over different parts of their kingdom notably Kamarupa and Darrang districts of Assam, Cooch Behar district of Bengal (western), and Koch Hajo, represented by the modern town of Hajo (eastern). They give accounts of the deeds and exploits of the different ruling families.

There are numerous old manuscripts which contain some accounts of the Koch royal dynasty, but by far the most detailed narrative yet brought to light is that contained in the Vaṁśāvalī or family history of the Darrāṅg *rājā*s.

The *Darrāṅg Rājavaṁśāvalī*[33] records that by the beginning of the sixteenth century (i.e. in 1515), Bisva Siṁha laid the foundation of the Koch kingdom on the ruins of the old kingdom of Kāmarūpa or Kāmatā. He died in 1540 after a reign of 25 years. He was succeeded by his son Nara Nārāyaṇa, who ruled the kingdom from 1540 to 1584. All the important political events of his reign, including the submission of Maṇipurī king to him, the defeat of the Kachārī

32. E. Gait, op. cit. (2003), p. 284.

33. Ed. by H.C. Goswami (Shillong 1917). Edward Gait caused a translation to be prepared of the said *vaṁśāvalī* while he was sub-divisional officer of Mangaldoi in the Darrāṅg district of Assam and gave analysis of its contents in a paper published in *JASB*, vol. LXII.

king by Chilarai, his (Nara Nārāyaṇa's) brother and general, and the Koch invasion of Ahom kingdom, are recorded in the Vaṁśāvalī. These two kings ruled the whole Koch kingdom. After the death of the famous king Nara Nārāyaṇa in 1584, the Koch kingdom was divided into different parts. Nara Nārāyaṇa's son Lakṣmī Nārāyaṇa became the ruler of the western part of this kingdom which included Cooch Behar and Jalpaiguri districts of Bengal. He ruled from 1584 to 1622. The two Koch kings, Raghu Deva (1581-1603) and his son Parīkṣit (1603-13) are said to have ruled the eastern part of the kingdom which included Koch Hajo. This Vaṁśāvalī also contains an account of some Koch kings of Darraṅg, Dharma Nārāyaṇa or Bali Nārāyaṇa and Sundar Nārāyaṇa (all predecessors of Samudra Nārāyaṇa). The Vaṁśāvalī ends abruptly with the death of Parīkṣit in 1613.[34]

Critically estimating the value of the Vaṁśāvalī of the Darraṅg *rājās*, E. Gait observes:

> . . . although at that time the memory of the events narrated must have been much fresher than it is now, there is clear internal evidence of a certain disregard of facts and of wild exaggeration, so it is impossible to rely on the narrative as fully as on the *burañjīs* of the Ahoms . . . it must be clearly borne in mind that absolute credence cannot be given to any statement which is not confirmed by the testimony of Ahom or Muhammadan writers.[35]

The said *Koch Rājavaṁśāvalī* deals with the history of the Koch kingdom ruled by different braches of the Koch royal family.

Manipur

The people living in the valley of Manipur callect Meitei have had the rich tradition of historical writing. This tradition

34. *Darraṅg Rājavaṁśāvalī* (*supra*), pp. 62-75, 83-120, 139-51.
35. Op. cit., p. 49.

virtually commenced in medieval period with the writing of historical chronicle — a chronicle containing an account of facts or events in a chronological order with dynastic genealogy and chronology. The writing of such chronicle began in the fifteenth century and further continued with little variation. There was a tradition of recording important events of the day-to-day life in chronicles of Manipur. The tradition was maintained throughout during the medieval period. A number of chronicles were produced during the period. Some of them were composed or compiled during the reign of a particular king by the court chronicler under the royal patronage, and some were compilations of the writings of different periods. It is undenible that several *puya*s (local Purāṇas) containing some historical facts and myths were written during the ancient period, similar to the ancient Indian tradition of writing Itihāsa–Purāṇa, but strictly applying the canon of historiography they cannot be considered historical works nor can they be called chronicles. The Meiteis' traditional concept of history finds the best expression in their own word *puwari* (narrative and illustrative story of forefathers or ancestors). The stories culled from some unreliable sources cannot, of course, be dignified with the name of history. The tradition of writing history as such had not fully developed in ancient Manipur. Some chronicles and other works were also written during the ancient period but they, like the *puya*s, are also of limited importance from the historical point of view. The *puya*s, chronicles and some other works composed during medieval period are, of course, historically important. They are more reliable than those composed during ancient period. The *puya*s, chronicles and other historical works of medieval period deserve our notice. The exact dates of composition and names of authors of some works are not known.

The *Cheitharol Kumbaba* — a royal chronicle of Manipur — is not the production of one age or one brain. It is rather a compilation of the writings of different times by different authors. It was first written during the reign of Kyamba (CE 1467-1508). The historical events of the period from CE 33 to 1484 (i.e. up to his own time) were recorded in it by the chronicler (anonymous). It was re-written by Chiron Shyamram and Oinam Anandaram in CE 1780 (at the palace of Canchipur by the order of King Bhāgyacandra, 1759-98) when the original copy was lost as stated in the text itself. In its present form (written in modern Manipuri language in Bengali script), it provides a detailed history of Manipur from the first King Pakhangba (who is said to have ascended the throne in CE 33) — the founder of the kingdom of Manipur — to the last King Bodhacandra (1941-55) as it contains the additions up to his time. The details of the events of the pre-fifteenth century period are not as authentic as those of the post-fifteenth century. The chronicle provides a good deal of information regarding the social, religious and cultural life of the Meitei people. The history recorded particularly after the declaration of Vaiṣṇavism as state religion by King Garibniwaj (CE 1709-48) is very very authentic.[36] A genealogical list of the kings who ruled Manipur in ancient, medieval and modern times is also given in the chronicle with their regnal years and total duration of their rule. The chronology of pre-Kyamba period is not fully reliable. The total duration of rule of some kings belonging to that period varies from 100 to 120 years which is unbelievable. These figures based on traditional Kali Era are no doubt inflated. The chronology from Kyamba period onwards in terms of regnal years and total duration of reigns of kings is trustworthy.[37] The dates of events recorded in Śaka Era are also accurate.

36. *Cheitharol Kumbaba*, ed. N. Khelchandra Singh and L. Iboongohal Singh (Imphal, 1967), pp. 1-174, 175 ff; see also G. Kamei, *History of Manipur*, vol. I, pre-colonial period (Delhi, 1991), pp. 34-37.

37. *Cheitharol Kumbaba*, pp. 691-95.

In spite of all its flaws, the *Cheitharol Kumbaba* may be considered an imporatant work from historiographical point of view. N. Lokendra Singh also observes:

> Despite all . . . limitations, *Cheitharol Kumbaba* continues to be an important source material for writing the history of Manipur. The various entries, reflecting the socio-economic, political, ecological, religio-cultural and many other aspects of Manipur society throughout the centuries could still be properly used through a scientific methodology.[38]

Another important chronicle *Ningthourol Lambuba*.[39] It deals with the dynastic history of Manipur from the time of Pakhangba down to the time of Garibniwaj. It is also a collection of writings of different periods. It was compiled probably during the reign of Garibniwaj. The genealogical lines are contained in it. But it is deficient in chronology. It may, however, be useful for reconstruction of the political history of Manipur from the first century to the time of Garibniwaj.

Both the above royal chronicles are historical records of the activities of the kings and the exploits of the warriors of Manipur.

The *Bijoy Pañcālī* or *Vijay Pañcālī*,[40] one of the famous native chronicles, was composed originally in Bengali by Kṛticandra and compiled by Dvija Sītārām Sharma (a court-chronicler) under the patronage of king Garibniwaj. It records the history of Manipur from the time of King Naothingkhong (CE 750) to the reign of King Garibniwaj (CE 1709-48).

---

38. "A Historiographical Study of some aspects of Cheitharol Kumbaba," in PNEIHA, IXth Session (Guwahati, 1988), p. 54.
39. Ed. O. Bhogeshwor Singh, Imphal, 1967 (1968).
40. Tr. from Bengali into English under the title *History of Manipur*, by M. Jhulon Singh, 2 vols., Imphal, 1936, 1941.

The *Bamon Khunthoklon*,[41] one of the important historical works, by an anonymous writer, contains valuable information regarding the immigration of brāhmaṇas in Manipur from different parts of India, Brāhmanisation, Sanskritisation and expansion of Brāhmanical culture in the valley of Manipur, etc. The recording of the events relating to the migration and settlements of brāhmaṇas, their religious activities including the propagation of Brāhmanical religion, etc. began in the fifteenth century and continued down to about the middle of the nineteenth century.

The *Bamon Meihaobarol* (MSS) also deals with the history of the brāhmaṇas of Manipur from the time of Kyamba to the time of Garibniwaj. It is useful for supplementing and confirming the account of the subject given in the work immediately preceding to it.

In the seventeenth century, specially during the reign of Khagemba (1597-1652), a number of works of historical value were written or rewritten in his court under his patronage, the most important of which is *Khagemba Nongshamei Puya*[42] which deals with migration of Muslims in Manipur. The tradition of historical writing further continued in the eighteenth century. The *Sanamahi Laiken*,[43] which was written by the local *paṇḍit* during the reign of Garibniwaj (1709-48), throws light on the traditional Sanamahi cult, coexistence of traditional religion and Brāhmanical religion, and Sanskritisation in Manipur during his time, etc. This work is useful for dealing with the religious history of Manipur. The two other historical works are *Shamshok Ngamba* and *Takhel Ngamba*, compiled during the reign of King Garibniwaj. They

41. Ed. H. Ibopishak Meitei, Imphal, 1987.

42. Ed. O. Bhogeshwor Singh and M.A. Janab Khan, Imphal, 1969.

43. Ed. O. Bhogeshwor Singh, Imphal, 1972.

deal with "the conquest of Shan states in Kabow Valley, war against Ava (Burma), Tripura, etc."[44]

The so-called pre-Pakhangba chronicle which deals with a line of rulers starting from Kangba is *Kangbaron* of Kangba dynasty. The *Kangla Shanglen Puba* (MSS) throws light on the political history of Manipur Valley before "emergence" of Pakhangba.[45] They do contain some facts, but cannot be considered as historical works.

Tripura

The tradition of historical writing in Tripura began in the fifteenth century with the composition of its royal chronicle known as *Rājamālā*. We learn from the text itself that its first part was composed in CE 1458 in parallel Sanskrit and Bengali (in verse) by a chief priest Durlabhendra and two brāhmaṇa scholars Bāṇeśvara and Śukreśvara who were in the court of Dharma Māṇikya (CE 1431-62). It contains an account of the rulers up to his time. It is the oldest specimen of Bengali composition extant. Its second part was added by Ranachatur Nārāyaṇa during the reign of Amar Māṇikya (1581-86), the third by Paṇḍit Siddhānta Vāgīśa during the reign of Govind Māṇikya (1660-76) and the fourth by Jayadeva during the reign of Kṛṣṇa Māṇikya (1760-83). It is a record of the continuous history of the royal family of Tripura. The entire *Rājamālā* was compiled by Durgamaṇi with alteration, revision and further addition of two more parts (fifth and sixth) during the reigns of Kāśī Candra Māṇikya (1826-29) and Kṛṣṇa Kiśore Māṇikya (1830-49) respectively bringing the narrative down to the time of the latter.[46]

44. Kamei, op. cit., p. 39.
45. Ibid., pp. 38-39.
46. See *Rājamālā*, pub. by the Directorate of Education, Government of Tripura, Agartala, 1967.

The original *Rājamālā* (consisting of four parts) in Bengali as a whole deals with the dynastic history of Tripura from the time of Druhya or Druhyu of Lunar dynasty to the eighteenth century. It has been rightly said that the original (unchanged) manuscript is of more historical importance. "It is a connected history of the kingdom of Tripura."[47] One of the laudable features of this chronicle is that it bears all the marks of antiquity. As early as 1850, Rev. James Long called it the most ancient work in Bengali and reasonably described it as a genuine historical record of the Ṭipperah family.[48] W.W. Hunter's *A Statistical Account of Bengal*, Vol. VI (Ṭipperah) published in 1876 was broadly based on Long's summary of the *Rājamālā*. He also reproduced a genealogy of the Ṭipperah kings on the authority of this source.[49]

The *Rājamālā* records in detail the deeds and glories of the kings. But it does not throw any light on the socio-economic condition of the people. Some information about the religious life of the people are, of course, contained in it. The genealogy of the kings of Tripura is given in it but without any chronology. The genealogy, however, contains some names of the kings, including the predecessors and successors of Tripur (the so-called founder of Tripura Kingdom), who actually ruled Tripura in ancient times. Their historicity can also be proved with the help of other reliable sources.[50] The *Rājamālā* contains very little information about ancient history of Tripura. The pre-fifteenth century history of Tripura provided in it is only partly reliable. But its history from the

47. See De Souza and Kulkarni (ed.), *Historiography in Indian Languages*, pp. 34-35.

48. "Analysis of Rājamālā", *JASB*, XIX, 1850, pp. 534-36.

49. W.W. Hunter, *A Statistical Account of Bengal*, vol. VI, p. 63.

50. See G.P. Singh, "The History and Culture of Ancient Tripura: A Re-Appraisement", PNEIHA, 1st Session (Shillong, 1980), pp. 30-36.

fifteenth century to the eighteenth is very very systematic and authentic. The history of Tripura of medieval period described in it is fully dependable. The views of some scholars are worth quoting here. Suniti Kumar Chatterji is of the view that "The historical value of this chronicle is not much for the period prior to the fifteenth century."[51] According to D.C. Sircar, the historical basis of its accounts cannot be doubted. The accounts of the period witnessed by the compilers are fairly reliable, but those of the earlier period are based on tradition, recorded or unrecorded. The details furnished by the earlier part of the present *Rājamālā* regarding the history of the Tripura royal family down to the eighteenth century requires verification from other sources.[52] ". . . the Tripura chronicles, on which the account of the kings was formerly based exclusively, were not composed before the close of the eighteenth century so that their account of the earlier rulers is unreliable,"[53] he said. D.C. Sen considered "the royal family of Tripura as one of the oldest surviving families and the *Rājamālā* as a great work, but he felt that the information recorded in the first part (till the fifteenth century) are not acceptable, though most of those in the later parts are reliable."[54] Differing from other scholars, R.C. Majumdar asserted that "the historical information recorded in the *Rājamālā* are on the whole dependable."[55] "From Śaka 1380 to Śaka 1850 we have a substantially correct history of the Ṭipperah Rāj which, in my opinion, presents materials far

51. *Kirāta-Jana-Kṛti*, p. 131.

52. *JASL*, XVII, 1-3, 1951, pp. 76-80; see also G.P. Singh, *The Kirātas in Ancient India*, p. 49.

53. N.R. Roychoudhury, *Tripura Through the Ages*, Foreword, iii.

54. Quoted in J.B. Bhattacharjee, "Rājamālā and the Historical Writings in Tripura", PNEIHA, 23rd Session (Tripura University, Agartala, 2002), p. 45.

55. *Bangladesher Itihas* (Madhya Yuga), p. 137 cf. Ibid.

more trustworthy than the *Rājataraṅgiṇī* (a chronicle of the kings of Kashmir) of Kalhaṇa. "The most attractive feature of the *Rājamālā* lies in the charm of its descriptions, where facts are recorded in a fascinating style lending a living interest to the account of events that have transpired in the different epochs of Tripura history,"[56] says D.C. Sen.

The original or old *Rājamālā* was used as one of the authentic sources by Kailash Chandra Sinha for writing his *Rajmala Ba Tripurar Itivritta* (*Rājamālā* or History of Tripura), published from Comilla in 1896; by E.F. Sandys for his *History of Tripura* (a compiled work), published from Calcutta in 1915; by Kaliprasanna Sen Vidyabhushan for his *Śrī Rājamālā*, published in four volumes (Agartala, vol. I, Tripura Era 1336 = CE 1926, vol. II, Tripura Era 1337 = CE 1927, vols. III & IV, Tripura Era 1341 = CE 1931); and by Nalini Ranjan Roychoudhury for his *Tripura Through the Ages — A Short History of Tripura from the Earliest Times to CE 1947*, published from Agartala in 1977.

The use of *Rājamālā* by these scholars for presenting history of ancient and medieval Tripura in their respective works bears witness to its historical value.

The *Rājamālā* in the words of E.F. Sandys is "one of the oldest continuous chronicles of any Indian reigning family."[57] He says: "Ancient history is usually veiled in myths and related in legends but facts in almost every case form the foundation of these stories."[58] He relied heavily on the *Rājamālā* for information regarding Tripura of Muhammadan period.[59] N.R. Roychoudhury also considers the *Rājamālā* as the "most

56. Quoted in N.R. Roychoudhury, op. cit., p. 2.

57. *History of Tripura*, p. 8.

58. Ibid., p. 9.

59. Ibid., pp. 12-23.

important source for the history of the Tripura Royal Family."[60]

"The *Rājamālā* is legitimately considered as an important source of the history of pre-colonial Tripura," says J.B. Bhattacharjee.[61]

From historiographical point of view the *Rājamālā* is no less important than any native, local or royal chronicle in India.

The *Tripura Vaṁśāvalī*, by Dvija Banga Chandra, is a genealogical record of the Tripura royal family based on *Rājamālā* and traditions. This Vaṁśāvalī gives reign periods of the kings who ruled Tripura in the fifteenth and sixteenth centuries. The date of composition of this work is not known to us.

The *Champaka Vijaya* written by Śaikh Mahaddi during the reign of Ratna Māṇikya II (1685-1712), and the *Kṛṣṇamālā* by Rāmagaṅgā Viśārada during the reign of Rājadhar Māṇikya (1785-1804), which form the part of historical literature of Tripura, also deserve our attention. The former gives a detailed account of the early phase of the reign of Ratna Māṇikya II and the latter gives that of the events of the reign of Kṛṣṇa Māṇikya (1760-83).

The tradition of historical writing further continued in Tripura but that does not fall within the scope of this work.

60. Op. cit., p. 1.

61. Op. cit., p. 41.

Book Six
The Tradition of Historical Writing in South India

Preliminary Remarks

IN south India, the tradition of historical writing first began in Tamiladeśa in the age of the third Saṅgam. The three successive Saṅgams (academies of learned writers, poets and scholars) existed in three different cities. The authors of the Saṅgam Age flourished under the royal patronage of the kings. The seat of the third Saṅgam was the city of Madurā (present Madurai), a centre of learning and capital of the Pāṇḍyas. The Pāṇḍya kings patronised the poets who produced poems on kings and their wars, and other important historical events. The poets of the second century CE were the first to initiate the tradition of historical writing. The Saṅgam works (anthologies of poems and epics or classics) of the second and third centuries are admittedly not historical works but they do contain kernel of historical truth. They are important not only for the political history of the Pāṇḍyas, Ceras and Coḷas but also for the social, religious and cultural history of the Tamils of the Saṅgam Age. Their historical value lies in the accurate description of the wars and conquests of the Pāṇḍya, Cera and Coḷa kings. The Saṅgam classics contain biographical references mainly about the rulers of the three dynasties — Cera, Coḷa and Pāṇḍya — and also some information about the commercial relations of the Coḷas with Greece and Rome during the period. The historical information contained in the Saṅgam works are, of course, scanty but reliable and valuable. They are, no doubt, deficient in chronology. The Tamil Saṅgam literature like the Purāṇic literature is partly historical and partly legendary.

During the period from the eleventh to the thirteenth centuries a number of works bearing historical character were produced in Tamiladeśa. The quasi-historical works of the Coḷa period include the biographies of Coḷa monarchs (imperial Coḷas) and also the dynastic history of the Coḷas. The study of these works supplements the information gleaned from the inscriptions of that period. Some Sanskrit works on Coḷa kings, some poems in Tamil about Pallava kings of Kāñcī and some Purāṇa type of works on socio-religious history of Tamiladeśa were also written during the period.

The tradition of historical writing further continued in Tamiladeśa. Some works of great historical value were composed during the medieval period. Some poems on the political history of the Pāṇḍyas (thirteenth-fourteenth centuries) were composed. The Tamil chronicle of the seventeenth century about the Rāṣṭrakūṭas, the dynastic rule of the Gaṅgas in Koṅgu region, the Coḷas, Coḷa and Hoysaḷa rule in Koṅgu and civil wars between Vijayanagara provincial governors (*nāyaka*s) in the early seventeenth century may be regarded as one of the historical works of the period.

Some of the historical ballads of the seventeenth century throw light on the military exploits of a general of a *nāyaka* (Vijayanagara viceroy) at Madurai. In the seventeenth century itself, some important works on the ruler of Jinji, the ruler of Madurai and the history of south India during Anglo-French conflict for power were produced.

In the seventeenth century, the traditional style of writing history in Tamiladeśa, no doubt, underwent changes to a considerable degree. Some ballads on Rājpūt prince Tej Singh of Jinji were written after his death in 1719 in the battle with the Nawāb of Arcot. His ballads are as famous in Tamiladeśa as that of Pṛthvīrāja Cauhāna in Rajasthan. The ballads of Tamiladeśa and the bardic literature of Rajasthan are of equal historical value.

In Karṇāṭadeśa (Karnataka), the historiographical tradition commenced with the writing of a biography of the founder of Kadamba dynasty towards the close of the fifth century CE. The works of the tenth century by the Kannada poets on different aspects of history of Karnataka in the ninth and tenth centuries, works by the court-poets of Rāṣṭrakūṭa kings (tenth century) and the court-poets of western Cāḷukya ruler of Kalyāṇī (tenth century), historical biographies of Rāṣṭrakūṭa and western Cāḷukya kings, works of general nature by the court-poets of the Cāḷukya king (eleventh century), some Kannada works (twelfth-thirteenth centuries) on some Jaina *tīrthaṁkaras* and a work under the western Gaṅga king (tenth century) of Mysore about history of Jainism constitute evidence of continuity in historical writing in Karṇāṭadeśa in both ancient and early medieval period.

The Hoysaḷa historiography forms an important phase of the subject under notice. The Hoysaḷas ruled Mysore with Dvārasamudra as their capital from the eleventh to the fourteenth centuries. They themselves preserved some historical records. The works by the court-poets of Hoysaḷa kings (twelfth-fourteenth centuries) including biographies of their patrons dealing with their political relations with the Pāṇḍya and Coḷa kings and other contemporary powers and their deeds and achievements are evidently of great historical value. Works on Hoysaḷa history continued to be written for centuries after the dynasty came to an end.

A number of historical and semi-historical works were written during the rule of Vijayanagara kings (1336-1565). The Vijayanagara rulers, the poets and scholars who adorned their courts, and some Vijayanagara princesses contributed to the development of historical writing. Some biographical poems on the life and achievements of Vijayanagara emperors were composed by their court-poets. Some of the Vijayanagara rulers and princesses themselves wrote works of historical importance. Some works dealing with Vijayanagara kings and their military exploits, wars and conquests and relations with Bījāpur and Bahamanī *sultāns* were also produced. Works in Sanskrit by the scholars under the patronage of Vijayanagara rulers about the life and deeds of the latter also bear historical character. During the rule of Vijayanagara kings works were composed in Kannada, Telugu and Sanskrit. After the fall of Vijayanagara empire several other works of historical importance were produced in the sixteenth and seventeenth centuries.

Seventeenth to eighteenth centuries may be considered as blooming period in the history of historical writing in Karṇāṭadeśa. Works of the period include biographies, chronicles, Vaṁśāvalīs, epic poems, prose works, etc. (all in Kannada) which are exclusively important for historical purpose. Some works on the dynastic history of Mysore were also written during the period.

The history of historical writing in Āndhradeśa can be traced from CE 1030 onwards. The works produced in the same year and further in 1150 (in Telugu) combined together are important for the study of the history of the Eastern Cāḷukyas of Veṅgī and the Rāṣṭrakūṭas in particular and the socio-religious and political history of Āndhradeśa during the period from the eighth to the eleventh centuries in general.

The tradition of historical writing further continued during the Kākatīya period. Some of the works in Telugu, Kannada and Sanskrit by the poets of that period are important for the political and religious history of

Āndhradeśa during the twelfth and thirteenth centuries.

Some of the works of the fourteenth and fifteenth centuries by the court-poets of Reḍḍī kings are important for the study of the history of the Reḍḍīs during the period. A biographical history of the Reḍḍī kings of Āndhra was written in Sanskrit in the early fifteenth century. The poets of Āndhradeśa who graced the court of kings of Vijayanagara (fourteenth-sixteenth centuries) composed some works which throw light on the history of Vijayanagara. The other poets wrote about Bahamanī ruler's invasion of Vijayanagara in the fifteenth century. Some poets in the service of Pusapati chieftains and of the Gajapatis (fifteenth century) presented the histories of Pusapatis, Gajapatis and Vijayanagara.

One of the important historical works (in Telugu) of the fifteenth century was about Paramāra king Bhoja of Mālwā. The Vaṁśāvalī or family record (first half of the sixteenth century) and a biographical history (of the later period) of the Kākatīyas of Warangal were composed in Telugu. During the seventeenth and eighteenth centuries, some historical *prabandhas* were also written in Telugu. The Telugu literature containing historical writings flourished mainly in southern part of Āndhradeśa.

The eleventh century marked the beginning of historiography in Kerala. That century first saw the production of a historical work known as *Muṣikavaṁśa.* During the medieval period (thirteenth-seventeenth centuries), several works including the Sandeśakāvyas, campūs, chronicles and ballads were composed in Malayalam which are important for the contemporary social, economic, political, religious and cultural history of Kerala. Some of the works, of course, suffer from the lack of historical accuracy.

6.1

Historical Writing in Tamiladeśa

SOUTH India has had its own tradition of historiography. This tradition first began in Tamiladeśa in the age of the third Saṅgam. The poets belonging to that age made notable contributions in the field of historical writing. It may be noted here that the third Saṅgam on the whole covers the first three centuries of the Christian Era, but it was the second century CE which marked the beginning of the tradition of historical writing in Tamiladeśa.

A number of works were produced in the second century CE by the poets of the third Saṅgam some of which are, of course, very important from a historical point of view. The earliest available work of considerable historical value composed in the second century CE in Tamil is the *Eṭṭuttogai* (eight collections) which contains some poems of historical interest. It is a treasure-house of useful information about the life and culture of the Tamils of the early age. Of these eight, *Puranānūru* and *Padirruppaṭṭu* supply in the forms of poetry valuable historical information. They deal with kings and their wars and other activities. The *Puranānūru* covers especially the Pāṇḍyas of Madurā and the Coḷas who ruled the tract to the north of them with their capitals at Uragapura (Uraiyur, near Trichinopoly) and Kāveripaṭṭanam (Puhār). It is very helpful for collecting information about the political exploits of the kings of these two dyansties during the period. The *Padirruppaṭṭu* provides material for a more continuous dynastic history of two main lines of the Ceras (Keralas) on the west coast ruling from Toṇḍī and Vañcī early in the second century CE. According to this work, the Koṅgu region, i.e. the district of Coimbatore, was also ruled by the Ceras in the second century CE. It also contains a reliable genealogy of the Cera kings of the Saṅgam Age. Uḍiyañjeral was one of the prominent Cera kings who was succeeded by his son, Neḍuñjeralādan. Seven other chiefs of this line are described in another group of poems. Another important ruler who is dealt with is Seṅguṭṭuvan, the son of Neḍuñjeralādan, whose glory was sung by another poet named Paranar. The biographical accounts of the Cera kings in the *Padirruppaṭṭu* highlighting especially their achievements are of exceptional value. Kapilar, a brāhmaṇa poet of the third Saṅgam, sang the glories of the Cera prince, Selvakkadungo Vali Ādan, who ruled in the second century CE. There are scattered references to historical subjects in the other collections of the aforesaid eight. The authors of the poems seem to be contemporary with the kings whose deeds they celebrate. In fact, the works of court-poets contain historical facts with poetic exaggeration.

The *Padirruppaṭṭu* (also called *Pathirruppathu*) — an anthology of poems on ancient Cera kings — is said to have belonged to the second century CE. It contains both facts and legends about the exploits of Cera kings. Some of the Cera kings have also been eulogised. This work can, however, be relied upon as a source of ancient history of the Cera kings.[1]

The two other available historical classics of the third Saṅgam are the *Pattuppaṭṭu* ("10 idylls" or an anthology of

1. P.L. Samy, "Sangam Period and Sources of the History of Tamil Nadu", in *Sources of the History of India*, vol. III, ed. N.R. Ray, p. 313; see also K.G. Sesha Aiyar, *Cera Kings of the Sangam Period* (London, 1937).

10 poems, descriptive in nature) and *Padineṇkīzhk Kaṇakku* (an anthology of "18 minor works"). The former was composed in the second century CE and the latter in the second and third centuries CE.

Some parts of the *Pattuppaṭṭu* relate to the Coḷa, Pāṇḍya and Cera kings. Of the 10 poems, the two — *Porunārrārruppaḍai* by poet Mutattāmakkaṇṇiyar and *Paṭṭinappālai* by poet Uruttiraṅ Kaṇṇanār — are very important. In both these poems, the Coḷa monarch, Karikāla (also called Karikālan), who ruled in the second century CE, finds mention. In the *Porunārrārruppaḍai,* he is described as having defeated the Pāṇḍya and the Cera kings and a number of minor chieftains allied with them in the battle of Veṇṇi (Kovil-Veṇṇi, near Tanjore). It is said that the Coḷa kingdom gained greatly both in territory and in influence during his reign. The old capital of the Coḷas was Uragapura, as noted before, and he founded his new capital named Kāveripaṭṭanam. He seems to be the greatest of all the early Tamil kings known to us from the works of the Saṅgam period. In the *Paṭṭinappālai,* we find a remarkable description of the deeds of this Coḷa king especially of his economic reforms. Of the 10 poems, the other two, *Maduraikkāñci* (the longest one) by poet Māṅgudi Marudanar and *Neḍunalvāḍai* by poet Nakkirar, are devoted to the activities of the Pāṇḍya rulers of whom Neḍuñjeliyan was the most famous. He ruled over the kingdom in the second century CE with his capital at Madurai. He is the hero of both the poems. He is described particularly in the former as having achieved a glorious victory over the two kings of the Coḷa and Cera dynasties and also five other chieftains in the famous battle of Talaiyālaṅgānam (modern Talai-alam-Kādu, Tanjore district). Being a poet himself he was a great patron of learning. The above-mentioned four poems do contain biographical references but they are very scanty. The second 10 of the said anthology was composed by

Kummattur Kannanar on the Cera king Neduñjeralādan. The poet has focused on Neḍuñjeral's war with the Coḷa ruler Valpah Tadakkai Peruvirarkilli in which both of them died.

The *Kalavazhi-nārpatu* (one of the said 18 poems) by Poygaiyar is on one of the early Coḷa kings, Koccenganān or Senganān, describing a battle with a Cera king. The date of the event and of the poet who appears as a contemporary has not been established. The event and the poet both may reasonably be assigned to the third century CE.

The *Śilappadikāram* and the *Maṇimekhaḷai*, the two epics composed in the age of the third Saṅgam, are of great historical importance.

The *Śilappadikāram* was written by a Buddhist monk named Ilaṅgovaḍigal (also called Ilaṅgo Aḍigal), brother of Cera king Senguṭṭuvan, in the second century CE. The exploits of Senguṭṭuvan have been immortalised in the Tamil classic by his own monk-brother. Among the Cera kings in Kerala Senguṭṭuvan figures prominently. He appears to have been a powerful potentate. He is said to have won several victories against the Coḷas and the Pāṇḍyas who were his political adversaries. He was a contemporary of the Coḷa king Karikāla and the Pāṇḍya king Neḍuñjeliyan. This epic as well as the colophons added to the poem *Padirruppaṭṭu* (one of the eight collections, already mentioned herebefore) establish the contemporaneity of Senguṭṭuvan (*c.* CE 173-95), Karikāla and Gajabāhu I of Ceylon and thereby solve the problem relating to their chronology. Both these sources also confirm that Koṅgudeśa formed pact of the Cera kingdom in the second century CE.

The Tamil Saṅgam works provide us with some information regarding the kingdom of the Coḷas. Both legendary and historical figures appear in them. The works testify to the rule of several Coḷa princes. It is one of the baffling problems to settle their chronology and order of succession. The most prominent among the Coḷa rulers who are celebrated in the works of the third Saṅgam, including the *Śilappadikāram,* are Ilañjeṭcenni and his son and successor, Karikāla, and Senganān.

The most celebrated Pāṇḍya king praised in several poems for his heroism is Neḍuñjeliyan. In the *Śilappadikāram,* he appears to have greatly increased the prestige and strength of the Pāṇḍyas by overpowering a formidable league of his enemies at Taliyālaṅgānam. The prominent Pāṇḍya kings whose glories were sung by the poets of the third Saṅgam were Neḍuñjeliyan and his remote ancestor, Mudukudumi. The Pāṇḍya kingdom and its capital Madurā are elaborately described in the poems of the Saṅgam Age. Many kings, who were contemporaries of Neḍuñjeliyan, and their achievements have also been touched upon by the poets of the Saṅgam Age. From the epic it appears that the Pāṇḍyas belonged to the Lunar dynasty.[2]

The *Maṇimekhaḷai* by a Buddhist poet named Sittalai Sāttanār, who is supposed to have been a merchant from Madurā and contemporary and friend of Ilangovaḍigal (author of the *Śilappadikāram*), is also not devoid of historical contents. The author mentions the legendary expeditions of the Cera king Senguṭṭuvan as far as the Gaṅga and the Coḷa realm. His prologue also refers to the Coḷas as a solar dynasty. The work shows the ascendency of Buddhism but tolerance of other religions, viz. Jainism, Ājīvikism and Lokāyata. It yields valuable information about ancient Tamil society.[3]

The Tamil Saṅgam works of the second and third centuries CE including the epics and other anthologies throw light on

2. *The Śilappadikāraṁ*, ed. V.R.R. Dikshitar (Oxford, 1939).

3. *Maṇimekhaḷai in Its Historical Setting,* by S.K. Aiyangar, pp. 3 ff.

many obscure aspects of contemporary political history of the Coḷas, Ceras and Pāṇḍyas. They yield us valuable information about the frequent wars which took place among the Coḷa, Cera and Pāṇḍya kings during the period for political supremacy and expansion of the frontiers of their respective kingdom and the resultant changes in the boundaries of their territories. The biographical references are mainly about the rulers of the three dynasties Coḷa, Cera and Pāṇḍya.[4] We also learn from the works of the third Saṅgam that there were several chieftains who either owed allegiance to these kings and fought for them or maintained an independent existence ruling over small principalities. There were also feudatories of one or the other of these kings. The glories and prosperity of the capital towns of chieftains and those of the extensive Coḷa and Pāṇḍya kingdoms have been sung by the poets of the third Saṅgam in their respective poems with some historical accuracy. The works contain trustworthy information about other aspects of the life of the Tamils in the early centuries of Christian Era.

There are some historical references in the Saṅgam classics to commercial intercourse of the Coḷas with the Greeks (called Yavanas) and the Romans which can further be confirmed by the evidences furnished in the *Periplus* by an unknown Greek merchant of the first century CE and in the *Geography* of Ptolemy who flourished about the middle of the second century CE. The Coḷas carried on their trade with these two foreign countries during the period from their famous port, Kāveripaddanam (Kāveripaṭṭanam), situated at the mouth of the Kāverī River. There are some other historical material in the classics of the third Saṅgam relating to the socio-economic life of the Tamils.

4. See also S.N. Padmanabhan, "Historical Biographies in Tamil Literature", in *Historical Biography in Indian Literature*, ed. S.P. Sen, p. 316.

The Saṅgam literature appears to be partly historical. It is very useful for the purpose of reconstructing the socio-economic, political and religious history of the Tamils of the Saṅgam Age. The works of the Saṅgam period despite containing historical truths possess all the defects of court-poetry. While critically estimating the historical value of the classical works of the third Saṅgam we find that they are deficient in internal evidence of chronology and coherence and continuity in the presentation of the subject matter. There are biographical information, though sketchy and scanty.[5]

Some works which include mainly the biographies of quasi-historical nature were produced between the eleventh and the thirteenth century CE. The historiography of the Coḷas during the period deserves special mention here. The *Rājarājacarita* or *Rājarājavijaya* on a great Coḷa monarch, Rājarāja I (CE 985-1014), and the *Kulottuṅgacolacarita* by one Tirunārāyaṇa on the Coḷa ruler, Kulottuṅga I (CE 1070-1118), were the two important biographical works but unfortunately they fell into oblivion after the collapse of the Coḷa dynasty. Both these works are believed to have been contemporary with their heroes. Jayagoṇḍan (better known as Jayaṅkoṇḍan) who flourished in the time of Kulottuṅga I (or in CE 1100) wrote the *Kaliṅgattupparani* (a Tamil war poem) which describes at length the victory of Kulottuṅga I over the Eastern Gaṅga king Anantavarman Coḍagaṅga (CE 1077–1147) of Kaliṅga in second Kaliṅga war which took place in about CE 1112. It also gives us a lot of useful information about the Coḷa genealogy. The work was written towards the end of the reign of said Coḷa king to celebrate his victories. By this time the practice of writing *praśasti* or composing

5. For details see V.R.R. Dikshitar, *Studies in Tamil Literature and History* (London, 1930); S.K. Aiyangar, *The Beginnings of South Indian History* (Madras, 1918).

song in praise of the king and genealogy of the king and achievements of his predecessor had become popular. Oṭṭakkūṭṭan graced the courts of three successive Coḷa emperors, Vikrama (CE 1118-33), Kulottuṅga II (CE 1133-47) and Rājarāja II (CE 1147-62) and composed poems on all of them. These include a war poem (*parani*) on Vikrama (about his Kaliṅga war) and peace poems (*ulā*s) on all three. The *ulā*s provide accounts of the achievements of the kings and of their predecessors with some exaggerations. The *Vikrama-Śolan-Ulā* not only highlights the deeds of Vikrama and the events which took place during his reign but also records a few interesting points bearing on earlier Coḷa history including the legend of Karikālan and an account of expedition of Kulottuṅga I deep into the realm of western Cāḷukya. The *Kulottuṅga-Śolan-Ulā* and the *Rājarāja-Śolan-Ulā* are on Kulottuṅga II and Rājarāja II who were immediate successors of Vikrama. The power of the Coḷas appears to have rapidly declined under them. Besides these three *ulā*s, Oṭṭakkūṭṭan wrote also a *Pillaittamil* on Kulottuṅga II which is popularly known as *Kulottuṅgan-Pillaittamil*. The historical significance of *parani*, *ulā*, and *pillaittamil* cannot be questioned. These are basically biographical works which can be utilised for the study of the history of the Imperial Coḷas. The *Coḷavaṁśacaritam* (whose author's name is not known to us) is more or less a dynastic history of the Coḷas. It contains the description of 16 Coḷa kings of the Solar race who ruled the kingdom with its capital at Tanjavur (Tanjore). The authenticity of the information contained in some of the works, particularly about the wars and conquests of the kings, can be proved by the inscriptional records of the Coḷa period.

The *Bṛhadīśvarmāhātmya* (*Sthalapurāṇa*) in Sanskrit of the later period also describes the history of 16 Coḷa kings and their capital Tanjore. The *Maduraittalavaralaru* (in Tamil) describes the history of the great Madurā temple. The *Nandikkalambakam* (a poem in Tamil) is on the Pallava king, Nandivarman III (*c.* CE 844-66), who ruled the kingdom with its capital at Kāñcī. The work was composed by his court-poet (anonymous) to celebrate the victory of his royal patron over the Pāṇḍyas who at the beginning of his reign tried to conquer his kingdom. Nandivarman after having defeated the Pāṇḍyas, who were the traditional opponents of his house, recovered the territories conquered by them. But towards the close of his reign he was defeated by the Pāṇḍyas and died soon after, some time in CE 866. The said work is the only evidence of historical writing on any Pallava king so far as ancient period is concerned. The *Nandikkalambagam*, the earliest among the *kalambakams*, is said to be of historical importance.[6]

The *Avantīsundarīkathā* of Daṇḍin (CE 635-700), who flourished at the court of Narasiṁhavarman II, the Pallava king of Kāñcī, towards the end of the seventh century CE (695-700), throw valuable sidelight on the history and culture of south India during the sixth and seventh centuries.

The *Periyapurāṇam* in 72 cantos of Sekkilār or Sekkizhār (twelfth century) is important for social and religious history of Tamiladeśa from the seventh to the twelfth centuries CE. The author in his work describes the lives of 63 Śaiva saints called Nāyanmārs (of the seventh and eighth centuries) who belonged to different castes and classes and also the social customs and religious beliefs and practices of the people during the period.[7] The religious works appearing from about the seventh century CE like *Devāraṁ*, *Tiruvācakam* and *Tiruvāymoli* are important for Śaivism, Vaiṣṇavism, Jainism and Buddhism.

6. S.N. Padmanabhan, op. cit., in S.P. Sen (ed.), op. cit., p. 318.
7. J.P. De Souza and C.M. Kulkarni (ed.), *Historiography in Indian Languages*, pp. 254-56.

The Tamil literary works containing historical writings (mentioned above) are, no doubt, of great value as sources of the ancient history of Tamiladeśa.

There are also some evidence of historical writing during the medieval priod.

Here mention may first be made of the *Kovai* which represents a collection of poems dealing with the battles fought by the successors of Kadungon. The most important Kovai is the *Tanjaivanan* (or *Thanjaivanan*) *Kovai* of Poyyamoli Pulavar which throws some light on the political history of the Pāṇḍyas of the Medieval Age. It describes the exploits of Vanan, a general of the Pāṇḍyan king Māravarman Kulaśekhara (1268-1308).

The historical traditions of the Koṅgu region or Koṅgudeśa (i.e. the district of Coimbatore and the southern portion of Salem) were collected in a Tamil chronicle *Koṅgudeśarājākkal*. It was compiled in the seventeenth century from older sources perhaps no longer extant. The said chronicle is repository of historical information. It begins with a Rāṣṭrakūṭa dynasty of seven kings dating back to the early centuries of the Śaka Era. If we accept that the Koṅgu region was ruled by the Ceras in the second century as stated in the *Padirruppaṭṭu* and *Śilappadikāram*, we may conclude that these Rāṣṭrakūṭas supplanted the Ceras in Koṅgu in the third century. The chronicle describes the reigns of this dynasty in general and conventional terms. "The last king Vikrama is said to have conquered the realms of the Coḷas, Pāṇḍyas and Ceras and to have been converted from Jainism to Śaivism." Whether he tried to conquer Karṇataka or ruled over it, the chronicle does not provide a clear picture about this and then abruptly goes on to the Gaṅga dynasty which ruled the Koṅgu region for several centuries beginning probably in the fourth century. The Gaṅgas were apparently Jainas. "An inscription even indicates that the first king of the line, Mādhava I or Koṅganivarman I, was made king by the Jaina monks. It is not very clear whether Vikrama was defeated in Karnataka or he was deposed by the Jaina leaders, or both these things happened. The chronicle tends to praise the Gaṅga rulers also in very general terms with some exceptions but pays careful attention to the exact line of succession such as adoption of a son by a childless king and other details. Though speaking of the successful wars of the Gaṅgas, it does not mention that at first they were feudatories of the Pallavas (as we learn from their own inscriptions). Afterwards they were of Karnataka. The chronicle mentions the invasion of Koṅgu at the end of the ninth century by the Coḷa emperor Āditya I when its capital (Talavanapura on the upper Kāverī) was captured and . . . then treats the Koṅgu country as part of the Coḷa empire providing incidentally some useful information about the Coḷas. Then it describes the conquest of Koṅgu by the Hoysaḷa king Vinayāditya in the later half of the eleventh century (Vinayāditya being a feudatory of the Cāḷukya king Vikramākitya VI). It further states that Vinayāditya took over the country gradually persuading the local rulers to accept his terms. This is an interesting note on the pacification of a conquered territory. From here the chronicle traces the rule of the Hoysaḷa kings in Koṅgu and sometimes in the Tamil country. From the fourteenth century, when the Hoysaḷa realm was annexed to the empire of Vijayanagara, the chronicle continues with the rulers of the new imperial line mentioning various campaigns and as usual paying attention to redistribution of fiefs. The last event mentioned are the civil wars between the Vijayanagara provincial governors (*nāyakas*) in the early seventeenth century when central imperial power declined."[8]

8. A.K. Warder, *An Introduction to Indian Historiography*, pp. 113-15.

This chronicle suffers to some extent from the lack of clarity, consistency and historical accuracy.

The work *Peddalagiri Vijayam* was dedicated to Muddalagiri, the reigning monarch of Madurā in the second half of the seventeenth century. "It is in *Utpalamala* metre in 530 lines carved on the four walls of Tanjore fort, describing the conquest of Ekoji, the Marāṭhā ruler."[9]

The *Ammānai* — a historical ballad — forms the part of bardic literature. The most prominent work of this class is the *Ramappaiyam* or *Ramayappan Ammānai* by an anonymous author. It is historical in nature. It dwells at length upon the military exploits of Ramayappan (also called Ramappaiyan), a general of Tirumalai Nayak (1653-59), the Vijayanagara viceroy of Madurai. The events narrated in this *Ammānai* relates to the subjugation of Sadakkai II Thevan, the Sethupathi of Ramnad, by the said general. This work is contemporaneous with the events described therein.[10] Another ballad, *Iravikkuttippillaipattu*, is about Iravikkutti Pillai, the courageous commander of the Venad froces. We are told that he was killed while he was valiantly fighting against the Nāyaka forces. The other two important ballads of historical value are the *Desingarājan Kadai* and *Khan Sahib Sandai*. The former deals with the exploits of Raja Jai Singh, the ruler of Jinji in the seventeenth century, and the latter with the life of Muhammad Yusuf Khan of Madurai, who fought under the command of the English during the siege of Trichinopoly in Karnatic wars. The latter work is relatively of greater historical value since it throws light on the

9. De Souza and Kulkarni (ed.), op. cit., p. 72.

10. N. Subrahmanian, "History in Tamil Literature", in *History in Modern Indian Literature*, ed. S.P. Sen, pp. 175-76; S.N. Padmanabhan, op. cit., S.P. Sen (ed.), op. cit., p. 318; De Souza and Kulkarni (ed.), op. cit., p. 88.

personalities and events in south India during the Anglo-French struggle for power.[11]

The Nāyakas of Tanjavur (Tanjore) and Madurā (both in Tamiladeśa under Vijayanagara rule) also produced some works of historical importance. They were the local rulers or provincial governors of Vijayanagara emperors. After the fall of Vijayanagara empire in 1565, they asserted their independence. The *Raghunāthābhyudaya*, a semi-historical poem in Telugu, by Vijayarāghava (1622-62), son of Raghunāth Nāyaka of Tanjore (1614-22), deserves mention here. The author of the work describes the Nāyaka rulers of both Tanjore and Madurā. While describing his ancestors (the Nāyakas of Tanjore), he focuses on the incidents that took place in his father's life in 1620. The genealogy of Nāyaka rulers of Tanjore is given in Rajacadamani's *Rukmiṇīkalyāṇa*.[12]

The tradition of historical writing in Tamiladeśa seems to have entered upon a new phase of orientation in the seventeenth century. There was complete departure from the traditional style of presenting the history. A new tradition of writing the history emerged which further continued after CE 1700.

The ballad composed on the life and deeds of Raja Tej Singh is worth mentioning here. Tej Singh, the son of Sarup Singh, was appointed Governor of Jinji (in south Arcot district) in 1700 by Zulfikar Khan. He successfully ruled there. The Nawāb of Arcot besieged Jinji in 1713. Tej Singh and his friend Mahemat Khan were defeated and killed in the battle. The heroic struggle of Tej Singh with the Nawāb of Arcot to preserve the independence of Jinji and his eventual defeat and death in the battle became the themes

11. De Souza and Kulkarni (ed.), op. cit., pp. 88 ff; S.N. Padmanabhan, op. cit., in S.P. Sen (ed.), op. cit., p. 318.

12. M. Krishnamachariar, *History of Classical Sanskrit Literature*, p. 229.

of the ballads. The heroic deeds of the Rājpūt prince dwelt upon in the ballads do have a historical basis. "The Tej Singh Rajan Ballad is a famous in Tamil Nadu as that of Pr̥thvīrāja Chauhāna is in Rajasthan."[13]

13. N. Subrahmanian, op. cit., p. 176.

6.2

The Tradition of Historiography in Karṇāṭadeśa

THE tradition of historical writing in Karṇāṭadeśa (Karnataka) seems to have been maintained right from ancient times. The *Mayūravarmacarita* (in prose in verse consisting of eight chapters) of unknown date and authorship is a biographical history of King Mayūraśarman (also called Mayūravarman), who founded the Kadamba dynasty of Jayantipura (Banavāsī) in Karnataka about the middle of the fourth century CE. It is an established fact that he set up an independent kingdom with its capital at Banavāsī and ruled in the third quarter of the fourth century CE. It is striking to note that some of the legends mentioned in the work concerning the king stands in comparison with a more sober account found in an inscription of the time of his great grandson (latter half of the fifth century CE). The work was presumably composed by a contemporary writer of the king or by someone else towards the close of the fifth century CE. The *Pārijātaharaṇa* (in ten cantos) of Kavirāja, a court-poet of Kāmadeva, one of the later Kadamba princes, is another important work. The poet in his work informs us that this king ruled over the province of Haṅgal (Dharwad district), Banavāsī and Puligere. He was a feudatory of the later western Cāḷukya king Someśvara IV (CE 1181-1219), and began to rule about CE 1182. The city of Haṅgal was besieged by the Hoysaḷa king Vīra-Ballāla II (CE 1173-1220) and after some vicissitude the Kadambas were completely subjugated and their territory annexed. The latter history has not been covered in the details provided in the work.

The Kannada work, *Vaḍḍārādhane* of Śivakoṭi, which is said to have been written in CE 920, throws light on social, religious and administrative condition in Karṇāṭadeśa in the ninth and early tenth centuries CE. The work also contains nineteen Jaina stories reflecting upon the doctrine of Jainism.

The biographical works (in Kannada) of three celebrated Jaina poets, Pampa, Ponna and Ranna, of the tenth century CE deserve special notice.

Pampa, the most eminent among the ancient Kannada poets, wrote *Ādi Purāṇa* and *Vikramārjuna Vijaya* (also known as *Pampa Bhārata*) in 941 or 942 under the patronage of Arikeśarī II (of Vemulavada), a feudatory ruler of the Rāṣṭrakūṭa king Indra III (CE 914-22). In his first work Pampa relates the history of Ṛṣabha, the first Jaina *tīrthaṁkara*. His second work is indeed *Arikeśarī Vijaya* since he highlights his heroic deeds. Pampa was not only a court-poet but also a general of Arikeśarī. As a fighter he took part in many battles of his patron. He was highly impressed by his patron's bravery, magnanimity and benevolent character. He was an eye-witness to the brave deeds and other marvellous feats of action of Arikeśarī in the battles. In compliance with the wish of his patron to get all the significant events of his life recorded, he composed the work as a memoir of the former. He identifies Arikeśarī with Arjuna, the hero of the *Mahābhārata*. The work contains several details of military organisation, weapons and warfare, etc. In the beginning of the work, the author gives the genealogy of Arikeśarī which is his pedigree for the last seven preceding generations. Its accuracy can be tested on the basis of the inscriptional records of the time. He has furnished a reliable account of various campaigns of Arikeśarī in which he also took part.

He tells us that Arikeśarī was a valiant warrior and actively participated in the campaigns of his imperial lords, the Rāṣṭrakūṭas. He gives "certain interesting details regarding the northern campaign of Indra III, in which Arikeśarī had taken part. Later, Arikeśarī fought with King Govinda IV (CE 923-36), son of Indra III and gave refuge to one Bijja, who had come to Vemulavada to save his life from the wrath of Govinda. He finally refused to accept the suzerainty of Govinda, led a war against him and secured the Rāṣṭrakūṭa throne to Baddega, the brother of Indra." The poet also informs us about the matrimonialties between the two families, those of Arikeśarī and the imperial Rāṣṭrakūṭas. He has thrown sidelight on the contemporary society. He has portrayed the vivid picture of the existing social system. He refers to the caste system but disapproves its rigidity. The Brāhmanical sacrifices also received his notice. The woman occupied an honourable position in the society. The institution of *gaṇikas* had flourished. Prostitution also appears to have existed. Its condemnation by Arikeśarī is well attested by the poet. He has touched upon many other aspects of contemporary history. He has provided a genuine historical account of the incidents which took place during the period. The facts are recorded without any exaggeration. The evidence adduced in the work about the important events of Arikeśarī's time is corroborated by his Vemulavada inscription dated CE 927 and Parabharaṇī copperplates of his grandson, Arikeśarī III, dated CE 966.[1]

Ponna, the court-poet of the Rāṣṭrakūṭa king Kṛṣṇa III (CE 939-68), wrote *Bhuvanaika Rāmābhyudaya* which contains, besides the events of his patron's time, many contemporary historical

1. H.V.S. Murthy, "Historical Biography in Kannaḍa Literature", in S.P. Sen (ed.), *Historical Biography in Indian Literature*, pp. 342-44; De Souza and Kulkarni (ed.), *Historiography in Indian Languages*, pp. 125 ff.

details. His other work, *Śānti Purāṇa*, deals with the traditional story of Śāntinātha, sixteenth Jaina *tīrthaṁkara*. Ranna, who flourished towards the end of the tenth century, continued the tradition of his two predecessors. He was the court-poet of the Western Cāḷukya ruler of Kalyāṇī, Satyāśraya (CE 997-1008), the son of Tailapa II (CE 973-97). He wrote *Sāhasabhīma Vijaya* in *c.* CE 1000 to glorify the achievements of his patron, Satyāśraya. The poet in his work mentions that Satyāśraya took part in the wars his father fought with the Śilāhāras of Koṅkaṇa and the Gurjaras further north. These campaigns as recorded by the poet are supported by the contemporary inscriptions. The poet identifies his patron with the hero Bhīma and gives him the title Sāhasa Bhīma. The work is of some help to us for tracing the relationship between the early Western Cāḷukyas of Vātāpī (Bādāmi) and the later Western Cāḷukyas of Kalyāṇī. We are told by the poet that the latter descended from the former, but this is doubted by some scholars. "This connection was, however, known to Ranna, but the genealogy that he gives in his work differs materially from what we get in the inscriptions that come slightly later."[2] The poet also throws some light though in an incidental manner on contemporary social life. His other work *Ajīta Purāṇa* (composed in 993) deals with the history of Ajīta, the second Jaina *tīrthaṁkara*.

Pampa and Ranna in their respective works, *Vikramārjuna Vijaya* and *Sāhasabhīma Vijaya*, "the two earliest historical biographies in Kannada literature,"[3] deal with the life and achievements of their patrons. The works of these two authors inspired the later writers to carry forward the tradition of composing biographies of historical personages.

---

2. Murthy, op. cit., p. 344; see also De Souza and Kulkarni (ed.), op. cit.

3. Murthy, op. cit.

Durgasiṁha, the court-poet of the Cāḷukya king of Kalyāṇī, Jayasiṁha II Jagadekamalla (CE 1016-42), wrote *Pañcatantra* in 1031 which throws a good deal of light on the social, religious and political life of the people during the period. Nāgacandra, popularly known as Abhinava Pampa, wrote *Mallinātha Purāṇa* about the beginning of the twelfth century CE describing the life of Mallinātha, the nineteenth Jaina *tīrthaṁkara*. About CE 1140, Karṇaparya wrote, besides other works, *Neminātha Purāṇa* depicting the life of Neminātha, the twenty-second Jaina *tīrthaṁkara*. Achaṇṇa, a Jaina poet of the twelfth century CE, wrote *Vardhamāna Purāṇa* which is a biography of Vardhamāna Mahāvīra, the last (twenty-fourth) Jaina *tīrthaṁkara*. In CE 1222, Pārśva Paṇḍita wrote *Pārśvanāṭha Purāṇa* which deals with the life and achievements of Pārśvanātha, the twenty-third Jaina *tīrthaṁkara*. Janna wrote *Anantanātha Purāṇa* on the life and teachings of Anantanātha, the fourteenth Jaina *tīrthaṁkara*. These Kannada works have considerable historical value. Many other works on Jaina *tīrthaṁkara*s were further composed in the thirteenth and fourteenth centuries.

Cāmuṇḍarāya, a devout Jaina and minister and general of the Western Gaṅga king, Rājamalla IV (CE 977-85), wrote *Triṣaṣṭi-Lakṣaṇa-Mahāpurāṇa,* popularly known as *Cāmuṇḍarāya Purāṇa* (in prose), in 978 which contains full biographical accounts of all the twenty-four Jaina *tīrthaṁkara*s. This work is very important for the history of Jainism. It also depicts the lives of 63 *śalākā-puruṣa*s (great men). It is worthy of note that the Western Gaṅgas (so called to distinguish them from the Eastern Gaṅgas of Kaliṅga) ruled over a large part of Mysore, called after them Gaṅgavāḍī. They were great supporters of Jainism.

The Hoysaḷa historiography also deserves our notice. The Hoysaḷas for all practical purposes ruled Mysore and adjacent lands with Dvārasamudra (Halebid) as their capital. Their rule virtually began in the early part of the eleventh century CE and continued till about the beginning of the fifth decade of the fourteenth century CE. It appears that they had preserved some records of historical importance with them. They described themselves in their records as "Yādavakulatilaka" or "Kṣatriyas of the Lunar race." Vidyācakravartin III, a court-poet of Vīra-Ballāla III (CE 1291-1342), while giving the genealogy of the Hoysaḷa kings in the first canto (historical introductory) of his epic poem, *Rukmiṇīkalyāṇa* (in 16 cantos) has also associated them with the Yādava *kula* or family.

There were three poets bearing the name Vidyācakravartin in the courts of the Hoysaḷa kings. Vidyācakravartin I, the court-poet of Vīra-Ballāla II (CE 1173-1220), was the author of many poetic inscriptions, engraved on stone during the reign of his patron.

The *Gadyakarṇāmṛta* of Vidyācakravartin II is an incomplete biography (*ākhyāyikā*) of the Hoysaḷa king, Someśvara (CE 1234-62), as it does not cover the entire details of his reign. The reason why the author could not incorporate all the events of the life of the king in his work is not known to us. The events described in the biography took place during the reign of his father, Narasiṁha II (CE 1220-34). The author calls himself "a new Bāṇa" and closely follows the model of *Harṣacarita*. He describes in detail the battle that took place at Śrīraṅgam (called Mahendramaṅgalam) between Narasiṁha II and the Pāṇḍya king, Māravarman Sundara (CE 1216-38), about a year before Someśvara's accession to the throne in CE 1234. The author says that the rivalry between the Pāṇḍya king and the Coḷa king, Rājarāja III (CE 1216-52) (then a vassal of the Hoysaḷa emperor) resulted in a battle between the Pāṇḍya and the Hoysaḷa kings. What the author says is a historical truth. As narrated by the author, the Pāṇḍya king Sundara invaded the Coḷa territory and defeated Rājarāja III. The latter fled and tried to reach the central Hoysaḷa territory (described in the work as Kuntala) for seeking the protection of Narasiṁha but was intercepted by the Kādava chieftain, Kopperuñjinga (called Nijahu) of the Pallava ancestry and an ally of Sundara, and then captured and imprisoned in the fortress of Jayantamaṅgalam (Sendamaṅgalam, South Arcot district). On hearing this news the Hoysaḷa prince Narasiṁha II hurriedly marched down into the Tamil territories and sent his army to Jayantamaṅgalam who defeated and slew the Kādava chief and set Rājarāja III free and then attacked the Pāṇḍya army at Śrīraṅgam (the place of the battle) and routed them. Thereafter the peace was concluded, and the Pāṇḍyas as well as the Coḷas became the tributary vassals to Narasiṁha II (also called Kuntaleśvara) who thus sought to establish a balance between the two main Tamil dynasties and maintain his hegemony or hold his sway over the whole region. The fall of the Pāṇḍyas and the revival of the Coḷas as recorded in the work are corroborated by the inscriptions of the Hoysaḷas. The author further relates that Someśvara was married to a princess Devikā, granddaughter of a king of Gurjara (Vallabha king of Gujarat). The ceremony was performed after Narasiṁha's victory. Someśvara was installed by his father as a ruler of the central part of the Tamil region strategically situated between the Pāṇḍya, Coḷa and Kādava domains. It appears that he began to rule from 1233, a year before he became the virtual emperor after the death of his father. The author concludes his biography with the attainment of royal fortune by Someśvara.[4] This biographical work appears to have been composed either

4. Warder, *An Introduction to Indian Historiography*, pp. 116-18; see also Krishnamachariar, *History of Classical Sanskrit Literature*, pp. 477-78.

much ahead of the end of Someśvara's reign or not much later than his accession. The information available in the standard works on ancient Indian history and the epigraphic records of the Hoysaḷas relating to the events concerned go to prove the historical accuracy of the statements of the author of the work. This is the reason why this work is regarded as historical.

"Works on Hoysaḷa history continued to be written for centuries after the dynasty came to an end apparently based on various surviving records and on tradition." The *Hoysaḷarājavijaya* and *Hoysaḷarājakulavaṁśa* are the two notable examples of such work. This shows the continuity in historical tradition of Karṇāṭadeśa. The *Stalapurāṇa*s describe the places of historical significance including those which formed parts of the Hoysaḷa empire during the imperial rule.

Lakṣmaṇaśāstrin's *Guruvaṁśamahākāvya* (early eighteenth century) provides some information about the last phase of the Hoysaḷas explaining the circumstances leading to the absorption of the Hoysaḷa domains into the new empire. This work also includes a brief historical account of the founding of Vijayanagara empire and the relations between some of its early rulers.

The great Vijayanagara kingdom which rose as a bulwark against the advancing tide of Muhammadan rule was celebrated in a series of biographical works on its successive kings. It is striking to note that the Vijayanagara rulers and the poets and scholars who adorned their courts and enjoyed the royal patronage and also some princesses equally contributed to the evolution of historiographical tradition in Karṇāṭadeśa. Some of them definitely had historical sense. They encouraged by all means the writing of historical works. They, no doubt, set a new tradition in the field of historical writing.

A celebrated brāhmaṇa scholar Mādhavācārya

Vidyāraṇya, spiritual preceptor of Harihara and Bukkā (two of the five sons of Saṅgama) who founded the Vijayanagara empire in 1336, wrote an epic poem, the *Rājakālanirṇaya*, which deals basically with the foundation of Vijayanagara and the life and achievements of its two founders Harihara (1336-42) and Bukkā (1343-79). Vidyāraṇya gives a date in May 1336 for the founding of the city. The main city was called Vidyānagara (city of knowledge) probably in honour of Vidyāraṇya the scholar and also Vijayanagara (city of victory). We are told by him that "when Pratāparudra II Kākatīya was taken prisoner (in 1323) by the Turkish army (the army led by Ulugh Khan) the two brothers fled to Kampilī, the southern part of the Sevuna kingdom where Kampiladeva, formerly a vassal of the Sevunas, had refused to submit to the Turks when his overlord did and asserted his independence. But a few years later the Turks made a determined attack on Kampilī and at the end of a hard and bitter struggle Kampiladeva was overwhelmed and died fighting. The two brothers were taken prisoner and carried off to Delhi. According to other sources, they were forcibly converted to Islam, then gained the confidence of the Turkish Emperor Mahamada (Muhammad), so that when the latter despaired in the face of the general uprising of the south of India against him he thought as a last resort of sending the two brothers back to Kampilī as governors, hoping they might be able to conciliate the people sufficiently to stabilise his rule there. Vidyāraṇya says simply that "Harihara and Bukkā impressed Mahamada by their upright conduct so that he freed them and appointed them to rule Kampilī, sending them with an army to suppress the rebels especially the Hoysaḷa ruler Vīra-Ballāla III (the strongest Indian power in the south). But Ballāla defeated their army whereupon they disappeared into Karnataka and wandered about until they chanced to meet Vidyāraṇya somewhere near the site of their future capital. On Vidyāraṇya's advice, they raised an army consisting of local people and succeeded in defeating Ballāla. They established a fortress or citadel for themselves at Anegoṇḍi (on the north side of the river Tuṅgabhadrā opposite Vijayanagara)." Ballāla III had now no option but to tolerate the presence of the new power or to agree to enter into an alliance. He afterwards marched to the south with an objective to exterminate or extirpate the Turkish army, still ensconced in the domains of the Pāṇḍyas. He inflicted a crushing defeat on them in 1342. His son Ballāla IV succeeded him, but many Hoysaḷa officers in Karnataka embraced the opportunity of shifting their allegiance to Harihara at Vijayanagara. Ballāla IV abandoned the struggle in the south and marched against Harihara, but was defeated and died in 1346. By 1348 the whole of the former Hoysaḷa empire passed under Vijayanagara administration[5] which is a historical fact. Harihara and Bukkā made Vijayanagara (Hampi) their capital.

Vidyāraṇya lived to see Harihara, who, having no son, was succeeded by his brother Bukkā and the latter by his eldest son Harihara II.

Soon after consolidating the empire, the two Hindu brothers Harihara I and Bukkā I thought of the final elimination of Turkish rule over the Pāṇḍya's dominion, a task left unfinished by the Hoysaḷas. First they extended Vijayanagara authority to the Pallava's realm, then Bukkā's second son prince Kampana (also called Kamparāya) was sent with an army to liberate Madhurā (Madurā, the capital of the Pāṇḍyas) from the Turkish rule and accomplish the task. Kampana was victorious. He killed the Turkish *sultān* in the battle, bringing the far south under Vijayanagara rule which is taken as one of the important historical events. His

5. Cf. Warder, op. cit., pp. 124 f.

victory is described in *Madhurāvijaya* (conquest of Madurā) or *Vīrakamparāyacarita* (biography of brave Kamparāya) by his wife, the princess Gaṅgā (also called Gaṅgādevī). Gaṅgā first describes the hero's father Bukkā, and the city of Vijayanagara with its temples and magnificence. Then she adds that Bukkā gave his son a long moral and political lecture and sent him with an army first to establish his authority in the Pallava capital at Kāñcī and then to liberate the Pāṇḍya capital Madurā from the Turuṣkas (Turks). Narrating the exploits of her husband Kampana or Kamparāya and his expedition to the south, Gaṅgā writes that he took five or six days to cross Karnataka and then in two battles attacked and routed the armies of a local Tamil ruler who opposed him. Emboldened by his success he further moved with his army in Kāñcī to extirpate the Musalmans (Muslims) and restore the city to its pristine glory. He fulfilled his mission, established his government there and ruled well. He advanced to the far south, killed the *sultāns* of Madurā and commemorated his victory by magnificent grants to the temples of the city. We are told by Gaṅgā herself that she was invited by him to display her poetic skill in a work to immortalise him. Complying with her husband's wish she composed an epic poem (under notice) of a great historical importance as is apparent from its very contents. She appears to have followed the traditions of the great writers of the court of Pratāparudra II Kākatīya and the courts of the Hoysaḷas. In her said work, she presents an eyewitness account of the desolate state of the Pāṇḍya capital Madurā occupied by the Turks. She says that the temples are in ruins, the river Kāverī has broken its banks and flooded the nearby areas. The survivors of the massacres by the Turks are still not relieved of their mental trauma and agony. Learning, good government, good deeds and nobility have all disappeared. The Tamils are in a pitiful state. She calls upon the prince to exterminate the Turks to rescue them handing him a sword which she says had belonged to the Pāṇḍya king. The battle with the Turks which follows is the climax of the epic and the climax of the battle between Kampana and Turkish *sultān* is the chopping off of the latter's head by the former (a great hero) with the sword of the Pāṇḍya king. She ends stating that peace is restored to the stricken Pāṇḍya kingdom, the remainder of the Turks surrendering.[6] Though the whole episode is described in a conventional literary style, its historical accuracy cannot be doubted. It very much forms part of medieval Indian history.

A number of historical and semi-historical works were written during the rule of Vijayanagara kings (1336-1565). In his *Nārāyaṇavilāsa*, Virūpākṣa II (1468-85), the last ruler of the Saṅgama dynasty, tells us that before he took the reign of Vijayanagara he acted as governor of Karnataka and Coḷa and Pāṇḍya provinces which were under Vijayanagara rule. The *Virūpākṣavasantotsava*, by a scholar named Ahobala, gives a historical description of Vijayanagara empire. It is the most important document for the social and political history of Vijayanagara. During the time of Virūpākṣa, Vijayanagara was on the decline. The Bahamanī *sultān* and the ruler of Kaliṅga invaded its western and eastern provinces respectively. Vijayanagara lost part of the eastern coastal region to Kaliṅga (formerly part of northern Deccan, Āndhra) after sustaining a defeat there and afterwards lost territory on the west coast to the *sultān* called Turks. The southernmost part of Āndhra (under Vijayanagara rule) was ruled by the Saluvas as Vijayanagara governors who were descended from one of Kampana's generals. Narasiṁha Saluva, who ruled there as a governor from 1456 to 1485, enlarged his territory and strengthened his position. He then came into conflict with

6. Cf. Warder, op. cit., pp. 125-27; Krishnamachariar, op. cit., p. 215.

the *sultān* and king of Kaliṅga and vanquishad them. He successfully repelled and expelled the invaders. He deposed Virūpākṣa, who failed to prove himself a worthy ruler. The latter was assassinated in 1485. Thereafter Narasiṁha reorganised the Vijayanagara empire, seized the throne, founded the Saluva dynasty and ruled the empire from 1486 to 1491. Rājanātha II who flourished under the patronage of Narasiṁha Saluva, wrote *Saluvābhyudaya* (a Sanskrit epic in 13 cantos) in about 1480 before the latter became an emperor of Vijayanagara. This work is of great historical importance. The deeds of Narasiṁha's ancestors and the former's victory in the wars against Gajapati, the king of Kaliṅga, and the Bahamanī *sultān* are well recorded therein. The work ends with the details of his majesty and prowess. After becoming an emperor, he recovered most of the districts occupied by the Bahamanī *sultāns* and the king of Kaliṅga and thereby retrieved the fallen fortunes of the empire. Narasiṁha Saluva himself wrote a poem, *Rāmābhyudaya*, at the request of poets and scholars of his court to describe the dynasty he founded. This work is included in historical manuscripts compiled by Taylor. Kṛṣṇadevarāya (1509-29) of Taluva dynasty was the greatest of all Vijayanagara emperors. He was a learned man, great warrior and powerful ruler. He waged many wars in all of which he was victorious. First of all, he subdued his refractory vassals or feudatory chiefs and reduced them to submission. Then he turned his attention towards his hostile neighbours. In 1513, he defeated Gajapati Pratāparudra, the king of Kaliṅga, and recovered from him those portions of the Vijayanagara territory which he had wrested from his weak predecessors and thereby restored Vijayanagara's old frontiers. He brought the recovered territories under his imperial sway. He defeated the *sultān* (of the Adilshahi dynasty) of Bījāpur in March 1520. He conquered the Raichur Doab from him. He ravaged Bījāpur territory and razed the fortress of Gulbargā (capital of the Bahamanī kingdom) to the ground. He was, thus, successful in humbling the pride of his hostile neighbours. His reign marked a glorious epoch in the history of Vijayanagara empire. The power and prestige of that empire reached the pinnacle of its glory during his rule. He left behind his name in the history of India as a powerful king. He was himself an accomplished scholar, a poet and writer and a great patron of art and literature, both Sanskrit and Telugu. His wars and conquests (stated above) are described in contemporary chronicles especially in a Telugu composition, *Kṛṣṇadevarāya Vijayamu*, by Kumāra Dhūrjaṭi.[7]

Vyāsarāya was a contemporary of Narasiṁha Saluva and the rulers of Vijayanagara down to Acyutarāya including Kṛṣṇadevarāya. He attended their courts and acted as a kind of spiritual head of the empire from 1486 until his death in 1539. His biography by Somanātha, the *Vyāsayogicarita* (stylistically on the borderline between an *ākhyāyikā* and a *campū*), contains much of the political history of the period. This biographical work (composed in 1535) is of considerable historical value. The writing style of Somanātha is exactly like that of Bāṇa (the court-poet-cum-historian of Harṣa of the seventh century). He notes that one of his ancestors was patronised by the emperor Bukkā, thus claiming an old family association with the rulers of Vijayanagara. He was born near Kāñcī. In his presentation of historical facts, Somanātha adopted the classical style of Indian historians. Towards the end of chapter IV of his work, he writes that after some years Narasiṁha consecrated his son Mārāya as an emperor. He gives a picturesque description of the imperial city Vijayanagara. The biography also says about reigns of Vīra Narasiṁha (1506-09) and Kṛṣṇadevarāya (1509-29).[8]

7. See also Warder, op. cit., pp. 127-29; Ibid., pp. 215 f, 222.

8. See ibid., pp. 129-30.

For the reign of Acyutarāya (1529-42), half-brother of Kṛṣṇadevarāya, we have two contemporary works in Sanskrit which also gives accounts of the Taluva dynasty to which these two rulers belonged. The princess Tirumalāmbā in a stylish *campū*, the *Varadāmbikāpariṇaya*, gives a genealogy of the dynasty as a branch of the original Lunar dynasty and then describes in some detail the deeds of Narasa Nāyaka (1505-06). We are told that he enters the city of Vidyāpurī (Vijayanagara) thus becoming the supreme ruler after which he campaigns in the east and south in order to consolidate his authority against rebellious vassals. He defeats the Turkish *sultān*. His marriage is described resulting in the birth of Acyuta. The main story of the *campū* from which it takes its title is the marriage of Acyuta with Varadāmbikā, a princess of Salaga. It ends with the consecration of their son, Venkaṭādri, as heir apparent.[9]

Rājanātha III composed a historical epic on Vijayanagara emperor Acyuta, the *Acyutarāyābhyudaya*. He first describes the reign of Narasa with some detail. He then gives a short sketch of the reigns of the earlier kings of the Taluva dynasty tracing their descent. After some account of the reigns of Vīra Narasiṁha and Kṛṣṇadevarāya, Rājanātha comes to his patron Acyutarāya. Rājanātha appears to be a fairly accurate historian, since most of the events he narrates are corroborated by inscriptions. He begins with the consecration of the new emperor (Acyuta) in his capital Vidyāpurī. Afterwards a minister brings news of a rebellion that some of the vassals are not paying their taxes. The emperor marches from his capital to collect taxes and gifts from some of his vassals forcing them to acknowledge his suzerainty and sends armies to various places in the south to assert his authority. The emperor undertakes a south Indian expedition to restore the

9. Warder, op. cit., pp. 130-31.

Pāṇḍya ruler to his dominions which he was dispossessed of. The epic closes with the description of the siege of Bījāpur and the victory over the *sultān* and the emperor's triumphal entry into his capital.[10]

Among other historical writings on Vijayanagara we may note the historical section of Bāsavarāja's encyclopaedia *Śivatattvaratnākara* (early eighteenth century) and the anonymous *Vibhāgaratnamālā* of about the same period. Both the works are in Sanskrit. The former provides us with the information that Rāmarāya was the *de facto* ruler of Vijayanagara during the reign of Sadāśivarāya. Its historical validity is beyond doubt in view of the fact that the throne of Vijayanagara passed to Sadāśiva in 1542, but the power was in the hands of his minister Rāmarāya who fought valiantly on the battlefield of Talikoṭa on 23 January 1565, but was captured and put to death by the *sultān* of Ahmadnagar. The latter work is a history of the Dindima family, brought from Vārāṇasī to the south by a Coḷa emperor and later supplying the Vijayanagara emperors with a succession of court-poets. From this work it appears that the Dindimas belonged to the Bhṛgavāṅgiras group of the clans of brāhmaṇas. Rājanātha II and III, the court-poets of Narasiṁha Saluva and Acyutarāya respectively, belonged to the Dindima family.

After the reign of Acyutarāya the Vijayanagara empire declined, its provincial governors (*nāyaka*s) and subordinate chiefs in due course gradually asserting their independence. Prominent among the hereditary lines of governors were those of Tañjanagara (Tanjavur, Tanjore) and Madhurā (Madurā) in Tamiladeśa who had also declared their independence. A variety of historical works in Sanskrit, Telugu and Tamil record the events of this period from

10. Warder, op. cit., pp. 131-32; Ibid., pp. 223-24.

middle of the sixteenth century to about the middle of the seventeeth century. The Tamil *Maduraittalavaralāru* — the history of the great temple in Madurai — is one of the main sources for this period. Towards the beginning of the last quarter of the seventeenth century the empire had ceased to exist. In 1675, the Marāṭhā rulers superseded the Vijayanagara emperors as the imperial power in south India.[11]

The *Vijayapurīkathā* (in Sanskrit) of unknown date and authorship is on Bījāpur *sultāns* of Adilshahi dynasty.

Saḍakṣarīdeva, a well-known Canarese poet, lived at Dhanugoor in Mysore in the beginning of the fifteenth century. In his *Mahācoḷarājīya* (in 10 cantos), he describes the history of the great Coḷa kings.[12] This work is of immense historical value.

The poem *Kumāraramaṇakathā* written about 1525 by Nañjunda Kavi is a historical biography of Kumāraramaṇa, prince of Kampila, who fought valiantly against the Muslims that had come to occupy Vijayanagara. The poet has exhaustively dealt with the heroic deeds of the prince.

A passing reference can be made to *Ghazi Muhamadacarita* (in Sanskrit), a biography of Mahmud of Ghazni (CE 998-1030), by R.G. Ramaraya.

In his *Rājavinoda* (composed probably in early seventeenth century), Udayarāja of Mysore describes the life and deeds of Bahamanī *sultān*, Muhammad III (1463-82). He gives his genealogy from Abdul Muzaffar Ala-ud-din Bahman who founded the Bahamanī kingdom in 1347 with its capital at Gulbargā and ruled there until his death in 1358.

The seventeenth and eighteenth centuries were fertile periods in the history of historical writing in Karṇāṭadeśa.

11. Warder, op. cit., pp. 132-33.
12. Krishnamachariar, op. cit., p. 274.

The Kannada literary works including the biographies, chronicles, Vaṁśāvalīs, memoirs, Kāvyas (epic poems) and the prose works (containing historical writings) composed during the period fairly attest to the rich historical tradition of Karṇāṭadeśa.

The *Kānthirāva Narasarājavijaya*, composed by Govinda Vaidya in 1648,[13] is a historical biography. It contains a lot of valuable information regarding the reign of Kānthirāva Narasarāja the ruler of Mysore (called Karṇāṭa by the author). Narrating his military exploits, the author (poet) informs us that Rāmadullā Khān, the commander-in-chief of the Bījāpur army attacked Mysore during the reign of Narasarāja but suffered a humiliating defeat at the hands of the Mysore forces. This event led to the development of hatred between the Bījāpur *sultān* and the Mysore Odeyar and the occupation of Samballi and Periyapaṭṭana by the Mysore forces. The circumstances that led to the invasion of Mysore are explicitly related in the said work. We are told that there existed hostility between Vīrabhadra Nāyaka, the chief of Ikkerī and Hanumānappā Nāyaka, the chief of Basavapāṭana. As the former was very powerful, the latter sought the help of Bījāpur *sultān* promising to pay rich tributes. The ambitious *sultān* taking it as an opportunity to extend his sway readily agreed and sent an army under the command of Rāmadullā Khān. No sooner had the Sultān's forces approached, the Ikkerī chief fled from the capital and took refuge in the hills. The defenceless city was ruthlessly and mercilessly plundered by the Muslim soldiers. Rāmadullā Khān returned to his kingdom with a rich war booty. Being emboldened by the success of his army chief, the *sultān* asked him to proceed to Mysore to invade it. The author has devoted nine of the 26 cantos of his work to the said Mysore campaign. We are told by him that

13. *Kānthirāva Narasarāja Vijayam* (Bangalore, 1971).

during the march towards the city of Śrīraṅgapaṭana "the strength of the Bījāpur army increased, the chief of Basavapaṭana and other minor chiefs joining it with their forces. The chiefs of Sira, Tumkur and Bangalore fell an easy prey to the invading force. Śāhajī, the father of Śivājī, was appointed as the governor of Bangalore. Many more chieftains in the neighbourhood were either defeated or voluntarily surrendered to the invading army. By the time the Bījāpur army reached Śrīraṅgapaṭana and comped on the outskirts of the northern side of the city, it had a series of spectacular success to its credit." Having felt elated at these victories, the army chief Rāmadullā Khān sent messengers to Nañjarāja asking him to submit and agree to pay annual tribute to the *sultān*. The king turned down the proposals as he was not prepared to "circumscribe the national honour." Consequently, the war ensued. The Mysore soldiers were known for their proficiency in guerrilla warfare. The author says that "they created havoc in the enemy camp. They killed many enemy soldiers and cut the nose of many more others. They thus struck terror in the rank and file of the enemy force. In spite of this, the enemy soldiers remained undaunted in their resolve to fight. Khan made a final attempt, but was decisively defeated by Narasarāja. The victorious king returned to the palace to the rejoicing of the people who hailed victory to Candavikrama, Trailokyavīraganda, Jayāṅganaramaṇa and Puṇḍarīkākṣasadṛśa. The king distributed the wealth captured in war among his soldiers." The author gives an account of the war camp of the enemy, the attire of the soldiers, and weapons of warfare. The war preparations of the Mysore king, the bravery of his soldiers and the guerrilla tactics have been described in greater detail. The Muslim rulers are said to have caused untold miseries to the people of Mysore and adjoining areas. There was no ruler who could put an end to their oppression. The victory of Narasarāja over the Bījāpur army made the people feel a sigh of relief. The story narrated by the author in this regard goes well in accord with the evidence we glean from other historical sources. The author also gives a description of the city of Śrīraṅgapaṭana. According to him, the city was well planned with broad streets, magnificent buildings, etc. The description of the market street recalls to our memory the splendour of the city of Vijayanagara. That part of the city where the king's palace was situated also finds mention. The different wings of the palace, the daily life of the king and courtiers, the dress of the people and their manners and customs are described in some detail. The author also focuses on the social life of the people of Karṇāṭadeśa of the time. He says that though the people belonged to different classes and castes, they "never suffered from the restrictions of caste. . . ."[14]

The author Govinda Vaidya further says that Kānthirāva Narasarāja (1638-59) encountered Madhurā's (Madurā's) Tirumala Nāyaka's (1623-59) force which had strength of 4,000 cavalry, 1 lakh foot-soldiers and few hundred elephants in his campaign against the Sambali chiefs."[15] The principality of Sambali is situated in between the kingdoms of Mysore and Madhurā. The Nāyakas of Madhurā are said to have instigated the chief of Sambali against the Mysore ruler in 1641.[16] With the cavalry the Madhurā's Nāyaka encircled the Mysore forces. But the latter inflicted a crushing defeat on the former.[17] Narasarāja constructed a separate stable at Śrīraṅgapaṭana to keep the captured horses and elephants of the Nāyaka of Madhurā.[18]

14. See Murthy, op. cit., pp. 345-48.

15. *Kānthirāva Narasarāja Vijayam*, XVII, v. 40, p. 320.

16. See ibid., XVII, v. 8, p. 315.

17. Ibid., vv. 44, 56-57 and 62, p. 321.

18. Ibid., VI, vv. 26, 29, pp. 88-89.

The *Kānthirāva Narasarājavijaya* is an invaluable work for the reconstruction of mainly the political history of Karnataka in the seventeenth century.

Nanjakavi's *Kānthirāva Narasarāja Caritre* also contains historical details of Narasarāja's wars and conquests and other events that took place during his reign.

There are some other biographical works of great historical value on the Mysore rulers. Besides these works, there are some Vaṁśāvalīs, etc. that deal with the dynastic history of Mysore.

In his *Devarājendra Sangatya Chamayya*, Krishnasarma gives us a biographical sketch of the Mysore ruler Devarāja Odeyar (1659-72).

The *Chikkadevarāja* Vaṁśāvalī and *Chikkadevarāja Vijayam* composed in 1680 and 1686 respectively by Tirumalarāya, the minister of the famous Mysore ruler Chikkadevarāja Odeyar (1672-1704), are two noteworthy historical works. The former describes the history of the Odeyars of Mysore from the days of Rājanripa giving their genealogies. Veṅkaṭa II's rule in Vijayanagara empire's southern portions (Tamiladeśa) with Candragiri as capital (from 1586 to 1614), his military expedition against the Madhurā Nāyaka and the treacherous activities of Tirumalarāya are also described in it.[19] It is the only work which refers to the predatory activities of the Adilshahi forces in the regions of Vellore and Candragiri. The latter work abounds in valuable information about the military strength of the Madhurā Nāyaka Cokkanātha, the successor of Tirumala. It further tells us that with the support of those who joined the military confederacy formed by him and his own armed forces, Cokkanātha besieged the fort of Erodu. But his forces suffered heavy casualty on the

19. R. Narasimhacharya, *Karnataka Kavi Carite*, II, p. 432; L. Basavaraja, *Tirumalarāja Matha Chikkadevarāj*, p. 6.

battlefield in their fight with forces of Cikkadevarāja, then prince of Mysore.[20] In his prose works, Cikkupadhya, the court-poet of Cikkadevarāja, throws light on a few aspects of the political history of Tamiladeśa after the fall of the Vijayanagara empire. He gives an account of the military expeditions of the Mysore rulers, including Devarāja and Cikkadevarāja Odeyar, against the Nāyakas of Madhurā and their victories over them. He also informs us of the forts, Paramatti, Malai, Muttamjati, Anantagiri, Amaduru, Kunthuru and Akkareddi in the kingdom of Madhurā, captured by the said rulers.[21] There are some epigraphic evidence to confirm it. Two Kannada inscriptions dated 1674 state that Cikkadevarāja routed the forces of the Madhurā Nāyaka Cokkanātha (1659-82) and captured Paramatti, Muttamjatti, and Anantagiri in the kingdom of Madhurā.[22] It may not, however, be denied that the heroic achievements of the Mysore rulers have been exaggerated to some extent in some of the above-mentioned works.

Under the patronage of Cikkadevarāja Odeyar, poet Ṣaḍakṣara wrote *Rājaśekharavilāsa*, *Vṛṣabhendravijaya* and *Sabaraśaṅkaravilāsa* which speak of the fundamentals of Vīraśaivism in Mysore in the seventeenth century.

The *Munivaṁśābhyudaya* written about 1680 by Cidānanda Kavi contains details of the Odeyar ruling family of Mysore, the rule of Cikkadevarāja Odeyar and the cordial

20. Tirumalayangar, *Chikkadevarāja Vijayam*, V, vv. 35, 37, 40-41, 81, 86, 88 and 90, pp. 107, 109, 114.

21. Narasimhacharya, op. cit., pp. 434, 436.

22. *MAR* 1906-11 (Bangalore, 1973), p. 133; *Ep. Car.*, V (revd. Mysore, 1976), 99. For details see K.G. Vasantha Madhava, "Kannaḍa Sources of the History of Tamil Nadu (Medieval period, 1336-1763)", in *Sources of the History of India*, vol. III, ed. N.R. Ray, pp. 388-90. The references now 15-22 given by me here have been cited by him in his article (pp. 390-91).

relation that existed between the Odeyars and the heads of Jaina *maṭha* at Śravaṇabeḷgoḷā.

Mysūrurājyada-Purvottara composed some time between 1734 and 1740 by an anonymous author gives a dynastic history of the Odeyars of Mysore from Rājā Odeyar, who founded this kingdom in 1612, to Kṛṣṇarāja Odeyar II who ruled the kingdom from 1734 to 1766.

Saundaryakāvya[23] written by Nuronda in about 1740 deals with the court of Kṛṣṇarāja Odeyar II, his conquest of Magadi and his victory against the Muslims in its vicinity. The poet also gives an account of the military exploits of Kalale Nañjarāja, the Senāpati (commander of the forces) of this ruler.

The *Keladi Nṛpavijaya* (in Kannada)[24] composed by poet Liṅganna some time after 1763[25] is a near historical work. It is written in *campū* style. It contains historical details of both Vijayanagara empire and the kingdom of Keladi that rose to prominence in the sixteenth century after the fall of the former.

The greatest Vijayanagara emperor Kṛṣṇadevarāya (1509-29) also finds mention in the *Keladi Nṛpavijaya*. This work supplements the information available in other sources regarding the history of Vijayanagara before and after the said emperor. According to this work, Chaudappā was appointed as the Nāyaka (local ruler or provincial governor as noted before) of Keladi in 1499 (ten years before the ascendancy of the said emperor). It is distinctly mentioned

23. Narasimhacharya, op. cit., III, p. 47.

24. *Keladi Nripa Vijaya*, ed. R. Shama Shastry, Bangalore, 1921.

25. No definite date of its composition can be suggested. The editor of the work is of the view that it was composed between 1763 and 1804 (ibid., p. vii). Whatever may be the date, the work is based on the historical records of the times of Keladi rulers which explains the reason for its inclusion here.

in this work that the title *Nāyaka* was conferred on Chaudappā by the Vijayanagara monarch. It is also stated therein that the change of capital from Keladi to Ikkerī took place during the rule of Chaudappā (in 1514). The work refers to Sadāśiva but wrongly synchronises him with Kṛṣṇadevarāya. As a matter of fact, the throne of Vijayanagara passed to the former in 1542. The work further relates that Chikka Saṅkanna, the contemporary of Rāmarāya, also took part in the battle of Rakkasa-Tangadi. Here we find only half truth. In fact, it was only Rāmarāya (minister of Sadāśiva) who took part in the famous battle of Talikoṭa (1565) which struck a severe blow to Vijayanagara empire. The earliest date known for the Nāyaka Chikka Saṅkanna is 1570 — the year in which Rāmarāya's brother, Tirumala, deposed King Sadāśiva and seized the throne of Vijayanagara. Critically estimating the value of this work, it may be pointed out that there are some discrepancies, inaccuracies and fallacies in it. Further, it suffers from anachronism. Some of the details available in the work regarding Vijayanagara empire do not tally with what we find in the medieval history of India.

The defeat of Vijayanagara ruler in the battle of Talikoṭa (1565) marked the fall and not the end of the empire. The Kingdom of Keladi came into existence sometime after 1565. Poet Liṅganna, the author of *Keladi Nṛpavijaya* gives a lucid account of that kingdom from its foundation to its final overthrow by Haider Ali in 1763. His account is absolutely based on the records left behind by the Keladi rulers including the *Rāja*Vaṁśāvalī containing their genealogical account. The information supplied by the poet about the Keladi kingdom is far more reliable than that about Vijayanagara empire. He throws a good deal of light on the system of administration of the kingdom. He dwells upon kingship system including coronation, succession and the position of the crown-prince, ministers and other officials, public works undertaken by rulers, successive capitals of the ruling chiefs, military organisation, political and diplomatic contacts of the rulers with other powers, etc. He provides some useful information about the gradual expansion of Bījāpur power in the rest of Karnataka.[26] The work is silent over the relations of the Keladi rulers with the rulers of Mysore.

It is the chronicle *Maisuru Arasugala Pūrvābhyudaya Kadattam* that deals with the history of Mysore with details of its relations with the Keladi kingdom.

The tradition of historical writing further continued. The chronicle, *Haidar Nāmā* (in Kannada), was written by Kacheri Krishniah (or Nalappa) in 1784. It is, no doubt, an important historical work containing details of the life and achievements of Haidar Ali who ruled Mysore from 1761 to 1782 with its capital at "Śrīraṅgapaṭṭanam." The chronicler records all the events that took place during the reign of Haidar Ali with fair amount of accuracy.[27] Another Kannada work, *Mysūru-rājara Caritre,* was written by Shanubhoga Veṅkaṭaramaṇa in about 1790. It deals with the history of Mysore rulers from 1776 to 1790. The author of the work himself admits that he wrote on the basis of earlier works on the subject.[28]

---

26. See also K.R. Basava Raja, "History in Kannaḍa Literature," in *History in Modern Indian Literature*, ed. S.P. Sen, pp. 195-97; De Souza and Kulkarni (ed.), op. cit., pp. 136-37.

27. See Basava Raja, op. cit., p. 199; De Souza and Kulkarni, op. cit., pp. 213-14.

28. The last two works have been added just to show the continuity in historiographical tradition. Their details are left out here since they do not fall within the scope of this work.

6.3

Historical Writing in Āndhradeśa

ĀNDHRADEŚA is one of those parts of south India which have had the distinction of preserving the records of historical value from very early times.

The kings of different dynasties ruled different parts of Āndhradeśa in ancient times and later. The Sātavāhanas were the first to rule it. They ruled in the Kṛṣṇā-Godāvarī region from the first century BCE to the close of the first quarter of the third century CE. The dynasty of the Sātavāhana was supplanted by that of the Ikṣvāku founded by Cāntamūla or Śāntamūla I. He ruled in the lower Kṛṣṇā Valley in the second quarter of the third century CE. The records of his son, Vīrapuruṣadatta, have been found at the three famous Buddhist sites, Amarāvatī, Jagayyapeṭa and Nāgārjunakoṇḍa, which are very important for the history of the Ikṣvāku family in general and growth of Buddhism in particular. This is the earliest evidence of preservation of historical records in Āndhradeśa.

A Śaiva poet, Nannecoḍu (CE 1150), in his *Kumāra Sambhavamu* (in 12 cantos in the form of *campū*, i.e. partly in prose and partly in verse) has presented a historical account of the struggle of Vijayāditya II (CE 799-847) and Vijayāditya III Gunaga (CE 848-92), the two Eastern Cāḷukya kings of Veṅgī (modern Peddavegi near Ellore), with the Rāṣṭrakūṭa king, Amoghavarṣa I (CE 814-78), for political supremacy. Vijayāditya II is said to have fought 108 battles in course of his prolonged struggle with the Rāṣṭrakūṭas, the Gaṅgas, and other contemporary powers extending over 12 years. He achieved victories against the Rāṣṭrakūṭas towards the close of his career. Ultimately the Rāṣṭrakūṭa king Amoghavarṣa defeated the Eastern Cāḷukya army and reasserted his supremacy over Veṅgī. The traditional hostilities between the Eastern Cāḷukyas and the Rāṣṭrakūṭas further continued during the time of Vijayāditya III, the most powerful ruler of the dynasty. Vijayāditya III obtained a glorious victory over the combined forces of Rāṣṭrakūṭa king Kṛṣṇa II (CE 875-911 or 878-914) and Kalacuri "Śaṅkaragaṇa" (Kokalla I of Tripurī, father-in-law of the latter) at the battle of Kiraṇapura (Bālāghaṭ), burnt Achalapura (Ellichpur), and overran the Rāṣṭrakūṭa kingdom. The work also deals with Vīraśaivism, the popular form of religion in Āndhra in the twelfth century. The historicity of the information supplied by the author of the work is well proven. Nannaya's *Āndhra Mahābhāratamu* written in CE 1030 in *campū* style at the instance of his patron Rājarāja Narendra, the Eastern Cāḷukya monarch of Veṅgī (CE 1018-60), is another literary work of historical importance. It gives a vivid and true picture of contemporary Āndhradeśa. It gives the genealogy of the Eastern Cāḷukyas with a description of their capital Veṅgī.[1] These two works in Telugu are authentic sources of information regarding socio-religious and political history of Āndhradeśa during the period. They are of invaluable aid for the historians.

The tradition of historiography further continued during the Kākatīya period. The Kākatīya ruler, Prola II (also called Prolarāja), himself used to preserve records of important happenings. One of his records is dated in the Cāḷukya-Vikrama *Saṁvat* 42 = CE 1117-18, which is the date of his

1. See also De Souza and Kulkarni (ed.), *Historiography in Indian Languages*, pp. 60-61.

accession. The seat of Kākatīya government at the time was Anmakoṇḍa (Hanamkoṇḍa). From the time of Gaṇapati (1198-99) onwards Oruṅgallu (Warangal) continued to be the capital of Kākatīyas till the end of their rule in 1323. One of the Śaiva poets, Pālakuriki Somanātha (1200-40) of the Kākatīya period, was the author of 25 works. He wrote in Telugu, Kannada and Sanskrit. His two major works, *Basava Purāṇamu* and *Paṇḍitārādhyacaritra*, are the biographies of the two Śaiva prophets, Basaveśvara and Paṇḍitārādya, respectively. The works are important for the religious history of Āndhradeśa during the twelfth and thirteenth centuries. The *Raṅganātha Rāmāyaṇam* in Telugu by Gona Buddha Reḍḍī (1200-50) is a work of considerable importance for the history of the "Gona Haihaye" dynasty in Telangana, subordinate to the Kākatīyas.

Pratāparudradeva (1295-1323), the last great king of the Kākatīya dynasty, was immortalised by Vaidyanātha's *Pratāparudrīya* — a literary work dedicated to him. Pratāparudra submitted to Malik Kafur who was sent by Ala-ud-din Khilji in 1308 to besiege Warangal, the capital city of the Kākatīya kingdom. He was finally defeated and made prisoner in 1323 by Ulugh Khan who was sent by Ghiyas-ud-din Tughluq to invade and occupy Warangal. And eventually the Kākatīya kingdom formed part of the Delhi Sultanate.

The Muslim invasion at the beginning of the fourteenth century led to dismemberment of the Kākatīya kingdom. The feudatories became independent and established small kingdoms. The eastern part of Āndhra was ruled by the Reḍḍī kings during the fourteenth and fifteenth centuries (1323-1450) and they extended patronage to their court-poets. It is worthwhile to mention here that most of this line took the name Vema. The local rulers (Reḍḍīs) had formerly served under Pratāparudra.

Errapraggada, the court-poet of Prolayavema Reḍḍī (1325-54) of Koṇḍaviḍu, wrote *Bhārata* and *Narasiṁhapurāṇam* — important for the history of the Reḍḍīs of Koṇḍaviḍu. The most famous poet Śrīnātha (1365-1440 or 1402-20) was at the court of Vema (Komati). In his *Palnativiracarita*, he describes the incidents in the war of Palnad fought at Karempudi in the twelfth century between the two branches of the Haihayas of Palnad headed by brāhmaṇa Yadu and Nayakuralu (Nagama) resulting in the destruction and desolation of the country. His many works are important for the history of Reḍḍīs in Āndhradeśa and their relations with the contemporary rulers in the Deccan and south India — Bahamanīs of Gulbargā, the Velamas of Telangana, the Rāyas of Vijayanagara and the Eastern Gaṅgas of Kaliṅga. A biographical history was also written of the Reḍḍī kings of Āndhra (1403-20). This was Vāmanabhaṭṭa's *Vemabhūpālacarita* in Sanskrit composed early in the fifteenth century. Vāmana's work was also known as *Vīra-Nārāyaṇacarita*, for it contained a detailed biography (*ākhyāyikā*) of Peta Komati Vema also called Vīra-Nārāyaṇa. The author calls himself a "new Bāṇa." He closely follows Bāṇa's style of writing the historical biography (*Harṣacarita*) of his patron Harṣa. He was remembered by the posterity as a historian. His aim of writing the biography was to show the absolute legitimacy of Vema's claim to the throne which was disputed by Kātaya Vema. After securing the throne, Vema proceeds on an imperial career of conquest of the four directions described with much exaggeration by the author (Vāmana) thus further justifying his position by his valour and prowess.[2]

The Telugu poets of Āndhradeśa contributed a lot to the historical writings both in the ancient and medieval period.

2. See also Warder, *An Introduction to Indian Historiography*, pp. 119-23; De Souza and Kulkarni, op. cit., pp. 62 ff.

Vinnakota Peddana at the court of King Viśveśvara of the Cāḷukya dynasty of Elamanchili composed *Kāvyālaṁkāra-Cūḍāmaṇi* which is important for the history of Cāḷukyas and the achievements of Viśveśvara.

The poets of Āndhradeśa who adorned the court of kings of Vijayanagara also composed some works of historical value under the royal patronage. Nachana Somanātha, a court-poet of Bukkā of Vijayanagara, wrote *Uttaraharivaṁśamu* which basically deals with the history of the Saṅgama dynasty of Vijayanagara. His description of Narakāsura corresponds to the Muslim invader invading Warangal and indulging in plundering activities. Allasani Peddana (1475-1535), the poet laureate at the court of Kr̥ṣṇadevarāya (1509-30), the greatest king of Vijayanagara, wrote *Manucarita* which is important for the political history of Vijayanagara of his patron's time. Another work, *Rāyavācakamu* (anonymous), also provides a historical account of events of Kr̥ṣṇadevarāya's times. It contains several other details relating to the history of Vijayanagara empire.

Bhairava Kavi belonged to a family of ministers who served the Velamas and later the Bahamanīs. In his *Śrīraṅgah-Māhātvamu*, he describes the Bahamanī ruler Ala-ud-din Ahmad Shah II's invasion of Vijayanagara in 1443-44. The author has also highlighted the role of Viṭhala, an elder brother of Rāmadeva and in service of Saipha Khan, played in the warfare with Vijayanagara. Rāmadeva, a great warrior particularly in Bahamanī *sultān*'s campaigns of Vijayanagara, has been praised in the said work. The poets of Adidem family for 33 generations were in the service of the Pusapati chieftains, of the Gajapatis and earlier of the Rāyas of Vijayanagara. Poet Nilādrī in the service of Pusapati Immadi Tammirāju, a general of Kapileśvara (1458), participated in the wars of his lord and enumerated all his achievements in his work *Ranaraṅgavijayam*. The work narrates his conflicts with the Aśvapatis, Narapatis and Padmanāyakas. There are some other works which contain historical writings. Gaṅgaya played a prominent role in the wars between the Gajapatis and the Rāyas of Vijayanagara. The capture of King Narasiṁha Saluva of Vijayanagara in Udayagiri fort (in 1486) by Puruṣottama Gajapati was rendered possible due to the valour of Gaṅgaya. Narasiṁha Saluva was engaged in the fight with the king of Orissa for recovering some of the districts occupied by him. The details thereof are provided in *Prabodha-Candrodayam*. The work is useful for the study of the history of Vijayanagara.[3]

Telugu literature covers part of Vijayanagara history as well as Āndhra itself. It also includes some works of the fifteenth century bearing on other parts of Indian history. One of such notable works is Ananta's *Bhojarājiyam* which contains valuable information about the famous Paramāra king Bhoja of Mālwā (eleventh century) about whom details are available in the Jaina work *Prabandhacintāmaṇi* of Merutuṅga, a Gurjara historian (already noted before). In various literary works composed by the poets of Āndhradeśa, there are historical chapters on the families of their authors and patrons — kings of Āndhra and Vijayanagara.[4]

The history of Āndhradeśa, particularly of the Kākatīyas and their successors, is preserved in local Vaṁśāvalīs and other records.

The *Kākatīyarāja-Vaṁśāvalī* (first half of the sixteenth century) by Kāśeśvarappā speaks of the prevalent religious tension, the triumph of Śaivism over Buddhism and Jainism, the destruction of 36 Jaina *bastī*s at Hanamkoṇḍa and the expulsion of the Jainas from the Kākatīya kingdom. The work is an important source for the Kākatīya period narrating the

3. De Souza and Kulkarni, op. cit., pp. 64-71.
4. Warder, op. cit.

history of the thousand years in 225 stories. The *Aśvarāyacarita* by Śrīnathuni Veṅkaṭaramayya describes the wars between the Palancha estate (Warangal district) and Jafaruddaula (1698).[5]

The tradition of historical writing further continued in Āndhradeśa. The *Kākatīyacarita* (a biographical work) by Narasiṁham deals with the Kākatīya kings of Warangal.

The aforesaid works deal with contemporary social, political and religious history of Āndhradeśa and other parts of south India. They are of great use for reconstructing the histories of the Eastern Cāḷukyas of Veṅgī, the Rāṣṭrakūṭas, the Kākatīyas, the Reḍḍīs, Vijayanagara rulers and Gajapatis.

Some of the works with a direct historical bearing composed during the period from the seventeenth to the eighteenth centuries in Telugu also deserve our notice. *Somadevarajiyamu* by Kuchimanchi Jaggakavi is a historical work describing the lineage of Pratāparudradeva, the Kākatīya ruler of Warangal.

> *Raṅgarāyacarita*, a historical *Prabandha* by Ditta Kavi Nārāyaṇa Kavi, is dedicated to Malraju Ramarayaningaru, the Padmanāyaka Lord of Bellankoṇḍa Fort. It describes the historical battle between the ruler of Bobbili and the ruler of Vijayanagaram supported by the French led by Bussy (1757). . . . In *Rāyalasima Yathaślokatātparya Rāmāyaṇamu* by the court-poet of Gadwala Estate (Kurnool district) under the rule of Somagiri or Somabhūpāla (1704), the preface describes the extent and territorial divisions of the estate.[6]

Several of the estates in Āndhradeśa have their histories written by their court-poets.

Among the Vaṁśāvalīs or family-records mention may

5. De Souza and Kulkarni, op. cit., pp. 72-75.
6. Yasoda Devi, "History in Telugu Literature", in *History in Modern Indian Literature*, ed. S.P. Sen, p. 188.

be made of *Gandikota Yadasdar* of Pemmasani family, *Surapuram Rājavaṁśāvalī* of Surapuram estate in Telangana, and *Bobbilimahārāja Vaṁśāvalī* by Maṇḍapalli Prabatiswarakavi. They contain a good deal of historical information.[7]

7. Yasoda Devi, "History in Telugu Literature", in *History in Modern Indian Literature*, ed. S.P. Sen, p. 194.

6.4

Historiography in Kerala

THE historiographical tradition in Kerala began in the eleventh century CE with the composition of *Muṣikavaṁśa* (a dynastic history of the Muṣikas) by Atula.

The *Muṣikavaṁśa* (an epic consisting of fifteen cantos) was composed by the poet Atula in the time of Śrīkaṇṭha, his contemporary and the last king of the Muṣika dynasty. It is one of the historical works of early south India. The poet in his work narrates the history of the kings who ruled over the Muṣika kingdom in the northern part of Kerala (north Malabar). Rāmaghaṭa was one of the prominent rulers of this dynasty. Several cantos are devoted to his life and achievements. He is said to have killed Mādhavavarman, the king of Magadha, in a battle and married his daughter Bhadragenā. He installed the son of Mādhavavarman on the throne of Magadha. Rāmaghaṭa had two sons. The elder Vatu was made king of Māhiṣmati (called Haihayadeśa) and the younger Nandana king of the Coḷa kingdom. A brief description of all the kings from Nandana down to Īśānavarman II appears in Canto XI. But in the absence of their synchronisms it is not possible to get an absolute chronology for the more historical part of Atula's work mentioning a few notable events such as wars with the Pallavas, the founding of temples, etc. There seems to be a historical basis for most of the events described in this canto. The records and traditions of the temples which cherished the memories of certain kings as their founders also appear to have been the sources of information for Atula. He may have utilised them along with the dynastic lists preserved in the royal archives for the purpose concerned. Canto XII appears more historical than the earlier ones. It deals with the activities of fifteen kings of the dynasty in a continuous and more detailed manner. Īśānavarman II married a princess of the Kalacuri family ruling in the Dāhala region on the upper Narmadā and also claiming descent from the ancient Haihayas. "It does not seem likely that he could interfere much in Kalacuri politics, with the Rāṣṭrakūṭa empire dominating the vast region between the two small kingdoms, yet Atula credits him with an expedition there to instate his father-in-law. He was then engaged in a war with the king of Kerala (i.e. the central region of Kerala, round Vāñci or Mahodaya of early medieval period) who was his brother-in-law, but eventually the two were reconciled and concluded peace. Afterwards Īśānavarman married a Coḷa princess who produced an heir to the throne." From the time of King Validhara (Īśānavarman's grandson via the Kalacuri princess) the dynasty switched over to the matriarchal system of succession, characteristic of medieval Kerala. Validhara repulsed an invasion by the Gaṅgas (of Talkāḍ or Talavanapura in the Mysore district of Karnataka) from beyond the mountains which formed his inland frontier. We are further told that his nephew Vikramarāma protected the famous Buddhist temple at Mūlavāsa from the waves of the ocean by erecting a sea wall. Of Jayamaṇi II it is noted that there was religious toleration in the kingdom of the Muṣikas during his reign. The poet elucidates that there was perfect harmony among the followers of opposite doctrines. Cantos XIII and XIV describe the events that took place during the reign of Valabha II, nephew of Jayamaṇi III. In Canto XIV, it is clearly stated that Jayamaṇi sent Valabha II as heir apparent with an army to join the king of Kerala in opposing the advance of Coḷa king towards Kerala. It is most likely that the Coḷa king referred to in the text was Rājendra I (*c.* CE 1014-44). While marching to the south, Valabha learnt of Jayamaṇi's death and of usurpation of the throne. Valabha II was succeeded by his younger brother, Śrīkaṇṭha, whose prosperous reign is described in the fifteenth and last canto of the work.[1] The credit goes to the author of the work for saving the history of the Muṣika kingdom from passing into obscurity by recording and preserving it.

In Kerala, except the *Muṣikavaṁśa* no other historical work worth the name was ever composed in ancient period as far as our knowledge goes.

Medieval period (thirteenth to seventeenth centuries) witnessed a spectacular progress in the field of historical writing in Kerala. The literary works — *Maṇipravāḷam* (the Sandeśakāvyas and the Kāvyas) — ballads, chronicles and other records composed in Sanskrit during the period contain historical writing to a considerable extent.

The three *Maṇipravāḷa* works of the thirteenth century include *Unniyacicaritam, Unnicirutevicaritam* and *Unnyadicaritam.* The first was composed by poets patronised by a northern Kerala king, the second by a poet of central Kerala and the third by a poet patronised by Cochin king. These three represent *campū* form of literary composition with an admixture of Sanskrit and Malayalam. They throw light on contemporary socio-cultural and political life of the people of Kerala. They refer to enmity of the petty chieftains. There are also some passing references to Hoysaḷa kingdom of Mysore.[2]

---

1. Warder, *An Introduction to Indian Historiography*, pp. 110-12; Krishnamachariar, *HCSL*, p. 170.
2. De Souza and Kulkarni (ed.), *Historiography in Indian Languages*, p. 114.

The latter half of the fourteenth century marked the beginning of a new phase in the history of historical writing in Kerala. That was the phase of paying serious attention to the presentation of historical facts in a literary composition.

Uṇṇunilisandeśam, the most celebrated of *sandeśa kāvyas*, was written by an anonymous author in about 1385. It throws light on the political achievements of the Venāḍa (south Travancore) rulers, Ravi Varmā (1350-75) and Āditya Varmā (1376-83). The work contains valuable historical information regarding the local kingdom of Venāḍa (with its capital at Quilon) and the petty principalities of Oḍanāḍa and Vaḍakkumkur. The author (poet) of this *kāvya* provides a lot of information about the fall of the second Cera empire, the attempt of Ravi Varmā of Venāḍa to carve out a southern empire, the Muslim attacks on the southern part of Kerala and the propagation of Hindu religion in the temples by depicting stories from the *Mahābhārata*. We are told that the brāhmaṇas were held in high esteem. The author portrays a vivid picture of the life of *devadāsīs*. We are informed that they enjoyed a high social status during the thirteenth and fourteenth centuries. The social institutions, agriculture and other professions, dress and ornaments of men and women, temples and festivals and religious beliefs and practices also received the attention of the author of the work. He has provided an accurate historical description of internal and external trade and commerce. We learn from this work that Quilon port was famous for its foreign trade especially with China. Art and architecture have also been focused upon in the work.[3] The description of the varied subjects reflects the historical perception as well as historical sense of the author of the work. The work on the whole gives us insights into socio-

3. De Souza and Kulkarni (ed.), *Historiography in Indian Languages*, pp. 114-16; also V. Kochu Krishnan, "History in Malayalam Literature", in *History in Modern Indian Literature*, ed. S.P. Sen, p. 217.

economic, political, religious and cultural life of the people during the period. It is, no doubt, of immense use for enriching our historical knowledge of the subjects dealt with.

Dāmodara (fourteenth century) was the court-poet of the prince Keralavarman of Kāyankula, a feudatory of the king of central Kerala (capital Mahodaya). He wrote an epic, the *Śivavilāsa*, in eight cantos. Though it preserves a picture of the political situation in Kerala in the fourteenth century, it is more important for social than for political history providing numerous incidental details of the life of the ruling families of the period, social life, the matriarchal system, cultural life and so on.

Kokasandeśam (one of the *sandeśa kāvya*s of the fifteenth century by an anonymous author) has a bearing on the history of northern Kerala in the fifteenth century. It provides historical information especially about the Zamorins (the Hindu *rājā*s of Calicut). We are told that one section of brāhmaṇas (Panniyur) lent support to one of the powerful Zamorin kings for the expansion of his empire. He had successfully extended the limits of his empire up to Cochin in the early quarters of the fifteenth century. During the fourteenth and in the beginning of the fifteenth centuries, the Zamorins of Calicut had several poets in their courts noted for their deep knowledge of Sanskrit. The only poet who composed poems in Malayalam was Punam Namboodari. His *Rāmāyaṇam* is in the *campū* form. The prose section of this work furnishes some historical data regarding social and cultural life in the realms of the Zamorians. The *Rājarathnavaliyam Campū* was composed by Nārāyaṇan in the latter half of the sixteenth century in praise of one Keśavarāja Varmā (1565-1601) of Cochin. It throws light on certain historical aspects of Cochin.[4]

4. De Souza and Kulkarni, op. cit., p. 117.

The *Keralolpatti* is another literary work of some historical value. It is in the form of a chronicle. It contains both historical facts and legendary tales. It appears to be based on old narratives current in Kerala and handed down, extended and revised through the centuries until we find it current in several different recensions in the modern Malayalam language. In modern form, it belongs to the sixteenth century and is often ascribed to Cunchat Ezhuttachan, the father of modern Malayalam literature. But, in fact, he is neither author nor editor of the *Keralolpatti*. It is of anonymous authorship. It serves to connect the ancient and medieval history of Kerala to the Purāṇic history of ancient India. It begins with the Paraśurāma tradition and Aryan settlements in 64 selected villages. It partly deals with the origin and early culture of Kerala. It records the colonisation of Kerala by brāhmaṇas and organisation of society there under their inspiration. The description of the early kingdoms of the Saṅgam period known to us from the other sources seems to be little vague. The information supplied to us about the political system in Kerala is, however, reliable to a considerable extent. The tradition recorded in the work tells us that the earliest form of government was monarchy, but some kind of popular revolution overthrew the kings and established a republic which elected rulers known as "protectors" (*rakṣāpuruṣa*). The state was governed by a cabinet of five protectors, one of whom acted as president and was elected for a term of 12 years, whilst the other four were elected for a period of three years and were responsible for smooth functioning of the republic. But after some time the republican system began to decline, because some of the protectorate assumed arbitrary powers and caused disaffection among the people leading to dissension and factions. Finally the protectorate lost the confidence of the people, and consequently a new system was introduced, according to which, the president given the title Perumāḷ was invested with power to rule the state. The first Perumāḷ Keya is supposed to have been appointed in CE 216, though date is contested. The Perumāḷ period, according to some, began much later. This system appears to have been successful and to have endured for a long period. At least 25 Perumāḷs are recorded in the tradition preserved in the said chronicle. The Perumāḷs and apparently the protectors before them seem to have ruled from Vāñci near medieval Mahodaya and modern Cochin. The *Keralolpatti* tradition does not carry the history beyond the last Perumāḷ Ceramān. The Perumāḷ kings of Kerala of whom little is authentically known find mention at least in this work. It appears that the Perumāḷs were followed directly by the kings of Kulaśekhara dynasty who ruled from Mahodaya but no connected history of this dynasty seems to have been preserved. The *Keralamāhātmya*, a collection of local antiquities, is more or less a recension of the *Keralolpatti*.[5]

The historical ballads of the seventeenth century also deserve mention here. One of the most important ballads of south Kerala is *Iravikkuṭṭipilla Pāṭṭu*. The story of the poem centres round Iravikkuṭṭi Pillai, a general of Ravivarmā Kulaśekharan of Travancore, who met a tragic end in his encounter with Ramappayyan, a general sent by Tirumāḷa Naikan of Madurai to conquer Travancore. The hero is depicted as a true patriotic warrior. The poem gives glimpses of the political history of the day. The second one is *Anchuthampurān Pāṭṭu* relating to the life of some seventeenth-century rulers of Travancore. The *Padapāṭṭu* composed by an anonymous poet during the period from 1646 to 1670 describes the struggle of succession among the princes of the Cochin dynasty. The poem tells us that of the five

5. Warder, op. cit., pp. 108-10; see also De Souza and Kulkarni, op. cit., p. 203.

princesses in the lineage of the Perumāḷs only the youngest had a son who secured the right to the throne of Cochin. It also deals with the political development of Cochin during the Dutch hegemony in Kerala. Katanceri Namboodari, the court-poet of Manavikrama, composed *Mamankam Kilipāṭṭu* which is an invaluable historical document giving much information regarding the early history of Calicut. The ballads of the north are important more for social than political history of northern Kerala. They provide detailed description of the feudal households, the daily life of the womenfolk of these households, the powers and rights enjoyed by women in a matriarchal society, etc. The feudal chieftains are said to have lived their life of luxury by levying various kinds of taxes. The ballads of north Malabar in particular are a mine of information on the social and political aspects of northern Kerala.[6]

It is to be noted here that except *Śivavilāsa* and *Keralamāhātmya* (the Sanskrit texts) all other works mentioned here were written in Malayalam.

6. V. Kochu Krishnan, op. cit., p. 218; De Souza and Kulkarni, op. cit., p. 118.

Book Seven
Chronological Traditions

Prefatory Remarks

CHRONOLOGY is an integral or important part of history. The former is not only an eye but also the backbone of the latter. Highlighting the importance of chronology in the context of historiography, P.K. Gode said: "Wrong chronology produced wrong history and want of chronology produced no history."[1] While dealing with history of historical writing in ancient and medieval India, we cannot keep aside the chronology. The ancient Indians had maintained both historical and chronological traditions. Different systems of chronology seem to have been followed by the Hindus, Buddhists and Jainas. The Hindus and Jains maintained their chronological tradition in medieval period too. The statement made by Sir William Jones in 1788 that the chronological system of the Hindus is neither authentic nor systematic[2] is no longer valid. John Bentley, while writing on the eras and dates of the ancient Hindus in 1796, also observed: ". . . the confusion and darkness that pervade the Hindu chronology" may precisely be attributed to the "ignorance of modern Hindus who are not able to discern the difference between the several eras and modes of dating which were made use of by their ancient historians. Brāhmaṇas and poets in recording past events have blended the whole together into one mass of absurdity and contradiction. It is not easy to describe the meaning of all the

1. Cf. S.R. Tikekar, *On Historiography*, p. 52.
2. "On the Chronology of the Hindus", *As Res.*, vol. 2 (Delhi, 1979), pp. 111-12; see also Bühler, "Hindu Chronology", in *En. Br.*, vol. 13 (211th edn.), pp. 499-500.

different modes of dating formerly in use."[3] His observation was obviously an attempt to prove that the chronological method applied by the ancient Hindu historians of India cannot be easily understood today by the modern Hindus because of its certain intricacies. But his attempt proved to be a failure. It is to be noted here that dates and eras were used in ancient and medieval India for chronological calculation and computation. It is unworthy of credence that "the chronology has been disturbed by the scholars of the Brāhmanical historical schools." The statement of a celebrated American Sanskrit scholar, W.D. Whitney, that "All dates given in Indian literary history are pins set up to be bowled down again"[4] is also not tenable. There is, however, some scope to re-examine the authenticity of Indian traditional chronology.

There were three traditions of chronology — Purāṇic, Buddhist and Jaina. There were definitely some chronologists amongst the *purāṇakāras*, Buddhists and Jainas as appears from the chronological data furnished by them. The chronological records were preserved by them. Their chronological conceptions are well reflected in the dates of the past events they have preserved. A critical combination of Purāṇic, Buddhist and Jaina chronology provides us the solid basis for chronological reconstruction of Indian history from the sixth century BCE to the early third century CE. By effecting compromise between different systems of chronology we can obtain positive result. The dates of some events given by the Jaina writers of Medieval Age are historically authenticated.

Some of the eras which were in use in ancient and medieval India have also chronological significance.

---

3. "On the Principal Eras and Dates of the Ancient Hindus", *As. Res.*, vol. 5 (Delhi, 1979), p. 315.
4. Cf. M. Winternitz, *HIL*, vol. I, p. 25; Tikekar, op. cit.

7.1

The Purāṇic Tradition of Chronology

ONE of the most important traditions of chronology is the Purāṇic one.

The regnal years of the kings of various dynasties of the post-Bhārata war period or so-called Kaliyuga and the total duration of each dynastic rule are given in the Purāṇas (*Vāyu, Viṣṇu, Matsya, Brahmāṇḍa* and *Bhāgavata*) which are helpful for chronological computation to fix the dates of the end of one dynasty and the beginning of the other and determine the reign-periods of the rulers and the dynasties.

The length of reign of all 22 kings of the Bārhadratha dynasty who ruled over Magadha is given separately in Purāṇas[1] with some variations. After having accepted the figures which appear reasonable we find that they altogether ruled approximately for 638 years. The length of reign of all five kings (from Pradyota to Avantivardhana) of Pradyota dynasty who ruled over Avantī kingdom are also given in the Purāṇas. They are said to have ruled for 138 years.[2] According to our calculation, they ruled either for 100 or 102 years (513-413 or 411 BCE).

The regnal years of kings of following six Magadhan

1. *Vy.*, 99.294-308; *Vṣṇ.*, IV.23, 1-13; *Mts.*, 271.18-30; *Bmd*; III.74, 107-21; *Bhāg.*, IX.22, 46-49.
2. *Vy.*, 99.308-14; *Vṣṇ.*, IV.24, 1-8; *Mts.*, 272.1-5; *Bmd.*, III.74, 121-25; *Bhāg.*, XII.I, 2-4; see also *EIHTA*, pp. 155-57; S.N. Pradhan, *Chro. Ancient India.*, p. 245.

dynasties are also given in the Purāṇas with total duration of rule of each dynasty.

The length of reign of all ten kings belonging to the dynasties of Bimbisāra and Śiśunāga are given with variations. It appears that they altogether ruled for 303, 360 or 362 years.[3] The total duration of their rule has gone high because of some bombastic or inflated figures. And this is the reason why it is not taken as trustworthy. It is generally believed that they ruled for not more than 200 years. The nine Nandas are said to have ruled for 40 or 100 years.[4] In reality, only two of them, the first (Mahāpadmānanda, the founder of the dynasty) and the last (Dhanānanda) were the reigning kings. We can reasonably assign 22 years to them, and accordingly 343-321 BCE can be taken as their reign period. According to Purāṇic tradition, a period of 1050 years had elapsed between the birth of Parīkṣit and the coronation of Mahāpadmānanda[5] which is the sheet-anchor of ancient Indian chronology. This figure is applied in various ways to fix the date of the Great Bhārata battle. For instance, some scholars taking 350 BCE as the date of coronation of Mahāpadmānanda fix (1050 + 350) 1400 BCE as the date of the battle.

Max Müller's statements that "Everything in Indian chronology depends on the date of Candragupta. . . . All the dates before him are to be considered only as hypothetical,"[6] and the observation made by E.M.

3. *Vy.*, 99.314-21; *Vṣṇ.*, IV.24, 9-19; *Mts.*, 272.5-13; *Bmd.*, III.74, 127-33; *Bhāg.*, XII.I, 5-7; see also *EIHTA*, pp. 162, 169; Pradhan, op. cit., p. 228; *PK*, p. 496; H.C. Raychaudhuri, PHAI, p. 228.

4. *Vy.*, 99.321-28; *Vṣṇ.*, IV.24, 20-24; *Mts.*, 272.14-21; *Bmd.*, III.74, 139-44; *Bhāg*; XII.I, 8-11; also *EIHTA*, pp. 170-71; *PK*, 407.

5. *Vy.*, 99.415; *Vṣṇ.*, IV.24, 104; *Mts.*, 273.36; see also *Bmd.*, III.74, 225-30; *Bhāg.*, XII.2, 26-32.

6. *HASL*, pp. 245, 268.

Elphinstone in 1839 that in ancient Indian history no date before the invasion of Alexander the Great (326 BCE) can be fixed with absolute certainty[7] contain some substratum of truth. V.A. Smith also for some time went on harping on the same tune,[8] but later he himself admitted that "the researches of multitude of scholars and antiquarians have rendered it possible to fix the considerable number of dates in pre-Alexandrian period (extending from 600 to 326 BCE) with approximate accuracy as well as to reconstruct the obscure history of ancient India . . . with the help of literary tradition."[9] There is no denying the fact that all the dates in ancient Indian history of pre-Bimbisāra period are either hypothetical or tentative but the dates of some kings of pre-Maurya dynasties of Magadha fixed on the basis of Purāṇic length of their reigns are reliable. It is true that the date of coronation of Candragupta Maurya can be taken as the starting point for calculating the Indian chronology.

The Purāṇas have provided authentic chronology of the Mauryas, Śuṅgas and Kaṇvas on the basis of which the reign period of each individual ruler of these three dynasties as well as the total duration of each dynastic rule can be worked out.

Of the 10 Mauryas, nine were the actual rulers whose regnal years are given almost uniformly in the Purāṇas. Candragupta is said to have ruled for 24 years (321–297 BCE), Bindusāra for 25 years (297–272 BCE), Aśoka for 36 years + 4 years before he was crowned and thus total for 40 years (272–232 BCE), Kuṇāla for 8 years (232–224 BCE), Daśaratha (or Bandhupālita) for 8 years (224–216 BCE), Samprati (or Indrapālita) for 10 years (216–206 BCE), (Śāliśuka, according to some Purāṇas, did not reign as the crown did not devolve

7. E.B. Cowell (ed.), *The History of India*, 9th edn. (London, 1911), p. 11.

8. *EHI*, 4th revd. edn., p. 1.

9. Ibid., pp. 4, 10-11.

upon him), Devavarman (or Somaśarman) for 7 years (206–199 BCE) and Bṛhadratha (the last king) for 7 years (191–184 BCE). They are said to have ruled for (133 + the said 4 years) 137 years (321–184 BCE)[10] which is perfectly accurate.

Puṣyamitra, the founder of the Śuṅga dynasty, is said to have reigned for 36 years (184–148 BCE), Agnimitra for 8 years (as a viceroy at Vidiśā during the lifetime or period of his father), Vasujyeṣṭha (or Sujyeṣṭha) for 7 years (148–141 BCE), Vasumitra for 10 years (141–131 BCE), Odraka for 2 years (131–129 BCE), Pulindaka for 3 years (129–126 BCE), Ghoṣa for 3 years (126–123 BCE), Vajramitra for 9 years (123–114 BCE), Bhāgavata for 32 years (114–82 BCE), and Devabhūti for 10 years (82–72 BCE). These0 10 Śuṅga kings (all brāhmaṇas) altogether reigned for (120–8 =) 112 years (i.e 184–72 BCE)[11] which is absolutely correct.

Vasudeva, the founder of the Kaṇva dynasty, is said to have reigned for 9 years (72–63 BCE), Bhūmimitra for 14 years (63–49 BCE), Nārāyaṇa for 12 years (49–37 BCE) and Suśarman for 10 years (37–27 BCE). The four Kaṇva kings (also brāhmaṇas) reigned exactly for 45 years (72–27 BCE).[12]

The reliability of Purāṇic tradition of chronology in respect of the Maurya, Śuṅga and Kaṇva dynasties can hardly be doubted. The length of reigns of the kings of these three dynasties and total duration of their rule as given in the Purāṇas are generally accepted by the historians of ancient India. Pargiter, while throwing light on early Indian

---

10. *Vy.*, 99.331-36; *Vṣṇ.*, IV.24, 29-32; *Mts.*, 272.22-26; *Bmd.*, III.74, 145-49; *Bhāg.*, XII.I, 12-15; also *EIHTA*, pp. 177, 180; *PK*, p. 434; R.S. Tripathi, *HAI*, p. 182; Pargiter, *PDKA*, pp. 28-30.
11. *Vy.*, 99.343-42; *Vṣṇ.*, IV.24, 33-37; *Mts.*, 272.26-33; *Bmd.*, III.74, 150-55; *Bhāg.*, XII.I, 16-18; also *EIHTA*, pp. 180-81; Tripathi, op. cit., p. 190.
12. *Vy.*, 99.343-47; *Vṣṇ.*, IV.24, 38-42; *Mts.*, 272.32-37; *Bmd.*, III.74, 155-60; *Bhāg.*, XII.I, 19-21; *EIHTA*, p. 182.

traditional history and chronology as recorded in Purāṇas, observes that the Purāṇas furnish details of dates to an extent that even in days of historical records may be surprising, for they mention even months and days in their computation. Whatever those ancient authors did or wrote, they did it with sincerity and accuracy, "truth" being the basis of accuracy. Our educational institutions are saturated with the teachings of modern scholars on the untruth of these Purāṇic accounts, but it is still hoped that time will come when truth will triumph and display a real orientation of ancient Indian history."[13]

The length of reign of each individual ruler of the Āndhra or Sātavāhana dynasty is also given in the Purāṇas with little variations. The total duration of reigns of 30 kings of this dynasty (from Śimuka to Pulumāvi IV) comes to 456 or 460 years.[14] It is further stated in some Purāṇas that a period of 836 years intervened between Mahāpadmānanda and the last Āndhra king Pulumāvi.[15] According to this chronological data, the Āndhras' rule began 376 years after the Nanda and lasted for 460 years (376+460=836). There is a great controversy among the authorities on ancient Indian history with regard to the dates of beginning and end of this dynasty. Some scholars relying on the Purāṇic testimony that the Āndhras ruled for about four centuries-and-a-half assign the beginning of their power to the last quarter of the third century BCE and its end to the first quarter of the third century CE. The generally accepted view is that their rule began some

13. "Earliest Indian Traditional History," *JRAS*, 1914, p. 267; see also his "Ancient Indian Genealogies and Chronology", *JRAS*, 1910, pp. 26 ff.

14. Vy., 99.348-58; *Vṣṇ.*, IV.24, 43-50; *Mts.*, 273.1-17; *Bmd.*, III.74, 160-70; *Bhāg.*, XII.I, 22-28; for details see *EIHTA*, pp. 183-85.

15. *Vy.*, 99.416-17; *Mts.*, 273.37; *Vṣṇ.*, IV.24, 105-07; *Bmd.*, III.74, 230-36; see also *EIHTA*, p. 186.

time in the first century CE and continued till about the end of the first quarter of the third century CE. Whatever may be the fact regarding the duration of their rule, the Purāṇic regnal years of some kings of proven historical identity are consistent with their inscriptions found in western India (Maharashtra).

The chronological data about various kings and dynasties of the post-Sātavāhana period supplied in the Purāṇas in an incidental or interspersed manner are not very credible. According to a tradition preserved in the *Bhaviṣya Purāṇa,* the seven Gupta kings reigned for 245 years. But the fact remains that in the imperial Gupta line there were 12 or 13 kings (from Śrīgupta to Bhānugupta who altogether reigned for 235 years (CE 275-510).

The Purāṇic chronology is partly reliable. And it has, no doubt, some historical value. Further, the length of reigns of some rulers and the total duration of rule of some dynasties given in the Purāṇas are absolutely correct.

Macdonell's view that the ancient Indian Sanskrit literature "suffers from an entire absence of exact chronology . . . and definite dates do not begin to appear in the Indian history till about CE 500,"[16] can outrightly be rejected.

J.W. McCrindle's statement that early Indian history of pre-Candragupta period "had not a single chronological landmark of its own,"[17] can also be disposed of.

---

16. *HSL*, pp. 10 f.
17. *AIMA*, p. 7, fn.

7.2

Chronological System in the time of Candragupta Maurya

THE information supplied by the classical (Greek and Roman) writers regarding the traditional chronological beliefs of the Indians in the fourth century BCE also deserves our notice. It was first the Greek historian Megasthenes who recorded in his *Indika* the chronological beliefs that prevailed in those days in India. Some of the Greek and Roman writers of the subsequent period derived their information about those beliefs from the said work of Megasthenes.

During his five years' stay (303-298 BCE) at the imperial court of Candragupta Maurya in Pāṭaliputra, the Greek ambassador Megasthenes gathered information from various sources about the ancient history of the Indians and their chronological system down to his time. Megasthenes' statement (*Indika*, Fragam, L.C.), that the reigns of 153 Indian kings down to the time of Alexander the Great extended over 6451 years and 3 months has been recorded by Pliny,[1] the Roman geographer and historian of the first century CE. The same statement has been recorded by a Roman writer, Solinus,[2] who flourished in the first half of the third century CE. He actually copied it from Pliny's *Naturalis Historia* (*Natural History*).

---

1. *Hist. Nat.*, VI, xxi, 4-5, J.W. McCrindle's *AIMA*, p. 115; also *Nat. Hist.*, VI, 17 (21), McCrindle's *AICL*, p. 108; R.C. Majumdar, *CAI*, p. 340.
2. *Collectanea Rerum Memorabilium*, 52.5, Majumdar, *CAI*, p. 457; McCrindle's *AIMA*, p. 115.

The famous Greek historian, Arrian (second century CE) informs us that from the time of Dionysos to Sandrakottos (Candragupta), the Indians counted 153 kings, and a period of 6042 years. Dionysos was earlier than Heracles by fifteen generations.[3] The said 153 kings, who had preceded Candragupta, are said to have reigned for a period of 6042 years, which is at variance with the period recorded by Megasthenes, Pliny and Solinus. The Purāṇic genealogies and chronology of pre-Candragupta period are, however, greatly supported by the classical evidence.[4]

McCrindle observes: "It is not known from what sources Megasthenes derived these figures, which are extremely modest when compared with those of Indian chronology."[5] He also states that "Pliny and Arrian were indebted for . . . details to Megasthenes, who evidently endeavoured to bring the chronology of the brāhmaṇas into some degree of correspondence with that of his countrymen."[6]

Dealing with traditional Indian chronology, R.C. Jain mentions the chronological date of the classical writers. He also asserts that Megasthenes knew the Indian tradition of chronology. He says: "It appears that the traditional history began to take some shape in the third century BCE."[7]

C.V. Vaidya is of the opinion that the historicity of Dionysos may be doubted but it is admitted by all that Heracles possessing two large cities, Methora and Cleisobara (Mathurā and Kṛṣṇapura of Vṛndāvana) was no other than Hari of Śrī Kṛṣṇa. According to him, "Since there were 153

3. *Indika*, I, IX, McCrindle's *AIMA*, pp. 203-04.
4. See also F. Wilford, "Chronology of the Hindus", *As. Res.* V (Delhi, 1979), pp. 291-2.
5. *AIMA*, p. 203, fn.
6. *AICL*, p. 108, note 1.
7. *EAB*, p. 203.

generations from Dionysos to Candragupta, and Dionysos was 15 generations earlier than Heracles, it follows that Heracles preceded Candragupta by 138 generations of kings. . . . Such was the tradition prevalent in India in 312 BCE (Candragupta's time), i.e. at a time when European scholars are agreed that the Indians had not learnt or discovered the methods of calculating the position of planets. That the inquisitive Greek ambassador at the court of Candragupta has left carefully sifted information about India without exaggeration or fabrication has also been admitted. The only possible way in which the above tradition may be impeached is by supposing that the Indians themselves had exaggerated notions about their antiquity."[8]

8. *The Mahābhārata: A Criticism*, p. 58.

7.3

The Buddhist Tradition of Chronology

THE Buddhist tradition of chronology is no less significant than the Purāṇic one. The chronology of Magadhan rulers from Bimbisāra to Aśoka is of special importance.

According to a Pāli commentary, *Sāmantapāsādikā*, Bimbisāra's son, Ajātasattu (Ajātaśatru), reigned for 24 years. The Buddha is said to have passed away in the eighth year of his reign. Udāyi Bhadda reigned for 16 years, Anuruddha and Muṇḍa jointly for 18 years, Nāgadāsaka for 24 years, Śiśunāga for 18 years, Kālāśoka for 28 years and his 10 sons, including Nandivardhana, altogether for 22 years, the Nandas for 22 years, Candagutta (Candragupta) for 24 years and Bindusāra for 28 years.[1] Asoka (Aśoka) is said to have reigned without coronation for four years.[2]

The chronology in the two Pāli chronicles, *Dīpavaṁsa* and *Mahāvaṁsa*, is little different from that in the said commentary.

According to the *Dīpavaṁsa*, Bimbisāra reigned for 52 years, Udāyi Bhadda for 16 years and ten sons of Kālāśoka for 22 years. Candragupta Maurya is said to have ascended the throne of Magadha 162 years after the death of Buddha (i.e. 483-162 = in 321 BCE) and ruled for 24 years (i.e. till 297 BCE).[3] We are also told that Aśoka was formally crowned as a

1. *Sāmantapāsādika*, I, pp. 72-73; see also B.C. Law, *The Magadhas in Ancient India*, p. 3, note 3.
2. *Sāmantapāsādika*, p. 41.
3. *Dīp.*, III, 50-60; V, 97.

king 218 years after the death of the Buddha (i.e. 483-218 = in 265 BCE).[4] The chronology given in this chronicle is apparently a broken one.

According to the *Mahāvaṁsa*, Bimbisāra ruled for 52 years (543-491 BCE) and his son, Ajātasattu, for 32 years (491-459 BCE). In the eighth year of the reign of the latter Buddha died (i.e. in 483 BCE). Ajātasattu's son and successor, Udāyi Bhadda, ruled for 16 years, Anuruddha and his son Muṇḍa for 8 years, Nāgadāsaka for 24 years, Śiśunāga (Śiśupāla) for 18 years, and his son Kālāśoka for 28 years and 10 sons of the latter, including Nandivardhana and Mahānandin, altogether for 22 years. These 10 kings in the line of Bimbisāra and Śiśunāga altogether ruled for 200 years. The nine Nandas are said to have reigned for 22 years. Candragupta Maurya reigned for 24 years and his son Bindusāra for 28 years.[5] This chronicle also states that Aśoka's coronation took place 218 years after the death of the Buddha (i.e. in 265 BCE).[6] There is another evidence to show that his coronation did not take place until 269 BCE.[7]

The Buddhist scholar, Aśvaghoṣa, gives the length of reign of the Magadhan rulers from Bimbisāra to Mahānandin which are as follows:

Bimbisāra (28 years), Ajātasattu (25 years), Darśaka (24 years), Udāyin (33 years), Nandivardhana (24 years) and Mahānandin (24 years).[8]

---

4. *Dīp.*, VI, 1.
5. *Mhv.*, ed. W. Geiger, II.28-32; IV.1-8; V.14-15; tr. Geiger, pp. 12, 15, 21, 163 f, 168 f; see also *EIHTA*, pp. 162, 178; S.N. Pradhan, *Chro. Ancient India.*, pp. 228, 245; P.L. Bhargava, *Chandaragupta Maurya: A Gem of Indian History*, pp. 6-7.
6. *Mhv.* (ed.), V, 21.
7. Ibid. (tr.) p. 28.
8. *Buddhacarita*, XI, 2.

Max Müller has correctly stated that there are "more than one system of Buddhist chronology," but his view, that "none of them can be considered authentic with regard to the times previous to Aśoka . . .,"[9] is untenable.

It is significant to point out that there is neither synchronism in the Purāṇic and Buddhist genealogical lists of kings of Bimbisāra and Śiśunāga dynasties nor parallelism between the two chronologies with regard to the regnal years of the kings of these two dynasties and duration of their rule. In fact, the Buddhist chronology in respect of these two dynasties and the Nanda dynasty is more reliable than the Purāṇic one. According to Buddhist chronology, the 10 rulers belonging to the dynasties of Bimbisāra and Śiśunāga reigned altogether for 200 years (543-343 BCE), and the nine Nandas for 22 years (343-321 BCE), which are corrective to the Purāṇic duration of their rule given before. Candragupta Maurya has been assigned 24 years (321-297 BCE) as a length of his reign which perfectly agrees with Purāṇic chronology. By striking a compromise between the two traditions of chronology — Purāṇic and Buddhist — we can fix the reign periods of two other Maurya rulers, Bindusāra and Aśoka. According to Buddhist historical tradition, Bimbisāra ruled for 28 years (297-269 BCE), and Aśoka ascended the throne in 269 BCE and ruled for four years as an uncrowned king and then further ruled after being formally crowned as a king in *c*. 265 BCE. In the Purāṇic tradition, Bindusāra is said to have reigned for 25 years (297-272 BCE) and Aśoka for 36 years (after his coronation). In case of Bindusāra, it is the Purāṇic length of reign which is acceptable and not the Buddhist one. Taking Aśoka's rule four years before and 36 years after his coronation we find that he ruled exactly for 40 years (272-232 BCE), as noted before.

9. *HASL*, p. 235.

7.4

The Jaina Tradition of Chronology

THE chronological traditions of the Jainas appear somewhat different from those of the Hindus and Buddhists. The Jaina chronology is not very systematic. It is rather fragmentary. It has, however, some considerable value.

> "... the ancient Jains seemed to have a love for dates and exactness which is evident from their numerous pontifical genealogies and dynastic chronologies, the dated colophons of their works and of the latter's successive manuscript copies, the historical and even pre-historical traditions recorded with corresponding dates and periods in later works, and from their inscriptional records which reach back to the fifth century BCE."[1]

> "In fact, the Jaina sources have a superiority over other sectarian sources in so far as chronology is concerned, especially for the history of ancient India. With their aid many an unknown or doubtful date can be fixed, while those already fixed can further be confirmed."[2]

K.P. Jayaswal once remarked that "among the Hindus the Jains alone have preserved a complete and admirable chronology for the two and a half thousand years or so after Mahāvīra's death."[3] Bühler also speaks very highly of the historical value and authenticity of Jaina traditions.[4]

---

1. J.P. Jain, *The Jaina Sources of the History of Ancient India (100* BCE *–* CE *900)*, p.3.
2. Ibid., pp. 3-4.
3. *JSS*, I, 4, p. 211, cf. ibid., p. 3.
4. "On the Authenticity of Jaina Traditions", in *The Indian Sect.*

→

The Jains themselves have preserved chronological records of ancient kings and dynasties. It seems that when their dynastic lists were put into their present form, the real date of Mahāvīra (599-468 BCE) had already either been forgotten or was at least doubtful. And his traditional date (599-527 BCE) was adopted. The traditional date of Mahāvīra's *nirvāṇa* on which the Jainas base their chronological calculations corresponds to the year 470 before the foundation of the Vikrama Era in 57 BCE, i.e. 527 BCE (ME). The Jains have given the dynastic chronology in this ME which is partly correct. It is only Hemacandra (CE 1125-72), the author of *Pariśiṣṭaparvan* (*Sthavirāvalīcarita*), who have applied different dates of Mahāvīra's *nirvāṇa*, including 468 and 467 BCE, for chronological calculations which give us better results than those based on traditional date.[5]

There are some Jaina records of dynastic chronology. The regnal years of individual rulers and total length of reigns of some dynasties are given therein.

According to Jaina tradition, simultaneously with *nirvāṇa* of Mahāvīra, Pālaka, the son of King Caṇḍapradyota of Ujjayinī, was crowned. In both Digambara and Śvetāmbara traditions, he is said to have ruled for 60 years. The former tradition is recorded in Yativr̥ṣabha's *Tiloyapaṇṇatti* (IV.95-96) and Jinasena's *Harivaṁśa* (60.487-88) and the latter in old Prākr̥t text, *Titthogāli-painna* (vv. 620-21), the *Tapāgaccha Paṭṭāvalī* (vv. 1-2) and some other *paṭṭāvalīs* (*Paṭṭāvalī-Samuccaya*, I, p. 197). The *Tīrthoddhāra-Prakaraṇa* also contains the same regnal years. We are also informed that in the period of 60 years allotted to Pālaka, Kūṇika (Ajātaśatru) and Udāyi were ruling at Pāṭaliputra (*Paṭṭāvalī-*

→ *of the Jains* (tr. Dr. Burgess, London, 1903). pp. 21-23, cf. Jain, op. cit., p. 3.

5. See also J. Charpentier, "The History of the Jains", in *CHI*, I, *Ancient India*, ed. E.J. Rapson, p. 139.

Samuccaya, I, p. 17). The contemporaneity of Pālaka of Avantī and Ajātaśatru of Magadha can be established also on the basis of Purāṇic chronology.

Hemacandra of Śvetāmbara school is in perfect agreement with all other Jaina scholars in stating that the rule of Nanda dynasty commenced 60 years after the death of Mahāvīra. He further says that this dynasty ruled for 95 years (*Pariśiṣṭaparvan*, VI.243). From the *Tapāgaccha-Paṭṭāvalī* (v. 2) and the *Tīrthoddhāra-Prakaraṇa* it appears that the rule of this dynasty ended 155 years after the *nirvāṇa* of Mahāvīra. Thus, the first king (Mahāpadmānanda) of this dynasty began his rule in (477-60) 417 BCE. He and his descendants continued to rule Magadha till the last king was deposed by Cāṇakya 155 years after the death of Mahāvīra which comes to (477–155) 322 BCE. They ruled from 417 BCE to 322 BCE which covers a period of 95 years (417–322 or 155–60). The *Paṭṭāvalī-Samuccaya* gives 155 years to the reign of the Nandas in ME.

Hemacandra differs from all other Jaina scholars, Digambara or Śvetāmbara earlier or later than himself, so far as the date of Candragupta Maurya's accesion to the throne of Magadha is concerned. According to him, he became king 155 years after the *nirvāṇa* of Mahāvīra (*Pariśiṣṭaparvan*, VIII, 339). Basing the calculation on the dates of Mahāvīra's *nirvāṇa* as given by him we find that his accession took place in (480–155) 325 BCE, (477–155) 322 BCE, (470–155) 315 BCE, (468–155) 313 BCE or (467–155) 312 BCE. Another Jaina tradition recorded in the *Vicāraśreṇī* (cf. *Prabandhacintāmaṇi*, composed in CE 1304 by Merutuṅga, a scholar of Śvetāmbara school) places his accession 255 years before the Vikrama Era (57 BCE) which dates back to 312 BCE. Some ancient Jaina scholars are of the opinion that his accession took place either 210 or 215 years after Mahāvīra's *nirvāṇa* (527 BCE) which comes to (527–210) 317 BCE or (527–215) 312 BCE. Some of the *paṭṭāvalīs* give 219 years as the interval between Mahāvīra's *nirvāṇa* (544 BCE) and the accession of Candragupta Maurya on the basis of which (544–219) 325 BCE is sometimes fixed as the date of the beginning of latter's rule which is not correct at all. All the dates except 322 BCE or 321 BCE are unworthy of acceptance. 317, 315 or 312 BCE should be taken as the dates of extension of his rule and not its beginning. It is true that in three different traditions — Purāṇic, Buddhist and Jaina — the date of his accession is calculated in different ways which varies from 322 BCE to 312 BCE. But generally 322 or 321 BCE is accepted by the historians of ancient India as the date of his ascendency.

The Mauryas are said to have ruled for 108 years (*Tapāgaccha-Paṭṭāvalī*, v. 2; *Tīrthoddhāra-prakaraṇa*) or 160 years (*Titthogāli-painna*, v. 621; *Paṭṭāvalī-Samuccaya*, p. 197) which is irreconcilable with Purāṇic duration of their rule.

Puṣyamitra (the founder of the Śuṅga dynasty) is said to have ruled for 30 years (*Tiloyapaṇṇati*, IV.96-97; *Harivaṁśa*, 60.489; *Tapāgaccha-Paṭṭāvalī*, vv. 2-3) or 35 years (*Titthogāli-painna*, vv. 621-22), and his successors, Vasumitra and Agnimitra for 60 years (*Tiloyapaṇṇati*, IV.96-97; *Harivaṁśa*, 60.489) and Balamitra and Bhānumitra also for 60 years (*Titthogāli-painna*, vv. 622-22; *Paṭṭāvalī-Samuccaya*, p. 197; *Tapāgaccha Paṭṭāvalī*, vv. 2-3).

The Gaddabha, Gaddabhilla or Gardabhilla dynasty ruled (over Ujjayinī) for 100 years (*c.* 74 BCE – CE 26) as appears from the *Tiloyapaṇṇati* (IV.97), the *Harivaṁśa* (60.490), the *Titthogāli-painna* (v. 622) and the *Paṭṭāvalī-Samuccaya* (p. 197).

According to the *Tiloyapaṇṇati* (IV.86 and 93), the Śakas' incursion into Ujjayinī took place 461 years after Mahāvīra's *nirvāṇa*, i.e. in (527–461) 66 BCE. It is further recorded in the *Tapāgaccha-Paṭṭāvalī* (v. 3) and the *Vicāraśreṇī* of Merutuṅga that they ruled for four years (*c.* 61-57 BCE). The Kṣatrapa of Ujjain, Caṣṭana, has been called Bhacchaṭṭhanān (Bhadra-Caṣṭana) in the Jaina tradition. Caṣṭana of Ujjain is probably identical with Ptolemy's Tiastenes of Ozene. The Śakas are said to have ruled (western India) altogether for 242 years (*Tiloyapaṇṇati*, IV.93, 97-98; *Harivaṁśa*, 60.490-91) which can be accepted without any hesitation. Nahavāhana (Nahapāna) of Śaka nationality was Kṣaharāṭa ruler of Saurāṣṭra and Maharashtra. He is said to have ruled for 40 years, i.e. from CE 26 to 66 (*Tiloyapaṇṇati*, IV.97; *Harivaṁśa*, 60.490; *Titthogāli-painna*, v. 622; *Paṭṭāvalī-Samuccaya*, p. 197; *Tapāgaccha-Paṭṭāvalī*, v. 3).

The Muruṇḍas (kingsmen of the Kuṣāṇas, also mentioned in some of the Purāṇas) are said to have ruled for 40 years (*Tiloyapaṇṇati*, IV.96; *Harivaṁśa*, 60.489). It is a fact of history that they had ruled a great part of central India for some time in the first half of the third century CE.

The traditions preserved in the *Tiloyapaṇṇati* and the *Harivaṁśa* bear witness to the fact that the Gupta rule virtually commenced at the expiry of 242 years of Śaka rule which gives us (78+242) CE 320, which marked the beginning of the rule of Candragupta I. The Guptas are said to have ruled for 231 years (*Tiloyapaṇṇati*, IV.98; *Harivaṁśa*, 60.491) or 255 years (*Tiloyapaṇṇati*, IV.94). The period of 231 years is in near approximation to the truth. This period covers 190 years of reigns of the early imperial Guptas in the line of Candragupta and 41 years of reigns of the three later Gupta rulers of Magadha in the line of Kṛṣṇagupta.

Kalkirāja called Kalki was a Hūṇa chief who is said to have ruled for 42 years (*Harivaṁśa*, 60.492; *Tiloyapaṇṇati*, IV.94). It is difficult to say as to who the said Hūṇa chief was?

The chronologies given in the *Dhavalā* of Vīrasena (CE 780), the *Jayadhavalā* of Jinasena Svāmī (CE 837), the *Uttarapurāṇa* of Guṇabhadra (CE 898), the *Trilokasāra* of Nemicandra (CE 973) and other Digambara works are almost identical with those in the *Tiloyapaṇṇati* and the *Harivaṁśa*. The chronology, which is given in the *Tapāgaccha-Paṭṭāvalī* (60 years of Pālaka's rule, the end of Nandas' rule 155 years after the death of Mahāvīra, 108 years of the Mauryas' rule, 30 years of Puṣyamitra, 60 years of Balamitra and Bhānumitra and 40 years of Nahavāhana), is preserved in the *Vicāraśreṇī* of Merutuṅga. The *Prabhāvakacarita* of Prabhācandra (CE 1277), the *Vividha-tīrthakalpa* of Jinaprabha Sūri (CE 1332) and other Śvetāmbara works are also important for the chronology of the rulers and the dynasties mentioned above.

The Jaina literature is rich in chronological data. But the data need a careful examination keeping in view some discrepancies. The chronology given in the Jaina traditions is not complete either in the case of kings or in the case of dynasties. In some cases the total length of reigns may not prove to be exact. But certain reign periods after the proper calculation of the data concerned have been found correct. The chronology of the rulers and the dynasties, particularly of Magadha and Ujjayinī, is useful for various purposes. In his *Vicāraśreṇī,* Merutuṅga is himself critical of discrepancies in the dynastic chronology.

Some of the Jaina writers of medieval period have given the reign periods of some Cāḷukya kings of Gujarat and Paramāra kings of Mālwā, and dates of historical events, including those of Muslim invasions of Gujarat, which are all historically authenticated.

In his *Prabandhacintāmaṇi* (CE 1304), Merutuṅga, one of the prominent Jaina scholars of Gujarat belonging to Śvetāmbara school, gives dates of accession and death of some Cāḷukya rulers of Gujarat in Saṁvat Era. He also gives regnal years of some Paramāra kings of Mālwā and Cāḷukya kings of Gujarat.

In his *Vividhatīrthakalpa* (CE 1332), Jinaprabha Sūri of Śvetāmbara school, gives the date of the sacking of Gūrjaradeśa (Gujarat) by "Gajjanavi" (Mahmud of Ghazni) in the time of the Cāḷukya ruler Bhīmadeva as "Vikrama

Saṁvat 1081" (CE 1025).[6] He also gives the date of Ala-ud-din Khilji's conquest of Gujarat as "Vikrama Saṁvat 1356"[7] = CE 1299. The accuracy of these two dates needs no test. The Muslim chroniclers and historians, and other authorities on medieval Indian history have accepted these dates without any controversy.

6. *Vividhatīrthakalpa*, ed. Jinavijaya, v. 29.
7. Ibid., v. 30.

7.5

Eras and Their Historical and Chronological Significance

No discussion of Indian chronological traditions will be complete without throwing light on some of the historical eras and their chronological significance.

The eras were introduced in ancient and medieval India to mark the historic events and to preserve the memory thereof, and were used to fix the date of accession of kings and the beginning and end of the dynastic rule, to determine the reign-periods of rulers and so on. Some of the eras were extensively used particulary in ancient Indian inscriptions to record the important events that took place during the reigns of kings.

Here we shall first begin with the Mahāvīra Era. Vardhamāna Mahāvīra occupies an important place in the history of ancient India. According to the popular tradition of the Jainas, 527 BCE, the date of his *nirvāṇa*, marked the commencement of Mahāvīra Era. The date "is one of the earliest landmarks in the chronology of ancient India while it is the very sheet-anchor of Jaina chronology."[1] There are some positive evidences in favour of this date. The Digambara tradition recorded in the *Tiloyapaṇṇati* (IV.1499) of Yativṛṣabha (CE 176), the *Dhavalā* of Vīrasena (CE 780), the *Harivaṁśa* (60.549

1. J.P. Jain, *The Jaina Sources of the History of Ancient India (100* BCE – CE *900)*, p. 32.

and 551) of Jinasena (CE 783), and the *Trilokasāra* (v. 850) of Nemicandra (CE 973), the Śvetāmbara and in *Titthogāli-Painna* (v. 623 cf. *Paṭṭāvalī-Samuccaya*, pp. 197 and 537) and the *Vicāraśreṇī* of Merutuṅga (CE 1304) show that there is an interval of 605 years and five months between Mahāvīra's *nirvāṇa* and the commencement of the Śaka Era (CE 78) which comes to (605–78) 527 BCE. Another class of Jaina tradition gives the same date in terms of the Vikrama Era. "The *Prākṛt Paṭṭāvalī* of the Nandī Saṁgha, which is one of the oldest Digambara *Paṭṭāvalīs*, the equally old Śvetāmbara *Tapāgaccha-Paṭṭāvalī*, Haribhadra's *Āvaśyakavṛtti* (CE 775), the *Tīrthoddhāra-prakaraṇa* and several other works unanimously state that Mahāvīra died 470 years before the commencement of the Vikrama Era (57 BCE)." The date is further confirmed by the traditional belief of the Jainas themselves, as recorded in some of their works, that Mahāvīra died 461 years before the first entry of the Śakas into the Ujjayinī region in 66 BCE. The statement recorded in some of the Pāli texts that the Buddha survived Mahāvīra by many years also proves that the latter died 44 years before the former's death in 483 BCE. The age of Mahāvīra at the time of his death is stated to have been "71 years, six months and seventeen days." He was born on "30 March 599 BCE." His renunciation on "11 November 570 BCE" and enlightenment "on 26 April 557 BCE" were two of the important events in his life. And his *nirvāṇa* took place on 15 October 527 BCE. The earlier use of this Mahāvīra Era is found in the *Paumcariu* (also called *Padma-Carita*) of Vimalasūri who gives his date ME 530 (CE 3).[2]

Hemacandra (aêŚvetāmbara scholar of the twelfth century CE) in his *Pariśiṣṭaparvan* has given different dates of Mahāvīra's *nirvāṇa*, as mentioned before, and accordingly fixed the dates of the accessions of some kings and the beginning and end

2. For details see ibid., pp. 36-54.

of rule of some dynasties. He has stated that Candragupta Maurya ascended the throne in ME 155 and the Nanda dynasty began in ME 60. His calculation is entirely based on the dates different from 527 BCE. But in one of his works, *Triṣaṣṭiśalākāpuruṣacarita* (X.12, vv. 45-46), he says that the accession of Kumārapāla (the Cāḷukya monarch of Gujarat) took place in ME 1669 = CE 1142 which is evidently a proof of his acceptance of the date 527 BCE.

Mahāvīra was a contemporary of Buddha and Bimbisāra but not Ajātaśatru. A Śvetāmbara tradition states that Mahāvīra attained *nirvāṇa* in the 16th year of the reign of Kūṇika (Ajātaśatru) which corresponds with 475 BCE. Such contradictory statements are there in some Jaina and other sources which sometimes create confusion in our mind about the date concerned. However, on the weight of the internal as well as external evidence 527 BCE can be accepted as the date of Mahāvīra's *nirvāṇa* and the commencement of Mahāvīra Era. We find that Candragupta Maurya ascended the throne of Magadha 205 or 206 years after Mahāvīra's *nirvāṇa* (i.e. in 322 or 321 BCE). The date 527 BCE does not affect the Mauryan chronology. The said era has been used mostly by the Jaina writers of ancient and medieval periods.

The popular Buddhist tradition places the Buddha's *nirvāṇa* in 483 BCE. This is the date which marked the beginning of the Buddha Era. It coincides with the eighth year of Ajātaśatru's reign which proves that he ascended the throne of Magadha in 491 BCE.

The other two eras — Vikrama and Śaka — are very important from both historical and chronological points of view.

According to Jaina historical tradition recorded in Merutuṅga's *Prabandhacintāmaṇi* (Vikramāṅkaprabandha section) and *Paṭṭāvalī,*[3] Rājaśekhara's *Prabandhakośa, Vikramāṅkasattvaprabandha* (in *Purātana-prabandha Saṁgraha*), Mahendrāditya, king of Ujjayinī (ME 453-466 = 74-61 BCE), was the father of Vikramāditya. The Śakas entered Ujjayinī in ME 461 = 66 BCE which marked the commencement of the first Śaka Era. After having consolidated their position they defeated Mahendrāditya in 61 BCE and thereafter occupied Ujjayinī and ruled over it until they were vanquished and expelled in ME 470 = 57 BCE by the Mālwā people led by Vikramāditya. After the expulsion of the Śakas, the latter was crowned as a king. In order to commemorate this event or his victory over the Śakas, Vikramāditya founded the era called Kṛta, Mālwā or Vikrama. After having regained the kingdom of Avantī (western Mālwā) with its capital Ujjayinī (Ujjain) in 57 BCE, he reigned for 60 years.[4] It is said that "He restored the Hindu monarchy to its ancient splendour."[5]

That Vikramāditya defeated the Śakas in 57 BCE and founded the Vikrama Era can also be corroborated by the statement of Prabhācandra Sūri (a Jaina writer who flourished in the last quarter of the thirteenth century) in his *Prabhāvakacarita.*

Raj Bali Pandey, an acknowledged authority on Vikramāditya and his times, has conclusively proved the historicity of Vikramāditya, the celebrated king of Ujjayinī in the first century BCE and founder of the Vikrama Era. The

3. *Paṭṭāvalī-Samuccaya*, ed. Muni Darśanavijaya, I, Appendix C, p. 199.

4. That Mahendrāditya of Gardabhilla dynasty was the father of Vikramāditya; that both were historical figures and ruled over the kingdom of Avantī with its capital at Ujjayinī and that the former was defeated by the Śakas who were later defeated, and expelled from Ujjayinī by the latter can also be proved by the statements of two Kāśmīrī *paṇḍits*, Kṣemendra and Somadeva of the eleventh century CE, in their respective works, *Bṛhatkathāmañjarī* (X.108-13) and *Kathāsaritsāgara* (XVIII.I).

5. B.C. Law, *Geographical Aspects of Kālidāsa's Works*, p. 26.

defeat of the Śakas and the founding of an era in 57 BCE, according to him, was an epoch making event in Indian history.[6] On the testimony of the Hindu and Jaina traditions, A.S. Altekar has also asserted that it was Vikramāditya who founded the era in 57 BCE known after him as Vikrama Era.[7]

The oldest name of the era that commenced in 57 BCE was Kṛta Saṁvat[8] which was in use from the third to the fifth centuries. It was later known as Mālwā Saṁvat, Mālwāgaṇa Saṁvat or Saṁvat of Mālaveśon. This Saṁvat was in use from the fifth to the ninth centuries. The Vikrama Saṁvat began to be used from the ninth century onwards. These three Saṁvats have been used in the inscriptions found in Rājpūtānā, Mālwā and other places.

The Yūpa inscription discovered at Nāndasa (Udaipur State) is dated Kṛta Saṁvat 282.[9] This is the earliest epigraphic evidence of the use of the Saṁvat. The Yūpa inscriptions of Barnala (Jaipur state) are dated Kṛta Saṁvat 284 and 335. The Yūpa inscription of Badawa (Kota) is dated Kṛta Saṁvat 295.[10] The inscription of Vijayagaṛh (Bharatpur state) is dated Kṛta Saṁvat 422 (or 428). In the Mandasor (ancient Daśapura, western Mālwā) inscription of Narovarman of 461, the Saṁvat is named both Kṛta and Mālwā. The Mandasor stone inscription of Kumāragupta I bears the date in Mālwā Saṁvat 493 = CE 436 which is the date of construction of the sun

6. *Vikramāditya: Saṁvat-pravartak* (Hindi tr. of his *Vikramāditya of Ujjayinī: Founder of the Vikram Era*), pp. 3-4, 35-36, 45; "Historicity of Vikramāditya," PTAIOC, 12th session, Banaras Hindu University, 1943-44, vol. II (Benares, 1946), pp. 503-11; see also his *Bhāratīya Itihāsa kā Paricaya* (*Introduction to Indian History*), pp. 71, 74.

7. "Who founded the Vikrama Era?" *PTAIOC*, vol. II (Benares, 1946), pp. 501-02.

8. *Ind. Ant.*, XIX, 1892, pp. 403-04.

9. *Ep. Ind.*, XXVI, pp. 118-25.

10. Ibid., XXIII, p. 43.

temple at Daśapura during his reign. The same temple was renovated in Mālwā Saṁvat 529 = CE 472 in the time of Kumāragupta II.[11] The Mandasor inscription of Yaśodharman is dated "Mālwāgaṇa Saṁvat 589."[12] The Kanasvā inscription of the Śivigaṇa (discovered from Koṭā of Rajasthan) bears the date 795 — the "Saṁvat of Mālaveśon."[13] The date of inscription of Gyārasapur (Gwalior state) is Mālwā Kāla (Saṁvat) 936.[14] It is significant to note that the era of 57 BCE was used by the Mālwāgaṇas for chronological computations.[15] The date of Dhaulapura stone inscription of Caṇḍamahāsena is Vikrama Kāla 898 = CE 841. This is an evidence of the earliest use of Vikrama Saṁvat in an inscription.[16]

In his *Vicāraśreṇī,* Merutuṅga has explicity stated that "Vikramāditya and his dynasty ruled for 135 years, and 605 years after Mahāvīra's *nirvāṇa* (i.e. in CE 78) came the Śaka king who displaced the dynasty of Vikramāditya." On the authority of this Jaina writer it is believed that the Śakas after 57 BCE again rose to power, reoccupied Ujjayinī and reasserted their authority. In order to celebrate it and to supersede the Mālwā Era they started a new era of their own, i.e. the second Śaka Era of CE 78. In the Jaina works, *Paṭṭāvalī-Samuccaya* and the *Prabhāvakacarita* of Prabhācandra also it is clearly stated that the Śakas after having conquered Ujjayinī second time

11. J.F. Fleet, *CII*, III, No. 18, pp. 79-88.
12. Ibid., nos. 33-34.
13. *Ep. Ind.*, XIX, p. 59.
14. *ASIR*, X (Report of Tours in Bundelkhand and Malwa in 1874-77 by A. Cunningham, Calcutta, 1880), pt. II.
15. See Fleet, op. cit., p. 154; *Ep. Ind.*, IX, p. 320; K.P. Jayaswal, *JBORS*, 1930.
16. For details of inscriptions in which Saṁvat, Kṛta, Mālwā or Vikrama have been used see R.B. Pandey, *Vikramāditya: Saṁvat-pravartak*, pp. 4-9; V.S. Agrawala, "Vikrama Saṁvat aur Vikramāditya", in *Itihāsa-darśana* (collection of his papers), collected and ed. P.K. Agrawala, pp. 120-21.

founded the Śaka Era in CE 78.[17] Some scholars regard Caṣṭana, a Kṣatrapa of Ujjayinī, as the founder of the Śaka Era of that year. But this goes against the truth, for his earliest known date is the year 52 in Śaka Era = CE 130. The Kuṣāṇa king, Kaniṣka, is generally credited with having founded the Śaka Era in CE 78. But his chronological position still remains uncertain. With regard to the year of his accession the choice lies between CE 78 and CE 125. Different other dates have also been suggested by the historians of ancient India. No definite date of his accession can be suggested with absolute certainty and accuracy. And we, therefore, do not take him as the originator of this era. Nor is there any ground to believe that an era founded by him in CE 78 was afterwards called the Śaka Era "in consequence of its long use by the Śaka princes of western India." E.J. Rapson is of the view that the era of CE 78 was originally founded by Kaniṣka and later called the Śaka Era. He says: "The Śaka Era, so called at a later date because it was used for more than three centuries by the Śaka kings of Surāṣṭra, originally Kṣatraps of the Kuṣāṇas. Probably marks the establishment of the Kuṣāṇa empire under Kaniṣka."[18] In fact, there was a separate Kaniṣka Saṁvat. It was used by the Kuṣāṇas during the period of their rule. It could not become widely prevalent.[19]

It is traditionally believed that it was Śālivāhana of Ujjayinī who conquered a group of the Śakas exactly 135 years after Vikramāditya (i.e. in CE 78) and celebrated his victory by commencing a new era called "Śālivāhana Śakābda." But the fact remains that an era of CE 78 founded by the Śakas after having reoccupied Ujjayinī was later changed to Śālivāhana Śaka Saṁvat to perpetuate the memory of

---

17. See also *JBBRAS*, XVI, p. 292.
18. *Ancient India from the Earliest Times to the First Century AD*, p. 105.
19. See also *JRAS*, 1914, pp. 973 f.

Śālivāhana. This new era, however, came into use. It may further be added here that some sections of the Śaka continued to occupy Ujjayinī. They ruled over Avantī and adjoining regions for over 300 years. The powerful Śaka kingdom, which had been established at Ujjayinī, was finally overthrown by Candragupta II about CE 390. He assumed the title "Vikramāditya." His name was long remembered as the "Vikram of Ujjain" in memory of Vikramāditya of the first century BCE. Some authorities[20] have mistaken him for Vikramāditya of Ujjain and attributed the Vikrama Era to him.

The two principal and very popular eras — Vikrama and Śaka — have been in use in terms of chronology since ancient times. Several dates in some of the historical works of ancient and medieval period are given in these two eras. Even Śālivāhana Śaka Saṁvat is still used for chronological computation, for instance, 135 years added to the date given in this Saṁvat is equivalent to date in Vikrama Saṁvat.

Another important era was the Gupta Era which began in CE 319 with the accession of the imperial Gupta ruler Candragupta I.[21] But according to the Jaina works, *Tiloyapaṇṇati* and *Harivaṁśa,* this era began in CE 320. And this is the reason why some scholars assign CE 319-20 to the commencement of the era.[22] This era was used in all parts of the Gupta empire except Mālwā where Mālwā Saṁvat was in use. The era has been used in the inscriptions of some Gupta rulers. According to the Sāñcī inscription, Candragupta II (CE 375-414) was ruling in the Gupta Era 93 = CE 412-13. The Bilsāḍ inscription dated Gupta Era 96 = CE 415-16 belongs to

20. See V.A. Smith, *The Oxford Student's History of India*, pp. 67-69; H.G. Rawlinson, *A Concise History of the Indian People*, p. 62.
21. See also *JIH*, LVI, I, 1978, p. 101.
22. See also S.P. Sen (ed.), *Historians and Historiography in Modern India*, pp. 37-39.

the time his son and successor Kumāragupta I (CE 414-55). The Girnār inscription of Skandagupta (CE 455-67) refers to the construction of a Viṣṇu temple in Gupta Era 138 = CE 458. According to Sārnāth inscription, Budhagupta was on the throne in Gupta Era 157 = CE 476-77. His accession may, therefore, be dated a year earlier. In post-Gupta times, the Gupta Era was changed to Valabhī Era. The Valabhī Era of CE 319-20 was first introduced in Saurāṣṭra (Kāṭhiāwāḍ). Both the eras were used for chronological purpose. The mention of the Cāḷukya chiefs of Saurāṣṭra in one of the Ūnā charters bearing the Gupta-Valabhī date 574 = CE 893 as feudatories of Mahendrapāla Pratihāra is an instance of their use in inscription by combining them together.

The traditional and historical eras of the Hindus also received the notice of the Arab writer Alberuni (CE 973-1048), who visited India during the time of Mahmud of Ghazni (CE 997-1030), learnt Sanskrit, studied Purāṇic and other ancient Indian Sanskrit literature and produced a scholarly work, *Tahqiq-i-Hind* (An Enquiry into India), in CE 1030. His description of the eras of Vikramāditya, Śaka, Valabha, Gupta and Harṣa is of utmost importance. He has unequivocally stated that "the epoch of the era of Śaka or Śakakāla falls 135 years later than that of Vikramāditya. . . . The epoch of the era of Guptas falls like that of the Valabha (the ruler of the town of Valabhī) 241 years later than the Śakakāla" which comes to CE 319. The Harṣa Era of CE 606 was used in Mathurā and Kannauj. The Vikrama Era was used in western and southern parts of India. All these eras, according to him, were used as cardinal points to fix the chronology which he calls "historic chronology."[23]

---

23. *Alberuni's India*, Eng. tr. of the Arabic text *Tahqiq-i-Hind* by E.C. Sachau, II, pp. 1-11; see also *Alberuni's Chronology of Ancient Nations*, tr. Sachau, pp. 6, 368, note.

In the north-east, it was only the ruling dynasty in Tripura that had an era of its own. It dated from CE 590. The dates of accession of some ancient kings of Tripura and those of some events have been fixed in this era.

The Cāḷukya-Vikrama Era was founded by Vikramāditya VI of Cāḷukya dynasty of Kalyāṇī in CE 1076 which marks his accession to the throne.

One of the most important eras of ancient India was the Laukika Era (also called Saptarṣi Saṁvat or Saptarṣi Laukika Saṁvat)[24] which was, from historical and chronological points of view, in use in Kashmir and its neighbourhood during the period extending from the twelfth to the sixteenth centuries or from the time of Kalhaṇa down to the time of Śuka. The 24th year of this era corresponds with the year 1070 of the Śaka Era (CE 1148). Kalhaṇa, a Kāśmīrī historian of the twelfth century, and his successors used this era for their chronological computations. They have supplied the chronology of the kings and rulers of Kashmir in this era adjusting it with other two eras — the Kali and Śaka or Śālivāhana — which can further be adjusted with the Christian Era.

Kalhaṇa has given the dates of accession of kings of different dynasties and their regnal years from Gonanda or Gonarda III to Siṁhadeva (also called Jayasiṁha) in Laukika Era with their equivalent dates in Kali and Śaka Era. His perfect sense of history and chronology is well reflected in Books IV-VIII of his work, *Rājataraṅgiṇī.* He has fixed the reign periods of all the kings who ruled the kingdom of Kashmir from about the end of the sixth century CE to about the middle of the twelfth century and the total duration of each dynastic

---

24. See also Colebrooke, "The Saptarṣi Era", *As. Res.*, IX (Ist pub. 1811, rept. Delhi, 1979), pp. 323 ff.

rule with perfect accuracy. The reign periods of 17 kings of the Karkoṭaka dynasty from Durlabhavardhana to Utpalapīḍa are given in Book IV. The rule of this dynasty is said to have begun in CE 598 and come to an end in CE 852. The reign periods of 15 princes of Utpala or Varman dynasty from Avantivarman to Sūravarman II are given in Book V. The rule of this dynasty commenced in CE 855 and ended in CE 939. The reign periods of ten princes from Yaśaskara to Diddā belonging to mixed dynasties are given in Book VI. The rule began in CE 939 and came to an end in CE 1003. The reign periods of six kings of the Lohara dynasty from Saṁgrāmarāja *alias* Kṣāmapati to Harṣa are given in Book VII. The rule of this dynasty commenced in CE 1003 and ended in CE 1101. The reign periods of all seven kings from Ucchala to Jayasiṁhadeva figure in Book VIII. In this Book, Kalhaṇa begins the chronology with CE 1101, which marks the commencement of the rule of Ucchala and ends with CE 1149, which marks the twenty-second year of the reign of Jayasiṁha.[25] The dynastic chronology provided by him in the said books of his work requires no modification. The dates given by him have been found correct and used by the historian of ancient India in their respective works while dealing with the history of Kashmir.

Judging the value of chronology given by Kalhaṇa in his *Rājataraṅgiṇī*, H.H. Wilson remarked:

> The chronology of the *Rājataraṅgiṇī* is not without its interest. The dates are regular, and for a long time both probable and consistent, and as they may enable us to determine the dates of persons and events, in other parts of India, as well as in kashmir.

---

25. *Kings of Kashmir*, Eng. tr. of *Rājatraṅgiṇī* of Kalhaṇa, and other Sanskrit works of Jonarāja, Śrīvara, and of Prājyabhaṭṭa and Śuka, by J.C. Dutt, I, Appendix A, i-ii, and xx-xxiii, II, xlv; H.H. Wilson, *HHK*, "Chronological Table", pp. 87-91.

> . . . The more recent the period, the more likely it is that its chronology will be correct.[26]

"Kalhaṇa Paṇḍita, the writer of the history, lived in 1148 CE and his dates are perfectly reliable, and have rightly been accepted by H.H. Wilson, up to five or six centuries previous to the time of the historian. Indeed there can be no doubt as to the correctness of Kalhaṇa's dates up to the reign of Durlabhavardhana, who ascended the throne in 598 CE," said R.C. Dutt.[27]

Applying the chronological method of Kalhaṇa, his four successors — Jonarāja, Śrīvara, Prājyabhaṭṭa and Śuka — have given the dates of accession of the rulers of Kashmir in Laukika Era with their equivalent dates in Kali and Śaka Era and their reign periods in their *Rājataraṅgiṇī*. The list of Jonarāja (from Jayasiṁha to Ali Shah) covers the period from CE 1127 to CE 1420. The list of Śrīvara (from Zain-ul-abidin to Muhammad Shah) covers the period from CE 1420 to CE 1486. His description of events embracing the period from Laukika 4538 = Śaka 1384 = CE 1462 to Laukika 4562 = Śaka 1408 = CE 1486 — the date which marks the deposition of Muhammad Shah and accession of Fatteh Shah as the next *sultān* of Kashmir — is very striking. The list of Prājyabhaṭṭa and Śuka (from Fateh Shah to Yākobha) covers the period from CE 1486 to CE 1587.[28] The said four chroniclers of medieval period were also the followers of the traditional chronology which had been in use in Kashmir since the time of Kalhaṇa.

The eras, which are not of historical or chronological significance, do not fall within the purview of the treatment of the subject.

---

26. *HHK*, chap. IV, "Remarks on the History and Chronology of Kashmir", p. 78.

27. "An Introductory Essay on the History of Kashmir," in J.C. Dutt, op. cit., II, ix.

28. See also J.C. Dutt, op. cit., III, xxi-xxiv.

Conclusions and Observations

Conclusions and Observations

THE tradition of historical writing in India began with the composition of *Bhārata Itihāsa* or *Bhārata Saṁhitā* and *Purāṇa Saṁhitā* or *Itihāsa Saṁhitā* by Vedavyāsa.

The writing of history began in Itihāsa–Purāṇa tradition which continued down to the end of the Gupta period. In the post-Gupta period, there was, no doubt, slight departure from the earlier tradition. However, some impact of that tradition is discernible on the historical writings of that period too. Some of the works composed between the seventh and the twelfth century CE bear the stamp of that tradition to a considerable extent. The traditional history of India was written purely in that tradition. The said tradition profoundly influenced the historical thoughts and writings in ancient India.

Various traditions of historiography evolved in India during ancient and medieval periods.

There were three phases of ancient Indian historical tradition — Vedic, epic and Purāṇic. The oldest Indian historical tradition is preserved in the *Ṛgveda*. The Ṛgvedic hymns about the Aryan people speak of the sense of history of those who composed them. These hymns constitute the earliest evidence of the historical sense of the Indians. The Purāṇic tradition is relatively of greater importance than the epic one. The Purāṇic tradition was one of the most important traditions of historiography in India. The *purāṇakāra*s made immense contributions to the development of the tradition of historical writing in ancient India. They were the first to record and preserve the dynastic genealogies and chronology — the two legitimate constituents or components of history. Their historical conception and chronological perception find reflections in the information they have supplied regarding the kings of different dynasties with length of their reigns. They have provided the dynastic history of India in a very systematic way up to the beginning of the Gupta rule. The details of the kingdoms and dynasties of the post-Gupta period furnished by them with some chronological data though not very systematic are also of considerable historical value. The Purāṇic historiography is important especially from dynastic, genealogical and chronological points of view. The Indian historical tradition gradually developed.

The other two important traditions of historiography were the Buddhist and Jaina. The Buddhists and Jainas also contributed to the evolution of the tradition of historiography in India, the former during the ancient period and the latter during ancient and medieval periods. They wrote the biographies, chronicles and other historical treatises and provided the dynastic genealogies and chronology. Their works virtually made the earlier history of ancient India richer. The contributions of the latter was, however, far greater than the former in respect of the writing of historical biographies and chronicles. They produced a number of such works during the medieval period. The historical writings of Jains are far superior to that of the Buddhists in terms of the richness of their contents and coverage of the subject matter. The Jains have presented the history within a wide compass covering a greater part of India. They made a more serious approach than the Buddhists to history as evidenced by the quality of their works. The Buddhist and Jaina historians of India, like their Hindu counterparts, gave impetus to the writing of history.

The Indian historiography took a new turn in the seventh century CE. The idea of history started changing to a reasonable extent from that century onwards. The period extending from the seventh to the twelfth centuries proved to be a blooming one in the history of historical writing in India. A number of biographical works were produced during the period. Some biographies are the productions of the historical schools that flourished in the post-Harṣa period under the patronage of the Pālas of Bengal, the Paramāras of Mālwā, the Cāḷukyas of Gujarat and Kalyāṇī, and the Cāhamānas of Śākambharī. Besides biographies, histories of kingdoms were also written.

The twelfth century was a landmark in the history of Indian historiography. Kalhaṇa, a celebrated Kāśmīrī brāhmaṇa historian of that century, was the first to initiate the tradition of examining all relevant past records thoroughly, objectively and critically for writing a true history. He was the forerunner of many Indian historians in the realm of debunking the truth from falsehood. His historical principles and laws were further followed by the Kāśmīrī chroniclers of the Medieval Age. It is a wrong notion that except the *Rājataraṅgiṇī* (a chronicle of kings of Kashmir) of Kalhaṇa there is no work in Sanskrit literature which merits the title of history. In fact, Kalhaṇa was the greatest of all ancient historians of India and his work the best of all historical works produced in ancient India. He may undoubtedly be called the father of Indian history.

The writing of historical biographies and that of historical chronicles and Vaṁśāvalīs in different parts of India in two different traditions between the seventh and the eighteenth century were the two significant stages in the evolution of Indian historiography.

The kings, rulers and emperors made significant contributions to the evolution of the tradition of historical writing in India during the aforesaid period by extending their patronage to the court-poets-cum-historians and chroniclers and by encouraging and inspiring them for writing their biographies to perpetuate the memory of their deeds or exploits, and chronicles to present the political or dynastic histories of the kingdoms. They deserve the credit for giving fillip to the productions of biographies, chronicles and other historical works. Archives were maintained where records were preserved and made available to the biographers, chroniclers and historians. The keeping of records of the past events testifies to the historical consciousness of record keepers.

The biographies and chronicles were also written independently without royal patronage. The biographies of kings who occupy important places in the annals of India and other historical personages include those of Mahāvīra, Buddha, Harṣa, Yaśovarman, Rāmapāla, Kumārapāla, Vikramāditya VI, Pṛthvīrāja Cauhāna, Guru Nanak, Śivājī and Guru Gobind Singh. The chronicles were written in Kashmir, Sindh, Punjab, Rajasthan and Nepal in northern India, Gujarat and Maharashtra in western India, and in Orissa, Assam, Manipur and Tripura in eastern India. The tradition of writing particularly the chronicle was handed down from generation to generation. Like the Hindus, Buddhists and Jainas, the native Muslim historians, and the Sikh historians of Punjab also contributed in the field of writing of biographies and chronicles maintaining the Indian tradition. The chroniclers were comparatively objective and critical than the biographers in presentation of the facts in their works. Not only the past events but also contemporary events, some of which based on eyewitness accounts, were recorded by them for the purpose of preserving them for the future.

Besides biographies and chronicles, many other historical

and semi-historical works of various kinds were produced in India during ancient and medieval period. The conventional beliefs that there were neither historians nor historiography in India before the dawn of modern age get falsified in the light of the facts stated above.

There were various schools of historical writing in ancient and medieval India. The historians of Rajasthan, Gujarat and Kashmir schools made proportionately greater contributions than those of other schools to the evolution of the tradition of historiography in India during the periods. The historians of these three prominent schools left indelible imprints of their writings on the historical thoughts and writings of the succeeding generations of Indian historians.

The tradition of historical writing in south India was no less rich than that in other parts of the country. Various kinds of historical and quasi-historical works were produced there during ancient and medieval periods which include histories of kingdoms and dynasties, biographies, chronicles and Vaṁśāvalīs.

There was neither poverty of historical knowledge nor dearth of historical records in ancient and medieval India. History was written in some form or the other in almost all parts of India during the periods. The works produced as a whole are very helpful for throwing light on various aspects of ancient and medieval Indian history and culture. Several missing links or broken chains in the history of ancient and medieval India can be restored with the help of the writings of the native historians of India. Some mistakes occurring in Indian history regarding dates of events, accession and death of the kings and length of reigns of the kings can also be rectified with the help of indigenous records. The view held by some scholars that the regular historical works on the part of the Hindus has long been a desideratum is not tenable.

Actually, there was an unbroken tradition of historiography in India.

The ancient Indians (the Hindus, Buddhists and Jainas) did possess the sense of history and chronology as evidenced by the works they produced. We, of course, do admit that only few of them were endowed with perfect sense of history and were critical historians.

The ancient Indians were acquainted more with the art than science of historiography. However, it would be too much to expect scientific, serious or absolutely genuine histories from the authors of ancient times. It has been aptly remarked that "The modern historian of ancient India unceremoniously discards the ancient forms and ideas — the very context of ancient historical works."[1] The ancient and medieval historians of India have presented histories whatsoever without distorting the facts. Every age had its own tradition of historiography. The prevailing attitudes in any age guide or influence the historian in the treatment of his subject.[2] The ancient and medieval concept of history and chronology was totally different from the modern one. The value of the works produced by ancient and medieval historians of India should be judged by the standard prevailing in a contemporary age and not by the modern standard of historiography.

It is not worthy of our acceptance that the ancient Indians did not produce political history.The heroic deeds of kings, the political events, including struggles between native princes for power and supremacy, attacks and invasions, battles and wars, conquests and annexations, rise and fall of

1. A.K. Narain, "Writing a new History of Ancient India: A Study in Problems, Sources and Methods", in *Problems of Historical Writing in India* (Proceeds. of the Seminar held at Delhi, January 1963), p. 8.
2. See also Narain, op. cit.; H.E. Barness, *A History of Historical Writing*, pp. 295-6; V.S. Pathak, *Ancient Historians of India*, p. 148.

kingdoms, etc. are described especially in the historical biographies and chronicles of the post-sixth century CE. The tradition of giving focus on political history of India further developed during the medieval period. The works of that period are full of details of political events. The details of Muslim invasions of Rajasthan and Gujarat during the Sultanate period are available in the biographical literature of the former and the chronicles and other historical works of the latter which can also be confirmed to a certain extent by the statements of Muslim chroniclers. Some of the works contain eyewitness accounts of events.

The early foreign invasions of India could not be recorded in ancient Indian literature not because of the lack of historical sense of the ancient Indians but because of non-availability of any dependable source material. The foreign invaders did not leave behind any record of their invasions either to be utilised by the Indian writers.

The historical and chronological traditions in India gradually evolved. The Purāṇic, Buddhist and Jaina traditions of chronology and the chronology given by Kalhaṇa and other historians or chroniclers of Kashmir are of great value. In some of the historical works composed by the Hindu and Jaina writers of the medieval period, the dates given of persons and events have been found absolutely correct. The Hindus and Jains continued to maintain their chronological tradition till late medieval period. However, it cannot be denied that the tradition of presenting history within a chronological framework had not fully developed in India in pre-modern age. In India, for the writers of ancient and medieval period the presentation of facts was more important than the chronology.

The Hindus, Buddhists, Jainas, native Muslims and Sikhs all contributed to the evolution of historiographical tradition in India.

There were historians and historiography in ancient and medieval India. But there was none among the ancient and medieval Indian historians to leave for posterity the complete history of ancient India and medieval India respectively. It may just be added here that the *Rājāvalī* written by Mṛtyuñjaya Vidyālaṅkār of Bengal in 1808 is a systematic history of India from the earliest period to the establishment of British rule.

Histories we have are the productions of different ages and of different brains. ". . . history is what the historian makes."[3]

The value of Indian historiography has not been properly judged by Western scholars with few exceptions. Marc Ferro's doubt about historiography in India is baseless. His statement, that "history in India is without identity,"[4] is unworthy of credence.

The Indian tradition of historiography is marked especially by its continuity and richness. The tradition of historical writing was maintained in India from the time of Vedavyāsa down to the end of the Medieval Age so far as the present study is concerned. That tradition further continued in modern India which does not fall within the scope of this work.

Any attempt to relegate to the background the contributions of the Indians to the making of history of India will be an injustice to history itself.

---

3. E.H. Carr, *What is History?* p. 26; see also P. Smith, *The Historians and History* (for his views on the subject).

4. *The Use and Abuse of History or How the Past is Taught*, Ch. IV, "India: History Without Identity", p. 34.

General Bibliography and Index

General Bibliography

Original Sources

Texts, Translations and Commentaries

Literary Sources

THE VEDAS

Atharvaveda Saṁhitā, ed. with Sāyaṇa's comm. by S.P. Pandit, Bombay, 1895-98; tr. with comm. by R.T.H. Griffith (*The Hymns of the Atharvaveda*), 2 vols., Varanasi, 1896-97; tr. W.D. Whitney (*On the Vedas*), HOS, Cambridge, 1905, 2nd Indian rpt., Delhi 1971, Calcutta, 1972; text with Hindi tr. and comm. by Dayananda Saraswati, Delhi: Dayananda Samsthan, VS 2032; ed. with Hindi tr. and Sāyaṇa's comm. by R. Sharma Acharya, 2 vols. Bareilly, 1973, 1975.

R̥gveda Saṁhitā, ed. with Sāyaṇa's comm. by F. Max Müller, 2nd edn., London, 1890-92; tr. R.T.H. Griffith, Benares, 1896-97; tr. H.H. Wilson, 6 vols., London, 1866-88; ed. with Hindi tr. and Sāyaṇa's comm. by R. Sharma Acharya, 4 vols., Bareilly, 1974-75.

THE BRĀHMAṆAS

Aitareya Brāhmaṇa, ed. and tr. M. Haug, Varanasi, 1976-77; tr. A.B. Keith, HOS, vol. XXV, Cambridge, Mass. 1920, rpt., Delhi 1971.

Gopatha Brāhmaṇa, ed. R.L. Mitra and H. Vidyabhushan, Calcutta, 1872.

Śatapatha Brāhmaṇa, ed. A. Chinnaswami Shastri and R.N. Dikshit, 2nd edn., Varanasi, 1984.

THE ĀRAṆYAKA

Taittirīya Āraṇyaka, ed. H.N. Apte, Poona, 1898.

THE UPANIṢADS

Bṛhadāraṇyaka Upaniṣad, ed. O. Bohtlingk, Leipzig, 1889.

Chāndogya Upaniṣad, ed. and tr. Swami Gambhirananda, Calcutta, 1983.

Upaniṣat-Saṁgraha (Containing 108 Upaniṣads), ed. J.L. Shastri, Delhi, 1980.

THE SŪTRAS

Gṛhya-Sūtras

Āśvalāyana Gṛhya-Sūtra, tr. H. Oldenberg, in SBE, vol. XXIX, pt. I, Oxford, 1892, rpt., Delhi, 1964.

Gobhila Gṛhya-Sūtra, tr. H. Oldenberg, in SBE, vol. XXX, pt. II, Oxford, 1892, rpt., Delhi, 1964.

Śāṅkhāyana Gṛhya-Sūtra, tr. H. Oldenberg, in SBE, vol. XXIX, pt. I, Oxford, 1886, rpt., Delhi, 1964.

Śrauta-Sūtra

Śāṅkhāyan Śrauta-Sūtra, ed. with comm. of Varadattasuta Anartiya and Govinda by A. Hillebrandt, Calcutta, 1888.

THE DHARMA-ŚĀSTRAS

Dharmaśāstra Saṁgraha, ed. J. Vidyasagar, Calcutta, 1876.

Manu-Smṛti, ed. with the *Manvartha-Muktāvalī* comm. of Kullūka Bhaṭṭa and the *Maṇiprabhā* Hindi comm. of H.G. Shastri by G.S. Nene, Varanasi, 1970.

Vasiṣṭha-Smṛti, cf. *Twenty Smṛties*, ed. with Hindi tr. R. Sharma Acharya, 2 vols., Bareilly, 1979-80.

Yājñavalkya-Smṛti, ed. A.F. Stenzler, Berlin, 1849; H. Apte, Anandashrama Sanskrit Series, Poona, 1903.

THE EPICS

Mahābhārata, ed. with Hindi tr. S. Damodar Satavalekar and Shrutishila Sharma, Pardi (Gujarat): Ādi Parva, 1968; Anuśāsana Parva, 1978; Āraṇyaka Parva, 2 vols., 1969; Āśramavāsika Parva, 1977; Bhīṣma Parva, 1972; Droṇa Parva, 1975; Karṇa Parva, 1973; Mahāprasthānika Parva, 1977; Mausala Parva, 1977; Sabhā Parva, 1982; Śalya Parva, 1973; Śānti Parva, 2 pts. 1979-80; Svargārohaṇa Parva, 1977; Udyoga Parva, 1969; Virāṭa Parva, 1969.

Vālmīki-Rāmāyaṇa, ed. D.R. Mankad, Oriental Research Institute, Baroda, 1965; tr. R.T.H Griffith, London, 1870.

Ayodhyā Kāṇḍa, ed. with Hindi tr. Akhilananda, Amritsar, VS 2019; Bāla Kāṇḍa, ed. with Hindi tr. Yudhishthira Mimamsaka by Akhilananda, Amitsar, VS 2025; Kiṣkindhā Kāṇḍa, ed. with Hindi tr. Akhilananda, Amritsar, VS 2021; Uttara Kāṇḍa, cf. *Vālamīki-Rāmāyaṇa Kośa* by R.K. Rai, Varanasi, 1965; Yuddha (Laṅkā) Kāṇḍa, text with Hindi tr. of Vijayapāla, Bahalagarh, VS 2029.

PURĀṆAS

Agni Purāṇa, ed. R.L. Mitra, BIS, ASB Calcutta, 1873-79; tr. M.N. Dutt, 2 vols., Calcutta, 1903-04; text with Hindi tr. of T. Jha and G.S. Tripathi, Prayag, 1986.

Bhāgavata Purāṇa, text with Hindi tr. and annotation, 2 vols., 8th edn., Gorakhpur, Saṁvat, 2040; ed. with Eng. tr. C.L. Goswami, 2 pts., 2nd edn., Gorakhpur, 1982.

Bhaviṣya Purāṇa, Venkateshwara Press, Bombay, 1910; ed. with Hindi tr. R. Sharma Acharya, 2 vols., Bareilly, 1978.

Brahma Purāṇa, ed. H.N. Apte, Anandashrama Sanskrit Series, Poona, 1895; text with Hindi tr. of T. Jha, Prayag, 1976.

Brahmāṇḍa Purāṇa, Venkateshwara Press, Bombay, 1913.

Brahmavaivartta Purāṇa, ed. with Hindi tr. T. Jha, Allahabad, 1985.

Garuḍa Purāṇa, Eng. tr. M.N. Dutt, Calcutta, 1908, rpt., Delhi, 1983.

Harivaṁśa Purāṇa, ed. N. Mukhopadhyaya, ASB, Calcutta, 1858; R. Kinjawadekar, Poona, 1936; text with Hindi tr. and comm., 4th edn., Gorakhpur, Saṁvat, 2044.

Kūrma Purāṇa, ed. with Hindi tr. of Shree Narayana Singh by Anandasvaroopa Gupta, Varanasi, 1972.

Liṅga Purāṇa, Venkateshwara Press, Bombay, 1927.

Mārkaṇḍeya Purāṇa, ed. K.M. Banerjee, BIS, ASB, Calcutta, 1862; ed. with Hindi tr. Dharmendra Nath Shastri, Meerut, 1983; tr. F.E. Pargiter, BIS, ASB, Calcutta, 1904.

Matsya Purāṇa, Anandashrama Sanskrit Series, Poona, 1907; text with Hindi tr., 2 vols., Gorakhpur, 1985; ed. with tr. of various oriental scholars and notes of B.C. Majumdar, S.C. Vasu, H.H. Wilson, Bentley, Wilford and others by J.D. Akhtar, vol. I, SBA, Delhi, 1972.

Padma Purāṇa, ed. V.N. Mandalika, Anandashrama Sanskrit Series, Poona, 1893-94; *Svargakhaṇḍa*, ed. Ashok Chatterjee Shastri, Varanasi, 1972.

Skanda Purāṇa, ed. Vasudeva Shastri, 3 pts., Anandashrama Sanskrit Series, Poona, 1893.

Vāmana Purāṇa, ed. with Hindi tr. of G.C. Vedanta Shastri, Shree Chaudhari Shree Narayana Singh and G.S. Rai by Anandasvaroopa Gupta, Varanasi, 1968.

Varāha Purāṇa, ed. P.H. Shastri, BIS, ASB, Calcutta, 1893.

Vāyu Purāṇā, Anandashrama Sanskrit Series, Poona, 1905; ed. R.L. Mitra, 2 vols. BIS, ASB, Calcutta, 1880-88; text with Hindi tr. of R.P. Tripathi Shastri, Prayāg, 1987.

Viṣṇu Purāṇa, ed. J. Vidyasagara, Calcutta, 1882; text with Hindi tr. of Muni Lal Gupta, 9th edn. Gorakhpur, Saṁvat, 2041; tr. M.N. Dutt, Calcutta, 1894, and H.H. Wilson, Calcutta, 1961.

Viṣṇudharmottara Mahāpurāṇa, Venkateshwara Press, Bombay, 1912.

Other Literary Works

Amarakośa of Amara Siṁha, text with the Maṇiprabhā Hindi comm. of H.G. Shastri, Varanasi, 1957.

Arthaśāstra of Kauṭilya, ed. R. Shamasastri, Mysore, 1909; tr. Vachaspati Gairola, Varanasi, 1984.

Kādambarī of Bāṇa, ed. K.P. Parab, Bombay, 1948; Eng. tr. C.M. Ridding. London, 1896; Hindi tr. M.C. Bharatiya, *Bāṇabhaṭṭa aur Unkī Kādambarī*, Ghaziabad, 1973-74; Hindi tr. V.S. Agrawala, *Kādambarī: Ek Sāṁskṛtika Adhyayana*, Varanasi, 1958.

Kāvyamīmāṁsā of Rājaśekhara, ed. with *Prakāśa*, Hindi comm. by G.S. Rai, Varanasi, 1964.

Mahābhāṣya (great comm. on Pāṇini's *Aṣṭādhyāyī*) of Patañjali, ed. F. Kielhorn, 3 vols. Bombay Sanskrit Series, Bombay, 1880-85.

Nirūkta of Yāska, ed. with Hindi tr. Uma Shankar Sharma, Varanasi, 1966; ed. with Durgācārya's comm. by V.K. Rajavade, Poona, 1921-26.

Buddhist Works

CANONICAL

Aṅguttara Nikāya, ed. R. Moris and E. Hardy, 5 vols., London, 1885-1900.

Apadāna, not yet edited.

Dīgha Nikāya, ed. T.W. Rhys Davids and J.E. Carpenter, 3 vols., London: Pali Text Society, 1890-1911, rpt. 1947-60; tr. T.W. and C.A.F. Rhys Davids (The Dialogues of the Buddha), 3 vols., London: Pali Text Society, 1899-1921.

Jātaka, ed. V. Fausboll, 6 vols., London, 1877-97; tr. various hands under the editorship of E.B. Cowell, 7 vols., Cambridge, 1895-1913.

Majjhima Nikāya, ed. V. Trenckner and R. Chalmers, 3 vols., London: Pali Text Society, 1888-99.

Milindapañha, ed. V. Trenckner, London, 1880; tr. from Pāli by T.W. Rhys Davids (*The Questions of King Milinda*), in SBE, XXXV, I Oxford, 1890, rpt. Delhi 1969; XXXVI, II Oxford, 1894, rpt. Delhi, 1969.

Saṁyutta Nikāya, ed. M. Leon Feer and Mrs Rhys Davids, 5 vols., London: Pali Text Society, 1884-1904.

Sutta Nipāta, ed. D. Anderson and H. Smith, London: Pali Text Society, 1913; ed. Rahul Sankrityayan, Rangoon, 1937; tr. V. Fausboll, SBE, X, II, 2nd edn., Oxford 1898.

Vinaya Piṭaka, ed. H. Oldenberg, 5 vols., London, 1879-83.

NON-CANONICAL

Asokāvadāna, ed. S.K. Mukhopadhyaya, Delhi, 1963.

Avadānaśataka, ed. J.S. Speyer, 2 vols., St. Petersburg, 1906.

Buddhacarita of Aśvaghoṣa, ed. and tr. E.H. Johnston, 2 vols., 2nd edn., Delhi 1972; tr. (cantos I-XVII) E.B. Cowell, in SBE, XLIX, I, Oxford, 1894, rpt. Delhi, 1972.

Buddhavaṁśa, ed. Morris, London: Pali Text Society, 1882; tr. B.C. Law, London: Pali Text Society, 1938.

Dīpavaṁsa, ed. and tr. H. Oldenberg, London, 1879, rpt. Delhi 1982.

Divyāvadāna, ed. E.B. Cowell and R.A. Neil, Cambridge, 1886, rpt. 1976.

Lalitavistara (or *Memoirs of the Early Life of Sakya Muni*), ed. R.L. Mitra, BIS, ASB, Calcutta, 1877; ed. S. Leftmann and A.S. Halle, 3 vols., London 1902, 1908, rpt. by P.L. Vaidya, Buddhist Sanskrit Texts Series, Darbhanga, 1958.

Mahāvaṁsa, ed. W. Geiger, London: Pali Text Society, 1908, rpt. 1958; tr. W. Geiger and M.H. Bode, London: Pali Text Society, 1912, rpt. 1950; tr. of both *Dīpavaṁsa* and *Mahāvaṁsa* by E.M. Coomaraswamy (*The Dīpavaṁsa and Mahāvaṁsa and their Historical Development in Ceylon*), Colombo, 1908.

Mahāvastu, ed. E. Senart, 3 vols., Paris, 1882-97; tr. J.J. Jones, 3 vols. (16, 18, 19), SBB, London, 1949-56.

Mañjuśrīmūlakalpa, ed. T. Ganapati Shastri, 3 vols. (70, 76, 84), Trivandrum Sanskrit Series, Trivandrum, 1920-25.

Sumaṅgalavilāsinī (comm. on the *Vinaya Piṭaka*), ed. J. Takakusu and M. Nagai, 4 vols., London: Pali Text Society, 1924-38.

Sumaṅgalavilāsinī (comm. on the *Dīgha Nikāya*), ed. Rhys Davids and J.E. Carpenter, 3 vols., London: Pali Text Society, 1886-1932.

Jain Works

CANONICAL

Ācārāṅga Sūtra, tr. H. Jacobi, SBE, XXII, I, Oxford, 1884, rpt. Delhi, 1973.

Bhagavatī Sūtra, with comm. of Abhayadeva, 3 vols., Bombay, 1918-21.

Kalpasūtra of Bhadrabāhu, ed. H. Jacobi, Leipzig, 1879; tr. H. Jacobi, SBE, XXII, I, Oxford, 1884, rpt. Delhi, 1973.

NON-CANONICAL

Ādi Purāṇa of Jinasena III, ed. Pannalal Jain, 1st edn. BGP, Kashi, 1951.

Harivaṁśa Purāṇa of Jinasena II, ed. Pannalal Jain, BGP, Kashi, 1962.

Jasahara-cariu of Puṣpadanta, ed. with notes by P.L. Vaidya, Karanja, 1931.

Jayadhavala of Jinasena III, BGP, Kashi, 1947.

Kuvalayamālā of Udyotanna Sūri, ed. A.N. Upadhye, pts. I & II, revd. edn., Bombay, 1970.

Mahāpurāṇa of Puṣpadanta, ed. D.K. Jain, 4 vols., MDJG, Delhi, 1979-83; P.L. Vaidya, 3 vols., Bombay, 1937-41.

Mahāvīracarita of Guṇacandra, Devchand Lalbhai Jain Series, No. 75, Bombay, 1929.

Nayakumāra-cariu of Puṣpadanta, ed. with notes by H.L. Jain, Karanja, 1933.

Nītivākyāmṛta of Somadeva Sūri, MDJG, Bombay, 1887-88; ed. S.L. Shastri, Delhi, 1950.

Padma Purāṇa of Ravisena, ed. Pannalal Jain, 3 vols., 1st edn., BGP, Kashi, 1958-59.

Pariśiṣṭaparvan (Sthavirāvalīcarita) of Hemacandra, ed. H. Jacobi, 2nd edn., BIS, Calcutta, 1932.

Pārśvanāthacarita (The Life and stories of the Jain Saviour Pārśvanātha), tr. M. Bloomfield, Baltimore, 1919.

Paṭṭāvalīs, Eng. tr. of the Digambara *Paṭṭāvalīs* by Hoernle, *Ind. Ant.*, XIX, pp. 233-42, XX, pp. 341-61, XXI, pp. 57-84; also in *Jaina Antiquary*, Arrah, XV, 2, pp. 1-7; *Jaina Siddhānta Bhāṣkara*, Arrah, I, 1, p. 37; I, 2-3, p. 32; I, 4, pp. 43, 51, 71, 78, 81, 103; *Paṭṭāvalī-Samuccaya* (a collection of Śvetāmbara Pattāvalis) ed. Muni Darshanavijaya, 2 vols., Viramgam, 1933.

Prabhāvakacarita of Prabhācandra, ed. H.M. Sharma, Bombay, 1909; ed. Jinavijaya, Bombay, 1940.

Rājāvalīs, Mss. in Jain Bhaṇḍāras at Delhi.

Rājāvalī-Kathe (A Compendium of Jain History) of Devacandra cf. Fleet, *Ind. Ant.*, 1892, pp. 157 ff.

Tilakamañjarī of Dhanapāla, ed. Bhavadatta Shastri, 2nd edn., Bombay, 1938.

Tiloyapaṇṇati of Yativṛṣabha, ed. A.N. Upadhye and H.L. Jain, Sholapur, 1951.

Triṣaṣṭiśalākāpuruṣacarita of Hemacandra, tr. H.M. Johnson, I-VI, Gaekwad's Oriental Series, Baroda, 1931-62.

Uttarapurāṇa of Guṇabhadra, ed. Pannalal Jain, 1st edn., BGP, Kashi, 1954.

Vardhamānacarita or *Mahāvīracarita* of Asaga, Sholapur, 1931.

Vasudevahiṇḍi of Sanghadāsagaṇi Vācaka, Bhavnagar, 1930; tr. B.L. Sandesaria, Bhavnagar, 1946; *The Vasudevahiṇḍi — An Authentic Jain Version of the Bṛhatkathā*, J.C. Jain, Ahmedabad, 1977.

Vividhatīrthakalpa of Jinaprabhā Sūri, ed. Jinavijaya, Bombay, 1934.

Yaśastilakacampu of Somadeva Sūri, ed. Sivadatta and K.P. Parab. Bombay, 1901-03; ed. with the Comm. of Śrutasāgara Sūri, vol. I, NSP, Bombay, 1916; ed. S. Shastri, Varanasi, 1960.

Historical Biographies

Alī Nāmā of Nusrati; *Āsaphvilāsa* of Jagannātha.

Badshah Aurangzeb ri Haqiqat; Bhera Śrī Guru Gobind Singh Kā.

Bhoja Prabandha of Ballāladeva, ed. J.L. Shastri, Delhi (undated).

Caitanya Bhāgavata of Vṛndāvan Dās; *Caitanya Caritāmṛta* of Kṛṣṇadāsa Kavirāja; *Caitanya Maṅgala* of Jayananda; *Campakavijaya.*

Delhi rī Pādshāh rī Yād.

Gauḍavaho of Vākpatirāja, ed. S.P. Pandit, Bombay Sanskrit & Prākṛt Series, No. 34, Bombay 1887.

Gorā Bādal Caupāī of Jatmal Nāhar; *Gorā Bādal Padminī Caupāī* of Hemaratna; *Gurbilās Pātshāhi Chevīn* of Sohan; *Gurbilās Pātshāhi Das* of Koer Singh; *Gurbilās Pātshāhi Dasween ke Caritar* of Bhāī Sukhā Singh; *Gyān Ratnāvalī Janamsākhī Guru Nānakjī dī.*

Hammīra Mahākāvya of Nāyacandra Sūri, ed. N.J. Kirtane, Bombay, 1878; ed. Jinavijaya, Jodhpur, 1968; also Jaganlal Gupta's article "Hammīra Mahākāvya", in *Nāgarī Pracāriṇī Patrikā*, Banaras, vol. 12, VS, 1988, pp. 259-309; abstract in *Ind. Ant.*, VIII, pp. 55 and 234; Eng. tr. C.H. Tawney, in *JBBRAS*, 1887.

Hammīra Rāso of Sāraṅgdhar; *Hammīra Rāso* or *Hammīrāyan* of Jodharāja; *Hammīra Caupāī* of Bhandav Vyasa; *Hammīra Haṭha* of Candraśekhar.

Harṣacarita of Bāṇa, ed. P.V. Kane, Bombay, 1918, rpt. Delhi, 1965; K.P. Parab, 3rd edn., Bombay, 1912; tr. E.B. Cowell and F.W. Thomas, London: Royal Asiatic Society of Great Britain, 1897, 2nd edn., 1929; Hindi tr. V.S. Agrawala under the title *Harṣacarita: Ek Sāṁskr̥tika Adhyayana*, Patna, 1964.

Janamsākhī of Bhāī Bala; *Janamsākhī* of Manohar Das Sodhi also called Manohar Das Meharbān; *Jaṅgnāmāh Śrī Guru Gobind Singh* of Ani Rai.

Kanhadade Prabandha of Padmanābha, ed. K.B. Vyas, Jaipur, 1953.

Khuman Rāso of Dalpat.

Kīrtilatā of Vidyāpati, ed. with Eng. tr. H.P. Shastri, Calcutta, 1924; ed. with Eng. tr. Umesha Mishra, Allahabad, 1960.

Kīrti-Samullāsa of Mahesh Thakur; *Kr̥ṣṇamālā*.

Kumārapālacarita (Prākr̥t *Dvāśraya Kāvya*) of Hemacandra, ed. S.P. Pandit, Bombay, 1900; A.V. Kathavate, 2 vols., Bombay, 1915-21; P.L. Vaidya, Poona, 1936.

Kumārapālacarita of Jayasiṁha Sūri, ed. Kṣntivijaya Gaṇi, Bombay, 1926.

Kumārapāla Prabandha of Jinamaṇḍana Gaṇi; *Kumārapāla Pratibodha* of Somaprabhā Sūri, ed. Jinavijaya, Gaekwad's Oriental Series, No. XIV, Baroda, 1920.

Mahārājā Ajit Singhji-ri-Khyāta; *Mahārājā Abhaya Singhji-ri-Khyāta*; *Mahima Prakash* of Sarup Das Bhalla; *Mānacarita*; *Marwar ra Pargana rī Vigat* of Nainsi, pt. I, ed. N.S. Bhati.

Nabākhānacarita of Mahesh Thakur.

Navasāhasāṅkacarita of Padmagupta, ed. V.S. Islampurkar, Bombay Sanskrit Series, Bombay, 1895.

Padmāvat of Malik Muhammad Jāyasī, ed. R.C. Shukla, Nagari Pracharini Sabha, Kashi, 1924.

Padmini Caritra Caupāī of Labhdodaya, ed. B.L. Nahata, Bikaner, VS, 2018.

Paramardi Rāso.

Prabhāvakacarita of Prabhācandra Sūri, ed. Jinavijaya, SJG, Bombay, 1940.

Pr̥thvīrāja Rāso of Canda Bardāī, ed. S.S. Das, Banaras, 1904, and Pandia and Das, Banaras, 1913.

Pr̥thvīrājavijaya of Jayānaka, ed. with comm. of Jonarāja by G.H. Ojha and C.S. Guleri, Ajmer, 1941; Hindi tr. in Nagari Pracarini Patrika, Banaras, 5, 1981, 133-83; Eng. abstract in *JRAS*, 1913, pp. 259-81.

Puruṣa Parikṣā of Vidyāpati, ed. and tr. Nerulkar, Bombay, 1914; Eng. tr. Grierson under the title *The Test of Man*, Royal Asiatic Society of Great Britain, London, 1935.

Rājaprakāśa of Kishordas; *Rājārāmacarita* of Keśava Paṇḍita.

Rājarūpaka of Ratanu Veer Bhana, ed. Pandit Rām Karan, Nagari Pracarini Sabha, Kashi, VS, 1998.

Rājavilāsa of Man, ed. M. Menaria, Nagari Pracarini Sabha, Kashi, 1957.

Rāmacarita (Pāla King Rāmapāla's *carita*) of Sandhyākara Nandi, ed. R.C. Majumdar, R.G. Basak and N.G. Banerjee, Rajsahi, 1939.

Raoji Amar Singhji-ri-Vāt; *Ratan Singh Mahesadasuta-ri-Vācanika* of Khiriya Jagga.

Samara Rāso of Ambadev Sūrī; *Śivabhārata* of Paramānanda; *Śrī Gur Sobha* of Chander Bhan also called Sainapat; *Surajanacarita* of Candraśekhar.

Veer Mayan of Bahadur Dhadhi.

Vikramacarita, HOS, vol. 26, Cambridge, Mass. 1926.

Vikramāṅkābhyudaya of Someśvara III, Mss. in the Jain Bhaṇḍāra, Paṭṭan.

Vikramāṅkadevacarita of Bilhaṇa, ed. G. Bühler, Bombay Sanskrit Series, no. 14, Bombay, 1875; tr. S.C. Banerjee and A.K. Gupta, Calcutta, 1965.

Viram de sonigara ki Vāt, ed. P.L. Menaria, Jodhpur, 1960.

Viśāladeo Rāso of Narpati, Nagari Pracarini Patrika, Banaras, vol. 45, no. 2, pp. 163-71.

Yaśodharacarita of Kanakasena Vādirāja, ed. T.A. Gopinatha Rao, Tanjore, 1912.

Chronicles, Vaṁśāvalīs and Other Historical Works

ASSAM

Ahom Burañjī (a chronicle of Assam from the earliest time to the end of Ahom rule), ed. and tr. G.C. Barua, Calcutta, 1930, rpt. Gauhati, 1985.

Assam Burañjī (a history of Assam from the beginning to the end of Ahom rule, an enlarged version of Kāśināth Tamuli Phukan's chronicle, by H.K. Barua), ed. S.K. Bhuyan, DHAS, Gauhati, 1930.

Assam Burañjī (a history of Assam from 1648 to 1681 based on old Assamese Manuscript chronicles), ed. S.K. Dutta, DHAS, Gauhati, 1938.

Assam Burañjī (a history of Assam from Sukāpha to Gadādhar Siṁha obtained from the family of Sukumar Mahanta), ed. S.K. Bhuyan, DHAS, Gauhati, 1945.

Darrāṅg Rājavaṁśavalī of Sūryakhari Daivajña (written in 1798), ed. H.C. Goswami, Shillong, 1917; also ed. N.C. Sharma, Pathsala, 1973.

Deodhai Assam Burañjī (with several shorter chronicles of Assamese Burañjīs), ed. S.K. Bhuyan, DHAS, Gauhati, 1932.

Jayantia Burañjī (a history of Jayantiā from the earliest times to 1744), ed. S.K. Bhuyan, DHAS, Gauhati, 1937.

Kachari Burañjī (a history of the Kachārīs from the earliest times to 1714), ed. S.K. Bhuyan, DHAS, Gauhati, 1936.

Kāmarūpar Burañjī (a history of Assam from ancient times to 1696 compiled from a number of old chronicles), ed. S.K. Bhuyan, DHAS, Gauhati, 1930.

Koch Rājavaṁśāvalī of Ratikānta Dvija, originally written in 1802.

Pādshāh Burañjī, an old Assamese chronicle originaly pub. by KAS, Gauhati, 1935, tr. into English by S.K. Bhuyan under the title *Annals of the Delhi Badshahate*, DHAS, Gauhati, 1947.

Purāṇī Assam Burañjī (a history of Assam from the beginning of the Ahom rule to 1696), ed. H.C. Goswami, KAS, Gauhati, 1922.

Satsari Assam Burañjī (a collection of seven old Assamese chronicles), ed. S.K. Bhyan, Gauhati University, Gauhati, 1960, 4th edn., 1974.

Tripurā Burañjī (a historical account of Tripurā with special reference to the events of 1710-15 by two Assamese envoys of King Rudra Siṁha), ed. S.K. Bhuyan, DHAS, Gauhati, 1938.

Tuṅgkhungia Burañjī (Eng. tr. of Śrīnāth Barbarua's Assamese chronicle dealing with history of Assam from 1671 to 1806 by S.K. Bhuyan with additions bringing down the account to 1826), OUP, London, 1933, rpt. DHAS, Gauhati, 1968.

BENGAL

Annadamaṅgala of Bharat Chandra; *Mahārāṣṭra Purāṇa* of Gaṅgārām; *Rājyacampati* of Govind Das; *Ratnasenakula-praśasti* of Bhavadatta.

GURJARADEŚA (GUJARAT)

Hammīra-madamardana of Jayasiṁha Sūri.

Kīrtikaumudī of Someśvara, Bombay, 1883.

Prabandhacintāmaṇi of Merutuṅga, ed. Jinavijaya, Shvetambara Jain Series, no. I, Santiniketan, 1933; Eng. tr. C.H. Tawney, The Asiatic Society, Calcutta, 1901.

Prabandha Kośa of Rājaśekhara Sūri II, ed. Jinavijaya, Svetambara Jain Series, Calcutta, 1935, SJG, Bombay, 1935.

Prabandhāvalī of Jinabhadra.

Purātana Prabandha Saṁgraha (a collection of some shorter Prabandha works), ed. Jinavijaya, Svetambara Jain Series, no. 2, Calcutta, 1936.

Sukr̥takīrti-Kallolinī of Udayaprabhā Sūri.

Sukr̥tasaṁkīrtana of Arisiṁha.

Vasantavilāsa of Bālacandra Sūri.

Vastupāla-Tejaḥpāla-praśasti of Jayasiṁha Sūri.

KASHMIR

Rājataraṅgiṇī of Kalhaṇa, ed. Durga Prasad, Bombay, 1892; Eng. tr. M.A. Stein, 3 vols., Westminster, 1900, rpt., 2nd edn., Delhi, 1961; Eng. tr. R.S. Pandit, Allahabad, 1935, rpt., Delhi, 1968; Eng. tr. J.C. Dutt under the title *Kings of Kashmir*, 2 vols., Calcutta, 1879, 1887, rpt. Delhi, 1997.

Rājāvalī or *Dvitīya Rājataraṅgiṇī* of Jonarāja, ed. P. Peterson, Bombay, 1896.

Jaina Rājataraṅgiṇī of Śrīvara, ed. with Hindi tr. Raghunath Singh, pt. I, Varanasi, 1977.

Rājataraṅgiṇī of Jonarāja and of Śrīvara, and *Rājāvalīpatākā* (also called *Rājāvalīpiṭaka*) of Prājyabhaṭṭa and Śuka, all tr. into English by J.C. Dutt under the title *Kings of Kashmir*, vol. III, Calcutta, 1898, rpt., Delhi, 1997.

MAHARASHTRA

Bal Bhonsle, *Marathi Bakhar*, *Manohar*, Poona, Oct. 1964.

H.A. Acworth, *Ballads of the Marāṭhās*, London, 1894.

H.A. Acworth and S.T. Shaligram, *Powadasas Historical Ballads of the Marāṭhās*, Poona, 1911.

Krishnaji Anant Sabhāsad's Bakhar — *Śiva Chatrapatichen Carita*, ed. K.N. Sane, 3rd edn., Poona, 1912; Eng. tr. S.N. Sen under the title *Śiva Chatrapati*, Calcutta, 1920.

Malhar Ram Rao, *Śiva Chatrapatichen Saptaprakaranātmak Caritra*, ed. M.J. Kirtane, 2nd edn., Poona, 1894.

N.J. Kirtane, *Marthyanche Bakharivar Ṭīkā*, Poona, 1926.

R.V. Hervadkar, *Marathi Bakhars*, University of Bombay Library, March 1955, Pune, 1957.

Śivadigvijaya, ed. P.R. Nandurbarkar and L.K. Dandekar, Baroda, 1895.

T.S. Shejwalkar, *Panipat*, 1761 (A critical evaluation of the *Bakhars*, including Raghunath Yadav's *Panipatanchi Bakhar* dealing with the third battle of Panipat 1761), Poona, 1946.

V.K. Rajwade, *Marathyanchya Itihasachi Sadhane*.

V.N. Kulkarni and Other (eds.), *Peshwanchi Bakhar* by K.P. Sohoni, Bombay, 1963.

V.S. Vakaskar (ed.), *Sabhāsad Bakhar*, 4th edn., Pune, 1973.

———, *Ninety-One Qalmi Bakhar* of Dattaji Trimal Waqnis (ed.), Pune, 1962.

MANIPUR

Bamon Khunthoklon, ed. H. Ibopishak Meitei, Imphal, 1987.

Bijoy (Vijaya) Pañchalī (originally composed by Krīticandra in Bengali and compiled by Dvija Sita Ram Sharma under the patronage of King Garībniwāj 1709-48), ed. M. Jhulon Singh and also tr. by him from Bengali into Manipuri under the title *Maṇipurī Itihāsa* (3rd edn. Imphal, 1947) and into English under the title *History of Manipur*, pts. I & II, Imphal, 1936, 1941; also tr. from Bengali into Manipuri by Mani Singh and Mangi Singh, Imphal, 1966.

Cheitharol Kumbaba (a royal chronicle), ed. N. Khelchandra Singh and L. Iboongohal Singh, Imphal, 1967.

Khagemba Nongshamei Puya, ed. O. Bhogeshwor Singh, M.A. Janab Khan, Imphal, 1969.

Ningthourol Lambuba, ed. O. Bhogeshwor Singh, Imphal, 1967 (1968).

Sanamahi Laiken, ed. O. Bhogeshwor Singh, Imphal, 1972.

NEPAL

Gopālarāja Vaṁśāvalī, in 3 pts. in Sanskrit and partly in old Newari compiled in CE 1390, discovered by C. Bendall in Darbar Library Kathmandu during 1884-85; ed. D.R. Regmi, *Mediaeval Nepal*, vol. III, pp. 112 ff, 158 ff. The chronicles and *vaṁśāvalī*s of Nepal are important for the study of its history of ancient and early medieval period.

Parbatīya Vaṁśāvalī (Originally written in Parbatīya with an admixture of Sanskrit and Newari), tr. Munshi Shiva Shankar Singh and Pt. Shri Gunanand in 1867; *History of Nepal*, ed. Daniel Wright (1st edn. Cambridge, 1877, rpt. Kathmandu, 1972) is totally based on the translation of this work; *Ind. Ant.*, vol. XIII, pp. 411 ff (for Bhagawanlal Indraji's writing on the Vaṁśāvalīs of Nepal).

Vaṁśāvalī, in Sanskrit (anonymous), 2 vols., composed in CE 1350.

ORISSA

Mādalā Pāñjī; *Gaṅgavaṁśānucarita and Rājavaṁśāvalī* (for history of Orissa since the establishment of the Gaṅga dynasty); *vaṁśāvalī*s of Orissa cf. *JASB*, vol. VI, pt. II, 1837, pp. 756 ff; *As. Res.*, XV, 1822 (for history and chronology of Orissa); *Samar Taraṅga* of Brajanāth Bade Jena.

PUNJAB

Nadir Shah di Var, by Najabat; *Vaṁśāvalī Nama Desan Patshahian Ka*, by Kesar Singh Chibbar; *Var Amritsar Ki*, by Darshan.

RAJASTHAN

Khyātas (comprehensive historical chronicles dealing with the histories of Rājpūt states in a chronological order), notably, the *Khyāta* compiled by Muhnot Nainsi known after him as *Mutha* or *Mūtā-Nainsi-ri-Khyāta*; *Deśavalīvivṛti*, by Jaganmohana.

SINDH

Cācanāmā also called *Chachnama* (a chronicle of Sindh), Eng. tr. in H.M. Elliot and J. Dowson's *The History of India as Told by Its Own Historians*, vol. I, pp. 138-211.

TRIPURA

Rājamālā (a royal chronicle), pub. by the Directorate of Education, Govt. of Tripura, Agartala, 1967.

Śrī-Rājamālā, by K.P. Sen, 4 vols., Agartala, vol. I, 1926, vol. II, 1927, vols. III & IV, 1931.

Rājamālā Ba Tripurar Itivritta (Rājamālā or History of Tripurā), by K.C. Sinha, Comilla, 1896.

Some South Indian Works

ĀNDHRADEŚA

Bhojarājiyam of Ananta; *Kākatīyacarita* of Narasiṁham; *Kākatīyarāja Vaṁśāvalī* by Kasesarvappa; *Kumārasambhavamu* of Nannecoḍu; *Manucarita* of Allasani Peddana; *Ranaraṅgavijayam* of Nilādru; *Raṅgarāyacarita* (a historical *Prabandha*) of Ditta Kavi Nārāyaṇa Kavi, *Somadevarājiyamu* of Kuchimanchi Jaggakavi; *Śrīrangah-māhātvamu* of Bhairava Kavi; *Uttaraharivaṁśamu* of Nachana Somanātha; *Vemabhūpālacarita* or *Viranārāyaṇacarita* of Vāmanabhaṭṭa.

KARṆĀṬADEŚA

Acyutarāyābhyudaya of Rājanātha III; *Chikkadevarāja Vaṁśāvalī* of Tirumalaraya, Dharwad, 1972; *Chikkadevarāja Vijayam* of Tirumalayanagar, Mysore, 1896; *Haidar Nāmā* of Kacheri Krishniah (or Nalappa) written in 1784; *Hoysaḷarājavijayam*; *Hoysaḷarājakulavaṁśa*; *Kanthirava Narasarāja Vijayam* of Govinda Vaidya, rpt. Bangalore, 1971; *Keladi Nṛpa Vijaya* of Liṅganna, ed. R. Shama Shastry, Bangalore, 1921;

Kṛṣṇadevarāyavijayamu of Kumāra Dhūrjaṭi; *Madhurāvijaya* or *Virakamparāyacarita* of Gaṅgā-devī; *Mahācoḷārājīya* of Sadak-Sarideva; *Mysuru-rājara-caritre* of Shanubhoga Veṅkaṭaramaṇa (written in or about 1790); *Mysururājyada-purvottara*; *Rājakālanirṇaya* of Vidyāraṇya; R. Narasiṁhācārya, *Karṇāṭaka Kavi Carite*, vol. II, rpt. Bangalore, 1973, vol. III, 1st edn., Bangalore, 1929 (for original literary works); *Sāluvābhyudaya* of Rājanātha II; *Vikramārjuna-Vijaya* or *Pampā Bhārata* of Pampā, ed. L. Rice, Bangalore, 1898; *Vijayapuri Kathā* (about Bijapur's Sultāns).

KERALA

Iravikkuttipilla Pāttu; *Keralolpatti*; *Kokasandeśam*; *Mamankam Kilipāttu* of Katanceri Namboodari; *Muṣikavaṁśa* of Atula; *Padapāṭṭu*; *Rājarathnavaliyam Campu* of Nārāyaṇan; *Śivavilāsa* of Dāmodara; *Uṇṇicirutevicaritam*; *Uṇṇiyacicaritam*; *Uṇṇunilisandeśam*; *Uṇṇyadicaritum*.

TAMILDEŚA

Coḷavaṁśacaritaṁ; *Kalavazhi-nārpatu* of Poygaiyar; *Kaliṅgattupparaṇi* of Jayangoṇḍān or Jayaṅkoṇḍān; *Kongudeśarājākkal*; *Kulottuṅgacoḷacarita* of Tirunārāyaṇa; *Kulottuṅgaṇ-pillaittamil* of Oṭṭakkūṭṭan; *Maduraikāñcī* of Māṅgudi Marudanār; *Maṇimekhalai* of Sittalai Sāttanār; *Maṇi-Mekhalai in Its Historical Setting*, by S.K. Aiyangar; *Nandikkalambakaṁ*; *Nedunalvādai* of Nakkirar; *Paṭṭinappālai* of Uruttiran Kaṇṇanar; *Periyapurāṇaṁ* of Sekkilār; *Porunārrārruppadai* of Mutattāmakkaṇṇiyar; *Rājarājacarita* or *Rājarājavijaya*; *Rājarāja-śoḷanuḷā*; *Ramayappan Ammanai*; *Śilappadikāraṁ* of Ilaṅgōvadigal, ed. V.R.R. Dikshitar, Oxford, 1939; *Tanjaivanan Kovai* of Poyyamoli Pulavar.

Classical (Greek and Latin) Sources

McCrindle, J.W., *Ancient India as Described by Megasthenes and Arrian* (tr. of the Fragments of the *Indika* of Megasthenes, and of the first part of the *Indika* (chs. I-XVII) of Arrivan, 1st edn., London, 1877.

———, *Ancient India as Described in Classical Literature*, Westminster, 1901, rpt. Delhi, 1984.

———, *Invasion of India by Alexander the Great*, 1st edn. Westminster, 1892, rpt. Delhi, 1989.

Majumdar, R.C., *Classical Accounts of India*, Calcutta, 1960, rpt. 1981.

Pliny, *Naturalis Historia* (*Natural History*), ed. C. Mayhoff, Leipzig, 1892-1909; tr., New York, 1962.

Chinese Work

Hiuen Tsang, *Si-Yu-Ki*, Eng. tr. S. Beal (*Buddhist Records of the Western World*), 2 vols., 1st edn., London, 1884, rpt. 1906, Delhi 1969, and by T. Watters (*On Yuan Chwang's Travels in India*) ed. T.W. Rhys Davids and S.W. Bushell, 2 vols., Royal Asiatic Society of Great Britain, London, 1904-05, 2nd Indian edn., Delhi, 1973.

Arabic Works

Al-Biruni, *Tahqiq-i-Hind*, Eng. tr. of the Arabic text by E.C. Sachau (*Alberuni's India*), 2 vols., 1st edn. Berlin, 1888, London, 1910, rpt. Delhi, 1964, 1989.

Cācanāmā (or *Chachnama*), Originally written in Arabic by an anonymous Muslim historian of Sindh, tr. into Persian by Muhammad Ali bin Abu Bakr Kufi in CE 1216, Eng. tr. in H.M. Elliot and J. Downson's *The History of India as Told by Its Own Historians*, vol. I.

Sachau, E.C. (tr.), *Alberuni's Chronology of Ancient Nations*, London, 1879.

Persian Sources

Khazain-ul-Futuh (The Treasure of victories), by Amir Khusrau, Eng. tr. M. Habib under the title *The Campaigns of Ala-ud-din Khilji*, Aligarh, 1931.

Futuh-us-Salatin of Isami, ed. Mahdi Hussain.

Siyar-ul-Mutakherin of Ghulam Hussain Khan.

Tārīkh-i-Ferishtā of Mahomed Kasim Ferishta, Eng. tr. of it in Briggs' *History of the Rise of the Mahomedan Power in India till the Year 1612 AD*, 2 vols. London, 1829.

Tārīkh-i-Ferozshāhī of Ziauddin Barani, tr. in Elliot and Downson's *The History of India as Told by its own Historians*, vol. III.

Coins and Inscriptions

Allan, J., *A Catalogue of the Indian Coins in the British Museum, Ancient India*, London, 1936.

———, *Catalogue of the Coins of the Gupta Dynasty and of Śaśāṅka, King of Gauda* (in the British Museum), London, 1914.

Cunningham, A., *Coins of Ancient India from the Earliest Times down to the Seventh Century CE*, London, 1891, rpt. Varanasi, 1971.

———, *Coins of Medievel India*, London, 1983.

Fleet, J.F., *Inscriptions of the Early Gupta Kings and Their Successors*, CII, III, Calcutta, 1888.

Rapson, E.J., *Indian Coins*, Varanasi, 1969.

Sircar, D.C. (ed.), *Select Inscriptions Bearing on Indian History and Civilization*, vol. I, Calcutta, 1965.

Smith, V.A., *Catalogue of the Coins in the Indian Museum, Calcutta*, vol. I: Coins of Ancient India, Oxford, 1906, rpt. Varanasi, 1972.

Modern Works

Agrawala, V.S., *Bhārata Sāvitrī* (a historical study of the *Mahābhārata*), vols. I and II, 2nd edn., Delhi, 1977, vol. III, 1st edn., Delhi, 1968.

Aiyangar, S.K., *The Beginnings of South Indian History*, Madras, 1918.

Aiyar, K.G.S., *Cera Kings of the Saṅgam Period*, London, 1937.

Altekar, A.S., "Can we Reconstruct Pre-Bhārata War History?", *JBHU*, IV, pp. 183-223.

Arora, R.K. *Historical and Cultural Data from the Bhaviṣya Purāṇa*, Delhi, 1972.

Bentley, J., "On the Principal Eras and Dates of the Ancient Hindus", *As. Res.*, vol. 5, Delhi, 1979, pp. 315-43.

Bühler, G., "On the Authenticity of Jaina Tradition", in *The Indian Sect of the Jains*, tr. Burgess, London, 1903.

———, "Hindu Chronology", in *EB*, vol. 13 (211th edn.), pp. 499-500.

Chakravorty, B.B., *Itihāsa of Bhāratavarṣa from the Bhāratīya Viewpoint (up to Gupta Period)*, Calcutta, 1995.

Das, A.C., *Ṛgvedic India: Cultural History of India as depicted in the Ṛgveda*, 2 vols., Calcutta, 1920, rpt. Delhi, 1980.

Dasgupta, K.K., "Historical Biography in Sanskrit Literature", in *Historical Biography in Indian Literature*, ed. S.P. Sen, Calcutta, 1979, pp. 3-28.

De, S.C., *Historicity of Rāmāyaṇa and the Indo-Aryan Society in India and Ceylon*, Delhi, 1976.

De Souza, J.P. and Kulkarni, C.M. (eds.), *Historiography in Indian Languages*, Bombay, 1972.

Devahuti, D. (ed.), *Bias in Indian Historiography*, Delhi, 1980.

———, *Harsha: A Political Study*, Oxford, 1970.

Dikshit, U.S., *Maharṣi Vedavyāsa: A Historical and Cultural Biography*, Varanasi, 1968.

Dikshitar, V.R.R., "The Purāṇa: A Study", *IHQ*, VIII, pp. 747-67.

———, *Studies in Tamil Literature and History*, London, 1930.

Dutt, R.C., "Kings of Kashmir", *Calcutta Review*, July 1880.

———, "An Introductory Essay on the History of Kashmira", in J.C. Dutt, *Kings of Kashmira* (Eng. tr. of the *Rājataraṅgiṇī* of Kalhaṇa), vol. II, Calcutta, 1887, rpt. Delhi, 1997, pp. iii-xxx.

———, "A Note on Kalhaṇa's *Rājtaraṇgiṇī*", in H.H. Wilson, *The Hindu History of Kashmir,* Calcutta, 1960, Appendix X, pp. 141-59.

Elliot, H.M. and J., Dowson, *The History of India as Told by Its Own Historians,* 8 vols. London, 1867-1877.

Ghoshal, U.N., *The Beginnings of Indian Historiography and Other Essays,* Calcutta, 1944.

———, *Studies in Indian History and Culture,* Calcutta, 1957.

———, "History and Historians of Ancient India in the Modern Age", in *Indo-Asian Culture,* IX, 1961, pp. 353-84.

Handiqui, K.K., *Yaśastilakacampu and Indian Culture,* Sholapur, 1949.

Jain, G.C., *Yaśastilaka kā Sāṁskṛtika Adhyayana,* Amritsar, 1967.

Jain, J.P., *The Jaina Sources of the History of Ancient India (100 BC – AD 900),* Delhi, 1964.

Jayaswal, K.P., "Chronology and History of Nepal, 600 BC – AD 800", *JBORS,* XXII, III, 1936, pp. 157-264.

Jones, W., "On the Chronology of the Hindus", *As. Res.*, vol. 2, 1st pub. 1799, rpt. Delhi, 1979, pp. 107-13.

Kennedy, J., "The Purāṇic Histories of the Early Aryas", *JRAS*, 1915.

Kumar, V., *Tilakamañjarī kā Ālocanātmaka Adhyayana,* Ujjain, 1978.

Majumdar, R.C., "Ideas of History in Sanskrit Literature", in *Historical Writing on the Peoples of Asia,* vol. I: Historians of India, Pakistan and Ceylon, ed. C.H. Philips, London, 1961, rpt. 1967, rpt. 1967 pp. 13-28.

———, *Historiography in Modern India,* Bombay, 1970.

Mankad, D.R., "Studies in Purāṇic History, Genealogies and Chronology in Modern Times", in *Purāṇa,* IV, I, 1962, pp. 3-22.

———, *Purānic Chronology,* Vallabh Vidyānagara, 1951.

Mirashi, V.V., "Some Purāṇic Passages corroborated by Inscriptional and Numismatic Evidence", in *Purāṇa,* I, I, pp. 31-38.

Mukhtar, J.K., *Jaina Sāhitya aur Itihāsa Parviśada Prakāśa,* Calcutta, 1956.

———, *Varṇi Volume,* Sagar, 1949.

Mukopadhyay, S.K., *Evolution of Historiography in Modern India,* Calcutta, 1980.

Munshi, K.M., *Glory that was Gurjaradeśa (AD 550-1300),* pt. II, Bombay, 1955.

Murthy, H.V.S., "Historical Biography in Kannada Literature", in *Historical Biography in Indian Literature,* ed. S.P. Sen, pp. 342-44.

Padmanabhan, S.N., "Historical Biographies in Tamil Literature", in *Historical Biography in Indian Literature,* ed. S.P. Sen, pp. 315-26.

Pandey, R.B., *Vikramaditya of Ujjayini: Founder of the Vikram Era*, Varanasi, 1951, tr. into Hindi under the title *Vikramāditya: Saṁvat Paravartaka*, Varanasi, 1960.

Pargiter. F.E., *Ancient Indian Historical Tradition*, 1st edn., London, 1922, rpt. Delhi, 1972.

———, *The Purāṇa Text of the Dynasties of the Kali Age*, Oxford, 1913.

———, "Ancient Indian Genealogies and Chronology", *JRAS*, 1910, pp. 1-56.

———, "Earliest Indian Traditional History", *JRAS*, 1914, pp. 267 ff.

Pathak, V.S., *Ancient Historians of India: A study in Historical Biography*, Bombay, 1966.

Patil, D.R., *Cultural History from the Vāyu Purāṇa*, Poona, 1946, rpt., Delhi, 1973.

———, "Gupta Inscriptions and Purāṇic Tradition", *BDCRS*, II, pp. 2-58.

Philips, C.H. (ed.), *Historians of India, Pakistan and Ceylon*, vol. I of *Historical Writing on the Peoples of Asia*, London: *SOAS*, 1961, rpt. 1967.

Pradhan, S.N., *Chronology of Ancient India*, Varanasi, 1979.

Premi, N.R. *Jaina Sāhitya aur Itihāsa*, Bombay, 1942, revd. edn., 1956.

Puri, B.N., "D.R. Bhandarkar and Indian Historiography", in *PIHC*, 42nd Session, Magadha University, Bodh Gaya, 1981, pp. 35-41.

———, *Ancient Indian Historiography*, Delhi, 1994.

Pusalker, A.D., *Studies in the Epics and Purāṇas*, Bombay, 1955.

———, "Conception of History in Ancient Indian Literature", in *Our Heritage*, XII, 2, 1964, pp. 35-52.

———, "Sanskrit Histories and Chronicles", in *Cul. Her. Ind.*, vol. V, ed. S.K. Chatterji, Calcutta, 1978, pp. 283-90.

Ray, S.N., *Historical and Cultural Studies in the Purāṇas*, Allahabad, 1978.

Reu, V.N., *Ṛgveda ek Aitihāsik Dṛṣṭi*, Delhi, 1967.

Santhanam, K. (ed.), *An Anthology of Indian Literatures*, Bombay, 1969.

Sarkar, Sir Jadunath, *Shivaji and His Times*, Calcutta, 1929.

Sarkar, J.N., "Ideas of History in Mediaeval India", *QRHS*, IV, 1-2, pp. 1-21.

Shastri, A. Banerji, "On Ancient Indian Historical Tradition", *JBORS*, XIII, pp. 62-79.

Shastri, N.C., *Ādi Purāṇa mein Pratipādita Bhārata*, Varanasi, 1968.

Sen, S.N., *Extracts and Documents relating to Maratha History*, vol. I, University of Calcutta, 1920.

Sen, S.P., (ed.), *Historians and Historiography in Modern India*, Calcutta, 1973.

———, (ed.), *History in Modern Indian Literature*, Calcutta, 1975.

———, (ed.), *Historical Biography in Indian Literature*, Calcutta, 1979.

Sieg, E., *Die Sagenstoffe des R̥gveda und die Indische Itihāsa Tradition*, Stuttgart, 1902.

———, "Itihāsa Tradition", in J. Hastings (ed.), *ERE*, vol. VII, pp. 46-62.

Singh, G.P., *Early Indian Historical Tradition and Archaeology*, Delhi, 1994.

———, *Ancient Indian Historiography: Sources and Interpretations*, Delhi, 2003.

———, "Sources of the History of Mediaeval Assam", in *Sources of the History of India*, vol. III, ed. N.R. Ray, Calcutta, 1980, pp. 119-32.

———, "A New Approach to the study of Historical Data in the Epic and Purāṇic Literature Regarding Ancient India", *Proceedings of the UGC Sponsored National Seminar on History and Literature*, Sardar Patel University, Vallabh Vidyanagar, Gujarat, February 1991, pp. 1-15.

———, "Historicity of Bilhaṇa's Account of Vikramāditya's Invasion of Kāmarūpa in the Eleventh century AD", *Shodhak, JHR*, XXVI, A, 76, 1997, pp. 3-5.

———, "Was Herodotus of Greece the Father of History?", *Adhyayan; JBIAS*, II, 1 & 2, 1993, pp. 1-10.

———, *The Purāṇic Tradition of Historiography in India*, XXXI, 1 & 2, January & July 2004, pp. 1-17.

Smith, R.M., *Dates and, Dynasties in Earliest India*, ed. J.L. Shastri, Delhi, 1973.

Thapar, R., "The Tradition of Historical Writing in Early India", in *AISH*, Hyderabad, 1984, pp. 268-93.

Tikekar, S.R., *On Historiography*, Bombay, 1964.

Tod, J., *Annals and Antiquities of Rajasthan*, vol. I, 1st edn., London, 1829, rpt., Delhi, 1971.

Upadhyaya, B., *Purāṇa Vimarśa*, Varanasi, 1965.

Vaidya, C.V., *The Mahābhārata: A Criticism*, Delhi, 1966.

Venkatachalam, K., *The Plot in Indian Chronology*, Vijayawada, 1953.

———, *Chronology of Ancient Hindu History*, 2 pts., Vijayawada, 1957.

Warder, A.K., *An Introduction to Indian Historiography*, Bombay, 1972.

Wilford, F., "Chronology of the Hindus", *As. Res.*, vol. V, Delhi, 1979, pp. 241-92.

Wilson, H.H., "An Essay on the Hindu History of Cashmir", *As. Res.*, XV, 1825, pp. 1-119.

———, *The Hindu History of Kashmir*, Calcutta, 1960.

General Works

Acton, L., *Lectures on Modern History*, London, 1906.

Agrawala, P.K. (ed.), *Itihāsa-Darśana* (Collection of papers of the late V.S., Agrawala), Varanasi, 1978.

Agrawala, V.S., *India as Described by Manu*, Varanasi, 1970.

Ali, S.M., *The Geography of the Purāṇas*, Delhi, 1983.

Allan, J., W. Haig, and H.H. Dodwell, *The Cambridge Shorter History of India*, Delhi, 1964.

Barnes, H.E., *A History of Historical Writing*, New York, 1963.

Barraclough, G., *History in a Changing World*, Oxford, 1955.

Basham, A.L., *The Wonder that was India*, London, 1969.

Baveridge, H., *A Comprehensive History of India*, vol. I, London, 1862, rpt., Delhi, 1982.

Bendall, C., *A Journey of Literary and Archaeological Research in Nepal and North India 1884-85*, Cambridge, 1886.

Bhandarkar, R.G., *A Peep into the Early History of India from the Foundation of the Maurya Dynasty to the Downfall of the Imperial Gupta Dynasty (322 BC – c. AD 500)*, Varanasi, 1978.

———, *Early History of the Dekkan down to the Mahomedan Conquest*, Delhi, 1979.

Bhargava, P.L., *Chandragupta Maurya: A Gem of Indian History*, Lucknow, 1935, rpt., Delhi: D.K. Printworld, 2007.

Burckhardt, J., *Judgements on History and on Historians*, Oxford, 1959.

Carr, E.H., *What is History?*, Harmondsworth, 1977.

Chakraberti, C., *Classical Studies in Ancient Races and Myths*, Delhi, 1979.

Chanda, R.P., *The Indo-Aryan Races: A Study of the Origin of Indo-Aryan People and Institutions*, Rajshahi, 1916, rpt., Delhi, 1978.

Chatterji, S.K. (ed.), *Cultural Heritage of India*, vol. V, Calcutta, 1978.

———, *Kirāta-jana-Kṛti*, Calcutta: The Asiatic Society, 1974.

Chaudhari, G.C., *Political History of Northern India from Jain Sources (AD 650-1300)*, Amritsar, 1963.

Collingwood, R.G., *The Idea of History*, London, 1946, rpt. 1973.

Croce, B., *The Theory and History of Historiography*, London, 1921.

———, *History as the Story of Liberty*, London, 1941.

Dey. N.L., *Civilization in Ancient India*, Delhi, 1972.

Devi, L., *Ahom-Tribal Relations (A Political Study)*, Gauhati, 1968.

Dutt, R.C., *A History of Civilization in Ancient India based on Sanskrit Literature*, vol. I (c. 2000 – 320 BCE), Mymensingh, 1888, rpt., Delhi, 1972.

———, *Ancient India* (*c. 2000* BCE – CE *800*), Delhi, 1980.

Elphinstone, M., *The History of India*, ed. E.B. Cowell, 9th edn., London, 1911.

Farquhar, J.N., *An Outline of the Religious Literature of India*, Oxford, 1920, rpt., Delhi, 1967.

Ferro, M., *The Use and Abuse of History or How the Past is Taught*, London, 1984.

Gait, E., *A History of Assam*, Calcutta, 1905, rpt., Delhi, 2003.

Geldner, K.F., *Vedische Studien*, Stuttgart, 1881-1901.

Gopalan, R., *History of the Pallavas of Kāncī*, Madras, 1928.

Gottschalk, L., *Understanding History: A Premier of Historical Method*, New York, 1958.

Gupta, S.P., K.S. Ramachandran (eds.), *Aspects of Indian History and Archaeology*, Delhi, 1977.

Gyani, S.D., *Agni Purāṇa: A Study*, Varanasi, 1964.

Hopkins, E.W., *The Great Epic of India*, New York, 1901, rpt., Calcutta, 1969.

Hunter, W.W., *A Statistical Account of Bengal*, vol. VI, London, 1876.

Hutchison, J., J. Ph. Vogel, *History of the Panjab Hill States*, vol. I, Lahore, 1933, rpt., Shimla, 1982.

Jacobi, H., *Das Rāmāyaṇa*, Bonn, 1893.

Jain, J.C., *Life in Ancient India as Depicted in the Jaina Canon and Commentaries (Sixth Century* BCE *to Seventeenth Century* CE*)*, Delhi, 1984.

Jain, R.C., *Ethnology of Ancient Bhārata*, Varanasi, 1970.

Jaiswal, S.K., *Polity and Administration in the Matsya Purāṇa*, Jaipur, 1996.

Jayaswal, K.P., *Hindu Polity*, Bangalore, 1981.

———, *History of India* (CE *150–350*), Lahore, 1933.

Kaegi, A., *Life in Ancient India (Studies in Rigvedic India)*, tr. from the German by R. Arrowsmith, Calcutta, 1950.

Kamei, G., *History of Manipur*, vol. I, *Pre-colonial Period*, Delhi, 1991.

Keith, A.B., *History of Sanskrit Literature*, Oxford, 1920, rpt., Delhi, 1973.

———, *The Religion and Philosophy of the Veda and Upanishads*, HOS, vol. XXXI, pt. I.

Kosambi, D.D., *The Culture and Civilisation of Ancient India in Historical Outline*, Delhi, 1972.

———, *An Introduction to the Study of Indian History*, Bombay, 1975.

Krishnamachariar, M., *History of Classical Sanskrit Literature*, 3rd edn., Delhi, 1974.

Law, B.C., *The Magadhas in Ancient India*, Varanasi, 1976.

———, *Geographical Essays Relating to Ancient Geography of India*, Delhi, 1976.

———, *Geographical Aspect of Kalidasa's Works*, Delhi, 1976.

———, *A History of Pāli Literature*, 2 vols., Delhi, 1983.

Levi, S., *Le Nepal Etude Historique dun Royaune Hindou*, vol. III, Paris, 1908.

Macdonell, A.A., *History of Sanskrit Literature*, 1st edn., Oxford, 1899, 3rd Indian edn., Delhi, 1972.

Macdonell, A.A., A.B., Keith, *Vedic Index of Names and Subjects*, 2 vols. 1st edn., London, 1912, rpt. 3rd edn., Indian Texts Series, Delhi, 1967.

Majumdar, A.K., *Early Hindu India: A Dynastic Study*, vol. I, 1st edn., Dhaka, 1917, rpt., Delhi, 1981.

Majumdar, R.C. (ed.), *The Vedic Age*, Bombay, 1965.

———, *Ancient India*, Delhi, 1977.

———, *Bangladesher Itihāsa (Madhya Yug)*, Calcutta, 1976.

Marushkin, B.I., *History and Politics*, tr. from Russian into English, Moscow, 1975.

Masson-Oursel, P & C., *Ancient India and Indian Civilisation*, London, 1951.

Max Müller, F., *A History of Ancient Sanskrit Literature*, 1st edn., London, 1859, revd. and ed. S.N. Shastri, Varanasi, 1968.

———, The Vedas (Collections of lectures and writings of Max Müller on the subject published in his various books), Varanasi, 1969.

———, *India: What Can It Teach Us*, London, 1883, and 1899.

Mishra, B.B., *Polity in the Agni Purāṇa*, Calcutta, 1965.

Mishra, B.P., *Nepal kā Itihāsa*, Bombay, 1904.

Mitra, R.L., *Sanskrit Buddhist Literature of Nepal*, Calcutta, 1882.

Mookerji, R. Kumud, *Ancient India*, Allahabad, 1956.

Muir, J., *Original Sanskrit Texts on the Origin and History of the People of India, their Religion and Institutions*, vol. II, 2nd edn., London, 1871.

Mukerjee, R. Kamal, *The Culture and Art of India*, London, 1959.

Nehru, J.L., *The Discovery of India*, Delhi, 1974.

Olmstead, A.T., *Assyrian Historiography: A Source Study*, Columbia, Missouri, 1916.

Pande, S.N., *Geographical Horizon of the Mahabharata*, Varanasi, 1980.

Pandey, R.B., *Bhāratīya Itihāsa kā Paricaya (Introduction to Indian History)*, Varanasi, 1963.

Phillips, M., *The Teaching of the Vedas*, London, 1894, rpt., Delhi, 1976.

Powicke, F., *Modern Historians and the Study of History*, London, 1955.

Prakash, O., *Political Ideas in the Purāṇas*, Allahabad, 1974.

Prasad, Rajendra, *Saṁskṛt aur Saṁskṛti*, Delhi, 1974.

Ragozin, Z.A., *History of Vedic India*, 1st edn., London, 1895, rpt., Delhi, 1974.

Rai, R.K., *Vālmīki-Rāmāyaṇa Kośa*, Varanasi, 1965.

———, *Mahābhārata Kośa*, Varanasi, 1982.

Rapson, E.J. (ed.), *The Cambridge History of India*, vol. I, *Ancient India*, Cambridge, 1922, rpt., Delhi, 1962.

———, *Ancient India from the Earliest Times to the First Century* CE, Varanasi, 1981.

Ray, H.C., *The Dynastic History of Northern India*, 2 vols., Calcutta, 1931, 1936.

Rawlinson, H.G., *A Concise History of the Indian People*, London, 1938, rpt., Madras, 1956.

Raychaudhuri, H.C., *Political History of Ancient India*, 6th edn., Calcutta, 1953.

Ray, N.R. (ed.), *Sources of the History of India*, vol. III, Calcutta, 1980.

Regmi, D.R., *Ancient Nepal*, 3rd edn. Calcutta, 1969.

Renier, G.J., *History: Its Purpose and Method*, Boston, 1950.

Renou, L., *Vedic India*, tr. from the French by Philip Spratt, *Classical India*, vol. III, Varanasi, 1971.

Rowse, A.L., *The Use of History*, 3rd edn., London, 1947.

Roy, B.P., *Political Ideas and Institutions in the Mahābhārata*, Calcutta, 1975.

Roychoudhury, N.R., *Tripura Through the Ages (A Short History of Tripura from the Earliest Times to 1946* AD*)*, Agartala, 1977.

Sandys, E.F., *History of Tripura* (compiled from authentic sources), Calcutta, 1915, rpt. (ed. R.G. Singh and A.D. Barma), Agartala, 1997.

Sarkar, J.N., *Thoughts on the Study of Indian History*, General President's Address, 37th Session, IHC, Calicut, 1976.

Shastri, J.L., *Political Thought in the Purāṇas*, Lahore, 1944.

Shastri, K.A.N., *The Coḷas*, vol. I, Madras, 1925, vol. II, pt. I, Madras, 1937.

———, *The Pandyan Kingdom*, London, 1929.

Sharma, R.P., *Paurāṇic Kośa*, Varanasi, VS 2028.

Sharma, S.R., *The Making of Modern India*, Calcutta, 1951.

———, *The Crescent in India: A Study in Mediaeval History*, Agra, 1937, rpt., 1983.

Shotwell, J.T., *Introduction to the History of History*, 2 vols., Columbia, 1939.

Singh, G.P., *The Kiratas in Ancient India: A Historical Study of their Life, Culture and Civilization*, Delhi, 1990.

———, *Political Thought in Ancient India*, Delhi, 1993.

———, *Republics, Kingdoms, Towns and Cities in Ancient India*, Delhi, 2003.

———, "The History and Culture of Ancient Tripura: A Reappraisement", PNEIHA, 1st session, Shillong, 1980, pp. 27-39.

———, "Trade and Commerce in Ancient India in the light of Jain and Buddhist Traditions bearing on its economic and cultural contacts with the Asian countries", *SHC*, IV, 1, March 1996, pp. 1-13.

Singh, M.G., *History of Himachal Pradesh*, Delhi, 1982.

Singh, M.R., *A Critical Study of the Geographical Data in the Early Purāṇas*, Calcutta, 1972.

Sircar, D.C., *Studies in the Geography of Ancient and Mediaeval India*, Delhi, 1971.

Smith, P., *The Historians and History*, New York, 1964.

Smith, V.A., *The Early History of India from 600 BCE to the Muhammadan Conquest*, revd. by S.M. Edwards, 4th edn., London, 1967.

———, *The Oxford History of India*, revd. by H.G. Rawlinson, Delhi, 1981.

Sorensen, *Index to the Names in the Mahābhārata*, 2 vols., London, 1904.

Srivastava, A.L., *The Sultanate of Delhi (CE 711-1526)*, Agra, 1959.

———, *The Mughul Empire (1526-1803)*, Agra, 1959.

Stem, F. (ed.), *The Varieties of History: From Voltaire to the Present*, New York, 1957.

Tandan, R.C., *Hindustān kī Kahānī* (Hindi tr. of Nehru's *Discovery of India*, Delhi, 1947.

Temperley, H.W.V. (ed.), *Selected Essays*, Cambridge, 1930.

Thapar, R., *A History of India*, vol. I, Baltimore: Penguin Books, 1966.

———, *The Past and Prejudice*, Delhi, 1975.

———, *Ancient Indian Social History*, Hyderabad, 1984.

———, *From Lineage to State*, Bombay, 1984.

Thompson, J.W., *A History of Historical Writing*, vol. I, *From the Earliest Times to the End of the Seventeenth Century*, New York, 1942 rpt., Gloucester, 1967.

Toynbee, A.J., *A Study of History*, abridged by D.C. Somervell, vols. I-VI, London, 1946.

Trevelyan, G.M., *Clio: A Muse and Other Essays*, London, 1930.

Tripathi, R.S., *History of Ancient India*, Delhi, 1985.

Trotter, L.J., W.H. Hutton, *History of India from the Earliest Times to the Present Day*, Delhi, 1975.

Usher, S., *The Historians of Greece and Rome*, London, 1969.

Wade, J.P., *An Account of Assam (Completed in 1800)*, ed. Benudhar Sharma, 1st edn., Gauhati, 1927, 2nd impression, Gauhati, 1972.

Weber, A., *The History of Indian Literature*, Eng. tr. from the second German edn. by J. Mann and Th. Zachariage, London, 1882, rpt. Delhi, 1981.

Wheelers, J.T., *India from the Earliest Ages (Hindu, Buddhist and Brahmanical Revival)*, vol. III of *The History of India*, Delhi, 1973.

Williams, M., *Indian Epic Poetry*, London, 1863.

Winternitz, M., *History of Indian Literature*, Eng. tr. from the original German by Mrs. S. Ketkar, vol. I, Calcutta, 1927, rpt. Delhi, 1977.

Journals and Periodicals

Adhyayan, Journal of the Bhāratīya Itihāsa Adhyayan Saṁsthān, Allahabad.

Annals of the Bhandarkar Oriental Research Institue, Poona.

Asiatic Researches, Calcutta, new rpt., Delhi.

Bulletin of the Deccan College Research Society, Poona.

Calcutta Review, Calcutta.

Epigraphia Carnatica.

Epigraphia Indica, Delhi.

Indian Antiquary, Bombay.

Indo-Asian Culture, Indian Council for Cultural Relations, Delhi.

Indian Historical Quarterly, Calcutta, new rpt., Delhi.

Indian Historical Review, New Delhi.

Journal of the American Oriental Society, New Haven, Connecticut, USA.

Journal of the Asiatic Society, Calcutta.

Journal of the Asiatic Society of Bengal, Calcutta.

Journal of the Asiatic Society, Letters, Calcutta.

Journal of the Banaras Hindu University, Benares.

Journal of the Bihar and Orissa Research Society, Patna.

Journal of the Bombay Branch of the Royal Asiatic Society, Bombay.

Journal of Indian History, Trivandrum.

Journal of the Numismatic Society of India, Varanasi.

Journal of the Royal Asiatic Society of Bengal, Calcutta.

Journal of the Royal Asiatic Society of Bengal, Letters, Calcutta.

Journal of the Royal Asiatic Society of Great Britain and Ireland, London.

Modern Review, Calcutta.

Our Heritage, Calcutta.

Purāṇa, Half-yearly Bulletin of the Purāṇa Department, All India Kashiraj Trust, Ramnagar, Varanasi.

Quarterly Review of Historical Studies, Calcutta.

Shodhak, A Journal of Historical Research, Jaipur.

Studies in History and Culture, Journal of the Postgraduate Department of History, Berhampur University.

Vienna Oriental Journal, Vienna.

Proceedings and Reports

Archaeological Survey of India Reports.

Archaeological Survey of Western India, G. Bühler's Report, vols. IV & V.

Bühler's *Report of a Tour in Search of Sanskrit Manuscripts, made in Kashmir, Rājpūtānā and Central India*, pub. as an extra No. of the *JBBRAS*, XXXIV, A, 1877, pub. also in *Ind. Ant.*, September 1877.

Mysore Archaeological Survey Reports, Mysore.

Problems of Historical Writing in India — Proceedings of the Seminar held at the India International Centre, New Delhi, 21-25 January 1963.

Proceedings of the Indian History Congress.

Proceedings of the International Congress of Orientalists.

Proceedings of North-East India History Association.

Proceedings and Transactions of the All India Oriental Conference.

Dictionaries, Encyclopaedias and Gazetteers

Dowson, *Hindu Classical Dictionary*, London, 1888.

Encyclopaedia Britannica, London & New York.

Encyclopaedia of Religion and Ethics, vol. VII, New York, 1914.

Geographical Dictionary of Ancient and Mediaeval India, by N.L. Dey, Calcutta, 1927.

Sanskrit-English Dictionary, by Monier-Williams, Oxford, 1899, rpt., Oxford, 1951.

The Imperial Gazetteer of India, vols. I-IV (Indian Empire), Oxford, 1907-09.

Index

A Statistical Account of Bengal (W.W. Hunter's), 383
Abdul Muzaffar Ala-ud-din Bahman, 424
Abdus Salam, 375
Abhaya Siṁha, 320
Ābhīras, 109, 274, 289
Abhidhamma Piṭaka, 131, 138, 144
Abhimanyu, 256, 277
Abhinanda (also called Gauḍābhinanda), 201
Abhinava Siddharāja, 294
Ābhīra Guptas, 289
Abhīra kings, 106
Abrahamkuli Khan, 320
Ābu, Paramāras of, 304
Ācārāṅga-Sūtra, 159
Achaṇṇa (a Jaina poet of the twelfth century), 412
Acyutarāya (half-brother of Kṛṣṇadevarāya), 421-22
Acyutarāyābhyudaya (by Rājanātha III), 422
Adhisīmakṛṣṇa, reign of, 87
Ādi Purāṇa, 175
Adilshahi dynasty, 424
Adil-Shahis, 235
Ādināthacarita, 173
Adis, 370
Āditya dynasty, 258
Āditya I, Coḷa emperor, 404
Āditya Varmā, 444
Ādityavardhana, 188
Afghanistan, 67, 263
Afghans, 360, 372
Afzal Khan, 336-37, 347
Agni dynasty, 209
Agni Purāṇa, 96
Agnidās, 346-47
Agnimitra, 456, 468
Agnivaṁśa (or Agnikula), 115, 208
Agra, 337, 339, 373
Agrahāras, 262
Agrammes (or Xandrammas), 102
Ahicchatra, 80
Ahmad Shah Abdali, 344
Ahmadnagar, 335, 423
Ahom(s), 371-72
 buraṅjī(s), 368-70
 kings, 367, 369, 372
 language, 365, 368

rule, 363-65, 368, 369, 372
rulers, 254
Ahom kingdom, Koch invasion of, 377
Ahom-Kachārī relations, 371
Ahom-Koch relations, 370, 372
Ahom-Mughal conflicts, 364, 372
Ahom-tribal relations, 364, 372
Ahwal-i-Mahbatjangi (Yusuf Ali's), 360
aitihāsika gāthā, 38, 356
aitihāsikas, 54, 89
Ajātaśatru/Ajātasattu (called Kūṇika also), 101, 131-33, 135-36, 144, 146, 149, 166, 168, 463, 467, 474
Ajayadeva, king of Madramaṇḍala, 273
Ajayameru (Ajmer), 216
Ajayapāla (Ajayarāja), 118, 292, 297, 314, 318
Ajīta (the second Jaina *tīrthaṁkara*), 411
Ajīta Purāṇa, 411
Ājīvikism, 398
Ajmer, 217, 294
Cauhāna rulers of, 117-18
Akbar, 230, 242, 276, 278, 326, 331
Akhairāja (a descendant of Kanhadade), 220
ākhyāna (narratives), 36, 51-54, 59, 61-63, 86
ākhyānavida, 53
ākhyāyikā, 36, 61-62, 187, 436
Akolā district, 113
Alakhāna, 262
Ala-ud-din Ahmad Shah II (Bahamanī ruler), 437
Ala-ud-din Khilji (the Sultān of Delhi), 216-22, 234, 242 316, 321-24, 435, 471
Alberuni (Arab writer), 7, 263, 480
Alexander the Great, 455, 459
Ālhā, 213-14
Ālhā Rāso, 214
Alī Nāmā (a long historical poem by Nusrati), 235
Alinas, 68
Alivardi (the Nawāb of Bengal), 355-56, 358-60, 361-62
Allahabad Pillar inscription, 107
Allahyar Khan, 372
Allakappa, 138
Allan, J., 15
Allasani Peddana (the poet laureate at court of Kṛṣṇdevarāya), 437
Alor (also called Aror), 284
Altekar, A.S., 100
Amar Das, 279
Amar Māṇikya, 382
Amara Siṁha, 62
Amarāvatī, 138
Ambadev Sur, 233
Ambaṣṭhas, 82, 122
Ambaṭṭha Sutta, 133
Amir Khusrau, 218, 220, 322-23
Ammānai (a historical ballad), 38, 405
Amoghavarṣa I, Rāṣṭrakūṭa king, 174-75, 433-34

Āmrabhaṭa, 313
Aṁśuvarman, 289
Anaṅgabhīma Deva, 243, 352
Anaṅgabhīma II, 351
Anaṅgapāla I, Tomara king, 117, 172, 210
Anaṅgapāla II, 118
Anaji Ranganath Malekar, 339
Ānandadeva, 118
Ānandapur, 280
Ānandavardhana, 262
Anant Phandi, 346, 348
Ananta Deva (King), 255, 265
Anantanātha, the fourteenth Jaina *tīrthaṁkara*, 412
Anantanātha Purāṇa (Janna's), 412
Anantavarman Coḍagaṅga, Eastern Gaṅga king, 350-52, 400
Ānartta, dynasty of, 119, 122
Āṇavas, 98
ancient court-poets, 246
ancient Indian literature, 15
ancient Indian traditions, 14
Andhaka-Vṛṣṇīs, 79, 82
Āndhra Mahābhāratamu, (Nannaya's), 434
Āndhradeśa (Āndhra), 39, 392, 433-34, 439
  dynasty, 95, 106, 457
  history of, 438
  kings (rulers) of , 115, 438
  poets of, 438
  political history of, 392
  Reḍḍī kings of, 393
  religious history of, 392
  rulers, 115
  Telugu poets of, 436
Āndhravṛtyas, 106
Aṅga kingdom, 101, 122, 133, 137, 149, 166, 204
Angad, 279
Aṅgarājā, 135
Aṅgiras (Bhāradvāja), 54, 89-90
Anglo-French conflict, 390, 406
Aṅguttara Nikāya, 132, 135
Anhilawāḍa, 169, 296, 298, 300-302, 307-09, 311-17, 322-23
  Cāḷukya dynasty of, 311
  Cāḷukya kings of, 318-19
Aniruddhadeva, 243
Anmakoṇḍa (Hanamkoṇḍa), 435
Annadamaṅgala (composed by Bharatcandra Ray), 354, 356-57
Annals of Livy or Tacitus of Rome, 12
Aṇu, 76, 79
Anugaṅgā, 114
Anuruddha, 146, 462
Anus, 68
Apadāna, 138
Aparānta, 122
Āpastamba Dharmasūtra, 95
āptasāmanta, 192
Arab conquest, 281
Arabian Sea, 81
Arabic, 26
Arabs, 4, 23, 196, 281, 283
Āraṇyakas, 55

Arikeśarī, 410
Arikeśarī II (of Vemulavada), 409
Arikeśarī III, 410
Arikesari, Cāḷukya prince, 164
Arisiṁha, 299
Ariṭṭhapura, 136
Ariyapariyesana Sutta, 134
Arjuna, Kṛtavīrya's son, 76
Arjuna, the hero of the *Mahābhārata*, 409
Arjunadeva, 315-16
Arjunavarman II, 316
Arṇorāja (the Cāhamāna ruler of Śākambharī), 202, 291, 302, 304, 312-13
Arrian, Greek historian, 460
Arthaśāstra, 60-61
Aryan(s), 66-67, 70, 74, 77, 79, 99, 119
    civilisation, 74
    culture, 68, 74, 84
    historical tradition of, 86
    kings, 58
    people(s), 47, 58, 68-69, 487
    settlements, 82, 446
    society, 75
Aryyarāja, 258
Āśāpallī, Bhīla king of, 311, 322
Asiknī (Cenāb), 67
Aśmaka kingdom, 122, 152, 194
Aśoka (Dhammāsoka), 102, 128, 139, 142-43, 145-49, 151, 154, 157, 169, 256, 258, 277, 288, 455, 464
    life history of, 156
Aśokan age, 138
Aśokasūtra, 149
Aśokāvadāna, 148-49, 151, 156
Assaka, 135
Assaka Jātaka, 136
Assam, 38, 243, 245, 254, 363, 369, 370, 372-74, 376, 490
    administrative conditions of, 370
    British occupation of , 364, 373
    history of, 364, 371-72
    kings, 372
    Mir Jumla's invasion of, 368-69
    Muslim invasions of, 364, 370
Assamese, 38
    burañjīs, 367, 369-70, 372
    historical literature, 366
    scholars, 366
Assam-Mughal conflicts, 373
Assam-Mughal relation, 373
Assyrians, 4, 11
Aśvaghoṣa, Buddhist scholar, 463
Aśvarāja, 303
Aśvarāyacarita (by Śrīnathuni Veṅkaṭaramayya), 439
Aśvasena, king of Vārāṇasī, 159
Atharvans, 54
Aṭṭhasālinī, 144
Atula, 442
Augustus, 184
Aurangabad, 331
Aurangzeb, 226, 235, 329-32, 337, 339
    death of, 172, 228, 320

avadāna(s), 36, 128, 148, 154
Avadānaśataka, 153
Avantī, 101, 115-16, 122, 135, 155, 166-67, 259
Avantideśa (western Mālwā), 307
Avantīpura, 138
Avantīsundarīkathā (of Daṇḍin), 402
Avantīśvara (or Śiva), 262
Avantivarman, 261-62, 482
Āvaśyakavṛtti (Haribhadra's), 165, 473
Ayodhyā, 77, 97, 194, 196
 kings of, 75
Azamshah, 172
Babur, 225
Babylonians, 4, 11
Bactrian Greeks, 140
Bādal, 220
Bāgaḍ-gaccha Paṭṭāvalī, 171
Bahadur Shah, Mughal Emperor, 228
Bahadurgarh, 332
Bahamanī,
 kingdom, 424
 sultān(s), 392, 419-20
Bāhlika region, 67, 122
Bahlol Lodi, Delhi Sultān, 273
Bahrām Khan, 273
Baijala (King), 286
Bājī Rāo II, 346, 348
bakhar(s), 38, 235, 254, 333, 342-43, 346, 349
*bakharkāra*s, 341-42
Balabhūti, 111
Bālāditya, 258
Balaji Vishwanath, the founder of the Peśawā dynasty, 344-46
Balamitra, 316, 468, 470
Ballāla III, 417
Ballāla IV, 417
Banerjee, Tarasankar, 28
Bāṇabhatta, court-poet-cum-historian of Harṣa, 18, 62, 165, 187, 190-95, 205
Bāṇeśvara, brāhmaṇa scholar, 382
Baṅga, 122
Barani, 322
Bārappa, the ruler of Lāṭa (southern Gujarat), 308
bardic tradition, 211
Barnala (Jaipur state), 476
Barraclough, G., 5
Basava Purāṇamu (by Pālakuriki Somanātha), , 435
Basaveśvara, Śaiva prophet, 435
Basham, A.L., 20, 267
Battle,
 of Giria, 356
 of Karnal, 280
 of Panipat, 344-45
 of Rakkasa-Tangadi, 431
 of Sāleri, 337
 of Talaiyālaṅgānam, 396
 of Talikoṭa, 334, 431
 of 10 kings, 68
 of Veṇṇi, 396
Bāveru Jātaka, 136
Benares, 356

Bengal, 38, 196, 198-201, 239, 254, 354-55, 357, 359
cauth of, 358-59
Lakṣmaṇasena of, 316, 318
Pālas of, 199, 489
socio-political condition of, 358
Bengali, 25
Beṅgālī writers, 354
Beṭ-Dvārakā, 81
Beveridge, H., 8
Bhadrabāhu I, 159
Bhadraśāla, 140
Bhāgavata Purāṇa, 94, 96, 453, 456
Bhagavatī-Sūtra, 159
Bhāgyacandra (King), 379
Bhāī Bālā, 236
Bhairava Kavi, 437
bhakti movement, 236, 239
Bhalānases, 68
Bhandarkar, D.R., 10
Bhandarkar, R.G., 9
Bhanno Shaloko (composed by Gaṅgādās Bhavā), 320
Bhānumitra, 468, 470
Bhāo Sāheb, the commander of the Marāṭhā forces at Panipat, 345
Bhārata Ākhyāna, 87
Bharata dynasty, 79, 84
Bhārata Itihāsa (or *Bhārata Saṁhitā*), 78, 86, 487
Bhāratas, 67-68, 80
Bharatcandra, 355-57
Bhārgava brāhmaṇas, 187
Bharukaccha, 121-22, 136, 140, 143, 145
Bharukaccha Śūrapāraka, 81
Bhāskar Paṇḍit, 355, 359, 362
Bhāskar Rām, 360
Bhāskaravarman, 191
Bhauṭṭas (Tibetans), 260
Bhavadatta, 111
Bhavanāga, 111
Bhaviṣya Purāṇa, 94-96, 108, 114-15, 458
Bhillama V, 324-25
Bhillas, 117
Bhilsā, 312-13
Bhīma, Cāḷukya king, 309-10
Bhīma, Kaivarta chief, 199-200
Bhīma I, Cāḷukya king of Gujarat, 232, 309, 311,
Bhīma II, Cāḷukya king, 178, 292-95, 297-300, 302, 305, 314
death of, 315
Bhinnamāla, kingdom of, 163
Bhinnmāl, Paramāras of, 164, 291, 304, 312
Bhīma-Bhoja-Prabandha (of Merutuṅga), 309
Bhīmadeva II, 296
Bhīmadeva, Cāḷukya ruler, 470
Bhīmanāga, 111
Bhīmasena Jātaka, 136
Bhoganagara, 138
Bhogeśvara, 240
Bhogin, 110
Bhoja, Paramāra king of Mālwā, 241, 309, 393, 438
Bhoja I, 116
Bhoja II, 116

Bhoja Prabandha (of Ballāla), 231
Bhojakaṭapura, 81, 121
Bhojarājiyam (Ananta's), 438
Bhojas, 79, 122
Bhoṅsalā Vaṁśāvalī (Veṅkaṭeśvara's), 332
Bhṛgavāṅgiras, 54, 90, 423
Bhṛgu (Bhārgava), 54, 89-90
Bhṛgukaccha (Broach), 233
Bhūmimitra, 456
Bhūpāldurga (or Bhūpālgaṛh), 330
Bhūteśa (Śiva), 260, 262
Bhūtīnandī, 110
Bhuvanābhyudaya (of Saṅkula of Kashmir), 256
Bhuvanaika Rāmābhyudaya (by Ponna), 410
Bhuvaneśvara (Śiva), worship of, 375
Bīdar, 335
Bihar, 38, 114
Bījāpur, 330, 335, 392, 420, 423, 426
  sultān(s), 424-25
  expansion of, 432
Bijoy Pañcālī (or Vijay Pañcālī), 380
Bikaner, 225
Bilhaṇa, 17, 18, 204-05
Bilsāḍ inscription, 479
Bimbisāra, 101, 131, 136, 142-46, 149, 163, 168, 454, 462-64, 474
  king of Magadha, 133, 135, 137, 159
Bindusāra, 102, 142, 147, 149, 151, 158, 168, 455, 463-64
biographical writing, traditions of, 184
Bisva Siṁha, the founder of the Koch kingdom, 376
Bobbilimahārāja Vaṁśāvalī (by Maṇḍapalli Prabatiswarakavi), 440
Bodhacandra (king), 379
Bodha-Gayā, 142
Bodhisattvāvadāna-Kalpalat (of Kṣemendra), 153
bodhi-tree, 156
Brahma, 96
Brahmadatta, king of Kāśī, 76, 131, 150
brāhmaṇa(s), 12-13, 55, 66, 72, 88-89, 91-92, 137-38, 141, 155, 203, 208, 259, 261-62, 264, 283, 297, 315, 381, 423, 444-46, 451, 460
  chroniclers, 277
  dynasty, 282
  of Manipur, 381
  rulers, 281
  text, 53
Brāhmaṇābād, 284
brahmāṇḍa, 55, 94-96
Brahmāṇḍa Purāṇa, 453
Brāhmanic literature, 90
Brāhmanic stories, 91
Brāhmanic tradition, 90-91
Brāhmanical culture, 381
Brāhmanical literature, 55, 91
Brāhmanical religion, 381
Brāhmanical sacrifices, 410
Brāhmanical temples, 304

Brāhmanisation, 381
Brāhmanism, 140, 193, 266, 297, 299, 304
Brahmavaivartta Purāṇa, 96
Bṛhadratha dynasty, 100
Bṛhaspatināga, 111
British rule, 494
Broach, 163
Buddhacarita (of Aśvaghoṣa), 155
Buddhaghoṣa, 141, 145
  commentaries of, 143
Buddhahood, 132
Buddhavaṁsa, 138
Buddhism, 131-32, 140, 145, 148, 150, 153-54, 157, 193, 258, 266, 275, 353, 398, 402, 438
  advent of, 48
  history of, 128, 132, 139
  rise of, 152
  schools of, 139
  spread of, 156
Buddhist(s), 3-4, 13, 17, 19, 43, 127-28, 140, 148, 157, 451-52, 465, 488, 490, 492-93
  bhikkhus, 143
  communities, 127, 132
  Councils, 132, 148
  historians, 130, 152, 179
  India, 154
  literature, 31, 53, 127, 157
  monks, 282
  rulers, 281
  Sanskrit texts, 140
  scholars, 127, 156
  schools, 156
  texts, 56
  tradition(s), 127, 146, 167, 468, 474
  tradition of chronology, 462
  vihāras, 260
Budhagupta, 480
Bühler, G., 129, 204, 465
Bukkā I, 417
Bundela history, 234
Bundelkhand, 116, 234, 291
burañjī(s), 38, 254, 363-71, 373-74, 376
Burckhardt, J., 5
Burdwan, 359-60
Burmese invasion, 364
Bury, J.B., 33
But-Shikan, 274
Cāca (generally spelled as Chach), 282
  death of, 282
Cācanāmā (or *Chāchnāmā*), 281-82, 285
Cāhamāna(s) (Cauhānas), 115, 202, 206, 208-09, 211, 214
  archives, 207
  dynasty, 216, 219
  independence of, 217
  kings (rulers), 119, 208, 217
Caitanya cult, 353
Caitanyadeva, Vaiṣṇava saint and religious reformer, 239, 353
caityas, 154
Cakṣu (or Oxus) river, 107
Calicut, history of, 448
Cāḷukya(s), 115, 119, 178, 209, 300, 302, 307, 311

dynasty, 291
history of, 291, 293
kingdom, 313
kings, 292, 297, 299, 308, 391
of Gujarat, dynastic history of, 290
of Kalyāṇī (in Karṇāṭadeśa), 203, 205, 308, 310, 489
period, 233
rulers of Anhilawāḍa, 309
Cāḷukya-Vikrama Saṁvat/Era, 42 434, 481
Cambay (called *Stambhatīrtha*), 233, 296, 302-04, 320, 323
cammakāra, 138
Campā, 81, 121, 132-34, 143, 166-67
Campaka, a minister of King Harṣa, 255
campū(s), 38, 393
Cāmuṇḍarāya, a devout Jaina, 308-09, 412
Cāṇakya (Kauṭilya), 56, 61, 89, 102, 140, 146, 157, 467
Canda, 214
Canda Bardāī, 211
Candagutta/Candragupta Maurya, 102,142, 145, 151, 157, 159, 166-67, 172, 241, 459, 462-64, 467-68, 462, 474
*cāṇḍāla*s, 274
Caṇḍamahāsena, 477
Caṇḍaprasāda, 303
Candavikrama, 426
Candella(s), 116
dynasty, 316
kingdom, 213, 312
kings, 214-15
Candradeva, founder of the Gāhaḍavāla dynasty at Kānyakubja, 241
Candragupta I, 469, 479
Candragupta II, 194, 289, 479
Candraprabhācarita (by Vīranandī) , 164
Candrātreya dynasty, 212
Candravarman, the first Candrātreya king, 213
Cāntamūla (or Śāntamūla I), 433
Cāpotkaṭa dynasty (also known as Cāvaḍā dynasty), 307
history of, 299, 307
carita(s), 36-37, 39, 128, 172
*carita-kāvya*s, 172
Cariyāpiṭaka, 138
Carlyle, 32, 34, 185
Carr, E.H., 5, 34
Caṣṭana, a Kṣatrapa of Ujjayinī, 468, 478
Caturavarga-cintāmaṇi, 325
Caturviṁśati-Prabandha, 318
caupāī, 36, 215
Cedī, 133, 155
Cedideśa, 98
Cellana, the daughter of Cetaka, 160
Central India, 177
Cera(s) (Keralas), 389, 395, 399, 403
empire, 444
kingdom, 397
kings, 395-97, 399

Cetaka, 159
Cetī, 135
Cetiya Jātaka, 136
Ceylon, 154, 156
    Gajabāhu I of, 397
Champaka Vijaya (by Śaikh Mahaddi), 386
Chandra Rao More, a Marāṭhā nobleman, 336
Chatrapati, 329
Chatraprakāśa (Lāl Kavi's), 234
Chatraśāla (king), 234
Chatta, 136
Chatterji, Suniti Kumar, 384
Chaudappā, 430-31
Cheitharol Kumbaba — a royal chronicle of Manipur, 378, 380
Chikka Saṅkanna, the contemporary of Rāmarāya, 431
Chikkadeva Vijayam (by Tirumalarāya), 428
Chikkadevarāja Odeyar, Mysore ruler, 428
Chikkadevarāja Vaṁśāvalī (by Tirumalarāya), 428
Chilarai, (Nara Nārāyaṇa's brother), 377
Chittor, 220
Choḍagaṅgadeva, 242
Christian Era, 139, 141, 152, 160, 289, 394, 399, 481
Chūtiya tribes, 370
Cidānandadeva, 374
Cikkadevarāja Odeyar, 429
Cikkupadhya, 429
Cina(s), (China), 122, 138, 140, 183-84
Clarendon, 32
Clio — the *Muse* of History, 4
Cochin dynasty, 447
Coimbatore, 395
Coḷa(s), 121-22, 389, 394, 399, 403, 414
    dynastic history of, 390
    dynasty, 396, 400
    historiography of, 400
    kings, 391, 396, 399, 401, 424
    monarchs, 390, 398
    period, 390
    princes, 398
Coḷa-rattha, 148
Coḷavaṁśacaritam, 38
court *khyātas*, 37
Cowell, 195
Croce, B., 35
Cullaniddesa, 138
Cullavagga, 132
Cunchat Ezhuttachan, the father of modern Malayala, 446
Cunningham, James, 343
Cutch, 309
Cyavana, 69
Dāhala region, 442
Dāhir, eldest son of Cāca, 282-83
Dakṣiṇāpatha, 122
Dalela (Diler Khan), 330
Ḍāmara(s), 261, 264-65, 309
Dāmodara, court-poet of Keralavarman of Kāyankula, 445

Dāmodaradeva, 243
Dāmodaragupta, 260
Dantidurga, 174
daṇḍanāyaka, 169, 312
Dara Shah (prince), 234-35
Daradadeśa (Dardistān, north-west of Kashmir), 259
Darbhaṅgā Rāj, 242
Dārdas, 123, 274
Darrāṅg Rājavaṁśāvalī (by Sūryakhari Daivajña), 376
Darśaka, 463
Darshan, a poet, 280
Darvābhisāra, 262
Das, Parimal Kumar, 9, 83
Daśapura, 81
Daśaratha (or Bandhupālita), 455
Daśārṇa, 122
Dāsas (or Dasyus), 68
Dasgupta, K.K., 75
Dattājī Trimal Waqnavis (or Waqianavis), 339
Dauhitra, 110
Davids, Rhys, 141
Debal, 283
Deccan, 106, 113, 196, 212, 305, 307, 324, 436
  Rāṣṭrakūṭas of, 129
Delhi (Dilli), 216-18, 285, 322-23, 329, 339, 356, 373, 416
  Cauhānas of, 117
  Sultanate, 435
  Sultāns of, 215
  Tomara dynasty of, 117, 172
Deshasthicha Powaḍā (Paraśurāma's), 349
Deśāvalīvivṛtti, (by Jaganmohana), 286
Devabhūti, 103, 194
*devadāsī*s, 444
Devagiri, 300
Devagupta (king), 190
Devala Devī, Rajā Karṇa's daughter, 323
Devanāga, 111
Devapāla of Mālwā, 304-05
Devarāja, 429
Devarājendra Sangatya Chamayya, (Krishnasarma's), 428
Devarakṣita, 200
Devavarman (or Somaśarman), 456
Devikā, princess, granddaughter of a king of Gurjara, 414
Dey, N.L., 22
Dhakkagiri, 161
dhamma, 143
Dhammapada-aṭṭhakathā, 144
Dhanānanda, Nanda Emperor, 140, 146, 159, 241, 454
Dhanañjaya, 138
Dhāra, 117, 197, 203, 300, 309-10, 312
  conquest of, 319
Dhārāvarṣa, 301
dharma, 171
Dharma Māṇikya, 382
Dharmadeva, 306
Dharmapāla, Gopāla's son and successor, 198, 201, 232
Dharma-Śarmābhyudaya (by Hariścandra), 165

Dharmaśāstra, 60-61
Dharmavarman, 110
Dharmavijaya (by Nala Bhuminātha), 333
Dhaulapura, 477
Dhavalā (of Vīrasena), 469, 472
Dhavalakapuri (modern Dholka), 294, 296
Dhruva Nirupama (also called Śrī-Vallabha), 176
Dhundhirāja, 333
Dīdārbaksha, 172
Diddā, granddaughter of Bhīma Śāhī, 264, 482
Digambara(s), 169
  *paṭṭāvalī*s, 169, 473
  school, 129, 162, 164, 175
  tradition, 170, 466, 472,
Dīgha Nikāya, 132, 134, 143
digvijaya, 247
Dikshit, Umashankara, 87
Dilel (Diler) Khan, a Mughal general, 337
Dillī kī Rājāvalī, 172
Dilwāṛā, 303
*dīnāra*s, 140
Dindimas, 423
Dionysos, 460
Dīpavaṁsa, Pāli chronicles, 145, 147, 462
Divākaramitra, a Buddhist monk, 191
Divodāsa, 69
Divyāvadāna, 140, 151
Dodwell, H.H., 15
Dṛṣadvatī, 83
Druhya(s) or Druhyu(s) of Lunar dynasty, 68, 76, 79, 98, 383
Durgācārya, 54
Durgasiṁha, the court-poet of the Cāḷukya king of Kalyāṇī, Jayasiṁha II Jagadekamalla, 412
Durlabhaka (alias Pratāpāditya), 259
Durlabharāja, 309
Durlabhavardhana, the descendant of Nāga Karkoṭa or Karkoṭaka, 259, 482
dussika, 138
Dutt, J.C., 269-70, 279
Dutt, R.C. 19, 21, 266
Dvāpara Age, 66, 86-87
Dvārakā (or Dvāravatī), 79, 81, 97, 121
  history of, 81
Dvārasamudra (Halebid), 391, 412
Dvyāśrayakāvya, 201
Egypt, 273
Egyptians, 4, 11
Eka, 332-33
Ekadeva (Nānadeva's son), 326
Elāra, Coḷa prince, 148
Elphinstone, M., 6
Erodu, fort of, 428
Errapraggada, the court-poet of Prolayavema Reḍḍī, 436
Eṭṭuttogai, 394
Farrukhsiyar, 228
Fatteh Shah, 271-72, 275-76, 483
Ferishta, Muslim chronicler, 293

Flavian emperors, 184
gacchas, 171
Gadādhar Siṁha (Ahom king), 244, 371-72, 374
Gaddabha, (Gaddabhilla or Gardabhilla) dynasty, 161, 170, 468
Gaddava kings of Ujjayinī, 177
Gāhaḍavāla dynasty of Kānyakubja (Kannauj) 118, 312, 316
Gait, Edward, 245
Gajapati(s), 393, 439
  dynasty, 352
  history of, 393
Gajapati Pratāparudra, the king of Kaliṅga, 420
Gandhāra, 122, 135, 140, 144, 188
Gandhāra Jātaka, 136
Gaṅgā (River), 67, 97, 150, 191, 198-99
  dynasty, 242, 350-52, 398, 403
  rulers, 404
Gaṅgārām, 357, 359-62
Gaṅgaya, 438
Gaṅgā-Yamunā doab, 98
Gangetic doab, 67, 98-99
Gangetic (Gaṅgā) Valley, 67, 80, 121
gaṇa form of government, 82
Gaṇapati, 435
Gaṇapatināga, 111
gaṇas, 134, 154
Gandharvasena Mahendrāditya, Gardabhilla king, 160
Gaṇeśvara (Bhogeśvara's son), 240
gaṇikas, institution of, 410
Gardabha princes, 107
Gardabhinas (or Gardabhillas), 107
Garibniwaj (king), 379-81
gāthās, 23, 54-55, 86
Gauḍa, 273
Gauḍavaho (Vākpatirāja's), 196
Gauṇa, 266
Gautama Buddha, 101, 128, 131-38, 139, 142-43, 145-47, 150-57, 259-60, 288, 463, 473-74, 490
  contemporaries of, 101
  death of, 145
  enlightenment of, 156
  Era, 474
  life of, 132
  parinirvāṇa of, 157, 474
Gautamīputra Śātakarṇi, 104
Geiger, L., 70
Geldner, K.F., 56
Geography (of Ptolemy), 399
Ghazi Muhamadacarita (in Sanskrit), (by R. G. Ramaraya), 424
Ghazni, 292
  empire, 265
Ghiyas-ud-din Tughluq, 435
Ghoṣa, 456
Ghoshal, U.N., 19, 25, 71
Ghulam Hussain Khan, 357
Gibbon, 32, 34
Girivraja (Rājagṛha), 77, 81, 121
Girnār, 178, 303
Gode, P.K., 451

Golcoṇḍā, 330, 335
Gomatī (Gomal), 67
Gona Haihaye dynasty, 435
Gonanda, Hindu king, 256-57, 481
Gonanda dynasty, 258
Gonanda I, 277
Gonanda or Gonarda III, 258, 481
Gopāla, Pāla ruler of Bengal, 157
Gopāla dynasty, 288
Gopāla III, Kumārapāla's successor, 200
Gopāladeva, 243
Gopālarājā Vaṁśāvalī, 286, 288
Gopālavarman, 263
Gopicandrer Pañcālī, a local chronicle of Cachar, 375
Gorā, 220
Gorā Bādal Caupāī (of Jatmal Nāhar), 219
Gorā Bādal Padminī Caupāī (of Hemratna), 219
Govind Māṇikya, 382
Govinda, 134
Govinda IV, king, son of Indra III, 410
Govinda Vidyādhara, 353
Govindacandra, 312
Govindarāja, Pṛthvīrāja's son, 216
Govindpant Bundale, 345
Govindrao Khanderao Citnis, 343
Grahavarman, the son of the Maukhari Prince Avantivarman of Kannauj, 189-90
Great Bhārata battle, 77, 81, 95, 454
Greece, 4, 13, 14, 30, 32-33, 183, 389
Greek(s), 11, 14, 23, 399
  historians, 13
  history, 12
Gṛhya-Sūtras, 55-56
Gujarat (Gurjaradeśa), 35, 44, 81, 97-98, 129, 177-79, 202, 212, 221, 232, 234, 291-94, 296-305, 307-08, 314-15, 319-25, 470, 490
  Cāḷukyas kings of, 129, 201, 295, 297, 299, 304-05, 307-08, 315, 319, 326, 470, 489
  chronicles of, 300
  economic history of, 233
  invasion of, 234
  Muslim invasions of, 470
  school, 254, 290, 306
  school, historians of, 491
  Sultān Muhammad of, 273
  Vāghelās of, 290, 294, 302, 315, 319, 321
Gujarati, 25, 38
Gulbargā (capital of the Bahamanī kingdom), 420, 424
  Bahamanīs of, 436-37
Guṇabhadra, 176
Guṇarūpaka (composed by Keshavadas), 226
Gunbiradsingar Prabandha (by Karnidanji Gadhavi), 320
Gupta(s), 157, 162, 166, 175, 177, 188, 258, 289, 469
  coins, 114
  dynasty, 114, 289
  empire, 192, 288, 479

Era (period), 64, 78, 479-80, 487
kings, 458
rule, 114, 120, 488
Gurbilās Pātshāhī Daswīṅ ke Caritar (by Bhāī Sukhā Singh), 239
Gurbilās Pātshāhī Dās (by Koer Singh), 238
Gurjara(s), 262, 411
Gūrjaradeśa (Gujarat), 163, 217, 290, 291, 302, 304, 306
Cāḷukya of, 308
Gurjara-Pratihāras, 178
Gurjaras of Bhinnamāla, 189
Guru Arjan Dev, 237, 279
Guru Gobind Singh, 236-38, 280, 490
Guru Nanak, 236, 238-39, 279, 490
Guru Ram Das, 237
gurukula, 63
Gurumukhi, 25
Guruvaṁśamahākāvya (Lakṣmaṇa-śāstrin's), 415
guruvāvalīs, 36, 128
Gyārasapur (Gwalior state), 477
Haidar Nāmā (by Kacheri Krishniah), 432
Haidar Shah, 272
Haider Ali 431
Haig, Wolseley, 15
Haihaya(s), 76-77, 79, 98, 436, 442
dynasty, 76
Haji Khan, a well-known general of Emperor Sher Shah, 230
Hamid Khan, 319
Hammīra, ancestors of, 216
Hammīra Deva, the Cāhamāna ruler of Raṇastambhapur, 216-17, 242 265, 292
Hammīra Haṭha (CE 1745) (by Candraśekhara), 218
Hammīra Mahākāvya (of Nayacandra Sūri), 216, 218
Hammīra Rāso (CE 1300) (by Śāraṅgdhar), 218
Hammīra-madamardana (of Jayasiṁha Sūri I), 299, 304
Hammīra-ra Chanda (VS 1798 = CE 1741) (by Rājarūpa), 218
Hammīrayān Caupāī (VS 1538 = CE 1481) (by Bhāndav Vyas), 218
Haṁsavega, a messenger of King Bhāskaravarman, 191
Hanamkoṇḍa, 438
Hanumānappā Nāyaka, the chief of Basavapāṭana, 425
haqīqat, 37, 229
Har Gobind, 238, 279
Har Kishan, 279
Har Rai, 279
Haṛappan period, 98
Hari, 260
Haribhadra Sūri, a Śvetāmbara scholar, 165
Harihara, 417
Harihara I, 417
Harihara II, 417
Harirāja (brother of Pṛthvīrāja), 217
Harivaṁśa Purāṇa (of Jinasena), 81, 175, 468-69, 472, 479

Hariyūpiā (Hariruda of Herat), 67
Harṣa, 191-93, 265, 490
  death of, 115
  Era, 480
Harṣacarita (of Bāṇabhaṭṭa), 187, 196, 413
Hasan Shah, 272
Hastikarṇa, 262
Hastināpura, (Capital of the Kuru kingdom) 77, 80, 100-101, 121, 151-52, 154
Helārāja, 256
Hemacandra (a Śvetāmbara scholar of the twelfth century), 166, 201, 292, 297, 313, 467, 473
Hemādri (or Hemādpant), 325
Heracles, 460
Herodotus, 4, 17, 32-33, 268
  Histories of, 12
Himalayan region, 192, 196
Hindu(s), 3-4, 7-8, 11, 19, 21, 23, 31, 36, 43, 127, 186, 221, 273-75, 278, 282, 451-52, 465, 480, 490-93
  army, 265
  gods, 274
  historians, 44
  ideals, 364
  pantheon, 262
  period, 278, 281
  religion, 444
  republics, 111
  saints, 236
  temples, 274
  traditions, 287, 476
  writers, 24, 43
Hinduism, 193, 258, 274-75, 364
  cults of, 266
Hindukuśa, 106
Historical biographies, 36
historical literature, 30
historiography,
  Indian tradition of, 239
  tradition of, 186
Hiuen Tsang, 20
Honaji Bala, 346, 348
Hopking, E.W., 60
Hoysaḷa(s), 324, 391, 412, 415, 417
  empire, 415
  historiography, 391
  history, 415
  kingdom, 443
  kings, 391, 404, 413
  kings, histories of, 39
  rule, 390
  Vīra-Ballāla II (king), 408
  Vinayāditya (king), 404
  Viṣṇuvardhana, 204
Hume, 32, 34
Hūṇa(s), 83, 107, 177, 189
  kingdom, 189
  territories, 188
Hussain Shah, 354
Hutchison, J., 253, 267
Hutton, W.H., 8
Huṣkapura, 260
Huviṣka, 258
Ibrahim Shah, the Turkish Sultān of Jaunpur, 240, 276
idol-worship, 274

Ikṣvāku, 68, 75
dynasty, 100
genealogies of, 97
Ilañjeṭcenni, 398
Iltutmish, Turkish Sultān of Delhi, 301-02
Imperial Coḷas, history of, 401
Indala (Ālhā's son), 214
Indian bardic literature, 212
Indian Buddhists, 157
Indian chronology, 15
Indian civilisation, 17
Indian literature, 28, 30, 52
Indian Muslim writers, 26
Indian scholars, 11
Indika, 459
Indra III, 410
Indraji, Bhagawanlal, 287
Indraprastha, 80, 117, 121
Indrāyudha (CE 783-84), the ruler of Kānyakubja, 176
Iraq, 273
Iravikkuṭṭi Pillai, a general of Ravivarmā Kulaśekharan, 405, 447
Iravikkuttippillaipattu (ballad), 405
Isami, 322
Īśānavarman II, 441-42
Islam, 224, 274-75, 416
Islam Khan, *sūbedār* of Bengal 356
Īśvara Singh (Jaya Singh's son). 228
Īśvaravilāsa (by Kr̥ṣna Śarmā), 229
itihāsa(s), 36, 51-56, 58-64, 78, 86, 88-89
tradition, 185
itihāsakāra, 90
itihāsakarttā, 87
Itihāsa-Purāṇa, 56-58, 88, 378
literature, 57
tradition, 41, 47, 51-52, 54-55, 59, 61-65, 90, 258, 487
Itihāsapurāṇaveda, 57
Itihāsa-Saṁhitā, 57, 60, 86
Itihāsaveda, 56
itivr̥tta (story of the past) 36, 61
Jacobi, H., 83
Jadumaṇideva, 243
Jafaruddaula, 439
Jagaḍucarita (Sarvānanda Sūri's), 233
Jagannātha, the son of Perubhaṭṭa Tailiṅga, 234
Jagannātha temple at Purī, 350-51
Jagatavilāsa, a biography of Mahārāṇā Jagat Singh, 227
Jai Siṁha, 373
Jai Singh (Dāhir's son), 284
Jai Singh, Sawāī Rājā, 228
Jaina(s), 3-4, 13, 17, 19, 31, 43-44, 127, 129, 160,168, 186, 202, 303, 314-15, 403, 438, 451-52, 465-66, 472, 488, 490, 492-93
and non-Jaina scholars, 290
authors, 177
bastīs, 438
canonical literature, 160
chroniclers, 297, 306
chronicles, 306, 314
community, 303

gurus, 36, 162
historians, 129-30, 179, 231, 290
historical writings of, 128
literature, 31, 53, 127, 129, 470
maṭha, 430
monks, 404
paṭṭāvalīs, 169, 171
prabandhas, 292, 297
purāṇakāras, 177
Purāṇas, 61
Rājataraṅgiṇī, 271
saints, 232
saṁghas, 170
scholars, 36, 127, 129, 172, 178, 232 298, 467, 470
shrines, 233
stories, nineteen, 409
Śvetāmbara tradition, 167
tīrthaṁkaras, 159, 391, 412
temples, 304, 314
tradition(s), 146, 159, 165, 307, 317, 465-68
traditions, historical importance of, 129
writers, 254
Jainism, 164, 173, 193, 201-02, 297, 299, 304, 313-14, 391, 398, 402-03, 412, 438
doctrine of, 409
growth of, 168
history of, 128, 159, 168, 176, 178
Jaitaran, 285
Jaitrasiṁha, the king of Medapāṭa, 301
Jālauka, 258, 277
Jālor, 221
Jambūdvīpaprajñapti-Saṁgraha (by Padmanandī), 165
Jammu, 273
Janakapura, the earlier capital of the Videha King, 289
Jānakīrām, 362
Janamsākhī(s), 236-37
janapadas, 74, 77, 81, 97, 120, 122
Janavasabha Sutta, 133
Janganāmāh Śrī Guru Gobind Singh (by Ani Rai), 237
Jātaka(s), 137
records, 135
jauhara, 222, 284
tradition of, 217
Java, 138
Jaya Itihāsa, 78
Jaya Singh II (1699-1743), the founder of Jayapura, 228
Jayacanda of Kānyakubja (Kannauj), 118, 209
Jayadeva, 289
Jayadhavalā (of Jinasena), 175, 469
Jayadissa, 138
Jayagoṇḍan (better known as Jayaṅkoṇḍan), 400
Jayagupta, 289
Jayakeśin, ruler of Koṅkaṇa, 204
Jayamaṇi II 442
Jayānaka, a Kāśmīrī brāhmaṇa 206-08
Jayāṅganaramaṇa, 426
Jayanta, king of Gauḍa, 260

Jayantiā,
history of, 370
rulers, 371
tribes, 370
Jayāpīḍa, 260, 273
Jayarāma, 327
Jayasena, 119
Jāyasī, 220
Jayasiṁha, the son of Sussala II, 255
Jayasiṁha, king of Rājapur, 273
Jayasiṁha Siddharāja, Cāḷukya ruler of Gujarat, 166, 168, 201, 291, 303, 311, 313, 318-19, 326
Jayasiṁha Sūri, 231, 266, 271, 291, 300-303, 311-12, 482
Jayasiṁha Sūri II, 202
Jayaswal, K.P., 162, 241, 465
Jayavarman, 297
Jehangir, 242
Jejākabhukti (Bundelkhand), 209, 212, 214, 316
Jhelum, 262
Jījāmbā (Jījābāī), Śāhajī Bhoṅsalā's first wife, 328
Jinaprabha Sūri, 322
Jinasena, 175
Jinasena II, (the author of the *Harivaṁśa Purāṇa*), 176, 466
Jinasena III, 175-76
Jinji, 332, 335, 337, 390, 405
Jīvitagupta II, 196
Jñātrikas, 159
Jodhpur, 285
Rāo Maldeo of, 226
Johiyās, 224
Jonarāja, Kāśmīrī historian, 208, 254, 270-71, 274, 276-78, 483
Jones, Sir William, 21, 99, 451
Joshi, Ram, 346, 348
Jyeṣṭha Rudra, 260
Kabul, 263
Kachārī(s), 371
kings, 371
tribe, 370, 375
Kachārī Burañjī, 371
Kadamba dynasty, 391, 408
Kaduha Sect Paṭṭāvalī, 171
Kadungon, 403
Kaegi, Adolf, 69
kaifiyat, 38, 345
Kaivartas, 199
Kākatīya(s), 325, 393, 435, 438-39
dynasty, 435
kingdom, 435, 438
kings, 439
period, 392, 434, 438
Kākatīyacarita (a biographical work by Narasiṁham), 439
Kākatīyarāja-Vaṁśāvalī (by Kāśeśvarappā), 438
Kākavarṇa (of Śiśunāga dynasty), 194
Kalacuri(s), 113, 324
of Cedi, 291
Kālaka, Jaina *ācārya*, 160-62, 233
Kālakācārya-Kathānaka, 160, 162
Kalale Nañjarāja, (commander of Kṛṣṇarāja Odeyar II), 430

kalambakam(s), 38, 402
Kālamukha, 137
Kālañjara, 209, 213, 291, 312
Kālāśoka (king), 132, 142, 145-46, 151, 156, 462-63
Kalavazhi-nārpatu, 397
Kalhaṇa Paṇḍit, a Kāśmīrī historian of the twelfth century, 17-18, 20, 24, 64-65, 254, 256-59, 264-71, 273, 276-78, 385, 481, 483, 489
Kali Era, 379, 483
Kaliṅga, 122, 138, 141, 194, 350-52, 419-20
  Eastern Gaṅgas of, 436
  Gaṅgas of, 325, 390, 403, 433, 442
  war, second, 400
Kāliñjar, 116
Kaliyuga, 87, 95-96, 100-101, 258, 277, 288
  Purāṇic history of, 99
Kaliyugarājavṛttānta, 95
Kalkirāja, 469
Kalpa-Sūtra, 159-60
Kalyāṇī, 203-04
  Cāḷukya capital, 205
  Cāḷukya ruler of, 203
  later Western Cāḷukyas of, 411
Kāmadatta, 111
Kamalā Devī, 323
Kamaluka, 263
Kāmarūpa, 122, 372
Kamboja, 81, 122, 135, 259
  kingdom, 137
Kāmeśvara, founder of Oinwar dynasty, 240
kammāra, 138
Kampana (or Kamparāya), Bukkā's second son, 417-19
Kāmpil (or Kāmpilya), 77, 81, 121, 152
Kampilī, 416
Kāmpilipurī (Kāmpilya), 76 (see also Kāmpil)
Kampilla, 137
Kāmpilya, 77, 81, 121, 152 (see also Kāmpil)
Kamran (Babur's son), 225-26
Kāmrūpar Burañjī, 371
Kāñcanadevī, Jayasiṁha's daughter, 312
Kāñcanapurī, 112
Kāñcī, 121, 402, 418, 421
  Pallava kings of, 390
Kangba dynasty, 382
Kanhadade (Kanhar Deva), the Cauhāna chief of Jālor, 220-21, 321
Kanhadade-Prabandha (of Padmanābha), 220, 222, 321
Kaniṣka,
  court of, 155
  Kuṣāṇa king, 258, 277, 478
  Saṁvat, 478
Kanjeevaram, 121
Kannada,
  literature, 411
  poets, 391
Kannauj (Kānyakubja), 115-16, 118, 187, 190-92, 196, 212, 258-59, 480

dynasties, 98
emperors of, 207
Rāṣṭrakūtas of, 325
Kānthirāva Narasarāja, 425, 427
Kānthirāva Narasarāja Caritre (Nanjakavi's), 428
Kānthirāva Narasarājavijaya (composed by Govinda V), 425
Kāntipurī (modern Koṭwār), 110-11
Kaṇva(s), 105, 455
dynasty, 103
kings, 456
Kapilar, a brāhmaṇa poet of the third Saṅgam, 395
Kapilavatthu (Kapilavastu), 132, 137-38, 143-45 153-54
Kapilendra Deva (1435-66), the founder of Solar dynasty, 243
Kappila (or Kampil), 138
Karikāla (also called Karikālan), Coḷa monarch, 396-97
Karkoṭaka(s), 261
dynasty (also called Karkoṭa), 259, 261, 482
Karkoṭaka, a Nāga chief, 76
Karṇa (king), 322
Karṇa (or Karṇadeva), 291, 321
Karṇa, Kalacuri king of Tripurī, 198
Karṇa, Vāghelā ruler, 323
Karṇāṭadeśa (Karnataka), 39, 177, 327-29, 331-32, 337, 343, 391-92, 403-04, 408-09, 417-19, 424-25, 427, 432
history of, 391, 428
tradition of, 415
Kārttika sudī, 313
Karvarman, 116
Kashmir, 8, 35, 37, 44, 141, 203, 208, 212, 254-58, 260-62, 264, 265-67, 270-71, 273-78, 319, 481, 483, 490
chronicle of, 16, 279
historians of, 17
history of, 20, 272
rulers of, 10
school, 153, 206, 267, 277
sultān of, 483
Kāśī (Vārāṇasī), 81, 101, 122, 133, 135-36, 152-53, 155, 194
history of, 80
kingdom of, 98, 137, 153-54
Kāśī Candra Māṇikya, 382
Kāśīpura, 145
Kāśika-Vastra, 155
Kāśmīrī chroniclers, 269, 489
Kāśmīrī soldiers, 265
Kāśmīr-Gandhāra kingdom, 137
Kaśyapa, 89
Katanceri Namboodari, the court-poet of Manavikram, 448
Kātaya Vema, 436
kathā, 36, 39, 59
Kathāgurucarita, 244
Kathāvatthu, 138
Katwa, 360, 361
Kātyāyana, 62
Kauśāmbī, 77, 80, 98, 101, 121, 152, 154
Kāverī (River), 259, 399

Kāveripaṭṭanam, 394
Kāvya(s) (epic poems), 39, 227, 425
Keith, A.B., 16, 56, 72, 83
Keladi kingdom, 431-32
Keladi Nṛpavijaya (Poet Liṅganna), 430-31
Kennedy, J., 212
Kerala(s), 39, 122, 441
    cultural history of, 393
    history of, 446
Keralolpatti tradition, 447
Keśavadeva, 243
Keśavadeva-Carita (of Ambarish Dvija), 244, 374
Keśavapaṇḍita, 235
Keśavarāja Varmā, 445
Khaduya, 262
Kharjūravāhaka (Khajurāho), 213, 234
Khasas, 123, 274
Khazain-ul-Futuh (Amir Khusrau's), 219, 323
Khuddaka Nikāya, 132, 135, 137
Khuddakapāṭha, 145
khyāta(s), 37, 215, 223, 285
Kilakila, kings of, 109
Kings of Kashmir, Chronicle of, 17
Kinnaras, 274
Kirāta(s), 122, 274, 288-89
    dynasty, 288
    kings, 288
Kirāteśvara Śiva, 375
Kīrtikaumudī (of Someśvara), 178, 290, 296-97
Kīrtilatā (by Vidyāpati Ṭhākura), 240
Kīrtipatākā (by Vidyāpati), 241
Kīrti-Samullāsa (by Mahesh Ṭhākura), 242
Kīrtisiṁha, the king of Mithilā, 241-42
Kīrttivarman, 116
Koccenganān, Coḷa king, 397
Koch(es), 372
    history of, 372
    kings (rulers), 254, 370-71, 374, 376
Koch Rājavaṁśāvalī (compiled in 1802 by Ratikānta Dvija), 376-77
Koṇḍaviḍu, Reḍḍīs of, 436
Koṅgu region (or Koṅgudeśa) 390, 395, 397, 403
    history of, 39
    invasion of, 404
Koṅgudeśarājākkal, Tamil chronicle, 403
Koṅkaṇa, 231, 325
    Śilāhāras of, 411
Kolhāpur, Śilāhāra realm of, 324
Koliyas, 136, 144
Koregaon, 332
Kosala kingdom, 77, 97, 100, 109, 122, 131, 133, 135-37, 141, 144, 149, 152-55
Kosala-Saṁyutta, 135
Kośāmba, 98
Kośāmbī, 132-34, 137-38, 144
Kosambi, D.D., 12

Koṭwār, 111
kovai, 39
Krishnamachariar, M., 301
Kṛta Saṁvat, 476
Krumu (Kurram), 67
Kṣaharāta, a predecessor of Nahapāna, 161
kṣatriya(s), 89, 91, 119, 154-55, 159, 321
  kings, 92
  tradition, 90-91
Kṛṣṇa (Lord), 81
  historicity of, 81
Kṛṣṇa Dvaipāyana Vyāsa, 66
Kṛṣṇa II, Rāṣṭrakūṭa king, 434
Kṛṣṇa III, Rāṣṭrakūṭa king, 164, 174
Kṛṣṇa Kiśore Māṇikya, 382, 386
Kṛṣṇā Valley, 433
Kṛṣṇadevarāya (1509-29) of Taluva dynasty, 420-22, 431
Kṛṣṇadevarāya Vijayamu (by Kumāra Dhūrjaṭi), 421
Kṛṣṇadevarāya, Vijayanagara emperor, 430
Kṛṣṇā-Godāvarī region, 433
Kṛṣṇagupta, 469
Kṛṣṇamālā (by Rāmagaṅgā Viśārada), 386
Kṛṣṇarāja Odeyar II, 430
Kṛvis, 68
Kṣudraka-Mālavas, 82
Kubhā (Kabul), 67
Kulacandra, the general of Bhoja Paramāra, 309, 311
Kulaśekhara dynasty, 447
Kulottuṅga I, Coḷa ruler, 400
Kulottuṅga II, Coḷa emperor, 401
Kulottuṅgacolacarita (by Tirunārāyaṇa), 400
Kulottuṅgan-Pillaittamil, 401
Kumāradevī, Licchavi princess, 201, 289
Kumāragupta, 189
  reign of, 109
Kumāragupta I, 476
Kumāragupta II, 477
Kumārapāla (CE 1143-73), the Caḷukya king of Gujarat, 166, 174, 177, 200-02, 294, 297, 302-04, 313, 318, 474, 490
Kumārapāla Prabandha (of Jinamaṇḍana Gaṇi), 231
Kumārapālacarita (of Hemacandra), 201-2
Kumārapāla-pratibodha (by Somaprabhācārya), 202
Kumbha, prince of Mewāṛ, 273
kumbhakāra, 138
Kumbhakāra Jātaka, 137
Kummattur Kannanar, 397
Kuṇāla, 149, 151, 455
Kunālāvadāna, 149
Kundagrāma, 159
Kuṇḍinapura, 81, 121
Kūṇika (Ajātaśatru), 170, 466, 474
Kuṇindas, 82
Kūrma, 96
Kuru(s), 68, 80, 98, 122, 134-35
  dynasty, 79

kingdom, 80, 152
kings, 154
Kurukṣetra, 83, 196
Great Battle of, 258
Kuruśravaṇa, 68
Kuśa (or Kuśāmba), 77
Kuṣāṇa(s), 111-12, 188
empire, 478
Kṣatraps of, 478
later, 112
Kuśāvatī, 77, 121, 138
Kuśinārā, 131, 133-34, 137-38, 143, 150
Kuvalayamālā (by Udyotana Sūri), 163
Lahore, 225
Lakṣmaṇa Sen, king of Vaṅga (Bengal) 241
Lakṣmī Nārāyaṇa (Nara Nārāyaṇa's son), 377
Lakṣmī Siṁha, Jayantiā Rājā, 370, 373
Lakṣmī-Karṇa, Kalacuri king of Tripurī, 203, 310-11
Lāl Koṭ (a Rājpūt citadel),210
Lalitāditya, king of Kashmir, 197, 259-60, 266, 273
Lalitapāṭan, 288
Lalitapura, 260
Lalitavistara, 154
Lalliya Shahi, 262
Lāṭa/Lāṭadeśa (southern Gujarat), 161, 231, 295, 310
Lāṭa(s), 188, 296, 302
Śaṅkha of, 300, 304-05
Laukika Era/Laukika Saṁvat (also called Saptarṣi Saṁvat or Saptarṣi Laukika Saṁvat), 275, 277, 481, 483
Lavaṇaprasāda (son of Arṇorāja), 294-95, 298, 318
Lāvaṇyasiṁha, (Tejaḥpāla's son), 304
Law, B.C., 157
Licchavī(s), 144, 150, 155, 287-88
dynasty, 289
Licchavīgaṇa, 143
Life of Julius Agricola, 184
Liṅga, 96
Livy, 4, 32
Lodhi dynasty, 273
Lohara dynasty, 264, 482
Lohicca Sutta, 133
Lokāyata, 398
Lokāyatika sect, 193
Lokottaravāda school, 152
Lunar dynasty, 209, 398, 422
Lunar family, kings of, 60
Macaulay, 32, 34
Maccha (Matsya), 134-35
Macdonell, A.A., 8, 56, 70, 458
Mādalā Pāñjī (the palm-leaf manuscripts preserved), 242
Mādalā Pāñjī, 350, 352
Madanapāla, 200
Madanavarman, Candella monarch of Bundelkhand, 312
Madanavarman, the Candella king of Jejākabhukti, 291, 318
Mādhava, 321

Mādhava I (or Koṅganivarman I), 404
Mādhavācārya Vidyāraṇya, brāhmaṇa scholar, 415
Mādhavadeva, 243
Mādhavagupta, 189
Mādhavavarman, the king of Magadha, 441
Madhunandī, 110
Madhurā (Madurā), 389-90, 423
  Nāyakas of, 406, 427, 429
  Pāṇḍyas of, 394
  sultāns of, 418
  temple, 402
Madhurā (Mathurā), 141
Madhurā Nāyaka Cokkanātha, the successor of Tiruma, 428-29
Madhurāvijaya (conquest of Madurā), 418
Madhya Pradesh, 212
Madhyadeśa, 76, 98, 116, 122
Madraka, 122
Madurā, 398, 418 (see Madhurā)
Maduraikkāñci (the longest one) (by poet Māṅgudi Ma), 396
Maduraittalavaralāru, the history of the great temple in Madurai, 424
māgadha, 89
Magadha, 90, 98, 101-03, 114, 122, 131, 135, 137-38, 140-43, 145-46, 151-56, 160, 166-67, 170, 196, 200, 204, 441, 462, 467, 470
  dynasties, 169
  empire, 133
  Gupta rulers of, 469
  imperial power of, 166
  kingdom, 80, 137, 149, 163, 168
Mahābhārata, 47, 50, 55, 57-63, 68, 74, 78-81, 84-87, 96, 122, 243, 444
Mahābodhivaṁsa (by Upatissa), 156
Mahācoḷarājīya, 424
Mahādeva, one of the Yādava kings of Devagiri, 325
Mahāgovinda Sutta, 134
mahājanapadas, 135, 152
Mahākosala, 135-36
Mahāli Sutta, 133
Mahamada (Muhammad Tughlaq), 242
Mahamada (Muhammad), Turkish Emperor, 416
mahāmaṇḍaleśvara rāṇaka, 294, 296
mahāmātya, 303, 321
Mahān, the uncle of Rāmapāla, 200
mahānagara, 154-55
Mahānāma, 146
Mahānandin, 463
Mahānasiṁha, 318
Mahānidāna Sutta, 134
Mahāniddesa, 137
Mahāpadmānanda, the founder of the Nanda dynasty, 102-03, 454, 457, 467
Mahāparinibbāna Sutta, 133
mahāparinirvāṇa, 156
Mahāpurāṇa (Puṣpadanta's), 174 176
Mahārāja Abhaya Singh of Mārwāṛ, 227-28

Mahārājā Amar Singh II, 228
Mahārājā Gaja Singh, 224, 226
Mahārājā Jaswant Singh, 229
Mahārājā Kīrtisiṁha, one of the rulers of Mithilā, 240
Mahārāja Kṛṣṇa Candra, 354
Mahārājā Śivasiṁha, a worthy descendant of Kīrtisi, 241
mahārājādhirāja and *paramabhaṭṭāraka* (titles), 188
Mahārāṇā Jagat Singh, 227
Mahārāṇā Rāj Singh of Mewāṛ, 226
Maharashtra, 38, 109, 235, 254, 324-26, 328, 330-33, 348-49, 358, 458, 490
Mahārāṣṭra Purāṇa (Gaṅgārām's), 356-57, 359-60, 362
Maharṣi Vedavyāsa, 87
maharṣis, 87
mahāsāmanta(s), 192-93
Mahāsatipaṭṭhāna Sutta, 134
Mahāsudassana Sutta, 134
Mahāvagga, 132
Mahāvaṁsa, 145-48, 462-63
Mahāvīra,
  death of (*nirvāṇa* of), 165, 167, 177, 466-68, 470, 473-74, 477
  Era, 472-74
  teachings of, 173
  the founder of Jainism, 134, 160, 162, 165, 167, 178, 232, 466, 473-74, 490
Mahāvastu-avadāna, 152
mahāvihāras, 142
Mahemat Khan, 406
Mahendra Māṇikya, 371
Mahendrāditya, king of Ujjayinī, 475
Mahendrapāla Pratihāra, 480
Mahendrapāla I Pratihāra, 263
Mahi River, 319
Mahim, history of, 334
Mahinda (Mahendra), 145, 148
Mahipāla, 199
Mahipāla II, 198
Māhiṣaka (Mysore), 122
Māhiṣmatī, 76-77, 113, 121
  regions, 109
Māhiṣmatīpur, 81
Māhissati, 137-38
Mahmud of Ghazni, 116, 470, 480
Mahobā (called Mahobaka), 209, 291, 312
Mahotsava (Mahobā), 213
maṅgala kāvya, 38
Maithili, 38
Maitraka dynasty, 316
Majjhima Nikāya, 132, 134
Majjhimadesa (Madhyadeśa), 131
Majumdar, A.K., 8
Majumdar, R.C. 19, 384
Mākandika-avadāna, 151
Mālavas, 123
Malaya (Malay Peninsula), 138
Malaya mountain, 196
Malayalam, 25
Malhar Ram Rao Citnis, 344
Malik Kafur, 435
Malla(s), 131, 133-35, 143-44, 150
Mallikārjuna of Koṅkaṇa, 202, 313

Mallinātha, the nineteenth Jaina *tīrthaṁkara*, 412

Mallinātha Purāṇa (by Nāgacandra), 412

Mālwā, 98, 107, 112, 116-17, 161, 188, 190, 197, 217, 291, 298, 300, 302, 309-11, 313, 475-76

annexation of, 312

conquest of, 192, 318

Era/Saṁvat, 476-77, 479

invasion of, 319

Paramāra Bhojadeva (Bhoja) of, 232

Paramāras of, 204, 304-05, 308, 312, 470, 489

rulers of, 325

Mālwāgaṇa Saṁvat, 476

Man Singh, 355

Mānacarita, anonymous, a biography of Rājā Mān, 229

Mānadeva I, 289

Mānava, 141

Maṇḍalas, 66

Mandasor (ancient Daśapura, western Mālwā), 476-77

Māṇḍavya (Mālwā), 273

maṇikāra, 138

Māṇikya Deva, king of Madra, 273

Maṇimekhaḷai, 397-98

maṇipravāla, 39

Manipur, 38, 245, 254, 363, 370, 377, 380-81, 490

migration of Muslims in, 381

Manipuri, chronicle in, 38

Maṇipurī kings, 371-72

Mañjuśrīmūlakalpa, 157

Manoja, king of Brahma-vardhana, 135

Mansur Khan, 370, 372

mantras, 54

mantrīpariṣad, 82

Manu, 62, 68

Manu Vaivasvata, 120

manvantara, 92

Mānyakheta, Rāṣṭrakūṭas of, 324

Marāṭhā(s), 235, 334-35, 337, 342, 344-49, 355, 359-62

army, 360

empire, 328

history of, 341

invasion(s), 357-58

invasions of Bengal, 355-56, 362

Kingdom, 332

rulers, 424

Marathi, 25, 38

bakhars, 330

historical literature, 333

Māravarman Sundara, Pāṇḍya king, 413

Mārāya, Narasiṁha's son, 421

Mārkaṇḍeya, 96

Mārtaṇḍa temple, 260

Marudeśa (or Rajasthan), 196

Mārwāṛ, 301, 305, 313, 321

Mārwāṛ ra Parganā ri Vigat (historical work by Nainsi), 230, 285

Marx, Karl, 9, 35

Maśaka, 81

Mathurā, 77, 79, 82, 110-11, 121, 149, 155, 163, 194

Matsya Purāṇa, 94-96, 122, 155, 453
Maukharīs, 157, 188
Maurice Winternitz (a German scholar), 16, 30, 56, 89, 186
Maurya(s), 100, 105, 157, 167-70, 232, 316, 455, 468
  dynasty, 102, 142, 147, 151-52
  dynasty, Bṛhadratha of, 98, 103, 151-52, 194, 456
  empire, 152, 178, 258
Mayamara *satra*, 374
Mayūragiri, 325
  Bagulas of, 326
Mayūraśarman, king (also called Mayūravarman), 408
McCrindle, J.W., 10, 458, 460
Medapāṭa (Mewāṛ), 219, 226, 285
  Guhilaputra Rājpūts of, 327
Medieval Age, 269-70, 403
medieval period, court-poets of, 246
Megasthenes, Greek historian, 459-60
Meghavāhana, 258
Mekala, 109
Menander, Bactrian Greek king, 139
Merta, 285
Merutuṅga, a scholar of Śvetāmbara school, 298, 306-17, 323, 467
Mewāṛ, 220
Midnapur, 359
Mihirabhoja, 263
Mihirakula, Hūṇa chief, 258
Mikir tribes, 370
Milinda (king), 139-41
Milindapañho, 139-41
Mīnaladevī, 318
Mir Habib, 361
Mir Jumla (Aurangzeb's General), 369-70, 372-73
Mir Kasim, 356
Mīrīs, North-Eastern Frontier tribes, 370
Mirja Nathan, 372
Mishra, Pandit Baladeva Prasad, 287
Mithi, 75
Mithilā (Janakapur/Bihar), 75, 77, 97, 121, 137-38, 150, 152, 154, 204, 240-41
mleccha(s), 119, 207, 258, 292, 321
  dynasty, 107
  kings, 265
Moamariyas, 374
Monier-Williams, Monier, 83
Mookerji, Radha Kumud, 19
Mount Ābu, 178, 292, 294, 303
Muddalagiri, 405
Mudgala, 69
Mudrārākṣasa (Viśākhadatta's), 194
Mudukudumi, 398
Mughal(s), 215, 225, 227-28, 234-35, 240, 273, 330, 332-33, 337-38
  empire, 235, 278
  period, 236
  rulers, 281
Muhammad Akbar (Aurangzeb's son), 330

Muhammad Ali bin Ābu Bakr Kufi, 281
Muhammad bin Qasim, 282-83
 death of, 284
Muhammad Ghori, 119, 210, 293, 300, 302
Muhammad III, 424
Muhammad Shah II, 276
Muhammad Shah Tughlaq (Mughal emperor), 228, 272, 275, 280, 285, 483
Muhammad Yusuf Khan, 405
Muhammadan(s)/Muslim(s), 3, 21, 119, 186, 274-75, 292, 300, 322-23, 342, 355, 369, 374, 418, 430, 493
 arrival of, 10
 attacks, 444
 chroniclers, 26, 218, 298, 322, 357, 471, 490, 493
 chronicles, 358
 conquest, 13, 15, 286
 historian of Sindh, 281
 historians, 226
 invader(s), 115, 207, 212, 216, 302, 375
 invasion(s), 130, 179, 298, 301, 314
 period, 12, 278
 rule, 270, 415
 rulers, 241, 426
 saints, 236
 sultāns, 275
Muir, 70
Mukerjee, Radhakamal, 19
Mukta Svāmin, 260
Mulaka, 138
Mūlarāja, the founder of the Cāḷukya dynasty of Anhilawāḍa, 291, 297, 308-9
Mūlarāja I, 299, 302
Mūlarāja II, Cāḷukya ruler, 292-93, 297, 300, 314
Mūlavāsa, 442
Müller, F. Max, 14, 30, 71, 454, 464
Muṇḍa (king), 151
Muṇḍa (Anuruddha's son), 462-63
Munivaṁśābhyudaya (by Cidānanda), 429
Muñja (or Muñjavarman), 117
 execution of, 310
Munśī Śiva Śaṅkara Singh, 286
Murshidabad, 361
Muruṇḍas, kingsmen of the Kuṣāṇas, 107, 469
Mustafa Khan, 362
Muṣika(s), 122, 442
 dynasty, 441
 kingdom, 441, 443
Muṣikavaṁśa (by Atula), 39, 393, 441
Mutha (or *Mūtā*) *Nainsi-ri-Khyāta* (by Nainsi), 285
Mysore, 212, 412, 424-25, 427, 429, 432, 443
 dynastic history of, 392
 history of, 428
 rulers of, 432
Mysore Odeyar, 425
Mysūru-rājara Caritre, (by Shanubhoga V), 432

Nabākhānacarita (by Mahesh Ṭhakura), 242
Nachana Somanātha, a court-poet of Bukkā of Vijaya, 437
Naḍḍula, Cāhamāna rulers of, 304, 311-12
Nādir Shāh dī Vār (by Najabat), 280
Nāga(s), 76
  Chūtiyā tribes, 370
  dynasties, 80, 110, 112
  kings, 110-12
  period, 111
Nāgabhaṭṭa, 163
Nāgacandra, (popularly known as Abhinava Pampa), 412
Nāgadāsaka, 146, 462-63
Nāgasena, of Nāga dynasty of Padmāvatī (Pavāyā), 194
Nāgasena, the learned Buddhist monk, 139
Nagauri Luṅkagacchiya Paṭṭāvalī, 171
Nahavāhana (Nahapāna) of Śaka nationality, 469
Nahavahana Gaddabhilla, 316
Nahuṣa, 68, 76
Naikādevī (also called Naiki), 292
nalakāra, 138
Nālandā, 196
Nānadeva, 326
Nanda dynasty, 142, 146-47, 167, 464, 467, 474
Nanda(s), 102, 104, 156-57, 167-68, 170, 316, 454, 457
  rule of, 470
Nāndasa (Udaipur State), 476
Nandī Saṁgha, 170
Nandikkalambagam, 402
Nandivardhana, (one of the sons of Kālāsoka), 156, 167, 462-63
Nandivarman III, Pallava king, 402
Nañjarāja, 426
Nannecoḍu, Śaiva poet, 433
Nānyadeva, king, the founder of Karṇāṭa dynasty, 241
Naothingkhong (king), 380
Nara Nārāyaṇa (king), 376-77
Narakāsura, 437
Narapatis, 438
Narasa Nāyaka, 422
nārāśaṁsīs, 52, 55
Narasarāja, 425-26, 428
Narasiṁha, Karṇāṭa prince, 242
Narasiṁha I, 352
Narasiṁha II (also called Kuntaleśvara), 413-14
Narasiṁha Saluva, king of Vijayanagara, 414, 419, 421, 438
Narasiṁhavarman II, the Pallava king of Kāñcī, 402
Naravardhana, 188
Naravarman, 117, 312
Nārāyaṇa, 456
Nārāyaṇa Śāha (king), 326
Nārāyaṇavilāsa (by Virūpākṣa II), 419
Narmadā, 76, 98, 112, 196, 442
Nasrat Khan, 322
Naturalis Historia (Natural History) (Pliny's) 459

Navasāhasāṅkacarita, 197
Nawāb Alikhan, 320
Nawāb Asaf Khan (a counsellor of Shahjahan), 235
Nawāb Aslam Khan, the Governor of Lahore, 280
Nawāb Ẓakariyā Khān, governor of Lahore 238
Nawāb of Arcot, 391, 406
Nayacandra, 216-18
Nāyaka Chikka Saṅkanna, 431
Nayakuralu (Nagama), 436
Nāyanmārs, Śaiva saints, 402
Nayapāla, 204
Nāzok Shah, 276
Neḍuñjeliyan, Pāṇḍya king, 396-98
Neduñjeralādan, Cera king, 397
Neḍunalvāḍai (by poet Nakkirar), 396
Nehru, Jawaharlal, 23
Neminātha, the twenty-second Jaina *tīrthaṁkara*, 412
Nepal, 254, 260, 286-89, 490
  history of, 158
  Valley, 287
Newārī, 37
New-York Daily Tribune, 9
Nicakṣu, 101
nikāya, 36
Nikāyas, 132
Nilādrī, a poet, 437
Nīlapurāṇa (of Nīlamuni), 256
Nilo Pant, 329
Nimi (Ikṣvāku's son), 75
Ningthourol Lambuba (chronicle), 380
Nirukta (by Yāska), 54
nirvāṇa, 146, 168, 175
Nisurata Khan (Nusrat Khan), 217
Nītivākyāmṛta (Somadeva Sūri's), 164
Nizam, 348
Nizam-ul-Mulk, 358
Noldke, 30
non-Aryan(s), 68, 79
  races, 83
  tribal groups, 68
  peoples, 47, 176
non-Buddhist ascetics and institutions, 143
North Pañcāla dynasty, 69
Nṛpāvalī, 255
Oḍambaras, 82
Odeyars of Mysore, 428, 430
Oḍradeśa or Oḍiśā (Orissa), 242, 254, 350-52, 355, 361, 438, 490
Oinwar dynasty, 240
Orissa, dynasties of, 351
Ormuz, 233
Oruṅgallu (Warangal), 435
Oṭṭakkūṭṭan, 401
Oxus, 106
Pañcāla(s), 80, 98, 101, 122, 134-35, 138
  dynasty, 79
  kingdom of, 152, 154
Pachet, 359
Padineṇkīzhk Kaṇakku, 396

Padirruppaṭṭu (also called *Pathirruppathu*), 394-95, 397, 403
padma (lotus), 81, 96
Padma Purāṇa, 175
Padmagupta, 197
Padmamihira, 256
Padmanābha (author), 221-22, 321
Padmanāyakas, 438
Padmāvat (of Malik Muhammad Jāyasī), 219
Padmāvatī, 111-12
Padminī, Rājpūt queen, 216, 219-20
Padminī Caritra Caupāī (of Kavi Labhdodaya), 219
Pādshāh Burañjī, 373
Pahalavas (Pārthians/Persians), 83, 122
Pakhangba (king), 379
Pakthas, 68
Pāla,
  dynasty, 198
  monarchy, 204
  supremacy, 199
  territories, 198
Pālaka, the son of King Caṇḍapradyota of Ujjayinī, 466-67
Pālakuriki Somanātha, Śaiva poet, 435
Pāli,
  canons, 128
  chronicles, 24
  literature, 30, 139
  texts, 142, 155
Pallava(s), 240, 441
  kings, 38
Pampa, Jaina poet, 409
Pamsupradanāvadāna, 149
Paṇḍitārādhyacaritra (by Pālakuriki Somanātha), 435
Panipat, 345
Paṇḍit Śrī Guṇānanda, 286
Paṇḍit Siddhānta Vāgīśa, 382
Pāṇḍya(s), 122, 389, 398-99, 402-03, 414, 417
  history of, 39
  king(s), 389, 391, 396, 398-99, 413
  kingdom, 398, 419
  political history of, 403
Paṇis (a trading class), 68
parakriyā, 63
Parallel Lives (by Plutarch), 184
Paramānanda, 328-29, 331
Paramāra(s), 115-16
  dynasty, 197
  kings/rulers, 117, 291
Paramardi, Candella king, 209, 214
Paramardi Rāso, 212-14
Paramardin (King), 292
Paramayona, 137
Paranar (a poet), 395
Parāśara, 66
paraṇī, 38
Pārasikas (Persians), 196
Paraśurāma, 346
  tradition, 446

Parbatīya Vaṁśāvalī, 286-88
parganās, 285
Pargiter, F.E., 48, 60, 71, 93, 111, 114, 456
Parihāsa Keśava (Viṣṇu), 260
Parihāsapura, 260
Pārijātaharaṇa (in ten cantos) of Kavirāja, a court-poet of Kāmadeva, 408
Parīkṣit, 102
Parīkṣit II, 80, 100
parinibbāna, 142
parinirvāṇa, 150
Pariśiṣṭaparvan (Hemacandra's), 166, 466
Parmāra, King of Avantī, 116
Parnāla (Panhāla, near Kolhapur), 331
Parnālaparvatagrahanākhyāna (Jayarāma's), 331
Pārśvanātha, the twenty-third Jaina *tīrthaṁkara*, 159, 173, 412
Pārśvanātha hills, 160
Pārśvanāṭha Purāṇa (by Pārśva Paṇḍita), 412
Pārśvanāthacarita, 173
Pārthivāvalī, 255
Paruṣṇi (Rāvī), 67-68
Parvagupta, 264
Pasenadi, King of Kosala, 133, 135-37, 144
Pāṭaligāma, 131, 133, 143
Pāṭaliputrakalpa (by Jinaprabha), 169
Pāṭaliputta (or Pāṭaliputra), 121, 131-32, 138-42, 145, 149-50, 167, 170, 459, 466
Pāṭan, 287
Patañjali, 62
Pathak, V.S., 65, 205
Patiṭṭhāna, 137-38
paṭṭāvalī(s), 17, 36, 128, 169, 171, 466-67
Paṭṭāvalī-Samuccaya, 467-69, 477
Paṭṭinappālai (by poet Uruttiraṅ Kaṇṇanār), 396
Pattuppaṭṭu, 395-96
Pauṇḍravardhana (north Bengal), 260
paurāṇika(s), 89
Paurava(s), 80, 90, 98, 100
Pāvā, 131, 138, 160
peninsular Gujarat, 311
Persian(s), 4, 11, 26
    chronicles, 342
    Gulf, 233
    invader, 281
    Tawārīkhs, 342
Perumāḷ Ceramān, 447
Perumāḷ Keya, 447
Perumāḷ period, 447
pesakāra, 138
Peśawā(s), 329, 334, 342-44, 346-48, 359
    period, 345-46, 349
Peśawā Bālājī Bājī Rāo, 344, 358
Peta Komati Vema (also called Vīra-Nārāyaṇa), 436
Phalodi, 285
Philips, C.H., 25
pillaittamil, 38
Piṇḍārīs, 348

Pipalak Śaka Paṭṭāvalī, 171
piṭaka, 132
Pithi, 200
Plassey, 356
Plutarch, Greek historian, 184
Pokaran, 285
Polybius of Greece, History of, 4, 12
polygamy, practice of, 83
Ponna, the court-poet of the Rāṣṭrakūṭa king Kṛṣṇa, 409-10
Popper, Karl, 35
Portuguese, 335
Porunārrārruppaḍai (by poet Mutattāmakkaṇṇiyar), 396
post-Babur (or Humayun) period, 226
post-Bhārata war period, 79, 100, 453
post-Gupta period, 64, 487-88
post-Harṣa period, 115, 489
post-Mahāvīra period, 178
post-Maurya dynasties, 178
post-Sātavāhana period, 106, 162, 458
post-Śuṅga period, 110
powaḍā(s), 38, 346-47, 349
Poygaiyar, 397
prabandha(s), 36-37, 39, 128, 179, 215, 231, 290, 292, 296, 298, 305, 307, 317-19, 393
Prabandhacintāmaṇi (of Merutuṅga), 306, 316-17, 438, 470, 474
Prabandhakośa (Rājaśekhara's), 318, 475
Prabandhāvalī (of Jinabhadra), 305
Prabhācandra Sūri (a Jaina writer), 475
Prabhākar, 346
Prabhākaradeva, 263
Prabhākaravardhana, 188
  kingdom of, 189
Prabhāsa, 323
Prabhāvakacarita (of Prabhācandra Sūri), 162, 232-33, 470, 475, 477
Prācyadeśa, 122
pradhānasāmanta, 192-93
Pradyota(s), 168
  dynasty, 101, 162, 166, 175-76, 194, 453
Prāgjyotiṣa, 122
Prāgjyotiṣapura, 77, 81
Prahlādana, 314
Prājyabhaṭṭa, 254, 276-78
Prākṛt, 31, 38
  text, 162
Prākṛt Paṭṭāvalī (of the Nandī Saṁgha), 169-70, 473
Prasad, Dr Rajendra, 23
praśasti-paṭṭa, 256
praśastis, 36, 38, 128, 177-78, 400
Prasenajit, 100, 149, 154
Pratāp (Nārāyaṇa's son), 326
Pratāpaditya, a local king of lower-Bengal, 240, 355
Pratāpāditya I, 258
Pratāparudra (king), 353
Pratāparudra II Kākatīya, 416, 418
Pratāparudradeva, the Kākatīya ruler of Warangal, 243, 435, 439

Pratāparudrīya (Vaidyanātha's), 435
Pratihāra Nāgabhaṭṭa II, 232
Pratihāras (Parihāras) 115-16, 209
pratisāmanta, 192
pratisarga, 92
Pratisarga Parvan, 108
Pratiṣṭhāna, 76, 77, 99
Pratiṣṭhānapura, 97, 121
Pravīra, 112-13
Prayāga, 97, 114
Prayāga-Praśasti (of Samudragupta), 193
pre- and post-Bhārata war period, 94
pre- and post-Buddha period, 135
pre- and post-Kaliyuga, traditions of both, 99
pre-Bhārata war period, 87, 97, 100, 165
pre-British period, 365
pre-colonial Tripura, 386
pre-Maurya period, 146, 169
pre-Nanda period, 156
pre-Pakhangba chronicle, 382
pre-Rāma period, 75
Prola II, Kākatīya ruler, 434
Pṛthvīcandra, 262
Pṛthvīrāja Cauhāna, 96, 118, 120, 206-07, 209-10, 391, 490
  death of, 119, 208
Pṛthvīrāja Cauhāna III, 207-08, 213-14, 318
Pṛthvīrāja Rāso (by Canda Bardāī), 208, 210, 212, 214
Pṛthvīrājavijaya (by Jayānaka), 206, 208
Ptolemy, 469
pūgas, 138
Pulindaka, 456
Pulindas, 122
Pulumāvī, Sātavāhana king, 103-04, 457
Pulumāvi IV, 457
Punjab, 44, 82, 188-89, 207, 225, 236, 239, 254, 259, 263, 265, 280, 490
Puṇḍarīkākṣasadṛśa, 426
Puṇḍra, 122
purākalpa, 36, 59, 63
Purāṇa(s), 7, 13, 16, 18, 24, 36, 38, 47-48, 50-64, 68, 71-72, 86-89, 91-97, 99-106, 109, 110-14, 116, 120-24, 128, 146, 151, 176, 453-58
  tradition, writers of, 52
  Veda, 55
Purananūru, 394
Purandar Siṁha, 369
purāṇakāras, 88, 92, 95, 124, 452, 487
purāṇam, 39
Purāṇa–Itihāsa (Purāṇa Saṁhitā), 57, 60, 86, 487
Purāṇī Assam Burañjī, 372
Purāṇic *ākhyānas*, 53
Purāṇic brāhmaṇas, 88, 91
Purāṇic genealogies, 17, 47
Purāṇic literature, 22, 30, 52, 57, 124, 390
Purāṇic *sūtas*, 88, 211
Purāṇic tradition(s) 47, 92, 146, 162, 167, 329, 464, 468, 487

of chronology, 456
Purūravā, 68, 76, 97
purātana-itihāsa, 59, 74, 94
Purātana-Prabandha-Saṁgraha, 319
purāvṛtta, 36, 59, 62
purdah system, 273
Purika, kingdom of, 112
Puru(s), 68, 76, 79
dynasty, 100
Purāṇic description of, 98
Puruṣa Parīkṣā (by Vidyāpati), 241-42
Puruṣadatta, 111
Puruṣottama, Kapilendra's son and successor, , 352
Puruṣottam Deva, 243
Puruṣottama Gajapati, 438
Pusalker, A.D., 19
Pusapati Immadi Tammirāju, a general of Kapileśvar, 437
Pusapatis, histories of, 393
Puṣkalāvatī, 121
Puṣpabhūti, founder of the kingdom of Śrīkaṇṭha, 187
Puṣyabhūtis, 157
Puṣyadharman (Śatadhanvan), 151
Puṣyamitra (the founder of the Śuṅga dynasty), 103, 109, 140, 152, 316, 456, 468, 470
Qutb-ud-din Aibak, 215, 217, 293-94, 298, 300, 302
Rā Kheṅgāra (Ābhira ruler), 168, 311
Rā Navaghana, 311
Raghuji Bhonsle, 358-59
Raghunāth Nāyaka of Tanjore, 406
Raghunath Shastri Datye, 334
Raghunāthābhyudaya (by Vijayarāghava), 406
Raghurajah, 355
Rāī family, 282
Rāī Siharas, a believer in Buddhism, 282
Raichur Doab, 420
Rāigaṛh, 337
Rai-Jetsi-Rau Chand (a Ḍiṅgal poem, composed by Vethu Sujo), 225
Rājā Bhoja, 117, 172
Rājadhar Māṇikya, 386
Rājagaha (Rājagṛha,the capital of Magadha kingdom), 131-34, 137, 144-45, 149-50, 152-53, 155, 160, 167
Rājā Jayasiṁha of Ambāvatī (Amber), 337
Rājā Kanhar Deva (Kanhadade), 222
Rājā Karṇa, 323
Rājā Kṛṣṇa-Māṇikya, 245
rajakāra, 138
rājakathās, 255
Rājamālā (compiled by Durgamaṇi), 382-86
Rājanātha, 422
Rājanātha II, 420, 423
Rājanātha III, 423
Rājā Odeyar, 430
Rājaprakāśa (a Ḍiṅgal *kāvya* written by Kishordas), 226

Rājapura (Rājorī) 81, 265
Rājarāja I, Coḷa monarch, 400
Rājarāja III, Coḷa king, 413-14
Rājarāja Narendra, the Eastern Cāḷukya monarch of, 434
Rajaram, N.S., 87
Rājārāma (Śivājī's second son), 235, 329, 332-33, 335, 338
Rājārāma, Marāṭhā *sūbedār*, 353
Rājārāmacarita (Keśava's), 332
Rājarathnavaliyam Campū (composed by Nārāyaṇan), 445
Rājarūpaka (by Ratanu Veer Bhāna), 227
Rājaśekhara Sūri, 63, 318-19
Rājaśekhara Sūri II, 318
Rājaśekharavilāsa, *Vṛṣabhend* (poet Ṣaḍakṣara), 429
Rajasthan, 35, 44, 129, 210, 211-12, 215-16, 222, 254, 285-86, 391, 490
  school, historians of, 491
Rājasundarī, daughter of Rājendra Coḷa, 350
Rājataraṅgiṇī (Kalhaṇa's), 10, 18, 23, 37, 64, 254-55, 257, 266-67, 270-71, 276, 385, 481-83, 489
rājāvalī(s), 36, 128, 171-72, 255, 271
Rājāvalī (written by Mṛtyuñjaya Vidyālaṅkār of Bengal), 494
Rājāvalī Kathā (an anonymous work of unknown period), 171
Rājāvalī-Dvitīya (second *Rājataraṅgiṇī*), 270
Rājāvalī-kathe (of Devacandra), 172
Rājāvalīpatākā, 276
Rājavaṁśa, 152
Rājavaṁśāvalī, 39, 352
rājavijaya, 39
Rājavinoda, 424
Rājendra I, 443
Rājpūt(s), 219-20, 224, 227, 229, 323, 326
  rulers, 115, 226, 285
  warriors, 218
Rājpūtānā, 116, 217, 284, 476
Rājpūtānā desert 188
Rājyābhiṣeka, 226
Rājyaśrī, 189-91
Rājyacampati (of the poet Govind, Das), 354
Rājyapāla, 116, 200
Rājyavardhana, 189-90
Ram Das, 279
Rām Siṁha, 370, 372-73
Rāmacandra (Lord), 75
Rāmacandra, Yādava king, 110, 316, 323, 326
Rāmacarita (Sandhyākara Nandī's), 197, 199-200-01
Rāmadatta, 111
Rāmadeva, a great warrior, 437
Rāmadullā Khān, the commander-in-chief of the Bījā, 425-26
Rāmagāma, 138
Rāmaghaṭa, 441
Rāmagupta, 194
Rāmapāla, one of the greatest Pāla kings of Bengal, 198-200, 490
Ramappayyan, a general sent by Tirumāḷa Naikan, 447

Rāmarāya (minister of Sadāśiva) 423, 431
Rāmāyaṇa (Vālmīki's), 47, 50, 59-61, 63, 68, 74-77, 83-84, 333
Rāmāyaṇam (Punam Namboodari's), 445
Ramayappan (also called Ramappaiyan), 405
Ranachatur Nārāyaṇa, 382
Ranaraṅgavijayam, 437
Rāṇā Hammīra of Mewāṛ, 285
Rāṇā Rāso (by Dayaldas), 223
Rāṇā Ratan Singh, the king of Mewāṛ, 216, 219
Raṇamalla Chanda (Śrīdhara Vyāsa's), 234
Raṇastambhapura (Raṇa-thambhor), Cāhamāna dynasty of, 216
Raṇathambhor, 217-18, 220
Rander, 323
Raṅganātha Rāmāyaṇam (in Telugu by Gona Buddha Reḍḍī), 435
Rānī Bāī, Dāhir's widow, 283
Rānī Lāḍī, another widow of Dāhir, 284
Rānīdīghī, 359
Ranke, German historian, 34
Ranna, Jaina poet, 409
Rapson, E.J., 12, 15, 85, 120
rāso(s), 36, 215, 222
Rāṣṭrakūṭa(s), 174, 178, 325, 390, 410, 433-34, 439
  dynasty, 403
  empire, 442
  kings, 129, 174, 391
Rāṣṭraudha, king of Kānyakubja, 326
Rāṣṭraudhavaṁśa (an epic poem of 20 cantos in Sanskrit), 325
Ratan Singh, 220
Ratan Singh Mahesadasota-ri-Vācanika is the most (by Khiriyk Jagga), 229
Ratna Māṇikya II (1684-1712), the rājā of Tripura, 245, 371, 386
Ratna Veer Bhāna, 228
Ratnasenakulapraśasti (of Bhavadatta), 354
Rāṭhor family, 118
Rāvī, 68
Ravi Varmā, 444
Rawar, 284
Ray, N.R., 185
Rāyagiri (Rāigaṛh), 328
Reḍḍī(s), 439
  kings, 435, 436
  kings, court-poets of, 393
  in Āndhradeśa, history of, 436
Renan, B. Croce (1866-1952),17 a historian of Italy, 34
Renou, Louis, 69
Ṛgveda, 30, 47-48, 50, 53, 58, 61, 66-72, 487
Ṛgveda Saṁhitā, 69
Ṛgvedic Age, 67-68
Ṛgvedic history, 72
Ṛgvedic hymns, 69
Rohiṇī (river), 136
Romaharṣaṇa (or Lomaharṣaṇa), 88

Roman(s), 4, 11, 399
historians, 13
Rome, 4, 13, 30, 32-33, 183-84, 389
Rowse, A.L., 32
Roychoudhury, N.R., 385
Ṛṣabha, the first Jaina *tīrthaṁkara*, 409
Rudra Siṁha (Ahom king), 369, 371
Rudramahālaya, temple of, 313
Rudrapāla, the powerful Kāśmīrī general, 265
Rukmiṇīkalyāṇa (Rajacadamani's), 406, 413
Rustam no Śaloko (poet Śāmal's), 234
Rustamkuli Khan, Nawāb of Surat, 319
Rustamno Shaloko (or *Abrāhamkulikhanno Shaloko*) (by Shamal Bhaṭ), 319
ṛṣis, 69, 87
Śabaras, 122, 191
Sabhāsad, 336, 338, 340
Sadācandra, 110
Sadakkai II Thevan, the Sethupathi of Ramnad, 405
Saḍakṣarīdeva, a well-known Canarese poet, 424
Sadāśiva, 431
Sadāśiva Rāo (the Bhāo Sāheb), 344
Sadāśivarāya, 423
Sāgala (Śākala = modern Sialkot), 139, 141
Sagan Bhāu (a Maharashtra Muslim), 349
Sagat Rāso (by Girdhar), 223
Śāha, 332-33
Śāhajī (founder of the Bhoṅsalā dynasty), 327
Śāhajī, the father of Śivājī, 426
Sāhasa Bhīma, 411
Sāhasabhīma Vijaya (by Rama)
Śāhendravilāsa (Ayyāvāḷ's epic), 332
Śāhīya dynasty, 263
Śāhu, the son of Śambhā (or the grandson of Śivājī), 344, 346, 359
Sāhyā mountains, 328
Śaiva,
cult, 123, 193, 266, 274
sect, 258
Śaivism, 313, 375, 402-03, 438
Sajjana, the Jaina minister, 312
Sajjanagiri, 330
Śaka(s), 83, 122, 161, 170, 177, 233, 307, 316-17, 469, 473, 475, 477-78
Era, 379, 403, 473-74, 477-78, 483
kingdom, 479
kings, 106, 108
Satraps, 161
Śākalapura, Madra's capital, 81, 121, 140
Śākambharī (or Sāmbhar), 202, 207-08
Cāhamāna dynasty of, 316
Cāhamāna rulers of, 305, 308, 314, 489
Śakasthān, 161

śakāvalī(s) (annals), 38, 349
Sāketa, 114, 132-34, 138, 141, 145
Śakti cult, 123, 193, 266
Śākya(s), 136, 144, 153-54
  clan, 101
  council, 155
Sakyma, the famous king of Māhiṣmatī, 109
śalākāpuruṣas, 174
Śālivāhana, 108, 234, 479
  dynasty, 108
  Śaka Era/Saṁvat, 108, 478-79
Śālivāhanacarita (of Śivadāsa), 234
Saluva(s), 419
  dynasty, 420
Saluvābhyudaya (Narasiṁha Saluva's), 420
Śambhājī (Śivājī's eldest son by his first wife), 329-32, 338
Śānti Purāṇa, 411
Śāntinātha, sixteenth Jaina *tīrthaṁkara*, 411
Samand (Śāmantadeva), 263
Sāmaññaphala Sutta, 132
sāmanta(s), 192-93
Sāmantapāsādikā, Pāli commentary, 142, 462
Sāmantasiṁha, Guhila chief, 314
Samar Taraṅga (Wave of War), of Brajanath Bada Jen, 353
Samara Ras (by Ambadev Sur), 233
Samara Siṁha of Pāṭan, 233
Samarasiṁha of Chittor, 321
saṁghas, 134
Saṁgrāma, 264
  dynasty, 271
Saṁgrāmarāja (alias Kṣamāpati), 264
Saṁgrāmasiṁha (also called Śaṅkha), the son of Sin, 300
Saṁhitās, 66, 72, 86
Samprati (or Indrapālita), 151, 455
Samrāṭ, a title, 112
Samudra Nārāyaṇa, the Koch king of Darraṅg, 376
Samudragupta, 107, 112
Saṁvaraṇa, 68
Saṁvat Era, 470
Saṁyutta Nikāya, 132, 135
Sanamahi cult, 381
Sanātana Dharma, 274, 304
Sāñcī inscription, 479
sandeśakāvya(s), 39, 393
Sandhyākara Nandī, 197, 200
Sandrakottos (Candragupta), 460
Sandys, E.F., 385
Saṅgam(s) (academies of learned writers, poets and scholars), 389
  Age, 389, 395, 398, 400
  classics, 399
  literature, 400
  period, 400, 446
Saṅgīti Sutta, 134
Śaṅkaradeva, 243
Śaṅkaravarman, 262-63
Sanskrit, 31, 37-38, 52, 56, 141, 148
  Buddhist text(s), 154-55
  literature, 11, 17, 23, 30-31, 48, 53, 127, 489

Śakakula, 161
texts, 156
Sanskritisation, 381
Sapādalakṣadeśa (northern Rajasthan), 207, 209
Sarabha (Sarabhojī), 333
Sarabharājavilāsa (Jagannātha's), 333
Sarabhojīcarita (Ananta Nārāyaṇa's), 333
Sarala Das, the celebrated Oriya poet, 243
Sāraṅgadeva, 316
Sārasvata,
valley of, 311
region, 68, 98, 122
Sarasvatī (River), 83, 98, 189
Sārasvat-maṇḍala, 308, 311
Sarayū (river), 153
Sarbuland Khan, the *sūbedār* of Gujarat, 227-28, 320
sardārs, 349
Sardesai, 358
Sarfaraz, 356-57, 359
sarga, 92
Sarkar, J.N., 270
Sarma, S.N., 244
Sārnāth, 132
inscription, 480
Sarup Das Bhalla, a descendant of the third Guru Amar Das, 239
Sarvasena, 113
Sarvāstivāda School, 148
Śaryātas, 97
Śaryāti, 97
śāsanapaṭṭikā, 168
Śāsanavaṁsa (of Paññāsāmi), 157
Śaśāṅka, Gauḍa king, 190-91
Śaśāṅkamaṇḍala, 190
Śātakarṇi II, 104
satī, custom of, 83, 273
Satārā, 355
Sātavāhana(s), 95, 100, 104, 305, 307, 317, 433
dynasty, 103
empire, 106
history of, 334
kings, 234
later, 106
satra, a religious institution of the Vaiṣṇavites, 374
satra chronicles, 374-75
śatrumahāsāmanta(s), 192-93
Śatruñjaya, 303-04
Satrusal Rāso (by Dungal Singh), 223
Satsari Assam Burañjī, 372
Satyāśraya (CE 997-1008), the son of Tailapa II, 411
Saundaryakāvya (by Nuronda), 430
Saurāṣṭra (Kāṭhiāwāḍ), 122, 168, 202, 233, 296, 300, 302, 311-13, 315, 318, 323, 480
Cāḷukya chiefs of, 480
conquest of, 168
Sauvīra, 122
Sāvatthī (Śrāvastī), 132-35, 138, 143-45

Sawāī Mādhavrāo, 346-49
Sāyaṇa, 54
Schubring, Dr Walthur, 170
Scythian(s), 161
    rule, 162
Second Buddhist Council, 148, 156
Selvakkadungo Vali Ādan, (Cera prince), 395
Seṅguṭṭuvan, the son of Neḍuñjeralādan, 395
Sen, D.C., 384
Sena dynasty, 354
Senguṭṭuvan, Cera king, 397-98
seṇis, 138
Śeṣadatta, 111
Śeṣanāga, 110
Sevuna(s), 416
    kingdom, 416
Shahir(s), 347-48
Shahjahan, Mughal Emperor, 234
Shahmir dynasty, 276
Shamsuddin I, 270
Sharma, S.R., 7
Shershah Suri, 230
Shias, 275
Shinde, Yashwantrao, 340
Siddharāja, Cāḷukya prince of Gujarat, 207
Sieg, Emil, 56
Sikandar (Zain-ul-Abadin's father), 274
Sikandar But-Shikan, 275, 278
Sikandar Lodi, 172
Sikh(s), 3, 186, 493
    gurus, 236-38, 279
    historians, 44, 490
    movement, 239
Sikhism, 236
Śilāhāra dynasty, 313
Śilappadikāram (by Ilangovaḍigal), 397-98, 403
Siṁha Era, 312
Siṁhadeva (also called Jayasiṁha), 481
Śimuka, 103, 457
Sindh, 122, 161, 196, 254, 282, 284, 490
    chronicle of, 26, 281
    conquest of, 281
    history of, 285
    political condition of, 281
    Sultān Qayamdin of 273
    women of, 283
Sindhu (Indus), 67
Sindhudeśa, 188
Sindhurāja Navasāhasāṅka, Paramāra king, 197
Sindhurāja, Paramāra king, 117, 305, 308
Siṅghana, Yādava ruler of Devagiri (modern Daulatābād), 295, 300, 304-5, 324-25, 334
Sinha, Kailash Chandra, 385
Sinhgad, 347
Siraj-ud-Daula, 356
Śiśuka (king), 110, 112
Śiśunāga (Śiśupāla), 142, 454, 462, 463-64

dynasties, 101
Śiśunandī, 110
Śītaldeva, Kanhadade's nephew, 221
Sittalai, Buddhist poet Sāttanār, 398
Śiva, 313
Śiva Bhārata (by Paramānanda), 235, 328, 331
Śiva Caritra (composed by Raghunasth Yadav Citre), 340
Śivā Chatrapaticen Carita (by Kṛṣṇājī Anant Sabhās), 335
Śiva Rāj Bhūṣaṇa (composed by Bhūṣaṇa), 235
Śiva Siṁha (Ahom king), 370
Śivadeva, Licchavi king, 289
Śivadigvijaya, one of the most valuable *bakhars*, 340
Śivājī (king), 327-33, 335-43, 347, 349, 490
bakhars on, 342
Era, 346
Śivanandī, 110
Śivarājarājyābhiṣeka Kalpataru (by Aniruddha), 331
Śivas, 68
Śivatattvaratnākara (Bāsavarāja's encyclopaedia), 423
Śivavilāsa (by Dāmodara), 445
Śivi kingdom, 136
Śivigaṇa, 477
Śivis, 82
Siwana, 285
Siyar-ul-Mutakh (Ghulam Hussain's), 360
Skanda, Pṛthvīrāja's general, 216
Skandagupta, 109, 480
Skandanāga, 111
Smith, R. Morton, 122
Smith, V.A., 93, 267, 455
Smṛtis, 58, 61
Sojat, 285
Solaṅkīs (Śuklas), 115
Solar dynasty, 207, 209, 326
Somadeva Sūri, 164
Somadevarajiyamu (by Kuchimanchi Jaggakavi), 439
Somaka of Paurava dynasty, 69, 194
Somanātha, 221, 299, 323
temple of, 304, 309, 315
Somapālavijaya (of Jalhaṇa), 206
Somasiṁha, 301
Somavaṁśīs, 287
Someśvara, 118, 178, 291-93, 295-99, 313-14, 318, 414
Someśvara II Bhuvanaikamalla, 203
Someśvara IV, Cāḷukya king, 324, 408
Śona (river), 187
Sonadaṇḍa Sutta, 133
Soṇṇabhūmi (Suvaṇṇabhūmi), 138
South Pañcāla kingdom, 76
Sovira (Sauvira), 141, 194
Soyarāmbā (Soyrā Bāī), 329
Śrauta-Sūtras, 55
Śravaṇabeḷgoḷā, 430
Śrāvastī, 121, 150, 153-55, 194

Śreṇika (Bimbisāra), 170, 174
Śrī Bhaṭṭa, 275
Śrī Gur Sobhā (by poet Chander Bhan), 238
Śrī Śātakarṇi I, 104
Śrīchavillākara (also called Śrīcchavillaka), 256
Śrīdhara, 178
Śrīgupta, 114
Śrīkaṇṭha (or Thāneśvar), 196, 441, 443
Śrīnagara, 258
Śrīnātha (poet), 436
Śrīparvatīya-Āndhras (of Telaṅgānā), 106
Śrīraṅgah-Māhātvamu (Bhairava Kavi's), 437
Śrīraṅgam (called Mahendra-maṅgalam), 413
Śrīraṅgapaṭana (Śrīraṅga-paṭṭanam), 426-27, 432
Śrīvara Paṇḍit, 254, 271-78, 483
Śr̥ṅgārapura (southern Maharashtra), 329-30
Sr̥ñjaya(s), 68-69
Srivastava, A.L., 219
Ssu-ma Chien, Chinese historian, 183
Stein, M.A., 18, 205, 268
Sthānavīśvara (modern Thāneśvar in Haryana), 187-88
stūpas, 154, 258
Subhatavarman, a Paramāra king of Mālwā, 300, 314
Sucavarman, 261
Sudarśanacarita (of Nayanandī), 173
Sudāsa, 68-69
śūdra, 109
Sūfīs, 275
Sujal Khan, 320
Śuka, 254, 276-77, 481, 483
    history, 277
Sukāphā (the founder of the Ahom dynasty in Assam), 369
Sūkar, 118
Śukreśvara, a brāhmaṇa scholar, 382
Sukr̥takīrti-Kallolinī (of Udayaprabha Sūri), 304
Sukr̥tasaṁkīrtana (of Arisiṁha), 298
Sūktimatipura, 81, 121
Sūktimuktāvalī (by Jalhana), 324
sultāns, history of, 373
Sultān Ābu-Sayyad of Khorasan, 273
Sultān Alauddin Khilji, 216-22, 234, 242, 316, 321-23, 435, 471
Sultān Feroz Shah Tughlaq, 240
Sultān Ibrahim Shah 241
Sultān Mahmud (Mahmud of Ghazni), 265, 309
Sultān Zain-ul-Abadin (called Jainollābhadina), 271, 273
Sultanate period, 44
Sulūva, 102
Sumaṅgalavilāsinī, 143
Sumati, 76
Sumerians, 4, 11
Sumitra of Śuṅga dynasty, 194
Śuṅga(s), 105, 110, 168, 455

dynasty, 103, 162, 166, 175-76
kings, 456
period, 78
rulers, 170
Sunidha, 131, 133, 143
Sunnis, 275
Surajanacarita (written by Sūdan), 219
Sūrapāla II, 199
Śūrasena, 101, 122, 135, 155, 163
kingdoms, 134
Surāṣṭra (Saurāṣṭra), 107, 161, 273
Surat, 323
surathot (by surathot), 178
Surathotsava, 297
Śūravarman II, 261-62, 264, 482
Śūrpārka, 121
Sūrya Prakāśa (composed by Karnīdān), 227
Sūryavaṁśa (by Paramānanda), 327
Sūryavaṁśī, 287
Suśarman, 103, 456
Susima (prince), 151
Sussala I, 265
Susunāga (Śiśunāga), 146
sūta(s), 89-90s
Sutta Nipāta, 137, 144
Sutta Piṭaka, 131
Suttas, 132
Śutudri (Sutlej), 67
Suvaṇṇabhūmi, 137, 141, 143
Suvāstu (Swāt), 67
Suvrata, 255
svayaṁvara, 118, 209
Śvetāmbara *Tapāgaccha-Paṭṭāvalī*, 169
Śvetāmbara(s), 169
*paṭṭāvalī*s, 170
scholars, 179
school, 129, 166, 168, 232, 305, 467, 470
sect, 160
tradition, 170, 466, 474
Swāmī Vīrasena, 174
Taccadeśa, 262
tacchaka, 138
Tacitus, Roman historian, 4, 32, 184
Tahqiq-i-Hind (An Enquiry into India), 7, 480
Tai language, 364
Takkaśilā (Takṣaśilā), 121, 136, 144 151, 153
Takkola, 137, 141
Tālajaṅghas, 77
Talikoṭa, battlefield of, 423
talisma, 283
Taluva dynasty, 422
Talwaṇḍī Rāī Bhoi (now called Nankānā Sāhib), 236
Tamali, 137
Tambapaṇṇi, 138
Tamil, 25
chronicle, 39
dynasties, 414
history of, 400
Saṅgam literature, 389
socio-economic life of, 399
Tamiladeśa, 38, 177, 328, 353, 389, 390-91, 394, 423, 428

history of, 390, 403, 429

Tāmradhvaja Nārāyaṇa, Kachārī Rājā 371

Tāmralipti, 81, 121-22

Tanjaivanan (or *Thanjaivanan*) *Kovai* (of Poyyamoli Pulovar), 403

Tañjanagara (Tanjavur, Tanjore), 332-33, 401, 423

Tanjavur (Tanjore), Nāyakas of, 406

Tāntric cult, 274

Tapāgaccha-Paṭṭāvalī, 467-69

Tarāīn (or Taroai),

first battle of, 207

second battle of, 119, 210

taraṅgas, 257

Tegh Bahadur, 280

Tej Singh, a Rājpūt prince, 390, 406

Tejaḥpāla (Vastupāla's brother), 296, 299, 302-04

Telangana, 435

Velamas of, 436-37

Telugu, 25

literature, 393, 438

Thakur-Atacarit — (a satra chronicle by Vidyānanda), 374

Ṭhākurī dynasty, 289

Thāneśvar, 189-92

Harṣavardhana of, 232, 259

Thapar, Romila, 22, 25, 123

Thera Moggaliputta Tissa, 139

Third Buddhist Council, 139, 148

third Saṅgam, 389, 394, 398-400

Thomas, 195

Thompson, J.W., 28

three Buddhist Councils, 156

Thucydides, 4, 12, 32, 268

Tibet, 289

Tilakamañjarī (by Dhanapāla, a Śvetāmbara poet), 165

Tilottamā (Saṁyogitā of *Pṛthvīrāja Rāso*), 207

Tiloyapaṇṇatti (of Yativṛṣabha), 162, 466, 468-69, 472

Ṭipperah kings, 383

Ṭipperah Rāj, 384

Tirabhukti, 241

tīrthaṁkaras, 162

Tīrthoddhāra-prakaraṇa, 166, 466-68

Tirumala (Rāmarāya's brother), 431

Tirumala Nāyaka, 427

Tirumalai Nayak (1653-59), the Vijayanagara viceroy, 405

Tirumalāmbā (princess), 422

Tissa, 143

Titthogāli-Painna, an old Prākṛt text 166, 466, 468-69, 473

Tod, James, 6, 13, 94

Tomara kings, 118

Toramāṇa, Hūṇa chief, 164

Toynbee, A.J., 34, 64

Trailokyamalla, 311

Trailokyavīraganda, 426

Trevelyan,G.M., 33

Triśalā, 159

Tribhuvanapāla, 315

Trichinopoly, 405
Trigartta(s), 82, 123, 262
Trilocanapāla (the Hindu Śāhī king of Lahore), 265
Trilokasāra (by Nemicandra), 166, 469, 473
Tripathi, R.S., 84
Tripiṭakas, 139
Tripura, 38, 254, 363, 382, 385-86, 490
  Era, 385
  history of, 383, 385
  kingdom of, 383
  kings of, 383, 481
  of Muhammadan period 385
  royal family, 384, 386
Tripura Burañjī, 371
Tripura Vaṁśāvalī (by Dvija Banga Chandra), 386
Tripureśvara, 262
Tripurī, 81, 121-22
Tritsus, 68
Triṣaṣṭiśalākāpuruṣacarita, 474
Trotter, L.J., 8, 72
Tuṅga, 265
Tuṅgabhadrā, 417
Tukāmbā (Tukābāī) Śāhajī's second wife, 328
Tukhāristān (the upper Oxus Valley), 259
Tulsīdās, 346-47
Tungkhungia Burañjī, 372
Turkish rule, 417
Turkish sultān, 419
Turks, 217, 292-93, 298, 316, 326, 418-19
Turuṣka(s) (Turks), 265, 274, 323, 418
Turvasa/s (Turvasu/s), 68, 76, 79, 98
Tuṣāras, 107, 122
Ucchala, 265-66
udāharaṇa, 61
Ūdala, 213-14
Udaya (Udayāditya) the founder of Udayapur, 117
Udayana (king), 101, 151-52, 154, 170
Udayaprabha Sūri, 304
Udayarāja, 424
Udayasiṁha, 213, 301
Udāyi Bhadda (Ajātasattu's son and successor), 142, 144-46, 151, 462-63, 466
Udāyin, 101, 167, 463
Udbhaṭa, 260
Uḍiyañjeral, 395
Ugraśravā, 88
Ujjain (Ujjayinī), 107-08, 115, 121, 137-38, 141, 161-62, 172, 229, 233-34, 307, 468, 470, 475, 477-79
  Gardabhilla of, 232
  Śālivāhana of, 478
Ulugh Khan, 322-23, 435
Unmattāvanti, 264
Upagupta, teacher of Aśoka, 149
*upākhyāna*s, 86
Upaniṣads, 55
Upatissa (monk), 156
Uragapura (Uraiyur, near Trichinopoly), 81, 394, 396
Uraśā (Haẓārā) region, 263

Utpala or Varman dynasty, 261, 264, 482
Utpalapīḍa, 259, 261, 482
Utpalas, 261
Uttamadatta, 111
Uttar Pradesh, 114, 212
Uttara Purāṇa, 175, 177
Uttarakuru, 260
Uttara-Pañcāla, 137
Uttarāpatha, 122, 151, 189
Uttarapurāṇa (of Guṇabhadra), 469
vācanika(s), 36, 215, 229
Vaḍḍārādhane (of Śivakoṭi), 409
Vaḍnagar Praśastis, 177
Vāghelā,
  history of, 295
  period, 233
  rulers, 234
Vāhlika kings, 109
Vaidya, C.V., 21, 78
Vaiśākha, 229
Vaiśāla dynasty, 75-76
Vaiśālī (also called Vaiśāla), 76-77, 97, 121, 143-45, 149-50, 152-55, 159
  Licchavīs of, 152
Vaiśālikas, 150, 154
Vaiṣṇava,
  cult, 123, 193, 266
  faith, 262
  revivalism, 375
  saints, 243-45
Vaiṣṇavism, 353, 379, 402
Vājapeya sacrifices, 112
Vajjī, 133, 135
Vajjians, 131, 133
Vajramitra, 456
Vajrasvāmī, 232
vākā (or chronicle of events), by Ṛṣi Rūghā, 36, 128, 172
Vākāṭaka(s), 113, 115
  dynasty, 112
Vākpati-Muñja, 308
Vākpatirāja Padmagupta, 17
Valabha II, nephew of Jayamaṇi III, 442-43
Valabhī,
  Era, 480
  Maitrakas of, 157
  Śilāditya of, 316
Validhara, king (Īśānavarman's grandson), 442
Vallabharāja, 309
Vālmīki, 74, 83
Valpah Tadakkai Peruvirarkilli, Coḷa ruler 397
Vāmana, 96, 260
Vaṁsa (Vatsa) 92, 133, 135
vaṁśacarita, 38
vaṁśānucarita, 92
Vaṁśāvalī(s), 20, 24, 37-39, 42-43, 88, 128, 253-54, 286-88, 349-52, 375-77, 386, 392-93, 425, 428, 438-39, 489, 491
  tradition 289
Vaṁsāvalī Nāmā Dasan Pātshāhianka (by Kesar Singh), 279
Vaṁśīgopāladeva, 243
Vanamālideva, 243

Vanan, a general of the Pāṇḍyan king Māravarman Kulaśekhara, 403

Vanarāja, 299

Vaneswar Vidyalankar, the court-poet of the Mahārā, 361

Vaṅgara, 110

Vaṅka, king of Sāvatthī, 136

Vār Amritsar Kī (by poet Darshan), 280

Varadāmbikā, a princess of Salaga, 422

Vārāṇasī, the capital of Kāśī kingdom, 121, 132-34, 136, 141, 143-44, 150, 152-55, 423

Varāṅgacarita (Jaṭila or Jaṭāsiṁhanandī's), 164

Vardhamāna Mahāvīra, the last (twenty-fourth) Jain *tīrthaṁkara*, 159, 412, 472

Vardhamāna Purāṇa, 175

Vardhamānapura (modern Vadhvān), 306

Vardhana dynasty, 188

Varman dynasty, 191, 261

varṇāśrama dharma, 123

Vārttā, 36, 215

Vasantavilāsa (a historical epic) of Bālacandra Sūri, 305

Vassakāra, 131, 133, 143

Vastupāla, 295, 298-99, 301, 303-05

Vastupāla-carita (of Jinaharṣa), 304

Vastupāla-Tejaḥpāla-Praśasti (by Jayasiṁha Sūri I), 302

Vasu (Uparicara Vasu), 77

Vasudeva, the founder of the Kaṇva dynasty, 103, 456

Vasudevahiṇḍi (by Saṁghadāsagaṇi Vācaka), 163

Vasudevaratha, 352

Vasujyeṣṭha (or Sujyeṣṭha), 456

Vasukra, a famous Kaśmīrī brāhmaṇa, 66

Vasumitra, 456, 468

Vāt(s) 223-24

Vātāpī (Bādāmi), Western Cāḷukyas of , 411

Vatsa, 155

kingdom, 152, 154

Vatsagulma, 113

Vatsarāja, 115

Vatsarāja Udayana (of Kauśāmbī), 194

Vayajaladeva (a Pratihāra), 314

Vāyu Purāṇa, 94-96

Veda(s), 47, 53-58, 60, 64, 71, 86

Vedavyāsa, 3, 28, 57, 64, 66, 86

Vedic Age, 52-54

Vedic Aryan culture, 70

Vedic hymns, 66

Vedic Itihāsa, 72

Vedic literature, 49, 52, 57, 71-72

Vedic period, 72

Vedic texts, 72, 92

Vedic traditions, 47, 92

Vedisā, 138

Veer Mayan (by Bahadur Dhadhi), 224

Vellore, 337

Vemabhūpālacarita (Vāmanabhaṭṭa's), 436

Veṅgī,
  Eastern Cāḷukya kings of, 433, 439
  Eastern Cāḷukyas of, history of, 392
Verāpatha, 137
Veraval inscription, 292
Vesāli (Vaiśālī), 132, 138
Vesuṅga, 137
Vibhanāga, 111
Vicāraśreṇī (of Merutuṅga), 321, 323, 467-68, 470, 477
Vidarbha, 113
Videha (Mithilā), 75, 97, 101, 122, 194
  dynasty, 75, 155
  kingdom of, 137, 150, 152, 154
Vidiśā, 110-11, 121-22, 137
Viḍūḍabha, 136
Vidyācakravartin, 413
Vidyācakravartin I, the court-poet of Vīra-Ballāla, 413
Vidyācakravartin III, a court-poet of Vīra-Ballāla, 413
Vidyāpati, 241
Vidyāpurī (Vijayanagara), 422
Vidyāraṇya, 417
vigat, 36, 215, 230-31
Vigrahapāla III, 198
Vigraharāja IV Viśāladeva (CE 1153-64), 223
vihāras, 149
Vijaya Govinda, 279
Vijayāditya II, 433
Vijayāditya III Gunaga, 433-34
Vijayagaṛh (Bharatpur state), 476
Vijayanagara, 390, 404, 416-18, 423, 427
  administration, 417
  empire, 334, 392, 406, 415, 419-20, 423, 428-31
  history of, 393, 430, 437-38
  invasion of, 393, 437
  kings, 391-93, 406, 419, 423, 437-39
  Nāyaka, 328
  political history of, 419
  princesses, 391-92
  Rāyas of, 436-38
  rulers of, 421
  Saṅgama dynasty of, 437
Vijayeśa, 262
Vijayasena, 200
Vikrama (CE 1118-33), Coḷa emperor, 401
Vikrama Era/Saṁvat, 108, 161, 307, 322, 467, 473-77, 479-80
Vikramāditya, King of Ujjaiyinī, 161, 233, 316, 319, 479
Vikramāditya (son of Mahendrāditya) 108, 161, 168, 234, 307, 317, 476
Vikramāditya V, 310
Vikramāditya VI of Cāḷukya dynasty of Kalyāṇī, 481
Vikramāditya VI Tribhuvanamalla, 203-5, 490
Vikramāṅkābhyudaya of Someśvara III Bhūlokamalla, 205
Vikramāṅkadevacarita (Bilhaṇa's), 202, 204

Vikramāṅka-Prabandha, 307
Vikramāṅka-Sattva-Prabandha, 319
Vikramarāma, 442
Vikramārjuna Vijaya (by Pampa)
vilāsa(s), 226-27
Vimala Prabandha (by Lāvaṇyasāmay), 232
Vinaya piṭaka, 131, 142
Vinayāditya, 404
Vindhya forest, 190-91
Vindhya region, 122, 191
Vindhyaśakti, 109, 112-13
Vindhyavarman, Paramāra king of Mālwā, 297
Vinnakota Peddana (at the court of King Viśveśvara), 437
Vipāśā (Beās), 67
Vīra Narasiṁha, 421-22
Vīra-Ballāla III, Hoysaḷa ruler, 416
Vīrabhadra Campū (Pasmanābha's), 234
Vīrabhadra Nāyaka, the chief of Ikkerī, 425
Vīrabhoja, 324
Vīradhavala (1219-38), the son of Lavaṇaprasāda, 295-96, 299, 301-02, 305, 315, 318
Vīradhavala, Vāghelā chief of Dholka, 303
Vīra-Nārāyaṇacarita (Vāmana's), 436
Vīrapuruṣadatta, 433
Vīra-Rājendra of Kāñcī, Coḷa monarch, 204
Vīraśaivism, 434
Vīrasiṁha, ruler of the kingdom of Tirabhukti (Tirhut), 240
Virāṭa, 121
Virāṭanagar, 81
Virūpākṣa, 419-20
Virūpākṣavasantotsava (by a scholar named Ahobala), 419
Viśāla (king), 76
Viśāladeva (son of Vīradhavala), 118, 296, 298, 303, 315
Viśāladeva, Vāghelā king of Gujarat, (1244-62), 318
Viśāladeva Rāso (by Narapati), 223
Viṣāṇins, 68
Vishnupur satra, 375
Viṣṇu Purāṇa, 94-95, 453
Viṣṇugupta (Cāṇakya), 167
Viśvakeśvara Kṣetra, 262
Viśvaksena, 119
Vitāśokāvadāna, 149
Vitastā (Jhelum), 67, 262
Viṭhala, an elder brother of Rāmadeva, 437
Vivasvān, 68
Vividhatīrthakalpa (of Jinaprabha Sūri), 168-69, 322, 470
Vogel, 253
Voltaire, 34
Vr̥jikas, 150
Vyāghranāga, 111
Vyas, K.B., 222
Vyāsa, 77, 84, 88, 95-96
Vyāsarāya, 421
Vyāsas, line of, 86
Vyāsayogicarita, (by Somanātha), 421

Warangal, 435, 437
Warder, A.K., 18, 71, 86-87, 114, 148, 242, 365
Weber, A., 18, 95
Western Gaṅgas, 412
Western Ghāṭs, 196
Western scholars, 31, 494
Wheeler, J.T., 48
Whitney, W.D. (American Sanskrit scholar), 452
Wilson, H.H., 269, 482
Wright, Daniel, 287
Xenophon, 4
yādāsta, 229
Yādava(s), 76, 79, 98, 324
  dynasty, 324
  kingdom, 325-26
  tribes, 82
Yadu(s), 68, 76, 79
  dynasty, 163
Yajña Śrī Śātakarṇi (king), 95, 104
Yamunā, 67, 82, 97, 212
  Valley, 112
Yaśaḥkarṇa, Kalacuri sovereign of Tripurī, 312
Yaśaskara, 264, 482
Yaśastilaka-Campū, 164
Yāska, 54
Yaśodharā, 160
Yaśodharman, 477
Yaśoharacarita (*Yaśodharacarita*) (of Kanakasena Vād), 197
Yaśonandī, 110
Yaśovarman of Kannauj, 196, 232, 259, 312, 490
Yaudheyas, 82
Yavana(s) (Bactrian Greeks), 83, 109, 140
  kings, 106
Yayāti, 69, 79
Yona, 137
Yuvarāja (king), 262
Zain-ul-Abadin, 272-76, 278
Zakariya Khan, governor of Lahore, 281
Zamorins (the Hindu *rājā*s of Calicut), 445
Ziauddin Barani, 218
Zulfikar Khan, 406